Driving Decentralization and Disruption With Digital Technologies

Balraj Verma
Chitkara Business School, Chitkara University, India

Babita Singla
Chitkara Business School, Chitkara University, India

Amit Mittal
Chitkara Business School, Chitkara University, India

IGI Global
PUBLISHER of TIMELY KNOWLEDGE

A volume in the Advances in Human and Social Aspects of Technology (AHSAT) Book Series

Published in the United States of America by
IGI Global
Engineering Science Reference (an imprint of IGI Global)
701 E. Chocolate Avenue
Hershey PA, USA 17033
Tel: 717-533-8845
Fax: 717-533-8661
E-mail: cust@igi-global.com
Web site: http://www.igi-global.com

Library of Congress Cataloging-in-Publication Data

Names: Verma, Balraj, 1985- editor. | Singla, Babita, 1988- editor. | Mittal, Amit, 1974- editor.
Title: Driving decentralization and disruption with digital technologies / edited by Balraj Verma, Babita Singla, Amit Mittal.
Description: Hershey, PA : Engineering Science Reference, [2024] | Includes bibliographical references and index. | Summary: "This book explores the digital revolution's impact on society, focusing on how it catalyzes decentralization and de-globalization, and disrupts traditional systems"-- Provided by publisher.
Identifiers: LCCN 2024002026 (print) | LCCN 2024002027 (ebook) | ISBN 9798369332535 (hardcover) | ISBN 9798369332542 (ebook)
Subjects: LCSH: Information technology--Economic aspects. | Information technology--Social aspects.
Classification: LCC HC79.I55 D755 2024 (print) | LCC HC79.I55 (ebook) | DDC 303.48/33--dc23/eng/20240118
LC record available at https://lccn.loc.gov/2024002026
LC ebook record available at https://lccn.loc.gov/2024002027

This book is published in the IGI Global book series Advances in Human and Social Aspects of Technology (AHSAT) (ISSN: 2328-1316; eISSN: 2328-1324)

British Cataloguing in Publication Data
A Cataloguing in Publication record for this book is available from the British Library.

Advances in Human and Social Aspects of Technology (AHSAT) Book Series

Mehdi Khosrow-Pour, D.B.A.
Information Resources Management Association, USA

ISSN:2328-1316
EISSN:2328-1324

Mission

In recent years, the societal impact of technology has been noted as we become increasingly more connected and are presented with more digital tools and devices. With the popularity of digital devices such as cell phones and tablets, it is crucial to consider the implications of our digital dependence and the presence of technology in our everyday lives.

The **Advances in Human and Social Aspects of Technology (AHSAT) Book Series** seeks to explore the ways in which society and human beings have been affected by technology and how the technological revolution has changed the way we conduct our lives as well as our behavior. The AHSAT book series aims to publish the most cutting-edge research on human behavior and interaction with technology and the ways in which the digital age is changing society.

Coverage

- Human Development and Technology
- Cyber Behavior
- Technology and Freedom of Speech
- Activism and ICTs
- Philosophy of technology
- Cyber Bullying
- ICTs and social change
- Digital Identity
- End-User Computing
- Gender and Technology

The Advances in Human and Social Aspects of Technology (AHSAT) Book Series (ISSN 2328-1316) is published by IGI Global, 701 E. Chocolate Avenue, Hershey, PA 17033-1240, USA, www.igi-global.com. This series is composed of titles available for purchase individually; each title is edited to be contextually exclusive from any other title within the series. For pricing and ordering information please visit http://www.igi-global.com/book-series/advances-human-social-aspects-technology/37145. Postmaster: Send all address changes to above address.

Titles in this Series

For a list of additional titles in this series, please visit: http://www.igi-global.com/book-series/advances-human-social-aspects-technology/37145

Considerations on Cyber Behavior and Mass Technology in Modern Society
Paolo Beneventi (Independent Researcher, Italy)
Engineering Science Reference • copyright 2024 • 271pp • H/C (ISBN: 9781668482285) • US $240.00 (our price)

AI and Emotions in Digital Society
Adrian Scribano (CONICET, University of Buenos Aires, Argentina) and Maximiliano E. Korstanje (University of Palermo, Argentina)
Information Science Reference • copyright 2024 • 321pp • H/C (ISBN: 9798369308028) • US $240.00 (our price)

Adoption and Use of Technology Tools and Services by Economically Disadvantaged Communities Implications for Growth and Sustainability
Alice S. Etim (Winston-Salem State University, USA)
Information Science Reference • copyright 2024 • 383pp • H/C (ISBN: 9781668453476) • US $225.00 (our price)

Philosophy of Artificial Intelligence and Its Place in Society
Luiz Moutinho (University of Suffolk, UK) Luís Cavique (Universidade Aberta, Portugal) and Enrique Bigné (Universitat de València, Spain)
Engineering Science Reference • copyright 2023 • 439pp • H/C (ISBN: 9781668495919) • US $215.00 (our price)

Cyberfeminism and Gender Violence in Social Media
Deepanjali Mishra (KIIT University, India)
Information Science Reference • copyright 2023 • 442pp • H/C (ISBN: 9781668488935) • US $215.00 (our price)

Investigating the Impact of AI on Ethics and Spirituality
Swati Chakraborty (GLA University, India & Concordia University, Canada)
Information Science Reference • copyright 2023 • 230pp • H/C (ISBN: 9781668491966) • US $225.00 (our price)

Applied Research Approaches to Technology, Healthcare, and Business
Darrell Norman Burrell (Marymount University, USA)
Information Science Reference • copyright 2023 • 455pp • H/C (ISBN: 9798369316306) • US $285.00 (our price)

Analyzing New Forms of Social Disorders in Modern Virtual Environments

IGI Global
PUBLISHER of TIMELY KNOWLEDGE

701 East Chocolate Avenue, Hershey, PA 17033, USA
Tel: 717-533-8845 x100 • Fax: 717-533-8661
E-Mail: cust@igi-global.com • www.igi-global.com

Table of Contents

Detailed Table of Contents

The chapter aims to show the development of the information society in the EU countries, its digital progress, and its repercussions on the economy of Serbia as a country that is a candidate for EU membership. The methodological concept and the analysis are based on the Digital Economy and Society Index (DESI), an official report of the European Commission. The DESI 2022 reports track the advancements made in the digital space in EU Member States and are primarily based on 2021 data. The findings of the study revealed that although Member States made progress in their efforts to go digital during the COVID-19 timeframe, they are still unable to address the gaps in digital skills, transform SMEs into digital businesses, or put out cutting-edge 5G networks. Also, the results show moderate progress in the development of the information society in Serbia in terms of the functioning of the internal market for electronic communications, the availability of modern electronic services, the development of information security, and the application of eGovernment and eCommerce.

The banking system serves as the central and essential component of a functional economy. A robust banking system is essential for fostering economic growth and facilitating development. However, the systems have certain drawbacks Numerous instances of fraudulent operations were reported, leading to clients experiencing theft and unauthorised access to their properties. With the progression of the digital era, there is an increasing exposure and scrutiny of these centralized systems, thereby leading to a shift in thoughts towards decentralised alternatives. This chapter provides a concise discussion of the necessity of decentralised financing and how it can be accomplished through the utilisation of blockchain technology. Firstly, the study examines the mechanics of decentralised banking systems and their potential to address the limitations of conventional banking systems. Further, a brief of various case studies has been given. Finally, the chapter discusses the transformation of the banking system using blockchain technology.

Conceptual research often lags in practice when firms disrupt business models. Immersive case studies help bridge this gap. This case explores the journey of a Hyderabad-based fashion-tech startup Ft.you. The fashion business is competitive and dynamic, saturated with players going head-to-head to stay relevant. Ft.you wants to change the way Indian women choose to dress with an innovative application that removes the hassles related to tailoring services, letting users customize the dress within an app, with input spaces for fabric selection and measurements. The case discusses the partnerships that Ft.you has established with fabric manufacturers and tailors and describes its marketing/sales strategies. It also documents the key decision points in the early stages of the journey of Ft.you.

Transparency, visibility, security, source-to-store traceability, and rising customer expectation are the critical points in the retail supply chain. The global supply chain involves a nexus of manufacturers and suppliers who urge for a robust network addressing the above challenges in the supply chain. A better provenance tool can benefit retailers, as customers are more concerned about the retail journey of the product start from its origin. Within the small span since its inception, blockchain has revolutionized the businesses and shown promising result in reshaping the supply chain. Blockchain in retail can provide evidence for the authenticity of product, tacking details for reliable retail delivery and enriching customer experience through product provenance. This chapter aims to explain to retailers the challenges, opportunities, and potential application of blockchain in the retail supply chain.

In the age of digitization, concerns about digital security and data ownership are paramount. The chapter investigates the cyber threatscape, noting the role of state-backed collectives. Essential defense tools, such as encryption and two-factor authentication, are contrasted with significant breaches like the 2014 Yahoo incident. The commodification of personal data by tech giants for advertising underlines the urgent need for clear data ownership guidelines. The balance between online utility and privacy is challenging, with corporations holding significant power due to vast data reserves. A proposed "digital bill of rights" could provide a universal rights-tech alignment. Future challenges lie in AI implications and the rise of quantum computing, leading towards "surveillance capitalism." Solutions involve quantum-resistant cryptography, AI-data safeguards, and enhancing digital literacy. The chapter advocates for balancing digital advancement with individual rights for a secure digital future.

Decentralized autonomous organizations (DAOs) represent a novel technology progress that could potentially challenge conventional organizations in terms of management and making choices. This chapter provides an introduction to decentralized finance (DeFi), situates DeFi within the framework of the conventional financial industry, establishes a connection of peer-to-peer transactions, and concludes with a discussion on policy implications. Decentralization has the capacity to weaken conventional mechanisms of accountability and diminish the efficacy of established financial regulations and enforcement. This study presents a thorough analysis of the current status of research on DAOs, highlighting the most important research areas and relevant works in the subject. Furthermore, it examines the performance of prominent decentralized finance in relation to these research areas, providing valuable observations on their real-world implementations and efficacy.

In the dynamic digital epoch, this exploration delves into the impact of technologies on decentralization, unraveling blockchain, AI, and IoT. It dissects their transformative influence on power structures, economic paradigms, and global interactions. From the transparency of blockchain to the decision-making of AI and the symphony orchestrated by IoT, the chapter explores technologies shaping a new decentralized reality. Blockchain disrupts traditional finance, extending its impact to healthcare and supply chain management. The intersection of AI and blockchain enhances security and governance. IoT transforms industries, ushering in real-time data exchange and automation. The chapter explores deglobalization, examining how digital platforms empower local entrepreneurship and decentralized digital identity systems enhance national security. Challenges, including security concerns and inclusive access, demand astute navigation, improved collaboration, and proactive governance. The chapter concludes with a call for collective wisdom and ethical stewardship to shape a decentralized future.

This study examines the growing problems that multinational corporations (MNEs) are facing as a result of a confluence of pandemics, environmental disasters, and the digital revolution. These problems appear as organizational, market, and geopolitical complexity, which institutional pluralism magnifies. As the nature of productive activity changes, so do the ways in which MNEs structure and manage their operations. Additionally, changing investor and consumer expectations are broadening the definition of value creation and having an effect on company strategies. They contend that these difficulties force MNEs to reevaluate the way in which they formulate, establish, and carry out their corporate purposes. In order to wrap up, they suggest a research agenda that stresses how critical it is for MNEs to take a purpose-driven approach.

This study aims to identify artificial intelligence and blockchain technology's publication productivity and intellectual structure in the healthcare industry. This study employs a bibliometric-content analysis technique to determine intellectual structure and publication productivity. The Scopus database analyses identified research articles from 2018 to 2023. The findings of the thematic mapping show that AI and blockchain are emerging techniques and topics such as "smart healthcare", "patient-centric", "healthcare management", "virtual & augmented reality", "decentralization", etc. are the potential and new dimensions that can be looked upon in future themes. This study advances knowledge by providing a current and future overview of AI and blockchain integration in the healthcare industry that would create new and enhance existing research streams.

The banking sector is transforming, with traditional banking focusing on personalization and quality of relationships, while digital banking focuses on simplicity of products. However, traditional banking must embrace technology to survive and compete. Technology has improved customer service, built trust, and created higher returns on investment. The future of banking lies in IT decentralization and deglobalization, which offer vast opportunities for effective customer service, timely product management, faster service delivery, information and risk management. The chapter covers IT infrastructure and decentralization in the Indian context, highlighting the paradigm shift and opportunities for financial institutions. Decentralizing IT can bring innovation, transformation, and customer agility, making traditional banking a competitor in the race. The chapter highlights the past, present, and future of IT decentralization in the Indian banking industry, emphasizing the role of new technologies like AI, blockchain in automation, integration, and global financial sector growth.

The millennial focus has shifted from mere consumption to sustainable consumption. Responsible and ethical buying is the primary focus. Millennial consumers are highly concerned about issues like environmental degradation and climatic changes and are ready to contribute to good causes. They are becoming more risk-averse and prefer to support businesses that emphasize pro-social messaging, environmentally friendly production, and moral business practices. The target consumer's perception of influencer marketing buzzwords like authenticity, credibility, and consumer involvement can be perceived as evolving. Influencers also power their voices to promote changes for good environmental causes. The study enlightens the development of the urge for ethical/sustainable buying to adopt moral influencer content as a basis to follow them and facilitate the consumer buying process. The people associated with the domain as influencers or aspiring to be one should focus on ethical influencing. The growing ethical consumerism is playing a vital role in behavioral adoption of ethical influencers.

Chapter 14
Determinants of Customer Analytics Capabilities: A Model to Achieve Sustainable Firm Performance 217
Meenal Arora, Chitkara Business School, Chitkara University, India
Amit Mittal, Chitkara Business School, Chitkara University, India
Anshika Prakash, School of Management and Commerce, K.R. Mangalam University, Gurugram, India
Vishal Jain, School of Engineering and Technology, Sharda University, India

Customer analytics is essential for creating insights from massive data that can be used to enhance management decision-making at various consumer levels, product creation, and service innovation. However, no studies have examined the potential of consumer analytics for achieving long-term corporate success. This research examines the structures of customer analytics capabilities in order to fill this gap by drawing upon a rigorous assessment of the big data literature. The interpretative framework for this study shows the concept of customer analytics, its significance, and the building blocks for consumer analytics capabilities. The research suggests a model of consumer analytics capabilities made up of four main constructs and some significant supporting sub-constructs. The study elaborates on developing a model to analyze sustainable firm performance through dimensions of customer analytics capabilities.

Chapter 15
Cyber Security in the Cloud: Harnessing the Power of Machine Learning and Cloud Cryptography231
Nahida Majeed Wani, Department of Mathematics, Amity University, Gwalior, India
Ajay Verma, School of Applied Sciences and Languages, VIT Bhopal University, India

In an era defined by digital interconnectivity, securing information in the cloud is paramount. By harnessing the power of present advanced technologies, organizations can fortify their defenses against evolving cyber threats while simultaneously embracing environmentally conscious practices. The model begins by integrating machine learning (ML) algorithms into fabric of cyber security. Anomaly detection, threat prediction, and adaptive response mechanisms enable a proactive defense, continually evolving to thwart emerging threats. Beyond the realm of cyber security efficacy, ML optimizes resource utilization, contributing to the sustainability of cloud operations. Complementing this adaptive intelligence, cloud cryptography emerges as a cornerstone for securing data at rest and in transit. From traditional encryption to quantum-resistant cryptographic techniques, the model ensures confidentiality and integrity of information. Sustainable cryptographic practices, coupled with efficient key management, further mitigate the environmental impact associated with cryptographic operations.

In an ever-evolving global landscape, the need for strategic foresight and innovative approaches to address contemporary challenges has never been more essential. This chapter delves into the profound transformations taking place in today's international relations and geopolitical dynamics. This comprehensive analysis examines the driving factors and practical implications of this reinvention, encompassing technological advancements such as Industry 4.0, blockchain, and cybersecurity. Furthermore, the exploration of governance models, including collaborative and participatory systems, highlights the means for states and non-state actors to engage in proactive dialogue and collective problem-solving. By dissecting the intricate links between digital sovereignty and data privacy, this chapter underscores the pivotal role of equitable access to resources and the protection of individual rights in a hyperconnected world.

This chapter intends to inform about the artificial intelligence intervention for enhancing the marketing of products as India is climbing new heights through the "Digital India" movement. Technologies lessen the market gaps globally. There are numerous domains where the digital arm can prove to be efficient. Online shopping and online educational facilities already proved to be sustained during the COVID-19 pandemic. The chapter discusses one of the segments of society among many segments that suffered during the pandemic: women's self-help groups. As a traditional means, women's self-help groups used to sell their products using exhibitions, but the pandemic and frequent lockdowns hampered the marketing strategy of such self-help groups. Digitalization can reach the smallest need, and research can provide need-based directions for application development. This chapter discusses how artificial intelligence can give wings to such women's self-help groups for marketing and market predictions.

Preface

As editors of *Driving Decentralization and Disruption With Digital Technologies*, we find ourselves at the forefront of a transformative era in human history. The past few years have witnessed a seismic shift propelled by the digital revolution, fundamentally altering the landscape of governance, commerce, and communication. In this edited reference book, we embark on a journey to explore the multifaceted impacts, challenges, and opportunities that arise from this unprecedented wave of change.

Edited by Balraj Verma, Babita Singla, and Amit Mittal, the book delves into the disruptive forces reshaping our world. It confronts the reality of power consolidation within large corporations, the erosion of privacy, and the exploitation of personal data – all consequences of the digital age. However, our narrative doesn't dwell solely on challenges; it illuminates a compelling path forward.

We argue that the same digital revolution that engenders centralization and globalization also holds the key to their antidotes: decentralization and de-globalization. Through the lens of decentralized technologies like blockchain and peer-to-peer networks, we advocate for a more democratic, equitable, and sustainable future. This book is a manifesto for shifting power dynamics from centralized institutions to individuals and communities, fostering innovation, reducing inequality, promoting social justice, and advancing the well-being of our planet.

Our exploration encompasses the vast landscape of the digital revolution's impact on society. From the catalyzation of decentralization and de-globalization to the transformative roles played by blockchain and decentralized finance (DeFi), we dissect the forces reshaping finance and empowering local communities. We scrutinize the effects of digital platforms on intermediaries, unraveling consequences for supply chains and global commerce.

Digital identity and data sovereignty complexities take center stage as we address personal data concerns and champion the cause of decentralized identification systems. Ethical considerations form a critical part of our analysis, delving into algorithmic bias, privacy issues, and advocating for digital inclusivity.

This reference book is designed for a diverse audience, including academic researchers, undergraduate and postgraduate students, MBA and executive education participants, practitioners, and technology industry professionals. Whether you're delving into the drivers and impacts of digital disruption, exploring blockchain-based platforms, or examining the rise of e-commerce and the decline of traditional manufacturing, our comprehensive coverage ensures relevance for all.

As we navigate through the intricacies of industry impacts, new forms of labor and production, digital privacy concerns, security risks, decentralized solutions, and their impact on social justice, we also address pressing issues like the concentration of wealth and power, job displacement, and the digital divide.

The book culminates in a discussion of policy solutions, emerging trends, technological advancements, and risk mitigation strategies. In essence, "Driving Decentralization and Disruption with Digital

Technologies" is a roadmap for understanding and navigating the complexities of our evolving digital landscape. Join us on this intellectual journey as we unravel the transformative potential of the digital revolution and shape the future of a decentralized world.

ORGANIZATION OF THE BOOK

Chapter 1: Digital Progress and Information Society – Evidence From EU Countries and Serbia

Ivana Domazet and Darko Marjanović provide a comprehensive exploration of the information society's development in EU countries, emphasizing digital progress and its impact on Serbia's economy. Using the Digital Economy and Society Index (DESI), the chapter unveils the advancements made in the digital space across EU Member States, highlighting the persistent challenges in digital skills, SMEs' transformation, and 5G network deployment. The findings extend to the moderate progress in Serbia's information society, covering areas such as electronic communications, modern electronic services, information security, eGovernment, and eCommerce.

Chapter 2: Blockchain Technology in Peer-to-Peer Transactions Emphasizing Data Transparency and Security in Banking Services

Authored by Isha Nag and Sridhar Manohar, this chapter focuses on the imperative need for decentralized financing in the banking sector. The authors discuss the limitations of traditional banking systems, emphasizing fraudulent operations and unauthorized access. Through the lens of blockchain technology, the chapter explores the mechanics of decentralized banking systems, presents case studies, and envisions the transformation of the banking sector.

Chapter 3: Fashion-Tech Disruption – The Ft. You Case Study

Sahithi Josyula, Birud Sindhav, Dale Eesley, and Shana Redd present a case study on the Hyderabad-based fashion-tech startup Ft.you. This chapter bridges the gap between conceptual research and practical disruption in the fashion business. The case explores Ft.you's innovative application, which allows users to customize dresses within an app, addressing challenges in tailoring services. It also delves into partnerships, marketing strategies, and key decision points in Ft.you's journey.

Chapter 4: Ensuring Robust and Secure Supply Chain Deploying Blockchain

Nishant Kumar, Pratibha Garg, Kamal Upreti, Sambhajiraje Patil, Amol Ohol, and Malleshappa Bhagawati delve into the critical aspects of retail supply chain, emphasizing transparency, visibility, and security. The chapter highlights the challenges faced by the global supply chain and proposes blockchain as a transformative tool. By providing evidence for product authenticity, tracking details, and enhancing customer experience, the authors advocate for the application of blockchain in reshaping the retail supply chain.

Chapter 5: Digital Footprints and the Battle for Data Sovereignty

Authored by Ishani Sharma and Arun Aggarwal, this chapter investigates digital security and data ownership concerns in the age of digitization. The authors explore the cyber threatscape, emphasizing encryption and two-factor authentication. The chapter calls for a "digital bill of rights" to address data ownership issues and advocates for balancing digital advancement with individual rights for a secure digital future.

Chapter 6: Traversing Technological Vistas in Decentralized Finance – A Bibliometric Approach

Divya Goswami and Balraj Verma provide an introduction to Decentralized Finance (DeFi) and its potential impact on conventional financial systems. The chapter analyzes the current state of research on Decentralized Autonomous Organizations (DAOs) and examines the performance of prominent DeFi projects. The authors discuss policy implications and highlight the challenges and opportunities associated with decentralization in finance.

Chapter 7: The Digital Shift – Unleashing Potential, Reimagining Power Dynamics

Umesh Chawla explores the impact of technologies such as blockchain, AI, and IoT on decentralization. The chapter dissects their transformative influence on power structures, economic paradigms, and global interactions. It covers the disruption of traditional finance by blockchain, the enhanced security and governance facilitated by the intersection of AI and blockchain, and the transformative role of IoT in industries. The chapter concludes with a call for collective wisdom and ethical stewardship to shape a decentralized future.

Chapter 8: Multinational Enterprises' Digital Transformation, Sustainability, and Purpose

Aarti, Swathi Gowroju, and Saurabh Karling examine the challenges faced by multinational corporations (MNEs) due to pandemics, environmental disasters, and the digital revolution. The chapter discusses how changing investor and consumer expectations are reshaping the definition of value creation and impacting company strategies. The authors argue for a purpose-driven approach for MNEs to navigate the complexities of the evolving global landscape.

Chapter 9: What Do We Know About Artificial Intelligence and Blockchain Technology Integration in the Healthcare Industry?

Sumit Oberoi, Sugandh Arora, Balraj Verma, and Krishna Kanta Roy conduct a bibliometric-content analysis to identify the publication productivity and intellectual structure of artificial intelligence and blockchain technology integration in the healthcare industry. The chapter highlights emerging themes such as "smart healthcare," "patient-centric," and "decentralization," providing an overview of current and future research streams in this domain.

Chapter 10: Future of Banking From IT Decentralization and Deglobalisation

Vijaya G. S., Divya Prabhu, Sandhya M., and Jehad Aldehayyat explore the transformation of the banking sector through IT decentralization and deglobalization. The chapter examines the paradigm shift in the Indian context, emphasizing opportunities for financial institutions. It discusses the role of new technologies like AI and blockchain in automating processes, integrating operations, and contributing to global financial sector growth.

Chapter 11: Ethical and Social Consequences of Accelerated Technology Adoption

Poornima Jirli and Anuja Shukla investigate the ethical and social consequences of rapidly adopting new technologies. Using empirical methods, the chapter explores the impacts of technological integration on societal norms, ethical considerations, and individual behaviors. The findings offer critical insights for policymakers, technology developers, and society at large, emphasizing the need for an ethically informed and socially conscious approach to technology adoption.

Chapter 12: The Issues and Challenges Faced by Faculty Members for Using Information Communication Technology

This chapter examines the challenges encountered by faculty members in integrating Information Communication Technology (ICT) into education. It delves into both moral and legal dimensions, shedding light on the multifaceted challenges that educators and learners must navigate in the dynamic digital classroom environment. Recognizing the increasing importance of incorporating modern technology in education, the discourse emphasizes the need for educators and students to possess a foundational understanding of the challenges associated with ICT use. The manuscript contends that individuals, regardless of their roles, should be equipped to navigate these challenges effectively. The chapter highlights significant opportunities for collaboration between teachers and students in the digital realm enabled by the integration of ICT into educational programs. However, it also acknowledges obstacles that may hinder teachers from embracing ICT and incorporating supplementary materials in the classroom. By scrutinizing these challenges, the chapter aims to provide insights that empower educators to seamlessly integrate technology into routine instruction, fostering a more technologically adept educational landscape.

Chapter 13: Influencer Marketing – Way to a Sustainable Marketing Approach

Focusing on the shift in millennial consumer behavior towards sustainable consumption, this chapter explores the landscape of influencer marketing as a pathway to a sustainable marketing approach. With a growing emphasis on responsible and ethical buying, millennial consumers prioritize issues like environmental degradation and climatic changes. The chapter delves into the consumer perception of influencer marketing buzzwords such as authenticity, credibility, and consumer involvement. It highlights how influencers leverage their voices to promote positive environmental causes and discusses the development of an urge for ethical and sustainable buying. The study emphasizes the role of ethical influencers in facilitating the consumer buying process, shedding light on the evolving landscape of ethical consumerism and its impact on behavioral adoption. As the chapter unfolds, it encourages those in the domain, influencers, or aspiring ones, to focus on ethical influencing in alignment with the growing trend of ethical consumerism.

Chapter 14: Determinants of Customer Analytics Capabilities

Meenal Arora, Amit Mittal, and Anshika Prakash focus on customer analytics as a crucial element for enhancing management decision-making in various aspects of business. The chapter presents a model of consumer analytics capabilities, highlighting its significance and building blocks. The research suggests that sustainable firm performance can be achieved through effective consumer analytics capabilities.

Chapter 15: Cybersecurity in the Cloud Harnessing the Power of Machine Learning and Cloud Cryptography

Nahida Wani and Ajay Verma address the paramount importance of securing information in the cloud in the digital era. The chapter integrates machine learning (ML) algorithms into cybersecurity, enabling proactive defense against evolving cyber threats. Cloud cryptography emerges as a cornerstone for securing data at rest and in transit, with a focus on sustainability through efficient key management and environmental impact mitigation.

Chapter 16: Reinventing the Global Order – Decentralization, Digital Sovereignty, and Empowered Supply Chains

Anuj Modgil and Marshall B delve into the profound transformations occurring in international relations and geopolitical dynamics. The chapter examines the driving factors and practical implications of reinventing the global order, encompassing technological advancements such as Industry 4.0, blockchain, and cybersecurity. It explores governance models, including collaborative and participatory systems, emphasizing equitable access to resources and the protection of individual rights.

Chapter 17: Potential of Digitalization for the Utilization of Artificial Intelligence Model for Uplifting Traditional Marketing Method – A New Sustainable Growth

This chapter unfolds a narrative on the intervention of artificial intelligence in enhancing product marketing, particularly in the context of India's "DIGITAL INDIA" movement. With technology bridging global market gaps, the chapter explores various domains where digitalization can prove efficient. It highlights the resilience of online shopping and educational facilities during the Covid-19 pandemic and addresses a segment that faced challenges: women's self-help groups. Traditionally relying on exhibitions for product sales, these groups encountered setbacks during lockdowns. The chapter delves into how digitalization, powered by artificial intelligence, can empower women's self-help groups in marketing and market predictions. By reaching the smallest needs, the research aims to provide need-based directions for application development, showcasing the potential of AI in fostering sustainable growth.

IN SUMMARY

As we draw the curtains on this comprehensive exploration, *Driving Decentralization and Disruption With Digital Technologies*, it is evident that the digital revolution is not merely a wave of change; it is a seismic shift reshaping the very fabric of our societies, economies, and interactions. Authored by a diverse group of experts, each chapter offers a unique lens through which to understand the multifaceted impacts, challenges, and opportunities embedded in digital transformation.

From the macro perspective of the EU countries' digital progress to the microcosm of a fashion-tech startup in Hyderabad, the book traverses technological vistas, financial landscapes, and ethical considerations. The chapters unveil a tapestry of disruptions: blockchain redefining banking, decentralized finance challenging traditional financial systems, and AI and blockchain integrating into healthcare. We journey through the intricacies of supply chain transparency, the battle for data sovereignty, and the reinvention of the global order through decentralization.

The collective wisdom shared by our esteemed contributors transcends disciplinary boundaries, providing a holistic view of the digital revolution's impact on various sectors. Whether it's the challenges faced by multinational enterprises, the future of banking in IT decentralization, or the ethical and social consequences of accelerated technology adoption, each chapter contributes to our understanding of the complex interplay between technology, society, and governance.

As editors, our goal was to curate a collection that not only captures the current state of affairs but also serves as a roadmap for navigating the uncharted territories that lie ahead. We believe that this edited reference book serves as a valuable resource for academics, students, practitioners, and technology professionals alike. It is a testament to the collaborative efforts of the authors who have dedicated their expertise to dissecting the digital revolution's nuances and implications.

The chapters not only diagnose the challenges but also prescribe solutions, advocating for a more democratic, equitable, and sustainable future. Whether it's the call for a "digital bill of rights" to safeguard individual data or the exploration of decentralized technologies to empower local communities, our contributors pave the way for a responsible and ethical integration of digital advancements into our societies.

In this dynamic digital epoch, we conclude with a call for collective wisdom, ethical stewardship, and proactive governance. As we stand at the intersection of technological advancements, societal transformations, and geopolitical shifts, the choices we make today will shape the decentralized future we envision. *Driving Decentralization and Disruption With Digital Technologies* is not just a book; it is an invitation to engage in the ongoing conversation about our digital destiny. We thank our contributors for their invaluable insights, and we look forward to the continued dialogue and exploration of the ever-evolving landscape of digital possibilities.

Balraj Verma
Chitkara Business School, Chitkara University, India

Babita Singla
Chitkara Business School, Chitkara University, India

Amit Mittal
Chitkara Business School, Chitkara University, India

Chapter 1
Digital Progress and Information Society:
Evidence From EU Countries and Serbia

Ivana Domazet
https://orcid.org/0000-0002-3493-4616
Institute of Economic Sciences, Belgrade, Serbia

Darko Marjanović
Institute of Economic Sciences, Belgrade, Serbia

ABSTRACT

The chapter aims to show the development of the information society in the EU countries, its digital progress, and its repercussions on the economy of Serbia as a country that is a candidate for EU membership. The methodological concept and the analysis are based on the Digital Economy and Society Index (DESI), an official report of the European Commission. The DESI 2022 reports track the advancements made in the digital space in EU Member States and are primarily based on 2021 data. The findings of the study revealed that although Member States made progress in their efforts to go digital during the COVID-19 timeframe, they are still unable to address the gaps in digital skills, transform SMEs into digital businesses, or put out cutting-edge 5G networks. Also, the results show moderate progress in the development of the information society in Serbia in terms of the functioning of the internal market for electronic communications, the availability of modern electronic services, the development of information security, and the application of eGovernment and eCommerce.

INTRODUCTION

Digital transformation and digital progress are closely intertwined concepts that represent the evolution, integration, and optimization of digital technologies, processes, and strategies within various sectors of society, business, and governance. Digital progress is the collective result of continuous advancements, innovations, and the integration of digital technologies across multiple domains. As digital transformation

DOI: 10.4018/979-8-3693-3253-5.ch001

occurs within sectors or organizations, it contributes to the overall digital progress of a region, industry, or society. Digital transformation initiatives undertaken by organizations, governments, and societies contribute to the larger picture of digital progress by driving technological advancements, enhancing capabilities, and improving services and experiences for individuals and businesses. Both concepts are integral in the current digital era, as they represent the ongoing efforts to leverage technology, innovation, and digital tools to enhance efficiency, create new opportunities, and address societal challenges. Digital transformation drives the changes in specific entities or sectors, while digital progress reflects the collective advancements and developments in the broader digital landscape, impacting societies, economies, and governance structures. An information society thrives on technological advancement, access to information, and the ability to adapt to and utilize digital technologies effectively. Digital transformation and progress are integral to achieving a more connected, efficient, and inclusive information society.

The emergence of cutting-edge digital technologies, the information space's revolution, and the speeding up of processes leading to economic globalization can all be used to identify the beginning of the twenty-first century. Digital technologies encompass a wide range of technologies and systems that use digital data and information in electronic form for various purposes. These technologies leverage digital signals or representations of data, often in the form of binary code (0s and 1s), to process, store, transmit, and manipulate information. Digital technologies have had a profound impact on various aspects of modern life, including communication, business, entertainment, education, healthcare, and more. The new economy of the twenty-first century is the digital global economic economy that runs on information technology, whereas the new society of the twenty-first century can be seen as a continuously evolving information society (Česnauskė, 2019). The advancement of information technology nowadays has a significant impact on both society and the economy. While information technology widens the spectrum of potential for all people, organizations, and states, a person and society constantly work to meet the expanding demands in one or more fields of endeavor. The rapid digital transformation of society, the economy, and the government is based on technology. The established order is altered by the digital transformation, which introduces new communication channels and methods as well as advances in company operations and state governance that take advantage of the new technologies' opportunities (Domazet et. al, 2023).

Technology drives today's world, and drives civilization forward; thanks to it, new, innovative solutions are constantly being created to optimize production processes and offer services in all sectors of the economy. One of the key factors in the development of the modern economy is digitalization. Digitization as a process is not just an addition to existing business processes but a complete change in the organizational structure and culture, i.e., the company's way of thinking. The key factor for the development of the digital economy is certainly the implementation and development of modern ICT solutions (Domazet, Zubović, Lazić, 2019). The application of digital technologies enables all companies, including small and medium-sized enterprises, to serve a large number of consumers in a cost-effective way, which has a direct impact on the growth of competitiveness of the observed economy.

Digital transformation refers to the process that begins the moment the company starts thinking about adopting digital technologies in all areas of business and continues until these technologies are fully integrated. The digital transformation of the EU economy and society harbors great growth potential for Europe as a whole. European industry can build on the benefits of connecting member states in the field of advanced digital technologies to capitalize on the many opportunities these technologies offer. At the same time, it is about reorganizing/improving business processes and business survival with the help of all available digital tools and technologies. All this is achieved with knowledge and skills that enable successful business management in a modern digital environment. It is a continuous process that is not always easy, but without it, doing business in today's world is no longer possible. Success in the market is reflected in the integration of digital transformation into the business strategy of any organization.

In the digital economy, information is becoming a fundamental resource that significantly impacts the value of companies with a digitally transformed business model. This value of information enables globalization and automation processes, and the marketing of products or services is no longer dependent on large investments. This creates the conditions for the emergence of more and more small companies that successfully compete with much larger and better-known competitors on the market with various innovative ideas and approaches. Physical distance is also no longer such an important parameter in business life, which further facilitates the marketing of products or services outside the borders of the domestic market.

The term "digital economy" refers to an economy built on digital technologies and the predominance of telecommunications, information technology, hardware, and software in all facets of the economy. The digital economy calls for a shift in perspective, moving away from the traditional state-centric development models and toward dynamic models based on continual improvement. Making the economy more competitive is one of the biggest challenges facing policymakers. There is no one-size-fits-all answer to this issue, but there are several areas where the adoption of various opportunities provided by the digital economy can significantly boost the efficacy and efficiency of the economy. Information and communication technology (ICT) is a key component in the growth of the digital economy. ICT not only has the potential to significantly increase each nation's competitiveness and shift production toward contemporary business processes, but it can also have a significant synergistic impact on micro-enterprises competitiveness.

The aim of this chapter is to determine the level of development of the information society and the digital progress of countries. The desk research is based on officially available secondary data, i.e. reports published by the European Commission. In this context, the Digital Economy and Society Index (DESI) was used for the analysis to show the digital progress of the analyzed countries. The research structure of this chapter is divided into two parts: The first part focuses on the European Union countries, while the second part focuses on Serbia as a country that is a candidate for EU membership.

BACKGROUND

Digital transformation is referred to as a process of change that involves implementing digital technology or creating new digital business models that maximize value for an organization (Fitzgerald et al., 2013; Kane et al., 2015; Verhoef et al., 2021). According to Vial (2019), digital transformation is a process that causes strategic and operational changes in businesses as a result of the advantages and disadvantages brought on by digital technologies. Other authors (Bresciani et al., 2021; Kraus et al., 2021; Westerman et al., 2011) focused on how digital transformation relates to the adoption of cutting-edge technology by agile businesses with the goal of dramatically enhancing their performance and broadening their horizons. Processes for digital transformation are necessary to keep ahead of technical innovation and to remain competitive in the market (Domazet et al., 2021). Although the adoption of digital technologies and the digitalization of organizations are naturally linked to the changes brought on by digital transformation (Verhoef et al., 2021), its implications are not solely focused on this aspect (Tabrizi et al., 2019; Vial, 2019). Companies may increase their flexibility and efficiency through digital transformation, improve their manufacturing processes, create value propositions for innovation ecosystems, and quickly adapt to market demands (Queiroz et al., 2020; Chen et al., 2018; Dedehayir et al., 2017).

Businesses all around the world are being totally redefined by digital transformation. To stay competitive in their respective marketplaces, established businesses from all sectors and in all shapes and sizes are urged to adapt their business models by typically utilizing digital technologies (D'Ippolito et al., 2019; Subramaniam & Piskorski, 2020; Kraus et al., 2021; Verhoef et al., 2021). Small and medium-sized businesses (SMEs) can successfully explore prospects in overseas markets, including those in emerging and developed nations, thanks to digital transformation (Bertello et al., 2021). Entry barriers have been lowered in many nations due to the development of digital technology, current trends toward globalization, and the opening of international boundaries, allowing new entrants into a market that is already very competitive on a global scale (Gefen & Carmel, 2008; Marjanović & Domazet, 2021). Business model innovation and digital transformation interact clearly, with digital transformation encouraging the reformulation and industry-specific adaptation of enterprises' business models (D'Ippolito et al., 2019). Operational and strategic digital transformation can be distinguished based on their applications. Operational digital transformation initiatives often focus on integrating digital technologies into systems and processes to achieve operational excellence (Sebastian et al., 2017; Warner and Wager, 2019). In order to add value, strategic digital transformation operations alter a wider range of organizational components, such as business models, organizational cultures, collaborative approaches, procedures, and systems (Kane et al., 2015; Cennamo et al., 2020; Gurbaxani and Dunkle, 2019; Loonam et al., 2018; Singh and Hess, 2017; Verhoef et al., 2021). The relevance and significance of digital transformation processes grow yearly, and this trend will likely continue in the near future depending on the influence of external factors (Poduyeva & Nechushkina, 2022; Domazet et al. 2023).

Digitalization is a contemporary worldwide economic and social development tendency that improves both the economy's efficacy and quality of life (Khalin & Chernova, 2018). A number of changes are brought about by the digitisation process and the use of new technologies in businesses, and these changes call for new managerial skills and approaches to human resource management (Sousa & Rocha, 2019; Bresciani et al., 2021; Simović & Domazet 2021). Businesses have undergone a change thanks to digital platforms, which have also given entrepreneurs a wealth of opportunities (Nambisan et al., 2019; Sturgeon, 2021; Bouncken & Barwinski, 2021). Global economic, financial, and social linkages are growing through digital platforms because of the expansion of data and information related to digital globalization (Schilirò, 2020).

Internationalization can be seen as an entrepreneurial opportunity that businesses may recognize and take advantage of since it offers the ability to introduce new products, services, or organizational methods to a market (Wood and McKinley, 2020). For SMEs, internationalization offers chances to increase sales and, if done properly, can lead to better business performance (Schwens et al., 2018). The most recent changes in technology and globalization have resulted in a dramatic increase in different regulatory functions, which strengthens the focus and importance of state industrial policy. Despite the disparities in their institutional makeup, the fourth industrial revolution, globalization, and human capital are thought to be the main forces behind today's economic growth (Romanova & Kuzmin, 2021; Marjanović & Domazet, 2023). Information and communication technology is one of the key factors enabling economic growth in the economy (Domazet et al., 2022a). According to the research's findings (Aristovnik, 2014), Eastern and Southern Europe in particular exhibits a rather low-efficiency rate when it comes to converting the advancement of the information society into educational outputs or outcomes.

Innovative technology can help accomplish the Sustainable Development Goals (SDGs) more quickly and successfully. Disparities in access to the usage of innovative solutions (including social innovation) and persistent, considerable wealth gaps between emerging and highly industrialized nations must be eliminated (Wysokińska, 2021). Businesses may use a variety of digital technologies to create the framework for quick product offering adaptation, ongoing cost reduction, as well as an increase and reinforcement of operational efficiency (Lanzolla et al., 2021; Mabey and Zhao, 2017). Due to their decreased communication and transaction costs, digital technologies have shown to have a significant impact on global learning and networking (Alcacer et al., 2016).

The ability to add value by utilizing the opportunities provided by information technology is what is meant by the term "digital economy" (Domazet et al., 2022). Information technology is increasingly determining a country's position in the world and luring investment from nations where such opportunities do not exist or do not exist in significant numbers (Marjanović et al., 2022). The digital economy fosters competition both domestically and internationally. As a result, any nation that wants to compete on the global market must effectively harness the potential of the digital economy and encourage technological advancement (Česnauskė, 2019).

RESEARCH METHODOLOGY AND OBJECTIVES

Digitization in the European Union (EU) is a multifaceted and comprehensive effort aimed at leveraging digital technologies to drive economic growth, enhance public services, and promote innovation and competitiveness within the region. The EU has set ambitious goals and strategies to foster digitization in various sectors. Digitization is a central theme in the EU's broader agenda to strengthen the region's global competitiveness, enhance the well-being of its citizens, and address emerging challenges. It reflects a commitment to harness the benefits of digital technologies while addressing the legal, ethical, and regulatory aspects that come with a digitalized society. EU policies and initiatives in digitization are designed to ensure a harmonized and forward-looking approach to the digital transformation of the European economy and society.

Digitization, a global economic and social movement, has varying effects on various nations. Indicators that measure digitalization are used to evaluate the level of digitization in any nation. Since 2014, the European Commission has tracked Member States' digital development and released yearly Digital Economy and Society Index (DESI) reports. The reports comprise thematic chapters that offer an EU-level analysis in the major digital policy areas as well as country profiles that assist Member States in identifying areas for priority action.

The main objective of this chapter is to determine digital progress, i.e. the development of the information society in the EU countries. In addition, the digital progress of Serbia is analyzed, as ICT, innovation, and digitalization are one of the main drivers of the Serbian economy. The desk research is based on officially available secondary data - reports (Digital Economy and Society Index - DESI) published by the European Commission for the period 2021-2022.

As shown in the Table 1 below, the DESI is a composite index that uses four components to measure advancement in digital performance (human capital, connectivity, integration of digital technology and digital public services), and includes a three-level structure. Based on this, we decided to use DESI in our study, considering that this index is a complex index that sums up relevant indicators of digital performance and follows the development of EU countries in digital competitiveness. It offers insight

Table 1. DESI structure

Dimension	Sub-Dimension	Indicator
Human capital	Internet user skills	At least basic digital skills; above basic digital skills; at least basic digital content creation skills
	Advanced skills and development	ICT specialists; Female ICT specialists; Enterprises providing ICT training; ICT graduates
Connectivity	Fixed broadband take-up	Overall fixed broadband take-up; At least 100 Mbps fixed broadband take-up; At least 1 Gbps take-up
	Fixed broadband coverage	Fast broadband (NGA) coverage; Fixed Very High Capacity Network (VHCN) coverage
	Mobile broadband	5G spectrum; 5G coverage; Mobile broadband take-up
	Broadband prices	Broadband price index
Integration of digital technology	Digital intensity	SMEs with at least a basic level of digital intensity
	Digital technologies for businesses	Electronic information sharing; Social media; Big data; Cloud; AI; ICT for environmental sustainability; e-Invoices
	e-Commerce	SMEs selling online; e-Commerce turnover; Selling online cross-border
Digital public services	ze-Government	e-Government users; Pre-filled forms; Digital public services for citizens; Digital public services for businesses; Open data

Source: European Commission (2022)

into the general performance of a country and makes it possible for the simple identification of areas in which it can be improved.

This chapter is divided into two parts:

1. Digital progress and the development of the information society in the countries of the European Union,
2. Digital progress and the development of the information society in Serbia.

Following a defined methodology and objectives, this chapter focuses on presenting the state of the EU economies in terms of their digital progress, as well as analyzing and detailing the digital performance of the Serbian economy, reflecting its competitiveness compared to the economies in its immediate vicinity.

Digital Progress and Development of the Information Society in the Countries of the European Union

The European Union (EU) has been actively promoting the progress and development of the information society among its member states. This effort is reflected in various initiatives, policies, and programs aimed at fostering digital transformation and ensuring that all EU countries benefit from the opportunities presented by the digital age. Digital progress and development refer to the advancements and improvements in digital technologies, digital infrastructure, and the integration of digital solutions in various aspects of society, the economy, and governance. It encompasses the growth and evolution of the digital ecosystem, including internet connectivity, digital skills, innovation in digital technologies, and the overall digital transformation of various sectors. Some key aspects of digital progress and the development of the information society in EU member states: (1) Digital Single Market (DSM), (2)

Connectivity, (3) Digital Skills and Education, (4) Research and Innovation, (5) eGovernment, (6) Data Protection, (7) Digital Health (eHealth), (8) Digital Economy and Society Index (DESI), (9) Artificial Intelligence (AI), (10) Blockchain and Cryptocurrencies, (11) Digital Cultural Heritage, (12) Smart Cities and (13) Cross-Border Data Flow.

Since 2014, the European Commission has tracked member states' progress in the digital sphere and has released yearly reports on the DESI. The study includes theme chapters that provide analysis at the EU level in significant areas of digital policy as well as national profiles, which are useful to member states in identifying areas that require priority actions. To represent the two key political initiatives that will affect the EU's digital transformation in the upcoming years—assistance for recovery and resilience, and the Digital Decade Compass—the EC adopted a new methodology for calculating DESI in 2021. The Commission made various revisions to the DESI 2021 edition in order to better methodology that would take into account the most recent political and technological developments, align DESI in four primary areas, and with the aims inside the Digital Compass. Eleven DESI 2021 indicators are used in Digital Compass to measure the objectives set forth in the primary four areas, replacing the old five-dimensional structure. To make sure that these objectives are covered in regular reports, DESI will be even more closely integrated with Digital Compass in the future. The DESI now adds a measure of how much help ICT-adopted enterprises provide for adopting eco-friendly practices (ICT for eco-sustainability) and employing gigabit services, in addition to the percentage of businesses that provide training and use ICT e-invoicing. For all nations, the DESI rankings from prior years have been revised to account for changes in the selection of new indicators and data corrections.

Figure 1 depicts how Member States have fared over the past five years in terms of the general degree of digitalization of their economies and societies. The figure displays the relationship between each nation's DESI 2017 scores (horizontal axis) and the DESI average annual growth between 2017 and 2022 (vertical axis). Like the conventional theory of economic growth, countries with lower initial digital development levels exhibit overall convergence when their growth rates accelerate (left side of the figure). Between 2017 and 2022, the EU will obviously exhibit a convergence pattern, according to DESI scores. The estimated pattern of convergence is represented by the blue line in the figure. The

Figure 1. Member States' relative progress (DESI) for the years 2017–2022
Source: EC (2022)

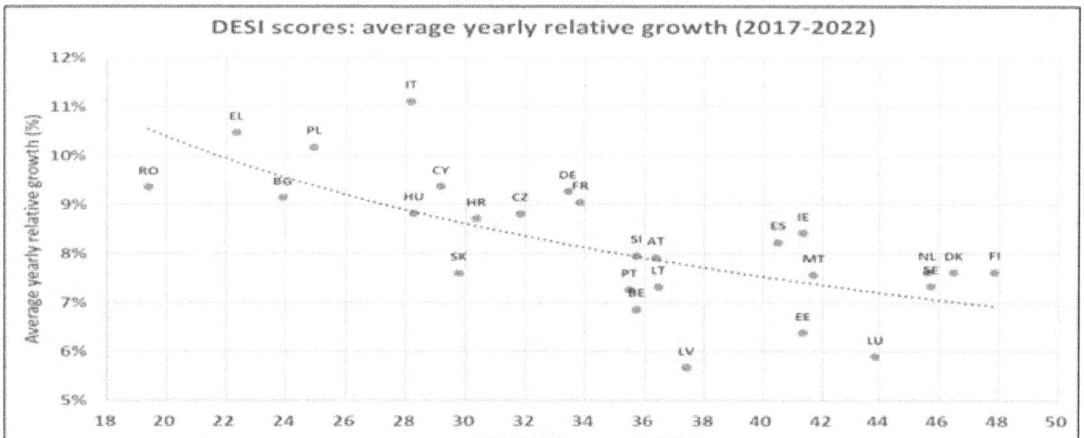

convergence curve predicted less growth for the nations above the blue line. Hence these nations are 'overperforming.' For the nations below the blue line, the opposite is true.

Denmark, Finland, Sweden, and the Netherlands have the most developed digital economies in the European Union in 2021, while Greece, Bulgaria, and Romania have the least developed economies. The target ranking for Serbia is 21st or higher to move ahead of the bottom 25% of nations and in front of the 7 (25%) EU member states with the lowest rankings. Serbia fall into the same group of nations like Romania, Bulgaria, Greece, Poland, Hungary, Slovakia, Cyprus, Italy, and Croatia that have generally poor performances. Serbia is above the clustered countries' average, according to the target index's value of 44, but still well behind the EU-27 average of 51.

The DESI 2022 reports, which track digital advancements in EU Member States, are primarily based on 2021 data. While Member States have made progress in their digitalization efforts during the COVID-19 timeframe, they are still unable to address the gaps in digital skills, turn SMEs into digital businesses, and put out cutting-edge 5G networks. The Member States' 2022 DESI rating is displayed

Figure 2. Digital Economy and Society Index, 2021
Source: EC (for EU countries) and RATEL (for Serbia)

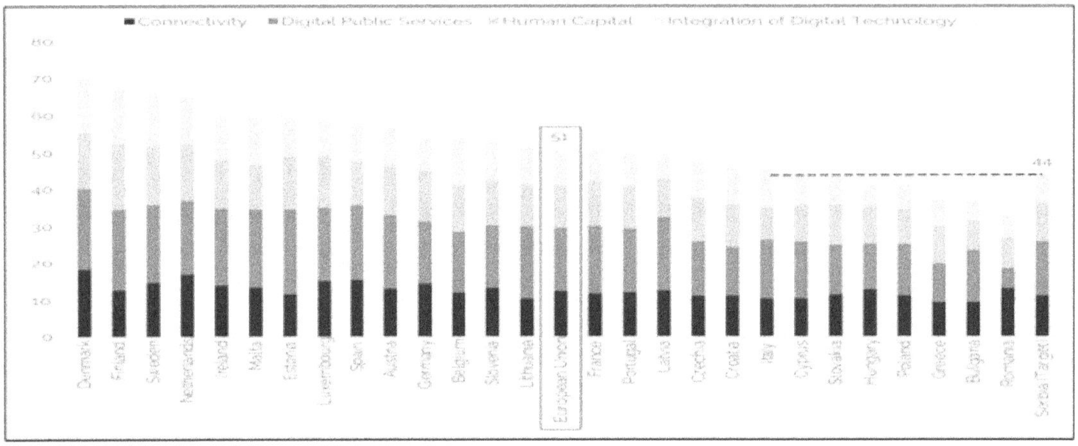

Figure 3. DESI, 2022
Source: EC (2022)

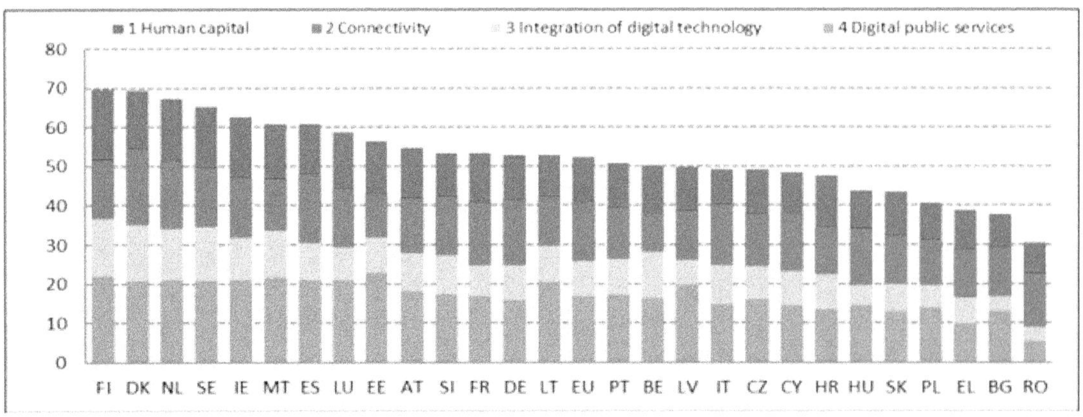

in Figure 3. The EU countries with the most developed digital economies are Finland, Denmark, the Netherlands, and Sweden, followed by Ireland, Malta, and Spain. Greece, Bulgaria, and Romania have the lowest DESI ratings.

Significant resources have been made available by the EU to aid in the digital revolution. Reforms and investments related to digitalization are allocated EUR 127 billion in national Recovery and Resilience Plans. This is a once-in-a-lifetime chance to use investments and reforms to speed up digitalization, strengthen the Union's resilience, and lessen its reliance on outside sources. Over and beyond the mandatory 20% threshold, Member States allocated an average of 26% of their Recovery and Resilience Facility (RRF) funds to the digital transformation. The following Member States have opted to allocate over 30% of their RRF to digital: Austria, Germany, Luxembourg, Ireland, and Lithuania.

Figure 4 displays the average DESI values for each category. Results for Serbia, the group of comparable nations, and the average of the EU-27 are displayed.

Serbia should report a close to average value (41) in category 1 (Human Capital), compared to the average in the group of comparable nations (39) and to demonstrate acceleration toward the average for the EU-27 (47). Serbia should strive to get the average score (45) of the group of comparable nations in category 2 - Connectivity. Serbia ranked near the bottom of the list of European nations in this category. The main cause was the meager 0.9% percentage of Internet subscribers who had at least 100 Mbps. The fact that infrastructure has been developed and 67.4% of homes now have fixed broadband connection at a speed of 100 Mbps or greater gives reason for optimism regarding this index's significant rise.

In comparison to the group of comparable nations, Serbia must keep its average score (30) in category 3—Integration of Digital Technology. For Serbia and the entire EU, there is a ton of space for improvement in this area. In category 4 - Digital Public Services, Serbia performed the worst among EU nations in 2018, according to earlier research. The current target value for this category is 57, which is markedly higher than the group of comparable countries' average (51), but also much lower than the EU average (68). The low values of e-government indicators, which indicate the sophistication of public services accessible on the Internet but also the extremely low amount of online medical service consumption, should be the reason for the earlier lower rank. For the section on open data access, Serbia attained the EU average, in contrast to all the other indicators in this category, where Serbia is below the European average.

Figure 4. Average DESI values and individual categories, 2021
Source: EC (for EU countries) and RATEL (for Serbia), 2022.

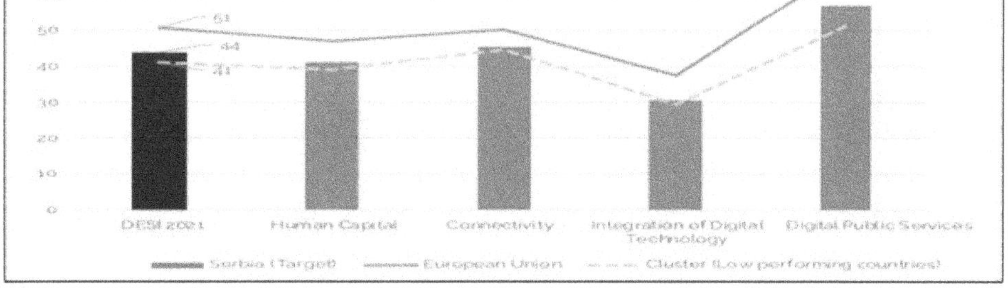

Digital Progress and Development of the Information Society in Serbia

The digitalization process is recognized as an important global trend in the world economy. Digitalization is not only a process of transformation of society and the economy as a whole but also a necessary condition for the survival of companies in the national and global market. The application of modern and innovative technological solutions based on ICT is now one of the fundamental tools for increasing the competitiveness, productivity and efficiency of the economy as a whole. With the fourth industrial revolution, digitalization is becoming the most important catalyst for innovation, modernization, economic growth, competitiveness, and comprehensive socio-economic progress and development. The Government of the Republic of Serbia has recognized the importance of digitalization and the development of e-government, which has led to significant development in this area in recent years. Digitalization, as one of the priorities of the Government of the Republic of Serbia, is changing the way public administration works and increasing its efficiency, transparency, and quality of work.

Although Serbia is not a member of the EU, it is making great strides towards the digitalisation of citizens and the economy and is more advanced than some EU members, especially in the field of e-government. In a survey conducted by the UN agency (Department of Economic and Social Affairs), Serbia is among the top 10 countries in the world in terms of the pace of e-government development. According to the latest published report (United Nations, 2022), it is ranked as a country with a very high EDGI (E-Government Development Index), just behind Belgium and ahead of Russia, the Czech Republic and Croatia. The improved ranking of e-government in Serbia is the result of the commitment to the e-government development programme of the Republic of Serbia 2020-2022 and the successfully implemented action plan for its implementation.

With a total WB (Western Balkans) DESI 2022 score higher than the WB average, Serbia is a digital top performer in the WB area. Serbia does well in every category while considering the WB DESI 2022, with scores higher than the WB averages.

According to the latest global report of the World Bank, which compares the progress of 198 economies in the world in the field of digital transformation, Serbia ranks 11th in the world, i.e. a high fourth place in Europe. In the report, Serbia is in the group "A", i.e. in the group of the world's leading countries in

Figure 5. Serbia's weighted score (0–100) for the WB DESI 2022
Source: EC (2022)

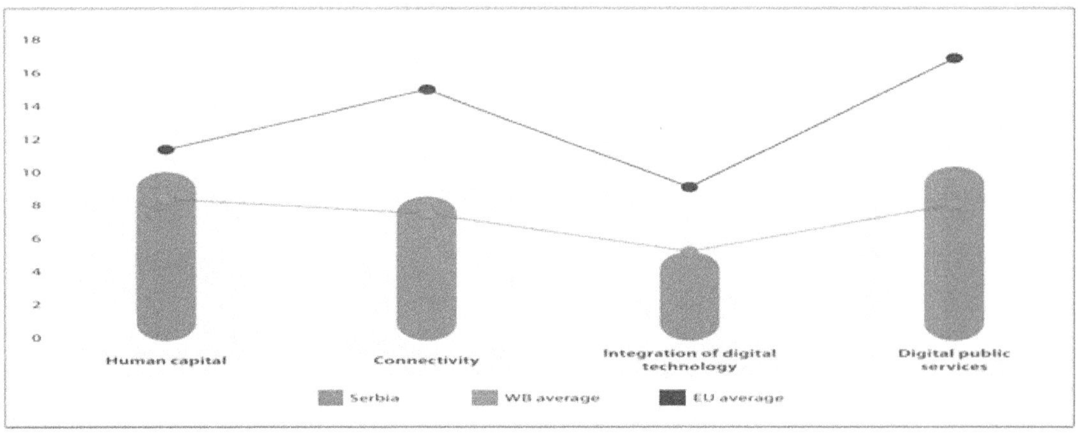

the field of digital transformation, both in terms of the value of the composite index of digital management maturity and in terms of each of the individual indices that assess the extent of the provision of key systems and technical-technological catalysts of digital transformation, the provision of digital services, the adequacy of regulations and policies, the level of digital skills, but also the existence of mechanisms for digital interaction and citizen participation, as well as the existence of other important prerequisites.

Human Capital

Human capital is at the core of a successful strategy to improve long-term inclusion, well-being and productivity. The Human Capital Index consists of two horizontal determinants - education and employment - drawn through five vertical columns organized by age (less than 15 years; 15 - 24; 25 - 54; 55 - 64; and 65 and older). In this way, the index assesses an individual country's success in developing people's skills and competencies through learning and in utilizing the knowledge acquired through productive employment. The first horizontal theme - education - contains several sub-themes relating to access to education, quality of education, knowledge acquired and learning in the workplace. The second horizontal theme - employment - covers several dimensions of employment, namely participation in the economy, skills and vulnerability.

When it comes to human capital, Serbia's economy is among the best performing in the WB. When it comes to those with basic and beyond basic digital abilities, it ranks first among WB economies. Additionally, compared to the WB average of 54%, Serbia has the greatest percentage of its citizens (64%), who possess at least rudimentary skills in creating digital material. Employees at 16% of Serbian businesses receive ICT training. The share has drastically decreased as compared to 2019, even if this is marginally greater than the WB average. In addition to having a greater percentage of female ICT professionals than the WB and EU levels (24% versus 19 in the WB region and 19% in the EU region), the share of ICT specialists is higher than the WB average (3.3% versus 2.6% in the WB region). Serbia outperforms the EU average in terms of the number of ICT graduates (7.1% versus 6.2% in the WB region and 3.9% in the EU region) and has experienced a 15% increase in this field over the last two years.

Connectivity

Serbia has the greatest connectivity score in the WB area, with faster-than-average coverage of VHCN, FTTP, and fast broadband (NGA) networks. Significantly higher than the WB average of 48%, Serbia reported fixed Very High-Capacity Network (VHCN) coverage of 59% of homes. With a steady increase, FTTP penetration currently stands at 50% of passing houses, which is higher than the WB average and on par with the EU average. Nevertheless, the overall fixed broadband adoption does not match this favorable fixed broadband coverage performance, as broadband penetration only reached 72% of all households—far below the WB average of 77%. Serbia does better than the WB average of 21% in terms of the percentage of homes with at least a 100 Mbps internet connection, with a penetration rate of 26% (up from 19% in 2020). Similar to the entire WB region, virtually little 1Gbps broadband is being used. Regarding mobile connection, the WB area saw the largest share of mobile broadband take-up, at 96% (as opposed to an average of 82% in the WB region). Although nearly all inhabited locations have 4G coverage by 2021, there are presently no formal plans for when the 5G spectrum will be allocated.

Integration of Digital Technology

The majority of Serbian businesses continue to struggle to take advantage of digital technology, and things will only get worse in 2021 as numerous indicators show declining numbers from 2020. In terms of fundamental digital technologies, 22% of businesses used social media in 2021 (down from 21% in 2019) and 29% of businesses used an enterprise resource planning system for electronic information sharing in 2021. These numbers are significantly lower than the WB averages. Adoption rates for sophisticated digital technologies are likewise low: only 1% of businesses said they used AI, and 4% said they used big data. Cloud computing is a much better scenario, with 22% of firms reporting adoption, higher than the WB average of 16%. 19% of businesses send electronic invoices that can be processed automatically, which is a little more than the WB average of 17%. Furthermore, according to 58% of businesses, using ICT allowed them to lessen their environmental impact.

Serbia adopted a number of significant strategic documents in 2020 and 2021, and if they are implemented properly, they should facilitate and hasten the corporate sector's digital transformation. The Industrial Policy Strategy 2021-2030 aims to increase industry-led development and competitiveness overall. The ICT sector is prioritized in the Smart Specialization Strategy 2020–2027 because it is Serbia's fastest-growing industry. The digitalization of services and commercial activities in the public and private sectors is given significant attention in Serbia's recently adopted Strategy for Development of Information Society and Information Security for 2021–2026. The primary goal of the 2020–2025 Strategy for Development of Artificial Intelligence is to make it easier for AI to be used for job creation, economic expansion, and overall quality of life enhancement.

Digital Public Services

When it comes to digital public services, Serbia leads among WB economies. 40% of Serbian internet users use e-government services, which is significantly higher than the WB average of 35%. Serbia scores highly on pre-filled forms (79), and on offering online services to businesses and citizens (43 and 68, respectively, versus the WB averages of 43 and 59). In open data, Serbia does better than the WB average as well. In 2020, Serbia updated its digital services platform, e-Uprava. More than 900 electronic services from various governmental authorities are offered to the more than one million active members of e-Uprava. In 2022, there were 2,060 more open data sets available on the government Open Data Portal, and 110 more institutions were releasing data on the portal over that same time frame.

CONCLUSION

The digital economy, also known as the "internet economy" or "online economy," refers to the portion of a country's or the world's economy that is based on digital technologies, the internet, and electronic commerce. It encompasses all economic activities, transactions, and interactions that involve digital technologies and the exchange of digital information. The digital economy is a rapidly growing and dynamic sector with a profound impact on various aspects of business, society, and daily life. The digital economy has brought about significant changes in business models, consumer behavior, and the way societies operate. It offers new opportunities for innovation, entrepreneurship, and economic growth while raising important challenges related to privacy, cybersecurity, regulation, and access to technology. As the digital economy continues to evolve, it plays an increasingly central role in global economic development and transformation.

The EU's commitment to fostering digital progress and development of the information society reflects its goal of enhancing the well-being of its citizens, strengthening its global competitiveness, and addressing emerging challenges. These initiatives aim to harness the benefits of digital technologies while addressing legal, ethical, and regulatory aspects of a digitalized society. While progress varies across member states, the overall vision is to create a digital Europe that benefits all its citizens.

Digital technologies are the backbone of the digital age, transforming how information is created, processed, shared, and utilized in various domains. They continue to shape the way individuals and organizations interact with the world and each other, and they play a central role in driving innovation and technological advancements in the 21st century. Digital technologies continue to evolve and have a profound impact on society and the economy. They offer new opportunities for innovation, efficiency, and connectivity, but also raise important ethical and privacy considerations. As they advance, they are likely to shape the future in various ways, from the way we work and communicate to how we address global challenges like healthcare and environmental sustainability.

The DESI 2022 results reveal that, despite most of the Member States making progress in their digital transformation, essential digital technologies like artificial intelligence and big data are still not widely adopted by businesses, even in the EU's leading nations. As more and more services, especially important ones, move online, low levels of digital literacy hinder possibilities for future growth, widen the digital divide, and raise the risk of digital exclusion. To achieve the complete deployment of the ubiquitous connection infrastructure—particularly 5G—necessary for highly creative services and applications, efforts must be increased.

Serbia is still positioned in the middle of the technological world. The gap caused by global information capitalism is far from shrinking as long as 20% of nations continue to account for 80% of all investments in new technology. As a result, smaller nations like Serbia continue to face issues from the growing digital divide. The governments of these nations still need to create the groundwork for more robust development and a chance to as much as possible reduce lagging. The overall goal of Serbia's Strategy for the Development of Digital Skills for the years 2020–2024 is to increase all citizens' digital knowledge and skills, including those of members of socially vulnerable groups, to monitor the advancement of ICT technologies across all fields and to meet the demands of the labor market.

The EU has a sizable digital gap, and currently, EU membership is not correlated with all information society levels. If the EU is to become a close-knit community and remain one of the world's most competitive economic powers, it must overcome the digital divide among its member nations. Finally, the EU may take into consideration the degree of the information society as an objective criterion in addition to the other objective and subjective criteria now used as EU membership criteria (Çilan et al., 2009). Serbia won't leave the digital divide until the overall IT investment remains constant at less than 2% of GDP. If IT investments reach 3% of GDP by 2025, Serbian society and economy have a possibility to link up on the route of accelerated recovery. The same objective becomes more difficult when converted to the amount of IT investment per person: The current per-capita investment should be doubled to €150. Serbia, therefore, requires the IT market to grow at a rate of over 10% annually until 2025 to close the digital divide.

Finally, it should be noted that this chapter has several limitations: (a) the research on the development of the information society and its digital progress was analyzed at the level of the EU and Serbia as a candidate country for EU membership, (b) the research conducted covered a shorter period of time (2 years) and (c) the analysis was conducted solely on the basis of secondary data, i.e. the Digital Economy and Society Index (DESI) report published by the European Commission. The first recommendation for future research would be regional coverage, i.e. the inclusion of more Western Balkan countries in the analysis. To make the analysis even more comprehensive and detailed, it is recommended to conduct the analysis over a longer period (5-10 years). Thirdly, the analysis should be conducted based on primary data and using a methodology appropriate to the nature of the study, with the aim of better understanding the digital progress of the countries analyzed.

ACKNOWLEDGMENT

The research presented in this paper was funded by the Ministry of Science, Technological Development and Innovation of the Republic of Serbia under contract number 451-03-47/2023-01/200005.

REFERENCES

Alcacer, J., Cantwell, J., & Piscitello, L. (2016). Internationalization in the Information Age: A new era for places, firms, and international business networks? *Journal of International Business Studies*, *47*(5), 499–512. doi:10.1057/jibs.2016.22

Aristovnik, A. (2014). Development of the information society and its impact on the education sector in the EU: Efficiency at the regional (NUTS 2) level. *The Turkish Online Journal of Educational Technology*, *2*(13), 54–60.

Bertello, A., Ferraris, A., Bresciani, S., & de Bernardi, P. (2021). Big data analytics (BDA) and degree of internationalization: The interplay between governance of BDA infrastructure and BDA capabilities. *The Journal of Management and Governance*, *25*(4), 1035–1055. doi:10.1007/s10997-020-09542-w

Bouncken, R., & Barwinski, R. (2021). Shared digital identity and rich knowledge ties in global 3D printing-A drizzle in the clouds? *Global Strategy Journal*, *11*(1), 81–108. doi:10.1002/gsj.1370

Bresciani, S., Ferraris, A., Romano, M., & Santoro, G. (2021). *Digital transformation management for agile organizations: A compass to sail the digital world*. Emerald Publishing Limited. doi:10.1108/9781800431713

Cennamo, C., Dagnino, G. B., Di Minin, A., & Lanzolla, G. (2020). Managing digital transformation: Scope of transformation and modalities of value co-generation and delivery. *California Management Review*, *62*(4), 5–16. doi:10.1177/0008125620942136

Česnauskė, J. (2019). Digital economy and society: Baltic states in the EU context. *Economics and Culture, 16*(1), 80-90.

Chen, B., Wan, J., Shu, L., Li, P., Mukherjee, M., & Yin, B. (2018). Smart Factory of Industry 4.0: Key Technologies, Application Case, and Challenges. *IEEE Access : Practical Innovations, Open Solutions*, *6*, 6505–6519. doi:10.1109/ACCESS.2017.2783682

Çilan, Ç. A., Bolat, B. A., & Coşkun, E. (2009). Analyzing digital divide within and between member and candidate countries of European Union. *Government Information Quarterly*, *26*(1), 98–105. doi:10.1016/j.giq.2007.11.002

D'Ippolito, B., Petruzzelli, A. M., & Panniello, U. (2019). Archetypes of incumbents' strategic responses to digital innovation. *Journal of Intellectual Capital*, *20*(5), 622–679. doi:10.1108/JIC-04-2019-0065

Dedehayir, O., Ortt, J. R., & Seppanen, ¨. M. (2017). Disruptive change and the reconfiguration of innovation ecosystems. *Journal of Technology Management & Innovation*, *12*(3), 9–21. doi:10.4067/S0718-27242017000300002

Domazet, I. (2023). Innovation and ICT: Key Factors of Successful Business. In Innovation, strategy, and transformation frameworks for the modern enterprise. IGI Global. doi:10.4018/979-8-3693-0458-7.ch014

Domazet, I., Marjanović, D., & Ahmetagić, D. (2022). The Impact of High-Tech Products Exports on Economic Growth: The Case of Serbia, Bulgaria, Romania and Hungary. *Ekonomika preduzeća, 70*(3-4), 191-205.

Domazet, I., Marjanović, D., Ahmetagić, D., & Antonijević, M. (2022). Does the Increase in the Number of Registered Patents Affect Economic Growth? Evidence from Romania and Bulgaria. *Economic Analysis: Applied Research in Emerging Markets*, *55*(2), 49–65. doi:10.28934/ea.22.55.2.pp49-65

Domazet, I., Marjanović, D., Ahmetagić, D., & Bugarčić, M. (2021). The Impact of Innovation Indicators on Increasing Exports of High Technology Products. *Ekonomika preduzeća, 69*(1-2), 31-40.

Domazet, I., Marjanović, D., Ahmetagić, D., & Simović, V. (2023). The influence of the number of patents on the economic growth of the country - evidence from Serbia and Hungary. *Strategic Management*, *28*(4), 41–52. Advance online publication. doi:10.5937/StraMan2300048D

Domazet, I., Zubović, J., & Lazić, M. (2018). Driving Factors of Serbian Competitiveness: Digital Economy and ICT. *Strategic Management*, *23*(1), 20–28. doi:10.5937/StraMan1801020D

European Commission. (2022). *Digital Economy and Society Index (DESI) 2022 - Methodological Note.* Available at: https://digital-strategy.ec.europa.eu/en/policies/desi

Fitzgerald, M., Kruschwitz, N., Bonnet, D., & Welch, M. (2013). Embracing digital technology: A new strategic imperative. *MIT Sloan Management Review*, *55*(2), 1–12.

Gefen, D., & Carmel, E. (2008). Is the World Really Flat? A Look at Offshoring at an Online Programming Marketplace. *Management Information Systems Quarterly*, *32*(2), 367–384. doi:10.2307/25148844

Gurbaxani, V., & Dunkle, D. (2019). Gearing up for successful digital transformation. *MIS Quarterly Executive*, *18*(3), 209–220. doi:10.17705/2msqe.00017

Kane, G. C., Palmer, D., Phillips, A. N., Kiron, D., & Buckley, N. (2015). Strategy, not technology, drives digital transformation. *MIT Sloan Management Review*, 1–25.

Khalin, V.G., & Chernova, G.V. (2018). Digitalization and its impact on the Russian economy and society: advantages, challenges, threats and risks. *Administrative Consulting*, (10).

Kraus, S., Jones, P., Kailer, N., Weinmann, A., Chaparro-Banegas, N., & Roig-Tierno, N. (2021). Digital transformation: An overview of the current state of the art of research. *SAGE Open*, *11*(3). doi:10.1177/21582440211047576

Lanzolla, G., Pesce, D., & Tucci, C. L. (2021). The digital transformation of search and recombination in the innovation function: Tensions and an integrative framework. *Journal of Product Innovation Management*, *38*(1), 90–113. doi:10.1111/jpim.12546

Loonam, J., Eaves, S., Kumar, V., & Parry, G. (2018). Towards digital transformation: Lessons learned from traditional organizations. *Strategic Change*, *27*(2), 101–109. doi:10.1002/jsc.2185

Mabey, C., & Zhao, S. (2017). Managing five paradoxes of knowledge exchange in networked organizations: New priorities for HRM? *Human Resource Management Journal*, *27*(1), 39–57. doi:10.1111/1748-8583.12106

Marjanović, D., & Domazet, I. (2021). Foreign Direct Investments: A Key Factor for Business Globalization. In Y. Bayar (Ed.), *Institutional, Economic, and Social Impacts of Globalization and Liberalization* (pp. 96–116). IGI Global. doi:10.4018/978-1-7998-4459-4.ch006

Marjanović, D., & Domazet, I. (2023). Economic Measures for Mitigation of the Consequences of COVID-19: Evidence From Serbia. In B. Marco-Lajara, A. C. Özer, & J. M. Falcó (Eds.), *The Transformation of Global Trade in a New World* (pp. 180–199). IGI Global.

Marjanović, D., Domazet, I., & Vukmirović, I. (2022). Social Environment as a Factor of Capital Investment in Serbia. *Eastern European Economics*, *60*(3), 247–264. Advance online publication. doi:10.1080/00128775.2022.2048181

Nambisan, S., Wright, M., & Feldman, M. (2019). The digital transformation of innovation and entrepreneurship: Progress, challenges and key themes. *Research Policy*, *48*(8), 103773. doi:10.1016/j.respol.2019.03.018

Poduyeva, O. N., & Nechushkina, E. A. (2022). Digital transformation as a tool of globalization. *Trade, Service, Food Industry, 2*(4), 362-370.

Queiroz, M. M., Fosso Wamba, S., Machado, M. C., & Telles, R. (2020). Smart production systems drivers for business process management improvement: An integrative framework. *Business Process Management Journal*, *26*(5), 1075–1092. doi:10.1108/BPMJ-03-2019-0134

Romanova, O. A., & Kuzmin, E. (2021). Industrial policy: A new reality in the context of digital transformation of the economy. *Digital Transformation in Industry*, 13-23.

Schilirò, D. (2020). Towards digital globalization and the covid-19 challenge. *International Journal of Business Management and Economic Research*, *2*(11), 1710–1716.

Schwens, C., Zapkau, F. B., Bierwerth, M., Isidor, R., Knight, G., & Kabst, R. (2018). International entrepreneurship: A meta–analysis on the internationalization and performance relationship. *Entrepreneurship Theory and Practice*, *42*(5), 734–768. doi:10.1177/1042258718795346

Sebastian, I., Ross, J., Beath, C., Mocker, M., Moloney, K., & Fonstad, N. (2017). How big old companies navigate digital transformation. *MIS Quarterly Executive*, *16*(3), 197–213.

Simović, V., & Domazet, I. (2021). An overview of the frameworks for measuring the digital competencies of college students: A European perspective. In *Stagnancy Issues and Change Initiatives for Global Education in the Digital Age* (pp. 259–283). IGI Global. doi:10.4018/978-1-7998-4993-3.ch012

Singh, A., & Hess, T. (2017). How chief digital officers promote the digital transformation of their companies. *MIS Quarterly Executive*, *16*(1), 1–17.

Sousa, M. J., & Rocha, A. (2019). Skills for disruptive digital business. *Journal of Business Research*, *94*, 257–263. doi:10.1016/j.jbusres.2017.12.051

Sturgeon, T. J. (2021). Upgrading strategies for the digital economy. *Global Strategy Journal*, *11*(1), 34–57. doi:10.1002/gsj.1364

Subramaniam, M., & Piskorski, M. (2020). How Legacy Businesses Can Compete in the Sharing Economy. *MIT Sloan Management Review*, *61*(4), 31–37.

Tabrizi, B., Lam, E., Girard, K., & Irvin, V. (2019). Digital transformation is not about technology. *Harvard Business Review*, *13*, 1–6.

United Nations. (2022). *E-Government survey: the future of digital government.* Available at: https://publicadministration.un.org/egovkb/en-us/Reports/UN-E-Government-Survey-2022

Verhoef, P. C., Broekhuizen, T., Bart, Y., Bhattacharya, A., Dong, J. Q., Fabian, N., & Haenlein, M. (2021). Digital transformation: A multidisciplinary reflection and research agenda. *Journal of Business Research*, *122*, 889–901. doi:10.1016/j.jbusres.2019.09.022

Vial, G. (2019). Understanding digital transformation: A review and a research agenda. *The Journal of Strategic Information Systems*, *28*(2), 118–144. doi:10.1016/j.jsis.2019.01.003

Warner, K. S., & Wäger, M. (2019). Building dynamic capabilities for digital transformation: An ongoing process of strategic renewal. *Long Range Planning*, *52*(3), 326–349. doi:10.1016/j.lrp.2018.12.001

Westerman, G., Calméjane, C., Bonnet, D., Ferraris, P., & McAfee, A. (2011). *Digital Transformation: A roadmap for billion-dollar organizations*. MIT Center for Digital Business and Capgemini Consulting.

Wood, M. S., & McKinley, W. (2020). The entrepreneurial opportunity construct: Dislodge or leverage? *The Academy of Management Perspectives*, *34*(3), 352–365. doi:10.5465/amp.2017.0162

Wysokińska, Z. (2021). A Review of the Impact of the Digital Transformation on the Global and European Economy. Comparative Economic Research. *Central and Eastern Europe*, *24*(3), 75–92.

ADDITIONAL READING

Appio, F. P., Frattini, F., Petruzzelli, A. M., & Neirotti, P. (2021). Digital Transformation and Innovation Management: A Synthesis of Existing Research and an Agenda for Future Studies. *Journal of Product Innovation Management*, *38*(1), 4–20. doi:10.1111/jpim.12562

Bertello, A., Ferraris, A., Bresciani, S., & de Bernardi, P. (2021). Big data analytics (BDA) and degree of internationalization: The interplay between the governance of BDA infrastructure and BDA capabilities. *The Journal of Management and Governance*, *25*(4), 1035–1055. doi:10.1007/s10997-020-09542-w

D'Ambra, J., Akter, S., & Mariani, M. (2022). Digital transformation of higher education in Australia: Understanding affordance dynamics in E-Textbook engagement and use. *Journal of Business Research*, *149*, 283–295. doi:10.1016/j.jbusres.2022.05.048

Feliciano-Cestero, M. M., Ameen, N., Kotabe, M., Paul, J., & Signoret, M. (2023). Is digital transformation threatened? A systematic literature review of the factors influencing firms' digital transformation and internationalization. *Journal of Business Research*, *157*, 113546. doi:10.1016/j.jbusres.2022.113546

George, G., & Schillebeeckx, S. J. D. (2022). Digital transformation, sustainability, and purpose in the multinational enterprise. *Journal of World Business*, *57*(3), 101326. doi:10.1016/j.jwb.2022.101326

Haddoud, M. Y., Onjewu, A. K. E., Nowinski, W., & Jones, P. (2021). The determinants of SMEs' export entry: A systematic review of the literature. *Journal of Business Research*, *125*, 262–278. doi:10.1016/j.jbusres.2020.12.017

Holzmann, P., & Gregori, P. (2023). The promise of digital technologies for sustainable entrepreneurship: A systematic literature review and research agenda. *International Journal of Information Management*, *68*, 102593. doi:10.1016/j.ijinfomgt.2022.102593

Kromidha, E., & Robson, P. J. (2021). The role of digital presence and investment networks signals the internationalization of small firms. *International Small Business Journal*, *39*(2), 109–129. doi:10.1177/0266242620958898

Kuhlmann, S., & Heuberger, M. (2023). Digital transformation going local: Implementation, impacts and constraints from a German perspective. *Public Money & Management*, *43*(2), 147–155. doi:10.1080/09540962.2021.1939584

Lahteenmaki, I., Natti, S., & Saraniemi, S. (2022). Digitalization-enabled evolution of customer value creation: An executive view in financial services. *Journal of Business Research*, *146*, 504–517. doi:10.1016/j.jbusres.2022.04.002

Luo, Y. (2022). A general framework of digitization risks in international business. *Journal of International Business Studies*, *53*(2), 344–361. doi:10.1057/s41267-021-00448-9 PMID:34075261

Mostaghel, R., Oghazi, P., Parida, V., & Sohrabpour, V. (2022). Digitalization driven retail business model innovation: Evaluation of past and avenues for future research trends. *Journal of Business Research*, *146*, 134–145. doi:10.1016/j.jbusres.2022.03.072

Pankov, S., Velamuri, V. K., & Schneckenberg, D. (2021). Towards sustainable entrepreneurial ecosystems: Examining the effect of contextual factors on sustainable entrepreneurial activities in the sharing economy. *Small Business Economics*, *56*(3), 1073–1095. doi:10.1007/s11187-019-00255-5

Park, I., Kim, D., Moon, J., Kim, S., Kang, Y., & Bae, S. (2022). Searching for New Technology Acceptance Model under Social Context: Analyzing the Determinants of Acceptance of Intelligent Information Technology in Digital Transformation and Implications for the Requisites of Digital Sustainability. *Sustainability (Basel)*, *14*(1), 579. doi:10.3390/su14010579

Popkova, E. G., De Bernardi, P., Tyurina, Y. G., & Sergi, B. S. (2022). A theory of digital technology advancement to address the grand challenges of sustainable development. *Technology in Society*, *68*, 101831. doi:10.1016/j.techsoc.2021.101831

Porfírio, J. A., Carrilho, T., Felício, J. A., & Jardim, J. (2021). Leadership characteristics and digital transformation. *Journal of Business Research*, *124*, 610–619. doi:10.1016/j.jbusres.2020.10.058

Trevisan, A. H., Lobo, A., Guzzo, D., de Vasconcelos Gomes, L. A., & Mascarenhas, J. (2023). Barriers to employing digital technologies for a circular economy: A multi-level perspective. *Journal of Environmental Management*, *332*, 117437. doi:10.1016/j.jenvman.2023.117437 PMID:36801533

Vadana, I. I., Kuivalainen, O., Torkkeli, L., & Saarenketo, S. (2021). The role of digitalization on the internationalization strategy of born-digital companies. *Sustainability (Basel)*, *13*(24), 14002. doi:10.3390/su132414002

Vaska, S., Massaro, M., Bagarotto, E. M., & Dal Mas, F. (2021). The digital transformation of business model innovation: A structured literature review. *Frontiers in Psychology*, *11*, 3557. doi:10.3389/fpsyg.2020.539363 PMID:33584396

KEY TERMS AND DEFINITIONS

Digital Economy: Together with technological development, the definition of a "digital economy" is constantly changing. The integration of digital technology, services, products, processes, and skills across economies is the emphasis of the modern digital economy. The adoption of information and communication technology (ICT) by all business sectors is supporting the growth of the digital economy and boosting its productivity.

Digital Technologies: Digital tools, systems, and resources that assist with data creation, archiving, and management are included in the concept of digital technology. Information technology (IT), which refers to the use of computers to process data and information, is a significant component of digital technology.

Digital Transformation: The integration of digital technology across all functions of an organization is known as "digital transformation," and it significantly alters how you do business and provide value to consumers. Additionally, it's a cultural shift that necessitates constant status quo challenge, experimentation, and comfort with failure on the part of organizations. The process of adopting and implementing digital technology by an organization to develop new goods, services, and operations, as well as modify existing ones, involves converting business processes into a digital format.

Information and Communications Technologies (ICT): Information and communications technology is an abbreviation for information technology (IT). It emphasizes the importance of unified communications and the integration of telecommunications (telephone lines and wireless signals) and computers as well as the enterprise software, middleware, storage, and audiovisual requirements that are required to enable users to access, store, transmit, understand, and manipulate information.

Information Society: A society is said to be an information society if significant economic, political, and cultural activities revolve around the creation, distribution, use, integration, and manipulation of information. A civilization where the use and knowledge of information and computer technology is at a high level is commonly regarded to be an information society.

Chapter 2
Blockchain Technology in Peer-to-Peer Transactions Emphasizing Data Transparency and Security in Banking Services

Isha Nag
Chitkara Business School, Chitkara University, India

Sridhar Manohar
https://orcid.org/0000-0003-0173-3479
Chitkara Business School, Chitkara University, India

ABSTRACT

The banking system serves as the central and essential component of a functional economy. A robust banking system is essential for fostering economic growth and facilitating development. However, the systems have certain drawbacks Numerous instances of fraudulent operations were reported, leading to clients experiencing theft and unauthorised access to their properties. With the progression of the digital era, there is an increasing exposure and scrutiny of these centralized systems, thereby leading to a shift in thoughts towards decentralised alternatives. This chapter provides a concise discussion of the necessity of decentralised financing and how it can be accomplished through the utilisation of blockchain technology. Firstly, the study examines the mechanics of decentralised banking systems and their potential to address the limitations of conventional banking systems. Further, a brief of various case studies has been given. Finally, the chapter discusses the transformation of the banking system using blockchain technology.

1. INTRODUCTION

Blockchain technology has gained significant attention in recent times. The utilization of this technology has been observed across several sectors, with the financial industry emerging as the primary

DOI: 10.4018/979-8-3693-3253-5.ch002

adopter. Blockchain and distributed ledger technologies have emerged as potent tools for facilitating decentralization through the promotion of trust and transparency. The centralized banking systems are commonly employed across the world for financial transactions; however, certain limitations, such as the lack of data openness and instances of fraud, have prompted an option towards decentralized systems (Nofer *et al.*, 2017). According to Tasatanattakool and Techapanupreeda (2018), blockchain is defined as "*a decentralized and distributed digital ledger that is used to record transactions across many computers so that the record cannot be altered retroactively without the alteration of all subsequent blocks and the collusion of the network*". It is composed of interconnected blocks, with each block containing several transactions. The blockchains are expanded by incorporating further blocks, resulting in a comprehensive record of transactions in the form of a complete ledger (Kaur, 2023). One of the primary benefits of utilizing a decentralized ledger is the inherent visibility of recorded data to all participants within the network. This characteristic fosters data transparency since it prevents any individual from altering or deleting the data (Sarmah, 2018). Consequently, the occurrence of data fraud is significantly minimized.

Blockchain technology has the capacity to facilitate decentralization through a range of mechanisms, including trustless transactions, decentralized applications (dApps), smart contracts, immutable records, supply chain transparency, democratic governance, resistance to censorship, global accessibility, data ownership, and financial inclusion, among other potential contributions Blockchain technology is rapidly being adopted in various sectors and is projected to grow even faster in the coming years. Nevertheless, it is crucial to acknowledge that the adoption of these technologies entails the disadvantage of heightened energy consumption and the necessity to overcome legislative obstacles to fully exploit their decentralized capabilities.

Sectors adopting blockchain technology range across banking and finance, retail, healthcare, telecom, travel and transportation, government, energy, entertainment and media, and others as with emerging technology and innovations, companies' growth opportunities in relation to digitalization also increases. It is to be noted that sizable investments from various companies across countries are being currently invested in blockchain. The chart below (Figure 1) shows the blockchain market globally is at USD 11.14 billion in 2022 and by 2030 it is expected to be at around USD 469.49 billion, which means a compounding increase of around 59% annually (Fortune Business Insight, 2023).

Among all other sectors, the financial sector has the potential to undergo transformation through the use of blockchain technology. The capacity to enhance security, efficiency, and transparency and foster novel inventions in the finance domain is supported by the technology. The use of robust security measures ensures the integrity of data, and hence minimising the likelihood of fraudulent acts performed by individuals. The integration of blockchain technology within financial institutions can yield cost savings by virtue of removing intermediaries and automating certain operations (Garg et al., 2021). The speed and convenience of the transactions contribute to an improved client experience. Blockchain technology serves as the fundamental infrastructure for decentralised finance, facilitated by the utilisation of smart contracts. Decentralized finance is a novel alternative to the existing finance system as it delivers financial tools to the customers without intermediaries like brokers or banks by using these smart contracts generated with blockchain technology (Zetzsche et al., 2020). Generally, smart contracts are contractual agreements that possess the ability to autonomously execute and exhibit programmable behaviour, functioning inside the framework of a blockchain. The contract is performed automatically, without the need for any middleman, when certain prewritten conditions set in code are satisfied.

Figure 1. Global blockchain technology market share, by industry, 2022
Source:https://www.fortunebusinessinsights.com/industry-reports/toc /blockchain-market-100072

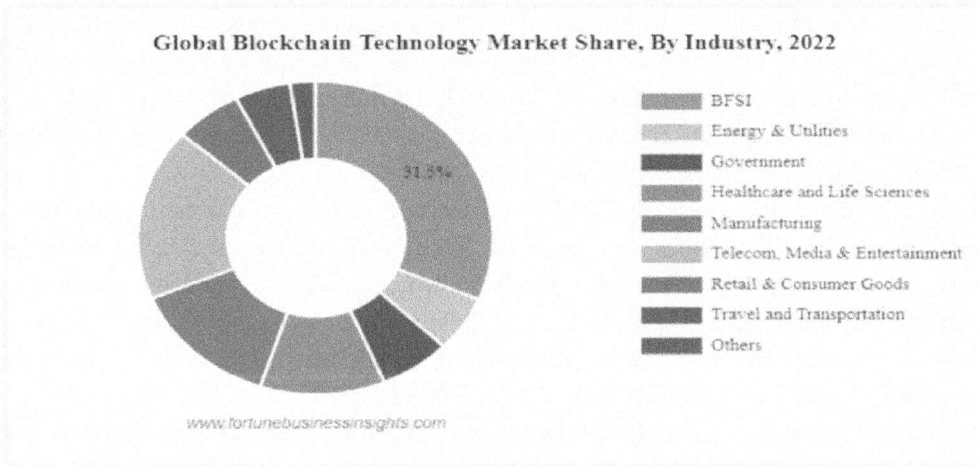

The identification of the true owner of assets within the finance services sector has proven to be a challenging task, resulting in financial firms, such as the US investment bank Bear Stearns, incurring losses. Due to the bank's lack of knowledge on the number of shares acquired by shareholders, an inadvertent loss was incurred as a result of providing additional shares to such shareholders (Tasatanattakool and Techapanupreeda, 2018). Therefore, with the advent of blockchain technology, it became feasible to maintain accurate and transparent records of all transactions (Sharma et al., 2023). It also presents various applications, encompassing both financial and non-financial domains.

2. BLOCKCHAIN AND DECENTRALIZED LEDGER FUNCTIONALITIES

The decentralized databases of blockchain technology exist on multiple computers and the copy on every system is the same. The blockchain architecture is divided into three layers namely Applications, Decentralized Ledger and Peer-to-Peer network (Ali et al., 2021). The application layer refers to the interaction between humans and machines, encompassing the application software that operates within the blockchain system. The application layer facilitates the monitoring of transactions by individuals, as it offers a user-friendly interface that is easily comprehensible to human users. The decentralized ledger, constituting the second layer of the blockchain, assumes the crucial role of providing a tamper-resistant global ledger. In this context, the formation of blocks occurs through the aggregation of transactions. The term "transactions" in this context refers to the transfer of tokens between two individuals. Prior to being deemed genuine, these transactions undergo a validation process. The process which is used to group the transactions is known as mining. The final component within the design of blockchain is the Peer-to-Peer Network. This layer is comprised of various nodes that engage in the exchange of diverse messages with the decentralized ledger.

2.1. Process of Decentralized Blockchain Transactions

A single transaction requires strict adherence to a series of consecutive steps. The first stage entails sending the necessary transaction to a peer-to-peer network through the nodes. The validation process is carried out by utilising a network of nodes and implementing a well-established algorithm. Upon completion of the verification procedure, the transaction is interconnected with other transactions to form a block within the ledger. Afterwards, the newly created block is added to the current block in a way that makes it unchangeable (Zarrin et al., 2021).

Similarly, within the financial system, when a consumer initiates a transaction, the transaction is transformed into a block. The blocks are disseminated as nodes to the blockchain and subsequently confirmed using the current algorithm. Once verified, the new block is appended to the previous block, resulting in an unaltered chain as shown in Figure 2 below.

Tiers of Blockchain: Based on different applications blockchain is categorised into three tiers: Blockchain 1.0, 2.0, and 3.0 (AbuNaseret al., 2010; Xu et al., 2019).

Blockchain 1.0: Initially, blockchain technology was predominantly utilised to facilitate transactions involving digital currencies. The utilisation of blockchain technology was first confined to the Bitcoin cryptocurrency, signifying its inaugural pragmatic deployment. The primary applications of Blockchain 1.0 were predominantly focused on digital currencies, specifically for foreign exchange and small-scale monetary transactions. Primarily, it served as a form of digital cash.

Blockchain 2.0: Blockchain 2.0 encompasses Bitcoin 2.0 and is mostly utilised in the realm of financial services. Blockchain 2.0 is mostly utilised for smart contracts, decentralised applications (Dapps), and Decentralised autonomous corporations (DACs). The finance industry encompasses a range of areas including securities trading, supply chain financing, banking instruments, payment clearing, anti-counterfeiting measures, credit system establishment, and mutual insurance. By leveraging smart contracts and blockchain technology, transactions are effectively safeguarded and decentralised, resulting in enhanced financial inclusivity and the elimination of the need for third-party approval. Banking systems for decentralized financing use Blockchain 2.0 for secure, transparent and efficient transactions.

Figure 2. Process of blockchain transaction
Source: https://link.springer.com/article/10.1007/s10586-021-03301-8/figures/4

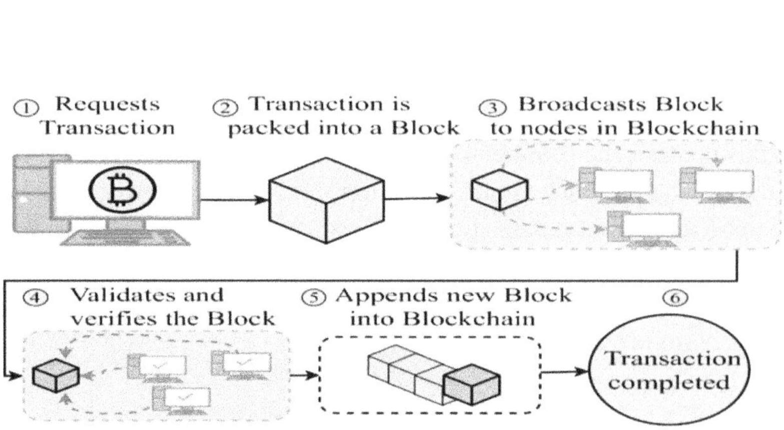

Blockchain 3.0: Blockchain 3.0 is characterised by enhanced security and sustainability due to its superior scalability and adaptability, in comparison to Blockchain 1.0 and 2.0. Blockchain 3.0 encompasses enhanced smart contracts that have broader applications outside finance, such as healthcare, science, governance, arts, and more. Blockchain 3.0 is the amalgamation of blockchain technology with tokens. Tokens serve as evidence of an individual's ownership of various digital assets, such as equities, bonds, and personal identity. The integration of Blockchain technology and tokens has the potential to catalyse a profound societal shift.

2.2. Types of Blockchain

Originally, Blockchain was categorised into two types: Public blockchains and Private Blockchains. However, another type called Hybrid Blockchain was later introduced based on additional factors (Shrivas and Yeboah, 2019; Paul et al., 2021).

- *Public Blockchain:* Public blockchains are universally available to all participants within the network. In the realm of public blockchains, also known as permissionless blockchains, universal access to data is provided to all members of the public without any limitations. Bitcoin and Ethereum are both examples of public blockchains. These blockchains have a range of capabilities, including complete transparency, flexibility, openness, and strong security and privacy. However, they also come with certain drawbacks such as slower transaction speeds, scalability issues, and high energy consumption.
- *Private Blockchain:* Authorization from the owning organisations is necessary to gain access to data in Private blockchains, as it is restricted. The blockchain grants transaction permission with the assistance of system administrators. The primary characteristics of a private blockchain are superior scalability in comparison to a public blockchain, expedited transaction processing, enhanced efficiency, improved scalability, and increased transaction speed. Furthermore, the energy consumption of these blockchains is reduced and the participants are carefully chosen in advance. Projects such as Multiledger and Hyperledger exemplify the concept of private blockchains. A significant concern in private blockchain systems is the diminished level of security. The security of a private blockchain is compromised when a third party acquires unauthorised access to the central administration system, making it more susceptible for a node to exploit the entire private blockchain system.
- *Hybrid:* A hybrid blockchain combines elements of both private and public blockchains, resulting in a system that incorporates both centralised and decentralised features. Performing the transactions necessitates improved control. It possesses both data transparency and integrity. The network is sufficiently adaptable to allow any individual to readily join openly. The hybrid blockchain provides extensive customisation by including attributes from both private (permission-based) and public (permissionless) chains. These blockchains improve both the security and transparency of the network.
- Consortium Blockchain: Energy Web Foundation and R3 are instances of consortium blockchains. Furthermore, these networks exhibit a semi-decentralized nature and are already being employed by government organisations and financial institutions. These blockchains have the capability to facilitate transactions within a single organisation. Such blockchains can be utilised for the purpose of overseeing a blockchain network.

2.3. Advantages and Disadvantages of Blockchain

Blockchain is a versatile technology that is being adopted in several sectors such as healthcare, data security, finance, arts, and research due to its numerous advantages. However, it is important to note that along with these advantages, there are also certain disadvantages associated with this technology (Golosova and Romanovs, 2018; Niranjanamurthy et al., 2019). Here are several benefits and drawbacks of Blockchain Technology:

Advantages

1. ***Data Transparency:*** Blockchain technology ensures complete data transparency, granting all participants in the network unrestricted access to the information stored on the distributed network.
2. ***Data Security:*** Due to the distribution of data among all users of the blockchain network, it is impossible for any individual to edit or tamper with the data. This significantly reduces the risk of fraud and ensures the security and safety of the data.
3. ***No need for intermediaries:*** In the traditional banking system, a central authority acts as a third party, which leads to increased transaction costs. However, in a banking system that utilises blockchain technology, intermediaries are not required, resulting in a reduction in the overall transaction costs.
4. ***Easy Audit:*** In a decentralised system, all data is accessible on the network from the past to the present, making audits straightforward.
5. ***High speed:*** In a decentralised banking system, the absence of a third party eliminates the need for data exchanges, resulting in increased speed and accuracy.

Disadvantages

1. ***Energy Consumption:*** A significant drawback of blockchain technology is its substantial energy consumption, which consequently results in environmental concerns.
2. ***Privacy Issue:*** Data stored on the blockchain is accessible to all participants in the network, which might potentially lead to privacy concerns due to the public nature of the data.
3. ***Lack of regulation:*** In a decentralised system, when there is no regulating authority such as the government involved, there is a higher likelihood of illicit actions occurring.
4. ***Initial Cost:*** Deploying blockchain technology can incur significant expenses, encompassing the aspects of development, training, and maintenance.
5. ***Irreversible Transactions:*** Reversing a transaction once it has been put to the blockchain is extremely difficult, which might pose challenges in situations involving human errors or fraudulent activities.

3. CENTRALIZED BANKING SYSTEM

Traditional banking systems have been the foundation of the financial industry for many years. However, they are now experiencing transformations with the emergence of digital transactions and challenges with decentralized banking systems. Galazova and Magomaeva (2019) emphasised that the digitalization of financial systems will result in the digitalization of the entire economy. Traditional banking systems possess distinctive attributes such as in-person transactions, regulatory frameworks, and a diverse array of loan and mortgage options. However, they also come with certain drawbacks, including high expenses, restricted operating hours, reliance on paper-based transactions, and susceptibility to fraudulent activities (Sood et al., 2022). In FY2023, the total number of fraud cases in the banking system were 13,530 in numbers (ENS Economic Bureau, 2023). Numerous research has concentrated on the function of central banks in identifying and thwarting fraudulent activities. Ghosh and Bagheri (2006) uncovered that deficiencies in rules and inadequate monitoring by central banks majorly contribute to fraud.

3.1. Gaps in Centralized Systems

Various shortcomings have been detected in the centralised financial system, leading people to seek superior alternatives such as blockchain and decentralised financial systems. The centralised financial system has several crucial gaps (Bolat, 2016):

4. *Limited Access:* Remote communities or underbanked individuals are unable to access centralised financial systems. Its physical location renders it inaccessible.
5. *Security Risk:* Centralised banking systems provide a significant security risk as hackers can simply infiltrate the protection measures, thereby gaining access to critical client information.
6. *Financial Inclusion issue:* Centralised financial systems are unable to deliver services to individuals or entities that do not have access to conventional financial systems. As a result, these individuals and businesses are excluded from the system's benefits and are not well served.
7. *High Transaction Cost:* The centralised banking system involves middlemen such as payment processors and clearing houses, which levy fees for transactions. These fees might be substantial, particularly for overseas transactions.
8. *Limited Transparency:* Centralised systems suffer from a lack of data transparency, which increases the likelihood of window dressing and fraud. Additionally, the absence of openness creates trust issues among consumers and service providers. Furthermore, this creates a difficulty for users in confirming the precision and reliability of the transactions.
9. *Slow settlement:* Conventional banking systems, such as centralised banking systems, have lengthy settlement periods for transactions, which can be particularly slow, especially for international transactions.
10. *Single point of failure:* Centralised financial systems rely on a singular point of control or authority, such as a clearing house or bank. If a technical malfunction or security breach occurs at the central control point, it will disrupt the entire interconnected system.
11. *Intermediary dependency and risk:* Since transactions rely on intermediaries in the centralised financial system, any problems or defaults by the counterparty can result in financial losses.
12. *Lack of innovation:* Conventional financial systems exhibit sluggishness and reluctance to embrace novel technology and ideas, hence impeding financial advancement.
13. *Geographical Boundaries:* Centralised financial systems, being limited to specific geographic regions, encounter difficulties in cross-border transactions due to varying regulatory demands and time zone disparities. In addition, individuals who are unable to physically access the bank or financial system are unable to utilise its services.

14. *Limited operating hours:* The centralised financial system functions within specific predetermined working hours, hence not providing round-the-clock service to their consumers.

4. NOTABLE CASE STUDIES ON BANKING SYSTEM FAILURES

Case 1: Global Financial Crisis (2008)

In 2008, individuals in the United States considered investing in an asset that may provide them with greater returns than the interest rates offered by banks or the stock market. Real estate investment came out to be the finest alternative. Financial institutions provided accessible mortgage loans, prompting individuals to engage in property investment with the intention of purchasing homes and subsequently selling them at inflated prices. However, due to a tax rate hike from 2.25% to 5.25%, clients could not repay their loans, leading to a rise in defaults. Property prices are decreasing due to an excess of supply compared to demand (Jones, 2009; Calvo, 2010). In the end, the worth of derivatives plummeted and banks ceased providing loans to one another. This event precipitated the financial crisis that resulted in the great recession.

Reason for the downfall: Lack of regulatory oversight was a major factor in the failure, as it did not adequately prevent or mitigate the risks associated with the complex financial element. Furthermore, as a result of insufficient data openness, only the bank itself was aware of its mortgage practices. Moreover, the failure of a single system has far-reaching consequences for all banks globally which highlights the issue of single system failure. The subprime mortgage crisis occurred when banks provided subprime mortgages to borrowers with a history of bad credit. This resulted in a credit freeze, as banks became hesitant to lend to one another. Consequently, enterprises and individuals encountered difficulties in obtaining loans, which ultimately had a global impact on economic activity.

Blockchain's Interference: On incorporating blockchain technology, regular oversight of transactions would be possible. Additionally, in the case of blockchain-supported systems, the occurrence of a single system failure would be eliminated, thus preventing any worldwide economic impact. Blockchains enable the execution of frequent audits, allowing regulatory authorities to monitor all actions conducted by banks.

Case 2: Wells Fargo Fake Accounts Scandal in the United States (2016)

The Wells Fargo scandal came to light in 2016 when it was discovered that the bank's employees had illicitly opened checking and savings accounts for customers without their authorization. The cause for this was discovered to be the employees' obligation to cross-sell additional products to their current customers. Cross-selling refers to the practice of offering multiple products to a customer during a sales transaction. Wells Fargo was the top-ranked bank at that time based on their cross-selling performance. A total of 1,534,280 unauthorised deposit accounts and 565,433 credit card accounts were opened due to both pressure and the incentives provided to staff. Customers became aware of the fraudulent activity when they received unsolicited credit cards, increased fees, and unfamiliar credits and debits in their accounts. In late 2016, reports of fraudulent activities emerged, leading to many regulatory organisations, including the Consumer Financial Protection Bureau (CFPB), imposing collective penalties of US$185 million on the company (Cavico and Mujtaba, 2017).

Reasons For Scandal: Several factors contributed to the incident, one of which was the imposition of sales pressure on bank workers to cross-sell products to current customers. Under this strain, customers began creating accounts on behalf of other customers, indicating a lack of control. There was a lack of enough supervision to identify and prevent these fraudulent operations and put an end to this unethical conduct.

Blockchain's Interference: By implementing blockchain technology in banking transactions, employees would be unable to fraudulently open accounts in customers' names. This is because blockchain networks ensure that data cannot be altered and transactions cannot be conducted without validation from other participants. Additionally, all transactions are transparent to all users in the network. Therefore, the use of blockchain technology can effectively eliminate such fraudulent activities.

Case 3: Kingfisher Airlines and Vijay Mallya's Loan Case (2016)

In 2005, a renowned Indian entrepreneur launched an airline service called Kingfisher Airlines. Malya obtained loans from various institutions, including Punjab National Bank and State Bank of India, in order to enter the aviation business. However, Kingfisher Airlines faced significant competition and encountered other challenges, which hindered its performance. As a result, Malya found it challenging to repay the debt. Furthermore, in the year 2012, the airline was forced to suspend its operations and began to fail in repaying the loans it had borrowed from banks. Subsequently, the banks officially designated Vijay Mallya as a deliberate defaulter, with an outstanding debt of $1.4 billion (Panigrahi et al., 2019). Mallya subsequently departed India and is currently residing in the United Kingdom. The Indian Government has levied several financial charges against him.

Reason for the Scandal: The bank granted the loan to Vijay Mallya without assessing his creditworthiness and financial standing. Under a centralised banking system, the decision to provide a loan is made by higher authorities and can be influenced based on their connection with the borrower. There was a lack of a sufficient regulatory structure in place to regulate the issuance of loans to individuals with poor credit history.

Blockchain's Interference: In blockchain-supported banks or decentralised financial systems, the absence of a centralised authority prevents transactions from being influenced by any particular party. Utilising technology, the process of "know your customer" can be executed with efficiency. Additionally, smart contracts will only carry out transactions if the predetermined conditions specified in the codes are met.

Case 4: Punjab and Maharashtra Cooperative Bank (PMC Bank) Failure (2019)

PMC was a notable cooperative bank in India. In 2019, the fraud case concerning PMC bank came to light when the Reserve Bank of India (RBI) uncovered that PMC had provided a loan of INR 4.355 Crore to a real estate developer named Wadhawan, who is the owner of Housing Development and Infrastructure Limited (HDIL). Additionally, PMC had created false accounts to hide this transaction. The bank extended loans beyond the established limit, and when HDIL failed to repay the loan, it resulted in non-performing assets for the bank. The auditors were unable to uncover these anomalies for a prolonged duration. Subsequently, the Reserve Bank of India (RBI) implemented additional regulations, including setting a maximum restriction on the amount of money depositors can withdraw (Singhal and Chauhan, 2021).

Reasons for failure: The reason for the bank's failure to provide a loan above the limit to an individual is due to their personal ties and the creation of fraudulent accounts to conceal their activity. This is a situation in which the banking system has not properly regulated transactions. Furthermore, due to the modifications made to the transactions, auditors faced significant challenges in promptly detecting them.

Blockchain's Interference: The aforementioned instance exemplifies the unethical conduct carried out by the bank authorities and the inadequacy of corporate governance. In addition, it was seen that auditors were unable to detect these irregularities for an extended period, indicating a lack of data transparency. By implementing blockchain technology, all transactions would be visible, eliminating any issues in conducting audits. Moreover, not only a select few individuals, but everyone in the network would have knowledge of the bank's activities. Consequently, such unethical practices may be effectively prevented.

Case 5: State Bank of Patiala (2005)

An incident was identified on March 5th, 2005, at the Dhuri Branch of State Bank of Patiala, concerning a sum of 8.75 crores. On February 10th, 2005, a surprise visit to the branch revealed that the branch had provided cash credit limits to 3527 sugar cane growers through a tie-up agreement with M/s Bagwanpura Sugar Mills, who served as a guarantor. However, it was disclosed that out of the total 3527 borrowers, only 1186 were truly from the villages and worked as agricultural labourers rather than being cane growers. The company engaged in impersonations and diversification of bank money, resulting in a significant number of borrowers being untraceable. The inquiry was carried out by the controller, and the findings were submitted by the Banking Division of the Ministry of Finance in New Delhi (Khanna and Arora, 2009).

Reason: Inadequate verification of borrower's credit history. There was a lack of transparency in the execution of transactions, and the bank faced difficulties in locating some of the borrowers.

Interference of Blockchain: In the aforementioned scenario, it is observed that a considerable proportion of borrowers were untraceable. This issue could have been mitigated by employing blockchain technology in decentralised financial institutions. Additionally, the data was not accessible to everyone, enabling a select few bank employees to make decisions without detection by others. Blockchain technology enables data transparency by securely storing all transactions on a chain, making it easy to track borrowers.

Case 6: A Sum of 9,000 Crore Has Been Deposited Into the Bank Account of the Cab Driver (2023)

On October 3, 2023, news emerged in the media regarding a fraudulent transaction of INR 9,000 crore that was attributed to the Chennai bank. An amount was deposited into the bank account belonging to a cab driver named Rajkumar. The cab driver provided a statement to the media indicating the amount of money involved. The debiting of the funds occurred within a span of 30 minutes following the wrong transaction. Meanwhile, Rajkumar transferred INR 21,000 to the bank account of one of his acquaintances. Rajkumar also reported that the bank employees assured me that they would handle the matter, but requested that I refrain from lodging any complaints or publicising the issue.

Reason for the transaction: The primary cause of the erroneous transaction was the lack of proper verification of the transaction. Additionally, while manually inputting client details, there is a possibility of similar errors occurring.

Interference of Blockchain: Blockchain technology mandates that all transactions must undergo verification by all network members, and ensures that stored data, such as consumers' personal details, remains unalterable.

5. **Evolvement of Peer-to-Peer Transactions:** Peer-to-peer transactions refer to the direct exchange of cryptocurrencies between users, without the need for any third party or middleman. Peer-to-peer transactions offer several significant benefits, including personalised offers, exemption from transaction costs, global accessibility, and a wide range of payment options. P2P exchanges not only facilitate the connection between buyers and sellers but also offer transaction security and mitigate the danger of fraudulent actions (Moenninghoff and Wieandt 2013). It employs escrow as a means of safeguarding the cryptocurrency. In addition to several benefits, there are also drawbacks such as limited liquidity and sluggish trade velocity. For peer-to-peer transactions, both sides must confirm the transaction. If there is a delay from any party, the transaction cannot proceed.
   5.1. Centralized vs Decentralized Banking Systems: Centralised banking systems and decentralised banking systems differ in various aspects such as regulatory power, transaction speed, and transaction cost (Klagge and Martin, 2005; Aysuna, 2019). Here are some of the differences:
6. **Implementation of Blockchain Technology In Banking:** Implementing Blockchain technology in Banking offers various advantages/benefits like more efficiency, security, high speed, data transparency etc (Garg et al., 2021). Following are the ways in which blockchain technology can be implemented in Banks:
   1. ***Auditing and Fraud Prevention:*** By leveraging blockchain technology in decentralised finance, it becomes effortless to identify and prevent fraudulent activities, while also facilitating more effective and streamlined auditing procedures.
   2. ***Customer Privacy and Authentication:*** Blockchain technology enhances consumer data security, hence providing customers with increased privacy and authentication.
   3. ***Central Bank Digital Currencies:*** Financial institutions are adopting blockchain technology to establish digital currencies in order to enhance the efficiency of transactions.

Table 1. Centralized vs. decentralized banking systems

Centralized Banking Systems	Decentralized Banking Systems
A centralized banking system is characterized by the presence of a central authority, typically a government or central bank, which exercises regulatory and supervisory control over the entirety of the financial system.	Decentralized systems work without a central governing authority, but instead rely on blockchain technologies and smart contracts.
Centralized banking is constrained by geographical limits due to the presence of physical branch sites and a limited geographic reach to its customers.	Conversely, decentralized financing enables universal access to financial services through the Internet, facilitating borderless transactions.
The fees and operational expenses associated with traditional banking systems are comparatively higher.	Decentralized banking systems provide clients with reduced operational expenses and fees.
Centralized banking can result in a monopoly where a few major banks dominate the market and restrict competition.	Decentralized banking systems foster an open and highly competitive market.
Centralized banks encounter the obstacle of being vulnerable to a single point of failure. In the event of a crisis, any issues faced by the central institution might have a substantial impact on the entirety of the banking system.	Decentralized financing utilizes a distributed ledger system, which mitigates the risk of a single point of failure by storing the ledger on multiple computers.

4. ***Supply Chain Finance:*** Blockchain technology can enhance supply chain financing by facilitating transparent documentation of products and transactions, hence mitigating the risk of fraud and enhancing transaction security and efficiency.
5. ***Digital Identity Verification:*** The utilisation of Blockchain technology can enhance the security and privacy of the identity verification process, hence increasing the efficiency of Know Your Customer (KYC) procedures.
6. ***Payments and Cross-Border Transactions:*** Utilising blockchain technology enables expedited and cost-effective cross-border transactions by eliminating the need for intermediaries, hence reducing transaction costs and enhancing speed.
7. ***Smart Contracts:*** Smart contracts, powered by blockchain technology, enable the automation of different financial processes such as loan approval and settlements of derivatives. These contracts execute transactions or agreements automatically based on prewritten scripts.
    7.1. **Addressing the Gaps in Implementations:** While there are numerous benefits to incorporating blockchain technology into the banking sector, it also presents certain challenges (Martino, 2019).

1. **Cost Of Implementation:** Smaller banks may face difficulties due to the substantial initial investment and continuous operational expenses involved in adopting blockchain technology. Therefore, the expense associated with using blockchain technology appears to be a significant obstacle.
2. **Customer Adoption:** It is necessary to teach both consumers and staff about blockchain technology, its advantages, and its functioning, as the current customers lack awareness of the latest technology. However, this task may provide a challenge. The stakeholders of the banks may exhibit resistance towards this cultural transformation within the organisation.
3. **Legal Issues:** The cross-border transactions must comply with various regulatory restrictions. Global blockchain transactions might give rise to intricate legal and jurisdictional concerns.
4. **Scalability Issue:** The addition of a larger number of transactions to the blockchain will inevitably give rise to issues and challenges related to scalability. Public blockchains experience increased congestion and reduced transaction speed as the number of transactions increases. Therefore, the primary focus is on scalability.
5. **Standardization and Governance:** Due to the absence of globally recognised standards for blockchains, ensuring interoperability and consistency across various systems becomes challenging.
6. **Energy Consumption:** The utilisation of blockchain technology poses a significant obstacle in terms of energy usage, hence giving rise to environmental apprehensions. Certain blockchain networks, particularly those that employ proof-of-work consensus, exhibit a significant energy consumption, making their utilisation somewhat problematic.
7. **Security and data privacy issue:** Although blockchain technology is mostly known for its robust security and data protection, it is not impervious to hackers when it comes to smart contracts. The utmost responsibility is to guarantee the security of the blockchain network and prevent any unauthorised access. Additionally, achieving a harmonious equilibrium between data transparency and data privacy poses a problem in this context. Ensuring the confidentiality of certain sensitive client data can be problematic, given that the data is accessible to all users on the network.

7. FUTURE SCOPE AND CONCLUSION

The future prospects of blockchain are highly intriguing since this technology offers numerous advantages that will potentially transform various aspects of the finance industry. The banking industry is confronted with a significant predicament of fraudulent activities, leading to substantial financial losses for firms, customers, and the overall economy on an annual basis. In order to avoid fraudulent activities and minimise their consequences, banks must implement a range of procedures, such as employing human analytics and utilising technical solutions. Albrecht (1996) asserts that ineffective internal controls heighten the likelihood of fraudulent activities. These include a deficient control environment, inadequate segregation of duties, insufficient physical safeguards, insufficient independent checks, improper authorization, inadequate documentation and record-keeping, control overrides, and an inadequate accounting system. The implementation of blockchain technology has the potential to revolutionise the banking sector by enhancing the speed, cost efficiency, and transparency of cross-border transactions and payments. By eliminating the need for third-party involvement, it reduces the fees involved with international money transfers. Smart contracts can automate financial operations such as trade settlements and loan approvals. This can aid in diminishing the necessity of intermediaries and optimising the processes. Blockchains can enhance the security and confidentiality of the identity verification process, hence bolstering the security of Know Your Customer (KYC) and other operations. Banks can have the ability to utilise blockchain technology to convert different assets, like equities, real estate, and art, into digital tokens. This process enhances their accessibility for both trading and ownership purposes. Blockchain technology has the potential to bolster the security and confidentiality of client data, granting customers greater authority over their personal information. The transparent ledger of Blockchain can facilitate banks in identifying and thwarting fraudulent activities, hence enhancing the efficiency of auditing procedures. In addition, banks have the opportunity to form partnerships with fintech businesses that utilise blockchain technology to provide cutting-edge financial services. Despite the numerous advantages, the implementation of blockchain in the banking system faces a significant difficulty due to the absence of a regulatory body or framework. This creates the potential for increased unlawful or immoral actions and disorder. To mitigate these risks, we propose the utilisation of a regulatory sandbox. The sandbox defines a limited scope with reduced criteria and processes for accessing the market. Under the premise that consumer rights are protected, FinTech innovation companies are authorised to swiftly carry out activities and are authorised to grow within the controlled environment of the regulatory sandbox. Also, semi-decentralized blockchains can be used to offer both private and public applications with permission base and permission-less features. Awareness programs and knowledge transfer strategies can be followed to make users aware and ready to adopt the technology.

REFERENCES

AbuNaser, M., & Alkhatib, A. A. (2019, April). Advanced survey of blockchain for the internet of things smart home. In 2019 IEEE Jordan international joint conference on electrical engineering and information technology (JEEIT) (pp. 58-62). IEEE. doi:10.1109/JEEIT.2019.8717441

Ali, O., Jaradat, A., Kulakli, A., & Abuhalimeh, A. (2021). A comparative study: Blockchain technology utilization benefits, challenges and functionalities. *IEEE Access : Practical Innovations, Open Solutions*, *9*, 12730–12749. doi:10.1109/ACCESS.2021.3050241

Aysuna, U. (2019). *Centralized versus Decentralized Banking: Bank-level evidence from US Call Reports* (No. 2019-03).

Bhagwani, S., & Govindaraj, P. (2020). Financial and Non-Financial Applications of Blockchain. *International Journal of Innovative Technology and Exploring Engineering*, *9*(6), 1050–1054. doi:10.35940/ijitee.F4117.049620

Bolat, A. (2016). Common models of banking System Regulation: advantages and disadvantages. *ХАБАРШЫ*, 314.

Calvo, S. G. (2010). The global financial crisis of 2008-10: A view from the social sectors. *UNDP-HDRO Occasional Papers*, (2010/18).

Cavico, F. J., & Mujtaba, B. G. (2017). Wells Fargo's fake accounts scandal and its legal and ethical implications for management. *S.A.M. Advanced Management Journal*, *82*(2), 4.

ENS Economic Bureau. (2023). *Banks saw highest number of frauds in digital payments in FY23: RBI*. Author.

Galazova, S. S., & Magomaeva, L. R. (2019). *The transformation of traditional banking activity in digital*. Academic Press.

Garg, P., Gupta, B., Chauhan, A. K., Sivarajah, U., Gupta, S., & Modgil, S. (2021). Measuring the perceived benefits of implementing blockchain technology in the banking sector. *Technological Forecasting and Social Change*, *163*, 120407. doi:10.1016/j.techfore.2020.120407

Golosova, J., & Romanovs, A. (2018, November). The advantages and disadvantages of the blockchain technology. In *2018 IEEE 6th workshop on advances in information, electronic and electrical engineering (AIEEE)* (pp. 1-6). IEEE. 10.1109/AIEEE.2018.8592253

Guo, Y., & Liang, C. (2016). Blockchain application and outlook in the banking industry. *Financial Innovation*, *2*(1), 1–12. doi:10.1186/s40854-016-0034-9

Jones, C. I. (2009). The global financial crisis of 2007–20. *A Supplement to Macroeconomics, 1*, 1-45.

Kaur, G. (2023). Blockchain Technology: Perspective From the Banking Sector. *Revolutionizing Financial Services and Markets Through FinTech and Blockchain*, 278-287.

Khanna, A., & Arora, B. (2009). A study to investigate the reasons for bank frauds and the implementation of preventive security controls in Indian banking industry. *International Journal of Business Science and Applied Management*, *4*(3), 1–21.

Klagge, B., & Martin, R. (2005). Decentralized versus centralized financial systems: Is there a case for local capital markets? *Journal of Economic Geography*, *5*(4), 387–421. doi:10.1093/jeg/lbh071

Martino, P. (2019). Blockchain technology: Challenges and opportunities for banks. *International Journal of Financial Innovation in Banking*, *2*(4), 314–333. doi:10.1504/IJFIB.2019.104535

Moenninghoff, S. C., & Wieandt, A. (2013). The future of peer-to-peer finance. *Schmalenbachs Zeitschrift fur Betriebswirtschaftliche Forschung = Schmalenbach Journal of Business Research, 65*(5), 466–487. doi:10.1007/BF03372882

Niranjanamurthy, M., Nithya, B. N., & Jagannatha, S. J. C. C. (2019). Analysis of Blockchain technology: Pros, cons and SWOT. *Cluster Computing, 22*(S6), 14743–14757. doi:10.1007/s10586-018-2387-5

Nofer, M., Gomber, P., Hinz, O., & Schiereck, D. (2017). Blockchain. *Business & Information Systems Engineering, 59*(3), 183–187. doi:10.1007/s12599-017-0467-3

Panigrahi, C. M. A., Sinha, A., Garg, A., & Mehta, A. (2019). A case study on the downfall of kingfisher airlines. *Journal of Management Research and Analysis, 6*(2), 81–84. doi:10.18231/j.jmra.2019.014

Paul, P., Aithal, P. S., Saavedra, R., & Ghosh, S. (2021). Blockchain Technology and its Types—A Short Review. *International Journal of Applied Science and Engineering, 9*(2), 189–200. doi:10.30954/2322-0465.2.2021.7

Sarmah, S. S. (2018). Understanding blockchain technology. *Computing in Science & Engineering, 8*(2), 23–29.

Sharma, R., Mehta, K., Sidhu, N. K., & Vyas, V. (2023). Extending UTAUT2 Model With Sustainability and Psychological Factors in Adoption of Blockchain Technology for the Digital Transformation of Banks in India. In Revolutionizing Financial Services and Markets Through FinTech and Blockchain (pp. 27-43). IGI Global. doi:10.4018/978-1-6684-8624-5.ch003

Shrivas, M. K., & Yeboah, T. (2019). The disruptive blockchain: Types, platforms and applications. *Texila International Journal of Academic Research, 3*, 17–39. doi:10.21522/TIJAR.2014.SE.19.01.Art003

Singhal, J., & Chauhan, V. (2021). Analytical study of PMC (Punjab & Maharashtra Co-operative bank) by considering financial failure of bank. *Globus-An International Journal of Management and IT, 12*(2), 6–10. doi:10.46360/globus.mgt.120211002

Sood, K., Kaur, B., & Grima, S. (2022). Revamping Indian non-life insurance industry with a trusted network: Blockchain technology. In *Big Data: A game changer for insurance industry* (pp. 213–228). Emerald Publishing Limited. doi:10.1108/978-1-80262-605-620221014

Tasatanattakool, P., & Techapanupreeda, C. (2018, January). Blockchain: Challenges and applications. In *2018 International Conference on Information Networking (ICOIN)* (pp. 473-475). IEEE. 10.1109/ICOIN.2018.8343163

Xu, M., Chen, X., & Kou, G. (2019). A systematic review of blockchain. *Financial Innovation, 5*(1), 1–14. doi:10.1186/s40854-019-0147-z

Zarrin, J., Wen Phang, H., Babu Saheer, L., & Zarrin, B. (2021). Blockchain for decentralization of internet: Prospects, trends, and challenges. *Cluster Computing, 24*(4), 2841–2866. doi:10.1007/s10586-021-03301-8 PMID:34025209

Zetzsche, D. A., Arner, D. W., & Buckley, R. P. (2020). Decentralized finance (defi). *Journal of Financial Regulation, 6*(2), 172–203. doi:10.1093/jfr/fjaa010

Chapter 3
Fashion-Tech Disruption:
The Ft.you Case Study

Sahithi Josyula
Carnegie Mellon University, USA

Birud Sindhav
University of Nebraska at Omaha, USA

Dale Eesley
University of Nebraska at Omaha, USA

Shana Redd
https://orcid.org/0000-0003-4342-9694
University of Nebraska at Omaha, USA

ABSTRACT

Conceptual research often lags in practice when firms disrupt business models. Immersive case studies help bridge this gap. This case explores the journey of a Hyderabad-based fashion-tech startup Ft.you. The fashion business is competitive and dynamic, saturated with players going head-to-head to stay relevant. Ft.you wants to change the way Indian women choose to dress with an innovative application that removes the hassles related to tailoring services, letting users customize the dress within an app, with input spaces for fabric selection and measurements. The case discusses the partnerships that Ft.you has established with fabric manufacturers and tailors and describes its marketing/sales strategies. It also documents the key decision points in the early stages of the journey of Ft.you.

INTRODUCTION

It was a bright, sunny afternoon in the city of Hyderabad. The businesswomen's expo was humming with announcements, and vendors were organising their stalls while trying to attract visitors and potential customers. This was second year of a businesswomen's expo at Hyderabad, which had been funded and supported by state agencies. Mrs. Rama Patlolla was not sure if enough people would stop by the booth

DOI: 10.4018/979-8-3693-3253-5.ch003

of her startup, Ft.you. Her app was aimed at women who wanted to take better control of their fashion choices. Rama's goal was to find paying subscribers.

At the expo, fewer than 100 customers signed up. It became evident to Rama that they did not have any form of digital marketing strategy in place, significantly complicating the customer acquisition process. Despite having some presence on social media, it failed to garner substantial followers. Given the product they offered and the value they provided, it was still essential to have a good social media presence and a carefully designed digital marketing strategy, notwithstanding the need to solve operational problems.

THE DEVELOPMENT OF FT.YOU

Setting the Stage

Before entering the realm of fashion and business, Rama served as a Vice President of software operation at Wells Fargo. While content with her job, she still wanted to create something of her own. In 2013, as she explored her options, she chose to collaborate with a few colleagues to develop an idea for a grocery delivery e-commerce platform. Unfortunately, the project stalled. Meanwhile, she joined another software engineering firm as a team leader. She managed it effectively, gaining extensive experience in overseeing large and diverse teams. This experience not only boosted her confidence but also fuelled her motivation to venture out on her own.

She ultimately made the decision to become her own employer and joined We Hub, India's first state-led incubator for women entrepreneurs. With a vision to provide women from diverse socio-economic backgrounds, demographics, and business scales with opportunities for entrepreneurship and economic empowerment, We Hub proved to be instrumental. While it offered invaluable assistance in establishing business relationships with various vendors, manufacturers, and stitching experts, it primarily focused

Figure 1. Internet and social media use in India

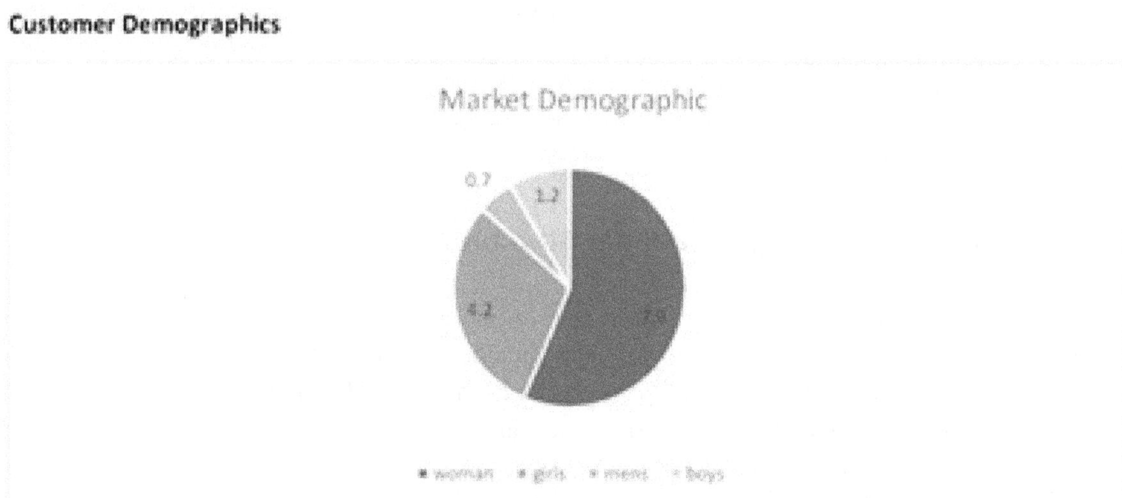

on providing networking opportunities as a startup incubator. However, the founders, including Rama, had to independently cultivate market access.

During her time at We Hub, Rama explored image processing but soon recognized that the entry barriers were excessively high. Consequently, she reverted to her original interest—a more feasible yet competitive option: e-commerce. Similar to many startup founders, the concept of Ft.you originated from the personal experiences of both the founders, Rama and Saraswathi, as they were having their garments tailored, including both traditional Indian attire and contemporary fashion. It is noteworthy that in India, selecting fabrics and opting for personalized tailoring remains commonplace especially for females. This practice is also prevalent among males, though they constitute a smaller segment, though most of the tailors are males.

Filling in the Gap

Ft.you endeavors to bridge the existing gaps among weavers/textile manufacturers, tailors, and potential customers. Many of the customers they have served expressed dissatisfaction with the quality of fabric from local boutiques and the inconvenience of finding suitable tailors. By providing an efficient online gateway through a mobile application, accessible from the comfort of one's home at a reasonable price, Rama aims to position Ft.you as a solution to these challenges.

For instance, in the vicinity of the Hyderabad Hitech district, home to numerous tech and fintech companies, tailoring costs are exceptionally high. This concerned Rama as she realized that the tailoring charges at her sister's boutique, located outside the main city, and those in the Hitech district were in different tiers.

Ft.you offers a diverse selection of fabrics, eliminating the need for potential customers to source cloth from a textile store. The extensive network of textile manufacturers ensures multiple fabric options are available, providing customers with choices that go beyond what is typically found in local shops. Recognizing the importance of fabric in determining the look, texture, drape, and overall quality of the dress, Ft.you collaborates directly with textile manufacturers to secure top quality and unique designs.

Moreover, many Ft.you customers tend to repeat their orders due to the simplified delivery mechanism. They highly value the time saved by avoiding visits to the tailor for custom fitment and measurements.

Ft.you is a dedicated application designed to address all clothing needs for women. The app is accessible on both the Google Play Store and the Apple App Store. Presently, while order fulfillment primarily occurs through online channels, Ft.you maintains a limited physical presence and relies on word-of-mouth advertising and customer outreach. Order requests are received through phone calls, online channels, and the app itself. As of 2022, they typically handle over 400 orders per quarter, generating revenue exceeding INR 0.5 million during that period.

Key Personnel and the Organizational Structure

As of 2023, the company boasts a team of six full-time employees, supplemented by several part-time staff members dedicating approximately 30 hours per month. The full-time workforce comprises remote developers and graphic designers. A notable challenge currently faced by the company is the absence of a dedicated marketing team, and they are actively seeking a UI/UX developer to enhance the application's user interface and experience.

The app, designed to replicate the boutique experience with detailed measurements, design ideas, customization options, and various material choices, has its alpha version available on both the App Store and Google Play Store.

In the initial stages of Ft.you, Rama was approached by numerous investors. However, she opted for managerial control, choosing not to dilute her investment by involving multiple stakeholders. Presently, the company is in the early revenue stage, with their first order processed in September 2022.

Ownership of the majority equity lies among friends and close relatives, with only one outside investor. Notably, no investments were sought until after the initial launch of the application in its alpha stage. Following the alpha version's debut in the last quarter of 2022, external investors expressed interest, and the company successfully raised about US $500,000 during that round. This funding is deemed sufficient to sustain lean operations for the next 12 to 18 months.

Rama explains, "Look, people approached me with a proposal of investing 20 lac rupees (about USD 24,000 in late 2023) and receive 5% stake in the company. That is not a fair amount. We need capital to operate, but I cannot raise equity at such low valuation".

Ft.you aims to keep the burn rate of the venture capital reasonable and focus on ramping up revenue generation to break even by the end of the year. Ft.you recognizes the need to hire marketing personnel, which would also mean an increase in expenditure. They are outsourcing their legal and corporate law affairs to an external legal firm, which assists with drafting agreements, privacy policies, and more.

Business Strategy

The company's current business plan revolves around being an E-commerce gateway, and it explicitly avoids investing in a physical shop network. Ft.you is committed to maintaining and bolstering its digital presence. To reassure customers about the legitimacy of the company and to provide them with a clearer understanding of its distinctive features compared to a traditional boutique, Ft.you is contemplating hosting information sessions at exhibitions and expos. When Ft.you was showcased on Aha (Telugu regional language) TV channel in a program called "Nenu Super Women", their app downloads happened to grow substantially. They have also appeared in the Telugu print media. They did marketing in their residential community and their network, by which they crossed 7-figure sales (in Indian rupees) in a year. As of the fourth quarter of 2023, apart from the warehouse dedicated to storing cloth and packaging materials, there is no physical store or center associated with Ft.you.

Ft.you actively engages in additional expos and summit events to cultivate relationships with manufacturers, broaden its network of suppliers, and connect with potential customers. The company places significant emphasis on meeting potential app users during these events to gather real-time feedback on the app's usability and navigational aspects. Ft.you considers this direct interaction crucial for enhancing the user experience and ensuring that the app meets the needs and expectations of its users.

Network of Suppliers and Tailors

In the initial stages of Ft.you, when it operated under the name Tailor Hub, the team actively sought contacts for tailors and manufacturers. They accomplished this through independent research at We Hub and by leveraging the personal contacts of the company's founders. During this phase, Ft.you aimed to comprehend the operational processes of tailors, recognizing the challenges and opportunities presented by the COVID-19 pandemic.

While the pandemic posed obstacles, it also served as an opportunity, as tailors were compelled to manage orders, design, and deliver items without in-person interactions—a practice integral to Ft.you's model as well. Overcoming the absence of face-to-face communication became a pivotal challenge, especially given that tailors traditionally operated in physical shops.

The Ft.you team diligently sought to gauge the effectiveness of interpreting outfit concepts through various channels, including pictures, verbal communication via phone calls, and text messages. Their objective was to determine how well they could capture customers' ideas and deliver a product that aligned with expectations, all in the absence of traditional face-to-face interactions.

In the pursuit of understanding the tailor and supplier aggregation side of the business, the team conducted surveys and engaged with around 100 fabric suppliers and tailors, many of whom possessed decades of experience in developing and sewing various garments. As part of the ideation and incubation process, they visited multiple boutiques and tapped into the knowledge of tailors and fabric suppliers.

Their approach centered on retaining suppliers and tailors by ensuring a viable amount of business for them. Subsequently, they adopted a strategy wherein different tailoring shops would reach out to Ft.you, providing images of the apparel they stitched along with detailed videos. This allowed Ft.you to evaluate whether the tailors would be a good fit for the platform.

Following their inquiries, the Ft.you team meticulously narrowed down and finalized their vendor list to 20. Through their analysis, they observed that tailor skills exhibited variations based on geographical locations. For instance, tailors situated away from the main city demonstrated greater proficiency in stitching traditional outfits as opposed to western ensembles.

Rama described the challenges of maintaining the supplier network, "We are still growing. Consumer tastes change rapidly in the fashion industry. I cannot buy 200-300 meters of fabric in a single order and get stuck with excess inventory. Unfortunately, some suppliers expect us to buy that much as minimum order while our requirement is 20-30 meters".

Sourcing Strategy for Manufacturer and Weavers

During their research, Ft.you recognized that obtaining fabric from local stores would be costly, potentially deterring customers unwilling to pay higher prices. Consequently, they delved into online directories of weavers and textile manufacturers to identify cost-effective yet reliable options. Their initial interactions and business transactions primarily occurred with manufacturers based in Surat, a city in the state of Gujarat.

Encountering minimum order quantity (MOQ) challenges during negotiations, Ft.you realized that, being a small company, investing in the manufacturers' required 100 meters of cloth wasn't feasible. Accumulating excess inventory of unused fabric posed a significant challenge, particularly since they consistently updated their fabric material stock on the app. After negotiations, they successfully persuaded a few manufacturers to supply 30 meters to the Ft.you warehouse.

The creative team is actively exploring various manufacturers and weavers nationwide to diversify their supplier base. Their upcoming target in the fabric domain is to establish relationships with weavers in Andhra Pradesh, Jaipur, and a few suppliers of khadi, a handmade fabric with a significant historical connection to India's struggle for independence. Future plans also include onboarding some weavers and tailors on a fixed-income basis, thereby expanding their engagement with skilled artisans.

Marketing Strategy

At present, Ft.you caters to a typical customer profile—females aged 18 to 60—who actively seek well-fitted apparel with diverse fabric options and prioritize timely delivery. This customer base is characterized by internet savviness and a preference for online ordering. Typically, these customers use the mobile application to purchase ethnic wear, especially during festivals, wedding seasons, and other special occasions. Beyond offering a variety of fabrics, Ft.you distinguishes itself by providing value-added services such as alteration and embroidery.

Ft.you faces competitors vying for the attention of customers with similar preferences and needs. Binks (getbinks.com) is backed by Y-combinator and based in Bengaluru, India. It was established in 2019 and already ships worldwide. However, a quick look at the Facebook page of the company reveals almost universally negative reviews posted by the customers. Apparently, it is not easy to provide mass-customization even with the current level of technological sophistication. Similarly, Cloud tailor serves 7 countries, backed by seasoned business people, and has a sophisticated online presence. However, unlike Ft.you, they seem to have no network of fabric suppliers. To stand out in this competitive landscape, Ft.you continually works towards enhancing its offerings and services, ensuring a seamless and satisfying experience for its customers.

Rama notes that "We need to fine tune our marketing. We have hired an agency, but we still need to be more focused in how we approach our audience. Hitech city is a prime area for us to target customers, and we could have some physical presence there or hold events to attract more attention of our target customers".

Competition

There is a Hyderabad based company named Cloud Tailor whose business and operating model are very similar to that of Ft.you and it is currently available on app store. Cloud tailor started in December 2020, they are currently past their initial learning curve and their market penetration is much higher in comparison to Ft.you.

Understanding the competitive landscape is crucial for Ft.you in navigating the challenges posed by similar businesses. It presents an opportunity for Ft.you to analyze Cloud Tailor's strategies, identify areas for differentiation or improvement, and refine its own approach to enhance market presence and customer satisfaction. Continuous monitoring and strategic adaptation can contribute to Ft.you's success and competitiveness in the evolving market.

Notable differences in the user interface (UI) of both applications were observed, with Cloud Tailor standing out for its more effective and well-designed UI. This discrepancy is somewhat expected, given that Cloud Tailor has been in operation for a longer duration and has undergone more iterations compared to the alpha version of the Ft.you application.

Cloud Tailor's apparent strength lies in its robust sales and marketing strategy, evident through collaborations with influencers, retail stores, and a strong presence on social media. Their sales and visibility experienced significant growth, especially after their appearance on Shark Tank India in the first quarter of 2023. This television exposure played a crucial role in enhancing Cloud Tailor's popularity among users and viewers.

However, the most striking disparity between the two lies in the extent of social media presence and the level of investment in marketing and digital strategy by Cloud Tailor. This suggests that, while

Figure 2. Key metrics for Cloud Tailor

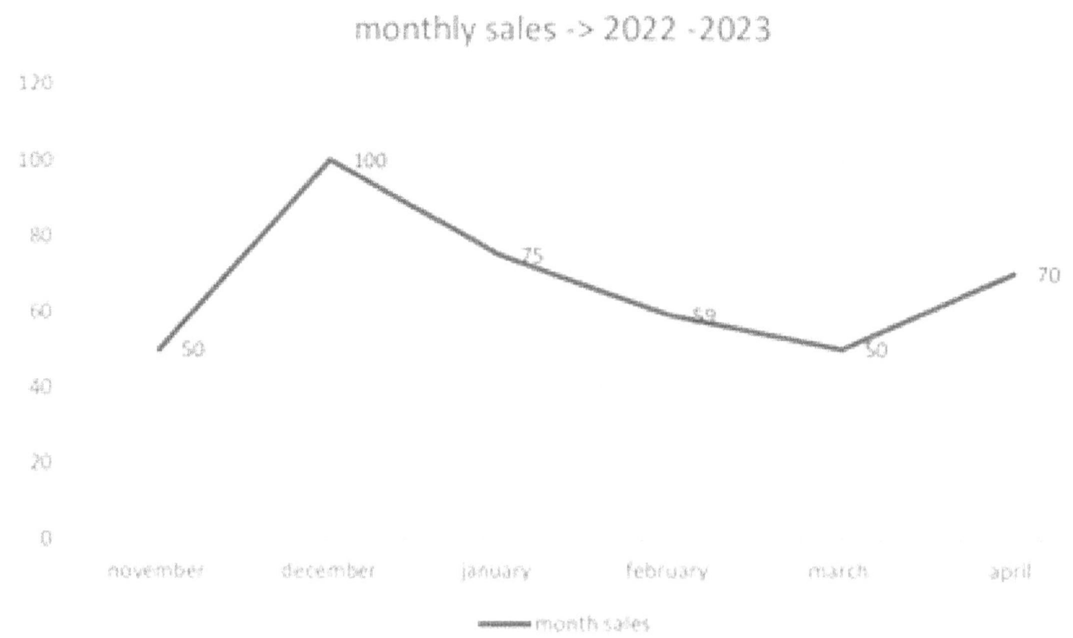

Ft.you may be in the earlier stages of its development, there is valuable insight to be gained from Cloud Tailor's approach to marketing and user engagement, providing an opportunity for Ft.you to refine its strategies for future growth and visibility. One striking difference between the two is that Ft.you is an eCommerce platform and Cloud Tailor is not. Ft.you communicates with its vendors through an app. So that the complete communication can be automated. It helps them in scaling. There are also other players like India-based getbinks.com eyeing the same market. Similarly, eShakti, Mtailor, and RedThreadCollection, all US-based, are major competitors when Ft.you thinks seriously about expanding globally. Ft.you should know that when going global, they will face a competitive landscape that has a different level of technological sophistication and financial resources. For example, Mtailor has developed a proprietary technology wherein a potential customers can put phone against a wall, take their own small video from 6-ft distance, and the software automatically translates that into custom measurements. Similarly, RedThreadCollection claims to create custom measurement from just a few pictures.

Ease in measurement is potentially connected to another issue: inclusivity in fashion. According to Kayla Marci, market analyst at retail and fashion technology firm Edited, inclusive sizing is necessary across all product types, as majority of US women are a size 14 and higher, and they also need fashionable clothes regardless of size. This need cannot be ignored by fashion companies (Howland, 2019). The fickle and constantly changing tastes of consumers is a structural feature of the fashion industry. Currently, sustainability is a big issue within the industry, signified by the movements such as save your wardrobe and circular fashion (Kourda, 2022). Ft.you should investigate such trends and incorporate within their company culture and operational strategy, if relevant.

Challenges

Delivery Challenges

In their early days, specifically during November and December 2022, Ft.you initially partnered with a delivery and logistics company. However, the experience proved to be unfavorable as they observed a lack of prioritization for small companies and startups like Ft.you. This resulted in delayed deliveries, leading to customer dissatisfaction. Faced with these challenges and the increasing volume of orders, Ft.you made the strategic decision to limit order intake, temporarily halt marketing activities, and seek a more reliable delivery partner.

The company has since successfully partnered with a different delivery service and is actively exploring collaborations with additional delivery services to diversify and mitigate risks. Given that many customers place orders for special occasions with the expectation of delivery within a week, Ft.you, which typically completes products in about 5-6 days, recognized the importance of addressing delays caused by delivery services. Consequently, they are cautious about committing to shorter deadlines due to the inherent risk associated with external delivery services.

These challenges highlight the inherent complexities and stressors that startups in the fashion industry, such as Ft.you, encounter in their day-to-day operations. Navigating logistical issues, especially in the realm of timely deliveries, is crucial for maintaining customer satisfaction and the overall success of the business.

Accuracy in Measurements Challenges

Capturing accurate measurements through the app has proven challenging for Ft.you, primarily because many users are not accustomed to taking measurements, and the team has noted that customers sometimes struggle to understand or follow written instructions. To address this challenge, the technical team at Ft.you is actively exploring the evaluation of AI/ML technologies to assist users in capturing precise measurements.

Despite serving over 200 customers, Ft.you has encountered some issues with fitting, particularly when customers enter incorrect measurements. Through analysis, it was observed that the most dissatisfied customers were those who had inputted inaccurate measurements. Recognizing the paramount importance of customer satisfaction, the Ft.you team is committed to addressing these concerns. They actively engage with dissatisfied customers, maintaining an ongoing correspondence to understand their specific issues and work towards resolution.

This commitment to customer satisfaction not only underscores Ft.you's dedication to quality service but also demonstrates their proactive approach in leveraging technology to improve the user experience and ensure accurate measurements for a more seamless fitting process.

App Side Challenges

The feasibility of the use of technology within fashion industry has enabled the startups like Ft.you. "In 2021, fashion companies invested between 1.6 and 1.8 percent of their revenues in technology. By 2030, that figure is expected to rise to between 3.0 and 3.5 percent" (McKinsey & Company, 2022, P. 2). For Ft.you, their app is a gateway for the customers to engage with Ft.you. The mobile application currently exhibits certain gaps that require attention. These gaps primarily pertain to design issues and logistical components that have yet to be fully integrated into the application. Addressing these aspects is crucial for enhancing the overall functionality and user experience of the app. The Ft.you team is actively working on closing these gaps to ensure a more comprehensive and streamlined mobile application for their users. Continuous improvement and refinement of these elements will contribute to the app's overall effectiveness and user satisfaction.

Vendor Outreach Challenges

Ft.you is confronted with a significant challenge in facilitating smooth communication among vendors across the country. Vendors and manufacturers situated in different regions are experiencing difficulties with video call services, and the identification of colors over video calls is compromised due to poor video quality. In response, Ft.you is exploring solutions such as maintaining a standardized color palette that can be shared with customers to overcome these challenges.

To enhance their design capabilities and ensure uniqueness in their offerings, Ft.you is planning to hire a fabric designer who will work exclusively with the brand. This designer will focus on creating prints and designs that are distinctively associated with Ft.you and are not available for retail or wholesale purchase.

In collaboration with the National Institute of Fashion Design (NIFT) in Hyderabad, the creative team at Ft.you is working on establishing effective channels for conveying design ideas to weavers and block-print manufacturers across the country. This strategic partnership aims to streamline communication, foster innovation, and bring unique designs to the market, showcasing Ft.you's commitment to delivering exclusive and high-quality products to its customers.

Decision Points

Rama is very eager to let others, especially women entrepreneurs, learn from her tough journey so far. "I see many people from my network get discouraged within months of being in an incubator, wind up their business, and leave, losing the money they have spent getting their business up to that point. I want people to understand the resilience and mindset needed to tough it out. It requires long hours and still, there will be a lot of disappointment. It is not easy to be an entrepreneur".

Ft.you has set its sights on reaching the global stage and is actively working towards refining its tailoring services. The company is dedicated to continuous improvement, actively seeking consumer feedback to incorporate the best practices into their services. Having reached a level of sophistication, Ft.you can now accurately assess whether manufacturing costs are precise or potentially overstated. Additionally, the company has established the capability to secure wholesale rates from cloth manufacturers.

Presently, Ft.you's focus is on optimizing marketing strategies and enhancing its online presence. The company is strategically aligning its efforts with seasonal requirements. For instance, during the November to December period, Ft.you is concentrated on acquiring party wear materials to meet the demands of the season. Similarly, for the summer months, the focus shifts towards acquiring cottons and khadi, aligning with consumer preferences for lightweight fabrics during warmer weather.

Recognizing their niche as a boutique specializing in unique clothing, Ft.you has come to the realization that engaging in mass production and maintaining a vast surplus inventory of cloth is not aligned with their business model. In response, they have decided to establish a small manufacturing and embroidery unit. This strategic move allows them to continually update their design library, staying distinctive and responsive in the dynamic fashion industry.

Presently, Ft.you has one or two members working in the embroidery unit and aims to expand this team by adding more skilled personnel. Furthermore, the company is in the process of calculating the costs involved in setting up an in-house block printing facility, complete with unique design concepts. This initiative aligns with Ft.you's commitment to maintaining exclusivity in their offerings while also controlling the production process, contributing to their overall business strategy and long-term sustainability.

In addition to their focus on women's wear, Ft.you has been exploring and designing clothing for boys and men. A recent success story involved the design of a wedding collection specifically tailored for grooms at a wedding event. Despite the app not initially featuring the required graphics and user interface (UI) to facilitate the design of men's wear as seamlessly as it did for the women's collection, Ft.you proactively accepted orders through the app and successfully crafted customized clothing for their male clientele (Wynn & Williams, 2012).

TEACHING NOTE: FT.YOU – AN APP FOR YOUR APPAREL

This case study explores the journey of Ft.you, a fashion-tech startup based in Hyderabad, India. The case delves into the challenges faced and decisions made by the founder, Rama Patlolla, as Ft.you aims to revolutionize how women choose and customize their clothing through a mobile application. Key aspects covered include the development of Ft.you, its business strategy, partnerships, marketing efforts, competition, challenges, and future plans.

Learning Objectives

- Understanding Fashion-Tech Startups: Explore the challenges and opportunities faced by fashion-tech startups, particularly in the context of tailoring services.
- Business Model and Strategy: Analyze the business model of Ft.you, focusing on its digital approach, supplier network, and marketing strategy.
- Partnerships and Networking: Assess the importance of partnerships in a startup's journey, with a specific focus on Ft.you's collaborations with fabric manufacturers and tailors.
- Competitive Analysis: Examine the competitive landscape by comparing Ft.you with Cloud Tailor, understanding the impact of UI, marketing strategies, and market penetration.
- Operational Challenges: Explore the challenges faced by Ft.you, such as delivery issues, accuracy in measurements, app design gaps, and communication challenges with vendors.

Analysis of Ft.you's Competitive Position

Ft.you operates in the competitive and dynamic landscape of fashion-tech startups, aiming to disrupt traditional tailoring services through its mobile application. The case provides insights into several factors influencing Ft.you's competitive position:

Business Model and Digital Presence

Ft.you's commitment to a digital-only presence is both a strength and a challenge. While it allows the company to offer convenience and customization to users, it faces competition from traditional boutiques and emerging fashion-tech players. The digital model allows for scalability but requires robust marketing and user engagement.

Supplier Network and Material Diversity

Ft.you's strategic partnerships with fabric manufacturers and tailors contribute to its unique value proposition. The diverse network ensures a wide range of fabric options, addressing the dissatisfaction customers often face with local boutiques. However, challenges in maintaining this network, especially regarding minimum order quantities, pose operational hurdles.

Competitive Landscape With Cloud Tailor

The presence of a competitor, Cloud Tailor, with a similar business model and higher market penetration, adds complexity. Cloud Tailor's effective UI, robust marketing, and social media presence, especially after appearing on Shark Tank India, highlight areas where Ft.you can improve to stay competitive.

Operational Challenges

Delivery delays, accuracy in measurements, and gaps in the mobile application are operational challenges that directly impact customer satisfaction. Addressing these issues is critical for retaining customers and differentiating Ft.you in the market.

Global Aspirations and Niche Focus

Ft.you's aspirations to reach the global stage indicate a forward-looking strategy. Focusing on unique, boutique-style clothing for women, experimenting with designs for men, and planning a small manufacturing unit contribute to a niche approach that can set Ft.you apart in the long run.

Important Actions for Success

Enhance Digital Marketing and UI/UX Design

Invest in a robust digital marketing strategy to increase brand visibility and user acquisition. This includes targeted social media campaigns, influencer partnerships, and participation in relevant expos.

Prioritize UI/UX improvements for the mobile application to match or exceed the standards set by competitors like Cloud Tailor. A seamless and visually appealing app enhances user experience, encouraging retention and positive word-of-mouth.

Optimize Supplier Relationships

Strengthen relationships with fabric manufacturers and tailors by addressing challenges related to minimum order quantities and variations in tailor skills. Negotiate flexible terms to accommodate Ft.you's dynamic business model.

Explore partnerships with weavers and tailors in different regions, expanding the diversity of fabric options and leveraging regional expertise in garment production.

Strategic Partnerships for Global Reach

Actively pursue strategic partnerships beyond local collaborations. Engage with international fabric suppliers, designers, or even influencers to broaden Ft.you's reach.

Leverage partnerships to enhance the cultural authenticity of designs, making Ft.you's offerings appealing to a global audience.

Implement AI/ML for Measurements

Accelerate the evaluation and implementation of AI/ML technologies to assist users in capturing accurate measurements. This addresses a critical pain point for customers and contributes to higher customer satisfaction.

Communicate the introduction of technology-driven measurement assistance as a unique feature, reinforcing Ft.you's commitment to innovation.

Streamline Logistics and Delivery Services

Diversify delivery service partnerships to mitigate risks associated with delays and prioritize those that align with Ft.you's commitment to timely deliveries.

Communicate transparently with customers about potential delays, managing expectations effectively. Implement strategies to ensure the most accurate and efficient delivery timelines.

Ft.you's success hinges on a combination of strategic refinement, technological adoption, and customer-centric operations. By addressing challenges, refining its digital strategy, optimizing supplier relationships, forging strategic partnerships, and innovating with technology, Ft.you can position itself competitively and achieve its aspirations for global recognition in the fashion-tech industry.

Five Forces Analysis for Ft.you

1. Threat of New Entrants

Low to Moderate: While the fashion-tech industry is dynamic, Ft.you has established a presence with an innovative app. The entry barriers include the need for technology expertise, supplier relationships, and understanding of the local fashion market.

2. Bargaining Power of Buyers

Moderate: The buyers (customers) have options in the market, and their bargaining power is influenced by factors such as fabric choices, prices, and delivery times. However, the personalized and convenient nature of Ft.you's service provides some degree of customer loyalty.

3. Bargaining Power of Suppliers

Moderate: Ft.you collaborates with various fabric suppliers and tailors. The bargaining power of suppliers varies; some may demand higher minimum orders, impacting inventory management. The diversity of suppliers mitigates this to some extent.

4. Threat of Substitute Products or Services

Moderate: Traditional boutiques and other online platforms offering similar customization services pose a threat. However, Ft.you's focus on an efficient app, diverse fabric options, and value-added services creates a unique value proposition.

5. Intensity of Competitive Rivalry

High: The fashion-tech industry is competitive. Cloud Tailor, a competitor, has a higher market penetration. Both companies are vying for the same customer segment. Ft.you needs to enhance its marketing strategies, digital presence, and user interface to stay competitive.

Ft.you operates in an industry with moderate threats from new entrants, buyers, and suppliers. The company faces competition from substitutes and experiences high competitive rivalry. Strategic focus on technology, supplier relationships, and differentiation will be crucial for Ft.you to maintain and improve its competitive position in the market.

SWOT Analysis for Ft.you

Strengths

- Digital-First Model: Ft.you operates in the digital space, offering users the convenience of customizing outfits through a mobile application. This allows for scalability, efficient order processing, and a broader reach.
- Diverse Supplier Network: The strategic partnerships with fabric manufacturers and tailors contribute to a diverse range of fabric options, giving customers more choices than traditional boutiques.
- Commitment to Niche and Unique Designs: Ft.you's focus on boutique-style clothing, experimentation with men's wear, and plans for a small manufacturing unit demonstrate a commitment to uniqueness, setting it apart in the fashion industry.
- Global Aspirations: The company aspires to reach the global stage, indicating forward-thinking and ambitious strategic goals. This global outlook positions Ft.you for potential expansion beyond regional boundaries.

- Customer Engagement and Feedback: Ft.you actively engages with customers, values feedback, and maintains correspondence with dissatisfied customers. This commitment to customer satisfaction contributes to building brand loyalty (Habel et al., 2020).

Weaknesses

- Limited Marketing Presence: Ft.you faces challenges in digital marketing and lacks the social media visibility seen in competitors like Cloud Tailor. This limits brand awareness and customer acquisition.
- Operational Challenges: The company encounters challenges in delivery services, measurement accuracy, and mobile application gaps. These operational issues directly impact customer satisfaction and retention.
- Competitive Disadvantage: Cloud Tailor, a competitor with a similar model, has a more effective UI, strong marketing, and higher market penetration. Ft.you's alpha version and marketing strategy need refinement to compete effectively.

Opportunities

- Strategic Partnerships: Exploring partnerships with international fabric suppliers, designers, or influencers can enhance Ft.you's global reach and bring cultural authenticity to its designs.
- AI/ML Technology Integration: Implementing AI/ML technologies for measurements addresses a critical customer pain point, improving accuracy and providing a unique selling point in the fashion-tech market.
- Regional Collaboration with NIFT: Collaborating with NIFT and other design institutes can streamline communication with weavers and manufacturers, fostering innovation and ensuring unique designs for Ft.you.
- Diversification into Men's Fashion: Ft.you's success with a wedding collection for men indicates potential in diversifying into men's fashion. Strengthening the UI for men's wear design could tap into a new market segment.

Threats

- Intense Competition: The fashion-tech industry is highly competitive, and Ft.you faces competition from established players like Cloud Tailor. Continuous innovation and strategic marketing are necessary to stay relevant.
- Logistical Challenges: Dependency on external delivery services poses risks to timely deliveries. Delays can result in customer dissatisfaction and impact Ft.you's reputation.
- Changing Consumer Preferences: Rapid changes in fashion trends and consumer tastes pose challenges for Ft.you. Flexibility in sourcing materials and staying ahead of trends is crucial.
- Minimum Order Quantity (MOQ) Issues: Negotiating MOQ with fabric manufacturers presents challenges. Suppliers expecting larger orders than Ft.you requires can lead to excess inventory and financial strain.

SWOT Summary

Ft.you's strengths lie in its digital model, diverse supplier network, commitment to uniqueness, and global aspirations. However, weaknesses in marketing, operational challenges, and competitive disadvantages need attention. Strategic partnerships, technology integration, diversification, and addressing logistical challenges are crucial for capitalizing on opportunities and mitigating threats in the dynamic fashion-tech landscape.

Discussion Questions Set 1 (for a 2.5 to 3 Hours Class Session)

1. Business Development Journey: Discuss Rama Patlolla's journey from a software engineering manager to the founder of Ft.you. What motivated her to transition into entrepreneurship, and how did her experiences contribute to the development of Ft.you?
2. Business Model: Evaluate Ft.you's business model. How does the app address the challenges in traditional tailoring services, and what value does it offer to customers? Discuss the decision to maintain a digital-only presence and avoid physical shops.
3. Partnerships and Supplier Network: Examine the importance of Ft.you's partnerships with fabric manufacturers and tailors. How did they build and refine their network? What challenges did they face in maintaining a diverse supplier base?
4. Competition: Analyze the competitive landscape, focusing on the comparison between Ft.you and Cloud Tailor. How does Cloud Tailor's longer presence in the market impact its strategies and market penetration?
5. Operational Challenges: Discuss the challenges faced by Ft.you, such as delivery issues, accuracy in measurements, and app design gaps. How are they addressing these challenges, and what role does technology play in overcoming them?
6. Global Aspirations: Explore Ft.you's aspirations to reach the global stage. How are they refining their tailoring services, and what strategic steps are they taking to achieve their global objectives?

Discussion Questions Set 2 (for a 1 to 1.5 Hours Class Session)

1. Since the competition for the current customer segment is intense, should Ft.you broaden its appeal to cater to men and children?
2. What recommendations will you make for enhancing marketing communication of Ft.you?
3. Would you advise Ft.you to open a physical store or an experience center? Why or why not?

Teaching Strategies

1. Case Analysis and Presentations: Divide students into groups to analyze specific aspects of the case (e.g., business model, partnerships, competition) and present their findings to the class.
2. Role Play: Conduct a role-playing exercise where students take on the roles of key stakeholders in Ft.you, discussing and making decisions on operational challenges, partnerships, and strategic planning.
3. Guest Speaker: Invite a guest speaker, preferably someone with experience in the fashion-tech industry or entrepreneurship, to share insights and engage in a Q&A session with students.

4. Industry Research Assignment: Assign students to conduct research on the current trends and challenges in the fashion-tech industry, focusing on startups similar to Ft.you.
5. Interactive Class Discussion: Foster an interactive class discussion by posing thought-provoking questions related to the challenges and decisions faced by Ft.you. Encourage students to share their perspectives and propose alternative strategies.

Assignments

Assess students based on their understanding of the fashion-tech industry, critical analysis of Ft.you's business model, effectiveness in addressing challenges, and creativity in proposing strategic solutions.

1. Business Model Analysis: Students can conduct a SWOT analysis of Ft.you's business model and propose potential improvements.
2. Technology Integration Plan: Develop a plan for the integration of AI/ML technologies in addressing measurement challenges and enhancing customer experience.
3. Strategic Marketing Proposal: Create a strategic marketing proposal for Ft.you, focusing on online presence, influencer collaborations, and other innovative strategies.
4. Global Expansion Strategy: Formulate a strategy for Ft.you to expand its operations globally. Consider market research, partnerships, and adaptation to different cultural preferences.

Additional Resources

1. Keep students updated on Ft.you's progress by following any recent developments, such as new partnerships, app updates, or expansions. This could lead to further class discussions or assignments on the evolving landscape of fashion-tech startups.
2. Explore case studies of other fashion-tech startups to provide a broader understanding of the industry and its challenges.
3. Discuss relevant articles and research papers on the intersection of technology and fashion, addressing topics such as user experience, market trends, and the impact of digital platforms.

REFERENCES

Habel, J., Kassemeier, R., Alavi, S., Haaf, P., Schmitz, C., & Wieseke, J. (2020). When do customers perceive customer centricity? The role of a firm's and salespeople's customer orientation. *Journal of Personal Selling & Sales Management*, *40*(1), 25–42. doi:10.1080/08853134.2019.1631174

Howland, D. (2019, February 11). *The plus-size era is over before it began.* https://www.retaildive.com/news/the-plus-size-era-is-over-before-it-began/547938

Kourda, H. (2022). *The Interview: Hasna Kourda, Founder, Save Your Wardrobe.* https://www.theindustry.fashion/the-interview-hasna-kourda-founder-save-your-wardrobe

McKinsey & Company. (2022, May 2). *State of Fashion Technology Report 2022*. https://www.mckinsey.com/industries/retail/our-insights/state-of-fashion-technology-report-2022

Wynn, J., & Williams, C. K. (2012). Principles for conducting critical realist case study research in information systems. *Management Information Systems Quarterly*, *36*(3), 787–810. doi:10.2307/41703481

APPENDIX 1

Figure 3.

Before Advertisement and Content recommendations

APPENDIX 2

Figure 4.

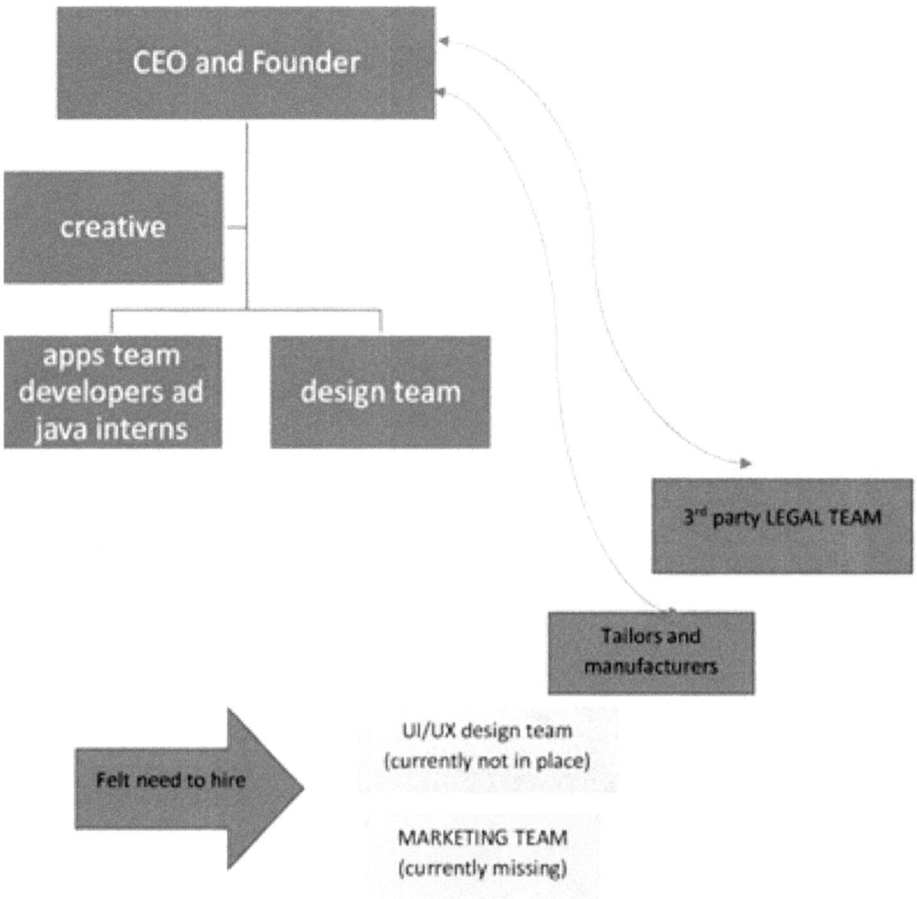

Table 1.

Name of product	Cost to make	Cost to sell	Cost to make with average cost of cloth from Ft.you	Cost to sell - customer with cloth	Margin
Indian Women's kurta	800 INR (500+300)	1200 INR	800 + 60*4 meters = 1040 INR	1200+800 = 2000 INR	33% and 48%
women's handwoven saree	8750 INR (from weaver)	20,000 INR	-	-	56%

Chapter 4
Ensuring Robust and Secure Supply Chain:
Deploying Blockchain

Nishant Kumar
Christ University, India

Pratibha Garg
Amity University, Noida, India

Kamal Upreti
Christ University, India

Sambhajiraje Patil
Dr. D.Y. Patil University, India

Amol Vasant Ohol
Dr. D.Y. Patil University, India

Malleshappa Bhagawati
Dr. D.Y. Patil University, India

ABSTRACT

Transparency, visibility, security, source-to-store traceability, and rising customer expectation are the critical points in the retail supply chain. The global supply chain involves a nexus of manufacturers and suppliers who urge for a robust network addressing the above challenges in the supply chain. A better provenance tool can benefit retailers, as customers are more concerned about the retail journey of the product start from its origin. Within the small span since its inception, blockchain has revolutionized the businesses and shown promising result in reshaping the supply chain. Blockchain in retail can provide evidence for the authenticity of product, tacking details for reliable retail delivery and enriching customer experience through product provenance. This chapter aims to explain to retailers the challenges, opportunities, and potential application of blockchain in the retail supply chain.

DOI: 10.4018/979-8-3693-3253-5.ch004

1 INTRODUCTION

Globalization and increasing supply chain interlinking have led to more uncertainty, intricacy, and susceptibility in supply chain. The scale of businesses, the number of geographical locations and product portfolios have expanded over the last few decades. Consequently, the traditional supply chain has grown to a gigantic modern network involving multiple products and need cooperation among various stakeholders (Farooq S, 2012). Moreover, demand for product traceability and visibility right from supplier to customer has increased. However, information gaps in recent supply chain networks has vividly affected the operations of all stakeholders involved right from suppliers, manufacturers, distributors, wholesalers and retailers and simplifying the process of tracking product histories and providing personalized goods. Supply chain needs to become smarter to meet these challenges. Efficient and effective supply chain management is vital for survival and accomplishment in this tempestuous world. To overcome these challenges, organizations have analysed innovative technologies which aid collaboration among various stakeholders, increase supply chain performance and make it more efficient and effective (Williamson EA, et. al. 2004).

A new technology called blockchain makes distributed ledger technology (DLT), a network in which all transactions are authenticated and apparent to all parties without involving intermediaries (Christidis K, Devetsikiotis M., 2016).

Blockchain technology has been utilized in several sectors, including financial services, manufacturing, food, agriculture, pharmaceuticals, hotels, airlines, healthcare, government, and supply chain management. Blockchain enhances the ability to track, observe, verify, validate, consolidate, automate, withstand challenges, make precise and prompt decisions, lower expenses, enhance supply chain efficiency, and increase customer contentment (Babich V, Hilary G., 2018). Blockchain reduces the transaction settlement and authentication time because the transactions are documented and distributed more efficiently along supply chains. Blockchain can be used as a means to track record of every movement of goods along the supply chain.

Though many contemplate about the effect of blockchain technology on supply chains but present awareness of its potential continues to be narrow. Given that the advancement and widespread adoption of blockchain technology is still in its early stages, conducting a comprehensive analysis of current developments in this field can provide valuable insights for both scholars and professionals in the sector. This chapter commences with a detailed discussion on the architecture of blockchain technology, supply chain overview and challenges, blockchain algorithm for retail application cases, trailed by a research framework, future directions and conclusion.

2 BLOCKCHAIN TECHNOLOGY

2.1 Basic Architecture

Blockchain technology is an innovative new technology which provides secure and efficient operations and also augments customer service. Blockchain got popularity with its use in cryptocurrency like Bitcoin and proved to be an effective and safe way of trading money. Blockchain is a revolutionary technology drastically improves transparency and security in transactions, generating innovative prospects for growth and reduces business operations risk and cost. Blockchain was conceptualized originally by (Nakamoto S, 2008) and then evolved its way into other application beyond cryptocurrency primarily on smart contracts and distributed ledger systems (Pilkington M., 2016). Blockchain facilitates the concept of distributed currencies named cryptocurrencies that are self-driven digital agreements called smart contracts and smart resources regulated upon internet named smart property (Wright A, & De Filippi P. 2015). Blockchain technology exploits a distributed data structure which is updated in real-time and manage transactions in moments with computer algorithms without third-party verification. It refers to distributed data ledger functioning across a network ensuing cryptanalytic hash function for recording and authentication of data. The network sustains an incontrovertible chain of data permitting agreement amongst un-trustable parties regarding persistence of information stored (Bashir I., 2016). Blockchain is a decentralized ledger comprise of records called blocks through various computers in a private or public network. Each transaction is stored in a block, which is then connected to the preceding block, forming an immutable chain that contains all the information from previous blocks. These blocks are permanently connected in a series which cannot be altered by a sole entity and authenticated using government conventions (Wang J, et. al. 2017). In blockchain, all transactions are apparent to all participants and each participant can check the record of the transaction of its partners without involving intermediaries (Chang, J., 2022, Viriyasitavat W,et. al. 2019, Wang Y, et. al. 2021)). The authentication process using recent encryption procedures can keep data safe on distribution ledgers contrary to tampering. As altering of prevailing blocks on blockchain is not possible so users can access complete track of activity (Miles C., 2017). Blockchain will be more tamper resilient if the blockchain network is larger (Zheng Z, et. al. 2017). Figure 1 shows the basic architecture of blockchain network.

2.2 Public vs. Private Blockchain

Blockchain can be public or private depending on access control. In public blockchain, transactions are non-permissioned where members are encouraged to join network and they can remain anonymous.

Figure 1. Basic architecture of blockchain network

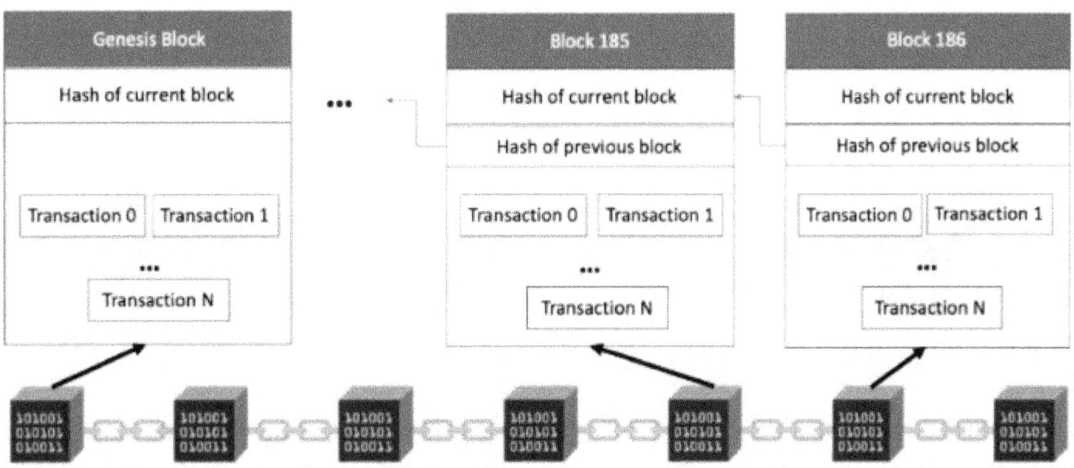

Within this network, trust is scarce among users. To address this absence, miners are introduced to verify the authenticity of transactions. The examples for public blockchains are Bitcoin and Ethereum. In contrast of this, in private blockchain admittance is regulated by a single organization or association of delegates called consensus and users need permission to join the network. This network facilitate transactional trust among users and costly miners are not required to authenticate transactions. Private blockchains exhibit Byzantine fault resistant consensus systems, which offer improved effectiveness, data authentication, increased network speed, and reduced transaction delay. Figure 2 show non permissioned public blockchain network.

2.3 Characteristics of Blockchain

Blockchain technology possesses numerous distinctive attributes that enable the establishment of a secure, transparent, verifiable, and trusted system for exchanging assets. It operates in a decentralized manner and maintains an unchangeable distributed ledger. The distinct qualities of blockchain that makes it different from traditional database are shown in Figure 3.

Figure 2. Non-permissioned public blockchain network

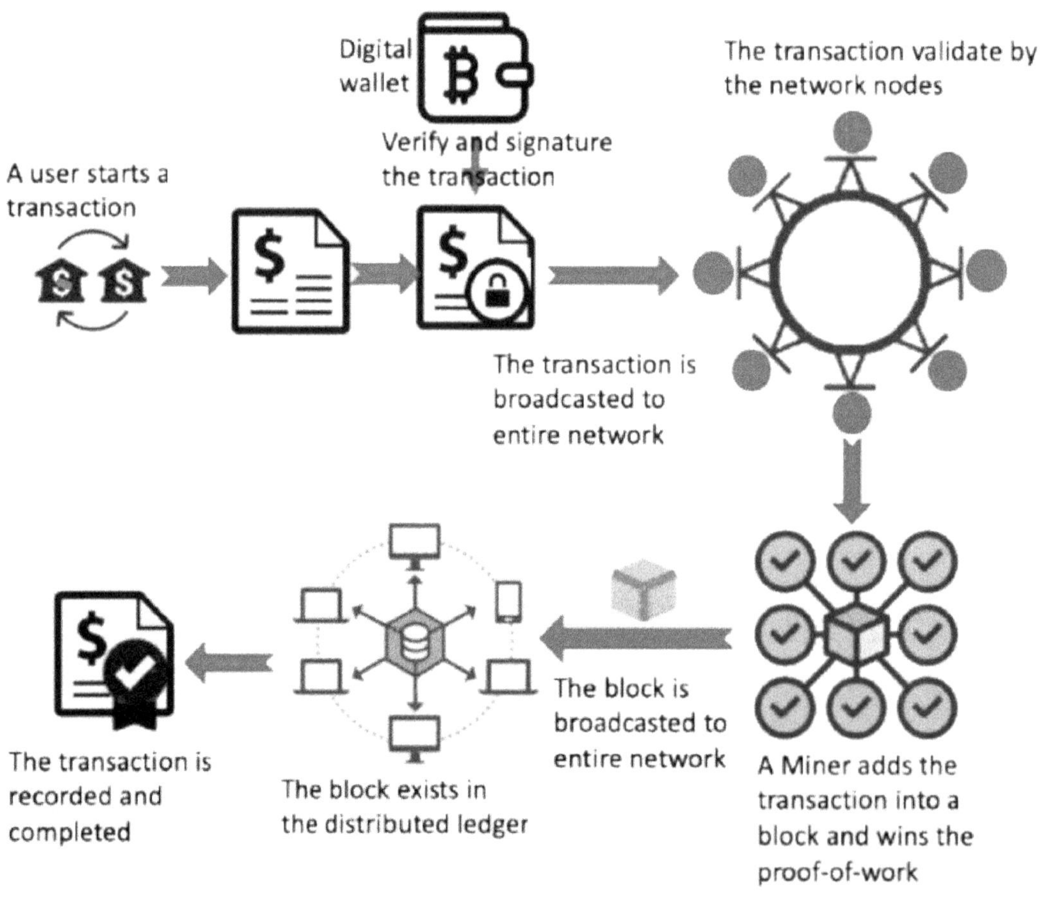

Figure 3. Distinct qualities of blockchain

2.4 Genesis of Blockchain Architecture: Consensus Algorithms

Blockchain is a distributed and decentralized network that operates without a central authority to check and approve transactions. Despite this lack of centralization, it is nevertheless regarded as a secure system. Reason behind the same is consensus algorithms that act as a base for blockchain network. A procedure of blockchain network through which all peers reach a common agreement and further establishes trust in distributed computing environment is consensus algorithm as shown in Table 1. Collaboration, co-operation, equal importance of every node and participation of every node are the key objectives of consensus protocol. There is no ideal consensus algorithm but the choice among various consensus algorithm represented in Figure 4 (Adapted from (Anwar et. al., 2023) depends on throughput, latency, block time and block size.

Figure 4. Types of consensus algorithms

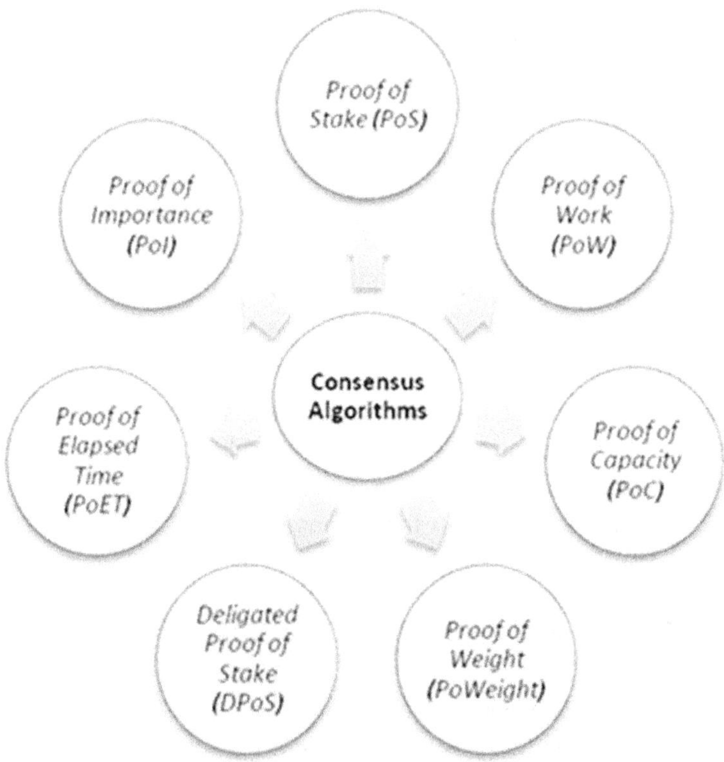

Table 1. Types of consensus algorithms

Proof of Stake (PoS): A user is encouraged to spend more to become a block creator.
Proof of Work (PoW): User initiates a transaction and miners try to a solve puzzle to verify it.
Proof of Capacity (PoC): Utilisation of capacity or usage of hard drive.
Delegated proof of stake (DPoS): Users with more coin will get to vote and elect witness.
Proof of weight (PoWeight): Similar as POS but the difference is that it depends on other factors like weight.
Proof of Elapsed Time (PoET): Similar to PoW but the difference is that it focuses more on consumption.
Proof of Importance (PoI): Users frequently send and receive transactions will get paid for it.

2.5 Smart Contract

A smart contract is a digital representation of a set of commitments and protocols that govern the execution of these commitments between parties (Szabo N., 1996). Nick Szabo was the first to anticipate it. The smart contract paradigm was integrated into Ethereum's blockchain network to streamline, verify, enforce, and enhance contract negotiations. Every participant is granted access to smart contracts, which are kept and shared in a distributed ledger. A smart contract delineates the responsibilities and entitlements among stakeholders prior to engaging in transactions within a blockchain network. The data is encoded as computer code to minimize ambiguity. These contracts are programmed to execute automatically once all predetermined circumstances in the blockchain network are met. Stakeholders that have reached a consensus on a smart contract experience enhanced trust and less likelihood of fraud and errors (Chu Y, 2018). Here are additional advantages of smart contracts:

- It reducing process time and save cost by eliminating intermediaries
- It is more accurate and efficient as all agreements are recorded in terms of computer Codes.
- It is real-time transparent and all participants have access to smart contracts.
- It executes automatically and speedily when all pre-defined conditions in blockchain network are satisfied.
- It is secure as distributed on all nodes of the blockchain network simultaneously and is stored using encryption

2.6 Popular Blockchain Platforms

Development and deployment of blockchain based applications are based on blockchain platforms. As shown in Table 2 (Adapted from (Purkayastha, 2023, Sharma TK. 2017) explains a brief overview of the application for some of the most popular blockchain platforms. Success of Bitcoin blockchain technology has raised inclination of organisation towards the adoption of other open source blockchain platform.

3 SUPPLY CHAIN OVERVIEW AND CHALLENGES

The Supply Chain Management concept was firstly introduced in 1980s, when organizations comprehended that by integrating different logistics processes into a complete whole system, distribution cost

Table 2. Popular blockchain platforms

Platform	Description	Network
Ethereum	Adaptable and flexible blockchain platform that can be used to develop decentralized application.	Public
Hyperledger (Sawtooth Lake)	Open source collaborative effort to create advanced business blockchain applications like distributed ledger, advanced contact engines and utility libraries.	Public and Private
Multichain	Advanced version of Bitcoin core software deployed for private financial transaction between or within the organisations.	Private
HydraChain	Ethereum platform that can be extended to create a permissioned distributed ledger.	Private
Factom	Converting blockchain capabilities into applications using Blockchain-as-a-service (BaaS).	Public and Private
IBM Blockchain	Enhancing Hyperledger by extending security and infrastructure facilities to enterprise.	Peer-to-peer through bitcoin
Azure BaaS	Assorted class of Blockchain platform in the form of Blockchain-as-a-service (BaaS) for enterprise.	Public and Private
IOTA	Support nano-payment without any fee and based on blockless distributed ledger (Tangle).	Public

can be reduced. The significant role of Supply Chain Management has become progressively larger during the decades as market dynamics continually change and companies look for optimizing efficiency in their operations (Camerinelli, E. 2009). A supply chain is a complicated vigorous network consisting of organizations, people, resources, activities, information involved in supplying goods or services to right consumers (Zhao J, 2020). It plays critical and unique role in determining the performance of organizations. Supply chain management encompasses the entire process of sourcing, procuring, manufacturing, distributing, and delivering raw materials, goods, information, and money. It aims to integrate these operations into a unified system that provides value to the client. (Kehoe L, 2017).

Supply chains turn out to be highly complex because of growing customer requirements highly competitive environment, widely spread geographic operations and adoption of new business models like ecommerce so the chance of disruptions and shudders intensely upsurges without sparing any business (Butner K., 2010). Supply chain function is currently facing various challenges related to transparency, visibility, security, manual errors, updating data, delay in processing, delivering of goods and services, tracing and tracking of various operations (Zhang J., 2019, Kadia, P., 2020, Scott,T., 2020). Supply–demand incompatibility difficulties like delay in delivery, stockouts and overstocking constantly retain the troubles in supply chains (Hyperledger, 2019). The increasing challenges in the supply chain are transforming it into more uncertain, complex, costly, and susceptible (Davis FD, 1989). Companies need real time accurate information regarding inventory, movement of products and supplies, and many others so as to take right decisions about supply chain operations and maintain productivity. The increasing supply chain cost due to increasing customer demand for better service level has impacted all the players including suppliers, manufacturers, retailers and distributors. Furthermore, the conventional technology employed in supply chain management lacks effective risk mitigation, cost reduction, and responsiveness to rapidly evolving market demands.

Today customers are extremely worried about source and quality of products they purchase.

Customers are highly concerned about ethical trade practices and truth behind the claims that retailers do about their products. So, improving the visibility of movement of goods and supplies from supplier to customer and building trust of customers has become one of the top priorities of companies. Retailers have to face the consequences when poor quality reaches to the market whether problem is due to any supply chain partner. Retailers have to do transactions with all supply chain partners mediated by financial institutions and banks using various documents, asset transfer note and agreement. These processes are usually exhibited by distrust and inefficiencies. Retailers have extensive supply chains problems concerning fake products, crumbling and forgery of data, improper storage environment, time consuming and expensive processes and lack of transparency. Studies show that counterfeit products sold by renowned retailers can be harmful to the health of consumers (Porter CE, 2006). Researchers have studied that sharing information related to demand and inventory level has significant effect on supply chain performance (Kayikci Y, 2018). Various challenges are witnessed for global supply chain because of following transformation:

- Increasing consumer demand for excellent service level
- Wholesalers are directly selling to consumers
- Replacement of physical inventory by digital inventory
- Lot of ecommerce companies are entering
- Security of data

4 BENEFITS AND CHALLENGES OF BLOCKCHAIN TECHNOLOGY TO SUPPLY CHAIN

4.1 Benefits to Supply Chain

Although blockchain is mostly known for providing the digital infrastructure for cryptocurrencies, its versatility extends much beyond that due to its inherent qualities. (P.W. Eklund, et. al. 2019, X. Xu, et. al. 2019). Blockchain applications have expanded beyond the realm of digital technology to encompass various aspects of business interactions, procedures, society, and products. (W.A.H. Ahmed, et. al. 2022). Blockchain technology has been utilized in diverse sectors like financial services, manufacturing, food, agriculture, pharmaceuticals, hotels, airlines, healthcare, and government. (F. Casino, et. al. 2019).

The blockchain can be employed in supply chain as a way of tracking the complete record of movement of goods from supplier to customers (Gupta, M., 2017). Information and Communication Technologies have transformed supply chain by providing platform for buyers and sellers as collaborators ensuring source and security of products (Subramanian N, et. al. 2020). In traditional supply chain, there is no simple way to track the authenticity and provenance of a product. Some systems like barcodes, RFID technology and unique electronic product codes are used to track items through the supply chain. But these sophisticated systems are basically insecure as they rely on centralized databases and centralized certificate authorities which have single points of failure which make them vulnerable to cyberattacks and insider fraud. Blockchain technology addresses various difficulties in supply chain management, such as ensuring authenticity, traceability, maintaining critical product information, making correct and fast decisions, reducing costs, enhancing supply chain performance, and increasing customer happiness. Research has been done on supply chain solutions grounded on blockchain to enhance traceability, transparency and auditability of flow of material throughout the supply chain from suppliers to customers. Blockchain presents improved transparency and traceability during the whole supply chain owing to its decentralized nature. Every transaction is added to the Blockchain, generating an auditable trail of all activities, involving appropriate documentation, the movement of goods and shifts in ownership. It has been recognized that blockchain based supply chain can reduce bullwhip effect by integration among all players lead to better product quality, customer positioning, fast financial payback, improved productivity and profits (Attaran M, et. al. 2007).

The blockchain act as an inter-organizational system in the supply chain starting with journey of products from raw material to end consumer (Paliwal V, et. al. 2020, Shah, 2021) and can significantly change supply chain management (SCM) (Treiblmaier H., 2018).

Figure 5 represents that as the item flow from manufacturer to customer, vital details are added in the blockchain making it convenient to trace the products journey and monitoring quality (Kim HM, et. al. 2018). It creates complete auditable stream of every item moving within the network from its origin to the customer.

Smart contracts can automate several activities in the supply chain right from compliance authentication to order accomplishment to payment processing, It lessens the requirement for manual processes, intermediaries and paperwork bringing about improved efficiency and cost reduction. Blockchain support companies to build customer trust by providing digital id to every product which secure all information regarding product life cycle. Technology can reduce risk in supply chain management by endowing authenticated podiums for people to register so as to govern their good and supplies movement and confirming that only registered members can access the system. So the blockchain-supply chain provide transparency in the product flow which helps businesses reduce frauds, counterfeiting and making better decisions (Min H., 2019). Immutability can be pronounced as one of the most advantageous features of blockchain technology as it eliminates the possibility of altering the transaction records. Further it makes auditing procedure more efficient and ensures trust and integrity in the data organizations (Lang J., 2017). Blockchain technology enable supply chain network to record tamper proof, complete and accurate details like timestamps, location, environmental conditions of all transactions ensuring data integrity and improved regulatory compliance.

Blockchain provides safer and secure mode of keeping a record of business transactions. It is not possible to hack blockchain technology as it is so structured that when there is attempt to hack particular block then all prior blocks in the past are tampered as well (Reyna A, et. al. 2018). Block chain technology makes transactions safer, secured and much faster by elimination of third-party intermediaries and reducing human intervention (Lang J., 2017). It increases flexibility by substituting outdated paper intensive manual processes with automated and self-regulated smart contract system (Zhang J. 2019).

Figure 5. Blockchain implementation throughout the retail supply chain

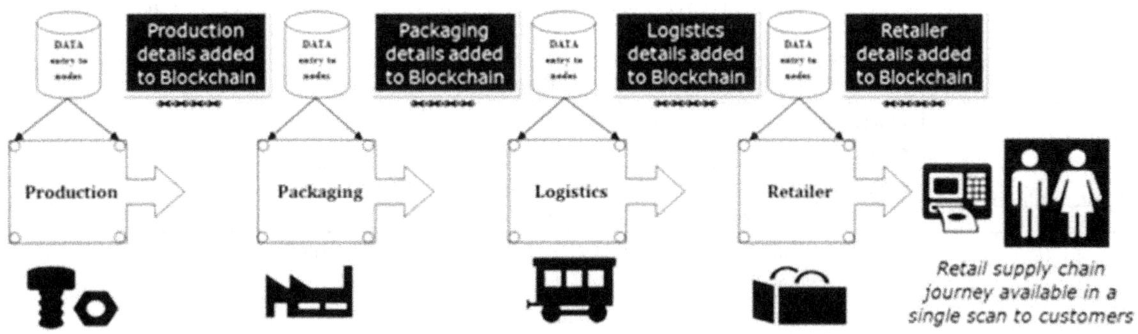

As Table 3 presents several benefits of blockchain application in supply chain (Narayanaswami et al., 2019, Shamout, 2019, Surjandy et al., 2019a).

4.2 Blockchain Technology Challenges

Even though blockchain is seemed as a favourable resolution for challenges related to supply chain but it needed substantial modifications in cultural and technological frameworks. Further, thorough valuation is desired to attend its challenges and realizing greatest ability of technology. Every transaction in a blockchain network is agreed by majority of nodes and hence limits the speed and processing power of network devices. So, it is essential to enhance the throughput of transactions by using a private blockchain network (Chang Y, et. al. 2020). There is no data standard existing which is fixed by the whole supply chain posing a challenge for implementation of blockchain. EPCIS has recommended GS1 to address this challenge but still it is not largely acknowledged and implemented in supply chain (GS1, 2014). Data recorded in blockchain cannot be altered because of immutable nature of blockchain (Ølnes S, 2020). Business executives' lack of awareness about blockchain technology serves as a barrier to their investment of time and money in this technology. (Jabbar S, 2020). Hence to handle this market acceptability challenge, the key stakeholders should be convinced with the benefits of blockchain. The ERP tools and existing systems in supply chain network do not support blockchain. So, it is necessary to either outsource or arrange in-house application development for specific supply chain (Queiroz MM, 2019). In first case organization's data privacy can be foremost concern and in the other case major investment is needed for long term.

Table 3. Benefits of blockchain application in supply chain

Benefits of Blockchain in Supply Chain	Description
Transparency	• Data analysis activities are automated • Provides end-to-end transparency created on permission level by means of hierarchy • Facilitates tracking of an item's status through a process
Data management	• It allows for standardization of data across a diverse supply chain which improve the accuracy of data analysis. • Enhances security of stored data. • Capturing the all information in real time
Response time	Facilitates the creation of a dynamic and real time supply chain which utilize its resources optimally.
Smart contract	• Allows for individual and customized contracts to be demarcated separately for each function which can be synchronized with each other. • Helps in process design of businesses • Enhances visibility while eliminating the requirement of intermediary
Efficiency	• Enhances end- to- end speed of supply chain processes • Early identification of bugs and issues helps to make the process more robust
Disintermediation	• This directs to an uninterrupted chain of transactions and enhances speed. • Enhances trust among various process stakeholders
Immutability	• A consensus mechanism is used for all the modifications in supply chain process. • Ensuring the security of all transactions involved.
Intellectual property	Ensuring the Intellectual Property registration and protection

5 USED CASES IN RETAIL SUPPLY CHAIN

Hyperledger Fabric: Blockchain Enabled Food Tracking System

Walmart developed a food traceability solution using Hyperledger Fabric technology to address issues in the decentralized food ecosystem. The choice of Hyperledger Fabric was based on the reason that food traceability system was mainly meant for many parties so the technology underneath it needs to be open-source vendor -neutral system. Walmart and its technology partner IBM collaborated to create two proof of concept (POC) projects for the purpose of analyzing the system. One proof of concept (POC) involved tracing the source of mangoes sold in Walmart stores in the United States, while the second POC aimed to monitor the origin of pork sold in Walmart stores in China. Research Team at Walmat claim the blockchain adoption in the system has been proved as an efficiency enhancer. For Mangoes in US the time spent to trace their provenance has gone down from 7 days to 2.2 seconds and for pork in china, it allowed to upload certificate of authenticity which further develops trust in the system. The success of two POC has given boost to expand the system outside Walmart and make it an open system. Walmart in collaboration with IBM and other food industry giants Nestle and Unilever launched IBM Food Trust. In continuation to the same, now company claims that Hyperledger Fabric based food traceability system has the ability to trace the genesis of more than 25 products like vegetables, fruits, meat and poultry, dairy products and multi-ingredient products from five different suppliers. Walmart have plans to roll out the Hyperledger Fabric traceability system for other product categories in near future (Hyperledger, 2019).

TradeLens: A Blockchain Based Shipping Solution

Maersk and IBM in 2018 introduced TradeLens: a blockchain enabled global trade platform with a goal to digitize global supply chain in 21st century. TradeLens intends to revolutionize the sector through: gathering all parties in supply chain on a common data sharing and collaboration platform in order to create value in the ecosystem, automation of cross organisational business process to foster trust, secured sharing of information across all supply chain partners and continuous improvement through an open API environment that allows third parties to deploy applications on TradeLens platform. Furthermore, smart contracts and IOT devices were coupled to record the interaction in the form of irreversible database. To evaluate the effectiveness of blockchain enabled global trade platform, TradeLens unfurl a beta project. Reduced paperwork, less operations cost, time and enhanced efficiency strengthen the concept of underpinning blockchain for shipping supply. Within such a small span of time TradeLens has become a leader in blockchain application in logistics industry. With its ground-breaking business model it has attracted interest of major players in the logistics sector. TradeLens has proved that implication of blockchain has enhanced the effectiveness and efficiency of supply chain (Kadia,P., 2023, Scott,T., 2023).

Intel: Blockchain Technology for Tracking Seafood in the Supply Chain

Intel looked into using blockchain technology to track seafood along the supply chain. A network was developed to facilitate many parties in managing food storage conditions, including temperature control and tracking the food supply chain from sea to table. Numerous records of this development which are public are accessible on the Blockchain website for traceability (Traceability, 2023). These records tell the usage of blockchain technology for collecting data on seafood product for example locations, temperatures, time-stamps, owners etc. within the whole supply chain network right from fishermen to transports and to restaurants. This blockchain technology enabled seafood supply chain can promote more trust between sellers and customers and further speed up and improve the safety of seafood supply chain network and augment consumer experiences.

6 THEORETICAL PERCEPTIONS USED FOR BLOCKCHAIN AND SUPPLY CHAIN MANAGEMENT RESEARCH

Utilizing blockchain in the retail supply chain offers numerous advantages and presents potential avenues for further research. Retail supply chain involves plenty of risk at manufacturer stage, freight transport and logistics. Various information theories can be implied to analyse the adoption intention and actual adoption behaviour of blockchain in retail supply chain.

The resource-based view (RBV) introduced by (Barney,1991 and B. Wernerfelt, 2018) tells the competitive advantage of an organization, ownership of resources, and competences that are unique, valuable and hard to replicate. Further Treiblmaier (H. Treiblmaier, 2018). recommended that for blockchain adoption, RBV can help to examine the organizational resource requirements.

Principal Agent Theory (PAT) given by Eisenhardt (K.M, 1989) reflects the usage and inference of information asymmetry and several interests between principals and agents. PAT may inspect how different groups relate in the blockchain structure in consideration of the transparency stipulated by blockchain (S. Kummer, 2020).

The information processing theory given by Galbraith (J.R. Galbraith, 1974) recognizes that companies must engage in information processing to reduce uncertainty. Organizations can implement information processing theory to estimate the competitiveness of different blockchain networks (S. Saberi, et. al. 2019), to investigate how blockchain transparency can enhance prevailing information processing competences and to find information processing requirements from blockchain adoption (V. Martinez, et.al. 2019).

Transaction cost analysis theory (TCA) given by Coase (R.H. Coase, 1987) and Williamson (O.E. Williamson 1981) explores the cost associated with organizational transactions and can be utilized to analyze the effects of distributed ledger technologies (DLT) in decreasing supply chain transaction costs, diminishing dependence on third parties, and modifying the allocation of work between suppliers and purchasers. (D. Roeck, et. al. 2020).

Institutional theory given by Hirsch (P.M. Hirsch, 1975) studies the influence of external pressures on organizations and norms by which organizations are ingrained. Institutional theory is used to examine whether external or internal pressures determine blockchain adoption (V. Martinez, et.al. 2019).

Social network theory given by Mitchell (J.C. Mitchell, 1969) explores the relationships and linkages among organizations and its effect on the network management. Social network theory is important to examine key drivers for blockchain adoption in the supply chain (M.M. Queiroz et. al. 2019).

Technology Adoption Model (TAM) introduced by Fred D. Davis (Davis FD 1989) is a widely used information system theory since its inception for examining user technology adoption. Decision variables at the core of TAM perceived simplicity of access and perceived effectiveness are subjective beliefs regarding a particular information system that have a substantial impact on an individual's attitude towards actually adopting the technology. (Porter CE, 2006). Perceived ease of use and perceived usefulness in TAM act as a focal point to measure individual belief. Belief act as an individual's cognitive response to use a specific technology, which further determines the individual attitude towards the use or dispose of technology (Kayikci Y et. al. 2018). Literature highlights extended TAM by addition of some new constructs for understanding user acceptance for particular information system or technology. On theoretical grounds the conceptual framework represented in Figure 8 is an extension of TAM by adopting additional variables on the basis of technology, organisational, environmental (TOE) factors given by Tornatzky (L.G. Tornatzky, et. al. 1990). TOE framework should be used for examining prominent factors behind adoption and actual use of blockchain in retail supply chain. Safety, security and privacy were integrated as social factors. Traceability and transparency was identified key behind application of blockchain technology (Subramanian N, et. al. 2020). Propositions could be formulated to examine causal relationship between constructs in the extended TAM model for blockchain adoption as shown in Figure 6.

Additional information technology theories employed to analyze key determinants of technology adoption and practical utilization of blockchain in the retail supply chain encompass the theory of planned behaviour (TBP) (I. Ajzen, 1991), task-technology fit (TTF) (D.L. Goodhue, 1995), technology readiness index (TRI) (A. Parasuraman, 2000) and unified theory of acceptance and use of technology (UTAUT) (V. Venkatesh 2003). Additionally, several researchers proposed the integration of a multitude of Theories of organizational information systems to provide a unified viewpoint. For instance, (S. Fosso et. al. 2020) adopted both the TAM and UTAUT theories to get a improved model which examined the relation between adoption of blockchain and supply chain performance.

7 RESEARCH IMPLICATIONS

Although there is an increasing amount of scholarly literature on the use of blockchain in supply chain management, research on the practical application and validation of blockchain-SCM ideas has been

Figure 6. Blockchain in retail supply chain adoption model

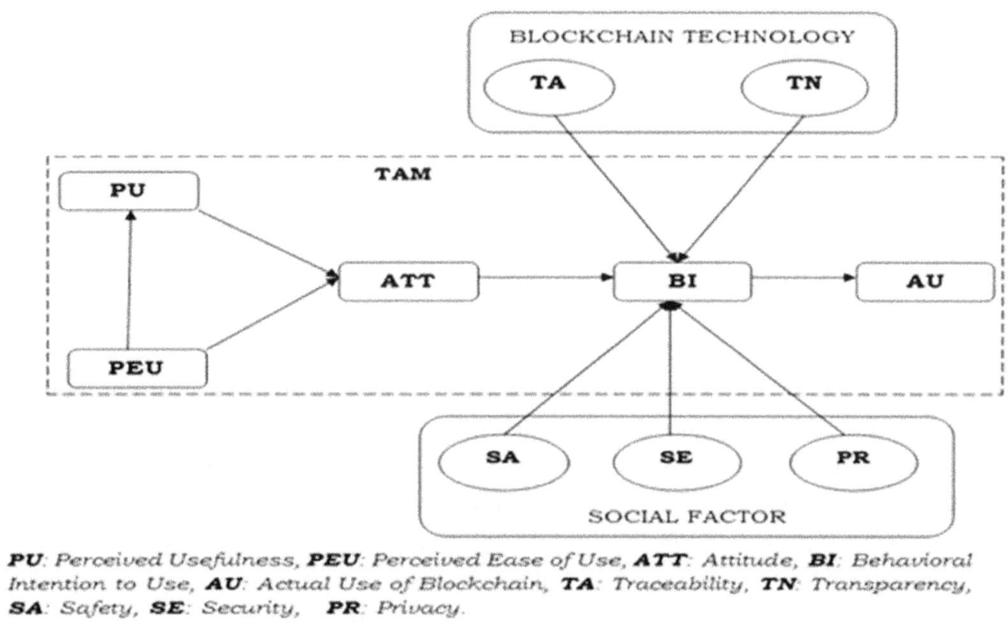

limited thus far. The previous literature examines many aspects and obstacles related to the acceptance and implementation of blockchain technology in the supply chain. Nevertheless, these investigations offer only restricted perspectives that can propel additional advancements in this domain of research. The implementation of blockchain technology as an interorganizational tool in distributed multi-tier supply chains necessitates thorough examinations regarding the technology, its potential, adoption prerequisites, advantages, and effects on various supply chain participants, in addition to supply chain architecture and management. As blockchain technology is being tested and used more frequently in academic and practical settings, it will provide more empirical evidence. This evidence can serve as a basis for additional research using various theoretical perspectives to promote the development of theories in this developing subject.

This study introduces a complete framework that serves as a foundation and direction for future research focused on the acceptance, implementation, and utilization of blockchain technology in the supply chain as a whole. The framework offers systematic direction on the optimal theoretical views that can be employed, either independently or in conjunction, in future research to develop the subject of blockchain-SCM. Although various theories have been proposed, the framework emphasizes the need to use multi-disciplinary research methods to address the limitations of individual studies. This approach will enable a more comprehensive understanding of the broader consequences of implementing and utilizing blockchain technology in the supply chain. The framework promotes the exploration of several theories to analyze the developing phenomenon, depending on the setting and aim of the research study. The primary objective of the framework is to provide guidance to academics regarding the diverse ideas that are pertinent to blockchain-SCM research. Nevertheless, there is a dearth of empirical evidence up to now. Hence, it is highly recommended for the research community to actively collaborate with practitioners, prominent corporations who are interested in blockchain applications, standards and regulatory authorities, as well as other agencies in order to advance and enrich knowledge (W.A.H. Ahmed 2022). The organized framework can assist in identifying the appropriate type and scope of involvement that would be advantageous in addressing certain research inquiries utilizing a specific theory or a mix of theories. Participating in established blockchain consortia and collaborating with commercialized blockchain platform providers can be beneficial for doing inter-organizational research. It may be beneficial to interact with regulator and consumer organizations to analyze the impact of the external environment on the adoption of blockchain technology.

8 CONCLUSION

Blockchain technology, a foundation for bitcoin introduced in the year 2009 has a capacity to revolutionize retail supply chain. At present bitcoin is not able to fulfil the role of money because of its current form. Based on the capabilities of blockchain discussed in chapter, undoubtedly it has the ability to bring transparency and security in retail supply chain. The decentralised platform to perform any form of transaction and making a permanent immutable record of it makes this technology a real game changer. Collaboration of channel partners, increase in efficiency of supply chain, transparency, traceability, security, safety and permanent historical record makes it the future of supply chain. Blockchain has the ability to make supply chain more robust for future challenges but an enterprise has to choose relevant use cases which have the ability to maximise the benefit. There is tremendous opportunity to study enterprise behavioural intent for blockchain adoption in retail supply chain based on the proposed research framework in cross cultural and longitudinal research context. Furthermore, the proposed model may be extended to investigate the influence of government intervention, current industry trend, organisational structure, peer pressure, management support in blockchain adoption and recent technological advancement like artificial intelligence, big data and cloud computing. An empirical analysis can also be performed to examine perceived benefit against perceived risk in adopting blockchain technology. Prior studies have found the importance of adequate training in technological context for dealing perceived risk and security in adopting blockchain technology (Amoako-Gyampah K, Salam AF 2004). Furthermore an extended research to understand individual viewpoint for drivers and barriers in adopting technology would add value for practitioners.

REFERENCES

Agarwal, S. (2018). *Blockchain technology in supply chain and logistics.* Massachusetts Institute of Technology.

Ahmed, W. A. H., & MacCarthy, B. L. (2022). Blockchain technology in the supply chain: Learning from emerging ecosystems and industry consortia. In S. Bauman (Ed.), *Handbook of digital business ecosystems: Strategies, platforms, technologies, governance and societal challenges* (p. 800). Edward Elgar Publishing. doi:10.4337/9781839107191.00032

Ajzen, I. (1991). The theory of planned behavior. *Organizational Behavior and Human Decision Processes, 50*(2), 179–211. doi:10.1016/0749-5978(91)90020-T

Amoako-Gyampah, K., & Salam, A. F. (2004, July 1). An extension of the technology acceptance model in an ERP implementation environment. *Information & Management, 41*(6), 731–745. doi:10.1016/j.im.2003.08.010

Anwar, H. (n.d.). *Consensus algorithms: The root of blockchain.* https://101blockchains.com/consensus-algorithms-blockchain/#prettyPhoto

Attaran, M., & Attaran, S. (2007, June 12). Collaborative supply chain management. *Business Process Management Journal, 13*(3), 390–404. doi:10.1108/14637150710752308

Babich, V., & Hilary, G. (2019). Blockchain and other distributed ledger technologies in operations. *Foundations and Trends® in Technology, Information and Operations Management, 12*(2–3), 152–172. doi:10.1561/0200000084

Barney, J. (1991). Firm resources and sustained competitive advantage. *Journal of Management, 17*(1), 99–120. doi:10.1177/014920639101700108

Bashir, I. (2017, March 17). *Mastering blockchain.* Packt Publishing Ltd.

Butner, K. (2010, January 5). The smarter supply chain of the future. *Strategy and Leadership, 38*(1), 22–31. doi:10.1108/10878571011009859

Camerinelli, E. (2009). *Measuring the value of the supply chain: Linking financial performance and supply chain decisions* (1st ed.). Gower Publishing Publishing.

Casino, F., Dasaklis, T. K., & Patsakis, C. (2019). A systematic literature review of blockchain-based applications: Current status, classification and open issues. *Telematics and Informatics*, *36*, 55–81. doi:10.1016/j.tele.2018.11.006

Chang, J. (n.d.). *Sidebench.* https://medium.com/@sidebench/blockchain-the-immutable-ledger-of-transparency-in-healthcare-technology-a4a64b1d5594

Chang, Y., Iakovou, E., & Shi, W. (2020, April 2). Blockchain in global supply chains and cross border trade: A critical synthesis of the state-of-the-art, challenges and opportunities. *International Journal of Production Research*, *58*(7), 2082–2099. doi:10.1080/00207543.2019.1651946

Christidis, K., & Devetsikiotis, M. (2016, May 10). Blockchains and smart contracts for the internet of things. *IEEE Access : Practical Innovations, Open Solutions*, *4*, 2292–2303. doi:10.1109/ACCESS.2016.2566339

Chu, Y., Ream, J., & Schatsky, D. (n.d.). *Getting smart about smart contracts*. Deloitte.

Coase, R. H. (1937). The nature of the firm. *Economica*, *4*(16), 386–405. doi:10.1111/j.1468-0335.1937.tb00002.x

Davis, F. D. (1989, September 1). Perceived usefulness, perceived ease of use, and user acceptance of information technology. *Management Information Systems Quarterly*, *13*(3), 319–340. doi:10.2307/249008

Farooq, S., & O'Brien, C. (2012). A technology selection framework for integrating manufacturing within a supply chain. *International Journal of Production Research*, *50*(11), 2987–3010. doi:10.1080/00207543.2011.588265

Fosso Wamba, S., Queiroz, M. M., & Trinchera, L. (2020). Dynamics between blockchain adoption determinants and supply chain performance: An empirical investigation. *International Journal of Production Economics*, *229*, 107791. Advance online publication. doi:10.1016/j.ijpe.2020.107791

GS1. (2014). *EPCIS*. https://www.gs1.org/standards/epcis

Galbraith, J. R. (1974). Organization design: An information processing view. *Interfaces*, *4*(3), 28–36. doi:10.1287/inte.4.3.28

Goodhue, D. L., & Thompson, R. L. (1995). Task-technology fit and individual performance. *Management Information Systems Quarterly*, *19*(2), 213–236. doi:10.2307/249689

Gupta, M. (2017). *Blockchain for dummies*. John Wiley & Sons.

Hirsch, P. M. (1975). Organizational effectiveness and the institutional environment. *Administrative Science Quarterly*, *20*(3), 327–344. doi:10.2307/2391994

Hyperledger. (n.d.). *Walmart turns to blockchain (and Hyperledger) to take on food traceability and safety*. https://www.hyperledger.org/blog/2019/02/21/walmart-turns-to-blockchain-and-hyperledger-to-take-on-food-traceability-and-safety

Jabbar, S., Lloyd, H., Hammoudeh, M., Adebisi, B., & Raza, U. (2020, November 20). Blockchain-enabled supply chain: Analysis, challenges, and future directions. *Multimedia Systems*, 1–20.

KadiaP. (n.d.). https://businessblockchainhq.com/business-blockchain-news/the-success-story-of-tradelens/

Kayikci, Y., & Subramanian, N. (2018). Feasibility of food loss reduction with blockchain in the emerging economy context. *Symposium on Logistics (ISL 2018) Big Data Enabled Supply Chain Innovations.*

Kehoe, L., O'Connell, N., Andrzejewski, D., Gindner, K., & Dalal, D. (2017). *When two chains combine supply chain meets blockchain.* Deloitte.

Kim, H. M., & Laskowski, M. (2018, January). Toward an ontology-driven blockchain design for supply-chain provenance. *International Journal of Intelligent Systems in Accounting Finance & Management, 25*(1), 18–27. doi:10.1002/isaf.1424

Kummer, S., Herold, D. M., Dobrovnik, M., Mikl, J., & Schäfer, N. (2020). A systematic review of Blockchain literature in logistics and supply chain management: Identifying research questions and future directions. *Future Internet, 12*(3), 60. doi:10.3390/fi12030060

Lang, J. (2017). *Three uses for blockchain in banking.* IBM.

Martinez, V., Zhao, M., Blujdea, C., Han, X., Neely, A., & Albores, P. (2019). Blockchain-driven customer order management. *International Journal of Operations and Production Management, 39*(6/7/8), 993–1022. doi:10.1108/IJOPM-01-2019-0100

Miles, C. (2017, December). *Blockchain security: What keeps your transaction data safe.* IBM. https://www.ibm.com/blogs/blockchain/2017/12/blockchain-security-what-keeps-yourtransaction-data-safe/

Min, H. (2019, January 1). Blockchain technology for enhancing supply chain resilience. *Business Horizons, 62*(1), 35–45. doi:10.1016/j.bushor.2018.08.012

Mitchell, J. C. (1969). *Social networks in urban situations: Analyses of personal relationships in Central African towns.* Manchester University Press.

Nakamoto, S., & Bitcoin, A. (2008). *A peer-to-peer electronic cash system.* Bitcoin.

Niranjanamurthy, M., Nithya, B. N., & Jagannatha, S. (2019). Analysis of Blockchain technology: Pros, cons and SWOT. *Cluster Computing, 22*(S6), 14743–14757. doi:10.1007/s10586-018-2387-5

Ølnes, S., Ubacht, J., & Janssen, M. (2017). Blockchain in government: Benefits and implications of distributed ledger technology for information sharing. *Government Information Quarterly, 34*(3), 355–364. doi:10.1016/j.giq.2017.09.007

Paliwal, V., Chandra, S., & Sharma, S. (2020, January). Blockchain technology for sustainable supply chain management: A systematic literature review and a classification framework. *Sustainability (Basel), 12*(18), 7638. doi:10.3390/su12187638

Parasuraman, A. (2000). Technology readiness index (TRI) a multiple-item scale to measure readiness to embrace new technologies. *Journal of Service Research, 2*(4), 307–320. doi:10.1177/109467050024001

Pilkington, M. (2016). Blockchain technology: Principles and applications. In Research Handbook on Digital Transformations. Academic Press.

Porter, C. E., & Donthu, N. (2006, September 1). Using the technology acceptance model to explain how attitudes determine Internet usage: The role of perceived access barriers and demographics. *Journal of Business Research*, *59*(9), 999–1007. doi:10.1016/j.jbusres.2006.06.003

Purkayastha, S. (n.d.). *Eight Blockchain platforms for rapid prototyping*. https://radiostud.io/eight-blockchain-platforms-comparison/

Queiroz, M. M., & Fosso Wamba, S. F. (2019, June 1). Blockchain adoption challenges in supply chain: An empirical investigation of the main drivers in India and the USA. *International Journal of Information Management*, *46*, 70–82. doi:10.1016/j.ijinfomgt.2018.11.021

Queiroz, M. M., Telles, R., & Bonilla, S. H. (2019). Blockchain and supply chain management integration: A systematic review of the literature. *Supply Chain Management*, *25*(2), 241–254. doi:10.1108/SCM-03-2018-0143

Reyna, A., Martín, C., Chen, J., Soler, E., & Díaz, M. (2018, November 1). On blockchain and its integration with IoT. Challenges and opportunities. *Future Generation Computer Systems*, *88*, 173–190. doi:10.1016/j.future.2018.05.046

Roeck, D., Sternberg, H., & Hofmann, E. (2020). Distributed ledger technology in supply chains: A transaction cost perspective. *International Journal of Production Research*, *58*(7), 2124–2141. doi:10.1080/00207543.2019.1657247

Saberi, S., Kouhizadeh, M., Sarkis, J., & Shen, L. (2019). Blockchain technology and its relationships to sustainable supply chain management. *International Journal of Production Research*, *57*(7), 2117–2135. doi:10.1080/00207543.2018.1533261

Scott, T., & IBM. (n.d.). https://www.ibm.com/blogs/think/2018/11/tradelens-how-ibm-and-maersk-are-sharing-blockchain-to-build-a-global-trade-platform/

Shah & Department of Health. (n.d.). *Unblocking the retail supply chain with blockchain*. https://www.tcs.com/content/dam/tcs/pdf/Industries/Retaillogistics/Abstract/Unblocking-retail-supply-chain-with-blockchain-1017-1.pdfRetrieved

Sharma, T. K. (2017). *List of best open source blockchain platform*. Blockchain Council.

Subramanian, N., Chaudhuri, A., & Kayıkcı, Y. (2020, May 27). *Blockchain and supply chain logistics: Evolutionary case studies. Springer.* Nature Publishing.

Szabo, N. (1996). Smart contracts: Building blocks for digital markets. *Extropy, 18*(16).

Tornatzky, L. G., Fleischer, M., & Chakrabarti, A. K. (1990). *Processes of technological innovation*. Lexington Books.

Treiblmaier, H. (2018, September 10). The impact of the blockchain on the supply chain: A theory-based research framework and a call for action. *Supply Chain Management*, *23*(6), 545–559. doi:10.1108/SCM-01-2018-0029

Venkatesh, V., Morris, M. G., Davis, G. B., & Davis, F. D. (2003). User acceptance of information technology: Toward a unified view. *Management Information Systems Quarterly, 27*(3), 425–478. doi:10.2307/30036540

Viriyasitavat, W., & Hoonsopon, D. (2019). Blockchain characteristics and consensus in modern business processes. *Journal of Industrial Information Integration, 13*, 32–39. doi:10.1016/j.jii.2018.07.004

Wang, J., Wu, P., Wang, X., & Shou, W. (2017). The outlook of blockchain technology for construction engineering management. *Frontiers of Engineering Management, 4*(1), 67–75. doi:10.15302/J-FEM-2017006

Wang, Y., Chen, C. H., & Zghari, A. (2021). Sales Designing a blockchain enabled supply chain. *International Journal of Production Research, 59*(5), 1450–1475. doi:10.1080/00207543.2020.1824086

Wernerfelt, B. (1984). A resource-based view of the firm. *Strategic Management Journal, 5*(2), 171–180. doi:10.1002/smj.4250050207

Williamson, E. A., Harrison, D. K., & Jordan, M. (2004). Information systems development within supply chain management. *International Journal of Information Management, 24*(5), 375–385. doi:10.1016/j.ijinfomgt.2004.06.002

Williamson, O. E. (1981). The economics of organization: The transaction cost approach. *American Journal of Sociology, 87*(3), 548–577. doi:10.1086/227496

Wright, A., & De Filippi, P. (2015). Decentralized blockchain technology and the rise of lex cryptographia. SSRN *Electronic Journal*. doi:10.2139/ssrn.2580664

Xu, X., Lu, Q., Liu, Y., Zhu, L., Yao, H., & Vasilakos, A. V. (2018). Designing blockchain-based applications a case study for imported product traceability. *Future Generation Computer Systems, 92*, 399–406. doi:10.1016/j.future.2018.10.010

Zhang, J. (2019, May 28). Deploying blockchain technology in the supply chain. In *Computer security threats*. IntechOpen.

Zhao, J., Ji, M., & Feng, B. (2020, March 19). Smarter supply chain: A literature review and practices. Journal of Data. *Information & Management, 2*(2), 95–110. doi:10.1007/s42488-020-00025-z

Zheng, Z., Xie, S., Dai, H., Chen, X., & Wang, H. (2017, June 25). An overview of blockchain technology: Architecture, consensus, and future trends. In *2017 IEEE international congress on big data (BigData congress)* (pp. 557–564). IEEE Publications. doi:10.1109/BigDataCongress.2017.85

Chapter 5
Digital Footprints and the Battle for Data Sovereignty: Digital Privacy, Security, and Ownership

Ishani Sharma
Chitkara Business School, Chitkara University, India

Arun Aggarwal
https://orcid.org/0000-0003-3986-188X
Chitkara Business School, Chitkara University, India

ABSTRACT

In the age of digitization, concerns about digital security and data ownership are paramount. The chapter investigates the cyber threatscape, noting the role of state-backed collectives. Essential defense tools, such as encryption and two-factor authentication, are contrasted with significant breaches like the 2014 Yahoo incident. The commodification of personal data by tech giants for advertising underlines the urgent need for clear data ownership guidelines. The balance between online utility and privacy is challenging, with corporations holding significant power due to vast data reserves. A proposed "digital bill of rights" could provide a universal rights-tech alignment. Future challenges lie in AI implications and the rise of quantum computing, leading towards "surveillance capitalism." Solutions involve quantum-resistant cryptography, AI-data safeguards, and enhancing digital literacy. The chapter advocates for balancing digital advancement with individual rights for a secure digital future.

1. INTRODUCTION

We stand at a pivotal juncture in history, an era profoundly characterized by the omnipresence of digital interactions. The emergence and rapid adoption of digital technologies, from smartphones' near-universal reach to the vast networks of social media platforms, has undoubtedly ushered us into the 'digital age' (Castells, 2011). A transformative period, this age presents us with unparalleled conveniences — instant communication, swift transactions, and a world of information at our fingertips. Yet, it's not without its

DOI: 10.4018/979-8-3693-3253-5.ch005

array of new and evolving challenges. Every online action, whether it's a tweet, a digital purchase, or an innocuous Google search, contributes to a complex matrix of digital traces. Collectively termed our "digital footprint", these traces are more than just bits and bytes; they serve as digital reflections of our behaviors, interests, and even our aspirations (Mayer-Schönberger, 2009). As technology continues to advance, the granularity and breadth of these footprints have only expanded, painting a detailed digital portrait of our lives. The very essence of these footprints offers a double-edged sword. On one side, these traces enable more personalized and streamlined online experiences. Algorithms utilize this data to tailor content, advertisements, and recommendations precisely to individual preferences, effectively enhancing user engagement (Haggart, 2019). However, the other edge of this sword poses critical challenges. Questions about the safety, privacy, and ownership of this data remain more relevant and contentious than ever.

Our digital footprints, as expansive as they are, have become a goldmine for numerous stakeholders. Tech giants, marketers, and even governments discern invaluable insights from these footprints. While this can lead to improved user experiences and insights for businesses, it simultaneously sparks concerns. Personal privacy stands at the frontline of these concerns. As revelations from events like the Facebook-Cambridge Analytica scandal showed, unauthorized data access can lead to significant manipulations, impacting democratic processes (Cadwalladr & Graham-Harrison, 2018). Moreover, the integrity and security of this data are under constant threat. Data breaches, often making headlines, highlight the vulnerabilities inherent in storing and managing massive amounts of personal data. Such breaches not only risk financial and personal information but also erode public trust in digital platforms (Romanosky, 2019).

Then there's the complex issue of data ownership. As users generate data, a debate rages on about who truly owns it. Is it the platform that collects and stores it, or the individual who produces it? This question becomes more intricate considering the vast monetization machinery that thrives on this data (Strassburg et al., 2020).

As we delve deeper into this chapter, our focus will remain affixed on understanding the myriad facets of digital footprints. We aim to dissect the quest for data sovereignty, a journey that encompasses individual rights, corporate interests, global policy considerations, and fundamental human rights in an increasingly digitized world (Polčák, & Svantesson, 2017).

By traversing this landscape, we hope to provide readers with a comprehensive grasp of the challenges, implications, and potential futures of our digital footprints in this age of interconnectedness.

2. UNDERSTANDING DIGITAL FOOTPRINTS

In the vast expanse of the digital universe, every individual action casts a shadow. This shadow, often referred to as a "digital footprint," embodies the data residue left behind as a result of our interactions on digital platforms. This concept is much more than just a metaphorical trace of our online presence; it encapsulates a myriad of information ranging from active online behaviors, like social media posts and email correspondences, to passive data collections such as IP address logs and the ubiquitous digital cookies (Mayer-Schönberger, 2009). Historically, the digital footprint of an individual during the early days of the internet was rather rudimentary. It predominantly comprised basic elements such as browsing records and email interactions. However, the digital revolution, characterized by the emergence of social media, e-commerce, and innovative tracking mechanisms, has rendered these footprints far more intricate. Today, they present a comprehensive, multi-dimensional snapshot of an individual's activities, choices, preferences, and even potential future behaviors (Boyd & Ellison, 2007).

Each digital platform plays a role in expanding this footprint. For instance, every interaction on social media, be it a 'like', 'share', or comment, not only showcases one's preferences but also maps intricate social networks and behaviors (Bingham, & Conner, 2010). Similarly, e-commerce sites meticulously record transaction details, browsing histories, and even the time spent viewing particular products. This granularity offers businesses insights into consumer behaviors and preferences. The locales and modalities of footprint creation are also worth noting. Beyond the obvious traces left on social media and online shopping platforms, even seemingly innocuous actions, such as reading an online article, can contribute. Furthermore, with the dawn of the Internet of Things (IoT) and wearable technologies, this footprinting isn't restricted to just PCs or smartphones. Smart appliances, wearable health monitors, and even connected vehicles gather vast amounts of data, adding depth and layers to our digital imprints (Kritzinger & Von Solms, 2010). The profound evolution of digital footprints over the years isn't merely a consequence of technological advancements. It's deeply intertwined with societal shifts and the changing nature of online interactions. As more people have integrated digital tools into their daily lives, there's been a corresponding increase in the volume and variety of data they produce (Rainie & Wellman, 2012).

However, the vastness and intricacy of digital footprints bring along a slew of concerns, primarily centered on privacy, security, and data ownership. As individuals become more digitally active, the potential for misuse of their data grows, leading to an increased emphasis on cybersecurity measures and data protection policies.To truly understand digital footprints, one must grasp their duality: on one hand, they enable a hyper-personalized digital experience, and on the other, they present challenges that our current legal and ethical frameworks are still grappling with. As we move forward in the digital age, the manner in which we manage, protect, and perceive these footprints will shape not only our online experiences but also our very identities in the digital world (Feher, 2021).

3. THE LANDSCAPE OF DATA SOVEREIGNTY

The notion of data sovereignty has swiftly risen to prominence in our increasingly digitalized world. At its essence, data sovereignty concerns the principle that digital information is beholden to the legal frameworks and governance structures of the country where it is physically stored (Barnard-Wills & Ashenden, 2012). This principle harks back to the interplay between information management, geopolitical dynamics, and the revolutionary leaps in digital storage capabilities over the years. Historically, the intersection of information governance and geopolitics was less intricate. The nascent days of the internet permitted a rather laissez-faire approach to data storage, allowing data to reside anywhere across the globe with minimal regulatory scrutiny. However, as the virtual realm burgeoned, so did the intricacies surrounding where and how data was stored. The increasing prevalence of cyber threats combined with an awakened understanding of data's monumental value resulted in nations acknowledging the pressing need to assert jurisdictional control over their citizens' data (Kuner, 2013).

Fast-forward to our contemporary digital milieu, and data has effectively been anointed as the "new gold." It's more than just strings of ones and zeros; it drives economies, shapes national policies, and significantly influences global geopolitics. The significance of data sovereignty in today's interconnected age touches upon myriad facets: from ensuring national security and preserving economic interests to safeguarding the privacy rights of individual citizens. This focus on data sovereignty can also be viewed as a reflection of nations' attempt to reclaim control in an environment where borders are increasingly nebulous (Cate & Mayer-Schönberger, 2013). The international regulatory framework further underscores the complex tapestry of data sovereignty. Various international laws and regulations have sprouted in recent years, attempting to set global standards for data handling, storage, and transfer. Notably, the European Union's General Data Protection Regulation (GDPR) serves as a testament to the global momentum towards tighter data control. By setting rigorous standards on data storage, transfer, and utilization, the GDPR exemplifies a broader international effort to anchor data sovereignty at the heart of global digital relations (Schwartz & Peifer, 2017).

However, while instruments like the GDPR are a step in the right direction, they also accentuate the challenges inherent in harmonizing data regulations across nations. Different countries, with their cultural, political, and economic nuances, view data sovereignty through varied lenses, leading to a patchwork quilt of regulations that global entities must navigate (Daskal, 2015). In wrapping up, understanding the vast and multifaceted landscape of data sovereignty requires a panoramic view. From its historic roots to its current-day implications and the international regulatory frameworks that shape its discourse, data sovereignty remains a crucial yet evolving frontier in the digital realm.

4. THE PRIVACY DILEMMA

Privacy, once a given in most societies, has evolved into a prized possession in today's digitally-driven era. The modern understanding of privacy goes beyond a mere right; it's a cornerstone of human dignity and a linchpin for individual autonomy. As Hoepman, (2014) postulates, privacy serves as a reflection of society's values, interwoven with nuances of freedom, individualism, and respect. As the tendrils of the digital realm spread further, they invariably draw users into a web of virtual interactions, each carrying its share of data footprints. Unfortunately, with the surge in online activities, vulnerabilities have also increased. Threats are multifaceted and relentless. One of the most alarming is the data breach, a phenomenon that has seen a meteoric rise in recent years. Romanosky's (2016) examination of cyber incidents shines a light on the startling frequency of these breaches, revealing the inherent risks of identity theft, financial fraud, and the unauthorized exposure of sensitive personal data.

Yet, as daunting as they are, data breaches are but one part of the privacy quagmire. The concept of surveillance, once associated primarily with Orwellian dystopias, is now a tangible reality. Both governmental bodies and commercial giants engage in pervasive monitoring of online behaviors. Strassburg et al. (2020) explores this in her seminal work on surveillance capitalism, highlighting how companies not only monitor but also commodify user data for profit, often without explicit consent or even awareness from the end-users. Responding to this digital onslaught, there have been concerted efforts to reclaim the sanctuary of privacy. Technological advancements have borne a suite of tools and applications tailored to safeguard user privacy. Encrypted messaging platforms, like Signal, allow for secure communications, while Virtual Private Networks (VPNs) mask online activities from prying eyes. Best practices have also been crystallized for the everyday netizen. Common advice now includes the routine updating of software, the use of strong, unique passwords, and the enabling of multi-factor authentication—steps that, while basic, provide a fortified defense against many online threats.

Parallel to these technological defenses, the legislative machinery worldwide has also whirred into action. Regulations have been crafted to provide users with legal recourses and rights concerning their data. A flagship example is the European Union's General Data Protection Regulation (GDPR). As

Kuner (2013) elucidates, the GDPR serves not merely as a directive but as a philosophical statement, emphasizing the primacy of individual rights in a data-driven age. This legislation, among others, aims to provide individuals with agency over their data, mandating transparency from companies and ensuring users have the right to know, edit, or even erase their digital footprints. In conclusion, the digital epoch presents a paradox. On the one hand, the conveniences and opportunities offered are unparalleled. Yet, on the other, these very advantages come intertwined with threats to the sanctum of personal privacy. As the dialogue on digital rights continues to evolve, understanding, navigating, and ultimately resolving the privacy dilemma remains paramount.

5. DIGITAL SECURITY: CHALLENGES AND SOLUTIONS

In our rapidly digitizing world, the conveniences and transformative possibilities presented by the internet are juxtaposed against a backdrop of emerging and constantly evolving cyber threats. Hackers, once depicted as lone wolves operating from shadowy basements, have metamorphosed into organized collectives, with some even enjoying tacit or overt state sponsorship (Anderson, 2020). These groups, alongside solo phishers and malicious actors, seek to exploit digital vulnerabilities, whether for monetary gain, political motives, or sheer mischief. Anderson's work shines a spotlight on this perilous game, emphasizing the continually shifting strategies employed by these malefactors and the defense mechanisms crafted in response. At the heart of defending against these cyber onslaughts lies a gamut of security measures, with encryption being paramount. Encryption is no longer a luxury or an afterthought; it's an essential first line of defense, scrambling data in a way that renders it incomprehensible to anyone without the right decryption key (Schneier, 2015). This cryptographic shield ensures that even if data is intercepted, its utility to the unauthorized recipient remains negligible.

Another significant evolution in the security domain is the widespread adoption of two-factor authentication (2FA). Beyond the realm of a mere password, 2FA necessitates a secondary verification step, which could range from a texted code to biometric verification. As Flores et al. (2014) point out in their study, this secondary layer not only bolsters security but also acts as a deterrent, with potential hackers often bypassing targets known to deploy 2FA in favor of easier prey. Yet, while individual users and companies work tirelessly to safeguard their digital real estate, the role of tech behemoths in shaping (and sometimes shaking) the digital security ecosystem cannot be overstated. Companies like Google, Apple, and Microsoft continuously refine their defensive mechanisms, pouring billions into research and the deployment of cutting-edge security protocols. Their efforts, while laudable, are not infallible. Consider the 2014 Yahoo breach—a cyber calamity that saw data from billions of users stolen. Perlroth, (2021) account of the incident offers not just a post-mortem but a dire warning of the vulnerabilities even the most fortified digital fortresses face.

Further complicating the landscape are the occasional alignments of interests between rogue states and hackers, with the former sometimes leveraging the latter's expertise for cyber-espionage or to wage proxy digital wars (Zetter, 2014). Such alliances make it clear that digital security is not just about safeguarding an individual's email—it's about defending national infrastructures, economies, and, by extension, ways of life. In summation, our hyper-connected epoch presents a unique paradox. The very tools that empower us, making our lives more interconnected and efficient, also expose us to risks that were unthinkable just a few decades ago. As the battlegrounds of digital security evolve, so must the strategies and tactics we employ to defend them.

6. OWNERSHIP OF DIGITAL DATA

The rapid digitization of our society has sparked fervent discourse around the intricate and often nebulous concept of data ownership. At its crux, data ownership delineates the legal entitlements and overarching dominion over data. Yet, as Lanier (2013) astutely observes, the multifaceted nature of data in the era of Big Data injects layers of complexity into what might seem, on the surface, a straightforward proposition (Arora et al., 2022). Central to this discourse is the pressing question: To whom does data truly belong? While the origin of data can be unequivocally traced back to individual users—be it through online interactions, consumption patterns, or even passive engagements—it's predominantly tech conglomerates and obscure data brokers that seize, dissect, and subsequently monetize it. Mayer-Schönberger, (2009) delves into this quandary, elucidating that despite individuals being the genuine authors of this data, their ownership rights often become obfuscated by the intricate web of user agreements and opaque data policies.

This massive data accumulation and subsequent commodification bear manifold implications. For starters, it has catalyzed the meteoric rise of a behemoth industry that prospers on the bedrock of targeted advertising, molding consumer behavior and steering decision-making processes. This commodification, as Strassburg et al. (2020) elaborates, is not a benign enterprise. By turning personal data—often sensitive—into a tradeable asset, the floodgates are opened for a gamut of potential misuse, encompassing grave concerns from privacy erosion to menacing threats like identity theft. Another angle to this conundrum is the power dynamic it establishes. Tech entities, by virtue of their unparalleled access to and control over data, exert a disproportionate influence over the digital ecosystem and, by extension, modern society. Singh, (2023) argues that this data-centric power can lead to systemic imbalances, whereby entities wielding this data can manipulate both markets and individual behaviors.

Additionally, the blurring lines of data ownership raise profound ethical questions. Should corporations profit from personal data without equitably compensating the individuals it stems from? Pasquale (2015) opines that this dynamic can lead to a disproportionate value capture, where entities profiting from the data rarely redistribute the accrued benefits to the data's true originators—everyday users. In light of these challenges, the criticality of charting the contours of data ownership becomes apparent. This isn't merely a legal or corporate conundrum. It's a foundational challenge for our digital era, intertwining with broader themes of individual rights, privacy, and the socio-economic fabric of our interconnected world.

7. STRIKING A BALANCE

In the current digital milieu, the luxuries of online conveniences stand juxtaposed against significant challenges associated with privacy and security. The digital experiences that permeate our daily lives, marked by instantaneous communication, personalized services, and a barrage of information at our fingertips, come at a palpable cost—compromising personal spaces and the potential erosion of trust (Baase, 2012). This dialectic, poised between digital luxury and the diminishing veil of privacy, lies at the heart of contemporary discourse on the digital age. The roles that governments, corporations, and individuals assume in this narrative are distinct yet interwoven. Governments, tasked with the Herculean responsibility of safeguarding citizen rights, find themselves in a challenging position. They must meticulously craft regulatory frameworks that strike a delicate balance: ensuring that while personal spaces remain inviolate, innovation and economic dynamics aren't stymied. As expounded by Greenleaf

(2012), data privacy laws are undergoing constant evolution, seeking to cater to this dual mandate and keep pace with technological advancements.

Simultaneously, corporations are often at the epicenter of these discussions, wielding considerable influence over how the story of data and privacy unfolds. These entities, driven by business imperatives, hold vast reservoirs of user data, positioning them at a vantage point. They dictate terms of service, algorithmic operations, and data monetization strategies. While some corporations project commitment to ethical data use, a holistic and universally adopted stance remains distant, as explored by Van Dijck (2014). For corporations, data isn't merely a byproduct—it's a valuable asset, often translated into significant revenue streams. However, the landscape is not merely shaped by institutional behemoths. Individuals, endowed with increasing cognizance of their digital footprints, rights, and the potential ramifications of data misuse, have become pivotal to reshaping this narrative. Their clamor for transparency, data control, and fair value exchange is forcing a recalibration of how data is perceived, treated, and transacted. This rising wave of individual agency suggests a more equitable digital future, but the journey is fraught with challenges.

Central to this debate is the concept of a "digital bill of rights." Such a foundational document seeks to enshrine the inviolable digital rights of individuals, providing an authoritative template for governments and corporations to align with. Tufekci (2017) critically assesses this proposition, noting its potential to bridge the chasm between technological advancements and fundamental rights. However, conceptualizing and realizing a universally accepted digital bill of rights is ambitious and would necessitate collaborative efforts transcending national boundaries and diverse interests. In sum, the journey towards a harmonized digital ecosystem—one that aligns convenience, privacy, and individual rights—is intricate. It demands concerted efforts from all stakeholders, accompanied by a recognition that individual rights and data-driven conveniences aren't necessarily mutually exclusive but require a reimagined framework for coexistence.

8. LOOKING AHEAD: THE FUTURE OF DIGITAL SOVEREIGNTY

The forthcoming chapters of digital sovereignty are being written in the light of explosive technological advancements. Pivotal among these are Artificial Intelligence (AI) and quantum computing (Mohana-Krishnan et al., 2023). As highlighted by Russell (2010), AI's capability to process and analyze colossal datasets presents both promise and peril. While AI has the potential to offer tailored digital experiences and drive innovation, it simultaneously exacerbates concerns regarding privacy due to its pervasive data collection and analysis mechanisms. Meanwhile, quantum computing, with its unprecedented computational power, might soon render current cryptographic systems obsolete, intensifying security apprehensions (Preskill, 2018). Predicting the trajectory of digital sovereignty, privacy, and ownership in this dynamic landscape requires an intricate interplay of technological foresight and societal considerations. Strassburg et al. (2020) posits that as technologies continue to evolve, there will be an amplified commodification of personal data, propelling society into an era of "surveillance capitalism." This paradigm, where personal data becomes the linchpin for economic growth, could fundamentally reshape perceptions of privacy and data ownership. Confronted with these profound shifts, there's a clarion call for proactive measures. Society, in tandem with policymakers, needs to lay down robust frameworks and guidelines. Preparing for this imminent future entails investing in research to develop quantum-resistant cryptographic techniques, bolstering legislative efforts for data protection in the age of AI, and fostering widespread digital literacy to empower citizens (Schneier, 2015). Only through such concerted efforts can society navigate the intricate maze of future digital sovereignty challenges and protect its denizens in an increasingly interconnected digital universe.

9. CONCLUSION

The intricate interplay of digital footprints, data sovereignty, and the quest for privacy underscores one of the defining challenges of our times. As delineated by Dingli, & Seychell (2015), the epoch of digital immersion affords us unprecedented conveniences. Nevertheless, each digital gesture, be it a 'like', 'download', or 'comment', etches an indelible mark in the vast digital cosmos, often unbeknownst to the user (O'Hara 2022). As we plunge deeper into this realm, the overarching conundrum emerges: To whom does this digital legacy truly belong? (Wang, Zhang, & Zhang, 2020). groundbreaking work on "data economies" proposes a paradigm wherein personal data transcends its simplistic definition, morphing into the lifeblood of a nascent economic order. This transformation of personal data into a pivotal asset, contrasted with the allure of bespoke digital experiences, presents a dilemma of herculean proportions. The luxury of digital facilitation stands juxtaposed against the stark reality of a digital self, constantly at the crossroads of encroachment, observation, and exploitation.Yet, the unfolding tale isn't merely one of caution but also of optimism and innovation. Pioneering endeavors, both at the technological and policy frontiers, are actively striving to redefine this balance. Concepts such as post-quantum cryptography (Bernstein, & Lange, 2017) and stringent data governance mechanisms shine as beacons in this intricate maze. As Dourish, & Bell, (2011) articulates, the path to a secure digital future necessitates a holistic, synergistic approach, binding stakeholders in a common, purpose-driven mission. Drawing this chapter to a close, it is evident that the pursuit of data sovereignty transcends transient debates; it is the linchpin upon which our digital destiny hinges. Informed by a tapestry of research and bolstered by collaborative fervor, our collective choices will shape this landscape. The journey, though complex, carries the promise of a digital ecosystem that marries progress with individual agency.

REFERENCES

Anderson, R. (2020). *Security engineering: a guide to building dependable distributed systems.* John Wiley & Sons. doi:10.1002/9781119644682

Arora, M., Prakash, A., Mittal, A., & Singh, S. (2022). Moderating role of resistance to change in the actual adoption of HR analytics in the Indian banking and financial services industry. In *Evidence-based HRM: a Global Forum for Empirical Scholarship.* Emerald Publishing Limited.

Baase, S. (2012). *A gift of fire.* Pearson Education Limited.

Barnard-Wills, D., & Ashenden, D. (2012). Securing virtual space: Cyber war, cyber terror, and risk. *Space and Culture, 15*(2), 110–123. doi:10.1177/1206331211430016

Bernstein, D. J., & Lange, T. (2017). Post-quantum cryptography. *Nature, 549*(7671), 188–194. doi:10.1038/nature23461 PMID:28905891

Bingham, T., & Conner, M. (2010). *The new social learning: A guide to transforming organizations through social media*. Berrett-Koehler Publishers.

Boyd, D. M., & Ellison, N. B. (2007). Social network sites: Definition, history, and scholarship. *Journal of Computer-Mediated Communication, 13*(1), 210–230. doi:10.1111/j.1083-6101.2007.00393.x

Cadwalladr, C., & Graham-Harrison, E. (2018). Revealed: 50 million Facebook profiles harvested for Cambridge Analytica in major data breach. *The Guardian, 17*(1), 22.

Castells, M. (2011). Network theory| A network theory of power. *International Journal of Communication, 5*, 773–787.

Cate, F. H., & Mayer-Schönberger, V. (2013). Notice and consent in a world of Big Data. *International Data Privacy Law, 3*(2), 67–73. doi:10.1093/idpl/ipt005

Daskal, J. C. (2015). *The un-territoriality of data*. Academic Press.

Dingli, A., & Seychell, D. (2015). *The new digital natives*. JB Metzler.

Dourish, P., & Bell, G. (2011). *Divining a digital future: Mess and mythology in ubiquitous computing*. MIT Press. doi:10.7551/mitpress/9780262015554.001.0001

Feher, K. (2021). Digital identity and the online self: Footprint strategies–An exploratory and comparative research study. *Journal of Information Science, 47*(2), 192–205.

Flores, W. R., Holm, H., Nohlberg, M., & Ekstedt, M. (2014). Investigating personal determinants of two-factor authentication adoption: Habit and complacency. *Proceedings of the 47th Hawaii International Conference on System Sciences*.

Greenleaf, G. (2012). Global data privacy laws: 89 countries and accelerating. *Privacy Laws & Business International Report,* (115).

Haggart, B. (2019). The age of surveillance capitalism: The fight for a human future at the new frontier of power. *Journal of Digital Media & Policy, 10*(2), 229-243.

Hoepman, J. H. (2014, June). Privacy design strategies. *IFIP International Information Security Conference,* 446-459.

Kritzinger, E., & von Solms, S. H. (2010). Cyber security for home users: A new way of protection through awareness enforcement. *Computers & Security, 29*(8), 840–847. doi:10.1016/j.cose.2010.08.001

Kuner, C. (2013). *Transborder data flows and data privacy law*. Academic Press.

Lanier, J. (2013). How Should We Think about Privacy? *Scientific American, 309*(5), 64–71. doi:10.1038/scientificamerican1113-64 PMID:24283017

Mayer-Schönberger, V. (2009). Can we reinvent the internet? *Science, 325*(5939), 396–397.

MohanaKrishnan, M., Kumar, A. S., Talukdar, V., Saleh, O. S., Irawati, I. D., Latip, R., & Kaur, G. (2023). Artificial Intelligence in Cyber Security. In Handbook of Research on Deep Learning Techniques for Cloud-Based Industrial IoT (pp. 366-385). IGI Global.

O'Hara, K. (2022). Digital Modernity. *Foundations and Trends® in Web Science*, *9*(1–2), 1-254.

Pasquale, F. (2015). *The black box society: The secret algorithms that control money and information*. Harvard University Press. doi:10.4159/harvard.9780674736061

Perlroth, N. (2021). *This is how they tell me the world ends: The cyberweapons arms race*. Bloomsbury Publishing USA.

Polčák, R., & Svantesson, D. J. B. (2017). *Information sovereignty: data privacy, sovereign powers and the rule of law*. Edward Elgar Publishing.

Preskill, J. (2018). Quantum computing in the NISQ era and beyond. *Quantum : the Open Journal for Quantum Science*, *2*, 79. doi:10.22331/q-2018-08-06-79

Rainie, H., & Wellman, B. (2012). *Networked: The new social operating system 10*. Mit Press. doi:10.7551/mitpress/8358.001.0001

Romanosky, S. (2016). Examining the costs and causes of cyber incidents. *Journal of Cybersecurity*, *2*(2), 121–135. doi:10.1093/cybsec/tyw001

Romanosky, S. (2019). Examining the costs and causes of cyber incidents. *Journal of Cybersecurity*, *2*(2), 121–135.

Russell, S. J. (2010). *Artificial intelligence is a modern approach*. Pearson Education, Inc.

Schneier, B. (2015). *Data and Goliath: The hidden battles to collect your data and control your world*. WW Norton & Company.

Schwartz, P. M., & Peifer, K. N. (2017). Transatlantic data privacy law. *Geological Journal*, *106*, 115.

Singh, P. (2023). Systematic review of data-centric approaches in artificial intelligence and machine learning. *Data Science and Management*, *6*(3), 144–157. doi:10.1016/j.dsm.2023.06.001

Strassburg, B. B., Iribarrem, A., Beyer, H. L., Cordeiro, C. L., Crouzeilles, R., Jakovac, C. C., ... Visconti, P. (2020). Global priority areas for ecosystem restoration. *Nature*, *586*(7831), 724–729.

Tufekci, Z. (2017). *Twitter and tear gas: The power and fragility of networked protest*. Yale University Press.

Van Dijck, J. (2014). Datafication, dataism and dataveillance: Big Data between scientific paradigm and ideology. *Surveillance & Society*, *12*(2), 197–208. doi:10.24908/ss.v12i2.4776

Wang, C., Zhang, Q., & Zhang, W. (2020). Corporate social responsibility, green supply chain management and firm performance: The moderating role of big-data analytics capability. *Research in Transportation Business & Management*, *37*, 100557. doi:10.1016/j.rtbm.2020.100557

Zetter, K. (2014). *An unprecedented look at Stuxnet, the world's first digital weapon*. Wired.

Chapter 6
Traversing Technological Vistas in Decentralized Finance:
A Bibliometric Approach

Divya Goswami
Chitkara Business School, Chitkara University, India

Balraj Verma
https://orcid.org/0000-0002-6542-3261
Chitkara Business School, Chitkara University, India

ABSTRACT

Decentralized autonomous organizations (DAOs) represent a novel technology progress that could potentially challenge conventional organizations in terms of management and making choices. This chapter provides an introduction to decentralized finance (DeFi), situates DeFi within the framework of the conventional financial industry, establishes a connection of peer-to-peer transactions, and concludes with a discussion on policy implications. Decentralization has the capacity to weaken conventional mechanisms of accountability and diminish the efficacy of established financial regulations and enforcement. This study presents a thorough analysis of the current status of research on DAOs, highlighting the most important research areas and relevant works in the subject. Furthermore, it examines the performance of prominent decentralized finance in relation to these research areas, providing valuable observations on their real-world implementations and efficacy.

1. INTRODUCTION

Decentralized finance, also known as DeFi, provides financial services, including credit, loans, and investing, directly on the blockchain without the need for a typical central commercial middleman (Werner et.,2021). DeFi applications aim to achieve disengagement and censoring resistance, demonstrating some degree of success (Carter et al., 2021).Open-source software is commonly used to implement these systems, which allow various stakeholders to take part in the decisions being made (Jensen

DOI: 10.4018/979-8-3693-3253-5.ch006

et al.,2021). Intermediaries frequently fulfill crucial functions in diminishing transaction expenses and broadening transaction opportunities. Mediators frequently facilitate financial interactions by connecting transactional parties, fostering confidence, and facilitating deal settlements (Roth, 2015). In the absence of intermediaries, transacting parties may encounter difficulties in establishing contacts, engaging in contract negotiations, and enforcing agreements. However, intermediaries frequently possess significant influence in structuring economic transactions, and they can exploit this influence to maximize their own interests, which raises worries about their monopoly status (Cohen et al., 2021). Despite being a global leader, the Indian financial industry faces challenges in its long-term development. (Goyal et al.,2019). The introduction of technology has brought about a significant transformation in the way financial services are planned, created, and utilized. Utilizing the technology of blockchain, decentralised financial services can expand financial accessibility, provide unrestricted access, foster innovation without requiring permission, and generate fresh prospects for investors and researchers. The finance industry is currently seeing a significant shift with the rise of decentralized financial institutions (DeFi). DeFi, based on the concept of blockchain, seeks to transform conventional financial systems by providing clear, accessible, and self-sufficient options to individuals worldwide. The incorporation of artificial intelligence (AI) in the fast changing environment has the capacity to unlock unparalleled prospects and redefine the prospects of finance in a decentralized manner. Artificial intelligence (AI), through its capacity to examine extensive quantities of information, detect trends, and generate smart forecasts, has the potential to enable decentralized finance (DeFi) systems to improve their activities, strengthen safety precautions, and offer customized solutions for customers. The uses of AI in DeFi are extensive and full of potential, ranging from artificially intelligent trading techniques and risk evaluation tools to fraud detection techniques and smart contracts audits.

However, the probable future expansion of DeFi is uncertain, as it is yet to be determined whether or not and to how much it will occur (Bank for International Settlements (BIS, 2022). The introduction of DeFi brings about significant technical and economic intricacy, which renders the understanding, assessments, and risk estimation of DeFi financial offerings progressively challenging. Financial firms and authorities handling DeFi (e.g., Aramonte et al., 2021 & Financial Stability Board, 2022) require a methodical assessment of these factors. There is a significant dearth of comprehensive information about DeFi among numerous groups, highlighting the need for a unique framework to enhance comprehension of the technology. The objective of this study is to offer a bibliometric analysis is "To know the key dimensions of DeFi, its evolution in the academic literature alongwith its financial capacities". Furthermore, we incorporate the latest discoveries and progressions that enhance comprehension of their operation, structure, and their ability to work together.

2. THEORETICAL UNDERPINNING

2.1 Decentralized Finance (DeFi)

Decentralized Finance (DeFi) is a financial ecosystems that operates without an authoritative body and lacks a layer of protection. It is characterized by its competitiveness, contestability, composability, and non-custodial nature, all enabled by technological advances (Auer et al., 2023). Decentralized finance, which is often known as DeFi, employs modern technology in order to eliminate intermediaries and centralized entities from financial transactions. DeFi comprises cryptocurrency, blockchain technology, and programs that facilitate money transfers among individuals. The DeFi sector is now in its early stages, making it vulnerable to hacking and theft due to inadequate software and insufficient checks for safety prior to the introduction of apps. These financial services lack oversight from conventional financial institutions or financial managers, so they do not provide protections against criminal conduct or investor fraud. A decentralized system is accomplished by employing consensus methods that motivate users to verify and uphold the blockchain (Buterin, 2014). Decentralization is a core characteristic of blockchain software that distinguishes it from conventional centralized systems. A centralized system is characterized by the presence of a sole entity or a collective of entities that exercise control over the system, overseeing all transactions and decisions that are made. These problems can arise, including a dearth of openness, suppression of information, and an increased susceptibility to deceit or misconduct. Conversely, a decentralized blockchain network facilitates a more open and accessible system, wherein each participant possesses an equitable responsibility in validating and upholding the network's integrity.

2.2 Blockchain

Blockchain technology has numerous potential applications across various industries, such as smart gadgets, a decentralized shared economic performance, business administration, and more (Yuan & Wang, 2018). Blockchain innovation is often linked to digital currency, notably Bitcoin, however its uses extend beyond just currencies and payments (Hsieh et al., 2018). The initial deployment of the blockchain system was pioneered by an anonymous individual or collective known as Satoshi Nakamoto in 2008, and subsequently activated on January 3, 2009. Bitcoins was initially launched as an innovative a peer-to digital currency system. Nakamoto's innovation constituted a significant advancement by amalgamating preexisting technology, namely encryption, distributed systems, and game theory, to establish a novel method for overseeing and validating transactions inside a decentralized network. Blockchains utilize different cryptographic techniques, including public/private key architecture and hash functions, to protect the databases and its users against assaults and criminal activities, such as overspending tokens. Every block in the Blockchain possesses a distinct hash that is generated according to what is inside of that specific block. If any effort is made to manipulate the contents in that specific block, the hash value will be altered. This alteration will be promptly detected as the hash in the subsequent block in the chain will no longer correspond. Digitally signed publicly accessible keys, and Merkle trees guarantee the integrity and security of the data. These methods contribute to the assurance of the security and transparency of the technology known as Blockchain (Beck et al., 2018).

2.3 Smart Contracts

Smart agreements are software programs that autonomously facilitate, validate, and enforce the creation and execution of electronic contracts between many parties, eliminating the requirement for middlemen or central authority. Smart contracts can enhance the velocity, effectiveness, and integrity of contract execution. Smart contracts has the capability to profoundly transform numerous conventional businesses by facilitating the automated execution of digital contracts, eliminating the necessity for an intermediary that is reliable (Wang, et al., 2019).

A basic smart contract can incorporate conditional statements that initiate execution when specific criteria are fulfilled. These tokens are usually recorded on a blockchain that supports this capability, and as a result, they possess the characteristics of the the distributed ledger, such as immutability, transparency, and security. Moreover, within the realm of supply chain management, smart agreements have the capability to guarantee adherence to specified conditions and terms by carrying out agreed-upon actions. Smart contracts have the potential to simplify property transactions and minimize the reliance on middlemen in the real estate sector (Tan et al., 2022).However, the utilization of smart contracts may restrict a company's ability to adjust to evolving conditions as a result of the blockchain's permanence, which could potentially lead to additional regulatory or legal expenses (Murray et al., 2021).

3. METHODOLOGY

Bibliometric analysis has become increasingly prevalent in corporate research in the past few years due to two main factors. Firstly, the development and widespread accessibility to bibliometric tools such as The Gephi program, Leximancer, VOSviewer, as well as scholarly databases like Scopus and Web of Science have contributed to its widespread acceptance (Donthu et al., 2021). Secondly, the cross-disciplinary adoption of bibliometric technique from science and technology studies in business study has further fueled its appeal. This study employed bibliometric techniques to identify prominent subjects within the realm of Decentralised Autonomous Organisations. The information was collected from Scopus, and a total of 256 pertinent publications were chosen through keyword-based searches. The analysis encompassed the identification of significant articles and clusters, as well as the identification of ideas and pivotal subjects in the field, such as administration, uses, safety, and legal obstacles. This methodology offers a comprehensive examination of Decentralised Autonomous Organisations that may act as a foundation for future study and organized advancement in the subject. This study investigates the precise content contained in the publication by analyzing the search terms supplied by the writers or frequently used in titles, descriptions, or whole texts (Methlagl, 2022).

3.1 Objectives of the Research

Defining the goals of the analysis is an essential stage in systematically examining the existing literature to initiate the process of research. Articulating research objectives showcases a comprehensive understanding of the overall topic matter and the specific research issue being investigated. A comprehensive investigation was undertaken to identify pertinent academic literature with the aim of enhancing comprehension of the research issue. The objectives were determined based on the study strategy outlined in the previously mentioned academic sources. The study seeks to investigate the current level of research maturity about *"What is DeFi and its goals in relation to ''DAO"? To understand the level of domination in the field of financing? Does the study topic have a particular emphasis on authors, countries, or journals?"*

After analyzing each summary of the articles in our bibliographical collection, we have identified three main areas of research. One category of articles centers on topics related to connections and behavior among individuals, while another category centers on the application of novel analytical techniques.

Table 1. Search protocol

Databank	Period	Type of Document	Search Standards	Keywords
Scopus	Until 19/12/22	Article, Conference Paper, Book Chapter, Review, Book	Article title, Abstract, Keywords	*"DAO*"*

These methods pertain to the estimation of profits and risks, the interpretation of financial indicators, and the optimization of investment portfolios.

3.2 Search Criteria

The investigation employed Scopus as its primary data source. Scopus, developed by Elsevier in 2004, is a database designed to record abstracts and citations. It is widely acknowledged as a prominent bibliographic reference library. In bibliometric analysis, the correctness of the keyword words used is an important component, in addition to the literature being utilized. The search parameters included any study articles that had the term "DAO*" in their heading, key words, and content. Has been restricted exclusively to the English language. In order to achieve a comprehensive comprehension of the data, it was imperative to do data cleansing, which involved rectifying any wrong or insufficient information. Researchers conducted a comprehensive investigation of the research inquiries to identify the essential terms employed in the search procedure. The writers participated in a collaborative conversation to establish and finalize the exact search criteria. Furthermore, they meticulously extracted the relevant data from the selected sources. A wide range of string types were manufactured, ultimately making major improvements to academic research.

("Decentralized decision making" OR "decentralized autonomous organization" OR "DAO*") AND ("Smart contracts")

Using the "AND," "OR," and "AND" operators to make connections between different search terms is how the key phrase strings are made. The chosen digital sources offer a search engine that is tailored to meet certain needs. Customized search methods are used in digital databases to carry out research strings.

3.3 Citation Analysis

A basic method for mapping scientific literature is citation evaluation, which is based on the idea that citations show intellectual connections between publications, which happen when a single article mentions another (Appio et al., 2014). The influence of an article is assessed based on the quantity of references it garners. The methodology allows for the identification of the most impactful papers in a specific scientific topic. Various measures, such as networking metrics, can be used to assess the significance of publications in a study field. However, a highly unbiased and direct measure of their influence is the number of citations they receive (Baumgartner et al., 2003, Stremersch et al., 2007). By employing citations, it is possible to examine the most impactful papers in a specific study domain in order to comprehend the cognitive structure of that topic (Donthu et al., 2021).

4. RESULTS AND DISCUSSION

The Bibliometric Analysis method enables researchers to discover the most prominent authors, institutions, and studies in a particular discipline, along with their interrelationships. Bibliometric analysis is an invaluable tool for evaluating the production and influence of researchers, institutions, and scientific fields. It demonstrates notable efficacy in evaluating scientific research, allocating funding, and devising strategic plans (Costa et al., 2019). In the end, bibliometric analysis helps scientists make better decisions about what to study and how to spread knowledge in a more efficient and effective way. VOSviewer is an application that is designed to create and display bibliometric networks. These networks might consist of several elements such as academic journals, researchers, or specific publications. They are formed by analyzing relationships such as citations, bibliographical coupling, co-citation, or the co-authorship. VOSviewer provides text mining capabilities to create and display co-occurrence networks of significant phrases taken from a collection of scientific literature. In the beginning, the VOS viewer got reference, bibliographical, and biographical terms from 256 publications. The VOS-viewer gives researchers powerful tools for seeing and analyzing bibliometric networks. Some of these features are network visualization, mapping and grouping, cocitation analysis, and bibliographic coupling analysis. Because of this, the VOS-viewer is an essential tool for researchers who want to get useful information from large datasets (Van Eck & Waltman, 2017).

Document citation involves examining the connections between publications by determining the most impactful articles in a specific study area.Citation functions as a means to acknowledge and attribute proper credit to the rightful source. Citing a document not only helps to acknowledge the original study work but also provides readers with a means to trace the evolution of data. In Table 2, the research document that is most frequently cited and occupies the top position is Jiang (2018), with a total of 396 citations. Subsequently, Liu (2018) contributed a document with a noteworthy 203 citations, while Mehar (2019) provided a paper with 173 citations. The document with the fewest citations on the list was authored by Nehai (2018) and Singh (2019), with 60 and 54 citations, respectively.

The VOS-viewer program was utilized to generate Table 3, which aims to highlight the key components that have had the greatest influence on the field of Decentralization in Financial services. The curated database consists of scholarly articles, compositions, and assessments. Authored by multiple individuals by 2023. The individuals who create written content Alex Norta is acknowledged as a distinguished researcher based on their high citation count and extensive publication record. The paucity of works, even from respected writers, suggests that this area of study is still in its early stages. Nevertheless, the increase in authorship and collaboration has the capacity to inspire greater enthusiasm in this field.

The VOSviewer program was utilized to compare different businesses based on their unique citation counts, with the aim of obtaining further insights. Table 4 presents data regarding the allocation of works of literature among various organizations. The text contains references to organizations that have received

Table 2. Citation of documents

S.No	Document	Citations	Links
1	Jiang (2018)	396	0
2	Liu (2018)	203	0
3	Mehar (2019)	173	1
4	Wang (2019)	143	7
5	Sayeed (2020)	130	0
6	Grossman (2018)	105	0
7	Norta (2015b)	82	1
8	Zamani (2018)	73	0
9	Nehai (2018)	60	2
10	Singh (2019)	54	3

Figure 1. Citation of documents

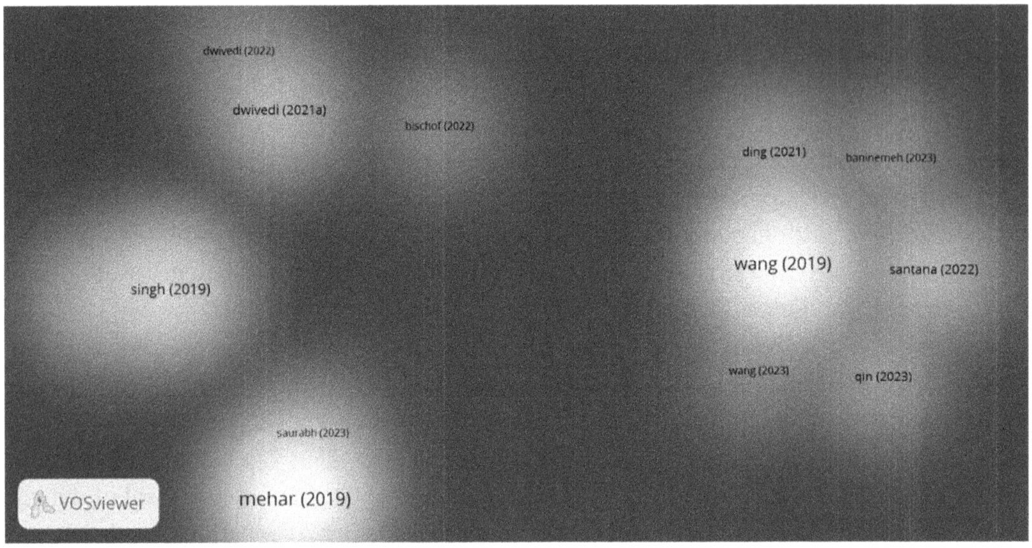

Table 3. Citation of authors

S.No.	Author	Documents	Citations	Total Link Strength
1	Alex Norta	8	252	10
2	Gabrielle Fletcher	2	173	6
3	Alana Giambattista	2	173	6
4	Elgar Gong	2	173	6
5	Henry M.Kim	2	173	6
6	Marek Laskowski	2	173	6
7	Muhammad Izhar Mehar	2	173	6
8	Ryan Sanayhie,	2	173	6
9	Charles Louis Shier	2	173	6
10	Yong Yuan	5	168	39

a significant number of citations. Harvard Law School in Cambridge, United States and York University in Toronto, Canada have the most amount of citations, totaling 173. The Institute of Automation, Chinese Academy of Sciences in Beijing, China, has accumulated 147 citations. Additionally, the Department of Software Science at Tallinn University of Technology in Tallinn, Estonia, has received 64 citations. The Institute of Systems Engineering at Macau University of Science and Technology in Macao has the lowest citation count, with a total of only 19 citations. The research elucidates that consistent invention inside the organization would assist administrators and managers at financial services in cultivating an excellent track record (Manohar, S., et al., 2020).

Table 5 indicates that China is the foremost country in terms of the worldwide distribution of literary works. It has generated 16 documents, accumulating a total of 797 citations, so ranking first among the top 10 countries. The leading countries in advancing knowledge in the field of decentralization in the

Figure 2. Citation of authors

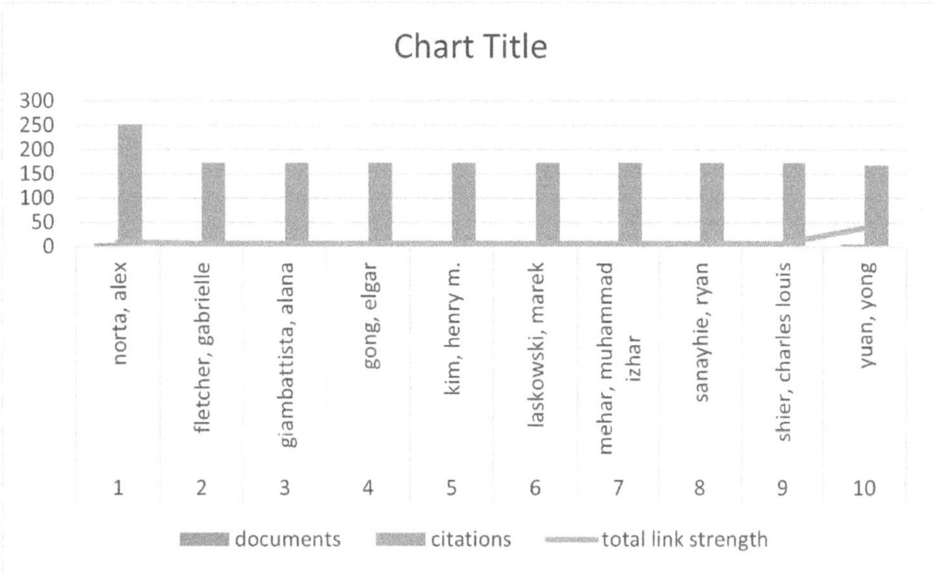

Table 4. Citation of organisation

S.No.	Organization	Documents	Citations	Total Link Strength
1	Harvard Law School, Cambridge, United States	2	173	0
2	York University, Toronto, Canada	2	173	0
3	State Key Laboratory For Management And Control Of Complex Systems, Institute Of Automation, Chinese Academy Of Sciences, Beijing, China	2	147	7
4	Department Of Software Science, Tallinn University Of Technology, Tallinn, Estonia	2	64	0
5	Institute Of Systems Engineering, Macau University Of Science And Technology, Macao	3	19	3

financial services sector are the United Kingdom, Hong Kong, United States, Estonia, Canada, Israel, Greece, France, and South Korea. China holds the top position with 16 research papers, 797 citations, and a link strength of 29. The VOSViewer software offers a graphical depiction, categorization, and clarification of the interrelationships across nations. Furthermore, every objective study has a unique approach to verify, examine, or define the research area. The study methodology utilized in understanding decentralization specifically in the field of finance, might vary depending on the researcher's specific objectives and degree of originality.

The geographical distribution of networking is determined by examining the country of origin of publications and using the VOS-viewer software, which is available for free. Figure 4 displays the results. The framework additionally reinforces the findings obtained from the bibliometric assessment of the top ten countries in terms of academic productivity in the field of DeFi. The varied assemblages of contrasting hues represent the discrete domains of investigation and their interaction with other areas of study encompassed by the research's scope.

Figure 3. Citation of organisation

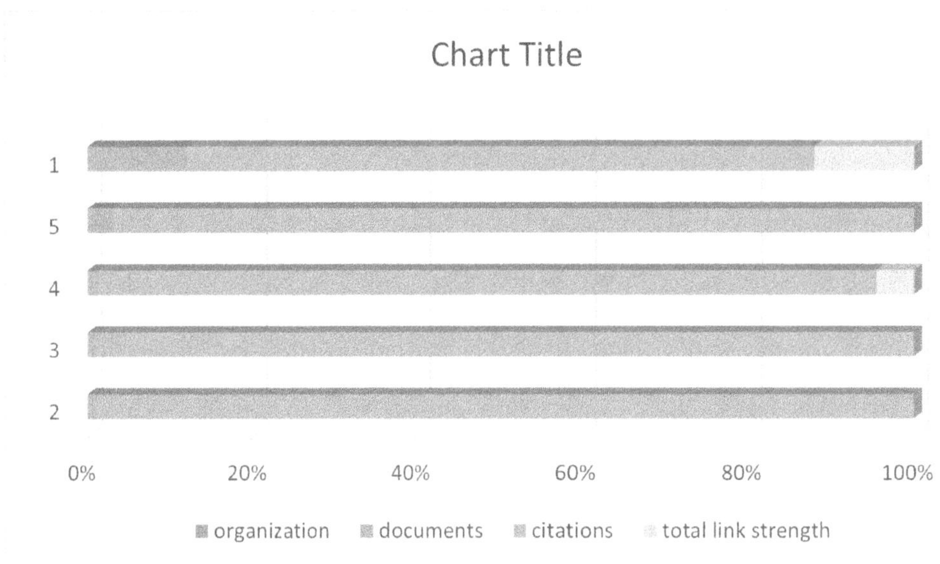

Table 5. Citation of countries

S.No.	Country	Documents	Citations	Total Link Strength
1	China	16	797	29
2	United Kingdom	7	430	8
3	Hong Kong	4	407	8
4	United States	16	354	12
5	Estonia	8	252	15
6	Canada	6	188	3
7	Israel	2	105	0
8	Greece	5	84	2
9	France	2	65	2
10	South Korea	4	63	8

The following table indicates that the top publications in the study field of financial guidance and individual investor differ in terms of their class, publication rate, and citations score. IEEE Access has the highest number of citations, with a total of 184. The IEEE Transactions on Computational Social Systems, on the other hand, has a reasonable number of citations, with a total of 149, placing it in second position among the selected sources. The data indicates that the Frontiers In Blockchain and Communications In Computer And Information Science are the further sources in the list with 64 and 57 number of citations that specialize in the area of Decentralized financial services. These figures indicate that journal papers and conferences are based on evidence have varying citation counts, implying their significance and influence.

Figure 4. Citation of countries

Table 6. Citation of sources

S.No.	Source	Documents	Citations	Total Link Strength
1	IEEE Access	7	184	1
2	IEEE Transactions On Computational Social Systems	2	149	7
3	Frontiers In Blockchain	3	64	0
4	Communications In Computer And Information Science	5	57	1
5	ACM International Conference Proceeding Series	7	38	1
6	IEEE Transactions On Systems, Man, And Cybernetics: Systems	3	19	3
7	Lecture Notes On Data Engineering And Communications Technologies	2	10	0
8	Blockchain: Research And Applications	2	7	1
9	Lecture Notes In Computer Science (Including Subseries Lecture Notes In Artificial Intelligence And Lecture Notes In Bioinformatics)	3	7	0
10	2022 IEEE International Conference On Omni-Layer Intelligent Systems, Coins 2022	2	5	2

Figure 5. Citation of sources

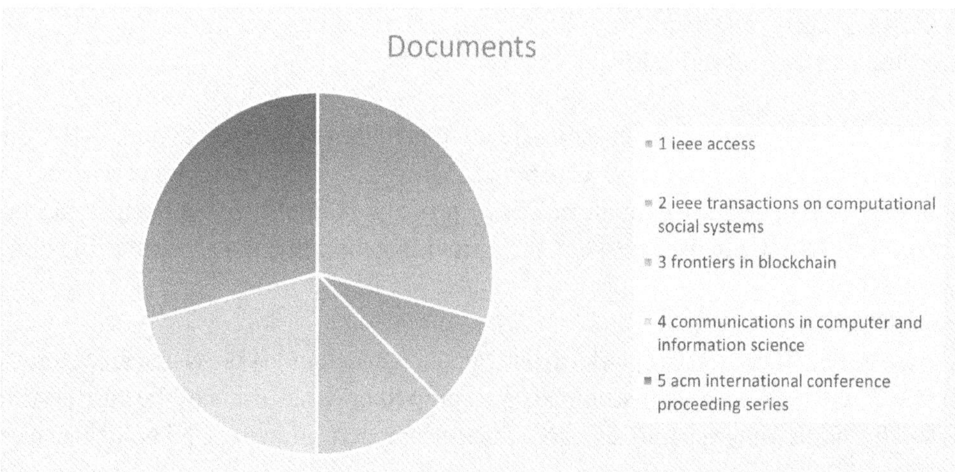

5. DISCUSSION

DeFi provides access to financial services for individuals who are unbanked, fostering financial globally. Decentralized financing is at the forefront of technological innovation, utilizing blockchain, smart contracts, and other cutting edge technologies, making it a fascinating area of study. Understanding the complete concept of DeFi, smart contracts is crucial for grasping how traditional financial systems are being disrupted, reducing reliance on centralized authorities and promoting more democractic and transparent financial ecosystem. This study clarifies that DeFi can empower individuals by allowing them to have greater control over their assets, eliminating the need for intermediaries and peer-to-peer transactions. The resulting research structure endeavors to offer a fundamental framework for forthcoming studies in a methodical and efficient manner. This work can serve as a foundation for enticing new researchers to investigate this topic, given the scarcity of prior scholarly research undertaken on DeFi services. It is morally necessary to promote greater scholarly interest in the progress of technology in the banking and finance sector in order to ensure the security and prosperity of future generations, given the rapid improvements in technology.

6. CONCLUSION

During our studies, we categorized the keywords and utilized them to retrieve 256 pertinent papers. The findings indicate a growing scholarly fascination with the application of in financial services, with a significant advancement has been advanced. Numerous studies have indicated that Decentralized Finance(DeFi) is a financial system that is build on Blockchain technology, that aims to provide inclusive, open, and permissionless financial services. The study further indicates that DeFi leverages smart contracts to automate and execute financial transactions without the need for traditional intermediaries like banks.China, United Kingdom and Honk Kong are the prominent countries for their extraordinary literary works and writers in this academic field. The findings were acquired through the process of records cleaning and categorizing the collection of data for network evaluation, utilizing the functionalities of MS Excel, VOS-viewer .In summary, studying decentralized finance offers insights into a transformative force in the financial landscape, combining technological innovation, financial inclusion, and the reshaping of traditional financial structures. The following are the real life examples of the successful projects of DeFi:

Top case studies of successful DeFi's:

1. BAL

The term "Balancer" refers to the cryptocurrency token known as BAL. Balancer is a functions as an autonomous investment platform and distributed exchange. Liquidity providers receive BAL tokens as a distribution, enabling users to earn incentives by providing liquidity to the balance sheet pools. The Balancer approach promotes active engagement in providing liquidity, thus guaranteeing the platform's depth of availability.

2. Uniswap (UNI)

Uniswap is a decentralized trading platform that implemented liquidity provision via automated market makers (AMMs). UNI tokens were distributed by airdrop to previous users of the site, ensuring a wide and inclusive allocation. Uniswap utilizes a governance approach, allowing UNI holders to participate in voting on ideas aimed at enhancing the protocol. This methodology has effectively fostered community engagement and facilitated the alignment of interests.

With the extensive use of smart contracts in DeFi, studying the technology involves examining security aspects and potential vulnerabilities, contributing to the improvement of overall robustness. This study also puts light on the assessment of the risks and challenges associated with the decentralized systems, helping the researchers and practitioners develop strategies for mitigating potential issues.

REFERENCES

Appio, F. P., Cesaroni, F., & Di Minin, A. (2014). Visualizing the structure and bridges of the intellectual property management and strategy literature: A document co-citation analysis. *Scientometrics*, *101*(1), 623–661. doi:10.1007/s11192-014-1329-0

Auer, R., Haslhofer, B., Kitzler, S., Saggese, P., & Victor, F. (2023). *The Technology of Decentralized Finance (DeFi)*. Bank for International Settlements, Monetary and Economic Department. doi:10.1007/s42521-023-00088-8

Baumgartner, H., & Pieters, R. (2003). The structural influence of marketing journals: A citation analysis of the discipline and its subareas over time. *Journal of Marketing*, *67*(2), 123–139. doi:10.1509/jmkg.67.2.123.18610

Beck, R., Müller-Bloch, C., & King, J. L. (2018). Governance in the blockchain economy: A framework and research agenda. *Journal of the Association for Information Systems*, *19*(10), 1. doi:10.17705/1jais.00518

Buterin, V. (2014). A next-generation smart contract and decentralized application platform. *White Paper, 3*(37), 2-1.

Cohen, L., Angelovska-Wilson, A., Strong, G., & Law, D. (2021). Decentralized finance: Ready for its "close-up"? *GLI–Blockchain & Cryptocurrency Regulation 2022*.

Costa, D. F., Carvalho, F. D. M., & Moreira, B. C. D. M. (2019). Behavioral economics and behavioral finance: A bibliometric analysis of the scientific fields. *Journal of Economic Surveys*, *33*(1), 3–24. doi:10.1111/joes.12262

Donthu, N., Kumar, S., Mukherjee, D., Pandey, N., & Lim, W. M. (2021). How to conduct a bibliometric analysis: An overview and guidelines. *Journal of Business Research*, *133*, 285–296. doi:10.1016/j.jbusres.2021.04.070

FSB. (2022). *Assessment of risks to financial stability from crypto-assets. Technical report*. Financial Stability Board.

Goyal, J., Singh, M., Singh, R., & Aggarwal, A. (2019). Efficiency and technology gaps in Indian banking sector: Application of meta-frontier directional distance function DEA approach. *The Journal of Finance and Data Science, 5*(3), 156-172.

Hsieh, Y. Y., Vergne, J. P., Anderson, P., Lakhani, K., & Reitzig, M. (2018). Bitcoin and the rise of decentralized autonomous organizations. *Journal of Organization Design*, *7*(1), 1–16. doi:10.1186/s41469-018-0038-1

Jensen, J. R., von Wachter, V., & Ross, O. (2021). How decentralized is the governance of blockchain-based finance: Empirical evidence from four governance token distributions. *arXiv preprint arXiv:2102.10096*.

Manohar, S., Mittal, A., & Marwah, S. (2020). Service innovation, corporate reputation and word-of-mouth in the banking sector: A test on multigroup-moderated mediation effect. *Benchmarking*, *27*(1), 406–429. doi:10.1108/BIJ-05-2019-0217

Methlagl, M. (2022). Mapping inclusive education 1980 to 2019: A bibliometric analysis of thematic clusters and research directions. *Issues in Educational Research*, *32*(1), 225–247.

Murray, A., Kuban, S., Josefy, M., & Anderson, J. (2021). Contracting in the smart era: The implications of blockchain and decentralized autonomous organizations for contracting and corporate governance. *The Academy of Management Perspectives*, *35*(4), 622–641. doi:10.5465/amp.2018.0066

Stremersch, S., Verniers, I., & Verhoef, P. C. (2007). The quest for citations: Drivers of article impact. *Journal of Marketing*, *71*(3), 171–193. doi:10.1509/jmkg.71.3.171

Tan, W., Zhu, H., Tan, J., Zhao, Y., Xu, L. D., & Guo, K. (2022). A novel service level agreement model using blockchain and smart contract for cloud manufacturing in industry 4.0. *Enterprise Information Systems*, *16*(12), 1939426. doi:10.1080/17517575.2021.1939426

Van Eck, N. J., & Waltman, L. (2017). Citation-based clustering of publications using CitNetExplorer and VOSviewer. *Scientometrics*, *111*(2), 1053–1070. doi:10.1007/s11192-017-2300-7 PMID:28490825

Wang, S., Ouyang, L., Yuan, Y., Ni, X., Han, X., & Wang, F. Y. (2019). Blockchain-enabled smart contracts: Architecture, applications, and future trends. *IEEE Transactions on Systems, Man, and Cybernetics. Systems*, *49*(11), 2266–2277. doi:10.1109/TSMC.2019.2895123

Yuan, Y., & Wang, F. Y. (2018). Blockchain and cryptocurrencies: Model, techniques, and applications. *IEEE Transactions on Systems, Man, and Cybernetics. Systems*, *48*(9), 1421–1428. doi:10.1109/TSMC.2018.2854904

Chapter 7
The Digital Shift: Unleashing Potential, Reimagining Power Dynamics

Umesh Chawla
HP PPS Sales Sdn Bhd, Malaysia

ABSTRACT

In the dynamic digital epoch, this exploration delves into the impact of technologies on decentralization, unraveling blockchain, AI, and IoT. It dissects their transformative influence on power structures, economic paradigms, and global interactions. From the transparency of blockchain to the decision-making of AI and the symphony orchestrated by IoT, the chapter explores technologies shaping a new decentralized reality. Blockchain disrupts traditional finance, extending its impact to healthcare and supply chain management. The intersection of AI and blockchain enhances security and governance. IoT transforms industries, ushering in real-time data exchange and automation. The chapter explores deglobalization, examining how digital platforms empower local entrepreneurship and decentralized digital identity systems enhance national security. Challenges, including security concerns and inclusive access, demand astute navigation, improved collaboration, and proactive governance. The chapter concludes with a call for collective wisdom and ethical stewardship to shape a decentralized future.

1. INTRODUCTION

The advent of digital technologies marks an era of unprecedented change, challenging traditional structures and fostering decentralization (Parker et al., 2016). This chapter embarks on an exploration of the multifaceted influence of digitalization on power dynamics, honing in on its role as a catalyst for decentralization and deglobalization. In a world where societies are diligently redefining norms, the purpose here is to dissect the implications of this digital shift, with a specific focus on the intersection of technology, decentralization, and deglobalization.

Digital technologies have seamlessly woven themselves into the fabric of our daily lives, altering the way we communicate, work, and conduct business. As this chapter unravels the intricate relationship

DOI: 10.4018/979-8-3693-3253-5.ch007

between these technologies and the shifting power dynamics in our globalized world, it invites readers on a journey to discern the subtle nuances and profound implications of the digital era.

Technological advancements have ushered in an era where the conventional models of power, economics, and global interactions are being reshaped. Decentralization, a central theme in this transformation, is being driven by key digital technologies, each playing a distinct role in redefining traditional paradigms.

1.1 The Evolution of Decentralization in the Digital Era

To comprehend the impact of the digital shift on decentralization, it is crucial to trace the evolution of decentralization itself. Traditional power structures were characterized by centralized control, where authority and decision-making were concentrated in a few entities. The advent of digital technologies, however, has introduced a new paradigm where power is distributed, and autonomy is decentralized.

Decentralization is not a novel concept, but its application and significance have been magnified in the digital age. The foundational principles of decentralization – transparency, security, and trust – are being reshaped and amplified through technologies such as blockchain, AI, and IoT. These technologies are not just tools; they are architects of a new decentralized reality.

The narrative of decentralization in the digital era is multifaceted. It extends beyond the realms of technology to encompass socio-economic and political dimensions. As we delve into the specifics of blockchain, AI, and IoT, it is imperative to recognize the interconnectedness of these technologies in shaping a decentralized future.

2. DIGITAL TECHNOLOGIES AND DECENTRALIZATION

2.1 Blockchain Technology: A Paradigm of Decentralization

Blockchain, the technology underpinning cryptocurrencies, challenges centralized models (Narayanan et al., 2016). Its decentralized ledger ensures transparency, security, and trust in transactions. This section explores blockchain principles and its transformative impact on various industries, illustrating real-world applications from financial systems to supply chain management.

Blockchain's disruptive potential is most evident in its ability to decentralize financial transactions. Bitcoin, the pioneering cryptocurrency, operates on a blockchain, enabling peer-to-peer transactions without the need for traditional banking intermediaries. This decentralized financial model has the potential to empower individuals in regions with limited access to traditional banking systems.

The principle of smart contracts, self-executing agreements written into code, further exemplifies the potential of blockchain. These contracts automate and enforce the terms of an agreement without the need for intermediaries, reducing the risk of fraud and manipulation. For instance, in supply chain management, blockchain ensures end-to-end transparency by recording every transaction and movement of goods on an immutable ledger (Narayanan et al., 2016).

Blockchain's impact extends beyond finance and supply chain. Its decentralized nature ensures tamper-proof data storage, making it applicable in areas such as healthcare, where patient records can be securely stored and shared among authorized entities without compromising individual privacy.

The implications of blockchain in reshaping industries are vast. Its transparent, secure, and decentralized nature holds the promise of not just disrupting existing systems but fostering a new era of trust and efficiency. As blockchain technology matures, its applications are likely to expand, leading to more profound transformations across various sectors.

2.2 Blockchain and Trust: The Cornerstone of Decentralization

Trust is a cornerstone of any functioning society, and the digital shift is redefining how trust is established and maintained. In traditional centralized systems, trust is often vested in institutions, governments, or intermediaries. Blockchain, however, introduces a novel approach to trust – one that is decentralized and distributed.

The decentralized ledger of blockchain ensures that trust is not concentrated in a single authority but distributed across a network of nodes. Each participant in the network has access to the same immutable record, creating a transparent and trustless environment. This shift from trusting a central authority to trusting a decentralized network marks a fundamental change in the dynamics of trust.

Moreover, blockchain's consensus mechanisms, such as proof-of-work and proof-of-stake, further enhance the trustworthiness of the system. Consensus mechanisms ensure that all participants agree on the validity of transactions, making it extremely difficult for malicious actors to manipulate the system. This consensus-driven trust forms the bedrock of decentralized systems, instilling confidence in users and stakeholders.

As blockchain continues to evolve, the concept of trust in digital interactions is undergoing a paradigm shift. It is not merely a technological evolution; it is a societal shift towards decentralized trust models. Understanding and embracing this shift is pivotal in navigating the complexities of the digital era.

2.3 Artificial Intelligence: Decentralized Decision-Making and Autonomy

AI, a cornerstone of the digital shift, has implications for decentralization (McMahan et al., 2017). This section explores decentralized AI applications, like federated learning, shifting from centralized machine learning models. Case studies in healthcare, finance, and other sectors highlight the benefits and challenges of this approach.

The advent of decentralized AI applications, particularly federated learning, represents a paradigm shift in machine learning. Traditional machine learning models rely on centralizing vast amounts of data for training, posing risks to privacy and security. Federated learning addresses these concerns by allowing models to be trained across decentralized edge devices without exposing raw data.

In healthcare, federated learning enables collaborative model training across different medical institutions without sharing sensitive patient data. This decentralized approach not only preserves data privacy but also enhances the diversity and representativeness of the training dataset. Decentralized AI models are also gaining traction in the financial sector, where privacy and security are paramount. By keeping data localized, these models reduce the risk of large-scale data breaches.

The decentralized nature of AI applications contributes not only to enhanced privacy but also to the democratization of AI capabilities. It allows smaller entities and individuals to leverage AI without the need for extensive resources. This democratization has the potential to drive innovation across diverse sectors, as AI becomes more accessible and adaptable to specific needs.

While the benefits of decentralized AI are significant, challenges such as ensuring model accuracy, addressing communication overhead, and managing security protocols in a decentralized framework need careful consideration. As decentralized AI continues to evolve, it holds the promise of not just transforming industries but also shaping a more inclusive and accessible future.

2.4 The Intersection of AI and Blockchain: Synergies for Decentralization

The convergence of AI and blockchain represents a powerful synergy that amplifies the decentralization narrative. Both technologies, while distinct in their functionalities, share common principles of transparency, security, and decentralization.

One notable application of this intersection is in enhancing the security of AI models. Blockchain's tamper-proof and transparent nature can be leveraged to trace the development and deployment of AI algorithms. This not only ensures the integrity of AI models but also provides a verifiable record of their evolution.

Moreover, the combination of AI and blockchain can address one of the challenges of decentralized systems – governance. AI algorithms can be employed to automate decision-making processes within blockchain networks, streamlining governance mechanisms. This automated governance ensures that the decentralized system operates efficiently and transparently.

Smart contracts, a feature of blockchain, can be enhanced with AI capabilities to create more dynamic and self-executing agreements. For example, in decentralized finance (DeFi), AI-powered smart contracts can autonomously assess and execute financial transactions based on predefined criteria. This intersection opens up new possibilities for automation and efficiency in various decentralized applications.

The collaboration between AI and blockchain is not limited to technical advancements; it extends to the philosophical underpinnings of decentralization. Both AI and blockchain embody the ideals of decentralization by redistributing power and control. Exploring and harnessing the synergies between these technologies can unlock novel solutions to the challenges posed by the digital shift.

2.5 The Internet of Things (IoT): Transforming Industries Through Decentralization

IoT's decentralized architecture connects devices, enabling real-time data exchange and automation. Case studies illustrate the transformative impact of decentralized IoT in smart cities, manufacturing, and agriculture, reshaping traditional industries.

The Internet of Things (IoT) represents a pivotal force in the ongoing digital shift, creating a decentralized network of interconnected devices. In smart cities, for instance, IoT applications facilitate the efficient management of resources and infrastructure. Decentralized sensors collect real-time data on traffic, energy consumption, and environmental conditions, enabling cities to make informed decisions without relying on centralized control systems (Atzori et al., 2010).

Manufacturing processes have also witnessed a transformation through decentralized IoT applications. By connecting machinery and production systems, manufacturers can achieve real-time monitoring and predictive maintenance. This not only reduces downtime but also optimizes resource utilization, contributing to overall efficiency.

In agriculture, decentralized IoT solutions have empowered farmers with data-driven insights. Soil sensors, drones, and connected machinery provide farmers with real-time information on crop health, weather conditions, and resource usage. This decentralized approach enables precise decision-making, leading to increased crop yields and sustainable farming practices (Atzori et al., 2010).

The decentralized nature of IoT not only enhances operational efficiency but also contributes to sustainability by enabling more precise resource management. As IoT ecosystems continue to evolve, the potential for further decentralization in areas like energy distribution, environmental monitoring, and healthcare holds significant promise.

3. DEGLOBALIZATION IN THE DIGITAL AGE

3.1 Digital Platforms and Local Economies: Empowering Local Entrepreneurship

Digital platforms, like Etsy and Airbnb, contribute to deglobalization by empowering local economies. This section explores how digital platforms enable direct connections between producers and consumers, disrupting traditional global supply chains (Parker et al., 2016).

The rise of digital platforms has redefined the way goods and services are exchanged, fostering a shift towards localized economies. Platforms like Etsy, known for handmade and unique products, connect artisans directly with consumers worldwide. This direct-to-consumer model eliminates the need for extensive global supply chains, enabling local entrepreneurs to reach a global audience.

Airbnb, a pioneer in the sharing economy, allows individuals to rent their properties directly to travelers. This decentralized approach challenges traditional hospitality models, providing economic opportunities for individuals while offering unique and personalized experiences for travelers. By facilitating direct interactions between hosts and guests, Airbnb contributes to the deglobalization of travel and accommodations (Parker et al., 2016).

The impact of digital platforms goes beyond facilitating transactions. It nurtures a sense of community and cultural exchange, as consumers have direct access to unique products and experiences from different parts of the world. This shift towards a more localized and personalized economy not only supports local businesses but also enhances cultural diversity in the global marketplace.

3.2 Digital Identity and National Security: Safeguarding Through Decentralization

Digital identity systems play a crucial role in national security by decentralizing citizen data. This section explores decentralized digital identity systems, built on blockchain principles, highlighting successful implementations in safeguarding national security (Swan, 2015).

Centralized databases storing citizen data pose significant risks, including the potential for large-scale data breaches and identity theft. Decentralized digital identity systems, leveraging blockchain's security features, offer a compelling solution to these risks. These systems distribute identity verification across a network of nodes, ensuring that no single point of failure exists.

Estonia, a pioneer in implementing decentralized digital identity, provides a noteworthy example. The country's e-Residency program, built on blockchain, allows individuals to establish a secure digital identity for online transactions and business activities. This decentralized approach not only enhances the security and privacy of citizen data but also facilitates efficient and transparent government services (Swan, 2015).

The decentralization of digital identity not only enhances security but also empowers individuals with greater control over their personal information. It shifts the paradigm from a centralized authority holding sensitive data to a distributed and secure network where individuals have sovereignty over their digital identities.

3.3 Cultural Impacts of Digital Decentralization

The shift towards decentralized digital platforms and identities has profound cultural implications. As individuals interact directly with producers and creators through digital platforms, cultural exchange becomes more authentic and diverse. Local artisans, empowered by digital platforms, can showcase their unique cultural products to a global audience, fostering appreciation and understanding.

Moreover, decentralized digital identities allow individuals to express their cultural identity in the digital realm securely. The preservation of cultural diversity is enhanced as people have control over how their identity is presented and shared. This stands in contrast to centralized systems where identity is often standardized and controlled by overarching authorities.

The cultural impacts of digital decentralization extend beyond economic transactions and digital interactions. They shape how we perceive and celebrate cultural differences, contributing to a more interconnected yet culturally rich global society.

4. CHALLENGES AND OPPORTUNITIES

4.1 Security Concerns: Navigating the Complex Landscape of Decentralized Security

While decentralization enhances security in many aspects, it presents new challenges. This section explores the evolving landscape of decentralized security, emphasizing the need for robust cybersecurity measures (Zissis & Lekkas, 2012).

The decentralized nature of blockchain and other distributed technologies inherently contributes to enhanced security. However, this does not make them immune to new and evolving threats. One notable challenge is the potential for 51% attacks in blockchain networks, where an entity controls the majority of the network's computing power. Such attacks can compromise the integrity of the blockchain, highlighting the importance of consensus mechanisms and ongoing research in securing decentralized systems.

Decentralized applications (DApps) also face unique security vulnerabilities. Smart contracts, while offering transparency and automation, can be exploited if not designed and audited rigorously. High-profile incidents, such as the DAO hack in 2016, underscore the importance of thorough security protocols in decentralized systems (Zissis & Lekkas, 2012).

As the digital landscape evolves, the need for comprehensive security measures becomes paramount. The dynamic nature of decentralized systems requires continuous innovation in cybersecurity to address emerging threats. Collaboration between industry stakeholders, researchers, and policymakers is essential to establish robust frameworks that ensure the security and integrity of decentralized technologies.

4.2 Inclusive Access: Bridging the Digital Divide in Decentralization

Ensuring inclusive access to digital technologies is a critical aspect. This section explores the potential for decentralized systems to bridge the digital divide. Case studies showcase initiatives leveraging decentralized technologies to empower marginalized communities (Warschauer, 2003).

The promise of decentralization extends beyond technological advancements to social impact. Inclusivity is a core principle that must guide the development and deployment of decentralized technologies. Initiatives focused on education and policy frameworks play a crucial role in ensuring that the benefits of the digital shift are accessible to all.

Decentralized finance (DeFi) platforms, built on blockchain, offer financial services to individuals who are excluded from traditional banking systems. These platforms enable anyone with an internet connection to access banking, lending, and investment services without relying on traditional financial institutions. This democratization of financial services has the potential to uplift communities that were previously underserved (Warschauer, 2003).

In the realm of education, decentralized technologies can empower learners in remote or underserved regions. Online educational platforms built on decentralized networks can provide access to quality educational resources, fostering a more equitable distribution of knowledge. Additionally, decentralized governance models can give communities a voice in shaping educational policies that cater to their unique needs.

4.3 Ethical Considerations in Decentralized Systems

The advent of decentralized technologies raises ethical considerations that demand careful examination. As power is distributed and control becomes more diffuse, ethical frameworks need to evolve to address potential pitfalls.

One critical aspect is the ethical use of AI in decentralized systems. The transparency and accountability afforded by blockchain can be instrumental in ensuring that AI algorithms operate ethically. However, the autonomy granted to decentralized AI models also necessitates robust ethical guidelines to prevent misuse.

Similarly, issues of digital identity and privacy in decentralized systems require ethical considerations. While decentralization enhances individual control, it also demands responsible stewardship of personal data. Striking a balance between individual empowerment and collective responsibility is paramount.

Ethical considerations extend to the environmental impact of decentralized technologies. Blockchain, in particular, relies on energy-intensive consensus mechanisms. The quest for more sustainable alternatives and eco-friendly blockchain solutions becomes an ethical imperative.

As the digital shift progresses, addressing these ethical considerations will be pivotal in shaping a decentralized future that aligns with values of fairness, accountability, and sustainability.

5. CONCLUSION

As digital technologies evolve, their impact on decentralization and deglobalization intensifies. This chapter underscores the need for proactive governance strategies to harness benefits and address challenges posed by the digital shift (Parker et al., 2016). In conclusion, the digital shift is reshaping societies, economies, and power structures, with the transformative potential of blockchain, artificial intelligence, and the Internet of Things driving decentralization and fostering deglobalization.

To navigate this transformative era successfully, collaboration between stakeholders, technological innovators, policymakers, and society at large is essential. The journey towards a decentralized future is laden with opportunities for progress, innovation, and inclusivity. By embracing the principles of transparency, security, and trust embedded in decentralized technologies, societies can navigate the complexities of the digital shift and harness its full potential.

The confluence of blockchain, artificial intelligence (AI), and the Internet of Things (IoT) has propelled the digital shift into uncharted territories, fundamentally altering the fabric of societies, economies, and power structures. The transformative potential of these technologies, while promising progress and innovation, also presents a landscape fraught with challenges and ethical considerations. As this chapter navigates the multifaceted implications of the digital era, it underscores the imperative for proactive governance to guide this profound transformation.

5.1 Necessity for Proactive Governance

The digital shift requires governance strategies that are as dynamic and adaptive as the technologies driving it. Proactive governance is the cornerstone of a successful transition into a decentralized future. Policymakers, industry leaders, and communities must collaborate to establish frameworks that balance innovation with responsibility.

Decentralized technologies demand governance that fosters transparency, accountability, and inclusivity. As blockchain, AI, and IoT continue to evolve, regulatory frameworks should be designed to encourage innovation while safeguarding against potential risks. Policymakers need to stay abreast of technological advancements, working in tandem with industry experts to enact laws that protect individual rights, prevent abuse, and ensure the ethical use of decentralized systems.

A study by Parker, Van Alstyne, and Choudary (2016) emphasizes the role of platform governance in transforming economies and suggests that regulatory frameworks need to adapt to the dynamics of decentralized networks. This highlights the importance of proactive governance in guiding the transformative potential of decentralized technologies.

5.2 Collaboration for a Decentralized Future

The journey towards a decentralized future necessitates collaboration on a global scale. Stakeholders, including technological innovators, policymakers, businesses, and society at large, must work together to harness the benefits and address the challenges posed by the digital shift.

Technological innovators play a pivotal role in this collaborative effort by developing solutions that prioritize user security, privacy, and ethical considerations. Policymakers, on the other hand, need to create an environment that encourages innovation while safeguarding societal interests. Open dialogue between these groups is crucial for developing regulations that strike the right balance.

A comprehensive review by Swan (2015) delves into the governance aspects of blockchain, emphasizing the need for collaboration between various stakeholders to create effective governance models. This collaboration is essential for establishing a balance between innovation and regulation, ensuring the responsible development of decentralized technologies.

Businesses also have a responsibility to adopt ethical practices in the deployment of decentralized technologies. Corporate responsibility extends beyond profit to include considerations of societal impact, environmental sustainability, and inclusivity. By adhering to ethical business practices, companies can contribute to the positive evolution of the digital landscape.

5.3 Embracing Principles of Transparency, Security, and Trust

At the core of the digital shift are principles of transparency, security, and trust. These principles, embedded in blockchain, AI, and IoT, should serve as guiding lights for societies navigating the complexities of decentralization.

Transparency ensures that actions within decentralized systems are open and accountable. Security safeguards against malicious actors and cyber threats, preserving the integrity of digital interactions. Trust, distributed across decentralized networks, replaces the reliance on single authorities, fostering a more democratic and resilient society.

In embracing these principles, societies can harness the full potential of decentralized technologies. Transparency builds confidence, security mitigates risks, and trust fosters collaboration. As decentralized systems become integral to daily life, these principles will shape the collective experience of navigating the digital frontier.

A recent survey by Zissis and Lekkas (2012) addresses the evolving landscape of decentralized security, emphasizing the need for robust cybersecurity measures in the face of new and emerging threats. This highlights the importance of continual innovation in cybersecurity to ensure the security and integrity of decentralized technologies.

6. FUTURE PROSPECTS AND EMERGING TRENDS

6.1 Interconnected Ecosystems: The Fusion of Blockchain, AI, and IoT

The intersection of blockchain, AI, and IoT marks the emergence of highly interconnected ecosystems. Future trends indicate a fusion of these technologies, creating synergies that amplify their individual impacts. This fusion holds the potential to revolutionize sectors such as healthcare, finance, and governance.

In healthcare, for example, the integration of blockchain ensures secure and transparent health records, while AI facilitates data analysis for personalized treatment plans. IoT devices, seamlessly connected to this network, provide real-time health monitoring, creating a holistic and decentralized approach to healthcare.

6.2 Sustainable Decentralization: Addressing Environmental Concerns

As the environmental impact of blockchain comes under scrutiny, the future of decentralized technologies will likely witness a concerted effort towards sustainability. Innovations in consensus mechanisms, such as proof-of-stake, aim to reduce energy consumption. Additionally, the integration of AI algorithms may optimize resource usage, making decentralized systems more environmentally friendly.

Sustainable decentralization aligns with global initiatives to combat climate change. By addressing environmental concerns, decentralized technologies can position themselves as not only drivers of innovation but also as contributors to a more sustainable and responsible future.

6.3 Decentralization and Social Impact: Redefining Communities

The evolution of decentralized technologies will redefine social structures and community dynamics. Initiatives leveraging decentralized platforms for community governance, resource sharing, and decision-making are likely to gain prominence. This shift towards decentralized community structures has the potential to empower individuals, giving them a more direct say in the matters that affect their lives.

Communities, both local and global, may form around decentralized platforms, fostering collaboration and inclusivity. Blockchain-based decentralized governance models can empower communities to make collective decisions, ranging from local policies to broader societal issues.

A seminal work by Atzori, Iera, and Morabito (2010) surveys the transformative impact of IoT, providing insights into its potential applications in smart cities, manufacturing, and agriculture. This underlines the significance of decentralized IoT in reshaping traditional industries.

7. FINAL REFLECTIONS

The digital shift, propelled by blockchain, AI, and IoT, is an ongoing saga that continues to unfold with profound implications. As societies navigate this transformative era, it is essential to reflect on the principles that guide this journey – transparency, security, and trust.

The decentralized future holds promises of a more inclusive, innovative, and interconnected world. However, these promises come with responsibilities. Proactive governance, collaboration, and a commitment to ethical considerations are essential for realizing the full potential of the digital shift.

In conclusion, the digital shift is not merely a technological evolution; it is a societal metamorphosis. It challenges existing power structures, redefines economic paradigms, and shapes global interactions. The journey towards decentralization and deglobalization is a collective endeavor, and how societies navigate this shift will define the contours of the digital era.

As we stand at the nexus of technology, decentralization, and deglobalization, the call is for collective wisdom, foresight, and ethical stewardship. The future is decentralized, and its trajectory rests in the hands of those who dare to embrace the transformative potential of the digital shift.

REFERENCES

Atzori, L., Iera, A., & Morabito, G. (2010). The Internet of Things: *A survey. Computer Networks*, *54*(15), 2787–2805. doi:10.1016/j.comnet.2010.05.010

McMahan, H. B., Moore, E., Ramage, D., Hampson, S., & Arcas, B. A. (2017). Communication-efficient learning of deep networks from decentralized data. In Artificial Intelligence and Statistics (pp. 1273–1282). Academic Press.

Narayanan, A., Bonneau, J., Felten, E., Miller, A., & Goldfeder, S. (2016). *Bitcoin and Cryptocurrency Technologies: A Comprehensive Introduction*. Princeton University Press.

Parker, G. G., Van Alstyne, M. W., & Choudary, S. P. (2016). *Platform Revolution: How Networked Markets Are Transforming the Economy and How to Make Them Work for You*. W. W. Norton & Company.

Swan, M. (2015). *Blockchain: blueprint for a new economy*. O'Reilly Media, Inc.

Warschauer, M. (2003). *Technology and social inclusion: Rethinking the digital divide*. MIT Press. doi:10.7551/mitpress/6699.001.0001

Zissis, D., & Lekkas, D. (2012). Addressing cloud computing security issues. *Future Generation Computer Systems*, *28*(3), 583–592. doi:10.1016/j.future.2010.12.006

Chapter 8
Multinational Enterprises' Digital Transformation, Sustainability, and Purpose: A Holistic View

Aarti
Lovely Professional University, India

Swathi Gowroju
Sreyas Institute of Engineering and Technology, India

Saurabh Karling
Lovely Professional University, India

ABSTRACT

This study examines the growing problems that multinational corporations (MNEs) are facing as a result of a confluence of pandemics, environmental disasters, and the digital revolution. These problems appear as organizational, market, and geopolitical complexity, which institutional pluralism magnifies. As the nature of productive activity changes, so do the ways in which MNEs structure and manage their operations. Additionally, changing investor and consumer expectations are broadening the definition of value creation and having an effect on company strategies. They contend that these difficulties force MNEs to reevaluate the way in which they formulate, establish, and carry out their corporate purposes. In order to wrap up, they suggest a research agenda that stresses how critical it is for MNEs to take a purpose-driven approach.

1. INTRODUCTION

Customers are currently working harder to maximize the specific benefits they get. The increasing demand for personalized products and the growing influence of customers on the development and production

DOI: 10.4018/979-8-3693-3253-5.ch008

processes are two examples of this (Bauernhansl et al., 2017). The adoption of digital technologies by factories is necessary to meet this problem. The phrase "Industrie 4.0" refers to the desired state in Germany. In order to ensure real-time information is available throughout the whole life cycle of products, processes, and manufacturing facilities, this entails improving information, communication, and automation technologies. Human resources, products, and production systems are all included in this network.

Additionally, the obtained large data sets are used for thorough optimization (Delgosha et al., 2020; Kagermann, 2017; Kar et al., 2019). Due to this exceptional situation, mechanical engineering companies face both opportunities and difficulties. By utilizing customer data, new opportunities for improving products and processes become available, such as improving machining techniques or anticipating the need for spare parts. At the same time, these businesses must deal with new consumer expectations; customers now demand not just to buy a physical machine but also service systems that include both hardware and software and offer value based on their individual needs (Bauernhansl et al., 2017; Kar et al., 2019; Lusch & Nambisan, 2015).

Examples used to illustrate this point include context-specific features and data that let machine operators quickly adjust to changing consumer needs. Such cases require tight cooperation between mechanical engineering companies and manufacturers. Information technology (IT) has evolved beyond its traditional function as a tool for increasing internal efficiency. Instead, it evolves into a crucial part of value generation and takes on a transformative function that provides a fresh source of competitive advantage (Lusch & Nambisan, 2015). Mechanical engineering businesses undergo a significant shift as a result of the imperative proliferation of goods with digital components, the development of cyber-physical systems, and their integration into service ecosystems. This transformation is known as the digital transformation journey.

It is praised that digitization will hasten the transition to sustainability. Services are now more affordable because to cloud computing, which lowers the cost of maintaining digital infrastructure. New capabilities are being introduced by artificial intelligence and machine learning (AI/ML), which have the potential to contribute 14% of the world's GDP by 2030 (PwC, 2017). The Internet of Things (IoT) will connect billions of gadgets with the help of 5G technology, increasing the intelligence of objects in homes, businesses, and factories. Additionally, the pandemic has sped up the manifestation of corporate purpose as stakeholders and employees alike wonder what purpose corporations serve in promoting social goals.

All of this takes place in the context of open and prompt social media reactions to multinational corporations' (MNEs') conduct (Zattoni & Pugliese, 2021). How profit-driven businesses, particularly MNEs, interact with their stakeholders is changing as a result of the convergence of the global health crisis brought on by the pandemic, the biodiversity crisis, and the climate catastrophe, as well as the calls for socioeconomic change (Hitt et al., 2021).

Multinational companies (MNEs) are facing new obstacles that force them to rethink how they use sustainability and digitization to accomplish their goals. First, MNEs must navigate a geopolitical landscape that is becoming more complex, where addressing climate change demands international cooperation in a time of rising nationalism and trade barriers (Lubinski & Wadhwani, 2020). Despite the acknowledged seriousness of the biodiversity and climate problems, there is a wide range of political readiness and capacity across nations to act and enforce strict rules. Digital technologies play a part in improving transparency and accountability as the regulatory landscape throughout the world changes, which has an impact on how MNEs evaluate potential for sustainable activities.

Furthermore, internal disagreements inside corporations are becoming increasingly common. Due to the increased use of remote work over the past few years by both employees and leaders, the pandemic has made it more difficult to coordinate operations. This is particularly obvious in the reconfiguration of workspaces (Barrero et al., 2021). Additionally, as the forces balancing localization and globalization have changed, there is a greater need for localization in areas like supply chain management and sustainability tactics.

Multinational companies (MNEs) are currently juggling competing dynamics as a result. While strengthening local resilience and tailoring sustainability initiatives may call for decentralizing authorities and involving local decision-makers, digital transformation necessitates investments and a uniform global plan. The organizational landscape is further complicated by the geopolitical tensions as businesses redesign their value chains and create their "China strategy," even if this results in job losses and higher costs (Delios et al., 2021).

This article examines the pressures that MNEs are under and proposes potential solutions. Management researchers can discuss the shifting nature of the multinational's organizational advantage and its implications for sustainability by comprehending, capturing, and assessing these initiatives.

For MNEs to preserve their competitive edge, corporate mission can:

- Encouraging stakeholders to evaluate and interact with the company in certain ways
- Setting the agenda for the topics that are important to the company
- Averting the complication brought on by varying stakeholder expectations and nationalist impulses

Management academics may aid in this knowledge by researching and analyzing MNEs' attempts to integrate purpose into their operations and the effects this has on their competitive advantage and sustainability.

Thirdly, key market participants like customers and investors are raising worries about climate change more frequently. The epidemic has exacerbated this trend even more. This circumstance raises concerns about the proper resource allocation for multinational corporations (MNEs) in order to generate and capture value related to sustainability. Investments in the development of natural reserves and other shared resources are required by the growing regeneration paradigm, which supports the sustainability paradigm. While operational efficiency and waste reduction have been the main focus of sustainability and environmental, social, and governance (ESG) efforts, these cost-cutting measures are not producing significant distinction. Thus, in order to optimize their beneficial influence while contending with budget constraints, MNEs are pressured to reevaluate their preferred geographies for corporate charitable contributions.

1.1. Enterprise Architectures Are Integrated Into the Digital Transformation Process

A digital business strategy serves as the starting point of digital transformation. This organizational strategy uses digital tools in its design and implementation to produce differentiating value. It goes well beyond the conventional IT strategy, which views IT as a tool for streamlining business operations. It includes sources of business value creation and capture as well as the scope, scale, and speed of the digital business strategy (Bharadwaj et al., 2013). More information is needed because the implementation of the digital transformation is a complicated procedure. The digital business strategy is what leads to the creation of a business model. In the past, firms operated in a setting that was largely stable and had few operational options.

In the past, business managers could create procedures straight from their strategy. But as digitization spreads, this has becoming more challenging. Not only have IT-based processes increased the range of possibilities, but they have also increased the complexity of the activities themselves (Al-Debi et al., 2008). To assist managers in putting their plan into practice, new approaches, frameworks, and instruments are required.

The creation of a digital transformation strategy is suggested by Matt et al. Making crucial choices about technology, structure, money, and value creation would be required (Al-Debi et al., 2008). Although it is currently at a somewhat abstract level, this method might aid in the clarification of key challenges in digital business strategy.

Business models offer another method for expressing strategy more clearly. A business model outlines the value creation process of a firm. Business models are made to explain how a company adds value, but they are not the best tools for organizing the delivery of operations and services (Al-Debi et al., 2008). As a result, a different strategy is required to plan, implement, and coordinate IT activities.

Enterprise architecture (EA), according to a number of academics in the field of information systems research, can be utilized to achieve business transformation (Gardner & Fehskens, 2012).

The enterprise architecture (EA) is a thorough representation of an organization. It outlines the core elements of the company and how they relate to one another. As a result, EA includes a range of guiding concepts, strategies, and models that help organizations create and implement their organizational frameworks, as well as the appropriate operational processes, IT infrastructure, and information systems.

By recording the current state of events within the company, the main goal of EA is to increase transparency. Its goal is to give the company the tools it needs to properly manage its intricate operations and information systems. It also has the function of assessing interfaces and data requirements.

Second, EA contributes to the management and preservation of the enterprise's key components by providing a thorough grasp of all of their essential components. Thirdly, EA makes it easier for strategic goals to be translated into routine operational procedures. The fourth goal of EA is to make sure that it is understandable and accessible to all parties concerned. The ability of EA to assist in the comprehensive optimization of operations and the identification of opportunities for simplification represents the fifth goal.

Various definitions and EA frameworks with different scopes and emphases exist in addition to this general description of Enterprise Architecture (EA) and the activities connected with it. The enterprise layers that they support, which include five potential tiers, are a key differentiator.

For example, EA specifies goods and outlines interactions with suppliers and customers in the strategic layer. Architects explore business procedures, information flows, and organizational responsibilities in the organizational layer. Applications, services, and interfaces are the focus of the integration layer. In contrast, the IT infrastructure layer defines hardware, network components, and software platforms, and the software layer defines data structures and program components.

1.2 Objective of Paper

- The paper presents a digital business strategy that goes beyond traditional IT methods and highlights the incorporation of enterprise architectures in the process of digital transformation.
- It recognizes the difficulties in putting digital transformation into practice and calls for new frameworks and methods, with an emphasis on using business models to communicate strategy.

- The introduction of enterprise architecture (EA) as a comprehensive organizational representation aims to manage key components, promote transparency, and make it easier to translate strategic objectives into operational procedures.
- The critique of EA is discussed, emphasizing its low adoption rate among SMEs, its connection to IT, and the difficulties in integrating it with agile approaches for digital transformation.
- In addition to highlighting agility, consumer-focused strategy, macro and micro cycles, and decision-making stages, the paper suggests a method for digital transformation in SMEs that puts an emphasis on user stories and iterative development.

2. CRITICISM ON ENTERPRISE ARCHITECTURES AS AN INSTRUMENT FOR DIGITAL TRANSFORMATION

Enterprise Architecture (EA) initially seemed to have the ability to considerably support small and medium-sized firms (SMEs) in the mechanical engineering industry in their efforts to undergo digital transformation. However, this strategy is currently not very popular in the field of corporate transformation. Only a few papers in the literature investigate the application of EA for company transformation. This is especially true for SMEs, where EA is underappreciated and generally unknown. EA is still relatively untapped, even in businesses that have previously synchronized their strategy and procedures.

There are a number of plausible explanations for this situation. Fostering collaboration amongst people from many disciplines and developing solutions that are understandable to all parties involved is one of the key goals of EA. Even while this is crucial during major transitions, business transformation and EA have very different approaches in practice. Each approach uses different languages, descriptive methods, and tools since they have different roots in different areas. While EA, despite its name, is strongly based in the field of Information Technology (IT), business transformation focuses a higher emphasis on processes. Little thought is often given to strategy and processes in favor of an IT-centric approach. As a result, the use of EA is primarily limited to IT departments (Aier et al., 2016; Majstorović & Terzić, 2018).

Small and medium-sized businesses (SMEs) have a limited understanding of EA frameworks. Consider TOGAF, which offers a thorough perspective on an enterprise but whose implementation is notably difficult. It requires rigorous training and certification in order to use. EA frameworks present management challenges because of their size and complexity. Although this problem is acknowledged, there aren't many remedies to it in the literature. Even the official TOGAF documentation advises simplifying the framework, but it doesn't specify which elements should be left out to make it appropriate for SMEs. Despite this situation, research rarely discusses the use of EA in SMEs.

In the context of digital transformation, additional difficulties arise in addition to those faced in business transformation. In the age of digitization, getting products to market quickly and involving customers in the creation of rapidly changing service systems are priorities. However, Enterprise Architecture (EA) follows a traditional waterfall methodology in which finalized, in-depth architectures are produced first, followed by implementation. This viewpoint makes the assumptionthat information systems are generally reliable. This methodology leaves minimal possibility for iterative development and quick corrections, clashing with more contemporary agile methodologies.

These agile methods decrease effort, boost speed, and improve customer satisfaction since they are based on incremental development and substantial client participation. Along with modifications to development methodologies, the scope of EA also evolves. A stronger focus on business alignment and the incorporation of digital strategies and business models is required in the context of digital transformation because there is a fundamental change in organizational structures and business processes. Currently, integration of applications and infrastructure tends to be the main focus, with this crucial alignment receiving comparatively less attention. Utilizing standardized platforms can aid in reducing these difficulties. Additionally, the distinctions between market participants are dissolving altogether in some instances.

In conclusion, Enterprise Architecture (EA) is a strong method for creating, maintaining, and documenting information systems. It is supported by a wide range of models and tools, and it has proven successful in various projects. The importance of EA, however, declines in the middle of the excitement around subjects like digital transformation. The main criticism derives from EA's widespread IT association and perceived complexity. Small and medium-sized organizations (SMEs) and businesses in the mechanical engineering sector frequently find it difficult to comprehend due to this complexity. A clear strategy that is easily understood by everyone is, however, clearly needed in the context of procedures that involve major change.

Another issue is that EA provides a comprehensive and rigid planning approach. Contemporary agile approaches are, nevertheless, redefining the design and development of software. New difficulties arise with the introduction of digital transformation, such as the growing integration of ecosystems and customers. This calls for strategies that enable an iterative development process and dig deeper into consumer requirements. As a result, there is a need for simple planning tools that have a strong business emphasis and are created to be understandable by all stakeholders.

3. APPROACH FOR DIGITAL TRANSFORMATION IN SMALL AND MEDIUM-SIZED ENTERPRISES

According to the analysis that came before, enterprise architecture (EA) has a lot of potential for bringing about digital transformation. Existing strategies do, however, have flaws, most notably their inability to successfully incorporate business. The increased significance of agile business development and the incorporation of ecosystems and smart products into the architectural framework are two additional difficulties for EA.

In this article, we outline the first phases of a revolutionary EA strategy designed for SMEs' (small and medium-sized firms) digital transformation. As was previously said, a strategy for implementing digital transformation must be far more nimble and tightly tailored to consumer needs. As a result, agile development approaches serve as the basis of the proposed approach.

The approach can be delineated into two distinct cycles: a macro cycle and a micro cycle. The macro cycle pertains to the architecture of the entire SME, while the micro cycle focuses on the implementation and testing of individual functions. In addition to these progressively developed macro and micro cycles, there are two relatively stable domains that serve to uphold the digital strategy of an enterprise.

The digital business strategy serves as the foundational element of this approach, encompassing fundamental decisions concerning the speed, scale, and scope of digital technology application within the enterprise. As proposed by Matt et al. (2015), it is imperative to derive a transformation strategy from the digital business strategy. Within this framework, technological and organizational principles for the implementation are established. However, in contrast to Matt et al. (2015)'s approach, this model does not regard value creation and financial aspects as sufficiently stable and therefore addresses them within the business model.

The business model is derived from the digital business strategy at the first stage of the macro cycle. This business model includes important details like the value proposition, client groups, and income streams, as was previously mentioned. The development of a perfect architecture is the next step. This stage seeks to provide a broad, conceptual overview of the business model. The ideal architecture contains explanations of fundamental procedures, essential IT services, and data required for implementation. Most importantly, this ideal architecture is unrestricted. Its goal is to provide architects the creative freedom to investigate novel concepts without being constrained by antiquated systems or strategic constraints.

The actual architecture is then created based on the ideal architecture while taking the transformation plan and the current architecture into account. There will always be legacy systems and interfaces to take into account because digital transformation often takes an incremental approach. But architects shouldn't keep using outdated systems indefinitely.

The Scrum methodology's product backlog and the architecture backlog both use the same basic idea. It requires developing user stories in light of the differences between the present design and the actual architecture. These user stories represent interfaces for encapsulated service systems. User stories can advance independently of one another during the micro cycle. Without going into specifics of the software or hardware, they outline the users, expected functionalities, and benefits. The development team has flexibility thanks to this method. User stories are prioritized in the backlog. Additionally, decisions are made regarding which user stories will be created inside by the company and which will be supplied by outside ecosystem partners.

The macro cycle can be finished before the micro cycle is started for the first time. The first step in this micro cycle is to choose user stories from the prioritized backlog, the number of which is determined by the desired rate of change for the organization. The next stage entails either creating or choosing services. Developers implement the selected user stories within a sprint during the building phase. However, choosing pre-existing services off the shelf is frequently the better choice, especially when a service is outside of the core competencies and is already present on the platform. In these situations, internal development should be avoided.

Each user story is tested after installation or acquisition; testing may be carried out with a test customer or inside a testbed offered by a variety of organizations (such as research institutes, universities, etc.). The I4KMU initiative in Germany assists SMEs in Germany in finding appropriate test environments for Industry 4.0-relevant technology.

After a review, one of three decisions can be made. The first choice is to mark the user story as finished, at which point the teams go on to the following user story. The second choice might call for modifications, which would force the micro cycle to restart. The third option can involve findings that have an effect on the overall architecture and cause the macro cycle to restart. The architecture is fairly basic in the first cycle of the macro cycle but gets increasingly intricate with each round. Decision-making in the micro cycle should always have plenty of room for flexibility in the macro cycle as shown in Fig 1.

4. OVERVIEW OF THE STUDIES

There are differences in the effects of the digital revolution on green growth of businesses at a local level, with pronounced regional heterogeneity, based on the data shown in various series in Al-Debi

Figure 1. Architecture of strategy

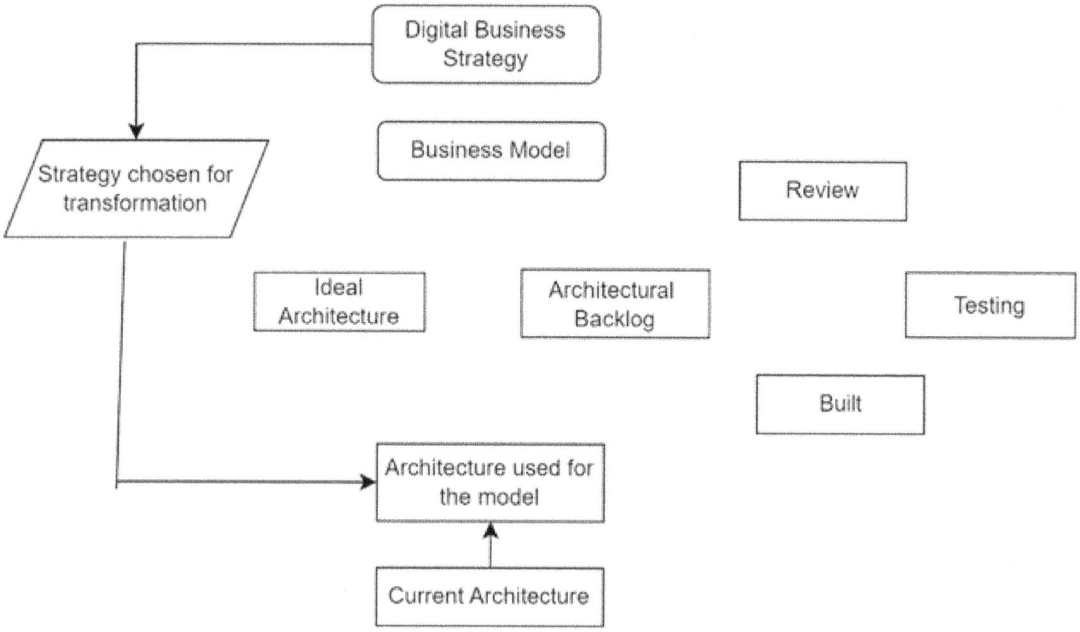

et al. (2008), Bauernhansl et al. (2017), Bharadwaj et al. (2013), Delgosha et al. (2020), Gardner and Fehskens (2012), Kagermann (2017), Kar et al. (2019), and Lusch and Nambisan (2015). Because the east was actively promoting digital China, smart societies, and the digital economy—using policy as a guide to achieve long-term goals—the effect of digitization on sustainable business growth in that region was particularly positive, indicating that digitalization in the towards the east exerted an encouraging impact on augmenting enterprise sustainability. As a kind of preparation, it gave regional businesses ideological direction and policy backing to fight the "long war" of digital transformation, significantly lessening the hindrance brought on by unfavourable circumstances encountered.

4.1 Digital Transformation, Sustainability All Over the World

The arithmetic coordination of the eastern region allows the original core enterprises and knowledge network to play a leading role. This results in the realisation of the knowledge spillover effect, the formation of a homogenous group effect, the constant attraction of companies to digital transformation, and the absorption of new members into the network. Due to disparities in information and production, businesses shifted from being geographically focused to creative collaboration, becoming demand-oriented for cooperation. This resulted in a decline in businesses during the early stages of the digital transition. Due to information asymmetry, this lessened the "misjudgment" made by businesses during the early phases of the digital transition. This enhanced businesses' capacity to seize opportunities and allowed the beneficial regulatory effect brought about by regional virtual agglomeration to fully manifest. There were few case studies shown in Table 1, that were collected from various cities, that worked on sustainability.

Table 1. Case studies collected from various cities

City of Vancouver, Canada - Greenest City	Vancouver, Canada, launched its Greenest City Action Plan with the goal of becoming the world's greenest city by 2020. They conducted a comprehensive analysis of sustainability indicators, including greenhouse gas emissions, waste diversion rates, and land use. The city collected and analyzed numerical data to track progress and identify areas of improvement, leading to policies and initiatives that promote sustainability.
São Paulo, Brazil - Environmental Monitoring	São Paulo, one of the largest cities in Brazil, faced significant environmental challenges, including air pollution and deforestation. The city utilized air quality monitoring stations to collect numerical data on air pollutants. By analyzing this data, São Paulo developed policies to reduce air pollution and improve environmental quality, particularly in low-income and heavily industrialized areas.
Yosemite National Park, USA - Ecosystem Diversity Analysis	Yosemite National Park implemented a long-term ecological monitoring program to assess the biodiversity and ecosystem health within the park. Researchers collected numerical data on plant and animal species diversity, as well as water quality and air quality measurements. This data informed management decisions to protect and restore the park's ecosystems, such as reducing the impact of air pollution and managing invasive species.
European Union - Regional Sustainability Assessments	The European Union (EU) conducts regional sustainability assessments to monitor and improve sustainability in member states. These assessments involve collecting and analyzing numerical data on factors like energy consumption, renewable energy adoption, waste management, and socioeconomic indicators. The EU uses this data to evaluate the progress of member states in achieving sustainability goals and to allocate funding and resources to support sustainability initiatives.
Indonesia - Forest Management and Conservation	Indonesia, home to vast tropical forests, faced significant challenges related to deforestation and biodiversity loss. The Indonesian government, in collaboration with environmental organizations, collected numerical data on forest cover, carbon emissions, and species diversity.This data informed policies and practices to address deforestation and promote sustainable forest management

4.2 Digital Transformation, Sustainability in India

India has undertaken various digital governance initiatives to streamline business processes for MNEs. This includes platforms like "Digital India" and "Make in India" that aim to provide a seamless and efficient interface for businesses to interact with government agencies.Several states in India have implemented single window clearance systems to facilitate a one-stop shop for MNEs to obtain permits and approvals, reducing bureaucratic red tape.The Goods and Services Tax (GST) regime in India is a significant digital transformation initiative that simplifies taxation for businesses, including MNEs, by replacing a complex tax structure with a unified system.The Indian government mandates that large companies, including MNEs, allocate a portion of their profits towards CSR activities. This encourages sustainable initiatives, such as environmental conservation, education, and healthcare, benefiting local communities. India is actively promoting renewable energy sources and green business practices. MNEs are encouraged to invest in renewable energy projects and implement sustainable manufacturing processes.

MNEs are encouraged to adopt sustainable practices in their supply chains, considering factors like fair trade, ethical sourcing, and minimizing environmental impacts. India's Securities and Exchange Board (SEBI) mandates that listed companies, including MNEs, report their sustainability efforts. Companies often use digital platforms to communicate their sustainability initiatives and performance transparently to stakeholders. India's Atmanirbhar Bharat (Self-Reliant India) initiative promotes innovation and self-reliance. MNEs are encouraged to invest in research and development and collaborate with Indian companies in technology transfer and knowledge sharing. India is actively engaging in international trade agreements and collaborations to foster foreign investments and cooperation. This includes bilateral and multilateral trade agreements that can benefit MNEs. India is also focusing on strengthening cyber security measures and data privacy regulations to ensure the safety and security of digital operations for MNEs. India is investing in education and skilling initiatives (Costa et al., 2022; Pappas et al., 2019;

Figure 2. Framework of sustainability

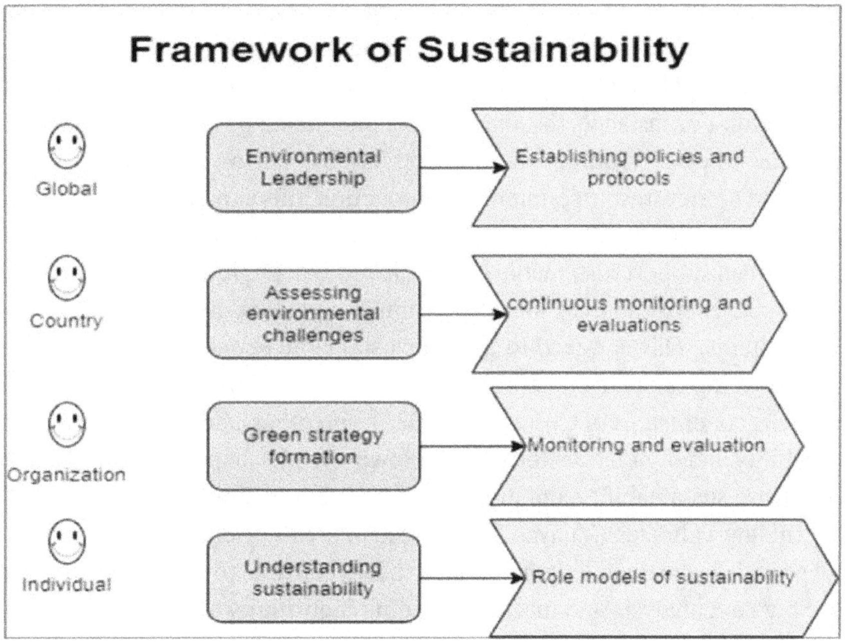

Rieger et al., 2022; Vijayan, 2019) to provide a skilled workforce for MNEs. Digital skilling programs and vocational training are essential for building a competitive workforce.

India's approach to taking care of multinational enterprises through digital transformation and sustainability is aimed at creating an environment where businesses can thrive, while also contributing to the country's socio-economic and environmental goals. This balance between digital transformation and sustainability is vital for both the prosperity of MNEs and the well-being of the nation and up to the individual human being as deployed in Fig 2.

Aiming to strike a balance between economic, social, and environmental factorsis the concept of enterprise sustainability. From an economic standpoint, enterprise sustainability is about promoting economic growth and efficiently using resources without compromising social and environmental well-being. In this regard, digital transformation can play a critical role in supporting businesses' ability to experience sustained economic growth.Deep learning facilitates digitization by excelling in tasks such as image and speech recognition, natural language processing, and data extraction. Through convolutional neural networks (CNNs) (Gowroju & Kumar, 2022; Gowroju et al., 2022; Narsimhulu et al., 2022; Swathi & Rani, 2019) and recurrent neural networks (RNNs), it enables efficient optical character recognition (OCR) for converting scanned documents into editable text and enhances information retrieval from unstructured data sources. Additionally, deep learning contributes to automation and robotics, predictive analytics, healthcare digitization, financial applications, and the development of smart cities by automating tasks, improving decision-making processes, and optimizing various operations. Its ability to learn patterns and make predictions aids in the transformation of industries, making processes more efficient and data-driven.

Enterprises can achieve sustainable economic growth through digital transformation by increasing operational efficiency and cutting costs. Businesses may optimise operations and save waste by utilising digital technologies (George & Simon, 2022) like automation, artificial intelligence, and data analytics. This leads to cost savings and higher productivity. Consequently, this can lessen the negative effects of corporate operations on the environment while promoting economic growth.

The process of digital transformation can also help create new business models that support long-term, steady economic growth. For instance, the sharing economy made possible by digital platforms enables people and companies to pool resources more effectively by sharing assets like lodging and cars. By decreasing the demand for new resource-intensive production, this can lower waste and advance sustainability (Liu et al., 2019). Additionally, by accelerating the development of renewable energy sources, digital transformation can support sustainable economic growth. Digital technologies facilitate the easier integration of renewable energy sources into the economy and allow for more effective management of renewable energy systems. This can lead to a more sustainable economic paradigm by fostering economic growth and lowering reliance on nonrenewable resources. This paper's empirical study, which is in accordance with the conclusions of Costa et al. (2022), and others, demonstrates a linear link between enterprise sustainability and digital transformation. However, a U-shaped curve illustrating the relationship between enterprise sustainability and digital transformation is revealed when the Chinese context is analysed. This finding validates (Vijayan, 2019) research and offers oblique empirical support for[] claim that digital growth is a patient, lengthy process that needs time to yield positive results. In practise, businesses utilise big data analysis and machine learning algorithms to help anticipate issues, optimise workflows, and better allocate resources.

Figure 3. Digital preservation idea

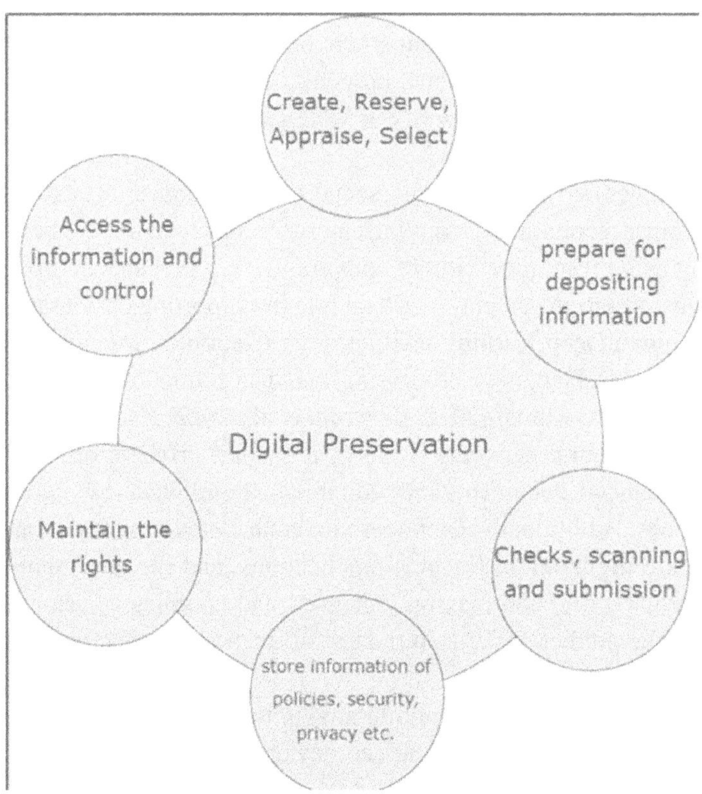

As a result, there is less waste, more sustainable growth, and wiser judgements.Better theoretical justification for this occurrence can be obtained from the study findings presented in this paper. The idea of circular economy can be aroused for further discussion, since enterprise carbon emissions, a proxy variable for robustness testing, have been utilised in this research as a measure of business sustainability (Pappas et al., 2019). As shown in Fig.3, Libraries, archives, and museums now rely on digital preservation and preservation systems to enable the collection, exploration, and long-term care of digital content as societal, significant, and scientific heritage is produced and shared in digital forms more often. However, a number of these tools and systems have significant sustainability issues, which makes their use more difficult for the historic preservation organizations that depend on them. The implementation of circular economy ideas is one significant way that digital transformation contributes to sustainable development. In a circular economy, resources are retrieved at the end of their useful lives, waste is reduced, and they are utilised and regenerated for as long as possible. Blockchain technology, for example, makes it easier for businesses to adopt circular economy ideas and track and handle resources more efficiently. Blockchain and other technologies (Rieger et al., 2022) can help businesses monitor and manage resources more efficiently. They can also make it easier for businesses to adopt the ideas of the circular economy, which can encourage the use of renewable energy sources and advance environmental sustainability. This entire study highlighted the following points:

- The study highlights beneficial impacts in the eastern region because of aggressive legislation and finds regional variances in the influence of digital transformation on company green growth.
- Case studies demonstrate how digital transformation globally forces a transition from geographically focused to demand-driven and collaborative business models.
- India has demonstrated a holistic approach through the implementation of digital governance initiatives, simplified taxation, and support of sustainable practices for multinational corporations (MNEs).
- Citing deep learning, automation, and data analytics for cost savings and environmental impact reduction, the study emphasizes the relationship between organizational sustainability and digital transformation.
- In the context of digital transformation, circular economy concepts—made possible by technology such as blockchain—appear to be important contributors to sustainable development.

5. MAJOR WEAKNESSES AND THEIR SOLUTIONS

The topic of the difficulties faced by multinational enterprises (MNEs) in the context of pandemics, natural disasters, and the digital revolution is presented in the research paper. Organizational, market, and geopolitical challenges are discussed, as well as the rising influence of institutional pluralism. The paragraph also discusses how productive activities are evolving, how investor and customer expectations are shifting, and how MNEs must reevaluate their business goals.

The following adjustments and ideas can be implemented to improve the proactive addressing of weaknesses:

- **Geopolitical Challenges**: Although the paper mentions some of the geopolitical difficulties MNEs encounter, it might go deeper by citing particular instances of businesses that have effectively managed geopolitical complications. Giving specific case studies or success stories would enhance the usefulness of the information.

- **Internal Organizing in Distance Learning Settings**:The paragraph recognizes the difficulties posed by internal conflicts and remote work, but it offers no concrete solutions. To improve this feature, include doable advice or case studies of businesses that have successfully handled coordination problems related to remote work.
- **Harmonizing Localization and Globalization**: Without going into particular tactics, the topic of harmonizing localization and globalization is touched upon in passing. It would be helpful to include case studies or examples of businesses that have effectively struck this balance and modified their business plans in response to shifting global conditions.
- **Purpose-Driven Strategy**: Although the paragraph stresses the significance of a purpose-driven strategy, it doesn't go into detail on how businesses may really incorporate purpose into their daily operations. This component would be improved by giving instances of businesses that have effectively matched their activities with a defined goal.
- **Stakeholder Engagement and Transparency:** Although these topics are briefly discussed in the conversation, there could be more precise instructions on how businesses can interact with stakeholders in an efficient manner. This component would be strengthened by giving examples of transparent practices or specialized communication tactics.

Concerning the research's shortcomings:

- **Absence of Empirical evidence**: The information offered in the highlighted paragraph may not be as credible because it lacks specific references to studies or empirical evidence. Robustness would be added to the discussion by offering empirical data or referencing pertinent studies.
- **Limited Analysis of Industry Variances:** While the paragraph covers MNEs' issues in general, it does not analyze possible differences between industries. Understanding that difficulties could vary depending on the sector or industry could give the analysis more depth.
- **Little Discussion of Regulatory Impacts:** The study could need a deeper investigation of how regulatory changes affect MNEs, especially in light of the digital revolution. This would help provide a more thorough comprehension of the difficulties encountered.

By talking about these issues, the conversation can become more in-depth, empirically supported, and offer a more thorough grasp of the problems and possible solutions facing multinational firms.

6. CONCLUSION

The study provided works on digitalization affects sustainable enterprise development and finds that the impact differs based on where in China a company is located. This leads to variations in economic and sustainable development outcomes across regions.In the eastern region of China, digitalization has a notably positive impact on sustainable enterprise development. This is primarily attributed to several factors, including supportive government policies, robust infrastructure, and a well-educated workforce. These factors create an environment conducive to digital transformation, which, in turn, positively affects the sustainability of enterprises in this region.In contrast, the central region of China experiences no significant impact of digitalization on sustainable enterprise development. This could be due to the dominance of heavy industry in this region, which might be less adaptable to digital transformation. Additionally, there might be less inherent attractiveness for businesses to cluster in this region, which can also affect the potential benefits of digitalization.The western region of China, while not heavily influenced by regional virtual agglomeration (the clustering of businesses in the same area), still shows a positive and significant relationship between digital transformation and enterprise sustainability. This suggests that digital transformation is beginning to have a scale effect and is contributing to the enhancement of enterprise sustainability in this region.The impact of digital transformation on enterprise sustainability varies due to a range of factors, including government policies, the quality of infrastructure, and the availability of skilled talent. These factors shape the overall environment for digital transformation and its potential impact on sustainable development.The conclusion emphasizes that regional governments and enterprises should customize their strategies for digital transformation investment and support based on their unique characteristics and development needs. In essence, a one-size-fits-all approach to digitalization may not work, and it's essential to consider the specific conditions and challenges of each region to foster sustainable enterprise development effectively.

The research paper focus on the following points:

- The study's goal is to demonstrate the local, national, and international implications of the digital revolution, with a focus on the legislative support in the eastern area and the varied repercussions worldwide.
- In line with the global trend toward sustainable practices, it highlights India's all-encompassing approach to digital governance, taxation, and sustainability for multinational enterprises.
- The paper focuses on the complex interplay between digital transformation and organizational sustainability, promoting the use of cutting-edge technologies like deep learning and blockchain to improve both the economic and environmental results.

REFERENCES

Aier, S., Weiss, S., Winter, R., & Rytz, B. (2016). Untangling EA's long path of becoming a partner for business transformation: The case of Swiss Federal Railways. In *2016 IEEE 20th International Enterprise Distributed Object Computing Workshop (EDOCW)* (pp. 1-7). IEEE. 10.1109/EDOCW.2016.7584394

Al-Debi, Mutaz, El-Haddadeh, & Avison. (2008). Defining the business model in the new world of digital business. *AMCIS 2008 Proceedings,* 300.

Barrero, J. M., Bloom, N., & Davis, S. J. (2021). *Why working from home will stick* (No. w28731). National Bureau of Economic Research. doi:10.3386/w28731

Bauernhansl, Hörcher, Röhm, & Bressner. (2017). Neupositionierungeinernationalen Technologieplattform. *Zeitschrift für wirtschaftlichenFabrikbetrieb, 112*(1-2), 7-11.

Bharadwaj, A., El Sawy, O. A., Pavlou, P. A., & Venkatraman, N. V. (2013). Digital business strategy: Toward a next generation of insights. *Management Information Systems Quarterly*, *37*(2), 471–482. doi:10.25300/MISQ/2013/37:2.3

Costa, I., Riccotta, R., Montini, P., Stefani, E., Roberto de Souza, G., Gaspar, M. A., & Martins, F. S. (2022). The degree of contribution of digital transformation technology on company sustainability areas. *Sustainability (Basel)*, *14*(1), 462. doi:10.3390/su14010462

Delgosha, S., Mohammad, N. H. H., & Saheb, T. (2020). The configurational impact of digital transformation on sustainability: A country-level perspective. In *ECIS2020 Proceedings*. Association for Information Systems AIS Electronic Library (AISeL).

Delios, A., Perchthold, G., & Capri, A. (2021). Cohesion, COVID-19 and contemporary challenges to globalization. *Journal of World Business*, *56*(3), 101197. doi:10.1016/j.jwb.2021.101197

Gardner, D., & Fehskens, L. (2012). Point-counterpoint: Enterprise architecture and enterprise transformation as related but distinct concepts. *Journal of Enterprise Transformation*, *2*(4), 283–294. doi:10.1080/19488289.2012.730813

George, G., & Simon, J. D. (2022). Digital transformation, sustainability, and purpose in the multinational enterprise. *Journal of World Business*, *57*(3), 101326. doi:10.1016/j.jwb.2022.101326

Gowroju, S., & Kumar, S. (2022). Review on secure traditional and machine learning algorithms for age prediction using IRIS image. *Multimedia Tools and Applications*, *81*(24), 35503–35531. doi:10.1007/s11042-022-13355-4

Gowroju, S., Sandeep Kumar, A., & Ghimire, A. (2022). Deep Neural Network for Accurate Age Group Prediction through Pupil Using the Optimized UNet Model. *Mathematical Problems in Engineering*, *2022*, 1–24. doi:10.1155/2022/7813701

Hitt, M. A., Holmes, R. M. Jr, & Arregle, J. L. (2021). The (COVID-19) pandemic and the new world (dis) order. *Journal of World Business*, *56*(4), 101210. doi:10.1016/j.jwb.2021.101210

Kagermann, H. (2017). *Chancen von Industrie 4.0 nutzen. In HandbuchIndustrie 4.0* (Vol. 4). Allgemeine Grundlagen.

Kar, A. K., Ilavarasan, V., Gupta, M. P., Janssen, M., & Kothari, R. (2019). Moving beyond smart cities: Digital nations for social innovation & sustainability. *Information Systems Frontiers*, *21*(3), 495–501. doi:10.1007/s10796-019-09930-0

Liu, Gailhofer, Gensch, Köhler, Wolff, Monteforte, Urrutia, Cihlarova, & Williams. (2019). *Impacts of the digital transformation on the environment and sustainability*. Issue Paper under Task 3.

Lubinski, C., & Wadhwani, R. D. (2020). Geopolitical jockeying: Economic nationalism and multinational strategy in historical perspective. *Strategic Management Journal*, *41*(3), 400–421. doi:10.1002/smj.3022

Lusch, R. F., & Nambisan, S. (2015). Service innovation. *Management Information Systems Quarterly*, *39*(1), 155–176. doi:10.25300/MISQ/2015/39.1.07

Majstorović, M. N., & Terzić, R. M. (2018). Enterprise architecture as an approach to the development of information systems. *Vojnotehničkiglasnik*, *66*(2), 380–398. doi:10.5937/vojtehg66-15850

Matt, C., Hess, T., & Benlian, A. (2015). Digital Transformation Strategies. *Business & Information Systems Engineering*, *57*(5), 339–343. doi:10.1007/s12599-015-0401-5

Narsimhulu, K., Santhosh Ramchander, N., & Swathi, A. (2022). An AI Enabled Framework with Feature Selection for Efficient Heart Disease Prediction. In *2022 5th International Conference on Contemporary Computing and Informatics (IC3I)* (pp. 1468-1473). IEEE. 10.1109/IC3I56241.2022.10073155

Pappas, I. O., Mikalef, P., Dwivedi, Y., Jaccheri, L., Krogstie, J., & Mäntymäki, M. (2019). *Digital transformation for a sustainable society in the 21st century*. Springer International Publishing. doi:10.1007/978-3-030-29374-1

Rieger, A., Roth, T., Sedlmeir, J., & Fridgen, G. (2022). We need a broader debate on the sustainability of blockchain. *Joule*, *6*(6), 1137–1141. doi:10.1016/j.joule.2022.04.013

Swathi & Rani. (2019). Intelligent fatigue detection by using ACS and by avoiding false alarms of fatigue detection. In *Innovations in Computer Science and Engineering: Proceedings of the Sixth ICICSE 2018* (pp. 225-233). Springer Singapore.

Vijayan, A. (2019). Digital India-A roadmap to sustainability. *International Journal of Innovative Technology and Exploring Engineering*, *8*(5), 571–576.

Zattoni, A., & Pugliese, A. (2021). Corporate governance research in the wake of a systemic crisis: Lessons and opportunities from the COVID-19 Pandemic. *Journal of Management Studies*, *58*(5), 1405–1410. doi:10.1111/joms.12693

Chapter 9
What Do We Know About Artificial Intelligence and Blockchain Technology Integration in the Healthcare Industry?

Sumit Oberoi
https://orcid.org/0000-0002-9989-2875
Symbiosis School of Economics, Symbiosis International University, India

Sugandh Arora
https://orcid.org/0000-0002-4740-5270
Sharda School of Business Studies, Sharda University, India

Balraj Verma
Chitkara Business School, Chitkara University, India

Krishna Kanta Roy
Symbiosis School of Economics, Symbiosis International University, India

ABSTRACT

This study aims to identify artificial intelligence and blockchain technology's publication productivity and intellectual structure in the healthcare industry. This study employs a bibliometric-content analysis technique to determine intellectual structure and publication productivity. The Scopus database analyses identified research articles from 2018 to 2023. The findings of the thematic mapping show that AI and blockchain are emerging techniques and topics such as "smart healthcare", "patient-centric", "healthcare management", "virtual & augmented reality", "decentralization", etc. are the potential and new dimensions that can be looked upon in future themes. This study advances knowledge by providing a current and future overview of AI and blockchain integration in the healthcare industry that would create new and enhance existing research streams.

DOI: 10.4018/979-8-3693-3253-5.ch009

INTRODUCTION

The term "*4IR*" or "*Fourth Industrial Revolution*" was first introduced in the CeBIT-2011 forum by German researchers (Majstorović et al., 2018). Since then, it has been a synonym to mention a process that empowers businesses and manufacturing facilities throughout all industries to connect with internet technology, including but not limited to AI (artificial intelligence), Big Data, CPS (*cyber-physical systems*), Deep Learning and other state-of-the-art tools. Though, digitization and internet-of-things (IoT) have already helped to transform business processes, logistics and supply chain management (Goyal et al., 2019; Manhoar et al., 2020; Ahsan & Siddique, 2022), the healthcare industry has also witnessed a significant transformation in last couple of decades with the proliferation of internet technology and AI-powered devices (Ochella et al., 2022; Verma & Srivastava, 2022). Healthcare technologies easily connect and exchange big data in a unique and secured manner.

According to Kumar et al. (2019), "*as the establishment of tools grows, the healthcare industry experiences radical and technical modification*". Artificial Intelligence (AI) and blockchain technologies are new and peculiar advancements in the healthcare industry (Vyas et al., 2022). On one hand, blockchain technology aids in storing encrypted electronic health records (EHR), whereas on the other hand, artificial intelligence requires this information to process outcomes. Blockchain technology facilitates healthcare practitioners to view the health records of the patient and artificial intelligence further uses numerous proposed combinations of "*Algorithms*", "*Decision-Making Capabilities*" and "*Big Data*" to prevent epidemiological transition (Kim & Huh, 2020). Innovative technologies like artificial intelligence (AI) can manage big data, enabling practitioners to swiftly detect, diagnose, and treat illness with automated options. At the same time, blockchain technology enhances communication and data transparency between healthcare professionals and patients.

AI plays a significant role in recognizing trends and patterns in the healthcare sector (Yi et al., 2022) and also helps in monitoring clinical trials (Kumar et al., 2023). It holds several advantages over traditional methods of making clinical decisions. AI algorithms predict precise health assessments and facilitate understanding patients' EHR data, which further aids in getting unprecedented insights into the care process, diagnostics and treatment variability results. While artificial intelligence has been recognized as a growing and prosperous area in the healthcare sector, the recent developments in blockchain technology systems have also opened new horizons for a decentralized environment. Blockchain technology, originally developed to understand the crypto-currency ecosystem (Oberoi & Kansra, 2021; Oberoi & Kansra, 2022; Verma et al., 2022), further started its integration into the healthcare sector. Blockchain accounts for various features, *viz.* decentralized control, automated micro-transactions, smart contracts, etc., for securing the privacy of patients' health records. These health records include medical reports, billing information and clinical trial results (Bach et al., 2018). Artificial intelligence and blockchain are powerful technologies that holds the potential to reform existing processes for greater efficiency and seamlessness.

Yet, till date there is a dearth of literature that highlights the trends and application of artificial intelligence (AI) and blockchain technology in healthcare industry. Therefore, this study aims to identify the publication productivity and intellectual structure of the research area. Following are the specific research questions (RQ) on application of both technologies in healthcare industry:

RQI: To highlight the research trends and publication productivity on application of artificial intelligence (AI) and blockchain technology in healthcare industry?

RQII: To identify highly influential articles on AI and blockchain in healthcare industry.

RQIII: To identify the prominent themes and areas of research that should be addressed in future research studies.

METHODOLOGY

This study employs bibliometric analysis technique to determine intellectual structure (i.e., themes, topics and application areas) and publication productivity from the existing literature on application of artificial intelligence and blockchain technology in healthcare. According to Donthu et al., (2021), "*Bibliometric analysis is a well-established scientific method for analyzing a body of literature, wherein bibliometric data are analyzed using quantitative tools*". Though, there exists various literature review techniques to exercise upon, but bibliometric analysis approach is the most preferred technique because of its dependence on review and quantitative analytical techniques (Lim et al., 2022).

Defining Study Scope

This study focuses on "bibliometric" & "intellectual structure" of the existing literature on blockchain technology and AI for the healthcare industry. The bibliometric structure of this study captures publication productivity. On the other hand, intellectual structure refers to the primary and niche themes of the research. The study scope is comparatively enormous, as both technologies are affluent research areas.

Data Collection for Analysis

To find the relevant articles, reviews and bibliographic data, authors identified appropriate keywords from the literature. Further, subject-matter experts and academicians working on artificial intelligence and blockchain technology in the healthcare industry were requested to check and rate the included keywords concerning relevance and clarity. To ensure that searched keywords extensively encapsulate concepts of AI and blockchain, a search string for data search covering two significant technologies is shown in Table 1.

The search string comprises keywords and terms such as "artificial intelligence", "AI", "applications", "blockchain technology", "health industry", and "electronic health records". The search criteria are limited to years (i.e., 2018-2023), document type (i.e., articles, reviews, book chapters and conference papers), source type (i.e., journals, conference proceedings, book and book series) and language (only English). Data for this study is retrieved from the "Scopus" database, as it accounts for the most extensive peer-to-peer reviewed research documents. Thus, 237 research documents were observed from the search string.

Data Analysis

For the eligible 237 research papers, a "*systematic methodological review*" (SMR) on artificial intelligence and blockchain technology in the healthcare industry was done, accompanied by bibliometric techniques embracing journal outcomes, co-citation analysis and author occurrence analysis. "*Visualization of Science (VOS)*" viewer software has been used in the study to visualize its output in a network and "*Biblioshiny*" by R-studio software has been used for cloud mapping, keyword analysis, co-citation analysis and author occurrence analysis. The features of the eligible research article were presented manually.

Table 1. Studies identified using search string

Search String	Search outcome
(("Artificial Intelligence") OR ("AI") AND "Blockchain" AND "Technology" AND "Healthcare" AND "Industry")	237

Source: Author's compilation

RESULTS

The study outcomes are observed using bibliometric and content analysis approaches grounded upon the three major research questions. The study results relate to publication productivity, research trends and intellectual structure.

Research Trends and Publication Productivity

To answer the foremost research question (RQ1), i.e., to highlight the research trends and publication productivity on the application of artificial intelligence and blockchain technology in the healthcare industry. This study examines the trends in total publications productivity over the years, citations, contributions by countries, contributions of institutions, etc. The data used for analysis is retrieved from the Scopus database and forms a big data set comprising of information *viz.* title, abstract, authors, journal citation count and keywords.

Two hundred thirty-seven research documents were retrieved from the online database comprising 92 articles, 59 conference articles, 56 reviews and 30 book chapters after meeting the SMR criteriais shown in Figure 1. The research trends on AI and Blockchain publications in healthcare industry have increased cumulatively from 9 publications in 2018 to 237 by January 2023 and still counting as displayed in Figure 2. As shown in the supplementary figure S1A, it was found that papers by (Chamola et al., 2020; Qadri et al., 2020 & Mamoshina et al., 2018) are the globally leading papers with total citations of 590, 320 and 254, respectively. Moreover, supplementary figure S1B highlights that the top 3 globally leading authors, namely Tanwar S, Gupta R and Gadekallu TR, working in this area of research are from India with 5(1.07), 4(0.94) and 4(0.61) articles and articles fractionalized values.

The distribution of published research documents is displayed on a world map. The colours on the map represent publication density values in Figure 3. A transformative shift in the number of research articles published from 2018 to 2023 for the top ten countries is displayed in Figure 3B. The analysis revealed that seventy-three countries contributed to the publications. India with 76 publications was observed to be the leading productive country followed by the United States (37), the United Kingdom (20), China (18) and Saudi Arabia (18). As presented in Figure 3C, apart from being the leading productive country in research publications, India has also turned out to be the top country with the most citations (797) followed by the United States (447), Korea (395), China (218) and South Africa (116). Figure 3D and 3E highlights the top ten most relevant academic affiliations and sources. Educational institutes such as INJE University of South Korea, Nirma University of India and the University of Electronic Science and Technology of China are the top three leading affiliations globally.

Additionally, Figure 4 displays the country collaboration map in the research area of AI and blockchain in the healthcare industry was created using both VoSviewer and Biblioshiny tool. The collaboration map illustrates two critical impressions, firstly the total number of research articles published by each

Figure 1. Flow diagram of literature search

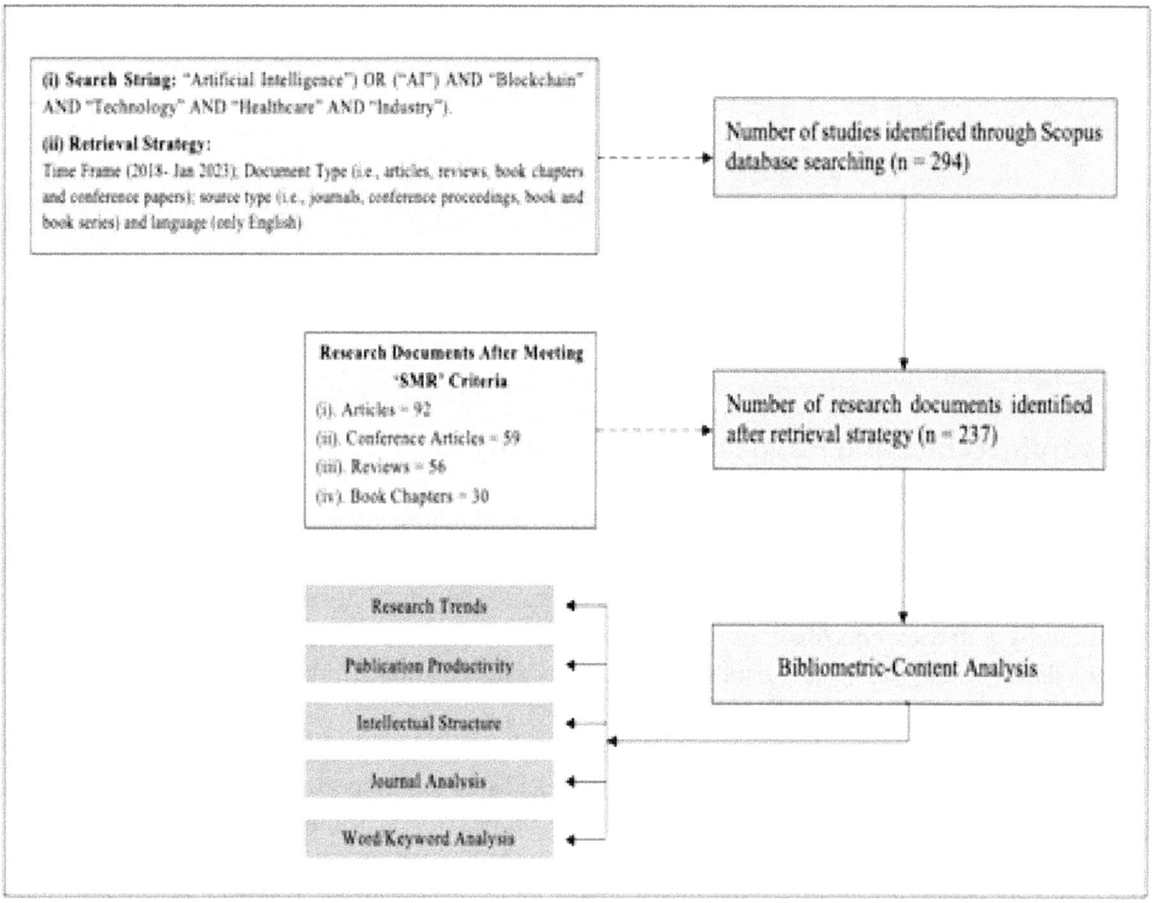

Figure 2. Global trend of annual publications on Al and blockchain in healthcare

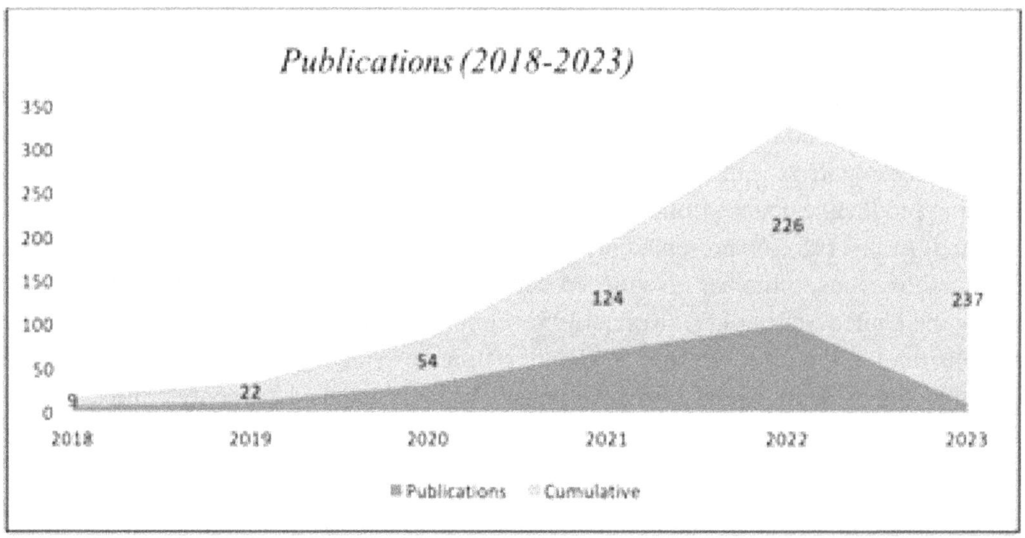

Figure 3. Research trends in AI and blockchain publications on healthcare industry

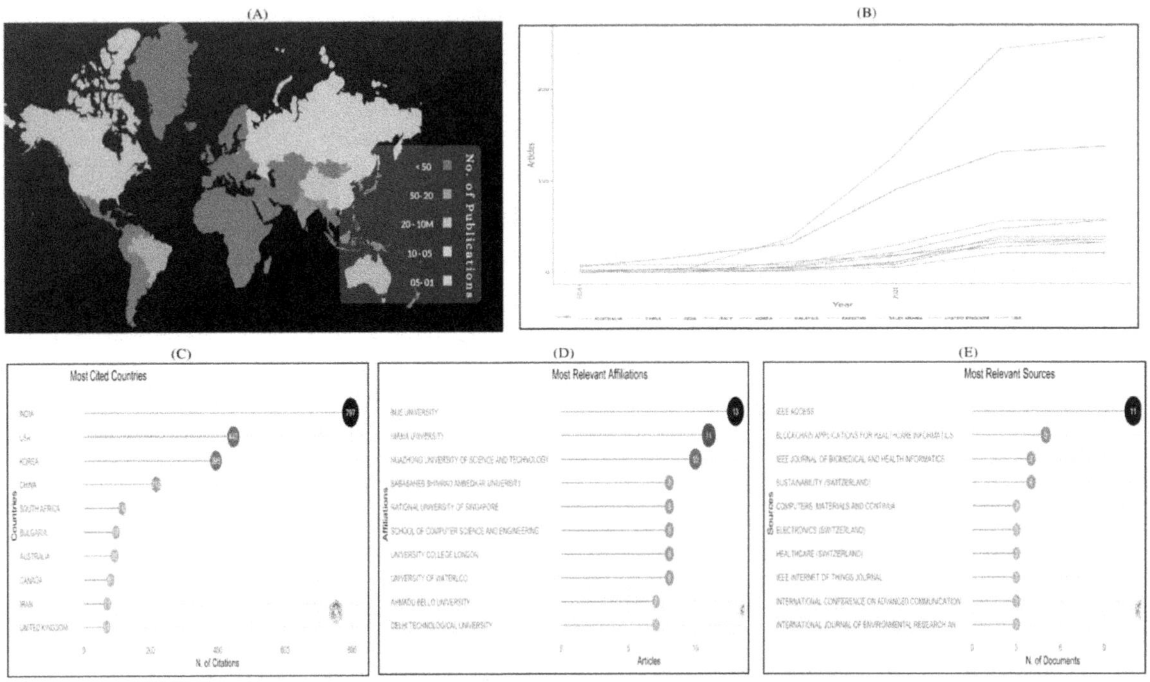

country i.e. depicted in blue, and secondly, the researcher's international collaboration, i.e. depicted with red lines. Countries with dark blue indicate increased articles output, whereas broader red lines denote increased collaboration between countries.

Figure 4B shows a solid and extensive collaboration between the countries like India, the U.S.A, U.K, China, Saudi Arabia, South Korea, Etc., on both metrics. Alternatively, Asian nations such as Bangladesh, Saudi Arabia, Malaysia, UAE, Pakistan, Etc., are also becoming emerging collaborators and publishers in this niche area of research (Figure 4A).

Influential Articles

To answer the second research question (RQ2), i.e., to identify the most influential research article on the application of AI and blockchain technology in the healthcare industry. This study conducted a "*performance analysis*" with the help of citation network for 43 articles. According to Ding and Cronin (2018) "*There are several metrics to measure the influence of a publication, but the most prevalent metric is citations*", wherein publication influence is estimated by the number of times the research document got cited by others. To retrieve the citation network VoSviewer software is used. Table 2 shows the top 15 influential research articles.

An article by Chamola et al. (2020) titled a comprehensive review of the covid-19 pandemic and the role of IoT, drones, AI, blockchain and 5G tops the list of influential articles with total citations of 590, followed by Qadri et al. (2020) article on the future of healthcare internet of things and Mamoshina et al. (2018) article on Converging blockchain and next-generation AI technologies to decentralize and accelerate biomedical research and healthcare with citations 320 and 254, respectively. Figure 5 of the

Figure 4. Graphical illustration of country collaboration map

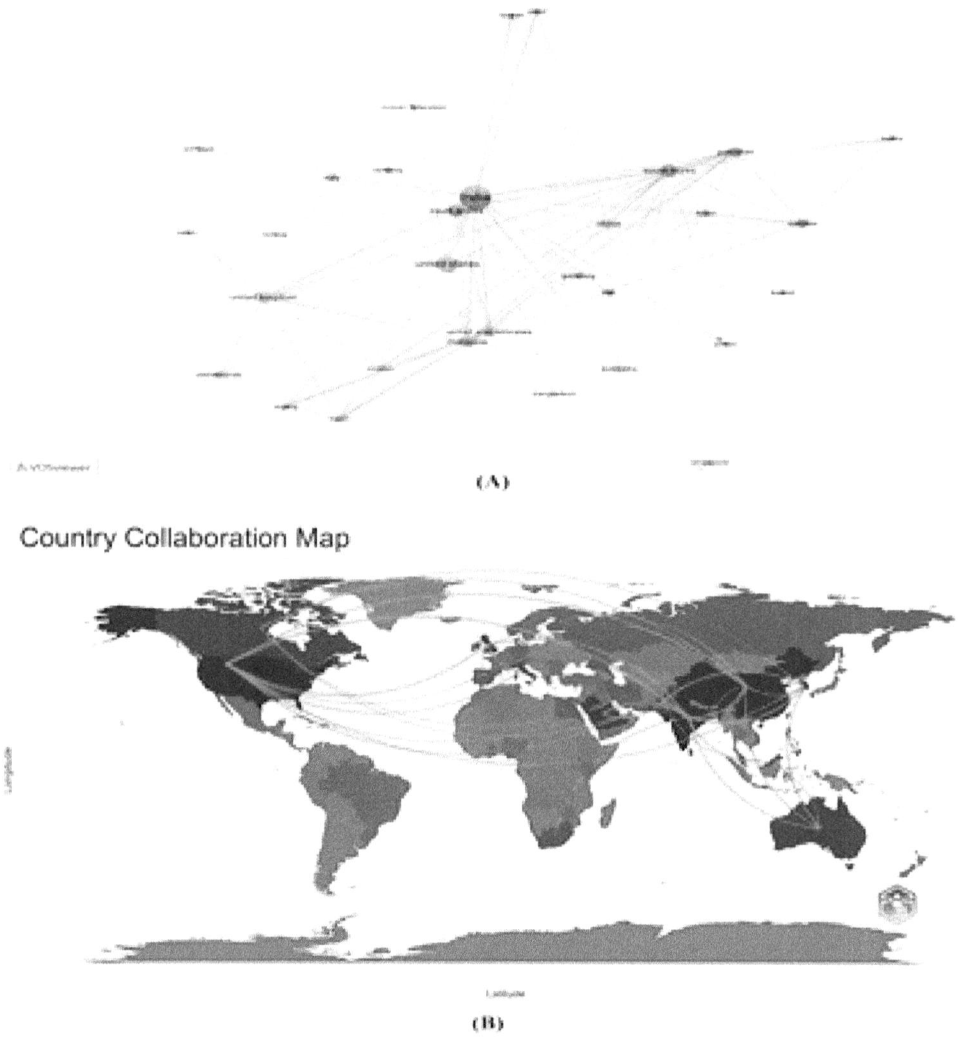

study displays the citation network amongst the different research publications. These publications' node size and colour represent a large number of citations and clusters of similar authors. Publications such as (Farahani et al., 2021; Nguyen et al., 2021; Elbadawi et al., 2021) are also among the most influential papers in this field, as observed through the normalized total citation values and node size to be bigger than research articles with rank 4, 5, 6, Etc.

Prominent Topics and Themes

Bibliometric tool "*Author Keyword Analysis*" is employed to identify the most pertinent research articles and trends in AI and blockchain technology in the healthcare industry (Yang et al., 2016; Wang et al., 2016). Additionally, author keyword analysis also helps increase the number of readers for the research document, which aids in getting more citations to the scholar. Figure 6 displays the Word Tree Map

Table 2. Top 15 influential articles on AI and blockchain technology in healthcare industry

Rank	Title	Year	Authors	Journal	Total Citations	TC per Year	Normalized TC
1	A Comprehensive Review of the COVID-19 Pandemic and the Role of IoT, Drones, AI, Blockchain, and 5G in Managing its Impact	2020	Chamola et al.	IEEE Access	590	147.50	12.03
2	The Future of Healthcare Internet of Things: A Survey of Emerging Technologies	2020	Qadri et al.	IEEE COMMUN SURV TUTOR	320	80.00	6.52
3	Converging blockchain and next-generation artificial intelligence technologies to decentralize and accelerate biomedical research and healthcare	2018	Mamoshina et al.	ONCOTARGET	254	42.33	3.75
4	Enabling technologies and sustainable smart cities	2020	Ahad et al.	SUSTAINABLE CITIES SOC	166	41.50	3.38
5	Blockchain-Powered Parallel Healthcare Systems Based on the ACP Approach	2018	Wang et al.	IEEE TRANS COMPUTAT SOC SYST	161	26.83	2.38
6	Blockchain-based Personal Health Data Sharing System Using Cloud Storage	2018	Zheng et al.	IEEE INT CONFE-HEALTH NETW, APPL SERV, HEALTHCOM	102	17.00	1.50
7	Blockchain Applications for Healthcare Data Management	2019	Dimitrov	HEALTHC INFORMATICS RES	97	19.40	4.59
8	Blockchain and Artificial Intelligence Technology for Novel Coronavirus Disease 2019 Self-Testing	2020	Mashamba-Thompson & Crayton	DIAGN	84	21.00	1.71
9	A Novel Smart Healthcare Design, Simulation, and Implementation Using Healthcare 4.0 Processes	2020	Kumar et al.	IEEE ACCESS	83	20.75	1.69
10	Disruptive Technologies for Environment and Health Research: An Overview of Artificial Intelligence, Blockchain, and Internet of Things	2019	Bublitz et al.	INT J ENVIRON RES PUBLIC HEALTH	59	11.80	2.79
11	The convergence of IoT and distributed ledger technologies (DLT): Opportunities, challenges, and solutions	2021	Farahani et al.	J NETWORK COMPUT APPL	50	16.67	4.70
12	Blockchain technology in the healthcare industry: Trends and opportunities	2021	Hussien et al.	J IND INFOR INTEGR	49	16.33	4.60
13	Blockchain and AI-Based Solutions to Combat Coronavirus (COVID-19)-Like Epidemics: A Survey	2021	Nguyen et al.	IEEE ACCESS	48	16.00	4.51
14	Harnessing artificial intelligence for the next generation of 3D printed medicines	2021	Elbadawi et al.	ADV DRUG DELIV REV	45	15.00	4.23
15	Blockchain for Business: Next-Generation Enterprise Artificial Intelligence Systems	2018	Swan	ADV COMPUT	43	7.17	0.63

Source: Authors compilation based on Scopus database.
Note: TC = Total Citation

that points out the top fifty used keywords in the study on AI and blockchain in healthcare for 2018-2023. The outcome of the Word Tree Map lucidly explains that concepts such as blockchain, artificial

Figure 5. Citation network among the different research publications on AI and blockchain

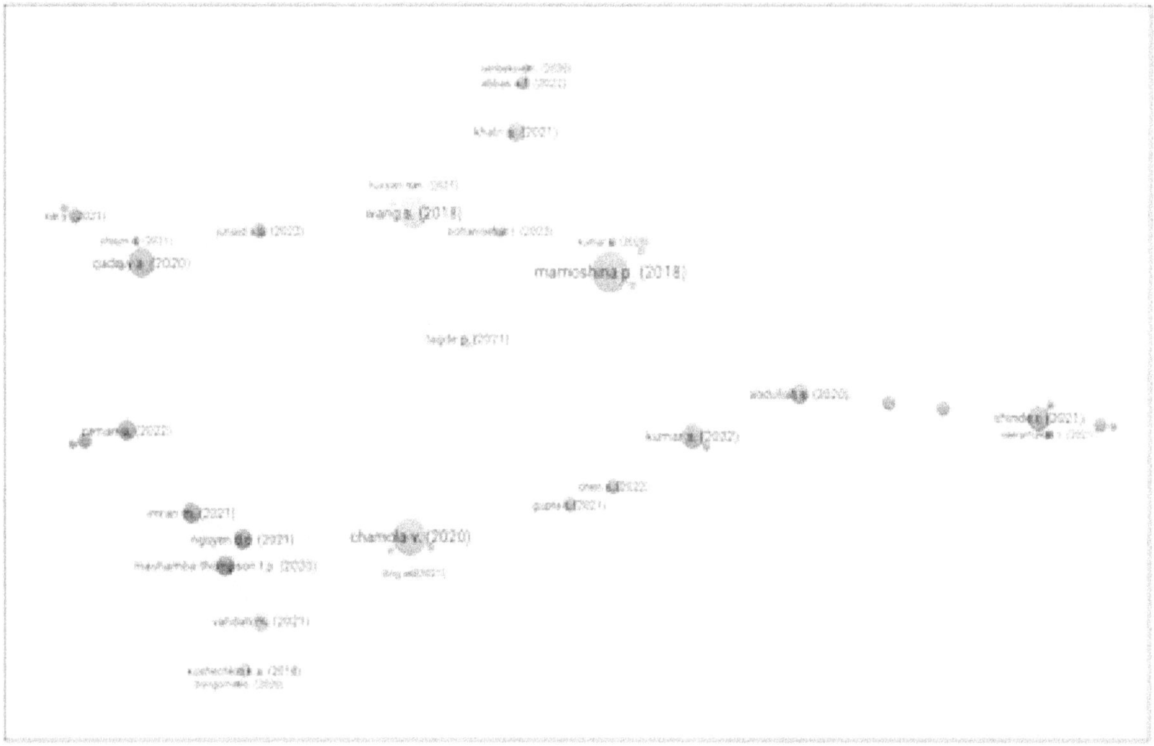

intelligence and healthcare are the top most cited keywords. Results during the 2018-2023 timespan indicate that the healthcare industry started integrating AI and blockchain technology. Keywords like machine learning, internet of things (IoT), deep learning, big data, security and covid-19 also highlight the emerging research trends in this area of research with a higher frequency of occurrence numbers.

Further, to answer the third research question (**RQ3**), i.e., to identify the prominent themes and areas of research that should be addressed in future research studies. Another analysis performed to answer RQ3 is the thematic mapping of intelligent learning environments. According to Agbo et al. (2021), "*Thematic mapping helps in gaining insight into the research field's current status and what its future sustainability holds*". This analysis technique helps disseminate knowledge and cognizance to the researchers about the potential future thematic areas of research within a field. Under thematic mapping analysis, a group of author keywords and interconnections are considered to obtain themes. Centrality and density are the two main criteria of these themes. Centrality criteria explain the importance of the theme to the area of research, and on the other hand, density refers to the theme's development within the field of study. Under the thematic mapping network approach, the map is divided into four different quadrants, namely Motor (Q1), Basic (Q2), Niche (Q3) and Emerging\Declining (Q4) focus zones in Figure 7.

Of the four themes, topics covered under the motor theme located in the upper right quadrant (Q1) are deemed the most relevant. Therefore, topics such as "smart data privacy", "security privacy", "computational modelling" and "digital twin's technology" are of utmost significance and established in this area of research. Themes under quadrant two (Q2), such as "smart contracts", "IoT", "healthcare", "blockchain", "medical services", Etc. in Figure 7 are established and proficient in structuring the research

Figure 6: Word tree map for 2018-2023

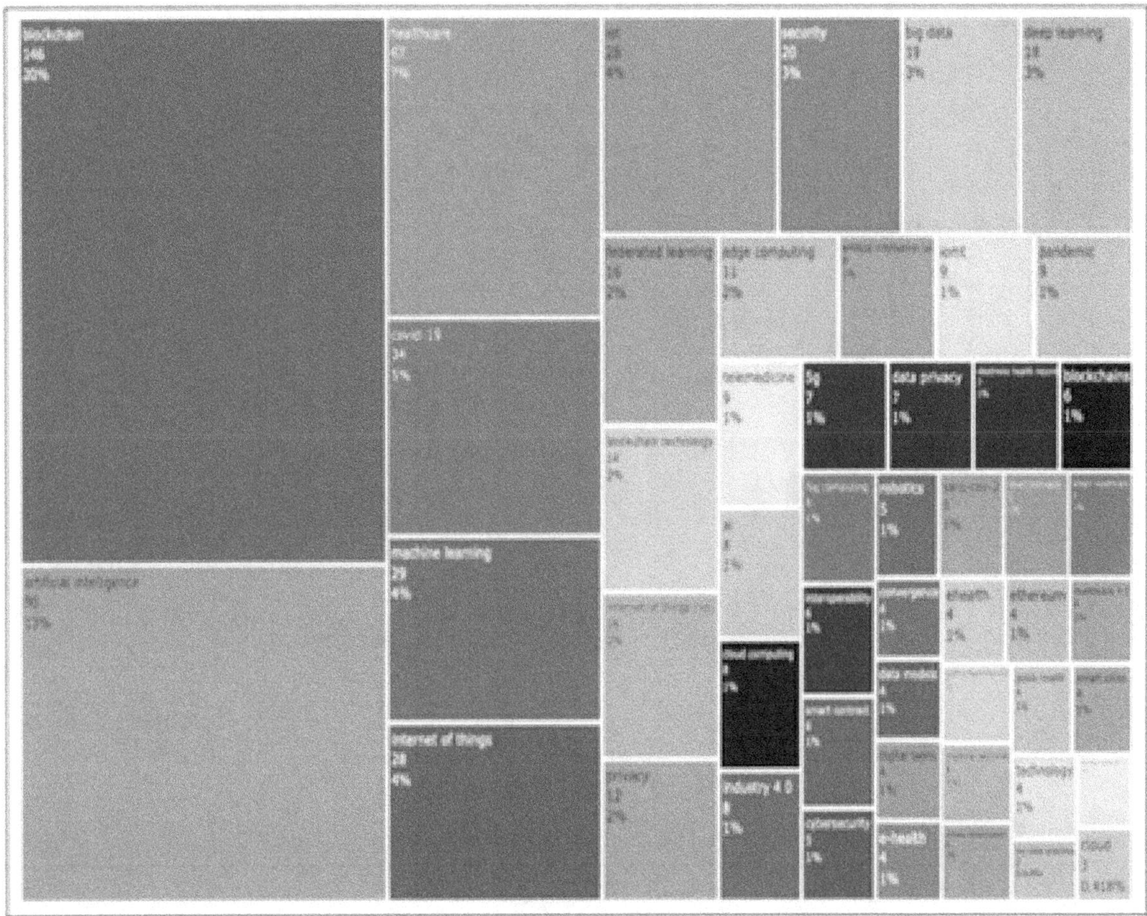

field. Literature on thematic mapping identifies themes under quadrant three (Q3) as very specialized and niche. The results of this analysis suggests that themes such as "smart healthcare", "patient-centric", "healthcare management", "virtual & augmented reality", "decentralization", Etc. are the potential themes that are required to be linked more with AI and blockchain technology. Lastly, themes presented under the declining/emerging quadrant (Q4), such as "challenges in public health" and "digital technologies", are pertinent but still in their emerging or developing stage.

Finally, identifying future research directions can help the healthcare industry to overhaul its approach and policy towards digital transformation. Therefore, to answer the research question and find the road for future research directions. This study performed Multiple Correspondence Analysis (MCA) which grouped the research documents retrieved from the Scopus database. The results of the multiple correspondence analysis are presented in Figure 8. It was found that keywords approaching the centre point have received close notice recently. Keywords are presented in two different coloured clusters, i.e., one in red emphasises upon the current status in the area of AI and blockchain and the blue coloured cluster highlights the directions for future research. Blue cluster focusses upon the need to include "deep learn-

Figure 7. Thematic mapping

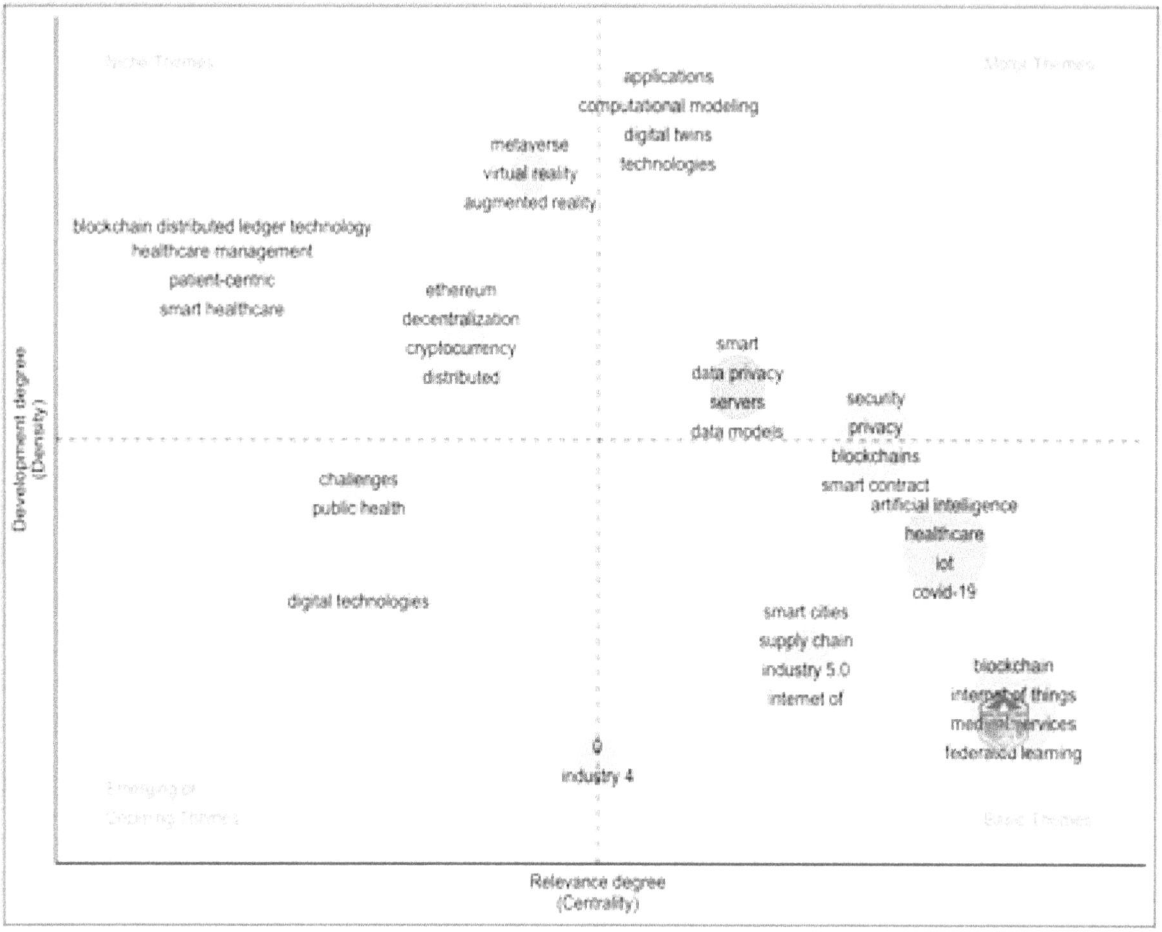

ing" in healthcare industry and develop tools that have potential to make changes in healthcare such as predict pediatric appointment no-shows, improve clinical decision, detect multiple disease.

CONCLUSION

Artificial intelligence and blockchain technology are different yet powerful technologies individually (Arora & Nabi, 2022). However, combining these two techniques in the healthcare industry has received significant attention among academicians, practitioners and providers to bolster innovation in developing IT infrastructure for healthcare and data management competencies. However, a need for more research examines the insight into research trends, prominent themes and future research directions. Therefore, this study performs a bibliometric-content analysis to address this research gap and provides major vital takeaways.

Firstly, research trends on AI and blockchain publications in the healthcare industry have increased from 9 publications in 2018 to 237 by January 2023. Secondly, an article by Chamola et al. (2020)

Figure 8. Conceptual structure map-method

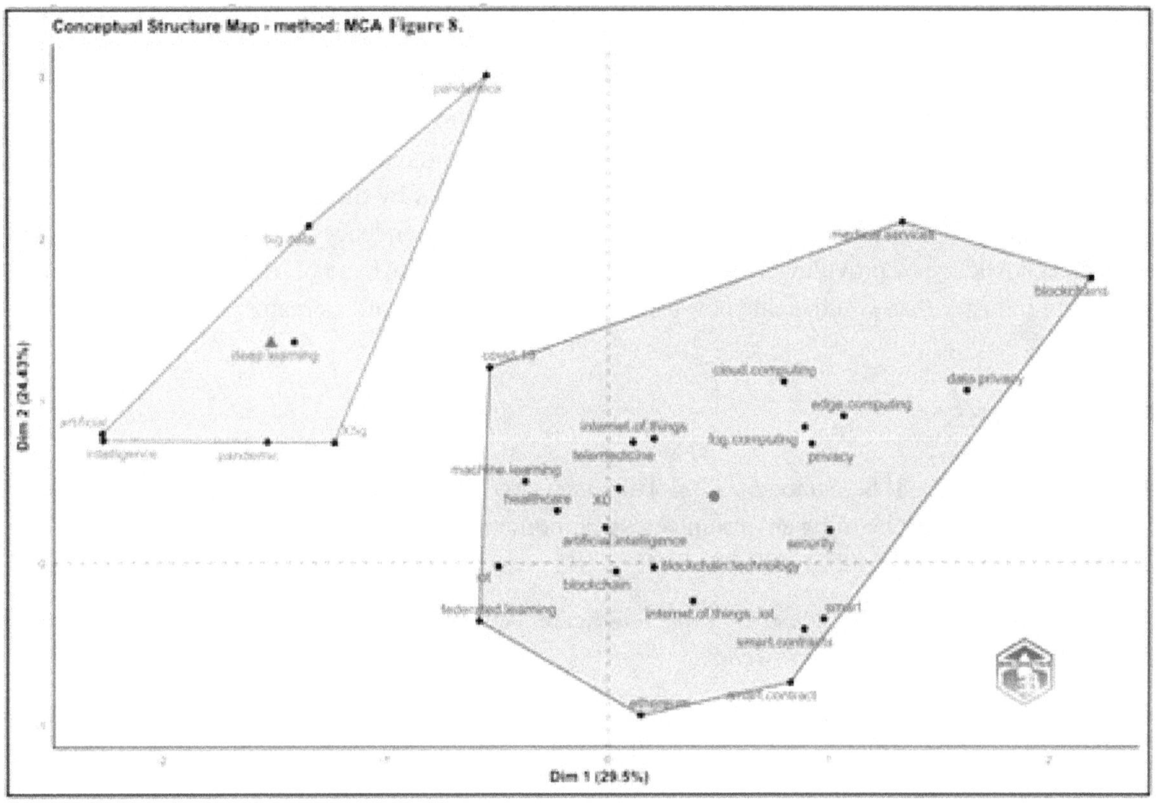

identified the role of IoT, AI, Blockchain and 5G in managing health catastrophes like Covid-19. Further, a research article by Qadri et al. (2020) discussed the future aspects of healthcare under emerging technologies. Lastly, Mamoshina et al. (2018) study on the convergence of Blockchain and AI in the healthcare industry is one of the top three most influential research articles discussing the integration of both emerging technologies. Prospective authors must be aware of the seminal research papers in this area to position and design future research articles in an original and new way to expand prior research knowledge.

Third, the results of the analysis revealed that "*blockchain*", "*artificial intelligence*", "*healthcare*", "*machine learning*", "*Internet-of-Things (IoT)*", "*Deep Learning*", "*big data*" and "*security*" are the most prominent research topics and keywords. Further, the revelation of "*Deep learning and Blockchain*" is the most relevant and sought-after link in the literature that highlights the potential and significance of artificial intelligence and blockchain technologies integration in the healthcare industry.

In short, this study has contributed in three significant ways. This research primarily outlined publication productivity in the healthcare industry using AI and blockchain technology. This highlights that this area of research is in its infancy stage and holds incredible scope for future research. Second, the present study identified the most significant research articles in this field, laying the foundation for future research. Third, this study has highlighted the prominent themes and potential topics on artificial intelligence and blockchain technology integration in healthcare, which permits prospective authors to achieve a one-stop insight.

The present study also provides substantial policy implications for stakeholders, including medical practitioners, AI and blockchain technology developers and research scholars. For medical practitioners, the cognizance regarding the application of AI and blockchain technology can help fetch encrypted patient records or big data, diagnosis and prevention of chronic diseases. Further, AI and blockchain technology developers also gain insights into the same by collaborating to advance automated and decentralized healthcare applications that offer superior prediction, treatment and data security of patients' electronic health records (EHR). Finally, this study helps research scholars by directing them to investigate the future research areas or themes identified using multiple correspondence analysis (MCA). This study advances knowledge by providing a current and future overview of AI and blockchain integration in the healthcare industry that would create new and enhance existing research streams.

REFERENCES

Agbo, F. J., Oyelere, S. S., Suhonen, J., & Tukiainen, M. (2021). Scientific production and thematic breakthroughs in smart learning environments: A bibliometric analysis. *Smart Learning Environments.*, *8*(1), 1–25. doi:10.1186/s40561-020-00145-4

Ahsan & Siddique. (2022). Industry 4.0 in Healthcare: A systematic review. *International Journal of Information Management Data Insights.*

Arora, S., & Nabi, T. (2022). Blockchain Adoption in Banking Systems: A Boon or Bane? In Applications, Challenges, and Opportunities of Blockchain Technology in Banking and Insurance. doi:10.4018/978-1-6684-4133-6.ch002

Bach, L. M., Mihaljevic, B., & Zagar, M. (2018). Comparative analysis of blockchain consensus algorithms. In *2018 41st International Convention on Information and Communication Technology, Electronics and Microelectronics*. 10.23919/MIPRO.2018.8400278

Chamola, V., Hassija, V., Gupta, V., & Guizani, M. (2020). A comprehensive review of the COVID-19 pandemic and the role of IoT, drones, AI, blockchain, and 5G in managing its impact. *IEEE Access : Practical Innovations, Open Solutions*, *8*, 90225–90265. doi:10.1109/ACCESS.2020.2992341

Ding, Y., & Cronin, B. (2011). Popular and/or prestigious? Measures of scholarly esteem. *Information Processing & Management*, *47*(1), 80–96. doi:10.1016/j.ipm.2010.01.002

Donthu, N., Kumar, S., Mukherjee, D., Pandey, N., & Lim, W. M. (2021). How to conduct a bibliometric analysis: An overview and guidelines? *Journal of Business Research*, *133*, 285–296. doi:10.1016/j.jbusres.2021.04.070

Elbadawi, M., McCoubrey, L. E., Gavins, F. K., Ong, J. J., Goyanes, A., Gaisford, S., & Basit, A. W. (2021). Harnessing artificial intelligence for the next generation of 3D printed medicines. *Advanced Drug Delivery Reviews*, *175*, 113805. doi:10.1016/j.addr.2021.05.015 PMID:34019957

Farahani, B., Firouzi, F., & Luecking, M. (2021). The convergence of IoT and distributed ledger technologies (DLT): Opportunities, challenges, and solutions. *Journal of Network and Computer Applications*, *177*, 102936. doi:10.1016/j.jnca.2020.102936

Goyal, Singh, Singh, & Aggarwal. (2019). Efficiency and technology gaps in Indian banking sector: Application of meta-frontier directional distance function DEA approach. *The Journal of Finance and Data Science, 5*, 156-172.

Kim, S. K., & Huh, J. H. (2020). Artificial neural network blockchain techniques for healthcare system: Focusing on the personal health records. *Electronics (Basel)*, *9*(5), 763. doi:10.3390/electronics9050763

Kumar, K., Zindani, D., & Davim, J. P. (2019). *Industry 4.0: Developments towards the fourth industrial revolution*. Springer. doi:10.1007/978-981-13-8165-2

Kumar, P., Chauhan, S., & Awasthi, L. K. (2023). Artificial intelligence in healthcare: Review, ethics, trust challenges & future research directions. *Engineering Applications of Artificial Intelligence*, *120*, 105894. doi:10.1016/j.engappai.2023.105894

Lim, W. M., Kumar, S., & Ali, F. (2022). Advancing knowledge through literature reviews: 'what', 'why', and 'how to contribute'. *Service Industries Journal*, *42*(7-8), 481–513. doi:10.1080/02642069.2022.2047941

Majstorović, V. D., Velimirović, M., Glišić, M., Kostić, J., Đura, E., Rančić, M., & Mitrović, R. (2018). Cyber-physical manufacturing in context of industry 4.0 model. In *Proceedings of 3rd International Conference on the Industry 4.0 Model for Advanced Manufacturing*. AMP.

Mamoshina, P., Ojomoko, L., Yanovich, Y., Ostrovski, A., Botezatu, A., Prikhodko, P., Izumchenko, E., Aliper, A., Romantsov, K., Zhebrak, A., Ogu, I. O., & Zhavoronkov, A. (2018). Converging blockchain and next-generation artificial intelligence technologies to decentralize and accelerate biomedical research and healthcare. *Oncotarget*, *9*(5), 5665–5690. doi:10.18632/oncotarget.22345 PMID:29464026

Manohar, S., Mittal, A., & Marwah, S. (2020). Service innovation, corporate reputation and word-of-mouth in the banking sector: A test on multigroup-moderated mediation effect. *Benchmarking*, *27*(1), 406–429. doi:10.1108/BIJ-05-2019-0217

Nguyen, D. C., Ding, M., Pathirana, P. N., & Seneviratne, A. (2021). Blockchain and AI-based solutions to combat coronavirus (COVID-19)-like epidemics: A survey. *IEEE Access : Practical Innovations, Open Solutions*, *9*, 95730–95753. doi:10.1109/ACCESS.2021.3093633 PMID:34812398

Oberoi, S., & Kansra, P. (2021). *Motivating Antecedents and Consequences of Blockchain Technology in the Insurance Industry*. Blockchain Technology and Applications for Digital Marketing. doi:10.4018/978-1-7998-8081-3.ch017

Oberoi, S., & Kansra, P. (2022). Blockchain Technology in the Insurance Industry. In Applications, Challenges, and Opportunities of Blockchain Technology in Banking and Insurance. doi:10.4018/978-1-6684-4133-6.ch009

Ochella, S., Shafiee, M., & Dinmohammadi, F. (2022). Artificial intelligence in prognostics and health management of engineering systems. *Engineering Applications of Artificial Intelligence*, *108*, 104552. doi:10.1016/j.engappai.2021.104552

Qadri, Y. A., Nauman, A., Zikria, Y. B., Vasilakos, A. V., & Kim, S. W. (2020). The future of healthcare internet of things: A survey of emerging technologies. *IEEE Communications Surveys and Tutorials*, *22*(2), 1121–1167. doi:10.1109/COMST.2020.2973314

Verma, B., & Srivastava, A. (2022). Dimensions of globalisation and economic growth of India: Exploring causal linkages. *International Journal of Economic Policy in Emerging Economies*, *15*(2/3/4), 197–213. doi:10.1504/IJEPEE.2022.121345

Verma, B., Srivastava, A., Mehta, R., & Chandel, J. (2022). FDI-linked Spillovers and the Indian Economic Growth: The role of Country's Absorptive Capacity. *IEEE Delhi Section Conference (DELCON)*. 10.1109/DELCON54057.2022.9753540

Vyas, S., Shabaz, M., Pandit, P., Parvathy, L. R., & Ofori, I. (2022). Integration of artificial intelligence and blockchain technology in healthcare and agriculture. *Journal of Food Quality*, *2022*, 1–11. doi:10.1155/2022/4228448

Wang, N., Liang, H., Jia, Y., Ge, S., Xue, Y., & Wang, Z. (2016). Cloud computing research in the IS discipline: A citation/co-citation analysis. *Decision Support Systems*, *86*, 35–47. doi:10.1016/j.dss.2016.03.006

Yang, S., Han, R., Wolfram, D., & Zhao, Y. (2016). Visualizing the intellectual structure of information science (2006–2015): Introducing author keyword coupling analysis. *Journal of Informetrics*, *10*(1), 132–150. doi:10.1016/j.joi.2015.12.003

Yi, J., Zhang, H., Mao, J., Chen, Y., Zhong, H., & Wang, Y. (2022). Review on the COVID-19 pandemic prevention and control system based on AI. *Engineering Applications of Artificial Intelligence*, *114*, 105184. doi:10.1016/j.engappai.2022.105184 PMID:35846728

Chapter 10
Future of Banking From IT Decentralization and Deglobalisation:
An Analysis of Its Possibilities

G. S. Vijaya
https://orcid.org/0000-0001-9185-9862
CMS Business School, Faculty of Management Studies, Jain University, India

Divya Prabhu
https://orcid.org/0000-0002-2880-4591
Government First Grade College, Mangalore University, Karkala, India

M. Sandhya
https://orcid.org/0009-0001-5552-9521
Government First Grade College, Mangalore University, Kaup, India

Jehad Aldehayyat
Al-Hussein Bin Talal University, Jordan

ABSTRACT

The banking sector is transforming, with traditional banking focusing on personalization and quality of relationships, while digital banking focuses on simplicity of products. However, traditional banking must embrace technology to survive and compete. Technology has improved customer service, built trust, and created higher returns on investment. The future of banking lies in IT decentralization and deglobalization, which offer vast opportunities for effective customer service, timely product management, faster service delivery, information and risk management. The chapter covers IT infrastructure and decentralization in the Indian context, highlighting the paradigm shift and opportunities for financial institutions. Decentralizing IT can bring innovation, transformation, and customer agility, making traditional banking a competitor in the race. The chapter highlights the past, present, and future of IT decentralization in the Indian banking industry, emphasizing the role of new technologies like AI, blockchain in automation, integration, and global financial sector growth.

DOI: 10.4018/979-8-3693-3253-5.ch010

INTRODUCTION

The banking sector is currently experiencing a significant transformation characterized by a dynamic interaction between conventional and digital methods. Both traditional banking, which prioritizes personalization, and digital banking, which prioritizes product simplicity, has a shared reliance on technology. The authors would like to state the coverage (scope) and the methodology used in framing this study. While this chapter will emphasize on the fundamental differences between traditional and digital banking, it will also highlight the emphasis on personal relationships in banking and of the product centric approach used in digital banking. In spite of these disparities, research indicates that technology serves as an indispensable conduit, facilitating the survival, competitiveness, and market penetration of conventional banks. In this article, we explore the ways in which technology has enabled banks to improve customer service, and thus the overall experience of their clients. Technology adoption promotes confidence and yields a significant return on investment. The discourse further encompasses the pivotal significance of information management, risk assessment, and the efficiency and convenience of service provision in influencing consumer contentment. This study would also cover the future of the banking business and how IT decentralization and deglobalization will play a big part in that. This chapter talks about the chances that financial institutions have ahead of them and stresses the importance of finding a balance between old-fashioned values and new technologies. A conceptual information on Indian banking sector's IT infrastructure is also highlighted here and there to look into the problems and chances banks face when they try to use autonomous IT systems. The authors conducted a thorough examination of the literature on globalization, deglobalization, and decentralization, as well as their meanings and benefits and drawbacks, trends, and recent events in the financial industry with regard to technology-driven operations. The ultimate objective of the study is to explore the transformation of banking industry from age old traditional banking to a highly decentralized digitized banking, highlighting opportunities and challenges, and the role of banks in embracing this shift. The chapter explores IT decentralization's role in fostering innovation and transformation in the financial sector, focusing on the Indian banking industry and its historical context. It also discusses the impact of emerging technologies like AI and block chain on automation and growth in the global financial sector. The chapter is meticulously crafted in terms of its intellectual and thematic elements. The writers have endeavored to sustain the readers' interest by avoiding an excessive focus on data and instead emphasizing the pertinent findings derived from the literature review and data analysis.

Traditional vs. Digital

Here is a concise explanation of the distinctions between traditional and digital in the context of banking:

1. Personal Relationships: Traditional banks have traditionally established trust by direct, in person encounters. Customers would physically visit nearby branches and interact with bank personnel to access a range of services. Today, we call it as relationship banking, which is characterized by the provision of personalized services tailored to individual financial needs, goals, and preferences.
2. Branch Networks: Traditional banks allocate significant resources to establish and maintain physical branch networks. India, for instance, witnessed a substantial increase in branches from 8321 in 1969 to 162904 in 2023 as mentioned in an RBI report (Business Line, 2023).

The report published by RBI in 2022 showed the Branch network and ATMs of selected banks by the end of March 2023 as follows:

3. Human Interaction: Traditional banking heavily relies on human interactions as a crucial component. Customers frequently seek guidance from bankers regarding financial matters, such as loan applications and intricate transactions. Individualized customer service cultivates loyalty, leading clients to frequently establish enduring ties with their nearby bank.
4. Documentation: Conventional banking transactions frequently necessitate substantial paperwork and documentation. This encompasses face-to-face account initiation, loan requests, and various other financial procedures.
5. Regulatory Compliance: Traditional banks encounter rigorous regulatory obligations, namely pertaining to customer authentication and adherence to anti-money laundering (AML) and know your customer (KYC) standards.

While the above points highlight the physical appeal of Traditional banking, the Digital mode has the following key features:

1. Technology Integration: Digital banks utilize technology to offer a smooth and effective customer experience. Customers can access services around the clock using online banking platforms, Smartphone apps and web-based interfaces.
2. Automation: Automation is a fundamental characteristic of digital banking. Automated systems frequently handle routine transactions, account administration, and customer assistance, thereby minimizing the necessity for manual involvement.

Figure 1. Details of branches and ATMs

Sl No.	Name of the Bank	Branches					ATMs and CRMs		
		Rural	Semi-urban	Urban	Metropolitan	Total	On-site	Off-site	Total
1	2	3	4	5	6	7	8	9	10
	Public Sector Banks	29,006	23,232	16,114	16,052	84,404	78,777	59,646	1,38,423
1	Bank of Baroda	2,568	2,067	1,473	1,780	8,188	8,786	2,615	11,401
2	Bank of India	1,867	1,467	822	932	5,088	5,325	2,889	8,214
3	Bank of Maharashtra	606	698	478	619	2,200	1,902	423	2,325
4	Canara Bank	3,061	2,737	1,989	1,923	9,700	8,098	4,032	12,130
5	Central Bank of India	1,696	1,330	772	795	4,493	2,609	326	2,935
6	Indian Bank	1,962	1,517	1,165	1,140	5,784	4,338	591	4,929
7	Indian Overseas Bank	904	961	653	684	3,202	2,783	693	3,476
8	Punjab and Sind Bank	673	281	362	321	1,637	814	21	835
9	Punjab National Bank	3,891	2,449	1,998	1,728	10,066	8,196	4,702	12,898
10	State Bank of India	8,041	6,516	4,022	3,827	22,406	25,682	39,945	65,627
11	UCO Bank	1,115	869	629	587	3,190	2,202	219	2,421
12	Union Bank of India	2,842	2,460	1,751	1,817	8,870	8,042	3,190	11,232

3. Mobile Banking Usage: Mobile banking has experienced a worldwide surge in popularity. As of 2021, the global Smartphone user base exceeds 3.8 billion individuals, leading to the extensive integration (James, 2018) of mobile banking applications.
4. Data Analytics: Digital banks employ data analytics to comprehend consumer behavior, preferences, and requirements. By utilizing data, this method enables customized product suggestions and focused marketing tactics.
5. Global Accessibility: Digital banking allows users to access their accounts and conduct transactions from any location worldwide, regardless of geographical limitations. This is especially advantageous for persons leading a cosmopolitan lifestyle.
6. Fintech Collaboration: Digital banks frequently engage in collaborations with fintech startups to augment their range of services. This collaboration results in the development of cutting edge financial solutions, such as digital wallets, rob advisors, and peertopeer lending platforms.
7. Cyber security Measures: Given the growing dependence on digital platforms, ensuring cybersecurity is of utmost importance. Digital banks allocate substantial resources to implement and maintain strong cyber security protocols in order to safeguard consumer data and uphold the reliability of online transactions.

Current Global Trends in the Banking Industry: A General Observation

1. Hybrid Models: Numerous conventional banks are embracing hybrid models, which merge the personalized approach of traditional banking with the efficiency of digital services. This exemplifies a worldwide pattern in which banks strive to offer a smooth and integrated omnichannel experience. Regulatory technology, sometimes known as RegTech, is gaining significance in the banking industry, encompassing both traditional and digital banks. It facilitates the optimization of compliance procedures, simplifying the adherence of banks to intricate regulatory mandates.
2. Open Banking Initiatives: Open banking, the practice of banks granting access to their data to external developers, is gaining worldwide momentum. This promotes innovation by enabling the integration of third-party applications and services with banks, thereby offering customers a wider array of financial instruments. The present chapter digs more of this aspect in the upcoming section.
3. The emergence of challenger banks, which are totally digital and often target certain niche markets, has been observed on a global scale. These banks disrupt conventional institutions by providing cutting edge services, frequently with reduced fees and improved customer experiences.
4. Several banks are currently investigating the incorporation of block chain technology and crypto currencies into their operations. The objective is to improve security, decrease transaction expenses, and take advantage of the increasing popularity of digital assets. More of this will be discussed in the coming sections.
    i) Technology a boon to Banking: Decentralizing is a self-regulating system that functions without an organized center or authority. In terms of banking, it completely negates the interference of the third party between two clients and ensures the smooth functioning of the transaction process with the help of agreements directly via computers and the internet. The chapter shall encompass the technology behind working of decentralized banking such as Block Chain, Smart Contracts and P2P systems
        a) Block chain Technology- Block chain technology is a chronological database used in ledger transactions and decentralized banks. It maintains transparency and control over

data, allowing users to view and control it without middlemen. The data is immutable, meaning it cannot be altered or reversed. When banks choose block chain technology, it causes debate about how this new technology can change the way standard banks work. The banking system is in danger because of many things, such as a decentralized system with no middlemen and groups that can't be trusted (Tanveer Kajla, 2022). This structured storage and transparency are key to the success of decentralized banking, ensuring secure transactions and transparency.

b) Smart Contracts- Block chain-based programs ensure smooth agreement initiation and completion, providing clients with better understanding of terms. Smart contracts in decentralized banks display terms transparently, controlled by lines of code. These processes, without middlemen, ensure smooth borrowing and lending across borders, allowing for transparent transactions..

c) P2P Systems- Peer to Peer (P2P) is the foundation of Decentralized Banks, enabling direct fund transactions without intermediaries. This system provides services like payment processing, buyer-seller information, and quality assurance, allowing clients to make independent financial decisions. Some services do not require transaction fees, promoting collective collaboration.

d) Virtual Assistants- In addition to all the above new technologies, mobile apps are changing the banking style altogether: The advent of mobile banking applications has brought about a significant paradigm shift in the realm of customer service. With more than 60% of the global population possessing a mobile phone by 2021, these applications provide banking services in a convenient and accessible manner. Digital banking platforms offer consumers access to their accounts and services continuously. This facilitates the ability of clients to oversee their financial matters, conduct transactions, and request support without hindrance, thereby augmenting overall consumer contentment. Then, there is Chat bots and Virtual Assistants: Banks are progressively adopting AIdriven chat bots and virtual assistants to deliver immediate replies to consumer inquiries. By handling routine inquiries, these technologies enable human agents to concentrate on more intricate matters.

Observe the following Infographics on Chatbot Adoption in Indian banking sector.

Chatbots can converse through text or voices and the above infographics as availed from RBI Progress report clearly highlighted that 11 out of 12 PSBs and 15 out of 21 PVBs had adopted the use of Chatbots in some or the other form. The charts also show the rising number and percentage of participation of banks in using the Chatbots.

Banks are also employing data analytics to facilitate personalization by acquiring valuable insights pertaining to consumer inclinations, actions, and requirements. This facilitates customized customer experiences, targeted marketing, and personalized product recommendations, thereby nurturing a sense of individualized service. As far as security issues are concerned, the consumer experience is optimized through the use of biometric authentication methods, including facial and fingerprint recognition. By utilizing biometric scans, users are able to log in to their accounts and authorize transactions, thereby reducing the need for conventional passwords. The utilization of automation tools empowers customers to effortlessly check their account balance, and notifications, transaction alerts, and budget monitoring are automated functions that give clients an up-to-date information on their financial transactions.

Figure 2. Showing ChatBot adoption

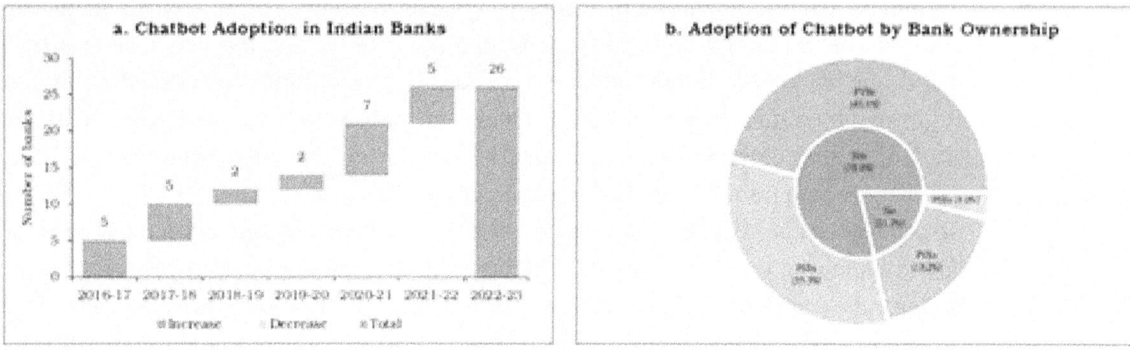

Figure 3. ChatBot usage in banking

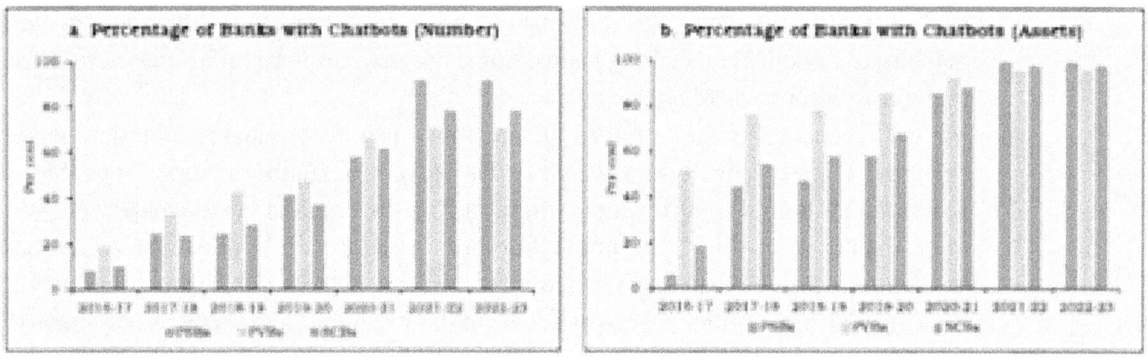

Today, banks are also offering Video banking services to enable clients to engage in live conversations with bankers. To mention few latest advances is that of Real-time transaction surveillance that is facilitated by technology in order to detect fraudulent activities and enhance security. Customers can receive automated alerts in the event of any suspicious activities, thereby implementing a proactive security strategy. Electronic signatures and digital documentation facilitates the streamlining of various processes, including account openings, loan applications, and other transaction related activities. By minimizing the amount of documentation, speeding up the processing times has taken banking industry to the next level in its operational efficiency.

The authors would be failing in their duty if the mention of Block chain and RS is not done here. The potential of block chain technology to improve banking transaction security and transparency has been found to be a valuable invention or addition to banking industry. The decentralized architecture of the system mitigates the potential for fraudulent activities, thereby instilling greater confidence among consumers. Augmented Reality (AR) and Virtual Reality (VR) have been experimented by some institutions in an effort to develop immersive banking experience..

Deglobalisation, Decentralization, and Banking

Globalization of finance can help the economy grow, but only if the market and financial system are strong. But as a result of globalization, financial crises and their consequences have spread around the world. As economies became more connected, the 2008 crisis hurt all of them, even those with strong banking systems. One reason for this is that making a country's finances stronger comes with a lot of financial threats. This means that financial deglobalization can be good for countries (Deniz SEVİNÇ, 2023) (Kose, 2009). They can speed up their economic growth by keeping their capital accounts closed and keep their finances stable by holding on to savings.

The process of deglobalization is making countries less connected and dependent on each other, especially when it comes to trade and economic ties. It means moving away from the globalized economic system, in which trade, investment, and the flow of goods, services, and cash connect countries very closely. Deglobalization can show up in many forms, such as trade hurdles, tariffs, and other protectionist measures that limit the amount of trade between countries. Also, foreign supply chains might need to be looked at again, and economic activities might shift toward being more local or regional. In an article by Citi Group that once stated with facts that Deglobalisation is far from real especially on Trades (Chua, 2022). The word is just a powerful narrative but the evidences on deglobalisation has been mixed, the same article has highlighted that Covid policies have negatively impacted more than 75% of European business and investment global plans. US companies in China when surveyed showed that 44% of them had planned a delay or decrease of investments towards the year end 2022. A disruption in trades and investments like this has a consequential and immediate effect on the financial industry especially banking. The shift toward less globalization can be caused by political choices, changes in public opinion, and economic factors (Tekbas, 2021). People often do this because they want to protect domestic businesses, keep the country safe, keep jobs, and fix what they see as unfair trade imbalances. That being said, it can have both good and bad effects, based on the rules and conditions. Some say that deglobalization can make economies more independent and resilient, while others say it could hurt economic growth and unity as a whole.

Deglobalization is the process of making countries less dependent on and linked to each other in terms of trade, investment, and business. It encourages people to focus on their own country's goals and help their own businesses while getting rid of competition from other countries. Moving away from global integration and toward a more self-sufficient way of building trade and business that will last is part of the process.

Deglobalization in banking refers to a change from a globalized strategy to a more localized or regional focus in terms of operations, investments, and client relationships. This shift occurs in the banking industry. Deglobalization is driven by a number of factors, including geopolitical conflicts, trade disagreements, and a desire for stronger economic independence. For the purpose of navigating shifting political and economic contexts, financial institutions reassess their global strategies.

Deglobalized and decentralized banking are two different ideas in the world of money. Because of things like economic nationalism and geopolitical conflicts, deglobalized banking makes it less possible for banks to connect with each other around the world. It means following stricter rules, locating activities closer to home, and relying less on global financial markets. Decentralized banking, on the other hand, moves financial activities and decisions away from a central authority. Crypto currencies and block chain technology are often used to make this possible. The financial industry is flexible and can change based on economic, technical, and geopolitical factors, so both trends can exist at the same time.

Factors that are driving deglobalization:

Risk Mitigation: Deglobalization can be a response to geopolitical concerns, which reduces a bank's exposure to the possibility of disruptions in foreign markets. Evolving regulatory regimes may drive banks to prioritize home markets over international expansion in order to comply with regulatory obligations. This is because domestic markets are more lucrative than international expansion. This has implications for the banking industry, specifically with regard to localized services. The process of deglobalization compels financial institutions to concentrate on adapting their services to the specific needs of local markets. Among them are the modification of product offers, marketing methods, and consumer involvement in order to cater to the particular requirements of any given location. One way to make a bank more resistant to the effects of global economic shocks is to adopt a more localized approach. Financial institutions may be better able to weather setbacks in a single market if they diversify their operations over multiple locations.

Striking a balance between decentralization and deglobalization of information technology: There is the possibility of a synergy between deglobalization and decentralization of information technology. Technology that is decentralized has the potential to facilitate transactions that are efficient, secure, and transparent across international borders, which is in line with a more localized operational focus. In such a situation, artificial intelligence and automation will play a significant part in the future of banking. By streamlining processes, improving client experiences, and contributing to efficiency gains, these technologies are becoming increasingly important.

In the past few years, people have lost faith in the traditional banking structure. People who are clients often get caught up in a web of scams. It is precisely this situation that has made decentralised banking important. However, looking at the history of decentralisation shows that this idea is not completely new.

The system was evident in the earliest days of commerce, when transactions were conducted directly between parties. Presently, the identical notion has undergone an evolution and is being efficiently implemented in decentralized banking. The advancement of technology has significantly simplified banking transactions.

In July 2018, the decentralized bank gained notoriety when the crypto currency exchange Binance announced an investment in Founder's Bank. It arose to become the first community-owned and decentralized bank in the globe. Upon the issuance of its European Union Bank License, the organization will grant cofounder ship to all other market participants. Eventually, a block chain governance model will be implemented.

Decentralized banks operate on the principle of lending crypto currencies through the efficient utilization of block chain technology. The institution in question is devoid of intermediaries. In lieu of this, peer-to-peer services and smart contracts ensure its seamless operation. Lenders and debtors from every region of the globe are eligible to join this banking system. The only prerequisites are a mobile phone and a well-connected desktop or laptop computer with an internet connection. You are completely prepared to join a decentralized bank with these.

Features: A decentralized bank offers several key features, including transparency, accessibility, improved data quality, security, cost effectiveness, digital currency, and circulation. Transactions are conducted through computers and the internet, allowing clients to interact directly. Transactions can be initiated from anywhere, eliminating geographical barriers. Innovative technology improves data storage and quality, preventing manipulation. Clients receive complete assurance about their transactions, and processing fees are nominal or even zero. Digital currency, such as electronic money, is available for

Figure 4. Features of decentralized banking
Source: https://www.solulab.com/decentralizedbanking/

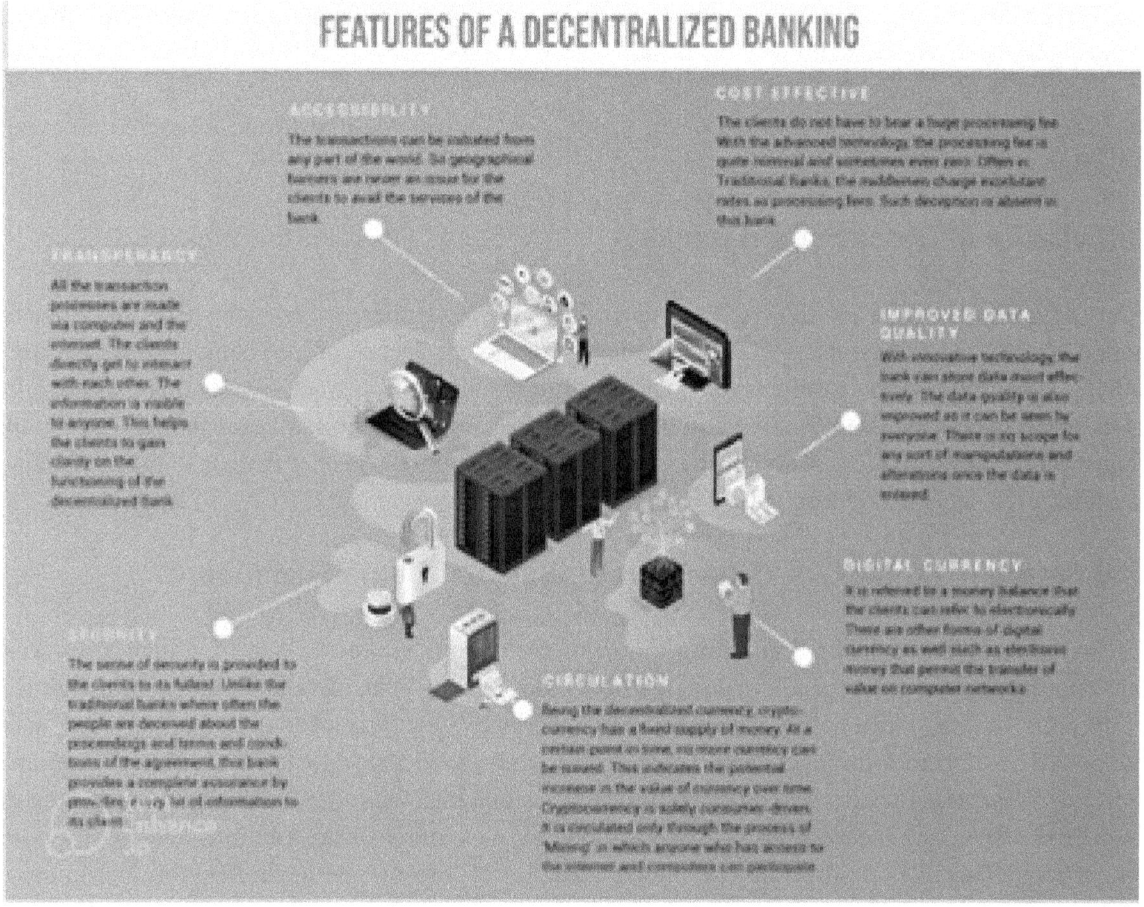

electronic transactions. Crypto currency, a decentralized currency, has a fixed supply and can only be circulated through mining, allowing anyone with internet and computer access to participate.

How is it different from Traditional banking?

The major point of difference between decentralized banks and traditional banks is the presence of middlemen in the operating process. Traditional banks cannot operate without the involvement of intermediaries. They do not provide their clients with financial freedom. Their technology is not that well advanced to ensure the democratization of the financial systems. Whereas, in a decentralized bank, a sense of lucidity and transparency remains because of the lack of intermediaries.

How has this benefitted the users?

Decentralized banks have revolutionized the lending process by eliminating geographical barriers and allowing clients to initiate transactions from anywhere. These banks provide full freedom to clients, as there are no middlemen and no one can influence their decisions. Transactions and agreement terms are transparent, ensuring clients feel secure. There are no meetings for loan approval or disapproval, and the sanctioning process is fast and easy. Automated financial history tracking is eliminated, and transaction fees are nominal or even zero, making the process even more beneficial for customers. Decentralized banking aims to generate trust, foster an open culture, and give people control over their money. It reduces the risk of systemic failure, as seen with the rise of digital currencies and user confidence. Decentralized banking counters the fading trust in central banks and government schemes, restoring the bond people share with the banking sector. It also allows people from all over the world to work incoherently, promoting economic development. Furthermore, decentralized banks provide users with knowledge about investment and lending processes, allowing them to choose their currency and maintain control over their finances.

Drawbacks of Decentralized Banks

Every coin has two sides and this banking is no exception. While there are so many benefits associated with it, there are certain cons as well that need to be discussed. Decentralized banking lacks oversight and monitoring authorities to address client errors. Middlemen provide guidance, but this is a core pillar of its success. Decentralized banking also poses challenges for regulators and legal enforcement, unlike centralized banks that offer clear paths for clients to take action. This lack of oversight and interference can hinder the success of decentralized banking.

The Future of Banking in IT Decentralization and Deglobalisation

Decentralization and deglobalization of information technology are the keys to the future of banking. Distributing control and decision-making authority throughout a business is an essential component of decentralization, which helps to develop agility and innovation. Deglobalization, on the other hand, (Kilic, 2015) refers to a shift away from a global focus and toward a local focus, hence lowering reliance on foreign markets. The next section examines the ways in which these developments are reshaping the landscape of banking, hence offering opportunities for customer-centric solutions and locally based innovations. Thus, Decentralization and deglobalization of information technology are the future of banking. The term "decentralization" in the banking industry (Lamba, 2021) is defined as it follows: In the banking industry, decentralization refers to the practice of dispersing control, decision making abilities, and operational procedures among multiple levels of the company. Block chain is a system that decentralizes ledgers, and it is at the forefront of decentralization in information technology. It also eliminates the requirement for middlemen by providing records of transactions that are safe, transparent, and impossible to alter. The implementation of decentralized information technology infrastructure in the context of Indian banking faces a number of particular problems. Frameworks for regulatory compliance, cultural aspects to take into account, and the requirement for interoperability with existing systems are all important concerns.

INDIAN BANKING INDUSTRY SCENARIO

Glaring Issues

1. The current state of the information technology infrastructure in Indian banking:
    a. Legacy Systems: A significant number of Indian banks employ legacy information technology systems that have been in operation for a number of years. When it comes to the quick

changes that are occurring in the modern financial industry, these systems frequently lack the flexibility and agility that are required.

b. Core Banking Systems: Core banking systems in India are essential to the management of operations; nevertheless, the shift to systems that are more modular and decentralized is a process that is taking place gradually.
c. Compliance with Regulations: The Reserve Bank of India (RBI) has severe regulatory standards for information technology infrastructure in order to guarantee the safety and reliability of financial systems.

2. Opportunities for Decentralized Systems in Indian Banking
    a. Financial Inclusion: Decentralized systems have the potential to make a contribution to the concept of financial inclusion by delivering banking services to places that are underserved and remote. One example of a technology that can assist safe and transparent transactions is block chain, which can be used in regions with poor infrastructure.
    b. Efficiency Gains: The implementation of decentralized systems has the potential to result in increased operational efficiencies, decreased transaction costs, and enhanced overall service delivery.
3. Techno Initiatives in Indian Banking and other related issues:
    a. Block chain Pilots: Block chain pilot projects for a variety of applications have been launched by a number of Indian institutions. Trade finance, supply chain finance, and transfers of money across international borders are all examples of this. Utilizing the decentralized nature of block chain technology in order to achieve better efficiency and transparency is the overarching goal.
    b. Partnerships with Fintech Companies: Collaboration with Fintech Companies For the purpose of improving their information technology infrastructure, Indian banks are increasingly working together with fintech startups. Partnerships in the financial technology industry have the potential to bring forward innovative solutions, such as apps for decentralized finance (DeFi) and digital identification solutions.
    c. Digital India Campaign as Government Initiatives - As part of its Digital India plan, the Indian government is working to encourage the widespread adoption of digital technologies across all industries, including banking. The implementation of these programs includes the promotion of digital literacy, the enhancement of internet infrastructure, and the facilitation of the transition to decentralized infrastructure.
4. Customer Centric Focus: The banking industry in India is undergoing a digital transition, with a particular emphasis on providing services that are centered on the client. Customers are able to exercise a greater degree of control over their financial transactions and data when decentralized solutions are utilized into the equation.
5. Future Hybrid Models& Hubs of innovation: In the future, the information technology infrastructure of Indian banks may incorporate hybrid models that combine parts of decentralized systems with those of their existing systems. This makes it possible to use the benefits of new technology while simultaneously allowing for a gradual transition. A number of Indian financial institutions are constructing innovation hubs in order to investigate and deploy new technology. In addition to collaborating with fintech companies and conducting experiments with decentralized solutions, these centers are primarily concerned with research and development.
6. Obstacles to Overcoming When Implementing Decentralized Information Technology Systems:

a. Interoperability: It is a very difficult task to integrate decentralized systems with preexisting infrastructure and to guarantee that interoperability is carried out without any interruptions. Careful planning is required in order to accommodate the coexistence of new and ancient systems.
b. Concerns Regarding Security: Decentralized systems require stringent security measures. The preservation of data privacy, the defense against cyber threats, and the adherence to regulatory standards are all essential requirements to take into consideration.
c. The implications for costs: As a result of the transition to decentralized information technology infrastructure, there may be large upfront expenses associated with the adoption of technology, training, and system integration.

7. Regulatory Considerations: As a way to make sure that banks follow a risk-based approach to IT and cyber security, the Reserve Bank of India (RBI) also gives advice on how to use new technologies. These standards must be followed at all times for any autonomous IT projects. New changes show that localizing data is becoming more important. For example, Indian regulators now require data to be stored within the country's borders. For decentralized systems that are stored in the cloud, this fact means something different.

The implementation of decentralized information technology infrastructure in the banking sector of India is fraught with difficulties, but it also has the potential to bring about considerable improvements in terms of efficiency, financial inclusion, and customer centric services. Banks that are navigating this transformative path must take into consideration a number of important factors, including regulatory compliance, partnership with fintech companies, and a gradual shift.

Challenges From Users' Perspectives

Several studies have shown that users express confidence in utilizing technology in banking say ATMs; however a notable proportion holds divergent opinions regarding the usage of phone banking. Although ATMs are widely used and easy to operate, phone banking lacks popularity and user-friendliness. Customers frequently encounter network or server issues, resulting in feelings of unease and concern. For instance, in the event that funds are debited from their account, they may need to contact customer service centers in order to retrieve the amount. This can lead to the loss of educational, commercial, or promotional opportunities. Banks should prioritize enhancing the user-friendliness and accessibility of phone banking services to cater to the needs of its customers. In addition, it is imperative to identify long-term resolutions for the recurring network and server issues. Establishing a robust infrastructure, particularly in remote regions, is essential for delivering uninterrupted services to customers while minimizing any potential disturbance. The authors would coin this as Self confidence factor for IT acceptance in banking. A survey conducted by the authors on 625 rural respondents in India indicated that individuals residing in rural areas exhibit a notable absence of endorsement for utilizing mobile phones for banking purposes, as evidenced by 367 respondents concurring that it is arduous. However, 209 individuals express dissent, indicating a lack of confidence in utilizing ICT even after observing others' usage. 81.30% of the participants believe that there is a moderate amount of assistance available, but it has to be increased. This is because there is still a difference between the bank's support system and the desired level of adoption of ICT. The authors would coin this as Bank support factor for accepting IT in banking. And finally the risk factor the survey revealed that fear and discomfort in using technology in banking often prevent knowledgeable users from embracing it. This fear stems from concerns about risk and costs. Banks must address this fear by providing risk-free, cost-effective techno services. Customers should not feel cheated, but rather have positive experiences with these services, reinforcing their continued use of technology. This will help rural people become more open to technology (Divya Prabhu, 2021). Thus, the authors would hereby suggest that Banks as a strong financial institution that connects economy to the lives of individual should look into tackling the Confidence, Support and Risk factor underlying the usage of IT in banking from the customers' perspective.

Paradigm Shift and Opportunities for FinTech: A Medium for Banking Decentralisation

India's economic and banking related policies are designed to integrate all banking services in a single area, making them accessible to all individuals regardless of their income, location, occupation, and other factors. In this environment, the decentralization of banking has emerged as the means by which a country might attain social equity and justice, even in terms of economic position. India's digital public goods and infrastructure surpass those of other nations (Dr GS Vijaya, 2023). This achievement has been made feasible by the integration of IT services and financial services by fintech enterprises. Consequently, this has led to the decentralisation of several banking operations. This can result in deglobalization. Adaptation is required of organizations that provide financial services as a result of the paradigm change in banking. Case studies based on real world activities highlight the elements that influence customers' acceptance of information technology. These factors include aversion to risk, resistance to change, and the role that banking institutions play in facilitating the shift. Within the context of the installation of decentralized information technology systems, this section offers a detailed understanding of the dynamics that must be considered.

1. An Acceleration of Digital Transformation: Companies that provide financial services around the world are continuing to speed up their attempts to convert their operations digitally by implementing cutting edge technology such as artificial intelligence, machine learning, and data analytics. There are chances for improved customer experiences, creative product offers, and efficient processes that are made possible by the shift toward digitalization for businesses.
2. The emergence of neobanks and the disruption caused by advancements in financial technology: Increasingly, traditional financial institutions are being challenged by neobanks and fintech companies, which are gaining popularity. Significant money has been secured by a number of fintech startups, which is an indication that investors are confident in the disruptive potential of these companies. Fintech organizations might examine the possibility of forming alliances with traditional financial institutions, invest in their own digital capabilities, or adopt solutions powered by fintech in order to maintain their competitive edge.
3. The Integration of Block chain Technology and Crypto currency: Large financial organizations are investigating the possibility of integrating block chain technology and crypto currencies into their operations. Services related to crypto currencies are being provided to customers by certain establishments. At the same time that they are contemplating the incorporation of digital assets into their service offerings, organizations that provide financial services can investigate block chain technology in order to make international transactions more effective (Macknight, 2022). At this time, the nation's central bank should intervene and anchor digital currency systems for monetary

and financial stability, managing them consistently and ingeniously, as the level of innovation observed in the digital asset world is crucial for the nation's banking watchdog to effectively monitor.

4. Remote Work and Digital Collaboration: As a result of the COVID19 epidemic, remote work trends have accelerated, which has an effect on the way financial services companies function. In order to keep operations running smoothly, digital collaboration tools and technology have gradually become indispensable. It is possible for businesses to improve their capabilities for working remotely, make investments in cyber security measures, and investigate technologies that allow virtual cooperation and communication (Manfredi-Sánchez, 2021 Retrieved from https://ijoc.org/index.php). At this point, the authors would like to discuss how the banking sector's adoption of digital payment systems has helped to strengthen the Indian economy by contributing to improved digital transactions made for payments of various kinds, such as RTGS, NEFT, UPI, Debit or Credit card, etc sourced from RBI.

This tremendous growth has, no doubt, facilitated ease of living, financial inclusion and growth of business and economy. This has been made possible due to the digital public infrastructure and digital public goods that are well developed in our country.

5. The application of artificial intelligence in risk management and fraud detection: The use of artificial intelligence in risk management and fraud detection is making progress. The use of artificial intelligence algorithms by financial institutions to examine massive datasets in order to identify potential dangers and fraudulent activity is becoming increasingly common. It is possible to increase risk assessment, expand fraud detection skills, and strengthen overall cyber security by implementing solutions that are driven by artificial intelligence. AI has been increasing used by the banks today for Asset management, algorithmic trading, credit underwriting, and to offer block chain based financial services as per a (RBI, 2022-23) recent report published by RBI.
6. Regulatory Technology (RegTech): There is still a significant emphasis placed on obeying regulations. The use of RegTech solutions is becoming increasingly popular as businesses look for effective ways to handle regulatory environments that are both complex and constantly changing. Companies that provide financial services have the opportunity to make investments in RegTech solutions in order to simplify compliance procedures, improve reporting accuracy, and reduce regulatory risks.

Table 1. Digital transactions per financial year

Financial Year	Total no of Digital Transactions (in Crore)	Volume of Digital Transactions (in Lakh cr)
2017-18	2071	1962
2018-19	3134	2482
2019-20	4572	2953
2020-21	5554	3000
2021-22	8840	3021
2022-23	9192**	2050**

Source: pib.gov.in/PressReleaseIframePage.aspx?PRID=1897272
**Data up to November 2022 only.

7. Initiatives for Financial Inclusion: An increasing number of people are beginning to acknowledge the significance of financial inclusion. Efforts are being made by governments and financial institutions to broaden access to financial services for people that do not have bank accounts or have inadequate bank accounts. In order to provide underprivileged populations with financial services that are both accessible and inexpensive, businesses have the opportunity to engage in initiatives to expand financial inclusion by utilizing technology.

The following section would highlight in support of the few of the above points.

The Chart below (Chart No. 01) shows the AI adoption index of banks in India, a clear growth picture is visible. A textual analysis performed on the annual reports of Indian banks also revealed that glossaries related to AI have been increasingly used in the last few years. The Chart num below is taken from a study report conducted by RBI

How About Innovating and Transforming Through IT Decentralization??

Decentralized information technology encourages creativity by providing employees at all levels with the ability to contribute to the production of ideas and the resolution of problems. This section investigates the ways in which the aforementioned change in organizational structure makes it possible to make transformative projects possible, such as the creation of new products, services, and experiences for customers. At the same time, it highlights the significance of leadership roles in the process of driving innovation within the financial industry.

Figure 5. Chart showing bank group wise AI adoption index

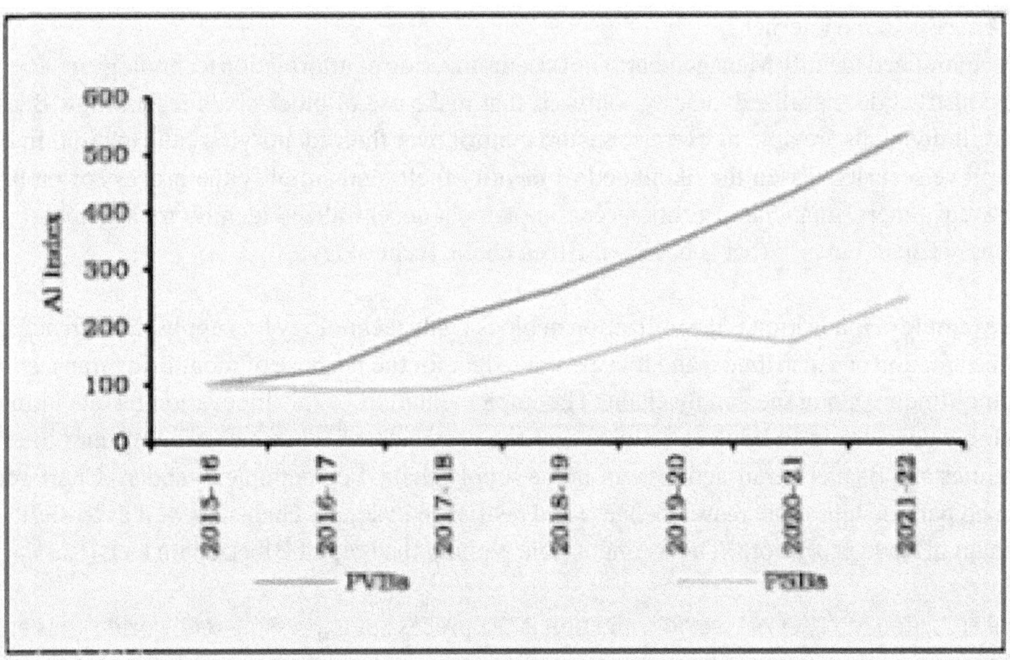

Figure 6. Chart showing AI related keyword mentions in bank reports

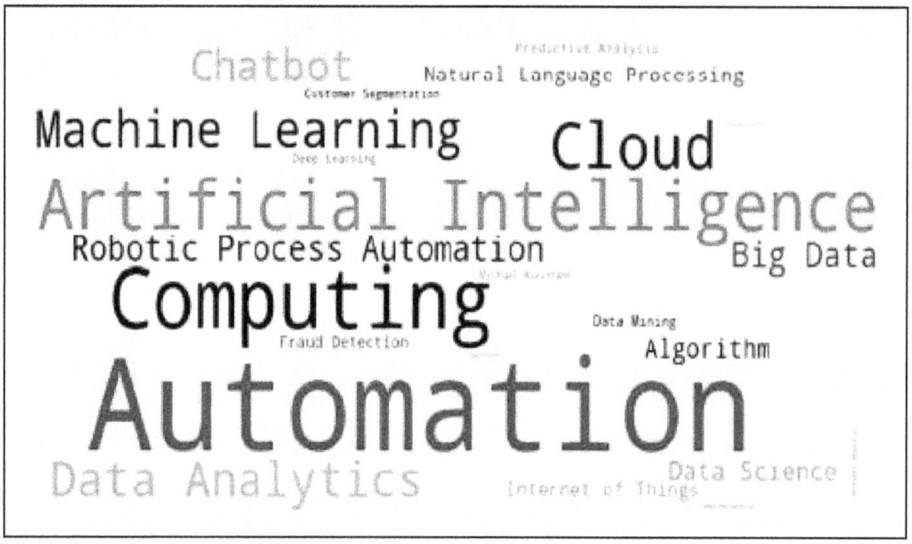

Source: RBI staff compilation using annual reports of banks.

1. Decentralized Finance (often known as "DeFi"): One significant example of innovation in banking caused by the decentralization of information technology is DeFi. Through the use of block chain technology, smart contracts make it possible to provide a variety of financial services, including lending, borrowing, and decentralized exchanges, without the need for traditional intermediaries. Through the provision of financial services that are more inclusive, transparent, and efficient, DeFi presents a challenge to the traditional banking model. These services are available to anybody who has access to the internet.
2. Decentralized Identity Management: The decentralization of information technology makes it easier to construct decentralized identity solutions that make use of block chain technology. Because of this, individuals are able to exercise secure control over their identifying information. In order to improve security, lessen the likelihood of identity theft, and simplify the process of on boarding new customers, financial institutions can implement decentralized identity management.
3. Supply Chain Finance that is based on Block chain Technology:

One example of innovation is the utilization of block chain technology for supply chain finance, which entails the creation of a distributed and transparent ledger for the purpose of monitoring transactions and facilitating funding along the supply chain. The implementation of this innovation results in increased efficiency, a decrease in fraudulent activity, and the provision of real-time visibility into the flow of commodities and financial transactions within the supply chain. For example, Standard Chartered Bank has formed partnerships to increase openness and resilience in supply chains, as well as to digitalize the entire chain of trade paperwork. This is impossible without the help of Block chain tech (Russia, 2018).

4. Tokenization of Assets: Asset tokenization is the process of expressing real world assets as digital tokens on a block chain. This concept enables fractional ownership and facilitates the efficient

transfer of ownership. Tokenization can be utilized by financial institutions for a wide variety of assets, including as real estate, art, or even corporate shares. This allows for historically illiquid assets to become more accessible and hence more tradable.

5. Smart Contracts for Automated Processes: Smart contracts, which are contracts that automatically execute themselves and have the terms of the agreement written directly into code, make it possible to automate a variety of financial procedures. Automation using smart contracts eliminates the need for middlemen, speeds up transaction processes, and guarantees the fulfillment of established conditions without the need for human interaction.
6. Payments and remittances that are not made across borders:

The decentralization of information technology, in particular through block chain, is bringing about innovation in international payments by offering an option that is quicker, more cost-effective, and even more transparent. Banks have the ability to embrace decentralized systems in order to enhance international transactions, hence reducing the associated settlement times and costs that are connected with traditional correspondent banking. From the Indian banking perspective, it is noteworthy to state that by the end of December 2022, the payment and settlement systems in the country has hugely extended and expanded enabling more billers to include in the cycle. The RBI's Digital Payment Index has substantially reached close to 400 by Mar 2023 from its base of 100 points in March 2018, which is a gap of merely 5 years. The following infographics are shared for the information of the readers on tremendous growth in the Index and the Value and Volume of the Digital Payment System in India.

Figure 7. RBI's digital payment index trend

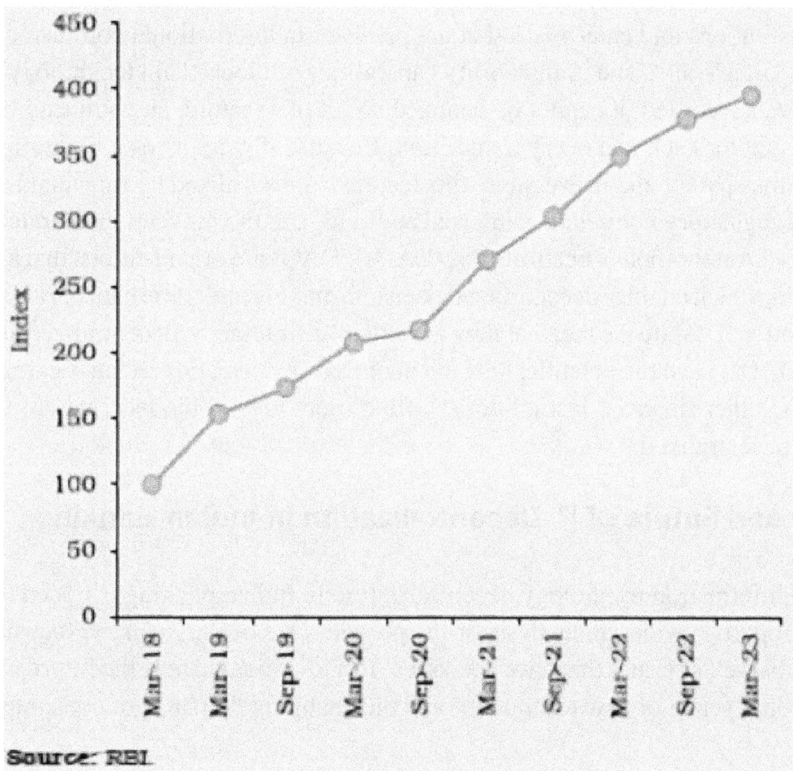

Figure 8. RBI's digital payment index trend: Value and volume of the payment system

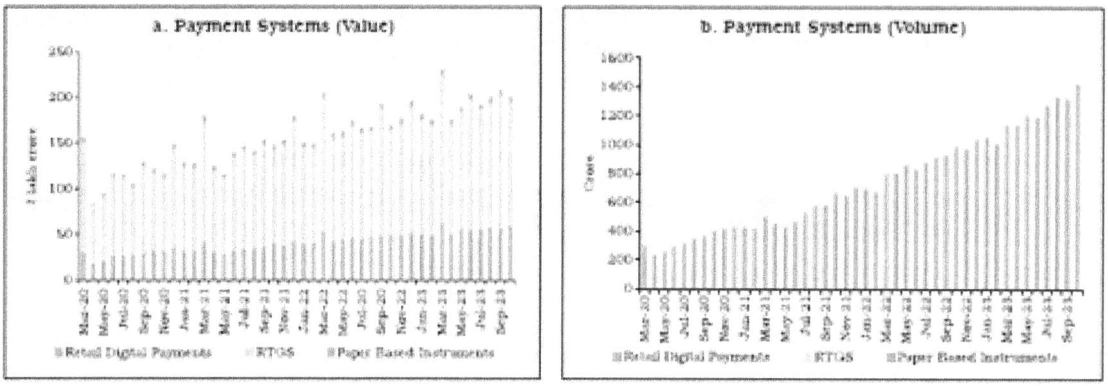

7. Collaboration with Fin techs and Startups: Banks are partnering with fin techs and startups to utilize their new solutions, especially those based on decentralized technologies. These relationships help to cultivate a culture of innovation within traditional banks, which enables these institutions to incorporate novel technology and maintain their competitive edge in a financial world that is always shifting.
8. Trade finance that is built on block chain technology is an example of innovation. Block chain technology makes it possible to create ledgers that are both decentralized and resistant to tampering, making it a perfect choice for trade finance. Smart contracts, which are used to automate operations like letters of credit, are included in this description. The transformation of trade finance procedures results in increased efficiency, transparency, and reduced risk of fraud, which is beneficial to both financial institutions and enterprises that are involved in international commerce.
9. Immutable Audit Trails: The immutability capabilities of block chain technology ensure that once a transaction is recorded, it cannot be changed. With this feature, an audit trail that cannot be altered is created for each and every transaction. Because it guarantees a record of all transactions that is both transparent and irreversible, this feature can be utilized by financial institutions for the purposes of regulatory compliance, internal auditing, and the prevention of fraud.
10. Decentralized Autonomous Organizations (DAOs): DAOs are organizations that are run by code on a block chain, which enables decentralized decision-making and governance. A DAO is an example of an innovation. Despite the fact that they are still in their infancy, decentralized autonomous organizations (DAOs) have the potential to bring about a transformation in the organizational structure of banks and other financial institutions, shifting them toward models that are more community driven and decentralized.

Present Past and Future of IT Decentralization in Indian Banking

The evolution of information technology decentralization in Indian banking is traced through a historical review. This report provides an analysis of the present state of the industry, focusing on successful implementations as well as issues that have been seen. It is investigated how the future will unfold, taking into account the emergence of new technology and the changing demands of consumers.

1. Olden days (not golden days for banking)

Legacy Systems: When Indian banks were in the past, they relied significantly on legacy information technology systems that were centralized and frequently complicated. However, these systems lacked the flexibility that was necessary to accommodate the rapid changes that were occurring in the banking industry.

Traditional Banking and Financial Practices: It was common practice to engage in face-to-face interactions and use physical branch networks. Traditional banking operations were not as widely connected with digital technology and the emphasis was placed on providing services in person.

Limited Adoption of Technological Developments: The early adoption of technology in the Indian banking industry was mostly concentrated on core banking solutions, automated teller machines, and fundamental internet banking services. The idea of a decentralized information technology infrastructure was not widely implemented.

2. The Now of banking

Adoption of Digital Channels: In order to provide consumers with services that are more easily available and convenient, financial institutions have progressively used digital channels, such as mobile applications and online banking.

Block chain Pilots: A number of Indian financial institutions have been conducting block chain pilot projects in order to investigate the possibilities that decentralized ledger technology has for enhancing the transparency, security, and efficiency of a variety of banking procedures.

Financial Technology Collaborations: Banks are now able to incorporate novel solutions, including those that are based on decentralized technologies, into their operations as a result of the increased prevalence of collaboration with tech businesses that specialize in financial technology.

Focus on Regulatory Matters: Regulatory organizations, in particular the Reserve Bank of India (RBI), have been putting a strong emphasis on the significance of having an information technology infrastructure that is both secure and efficient. The emphasis placed on ensuring compliance with regulations has had an impact on the implementation of new technology.

3. The Tomorrow

   a. Decentralized Finance (popularly known as "DeFi"): A greater study of decentralized finance (DeFi) solutions, which offer financial services without the use of traditional intermediaries, may be in store for the future of information technology (IT) decentralization in Indian banking. The baby steps in the technological development in India perhaps began with the gradual adaption and usage of Debit and Credit cards and the availability of ATMs. Before we could guess what could be the future of technology usage in Banking, the authors here would like to mention that the country has witnessed a tremendous growth or variation in the total number of Credit cards, Debit cards and the ATMs between 16-19%, 3-5% and 3-6% respectively (RBI, 2022-23) between two financial years as reported by RBI in its bulletin having a gap of nine months only (as it was provisionally published with data upto November 2022).

b. Expanded Integration of Block chain Technology: Not only in pilot projects, but also in practical applications like supply chain finance, trade finance, and secure data management, it is anticipated that block chain technology will play a more prominent role in the future.
c. Models that are Hybrid: One of the possible future scenarios involves the implementation of hybrid models, which are characterized by the coexistence of traditional centralized systems with decentralized alternatives. While taking use of the benefits that new technologies have to offer, this strategy makes it possible to make a smooth shift.
d. An Acceleration of Collaboration: In order to take advantage of innovative solutions, financial institutions are expected to continue their collaboration with FinTech startups and technology companies. Collaborations may extend to include decentralized identity management, services driven by artificial intelligence, and applications based on block chain technology.
e. The importance of putting the customer first: It is expected that future innovations will place a priority on improving the experiences of customers. It is possible for decentralized systems to contribute to the provision of personalized services, the acceleration of transactions, and an overall improvement in consumer satisfaction.
f. The Development of the Regulatory Framework: It is anticipated that the regulatory framework will develop in order to give clear standards for the incorporation of decentralized technologies into the banking sector as the use of these technologies becomes more widespread. This is going to be extremely important in order to guarantee trust, compliance, and security.
g. Financial inclusion initiatives: It is possible that decentralized systems could play a part in improving efforts to achieve financial inclusion by reaching out to groups that are not banked or under banked through the use of digital solutions that are both innovative and accessible.
h. Technologies shaping the future: AI, Block chain and 5G

i) Artificial Intelligence (AI):

Chat bots and Customer Service: Customers' Needs- In the field of customer service, artificial intelligence is presently being utilized for chat bots and virtual assistants, which provide immediate solutions to inquiries. In the future, advanced artificial intelligence algorithms will make it possible to process more natural language, which will result in interactions with customers that are both more sophisticated and more effective.

Individualized Banking: Artificial intelligence analyzes customer data to provide individualized product suggestions and targeted marketing. Today, AI is used to provide personalized banking services. In the future, a significant part in the creation of highly personalized banking experiences, the anticipation of consumer needs, and the provision of tailored financial advice will be played by artificial intelligence.

Risk Management: Artificial intelligence is utilized for all aspects of risk management, including credit scoring, fraud detection, and risk analysis today. Tomorrow, Enhanced artificial intelligence algorithms will provide risk evaluations that are more accurate, which will contribute to proactive risk management and the avoidance of fraud.

Automation: Artificial intelligence automates routine procedures, thereby lowering the amount of manual labor required in areas such as account management and transaction monitoring. When artificial intelligence is more widely integrated, it will result in the automation of processes from beginning to end, simplifying complicated financial activities and increasing overall efficiency in the future days to come.

ii) Block chain Technology – Today & Tomorrow:

Cross Border Payments: In order to improve both the speed and transparency of cross border payments, certain financial institutions are utilizing block chain technology. A worldwide network that facilitates transactions across borders that are both quicker and more cost-effective will be created if block chain technology is adopted more widely in the later days.

Digital Identity Management: Block chain technology offers a framework that is both decentralized and secure for the management of digital identities. The future will see the widespread use of blockchain based digital IDs, which will protect individuals' privacy and lessen the likelihood of identity theft.

iii) The Development of 5G Technology:

Real-time financial services, improved mobile banking experiences, and Internet of Things applications will all be supported by the introduction of 5G infrastructure, which will enable quicker and more dependable communication. In the future, quantum computing will be more prevalent. There is a possibility that quantum computing may revolutionize data encryption and solve difficult financial modeling problems, which will have an effect on the management of risk and security in the banking industry. When it comes to biometric authentication, the future is bright. For the purpose of providing a secure and convenient authentication method for banking transactions, biometric technology such as fingerprint scanning and facial recognition will eventually become the norm. Internet of Things (IoT) devices will play a role in the collection of data for tailored banking services, and smart gadgets will make it possible to conduct financial transactions in a way that is both seamless and secure. Processing power at the device level will be increased through the use of cutting edge computing, which will make it possible for real-time banking applications to process data more quickly and securely.

Collectively, these technologies contribute to the creation of banking experiences that are more efficient, safe, and personalized for clients as well as for financial institutions.

Time to Deglobalise Indian Banking

Deglobalization in the banking industry refers to reducing reliance on global markets and institutions, focusing on more localized or regional approaches. In the Indian context, the banking industry can undergo deglobalization through various strategies and initiatives:

1. Localized Operations: Banks can focus on expanding their branch networks within specific regions, catering to the needs of local communities. This allows for a more personalized approach to banking services.
2. Regional Collaboration: Collaboration with other regional banks or financial institutions can strengthen the regional banking ecosystem. Shared infrastructure and services can enhance efficiency and reduce dependence on global players.
3. Promotion of Financial Inclusion: Banks can play a crucial role in promoting financial inclusion by extending their services to rural and underserved areas. This ensures that a larger segment of the population participates in the formal banking system.

4. Emphasis on Local Economic Development: Banks can actively support and invest in local businesses and industries. This approach fosters economic growth at the local level and reduces reliance on global markets.
5. Digital Transformation for Local Markets: Implementing digital platforms and solutions tailored to local needs can contribute to deglobalization. This includes digital banking services, payment solutions, and other technology driven offerings designed for the Indian market. In India, there is this concept of DBU i.e. Digital Banking Units, for instance. In total there are 75 DBUs in the country which is a specialized fixed point business unit or hub with the necessary digital infrastructure to offer digital banking products and services and to support current digital financial products and services, both for self-service and with help. While states like Goa, Chandigarh, Arunachal is allotted only 1 DBU, larger States like TamilNadu, Uttar Pradesh, and Karnataka are allotted 4 DBUs as per data retrieved from RBI.
6. Regulatory Measures: Regulatory bodies, such as the Reserve Bank of India (RBI), can encourage banks to comply with regulations that prioritize domestic interests over global expansion. This may involve revisiting licensing and regulatory frameworks to align with deglobalization objectives.
7. Encouraging Regional Innovation Hubs via Fintech Collaboration: Establishing regional innovation hubs that foster collaboration between banks and local fintech companies can drive innovation tailored to the specific needs of the Indian market.
8. Diversification of Investments by focusing on Domestic Investments: Banks can prioritize investments in domestic projects and infrastructure, reducing exposure to international markets. This could include investments in sectors such as agriculture, manufacturing, and technology.
9. Promoting Regional Trade Finance: Banks can support and facilitate regional trade by establishing and promoting trade finance solutions that cater to local businesses. This approach strengthens regional economic ties.
10. Cyber security Measures: Implementing robust cyber security measures, including data localization, ensures that sensitive financial data remains within the country, reducing dependence on global data centers.
11. Customer Education and Engagement: Banks can contribute to deglobalization by actively engaging in initiatives to enhance financial literacy at the local level. Educated consumers make informed choices that align with local economic interests.
12. Balancing Global Integration with Local Priorities: While focusing on deglobalization, banks can strategically engage in global partnerships that align with local interests without compromising the overall objective.

It's important to note that a balanced approach is crucial, ensuring that deglobalization efforts do not hinder the industry's ability to leverage global best practices, technological advancements, and necessary collaborations for sustainable growth. Additionally, regulatory support and clear policy frameworks play a vital role in shaping the direction of the banking industry in India.

Before We Conclude

In conclusion, there is a positive outlook towards deglobalization and the adoption of decentralized information technology in the banking sector in India. Several factors contribute to this optimistic perspective:

1. Localized Resilience: Deglobalization fosters a more localized and resilient banking ecosystem in India. By focusing on regional strengths, banks can better withstand global economic uncertainties and tailor their services to the unique needs of local communities.
2. Financial Inclusion: The shift towards decentralized technology allows for innovative solutions that promote financial inclusion. By leveraging technology, banks can reach unbanked and underserved populations, providing them with access to essential financial services.
3. Efficiency and Innovation: Decentralized information technology, including block chain and AI, brings efficiency and innovation to banking operations. Smart contracts, automated processes, and advanced analytics contribute to streamlined services, reducing costs and enhancing customer experiences.
4. Cyber security and Data Sovereignty: Embracing decentralized systems enhances cyber security measures, ensuring the protection of sensitive financial data. Data localization practices contribute to better control over data sovereignty, addressing concerns related to privacy and security.
5. Regional Economic Development: Deglobalization encourages banks to actively participate in regional economic development. By supporting local businesses, investing in regional projects, and fostering innovation hubs, banks contribute to the growth of the communities they serve.
6. Adaptability to Regulatory Frameworks: A positive outlook is reinforced by the adaptability of the banking industry to evolving regulatory frameworks. Regulatory support for deglobalization initiatives provides a clear path for banks to align with local priorities while ensuring compliance. At the World Economic Forum in Davos, people are talking about "deglobalization" and "reshoring" or "near-shoring," (Chiu, 2022) which means bringing goods back to the country where they are made. In the context of our study, the deglobalisation would also have an impact on the flow of money between countries, the challenge is not only to develop a regulatory framework that is compatible with the international financial or banking system but also making it an adaptable globally is a formidable task.
7. Customer Centric Services: Decentralized technology enables banks to offer more customer centric services. Personalized experiences, efficient digital channels, and tailored financial products contribute to higher customer satisfaction and engagement.
8. Balanced Global Integration: While embracing deglobalization, the positive outlook is reinforced by the industry's ability to strike a balance between local priorities and global integration (Reenu Kumari, 2023). Strategic global partnerships that align with local interests can contribute to a well-rounded and sustainable banking landscape.
9. Innovation in Financial Inclusion: The positive outlook is further amplified by the potential for innovative financial inclusion initiatives. By leveraging decentralized technologies, banks can extend their services to remote areas, empowering individuals and contributing to broader economic development.

India's Path to Inclusive Growth-Oriented Deglobalisation Through Decentralized Banking

In their voluminous research-supported writings, global financial specialists have identified the transition from globalization to deglobalization across all sectors as a result of trade wars between China and the United States, supply chain disruptions caused by the COVID-19 pandemic (Antràs, 2020), and the recent Ukraine conflict, among other factors. All of these megatrends are causing an explosion in international finance, investment, and trade, which is reshaping the banking system in a way that is inextricably linked to information technology. Thus, India can't be left behind in this race. To achieve inclusive growth in India's banking sector, it is crucial to focus on local economic growth, financial inclusion, and giving power to underprivileged groups. To achieve this, there are several key strategies that can be implemented.

1. Focus on Financial Inclusion: Expand branch networks to reach rural and underserved areas, promoting digital financial services and microfinance and small loans.
2. Support small businesses in your area: Provide easy access to credit and specialized financial products for MSMEs, encouraging them to start their own businesses and supporting the local economy.
3. Implement community banking initiatives and cooperative banks: Encourage community-based cooperative banks and credit societies to grow and better meet the needs of their local communities.
4. Implement financial literacy programs: Start educational initiatives to help people learn about banking services, financial planning, and investment possibilities.
5. Align banking strategies with regional economic hubs: Align banking strategies with plans for regional economic growth, helping businesses important to each region's economic strengths.
6. Promote socially responsible banking: Adopt Environmental, Social, and Governance (ESG) practices and push for ethical banking practices that prioritize customer health and communities over short-term profits.
7. Work with the government to make policy changes that support growth for everyone, promote responsible banks, and create a good regulatory environment.
8. Utilize new technologies: Utilize fintech solutions to make financial goods accessible to everyone, such as digital wallets, micro-insurance, and investment platforms.
9. Encourage employee diversity and inclusion: Encourage diversity in banks to reflect the areas they serve and provide cultural sensitivity training for bank staff.
10. Measure and report social impact: Create and use metrics to track how banking activities affect society, with a focus on positive results for people, companies, and communities.

Deglobalization is not just a shrinking back from international integration, but can be viewed as shifting economies from the output for export to the local market (Bello, 2004). Currently, banks in the country have the capability to utilize the technological infrastructure of the business environment to offer smooth banking services and enable this shift or movement to local markets as mentioned in the earlier paragraphs. These services include credit, deposits, various types of loans (such as vehicle and personal loans), government schemes like MUDRA loans, mandatory payments, tax filings, as well as a wide range of basic, advanced, and general financial services. All of these services can be accessed easily through the user's smart phones or applications, or through net banking. Therefore, financial operations can be expediently and effectively executed without the need for staff or any intermediary. This has established a potent and advantageous method for banks to distribute their operations and services in a decentralized manner, regardless of the user's location, position, or time of application. Information technology has facilitated the decentralization of banking. Consequently, this has facilitated the rapid circulation of money around the entire globe. India is a densely populated nation. Nevertheless, the majority of the population is predominantly rural or semi-urban, with a low to moderate economic status. The majority of individuals operating small, medium, and indigenous businesses including roadside shops play a significant role in contributing a relatively modest yet substantial portion of the overall money circulation throughout the country. Although the wealthy or affluent individuals and high-income groups often allocate their funds towards foreign brands and products, resulting in a decrease in domestic wealth and repatriation of capital, it is ultimately the low-income groups in the country who truly contribute and distribute capital within India.

In meeting the challenges arising from a hostile global environment, the Central bank of the country should not lose sight of the task of improving the long-term potential of our country. The future tasks to be addressed includes Green transition, reconfiguration of supply chains and logistics, production-linked incentive schemes, digital banking and financial services, and innovative technologies (Dayal, 2022) that can offer immense opportunities for the Indian economy to go global but remain local.

By working together, banking organizations, government agencies, and local communities can achieve inclusive growth in the banking sector through deglobalization. In this chapter, the writers have attempted to conduct a conceptual analysis of the past, present, and future of the Indian banking sector in the context of IT deglobalization. The analysis indicates a bright outlook for achieving IT decentralization in banking and, as a result, financial deglobalisation of the country via the banking pillar. The chapter has emphasized the notion that by deglobalizing the IT and financial industries, the country may achieve inclusive growth. The authors argue that a country might effectively disengage from global trade while still maintaining connections through a decentralized banking system facilitated by an efficient information technology platform. When banks successfully decentralize their services using IT, a significant portion of their operation becomes automated, resulting in cost savings, time efficiency, and speedier movement of capital domestically and internationally. Therefore, this chapter has emphasized the significance of banks in the process of deglobalization and in ensuring a country's long-term economic strength.

REFERENCES

Al, R. N. (2019). Financial deglobalisation in banking? *Journal of International Money and Finance*, *94*, 116–131. doi:10.1016/j.jimonfin.2019.01.011

Antràs, P. (2020). *De-globalisation? Global value chains in the post-COVID-19 age*. National Bureau of Economic Research Working Paper 28115. https://www.nber.org/papers/w28115

Bello, W. (2004). *Deglobalization: Ideas for a new world economy*. Zed Books.

Bremus, F., & Fratzscher, M. (2015). Drivers of structural change in cross-border banking since the global financial crisis. *Journal of International Money and Finance*, *52*, 32–59. doi:10.1016/j.jimonfin.2014.11.012

Chiu, I. H.-Y. (2022). Prospects for international financial deglobalisation and its potential impact on international financial regulation. *Law and Financial Markets Review, 16*, 1-19. . doi:10.1080/17521440.2023.2204991

Chua, J. (2022, Oct 13). *citigroup.com*. Retrieved January 16, 2024, from Global Insights: https://www.citigroup.com/global/insights/global-insights/deglobalization-is-a-convenient-narrative-but-the-data-doesn-t-support-it

Dayal, Y. (2022). *RBI Press Release 2022-2023/1319*. www.rbi.org.in

Deniz, Sevinç, A. P. (2023). How does deglobalization affect economic growth? *Journal of Research in Economics, Politics & Finance*, *8*(1), 1–19.

Divya Prabhu, D. G. (2021). *Shodhganga Inflibnet.* Retrieved Dec 2023, from http://hdl.handle.net/10603/346873

Dr, G. S., & Vijaya, D. P. (2023). Financial Inclusion – an Assessment of Progress via Rural Banking System and Way Forward. In The Sustainable Fintech Revolution. IGI Global.

Giannetti, M., & Laeven, L. (2012). The flight home effect: Evidence from the syndicated loan market during financial crises. *Journal of Financial Economics*, *104*(1), 23–43. doi:10.1016/j.jfineco.2011.12.006

James, H. (2018). Deglobalization: The Rise of Disembedded Unilateralism. *Annual Review of Financial Economics*, *10*(1), 219–237. doi:10.1146/annurev-financial-110217-022625

Kilic, C. (2015). Effects of globalization on economic growth: Panel data analysis for developing countries. *Economic Insights - Trends and Challenges*, *67*(1), 1–11.

Kose, M. P., Prasad, E., Rogoff, K., & Wei, S.-J. (2009). Financial globalization: A reappraisal. *IMF Staff Papers*, *56*(1), 8–62. doi:10.1057/imfsp.2008.36

Lamba, H. (2021). Deglobalization: Review and research future agenda using PAMO framework. In J. Paul and S. Dhir (Eds.), Globalization, deglobalization, and new paradigms in business. doi:10.1007/978-3-030-81584-4_1

Macknight, J. (2022, April 11). *Is this the beginning of a deglobalisation trend?* Retrieved January 2024, from TheBanker.com: https://www.thebanker.com/Is-this-the-beginning-of-a-deglobalisation-trend-1649681217

Manfredi-Sánchez, J. (2021). Deglobalization and public diplomacy. *International Journal of Communication*, *15*, 905–926. https://ijoc.org/index.php

MicroSave. (2022, Sept). Retrieved 2023, from microsave.net: https://www.microsave.net/library/

RBI. (2022-23). *Trend and Progress of Banking in India.* New Delhi: RBI.

Reenu Kumari, A. S. (2023). The Transformation of Global Trade in a New World: Deglobalization and Its Risk in International Trade Post COVID-19. In The Transformation of Global Trade in a New World. IGI.

Russia, B. o. (2018). Globalisation and deglobalisation. *BIS Papers*, (100), 291–310.

Tanveer Kajla, V. S. (2022). Blockchain in the Banking Sector: Revolution or Digital Disruption? In *Applications, Challenges, and Opportunities of Blockchain Technology in Banking and Insurance*. IGI Global. doi:10.4018/978-1-6684-4133-6.ch008

Tekbas, M. (2021). The impact of economic, social and political globalization on economic growth: Evidence from BRICS-T countries. *Gaziantep University Journal of Social Sciences*, *20*(1), 57–71. doi:10.21547/jss.796472

The NPCI. (2023). Retrieved May 2023, from npci.org: https://www.npci.org.in/statistics

Usha, S. D. J. (2014). Role of information technology in the globalized banking sector. *Shanlax International Journal of Arts, Science & Humanities, 1*(4), 107-113.

Chapter 11
Ethical and Social Consequences of Accelerated Technology Adoption

Anuja Shukla
Jaipuria Institute of Management, Noida, India

Poornima Jirli
https://orcid.org/0009-0000-3796-6974
SSBM, India

ABSTRACT

This study examines the ethical and social consequences of the accelerated adoption of new technologies. An empirical approach is employed to explore the impacts of rapid technological integration on societal norms, ethical considerations, and individual behaviours. Responses from 305 participants are analysed using partial least squares structural equation modeling (PLS-SEM), focusing on perceived usefulness, ease of use, relative advantage, personal innovativeness, and fear of missing out (FOMO). The findings unveil intricate interactions between technological advancements and ethical-social dynamics, underscoring challenges and opportunities. Critical insights are offered by this study for policymakers, technology developers, and society at large, aiming to encourage a more ethically informed and socially conscious approach to technology adoption.

1. INTRODUCTION

In the contemporary era, embracing technology, especially artificial intelligence (AI), marks a pivotal shift in individual and organisational growth (Castells, 2009). The AI sector's valuation, reaching a staggering $207 billion in 2023, indicates its profound influence across diverse domains, including commerce and healthcare, reflecting the sector's potential for transformation and investor confidence in its ongoing innovation (Statista, 2023). However, the rapid adoption of Generative AI, surpassing historical, technological milestones like smartphones and tablets, introduces a spectrum of ethical and

DOI: 10.4018/979-8-3693-3253-5.ch011

social quandaries alongside its opportunities (Dignum, 2018). AI's deep integration into everyday life, while demonstrating its utility, also brings critical ethical considerations to the forefront. Technologies such as ChatGPT risk mirroring and perpetuating societal biases, necessitating an in-depth exploration of their wider ramifications, as these biases and AI-influenced decisions could profoundly impact the ethical and social landscape (Hurlburt, 2023; UNESCO, 2023; Schlagwein & Willcocks, 2023).

The rapid rate of AI's incorporation highlights the urgency for its development and utilisation to be guided by a responsible ethos. The diffusion of traditional media was shaped by socioeconomic elements and infrastructure availability (Chaffee & Metzger, 2001). This evolution presents new challenges in a hastened context in the modern digital age. Despite democratising technology access through the internet and smartphones, disparities persist, with a significant global population still excluded due to various barriers (Warschauer, 2004). This context sets the stage for this study, which aims to dissect the factors contributing to the soaring adoption rates of technology in recent times while critically examining the ethical and social repercussions stemming from this accelerated technology adoption.

As we navigate the complexities of technological integration, we must discern both the social and ethical repercussions. The shift in trust dynamics, information overload, and altered social behaviours underscore the profound social changes we are witnessing (Danaher & Sætra, 2022; Lee & See, 2004). Ethically, the erosion of truth, redistribution of power, and impacts on human identity present challenges that require careful consideration and ethical foresight (Horwich, 2006; Danaher, 2020). These transformations necessitate a holistic understanding of how technology reshapes our societal fabric and ethical principles.

2. LITERATURE REVIEW

The credit for understanding the adoption of technology historically is attributed to the theory of diffusion of innovation by Everett M. Rogers (1963), which explains how new ideas and technologies spread within a social system (Davis, 1989). Over the years, this theory has been applied across various fields to study the adoption of new technologies.

Initially proposed in 1962, Rogers's diffusion of innovation theory aims to elucidate how new ideas, practices, or technologies are spread and eventually integrated into social systems (Rogers, 1962). The theory highlights the significance of communication channels, social networks, and adopter categories in adoption (Davis, 1989). Additionally, several factors contribute to adoption, including relative advantage, compatibility, complexity, trialability, and observability (Davis, 1989). In 1962, sociologist Everett Rogers consolidated these studies into a series of generalisations forming the foundation of the current diffusion model, utilised globally in industrialised and developing countries. The diffusion process is often represented by "bell-shaped" curves (Rogers, 1962).

In the diffusion curve depicted in Figure 1, five segments represent distinct groups within a social system: innovators, early adopters, early majority, late majority, and laggards (Rogers, 1962). It is noted that innovators are characterised by high education levels, a propensity for risk-taking, access to funding, specialised skills for understanding and applying technical knowledge, and exposure to diverse information sources. The diffusion of innovation within a social system is a temporal process (Rogers, 1962). Drawing upon Lazarsfeld's (1963) theories, Rogers highlights the importance of personal influence over media influence in this process (Lazarsfeld & Menzel, 1963). The diffusion process is significantly shaped by private information and media influences, yet it is inseparable from the social environment in

Figure 1. Theory of diffusion
(Source: Rogers, 1962)

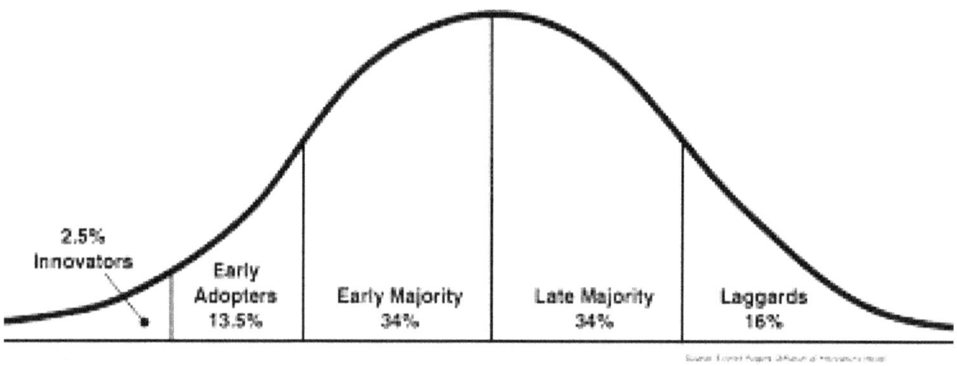

which it occurs. Factors such as prevailing social norms, the role of opinion leaders, and the presence of change agents and aides critically influence the rate of diffusion of an innovation. Initially formulated in the early 20th century, the diffusion model originated from the industrialised Western world, reflecting its specific social, cultural, economic, and communicational contexts. Given the rapid technology adoption rates in contemporary times, there is a recognised need to reassess the Rogers diffusion model.

The adoption and usage of technology have been extensively researched across various contexts, including individual users (Thong et al., 2006), groups (Sarker et al., 2005; Sia et al., 2002), organisations (Sia et al., 2004; Thong, 1999), and multiple levels (Magni et al., 2012; Maruping & Magni, 2012; Yen et al., 2015). A significant increase in the diffusion of new digital technologies has been observed over the past decade (OCED, 2021). The emergence of these technologies is anticipated to lead to the decline of several sectors and firms, altering their organisational structures, competitive strategies, and customer interactions (Iansiti & Lakhani, 2020; DeStefano et al., 2020; Agrawal et al., 2018). This convergence of complementary digital technologies is often called "Industry 4.0" (Bradford & Florin, 2003). The literature identifies Nine technologies as Next Generation Disruptive Technologies (NGDTs), including IoT, mobile devices, big data, cloud computing, artificial intelligence, blockchain, virtual/augmented reality, robotics, and 3D printing (OCED, 2021). In the latter half of the 20th century, digital technologies have progressively replaced analogue technologies. NGDTs enable more effective generation and utilisation of data, thus facilitating process automation and aiding firms in making more accurate decisions (Agrawal et al., 2018; Cho et al., 2023). Despite widespread study, most current research examines these NGDTs in isolation (DeStefano et al., 2020).

It has been observed that certain firms exhibit a higher propensity for technology adoption compared to others, according to firm-level data (Cho et al., 2023). This tendency is particularly notable with traditional digital technologies, which are biased towards more prominent firms. Larger firms possessing more knowledge-based capital and accumulated technology find it easier to adopt emerging technologies (Agrawal et al., 2018). Large firms' adoption of modern technologies may have initiated dynamics that benefit a select group of leading frontier firms, thereby exacerbating disparities across businesses (Brynjolfsson & McAfee, 2014). Additionally, Enterprise Resource Planning (ERP) software is advantageous for large multinational corporations, enabling them to efficiently coordinate and capitalise on extensive production networks (OCED, 2021; Cho et al., 2023).

It is theorised that younger firms, often equipped with newer assets, are more likely to be compatible with recent technologies (Cho et al., 2023). Young firms experiencing rapid growth are more likely to own a website (Agrawal et al., 2018; Castells, 2009). Additionally, these firms adopt certain types of hardware more readily than their older counterparts (DeStefano et al., 2020). Furthermore, young firms have the potential to adopt emerging technologies even while they are still relatively small (Bradford & Florin, 2003; Cho et al., 2023).

Frontier digital technologies are increasingly being diffused as firms become more reliant on assets such as data, highlighting the significance of intangible investments in these technologies (DeStefano et al., 2020). Lopez-Acevedo and Griffith (2002) have noted that foreign-owned firms typically exhibit higher productivity and more effective use of technology (DeStefano et al., 2020). Multinational corporations, maintaining stringent productivity and production standards, are often inclined to share new technologies readily (Thong et al., 2006; Iansiti & Lakhani, 2020).

Bedué and Fritzsche (2022) state that artificial intelligence (AI) represents one of the most rapidly advancing areas in the field of technology, encompassing a diverse array of applications in sectors such as finance, healthcare, the internet, and marketing. Due to its profound impact on society, organisations, and individuals, artificial intelligence has been a subject of extensive discussion across various research domains (Agrawal et al., 2018). Within information systems, scholars have shown a particular interest in examining the acceptance and adoption of artificial intelligence (AI) technologies (Brynjolfsson & McAfee, 2014).

The utilisation of AI technologies presents several potential benefits, yet the extent of AI's capabilities has not been fully realised in current implementations (Bedué & Fritzsche, 2022). Adopting AI at an individual level is influenced by various factors, including trust, social influence, hedonic motivation, and effort expectations (Agarwal & Prasad, 1998). Additionally, the broader socioeconomic context significantly shapes AI adoption, distinguishing it from other technological advancements (Agrawal et al., 2018; Castells, 2009). Despite acknowledging the potential and functionalities of AI, industry decision-makers face uncertainties regarding its future applications (Bengio, 2017), and there is a reliance on trustworthy sources for information about the risks and benefits associated with AI (Alutaybi, Al-Thani, McAlaney, & Ali, 2020).

In artificial intelligence, generative AI, a specialised subfield, has been developed to automate the creation of textual, visual, and musical content. This is achieved by utilising deep learning techniques to generate new outputs informed by patterns identified in training data (Goodfellow, Bengio, & Courville, 2016). Over the past decade, there has been a significant advancement in generative AI technology, exemplified by sophisticated models such as GPT-4 from OpenAI.

According to the Diffusion of Innovations (DOI) theory, the adoption of generative AI has progressed beyond the initial stage of 'innovators', typically comprising tech enthusiasts and AI researchers. It has entered the 'early adopters' phase. In this phase, business organisations increasingly implement generative AI for diverse purposes, such as content creation, chatbot development, and data analysis (Perez, 2022). Many potential adopters are currently positioned in the 'early majority' stage, awaiting further proof of the technology's effectiveness. Challenges like discrimination in AI applications, misuse of AI technologies, and concerns about AI ethics and regulatory aspects are some obstacles impeding its broader acceptance (Bengio, 2017).

Recognised as an innovative breakthrough, generative AI is distinguished by its unique attributes, notably its unpredictability and capability to produce novel outcomes (Bengio, 2017). In early adoption, generative AI models are utilised across various applications, including automated journalism and the creative arts (Knight, 2019). The role of communication channels in disseminating information about advanced artificial intelligence has been emphasised in numerous studies. Online platforms such as Medium, arXiv, and Github have played a pivotal role in enhancing awareness of generative AI within technology communities and business sectors (Santos, 2020).

The broader implementation of generative AI is currently nascent, with expectations of increased acceptance as technology develops and its societal advantages become more evident (Wirtz, Weyerer, & Geyer, 2019). The social ecosystem encompassing the diffusion of generative AI comprises various stakeholders, including developers, researchers, business entities, and end-users. These actors exhibit varying degrees of readiness for adopting advanced artificial intelligence. Within this social framework, policymakers play a crucial role in either facilitating or hindering the dissemination of this technology through their regulatory actions (Scherer, 2020).

Recent technological advancements, particularly in digital platforms and artificial intelligence-based services, have notably accelerated adoption rates. The Generative AI model, ChatGPT, exemplified this trend by attracting one million users within just five days of its launch in 2022. This rapid user acquisition contrasts with older platforms like Instagram, which took around 2.5 months to reach the same user milestone after its 2010 launch. Furthermore, traditional media platforms such as Facebook and Twitter took even longer to gather a similar number of users (Exploding Topics, 2023; The Guardian, 2023).

This trend of swift growth is also evident in the rise of social media platforms. By 2021, YouTube reported over 2 billion monthly active users, while Instagram had over one billion. The transformation in communication, information sharing, and consumption facilitated by these platforms has significantly contributed to their rapid adoption (Statista, 2021).

The quick expansion and user engagement with OpenAI further underscores the accelerated adoption of AI technologies (SimilarWeb, 2023). In this rapidly evolving landscape, factors like perceived usefulness, ease of use, relative advantage, personal innovativeness, and the fear of missing out (FOMO) are increasingly influential in the diffusion of new technologies.

The Growing Economic Footprint of AI

The economic footprint of artificial intelligence (AI) is expanding rapidly, as evidenced by critical insights from the global AI market (Statista, 2023). In 2023, the market will reach an impressive $207 billion, signifying AI's substantial influence on the global economy and its pivotal role in driving innovation across various sectors. This remarkable market valuation reflects the widespread integration of AI technologies into business operations, healthcare, finance, and consumer applications, underscoring the importance of understanding the factors influencing the adoption of such transformative technologies (Statista, 2023).

Financial commitments toward chatbot and conversational AI startups are strong indicators of the sector's significance and potential. As of 2023, leading startups in this domain have garnered impressive funding, reflecting investor confidence in their technological advancements and market potential. For instance, ASAPP leads with funding of $380 million, followed by Observe.ai at $214 million and Ada at $191 million, among others. The funding these companies have received is a testament to their business models and broader investment trends within the AI industry (refer to Figure 2).

Such funding highlights the competitive edge and innovative strides that these startups are making. With significant financial backing, these companies are well-positioned to advance the development

Figure 2. AI start-ups, 2023
Source: Statista, 2023

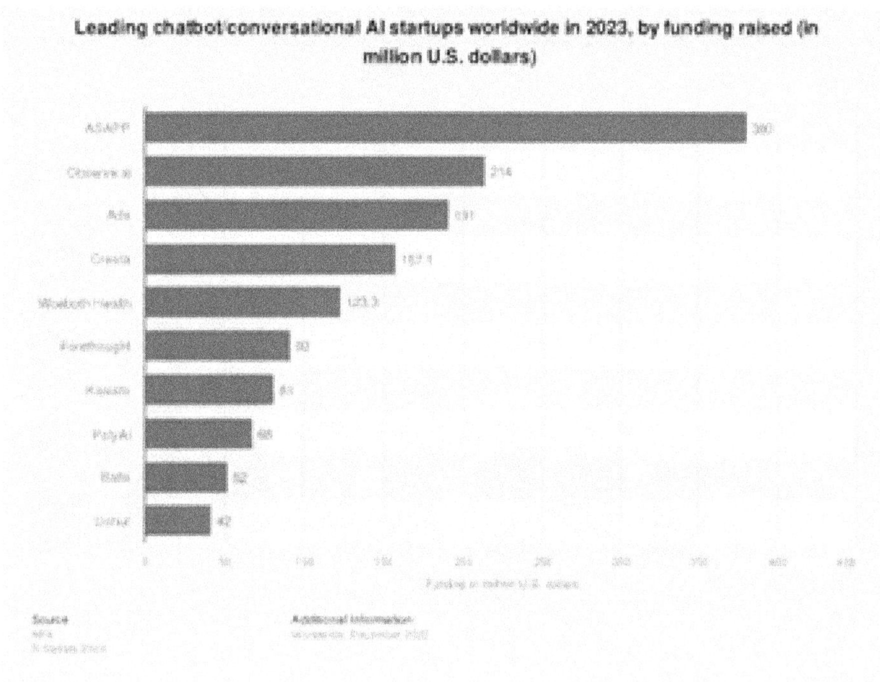

and integration of AI technologies in various customer service applications, signalling a transformative shift in how businesses interact with their clients.

In the context of technology adoption, these investments are a prelude to the broader acceptance and integration of conversational AI technologies into the mainstream market. The support from venture capital and other investment forms underscores the anticipated role of chatbots and AI in enhancing operational efficiencies and customer experiences across sectors.

Furthermore, investment in AI startups remains robust, with global funding reaching $12.1 billion in the second quarter of 2022 alone (Statista, 2023). This substantial investment underscores AI startups' vitality and growth potential and reflects investor confidence in AI as a leading sector for technological advancement and economic opportunity (Statista, 2023).

The global explainable artificial intelligence (XAI) market is experiencing significant growth, valued at $5.1 billion in 2022, with projections indicating a rise to over $24 billion by 2030 (Thormundsson, 2023) (refer to Figure 3).

Ethics

In discussing AI ethics, the UNESCO report (2023) brings attention to the ethical intricacies within artificial intelligence, notably its ability to amplify societal biases, as illustrated by gender disparities in search engine outcomes. The report raises concerns about the integration of AI in judicial systems, highlighting the potential lack of transparency and intrinsic biases that could undermine fairness and human rights (UNESCO, 2023). UNESCO advocates for stringent ethical frameworks to address the

Figure 3. AI expansion
Source: Statista,2023

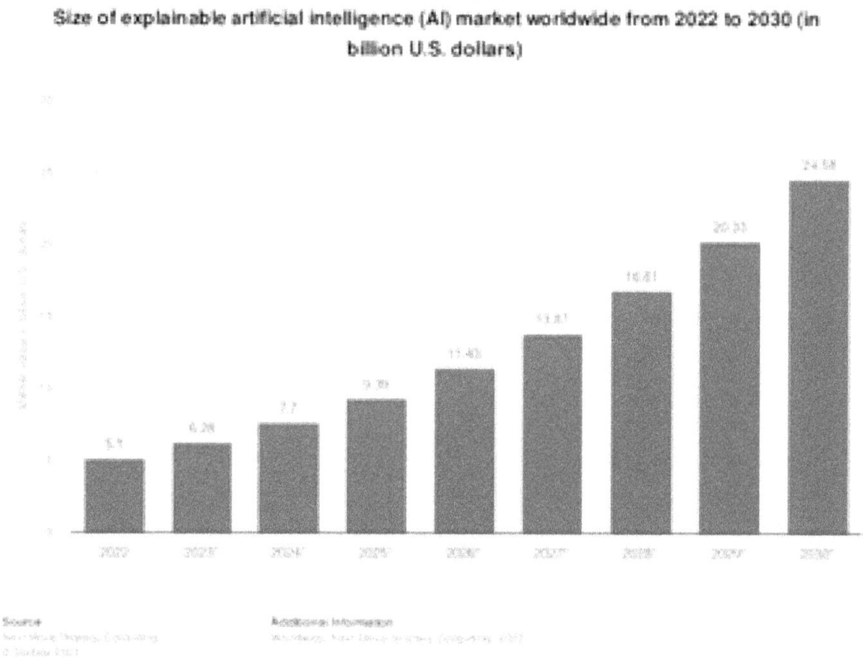

profound societal effects of AI (UNESCO, 2023). Hurlburt (2023) offers a critical perspective on AI, noting its lack of accurate intelligence attributes such as consciousness and free will, which raises questions about its ethical decision-making capabilities (Hurlburt, 2023). He identifies shortcomings in Large Language Models like GPT, particularly their failure to meet FAIR data principles, leading to possible misinformation (Hurlburt, 2023). Hurlburt also discusses the ethical complications in AI-driven content moderation, emphasising the difficulty of eliminating bias and the impact on content moderators, as well as the equity issues within the generative AI field due to high operational costs that could lead to business-induced biases (Hurlburt, 2023). Schlagwein and Willcocks (2023) explore the ethical biases embedded in AI systems, especially in generative models like ChatGPT, which often reflect the biases in their training data. This can significantly affect AI-generated content and decisions, reinforcing existing societal prejudices (Schlagwein & Willcocks, 2023). To address these challenges, Srinivasan and Parikh (2021) suggest employing generative artworks as pedagogical tools to bridge the communication gaps in AI ethics. They propose that such artworks could depict a variety of ethical viewpoints, visualise hypothetical scenarios and mismatches in AI systems, and convey non-Western perspectives, thus fostering greater comprehension and empathy among diverse AI stakeholders (Srinivasan & Parikh, 2021).

The technological shift in trust dynamics raises pivotal ethical questions. As technology, particularly AI and robotics, assumes roles traditionally held by humans, it redistributes power and accountability, creating a complex moral landscape where determining responsibility for autonomous systems' actions becomes increasingly challenging (Danaher, 2020; Levine & Schweitzer, 2015). This shift affects interpersonal relations and challenges our understanding of autonomy and self-determination (Sætra, 2021c).

Moreover, the growing difficulty in discerning truth in the digital age, exacerbated by the proliferation of misinformation, poses significant ethical concerns. The blurring of factual accuracy impacts societal discourse and decision-making, potentially leading to increased polarisation (Fallis, 2021; David, 2020). This erosion of the ethical value of truth and integrity in communications and media highlights the need for critical evaluation and ethical frameworks to navigate this 'post-truth' era (Horwich, 2006; Appiah, 2010).

Furthermore, the concept of robotomorphy, where human traits are ascribed to technology and vice versa, presents unique ethical challenges. This blurring of the lines between human and machine capabilities requires re-examining traditional moral concepts, particularly regarding autonomy, agency, and the nature of human identity in a technologically integrated society (Sætra, 2021). These evolving ethical landscapes underscore the importance of adapting ethical frameworks to account for the profound societal effects of AI and technology, ensuring that they align with values conducive to a just and equitable society.

Social Impact

Solaiman et al. (2023), for assessing the societal impacts of generative AI, underscores the need for standardised evaluation protocols. It is noted that without careful moderation, AI may reinforce societal biases and stereotypes, potentially exacerbating inequality and marginalisation issues (Solaiman et al., 2023). Furthermore, the paper articulates concerns regarding AI's influence on user autonomy and trust and the risks of centralising power through AI in authoritative domains such as surveillance and military applications (Solaiman et al., 2023).

Sætra's analysis underscores the complex societal ramifications of generative AI across different levels. At the macro level, he expresses concern over the technology's ability to undermine democratic processes by generating a profusion of political content, raising the risks of misinformation and societal polarisation (Danaher & Sætra,2022). Additionally, he notes the potential displacement of "knowledge workers," leading to changes in labour dynamics and the nature of work (Edwards,2022). Sætra also highlights the perpetuation of societal biases and discrimination by generative AI (Bender et al.,2021) and its significant contribution to environmental challenges through high energy consumption (Brevini,2021). From a meso perspective, Sætra identifies challenges generative AI poses in various professions and sectors. The technology's capability to replicate human-produced content without permission or remuneration poses ethical dilemmas (Zuboff,2019). He also notes the disproportionate impact of AI biases on marginalised communities (Bender et al.,2021).

At an individual level, Sætra raises concerns about the potential decline in cognitive skills due to over-reliance on AI for mental and creative tasks(Sætra,2019). Additionally, the increasing persuasiveness of generative AI could lead to manipulation risks (Sætra & Mills,2021). He also cautions about the possibility of AI supplanting human partners, with implications for personal relationships and social skills (Sætra,2021). Sætra emphasises the necessity of aligning generative AI's development and use with values essential for a beneficial society, including freedom, democracy, sustainability, well-being, and justice(Brey,2018). He advocates for a proactive human role in guiding and regulating generative AI to prevent adverse societal impacts (Griffy-Brown, Earp & Rosas,2018).

The transformation of trust from human entities to technological systems, as analysed by Danaher and Sætra (2022), fundamentally changes the dynamics of social relationships and dependencies. According to Lee and See (2004), this transition significantly affects how individuals interact among themselves and with technological tools, potentially paving the way for a society where technology increasingly mediates or suppresses human interactions. Moreover, the rapid expansion of digital information and the accompanying challenges in distinguishing truth profoundly affect social discourse and decision-making processes. Fallis (2021) and David (2020) note that this trend could exacerbate societal polarisation and the spread of misinformation, influencing various aspects, from political ideologies to individual beliefs. Furthermore, integrating artificial intelligence and robotics is reshaping social norms and behaviours. As Sætra (2020) points out, individuals are likely to modify their interactions to align with the capabilities and constraints of technology. This adaptation could lead to a redefinition of social etiquette and norms, reflecting the evolving landscape of human-technology interplay.

3. CONCEPTUAL MODEL AND HYPOTHESIS DEVELOPMENT

The significance of theoretical underpinnings in model development is widely acknowledged, with the understanding that various models depend on foundational theories due to the potential interconnectivity of different variables (Greenhalgh et al., 2004). The diffusion of innovations theory, formulated by Rogers, has been a pivotal tool in comprehending technology adoption. Concurrently, other models like the Technology Acceptance Model (TAM) and the Unified Theory of Acceptance and Use of Technology (UTAUT) have offered further perspectives. The TAM, proposed by Davis in 1989, underscores perceived usefulness and ease of use as crucial determinants of technology acceptance (Alutaybi, Al-Thani, McAlaney, & Ali, 2020). Integrating eight distinct models, including TAM and DOI, the UTAUT model aims to predict behaviours related to technology acceptance (Ajzen & Fishbein, 1980).

Recent scholarly efforts have been directed towards updating and reinterpreting traditional adoption theories for the digital age. Tarafdar and Vaidya (2006) highlighted the necessity to revise the Diffusion of Innovations theory, particularly regarding cloud computing adoption, to reflect the evolving nature of information technology. Consequently, the Stimulus Organism theory is utilised (Figure 4, Pavlov, 1927a). Based on Pavlov's stimulus-response framework, the process of innovation diffusion, leading to an accelerated technology adoption, could be represented as follows:

1. Stimulus (Technology): When new technologies are introduced, they act as stimuli (Pavlov, 1927a; Pavlov, 1927b).
2. Response (Adoption/Resistance): Users respond to the stimulus by adopting or resisting the technology. Several factors influence this response, such as perceived usefulness, ease of use, and previous experiences (Valente, 2012; Berwick, 2003; Venkatesh et al., 2003; Venkatesh & Davis, 2000).

3.1 Usefulness and Adoption Rate

The notion of "usefulness" has become increasingly prominent in recent studies on technology adoption. It is observed that potential users are more inclined to adopt a technology when they perceive it as advantageous for executing specific tasks or enhancing their performance (Davis, 1989; Venkatesh et al., 2003). This trend is evident across various technologies and settings, underscoring the significance of perceived usefulness as a pivotal determinant in the acceptance of technology (Valente, 2012; Berwick,

Figure 4. Conceptual model framework

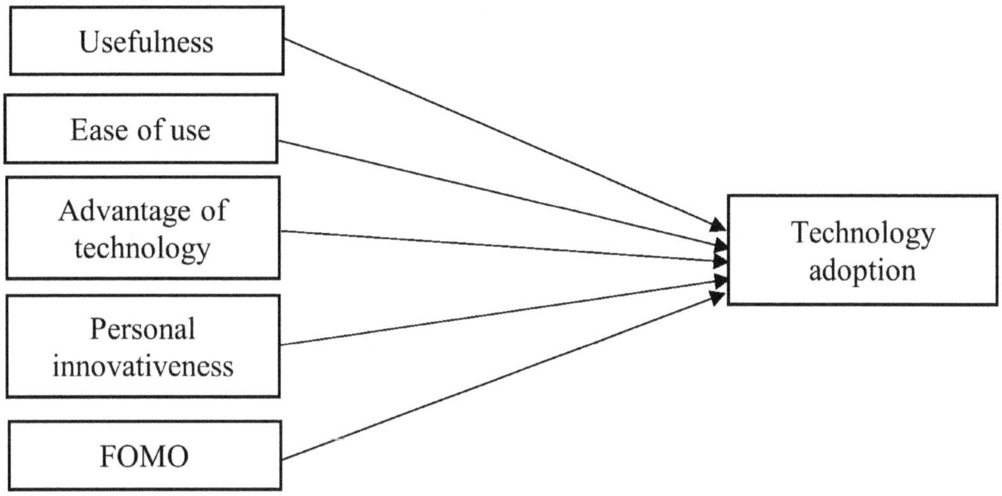

2003; Venkatesh et al., 2003; Venkatesh & Davis, 2000). Moreover, it is crucial to acknowledge that perceptions of usefulness are not isolated; they are subject to influences from multiple factors, such as an individual's technological expertise, the specific context in which the technology is used, and the inherent characteristics of the technology itself (Taylor & Todd, 1995; Chaffee & Metzger, 2001; Russell & Norvig, 2020). Grasping the nuances of how usefulness impacts technology adoption remains a crucial area of research in the digital era. This review of literature, accentuating the role of "usefulness" in the adoption of technology (Taylor & Todd, 1995; Chaffee & Metzger, 2001), leads to the formulation of the following hypothesis:

H1: The usefulness of a technology positively impacts its adoption rate.

The proposed hypothesis suggests that the perception of a technology's utility significantly influences its adoption rate. It is postulated that users are inclined to adopt a technology when they perceive it as advantageous or efficient for particular tasks. Consequently, enhancing the perceived utility of a technology is likely to impact its adoption rate positively.

3.2 Ease of Use and Adoption

The perception of a technology's "ease of use" is acknowledged as a crucial determinant of its adoption rate, akin to its practicality. The Technology Acceptance Model (TAM), as proposed by Davis (1989), suggests that a user's decision to adopt new technology is significantly influenced by its perceived ease of use and usefulness (Alutaybi, Al-Thani, McAlaney, & Ali, 2020). Consequently, user-friendly and straightforward technologies are more likely to be adopted (Venkatesh et al., 2003; Venkatesh & Davis, 2000; Venkatesh et al., 2012).

Subsequent research has consistently corroborated the impact of perceived ease of use on adopting technology (Zhou, 2011). In the context of the evolving digital landscape, the ease with which technology can be used plays a pivotal role in the diffusion of innovation. Reflecting on the literature review that underscored the significance of "usefulness" in adopting technology (Venkatesh & Davis, 2000; Venkatesh et al., 2012), a hypothesis is thus formulated.

H2: The ease of use of technology positively impacts its adoption rate.

According to this hypothesis, users are more likely to adopt technologies perceived as simple to use (Davis, 1989). Consequently, user-friendly and intuitive technologies tend to be adopted more rapidly compared to less user-friendly options. This hypothesis underscores the critical role of ease of use in facilitating technology adoption.

3.3 Advantage of Technology and Adoption Rate

It is hypothesised that a technology's perceived "advantages" are crucial in influencing its adoption rates. According to Rogers' Diffusion of Innovation Theory, potential users are more inclined to adopt new technology if they perceive it as offering superior benefits than its predecessors (Rogers, 1962). These benefits could include enhanced convenience, efficiency, cost reduction, or other advantages. Numerous studies across various technological fields have affirmed that the perceived benefits of technology significantly sway users' decisions to adopt it (Mathieson, 1991). Therefore, for effective adoption and diffusion, the perceived benefits of a technology must be identified and communicated.

H3: The advantage of a technology significantly impacts its adoption rate.

According to this hypothesis, the adoption rate of a technology is significantly impacted by its perceived benefits or advantages. It is suggested that a technology is more likely to be adopted by users when they recognise distinct advantages, such as enhanced efficiency or effectiveness, in its use (Rogers, 1962).

3.4 Personal Innovativeness and Adoption Rate

In the realm of technology adoption, "Personal Innovativeness" is defined as an individual's propensity to engage with novel technologies. According to Rogers' Diffusion of Innovation Theory, individuals with higher innovativeness are inclined to adopt new technologies earlier than their less innovative counterparts (Rogers, 1962).

Investigations undertaken by Agarwal and Prasad (1998) have corroborated that an individual's readiness to embrace new technologies is substantially influenced by their degree of innovativeness (Agarwal & Prasad, 1998). Similarly, Lu, Yao, and Yu (2005) have argued that personal innovativeness is a critical factor in accepting and utilising new technologies (Lu, Yao, & Yu, 2005). The significance of personal innovativeness in expediting the adoption of new technologies is thus emphasised. This hypothesis emerges from a synthesis of the extant literature.

H4: An individual's innovativeness positively correlates with the adoption rate.

The hypothesis suggests that the inclination of an individual towards adopting new technologies, termed personal innovativeness, may bolster the adoption rate of a technology (Thakur & Srivastava,

2014). It is posited that individuals who exhibit innovative traits are more inclined to experiment with new technologies, thereby contributing to an increased adoption rate.

3.5 Fear of Missing Out (FOMO) and Adoption Rate

Recently, the notion of "FOMO" (Fear of Missing Out) has garnered attention in the context of technology adoption. This phenomenon is characterised by individuals' apprehension that they are missing out on rewarding experiences available to others. Such fear may prompt people to adopt new technologies, particularly within social media platforms (Goodfellow, Bengio, & Courville, 2016). The potential of FOMO to considerably influence the adoption of wearable technologies has been noted. Consequently, a hypothesis has been formulated based on the literature surrounding FOMO.

H5: The fear of missing out (FOMO) significantly impacts the adoption rate.

The psychological phenomenon known as Fear of Missing Out (FOMO) is the foundation for this hypothesis. It is theorised that individuals may be compelled to adopt technology due to a fear of being left behind, significantly impacting its adoption rate (Przybylski et al., 2013).

4. RESEARCH METHODOLOGY

This research employed a descriptive study design, targeting digital users. Data was gathered from a deliberately selected sample of 380 respondents (Shukla & Mishra, 2022). The survey instruments were adapted from scales previously established in relevant literature (Table 3). Responses were quantified using a five-point Likert scale, where a score of 1 denoted "Strongly disagree" and five denoted "Strongly agree." Partial least squares structural equation modelling (PLS-SEM) was utilised for data analysis. A total of 380 responses were collected. Any incomplete reactions were excluded from the final dataset, resulting in 305 usable responses.

4. DATA ANALYSIS

Respondents' demographic characteristics, such as gender, age, and occupation, are classified. These characteristics are summarised in Table 2. Females comprise the majority of the respondents, representing 58.1%, while males account for 41.9%. Regarding age distribution, the predominant group is those aged between 18 and 29, constituting about 57.8% of the total respondents. The occupational backgrounds of the respondents are diverse, with a significant proportion being salaried employees.

5.1 Assessment of Measurement Model

The robustness of the survey was examined through Confirmatory Factor Analysis (CFA), which focused on evaluating the measurement model. This evaluation involved analysing the connections between indicators and constructs, a crucial aspect of assessing a measurement model. To achieve this, tests for internal consistency, convergent validity, and discriminant validity were employed. Internal consistency

Table 1. Constructs and definitions

Constructs	Definition	Relevant Studies
Ease of use	The notion of ease of use, often termed as perceived ease of use, plays a crucial role in models of technology adoption. It pertains to the extent to which an individual perceives a specific system or technology as easy to use. Generally, it is observed that the simplicity with which users can adopt a technology correlates with the speed of its adoption.	Gao, Kortum, & Oswald, 2018;Davis, F.D., 1989;Lund, A.M., 2001;Davis, 1989;Venkatesh et al., 2003
Usefulness	In the context of technology adoption, the term "usefulness," frequently identified as perceived usefulness, is defined as the extent to which an individual believes that utilizing a specific technology or system will improve their job performance or productivity. According to the diffusion of innovation theory, technologies that are perceived as useful are expected to be adopted more swiftly.	Gao, Kortum, & Oswald, 2018;Davis, F.D., 1989;Lund, A.M., 2001;Rogers, 2003
Advantage of Technology	In the discourse on technology, the term "technology advantage," or relative advantage, is used to describe the extent to which an innovation is regarded as better than the concept, product, or technology it supersedes.	Gao, Kortum, & Oswald, 2018;Nayak & Narayan, 2019;Kaya & Balta, 2016;Davis, F.D., 1989;Couper, M.P., 2008;Moore & Benbasat, 1991;Rogers, E. M. 2003
FOMO	FOMO, an acronym for Fear of Missing Out, denotes the apprehension associated with the possibility of being excluded from rewarding experiences that others might be enjoying. This fear of missing out can lead to a situation where individuals are more inclined to adopt new technologies swiftly in order to maintain connectivity and stay informed.	Riordan et al., 2020;Aitamurto et al., 2021;Kärkkäinen, T., 2023;Alutaybi et al., 2020;Przybylski et al., 2013;Riordan et al., 2020
Personal Innovativeness	Within the framework of technology adoption, "Personal Innovativeness" is defined as the propensity of an individual to undertake risks through the exploration of new technologies. As outlined by Rogers (2003), this concept embodies an individual's readiness to engage in new experiences, particularly those associated with the adoption of novel technologies.	Jackson et al. (2013);Wang, W.T. and Lin, Y.L., 2021;Alkawsi, G., Ali, N.A. and Baashar, Y., 2021;Parveen, F. and Sulaiman, A., 2008;Rogers, 2003;Jackson et al., 2013;Agarwal & Prasad, 1998

Table 2. Descriptive results

Variable	Category	Frequency	Percentage
Gender	Male	145	41.9
	Female	201	58.1
Age	18-30	200	57.8
	30-40	70	20.23
	40-50	40	11.56
	Above 50	36	10.5
Occupation	Private job	160	46.2
	Government	08	2.3
	Job	120	34.6
	Student	32	9.2
	Homemaker	26	7.5

was evaluated using a composite reliability test and Cronbach's alpha. As detailed in Table 3, Cronbach's alpha values surpassed the recommended threshold of 0.7 (Pavlou, 2018). Furthermore, the composite reliability values, ranging from 0.81 to 0.91, were deemed acceptable (Shukla & Mishra, 2022; Sharma & Shukla, 2017) (Refer to Table 4).

The assessment of convergent validity in the model involved scrutinising the average variance extracted (AVE) and outer loadings (Refer to Table 7). Factors such as EU4, U4, AT4, FOMO4, and PI4 were excluded from the model because their values did not meet the acceptable threshold of 0.7. This exclusion led to a notable enhancement in the AVE values (refer to Table 3), affirming the validity of the concurrent model.

Additionally, an analysis for discriminant validity was conducted, utilising cross-loadings and the Fornell-Larcker Criterion (1981). The results indicated that the factors did not demonstrate cross-loading, as they showed more substantial loadings on their respective constructs than on others (Sia, Tan, & Wei, 2002). According to the Fornell-Larcker criterion (1981), the AVE values surpassed the squared correlations with other constructs, establishing discriminant validity (Shukla & Mishra, 2022; Sharma & Shukla, 2017).

Table 3. Summary of results of evaluation of measurement model.

Construct		Items	Outer Loadings	Cronbach's Alpha	Composite Reliability	AVE
Ease of use (Davis, 1989)	EU1	Generative AI is easy to use.	0.787	0.755	0.824	0.535
	EU2	Generative AI is simple to use.	0.875			
	EU3	Generative AI requires the fewest steps possible to accomplish what I want to do with it.	0.709			
	EU4	Generative AI is easy to master	0.565			
Usefulness (Davis, 1989)	U1	Generative AI helps me to more effective	0.757	0.831	0.871	0.643
	U2	Generative AI saves me time when I use it.	0.845			
	U3	Generative AI is useful	0.785			
	U4	I am effective and efficient				
Advantage of Technology (Aitamurto et al., 202)	AT1	I am glad to share the benefits of latest technology like Generative AI	0.795	0.776	0.931	0.731
	AT2	I will be able to maximise my reach with the technology	0.782			
	AT3	Using Generative AI kind if technology, I find it easy to do what I want it to do.	0.758			
	AT4	Using Generative AI technology will provide mean possibility of reducing human work.	0.407			
Fear Of Missing Out (Wang & Lin, 2021)	FOMO1	When others do not interact with me as expected using the latest social media technology, I may be concerned that my reputation among my friends has declined	0.723	0.842	0.871	0.821
	FOMO2	When others do not interact with me as expected using the latest social media technology, concerned with my profile being less active so that others lose interest	0.813			
	FOMO3	When I am unwilling to engage in technology for social interaction (e.g., group chat), I may be concerned about losing the benefits of being in the online group	0.856			
	FOMO4	Following online news make me feel better	0487			
Personal Innovativeness	PI1	In technology, I have heard about it	0.79	0.851	0.731	0.867
	PI2	My peers make the most use of Generative AI technology.	0.779			
	PI3	I am curious about latest trends and like to experiment	0.747			
	PI4	Personal Innovativeness will positively effect on attitude.	0.637			

Convergent validity was established by evaluating the average variance extracted (AVE) and outer loadings. The AVE values were determined to exceed the threshold of 0.5 ([Table 4]), thereby confirming the establishment of convergent validity.

5.2 Assessment and Evaluation of Structural Model

A collinearity assessment was performed on the model, with the calculated Variance Inflation Factor (VIF) values all exceeding 5, thus indicating the absence of multicollinearity concerns. The model underwent evaluation using PLS-SEM, incorporating bootstrapping on 5,000 subsamples (Shukla & Mishra, 2022; Sharma & Shukla, 2017).

The structural model delineates the relationships between constructs for hypothesis testing. Five hypotheses were proposed in this study. Notable results were observed for hypotheses H1, H2, H3, H4, and H5, underscoring the significant influence of factors such as "Ease of use, Usability, Technology Advantage, FOMO, and Personal Innovativeness" in accelerating technology adoption. Consequently, hypotheses H1, H2, H3, H4, and H5 received support. The R square value was computed at 0.789, and the adjusted R square at 0.796. Additionally, the f-square values were found to range between 0.146 and 1.582. Based on its SRMR (Standardized Root Mean Square Residual) rating of 0.105, the model possessed high predictive capacity.

The internal structure analysis validated all five hypotheses, as indicated in Table 5, with the t-values being significant ($t > 1.96$). The most robust relationship was observed between the Advantages of technology and the Adoption rate ($\beta = 0.647$, $p = 0.000$), suggesting that the benefits or advantages of technology are critical in determining its adoption rate by users and industries. Technologies with clear and substantial advantages will likely be adopted and implemented more rapidly. The next most substantial relationship was between the usefulness of technology and the Adoption rate ($\beta = 0.641$, $p = 0.000$), indicating that the more beneficial and practical technology is perceived, the more likely it is to be adopted swiftly and broadly. The relationship between FOMO and Adoption rate ($\beta = 0.478$, $p = 0.000$) was also significant, implying that the fear of missing out can significantly influence the speed of adoption of new technologies or trends. The significance of the relationship between Ease of use and Adoption rate ($\beta = 0.423$, $p = 0.000$) suggests that user-friendly technologies are more readily and widely adopted as they lower the barriers to acceptance. Lastly, the relationship between Personal Innovativeness and Adoption rate ($\beta = 0.417$, $p = 0.000$) was significant, indicating that individuals who are more innovative and open to new experiences tend to adopt new technologies or innovations more quickly and readily.

Table 4. AVE

Constructs	AVE
EU	0.85
U	0.714
AT	0.876
FOMO	0.786
PI	0.659

5. RESULTS AND DISCUSSION

The findings of this research indicate that various elements, including perceived ease of use, usefulness, personal innovativeness, fear of missing out (FOMO), and technological advantages, significantly influence the acceleration of technology adoption. As per Davis's study (1989), the acceptance and adoption of technology are profoundly affected by perceived ease of use and usefulness (Alutaybi, Al-Thani, McAlaney, & Ali, 2020; Agarwal & Prasad, 1998). Our survey validated several of these factors, affirming their relevance in a context where the technology landscape continuously evolves. The importance of personal innovativeness in adopting technology was also substantiated, aligning with the observations of Rogers (1995). Consistent with Thakur and Srivastava's findings (2014), participants who exhibited a high level of innovativeness showed a greater tendency towards adopting new technologies (Thakur & Srivastava, 2014). The influence of the fear of missing out (FOMO) on technology adoption was significant (Przybylski et al., 2013), with a higher FOMO level correlating with a faster adoption of new technologies among participants.

Additionally, the relative advantage of a technology plays a pivotal role in its adoption, according to Rogers' theory (Rogers, 1962). The survey results further revealed that technologies offer discernible effort reduction and performance benefits. The survey results substantiate Hypothesis H1, which posits that the perceived usefulness of technology has a direct effect on its adoption rate. This aligns with Davis's Technology Acceptance Model (1989), suggesting that perceived usefulness is critical to technology acceptance (Alutaybi, Al-Thani, McAlaney, & Ali, 2020). Furthermore, Hypothesis H2, regarding the impact of technology's ease of use on adoption rates, received affirmation from the survey participants. The data reveal a positive correlation, supporting the notion advanced by Venkatesh and Bala (2008) that ease of use significantly influences users' acceptance of technology (Venkatesh & Davis, 2000) (Venkatesh et al., 2012)(Venkatesh et al., 2003).

To Hypothesis H3, the survey confirms that the relative advantage of technology markedly influences its adoption rates, which is consistent with Rogers's Diffusion of Innovations Theory (2003), underscoring the importance of perceived comparative advantage in adoption decisions. Concerning Hypothesis H4, the survey indicates a positive correlation between personal innovativeness and technology adoption, aligning with the findings of Thakur and Srivastava (2014)(Thakur & Srivastava, 2014). Lastly, Hypothesis H5, which associates the fear of missing out (FOMO) with the impetus for technology adoption, found robust support in the survey data. FOMO has been identified as a significant factor affecting the behavioural intent to use technology (Przybylski et al., 2013).

Table 5. Results of PL-SEM

Hyp	Hypothesis	t-Values	p-Values	Beta	Result
H1	The usefulness of a technology positively impacts its adoption rate.	18.981	0.000	0.641	Supported
H2	The ease of use of technology positively impacts its adoption rate.	8.539	0.000	0.423	Supported
H3	The advantage of a technology significantly impacts its adoption rate.	16.25	0.000	0.647	Supported
H4	An individual's innovativeness positively correlates with adoption rate.	4.872	0.000	0.417	Supported
H5	The fear of missing out (FOMO) significantly impacts adoption rate.	6.372	0.000	0.478	Supported

Source: Authors' compilation.

The conclusions derived from the survey results corroborate that these pivotal factors – perceived ease of use, usefulness, personal innovativeness, FOMO, and the relative advantage of technology – significantly influence the rate of technology adoption.

6. CONTRIBUTION OF THE STUDY

This study has yielded essential insights into the factors that expedite technology adoption, benefiting individuals, organisations, and society. The findings indicate that perceived usefulness, ease of use, relative advantage, personal innovativeness, and fear of missing out are substantial influencers in the adoption process. The information presented in this article equips individuals with the necessary knowledge to make more informed decisions when considering the adoption of new technologies.

Organisations, especially those developing and marketing new technologies, can use these insights to refine product quality and communication strategies. They can expedite the adoption process by highlighting the utility and user-friendliness of their products and clearly presenting their advantages over existing technologies. Moreover, recognising the significance of individual innovativeness and the fear of missing out can aid companies in targeting the most suitable demographic groups to boost adoption.

This research offers policymakers, educators, and society a thorough comprehension of the patterns in technology adoption. The insights gleaned can inform the development of policies, educational programs, and public discourse regarding technology adoption, particularly in sectors where rapid technology adoption is vital, such as advancing digital literacy or sustainable technologies. This study deepens the understanding of technology adoption and lays the groundwork for future research. A more intricate grasp of the various factors influencing technology adoption could result in the evolution of more detailed theories and models.

7. CONCLUSION

A study was conducted to ascertain the factors that accelerate technology adoption. This empirical investigation centred on perceived usefulness, ease of use, relative advantage, personal innovativeness, and fear of being left behind, identified as crucial determinants in the adoption process.

The study's results underscore that technology's perceived usefulness and ease of use are instrumental in promoting higher adoption rates. Technologies perceived as easy to use and beneficial are more likely to be adopted quickly, supporting previous research in this domain. Furthermore, the study validates Rogers' (2003) diffusion of innovations theory, which asserts that their relative advantage over existing ones primarily drives the adoption of new technologies. The study also contributes significantly to understanding the psychological factors in technology adoption, revealing that personal innovativeness and the fear of missing out play vital roles in influencing adoption decisions. It highlights that both individual characteristics and social dynamics are influential in shaping patterns of technology adoption. Overall, the study significantly enriches the literature on technology adoption and offers valuable insights for those involved in technology design, marketing, policy-making, and individual users.

8. LIMITATIONS AND FUTURE RESEARCH

Acknowledging constraints in research endeavours is essential for transparency and identifying areas for future enhancement. The limitations of this study include the possibility that the sample of 380 respondents may not fully represent the broader population's sentiments, with the demographic distribution potentially not capturing the full diversity of digital users. Secondly, being a cross-sectional study, it offers insights at a specific point in time, whereas longitudinal studies could reveal changes in perceptions over time. Thirdly, the responses might be subject to recall bias or influenced by the respondents' desire to conform to socially acceptable norms. Fourthly, the study's focus on specific geographical locations may not encompass cultural variations across different regions.

The findings of this study lay the groundwork for understanding the factors that drive rapid technology adoption. Future research should consider expanding the sample size to include a more diverse range of age groups, professions, and geographical locations. Longitudinal studies tracking the same participants over time could shed light on evolving technology adoption dynamics and the sustained impact of factors like perceived usefulness and FOMO. In addition to FOMO and personal innovativeness, other psychological aspects such as tech-savviness, cognitive load, or trust in technology could be explored. Considering the global reach of technology, investigating how cultural norms and regional peculiarities affect adoption could yield valuable insights. While this study addresses general technology adoption, future research could focus on specific innovations like augmented reality, blockchain, or quantum computing, examining unique adoption factors associated with these technologies. Moreover, understanding how global events, such as pandemics or economic downturns, impact technology adoption rates could also be a significant area of study.

REFERENCES

Agarwal, R., & Prasad, J. (1998). A conceptual and operational definition of personal innovativeness in information technology. *Information Systems Research*, *9*(2), 204–215. doi:10.1287/isre.9.2.204

Agrawal, A., Gans, J., & Goldfarb, A. (2018). *The Economics of Artificial Intelligence: An Agenda*. University of Chicago Press.

Ajzen, I., & Fishbein, M. (1980). *Understanding attitudes and predicting social behaviour*. Academic Press.

Alutaybi, A., Al-Thani, D., McAlaney, J., & Ali, R. (2020). Investigating the Role of Fear of Missing out (FOMO) in the Relationship between Social Network Services Use Intensity and Nomophobia. *International Journal of Environmental Research and Public Health*, *17*(13), 4712. PMID:32629997

Amoroso, D.L., & Lim, R.A. (2015). Exploring the personal innovativeness construct: the roles of ease of use, satisfaction and attitudes. *Asia Pacific Journal of Information Systems, 25*(4), 662-685.

Bedué, P., & Fritzsche, A. (2022). Can we trust AI? An empirical investigation of trust requirements and guide to successful AI adoption. *Journal of Enterprise Information Management*, *35*(2), 530–549. doi:10.1108/JEIM-06-2020-0233

Bender, E. M., Gebru, T., McMillan-Major, A., & Shmitchell, S. (2023). On the dangers of stochastic parrots: can language models be too big. *Proceedings of FAccT*. Retrieved from https://explodingtopics.com/blog/chatgpt-users

Bengio, Y. (2017). Deep Learning and the Future of AI. *arXiv preprint arXiv:1705.07798.*

Bradford, M., & Florin, J. (2003). Examining the role of innovation diffusion factors on the implementation success of enterprise resource planning systems. *International Journal of Accounting Information Systems*, *4*(3), 205–225. doi:10.1016/S1467-0895(03)00026-5

Brevini, B. (2021). Is AI good for the Planet? *Polity*.

Brown, I. T. J. (2002). Individual and Technological Factors Affecting Perceived Ease of Use of Web-based Learning Technologies in a Developing Country. *The Electronic Journal on Information Systems in Developing Countries*, *9*(1), 1–15. doi:10.1002/j.1681-4835.2002.tb00055.x

Brown, T. B. (2020). *Language Models are Few-Shot Learners*. OpenAI.

Brynjolfsson, E., & McAfee, A. (2014). *The Second Machine Age: Work, Progress, and Prosperity in a Time of Brilliant Technologies*. WW Norton & Company.

Cakmak, P. I., & Tas, E. (2012). The use of information technology on gaining competitive advantage in Turkish contractor firms. *World Applied Sciences Journal*, *18*(2), 274–285.

Castells, M. (2009). The Rise of the Network Society: The Information Age: Economy, *Society and Culture*. Wiley-Blackwell.

Chaffee, S. H., & Metzger, M. J. (2001). The End of Mass Communication? *Mass Communication & Society*, *4*(4), 365–379. doi:10.1207/S15327825MCS0404_3

Cho, J., DeStefano, T., Kim, H., Kim, I., & Paik, J. H. (2023). What's driving the diffusion of next-generation digital technologies? *Technovation*, *119*, 102477. doi:10.1016/j.technovation.2022.102477

Chui, M., Issler, M., Roberts, R., & Yee, L. (2023). Technology Trends Outlook 2023. Academic Press.

Danaher, J., & Sætra, H. S. (2022). Technology and moral change: The transformation of truth and trust. *Technology in Society*, *75*, 102372.

Danaher, J., & Sætra, H. S. (2022). Technology and moral change: The transformation of truth and trust. *Ethics and Information Technology*, *24*(3), 35. Advance online publication. doi:10.1007/s10676-022-09661-y

David, M. (2020). The correspondence theory of truth. In *The Stanford Encyclopedia of Philosophy* (Winter 2020 Edition). Available at: https://plato.stanford.edu/archives/win2020/entries/truth-correspondence/

Davis, F. D. (1989). Perceived usefulness, perceived ease of use, and user acceptance of information technology. *Management Information Systems Quarterly*, *13*(3), 319–340. doi:10.2307/249008

DeStefano, T., Kneller, R., & Timmis, J. (2020). *Cloud Computing and Firm Growth*. CESifo Working Paper No. 8306.

Digital, O. E. C. D. (2020). *Economy Outlook 2020*. OECD Publishing. doi:10.1787/bb167041-

Dignum, V. (2018). *Responsible Artificial Intelligence: How to Develop and Use AI in a Responsible Way*. Springer.

Edwards, B. (2022). Artists stage mass protest against AI-generated artwork on ArtStation. Ars Technica.

Fallis, D. (2021). The epistemic threat of deepfakes. *Philosophy & Technology*, *34*(4), 623–643. doi:10.1007/s13347-020-00419-2 PMID:32837868

Feder, G., & Umali, D. L. (1993). The adoption of agricultural innovations: A review. *Technological Forecasting and Social Change*, *43*(3-4), 215–239. doi:10.1016/0040-1625(93)90053-A

Goodfellow, I., Bengio, Y., & Courville, A. (2016). *Deep Learning*. MIT Press.

Greenhalgh, T., Robert, G., Macfarlane, F., Bate, P., & Kyriakidou, O. (2004). Diffusion of innovations in service organizations: Systematic review and recommendations. *The Milbank Quarterly*, *82*(4), 581–629. doi:10.1111/j.0887-378X.2004.00325.x PMID:15595944

Griffy-Brown, C., Earp, B. D., & Rosas, O. (2018). Technology and the good society. *Technology in Society*, *52*, 1–3. doi:10.1016/j.techsoc.2018.01.001

Horwich, P. (2006). The value of truth. *Noûs (Detroit, Mich.)*, *40*(2), 347–360. doi:10.1111/j.0029-4624.2006.00613.x

Hurlburt, G. (2023). What If Ethics Got in the Way of Generative AI? *IT Professional*. . doi:10.1109/MITP.2023.3267140

Iansiti, M., & Lakhani, K. R. (2020). *Competing in the Age of AI: Strategy and Leadership when Algorithms and Networks Run the World. Harvard Business Review.*

Knight, W. (2019). *AI is helping reporters write news. But is it creative?* MIT Technology Review.

Lazarsfeld, P. F., & Menzel, H. (1963). Mass media and personal influence. In *The Science of Human Communications*. Basic Books.

Lee, J. D., & See, K. A. (2004). Trust in automation: Designing for appropriate reliance. *Human Factors*, *46*(1), 50–80. doi:10.1518/hfes.46.1.50.30392 PMID:15151155

Levine, E. E., & Schweitzer, M. E. (2015). Prosocial lies: When deception breeds trust. *Organizational Behavior and Human Decision Processes*, *126*, 88–106. doi:10.1016/j.obhdp.2014.10.007

Lu, Y., Yao, J. E., & Yu, C. S. (2005). Personal innovativeness, social influences and adoption of wireless Internet services via mobile technology. *The Journal of Strategic Information Systems*, *14*(3), 245–268. doi:10.1016/j.jsis.2005.07.003

Magni, M., Angst, C. M., & Agarwal, R. (2012). Everybody needs somebody: The influence of team network structure on information technology use. *Journal of Management Information Systems*, *29*(3), 9–42. doi:10.2753/MIS0742-1222290301

Manning, L., Brewer, S., Craigon, P. J., Frey, J., Gutierrez, A., Jacobs, N., Kanza, S., Munday, S., Sacks, J., & Pearson, S. (2022). Artificial intelligence and ethics within the food sector: Developing a common language for technology adoption across the supply chain. *Trends in Food Science & Technology*, *125*, 33–42. doi:10.1016/j.tifs.2022.04.025

Maruping, L. M., & Magni, M. (2012). What's the weather like? The effect of team learning climate, empowerment climate, and gender on individuals' technology exploration and use. *Journal of Management Information Systems*, *29*(1), 79–114. doi:10.2753/MIS0742-1222290103

McElheran, K. (2018). *Economic Measurement of AI*. Presented at the NBER Economics of AI Conference, Toronto, Canada.

McKinsey & Company. (2023). *The state of AI in 2023: Generative AI's breakout year*. Available at: https://www.mckinsey.com/capabilities/quantumblack/our-insights/the-state-of-ai-in-2023-generative-ais-breakout-year

Pavlou, P. A. (2018). Internet of things–will humans be replaced or augmented? *NIM Marketing Intelligence Review*, *10*(2), 42–47. doi:10.2478/gfkmir-2018-0017

Pavlov, I. (1927a). *Conditioned Reflexes*. Oxford University Press.

Pavlov, I. P. (1927b). *Conditioned reflexes: An investigation of the physiological activity of the cerebral cortex*. Oxford University Press.

Perez, S. (2022). *The rise of generative AI in the business sector*. TechCrunch.

Przybylski, A. K., Murayama, K., DeHaan, C. R., & Gladwell, V. (2013). Motivational, emotional, and behavioral correlates of fear of missing out. *Computers in Human Behavior*, *29*(4), 1841–1848. doi:10.1016/j.chb.2013.02.014

Rijanto, A. (2021). Blockchain Technology Adoption in Supply Chain Finance. *Journal of Theoretical and Applied Electronic Commerce Research*, *16*(7), 3078–3098. doi:10.3390/jtaer16070168

Rogers, E. M. (1962). *Diffusion of innovations*. Free Press.

Russell, S., & Norvig, P. (2020). *Artificial Intelligence: A Modern Approach* (4th ed.). Pearson.

Sætra, H. S. (2019). The Ghost in the machine. *Human Arenas*, *2*(1), 60–78. doi:10.1007/s42087-018-0039-1

Sætra, H. S. (2020). The parasitic nature of social AI: Sharing minds with the mindless. *Integrative Psychological & Behavioral Science*, *54*(2), 308–322. doi:10.1007/s12124-020-09523-6 PMID:32185700

Sætra, H. S. (2021). Robotomorphy: Becoming our creations. *AI and Ethics*. Advance online publication. doi:10.1007/s43681-021-00092-x

Sætra, H. S. (2023). Generative AI: Here to stay, but for good? *Technology in Society*, *75*, 102372. doi:10.1016/j.techsoc.2023.102372

Sahin, I. (2006). Detailed review of Rogers' diffusion of innovations theory and educational technology-related studies based on Rogers' theory. *The Turkish Online Journal of Educational Technology*, *5*(2), 14–23.

Santos, C. (2020). *How Medium, arXiv, and Github Are Disrupting the Dissemination of AI Knowledge*. Towards Data Science.

Sarker, S., Valacich, J. S., & Sarker, S. (2005). Technology adoption by groups: A valence perspective. *Journal of the Association for Information Systems*, *6*(2), 37–71. doi:10.17705/1jais.00064

Scherer, M. U. (2020). Regulating Artificial Intelligence Systems: Risks, Challenges, Competencies, and Strategies. *Harvard Journal of Law & Technology*, *29*(2), 353–398.

Schlagwein, D., & Willcocks, L. (2023). 'ChatGPT et al.': The ethics of using (generative) artificial intelligence in research and science. *Journal of Information Technology*, *38*(3), 232–238. doi:10.1177/02683962231200411

Sharma, S. K., & Shukla, A. (2017). Impact of electronic word on mouth on consumer behaviour and brand image. *Asian Journal of Management*, *8*(3), 501–506. doi:10.5958/2321-5763.2017.00081.6

Shukla, A., & Mishra, A. (2022). *Role of review length, review valence and review credibility on consumer's online hotel booking intention*. FIIB Business Review.

Sia, C. L., Tan, B. C. Y., & Wei, K. K. (2002). Group polarization and computer-mediated communication: Effects of communication cues, social presence, and anonymity. *Information Systems Research*, *13*(1), 70–90. doi:10.1287/isre.13.1.70.92

Sia, C. L., Teo, H. H., Tan, B. C. Y., & Wei, K. K. (2004). Effects of environmental uncertainty on organizational intention to adopt distributed work arrangements. *IEEE Transactions on Engineering Management*, *51*(3), 253–267. doi:10.1109/TEM.2004.830859

Silva, Menon, Falco, & MacDonald. (2019). Structural adjustment, mass lay-offs and employment reallocation. *OECD Science, Technology and Industry Policy Papers*, 72.

SimilarWeb. (2023). *Website Analysis: Chat.openai.com*. Retrieved from https://pro.similarweb.com/#/digitalsuite/websiteanalysis/overview/website-performance/*/999/3m?webSource=Total&key=chat.openai.com

Solaiman, I. (2023). Evaluating the Social Impact of Generative AI Systems in Systems and Society. *arXiv preprint arXiv:2306.05949v2*. Available at: https://arxiv.org/abs/2306.05949v2

SrinivasanR.ParikhD. (2021). Building Bridges: Generative Artworks to Explore AI Ethics. *Fujitsu Research of America & Georgia Tech and Facebook AI Research*. arXiv:2106.13901v1

Statista. (2021a). *Number of Instagram users worldwide from 2016 to 2021*. Retrieved from https://www.statista.com/statistics/253577/number-of-monthly-active-instagram-users/

Statista. (2021b). *Number of YouTube users worldwide from 2016 to 2021*. Retrieved from https://www.statista.com/statistics/805656/number-youtube-viewers-world/

Statista. (2023). *Leading chatbot/conversational AI startups worldwide in 2023, by funding raised*. Available at: https://www.statista.com/statistics/1359073/chatbot-and-conversational-ai-startup-funding-worldwide/

Tarafdar, M., & Vaidya, S. D. (2006). Challenges in the adoption of E-Commerce technologies in India: The role of organizational factors. *International Journal of Information Management*, *26*(6), 428–441. doi:10.1016/j.ijinfomgt.2006.08.001

Taylor, S., & Todd, P. A. (1995). Understanding information technology usage: A test of competing models. *Information Systems Research*, *6*(2), 144–176. doi:10.1287/isre.6.2.144

Thakur, R., & Srivastava, M. (2014). Adoption readiness, personal innovativeness, perceived risk and usage intention across customer groups for mobile payment services in India. *Internet Research*, *24*(3), 369–392. doi:10.1108/IntR-12-2012-0244

The Guardian. (2023). *ChatGPT reaches 100 million users, making it the fastest growing app*. Retrieved from https://www.theguardian.com/technology/2023/feb/02/chatgpt-100-million-users-open-ai-fastest-growing-app

Thong, J. Y. L. (1999). An integrated model of information systems adoption in small businesses. *Journal of Management Information Systems*, *15*(4), 187–214. doi:10.1080/07421222.1999.11518227

Thong, J. Y. L., Hong, S. J., & Tam, K. Y. (2006). The effects of post-adoption beliefs on the expectation-confirmation model for information technology continuance. *International Journal of Human-Computer Studies*, *64*(9), 799–810. doi:10.1016/j.ijhcs.2006.05.001

Thormundsson, B. (2023). Explainable AI market revenues worldwide 2022-2030. *Statista*. Available at: https://www.statista.com/statistics/1256246/worldwide-explainable-ai-market-revenues/

Tomczyk, Ł., & Szotkowski, R. (2023). Sexting, fear of missing out (FOMO), and problematic social network use among adolescents. *Human Technology*, *19*(2), 283–301. doi:10.14254/1795-6889.2023.19-2.8

UNESCO. (2023). *Artificial Intelligence: examples of ethical dilemmas*. Available at: https://www.unesco.org/en/artificial-intelligence/recommendation-ethics/cases

Valente, T. W. (2012). Network interventions. *Science, 337*(6090), 49-53.

Venkatesh, V., & Davis, F. D. (2000). A theoretical extension of the technology acceptance model: Four longitudinal field studies. *Management Science*, *46*(2), 186–204. doi:10.1287/mnsc.46.2.186.11926

Venkatesh, V., Morris, M. G., Davis, G. B., & Davis, F. D. (2003). User acceptance of information technology: Toward a unified view. *Management Information Systems Quarterly*, *27*(3), 425–478. doi:10.2307/30036540

Venkatesh, V., Thong, J. Y., & Xu, X. (2012). Consumer acceptance and use of information technology: Extending the unified theory of acceptance and use of technology. *Management Information Systems Quarterly*, *36*(1), 157–178. doi:10.2307/41410412

Warschauer, M. (2004). *Technology and Social Inclusion: Rethinking the Digital Divide*. MIT Press.

Wejnert, B. (2002). Integrating models of diffusion of innovations: A conceptual framework. *Annual Review of Sociology*, *28*(1), 297–326. doi:10.1146/annurev.soc.28.110601.141051

Wirtz, B. W., Weyerer, J. C., & Geyer, C. (2019). AI-driven technologies and their implications for consumers. *Electronic Markets*, *29*(4), 631–649.

Yen, H. R., Hu, P. J. H., Hsu, S. H. Y., & Li, E. Y. (2015). A multilevel approach to examine employees' loyal use of ERP systems in organizations. *Journal of Management Information Systems*, *32*(4), 144–178. doi:10.1080/07421222.2015.1138373

Zhou, T. (2011). An empirical examination of initial trust in mobile banking. *Internet Research*, *21*(5), 527–540. doi:10.1108/10662241111176353

Zuboff, S. (2019). *The Age of Surveillance Capitalism: the Fight for a Human Future at the New Frontier of Power*. PublicAffairs.

Chapter 12
The Issues and Challenges Faced by Faculty Members for Using Information Communication Technology

Simerjeet Singh Bawa
Chitkara Business School, Chitkara University, India

Rajit Verma
MM Institute of Management, Maharishi Markandeshwar University, India

Sunayna Khurana
MM Institute of Management, Maharishi Markandeshwar University, India

Ram Singh
https://orcid.org/0000-0002-6565-3091
MM Institute of Management, Maharishi Markandeshwar University, India

Vinod Kumar
https://orcid.org/0000-0002-3578-8155
MM Institute of Management, Maharishi Markandeshwar University, India

Meenu Gupta
MM Institute of Management, Maharishi Markandeshwar University, India

Mandeep Kaur
https://orcid.org/0000-0002-4736-8991
MM Institute of Management, Maharishi Markandeshwar University, India

Makarand Upadhyaya
Department of Management and Marketing, College of Business Administration, University of Bahrain, Bahrain

ABSTRACT

There are several challenges with ICT use in education, notably moral and legal ones. Both educators and learners ought to have a basic awareness of the challenges and issues related to using ICT in the classroom. In respective capacities as teachers, students, or potential teachers, they must be beyond criticism. Incorporating modern technology in education is essential in the digital world, according to an increasing number of studies. Teachers and students have a lot more opportunities to collaborate online since educational programmes incorporate information and communication technology (ICT). However, various obstacles could make teachers hesitant to use ICT in the classroom and hinder them

DOI: 10.4018/979-8-3693-3253-5.ch012

from introducing supplementary materials. Examining the challenges associated with implementing ICT in education can help educators get over them and incorporate the technology into routine instruction. The objective of this chapter is to learn more about how teachers view the obstacles and difficulties that impede them from integrating ICT in the classroom.

I. INTRODUCTION

Information and communication technologies (ICTs) have developed quickly in recent years and have a profound impact on how the world functions and communicates. Due to rising temptation to invest in new technology, this seems to have had an impact on the demand for educational and training services in terms of both material and delivering manner. ICT choices are emerging, allowing decision-makers a broader choice from which to pick when integrating ICT into education and training. Technology's use as a tool to improve the various linguistic competence has attained a lot of attention because teachers are frequently exposed to new ways. In addition to syllabus updates that are formally approved—typically by the Ministry of Education in each country—workshops and brief training sessions offer novel techniques and activities or encourage new content. This indicates that, despite the fact that teachers are exposed to frequent subject changes, it does not necessarily make them more imaginative or receptive to novel concepts. According to Roy and Swargiary (2023), a great deal of international research has demonstrated that many IRI programs have a favorable effect on educational equity and learning outcomes. And in comparison to other interventions, it has shown to be a cost-effective technique thanks to its economies of scale.

II. ISSUES IN INFORMATION COMMUNICATION TECHNOLOGY

According to Tinio (2012), there are four major interconnected issues that must be considered when assessing the overall impact of the application information and communication technologies (ICTs) in the teaching. These issues include effectiveness, cost, equity, and sustainability.

1. Effectiveness

How effectively ICTs are used in education is influenced by their application and purposes. ICTs aren't always, for everyone, or in the same way effective as traditional educational tools or teaching methods. The following viewpoint could be adopted regarding efficient (Singh et al., 2022).

a. *Increasing access*: There is certain proof that opportunities for higher education and vocational training are being broadened to include individuals and groups who are unable to attend regular institutions. 14 million students enrollment is there in around 3500 educational institutions in the USA (Potashnik & Capper, 1998).
b. *Raising quality:* Although there is limited information about how educative broadcasting and television programmes affect the quality of primary education, the strategies appear to be equally successful as conventional classroom instruction. (Hannafin, & Savenye, 1993). The Interactive

Radio Instruction has undergone the most in-depth research of all the educational radio programmes, claim Perraton and Creed (2002). Findings show strong indication of the successful project in enhancing education quality, as seen by better outcomes on standardized assessments and improved attendance.

2. Cost

Digital learning, computer-based learning, and instructive TV programs are typically cost more than radio programmes (Blurton, 2002). Blurton noted that there is strife about whether watching television programmes is more economical than pursuing an education digitally or using a computer. Despite this, classification It is challenging to conduct cost-effectiveness studies since there is a paucity of data, programme variations, generalizations concerns, difficulties measuring academic performance, and opportunity costs. Specifically speaking regarding the use of computers and the web, Blurton argues that there are a variety of factors that make it difficult to determine if ICT is "cost-effective" in academic contexts. Yet, when contrasted to the alternatives of expanding basic infrastructure, conserving money by sharing capabilities, and the cost to society of not allowing access, using ICT to facilitate learning looks to be a preferred (Sharma, 2023).

3. Equity

There are serious worries that the adoption of educational technology will widen already existing disparity along economic, social, cultural, geographic, and gender lines given the significant differences in access to ICTs between rich and poor countries as well as between various factions within countries. Everyone would be given equal chances to engage in an ideal world. Access, though, varies depending on the individuals involved—both as users and creators. Early discrepancies are so commonly reinforced, exacerbated, and even reproduced. As a result, remains a sizable obstacle in the way of global education policymakers defining the problem and providing development assistance (Hernes, 2002).

4. Sustainability

Resilience is a factor that development programmes typically ignore. The lengthy history of development assistance has demonstrated that many initiatives and programmes get off to a great start but wind up having little long-term impact. This also applies to numerous ICT-based educational initiatives. A framework that enables the educational institution or society to carry out the initiative independently or in collaboration with other interested parties after the activating sponsor revokes is rarely put in place for these initiatives, which are frequently started by external donors such as businesses or international aid organisations.

III. PROBLEMS AND ISSUES ARISE WHILE UTILIZING ICT IN EDUCATION

The efficient use of ICT in education is hampered by a variety of problems. The following categories have been created using these variables.

a. Issues Relating to Infrastructure

A country's national educational framework is built on pinnacle of the nation information and communication infrastructure. Before starting any ICT-based endeavour, authorities and strategists must carefully take the following into account.:

Are there areas or buildings that can accommodate the available technologies, first and foremost? Significant renovation would be necessary in countries with a large amount of out-of-date college structures to ensure proper wiring, air conditioning and heating, and overall security.

The provision of telephone service and electricity is another fundamental prerequisite. Large portions of poor nations continue to lack a consistent electrical source, and the closest phones are located far away.

b. Financial Challenges Associated With ICT Use

Pivot problems with the usage of ICT in education are integrating academic goals with real-world economic factors. Technology use in educational initiatives demand significant financial inputs, so developing nations must exercise caution when deciding which ICT use models to deploy and keep in mind sustaining economies of scale.In the end, it comes down to whether the value produced by using ICTs outweighs the expense in comparison to alternatives In other terms, is ICT-based training the most effective technique, given the available financial, human, and other resources, for achieving the specified academic goals, and if so, what is the modalities and extent of deployment that can be backed? For ICT use programmes, Whyte, as referenced by Cisler (2002), identified the following prospective funding and resource sources:

- Public funding; private contributions; and fundraisers
- Initiation costs
- Grants
- Revenues from the primary business
- Direct computer accessories
- connectivity
- Office services
- Profits from auxiliary activities

The educators have categorized the obstacles to instructors using ICT in the classroom using a variety of categories. Extrinsic and intrinsic obstacles are the two main groups into which researchers have divided the hurdles. Access, time, support, resources, and training were identified by Ertmer as first-order extrinsic barriers, while second-order internal barriers were referred to as attitudes, beliefs, habits, and resistance (Zhang et al., 2021).

IV. RESEARCH METHODOLOGY

The teachers conducted study on the difficulties and barriers preventing teachers from integrating ICT in the classroom using a standardized questionnaire. 30 teachers (Out of this 18 males and 12 women) were randomized selected from the city's five colleges to take the survey. The bulk of the respondents were already comfortable with using the Internet because they did so frequently for information gathering, emailing, and networking sites. Two distinct sections present the findings and results. The analysis of the information gathered from the second section, which addresses instructors' proficiency with ICT, is first presented. The outcomes and results are divided into groups in the second section based on the difficulties and obstacles that prohibit teachers from utilizing ICT in the classroom.

Analysis

The findings and outcomes are presented in two separate sections. First up is a study of the data acquired from the second component, which deals with familiarity of teachers with ICT. The second part of the outcomes is separated into groups based on the difficulties and obstacles that prohibit teacher's fromutilizing ICT in the classroom.

The three items in this section of the questionnaire pertained to the teachers' knowledge with ICT. According to Table-1, the majority of college teachers (70%) who were questioned regarding their own experiences with ICT saw themselves as regular or confident users of the technology. Although it is obvious from this premise that teachers are conversant with ICT, it does not imply that they will incorporate it into the syllabus. Only two teachers, compared to around 27% of respondents, have

never utilized ICT on their own. When asked to evaluate their own usage of the technology, the majority of instructors (70%) claimed they either never use ICT in the classroom or only use it occasionally. Table-1 shows that the majority of instructors (76%) thought that their coworkers were either unfamiliar with ICT or used it sparingly. According to the surveyed teachers, 17% of them use ICT frequently or with confidence.

Table-2 lists the eight causes why they are unable to apply ICT in the classroom. Also, most prominent hurdles are reflecting in Table-1 based on mean ratings. It can be observed, only three attributes had mean ratings that were equal or higher than 3.5, reflecting the teachers' perception of concerned three attributes as primary obstacles standing in the way of their application of ICT in instructional activities. Teachers said that they were unable to use ICT in the classroom due to a lack of technical support and

Table 1. Teacher's familiarity with ICT

Items	Variables	Frequency	Percent
Individual experience with ICT	Never before used	1	3
	Less usage	8	27
	Regular User	16	53
	Confident user	5	17
Rate yourself in the use of Technology in the classroom	Never before used	9	30
	Less usage	12	40
	Regular User	7	23
	Confident user	2	7
What do you think about other teachers' ICT knowledge	Never before used	10	33
	Less usage	13	43
	Regular User	5	17
	Confident user	2	7

restricted access to the Internet and other ICT. Lack of class time was another significant barrier to the instructors' use of ICT in the curriculum.

Nonetheless, more than two-thirds of the respondents thought that their perspectives of using ICT in the classroom were unaffected by the unfavourable sentiments of their colleagues and the college

Figure 1.

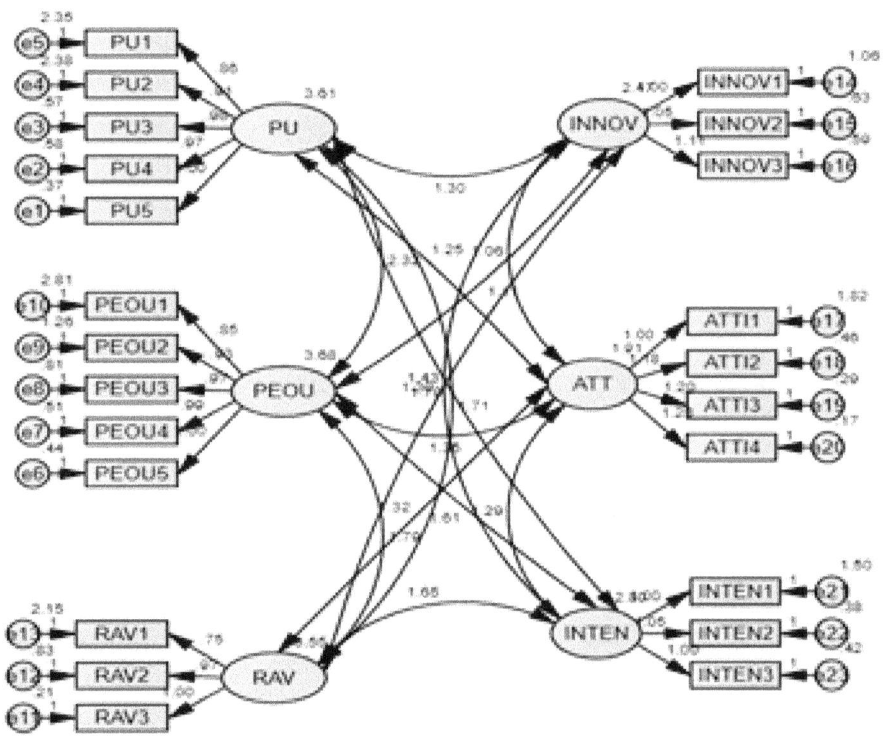

Table 2. Barriers preventing teachers to use ICT

	Strongly Disagree & Agree		Undecided		Agree & Strongly Agree	
Statements	**F**	**%**	**F**	**%**	**F**	**%**
Lack of class time makes it difficult to use ICT	9	30	1	3.3	20	66.6
inability to access ICT prevents me from using it	1	3.3	6	20	23	76.6
The lack of technical support for ICT at institutions deters me from using it	2	6.6	4	13.3	26	86.6
Social perceptions of ICT prevent me from using	14	46.6	5	16.6	11	36.6
Unfavorable opinions of coworkers prevent me from using	20	66.6	6	20	4	13.3
My college's perspective on ICT deters me from using	19	63.3	5	16.6	6	20
Time spent learning IT prevents me from using ICT	16	53.3	4	13.3	10	33.3
Eligibility Requirements Make It Difficult For Me To Use	16	53.3	4	13.3	10	33.3

Figure 2. Barriers preventing teachers to use ict according to the mean scores

Model Fit Summary

CMIN

Model	NPAR	CMIN	DF	P	CMIN/DF
Default model	61	616.171	215	.000	2.866
Saturated model	276	.000	0		
Independence model	23	13521.757	253	.000	53.446

RMR, GFI

Model	RMR	GFI	AGFI	PGFI
Default model	.117	.917	.893	.714
Saturated model	.000	1.000		
Independence model	1.718	.179	.104	.164

Baseline Comparisons

Model	NFI Delta1	RFI rho1	IFI Delta2	TLI rho2	CFI
Default model	.954	.946	.970	.964	.970
Saturated model	1.000		1.000		1.000
Independence model	.000	.000	.000	.000	.000

Parsimony-Adjusted Measures

Model	PRATIO	PNFI	PCFI
Default model	.850	.811	.824
Saturated model	.000	.000	.000
Independence model	1.000	.000	.000

NCP

Model	NCP	LO 90	HI 90
Default model	401.171	330.757	479.222
Saturated model	.000	.000	.000
Independence model	13268.757	12891.179	13652.651

administration. The opinions of society regarding ICT and the requirements for qualifications, according to more than half (46.6%) of the questioned teachers, do not prevent them from using ICT applications in the classroom.

V. CONCLUSION

A range of tactics and pedagogical theories can be used to improve teaching and learning with information and communications technology. However, using ICT as a teaching tool is significantly more challenging because it necessitates teachers having more specialised knowledge. Yet, a variety of difficulties and barriers impede teachers from integrating ICT into the classroom or using it to augment their lesson plans. According to this survey, even while college instructors are knowledgeable of ICT and its uses, they don't always include it into their curricula. A further barrier to instructors adopting ICT in the classroom is the lack of adequate technical support at colleges and restricted access to the Internet and ICT. Two other significant obstacles that teachers must overcome in order to integrate ICT into the curriculum were identified, namely a lack of class time and the amount of time required for studying and using ICT.

On the one hand, teacher training programmes need to give educators the necessary and appropriate assistance so they can include into the curriculum. Nevertheless, educators also need to be aware of what is occurring in the classroom and how it is changing. ICT can therefore be used to improve academic endeavours by possibly effective means in teaching and learning.

REFERENCES

Blurton, C. (2002). *New directions of ICT use in education.* http://www.unesco.org/education/educprog/lwf/dl/edict.pdfs

Cisler, S. (2002). Letter from San Francisco: The Internet Bookmobile. *First Monday*, *7*(10).

Hannafin, R. D. & Savenye, S. (1993). *Technology in the classroom: The teacher's New role and resistance to I.T.* Academic Press.

Perraton, C., & Creed, F. (2002). *Computers as tutors: solving the crisis in education.* http://www.cris.com/faben1/html

Roy, K., & Swargiary, K. (2023). ICT in Education Implementation in India: Advancements and Oppurtunities. *Dogo Rangsang Research Journal*, *13*(5), 91–96.

Sharma, P. (2023). Futuristic Trends in Higher Education: Role of ICT and E-Learning. *European Chemical Bulletin.*

Singh, V., Dubey, A. & Sonkar, C. (2022). Role of Information and Communication Technologies (ICT) in Education Sector in India. *International Journal of Creative research Thoughts*, *10*(1), 131-149.

Zhang, X., Rane, K. P., Kakaravada, I., & Shabaz, M. (2021). Research on vibration monitoring and fault diagnosis of rotating machinery based on internet of things technology. *Nonlinear Engineering*, *10*(1), 245–254.

Chapter 13
Influencer Marketing:
Way to a Sustainable Marketing Approach

Sayantan Mukherjee
Alliance School of Business, Alliance University, Bangalore, India

Ajay Verma
https://orcid.org/0000-0002-0994-4812
School of Applied Sciences and Languages, VIT Bhopal University, India

Shromona Neogi
Alliance School of Business, Alliance University, Bangalore, India

ABSTRACT

The millennial focus has shifted from mere consumption to sustainable consumption. Responsible and ethical buying is the primary focus. Millennial consumers are highly concerned about issues like environmental degradation and climatic changes and are ready to contribute to good causes. They are becoming more risk-averse and prefer to support businesses that emphasize pro-social messaging, environmentally friendly production, and moral business practices. The target consumer's perception of influencer marketing buzzwords like authenticity, credibility, and consumer involvement can be perceived as evolving. Influencers also power their voices to promote changes for good environmental causes. The study enlightens the development of the urge for ethical/sustainable buying to adopt moral influencer content as a basis to follow them and facilitate the consumer buying process. The people associated with the domain as influencers or aspiring to be one should focus on ethical influencing. The growing ethical consumerism is playing a vital role in behavioral adoption of ethical influencers.

INTRODUCTION

Influencers have the power of their voices, and many prefer to use their voices to urge people to learn more about a worthwhile cause or advocate for change (Fuxman et al., 2022). The study aims to understand millennial consumers' preference in adopting ethical influencers and the role of authenticity,

DOI: 10.4018/979-8-3693-3253-5.ch013

credibility, social impact, and consumer engagements of the brands led by the urge for ethical buying. E-influencers are persons who have developed a reputation for their subject-matter expertise (Berne-Manero & Marzo-Navarro, 2020). They frequently post about that subject on their preferred social media platforms, where they amass sizable fan bases of enthused, active individuals who pay close attention to their opinions. They have potential to start trends and persuade their followers to purchase the things they advocate, social media influencers are adored by brands (Atiq et al., 2022).

As brands continue to allocate more in influencer marketing, they must carefully consider whether their approach meets the industry's ethical and equality-driven expectations (Marín-García et al., 2022). Failure to develop an ethical strategy can damage your brand's reputation, cost you money, and prevent you from building a strong community of advocates. When it comes to maintaining brand loyalty, a brand's ethics and core values are now more important than ever, and prioritizing an ethical influencer marketing strategy is non-negotiable (Risitano et al., 2022). The need for ethical influencers in the domain has enhanced immensely. Instead of pressuring others into doing something, ethical influence involves winning their approval and making the decision to do it. The ultimate goal of the ethical influencer is to make people truly "desire" to do something, which is obviously the most powerful form of persuasion (Haider et al., 2022).

People are paying more attention to the products being sold, how they are getting produced and proper communication about ethical production is helping the brands to connect the target consumers and in turn people help them grow by associating (Sahadev et al., 2022). Consumers, especially millennials, are paying more attention to where they spend their money. The customers intend to place a greater emphasis on social and environmental issues while making purchasing decisions (Risitano et al., 2022).

Influencer marketing is becoming more powerful in the ever-changing world of digital marketing, with the potential to influence customer behavior towards more sustainable and ethical choices(Rathore, 2018). Brands may lead the way in sustainable marketing by carefully associating with influencers that demonstrate and promote ethical principles (Rathore, 2018). Through their carefully selected material and genuine interactions, ethical influencers can impact consumer mindsets and encourage conscientious buying practices. A change in consumer behavior is accelerated when these influencers promote companies who are serious about doing the right thing for the environment and their followers (Topalova, 2021). Their support encourages people to think about the impact of their purchasing decisions and highlights the value of products made in an ethical manner. Inspiring a societal embrace of responsible consumerism, the ripple impact of ethical influencers goes beyond conventional product promotion. A more positive and responsible consumer culture can be fostered through the use of influencer marketing, which in turn promotes the broad adoption of ethical and sustainable principles (Mutum & Ghazali, 2023). Thus, the first research objective is:

RO_1: The influence of ethical purchase intention of consumers on behavioral adoption of ethical influencers

The mediating roles of social responsibility, authenticity, and credibility in influencer marketing create an attractive pathway for the promotion of sustainable practices. Ethical influencers provide a mediating role between consumers' intentions to buy and their actual conduct in an ethical manner (Kushwah et al., 2019). By projecting an authenticity that is based on true belief and congruence with ethical principles, these influencers help link customers with sustainable brands. An essential component of influencer marketing, credibility increases the persuasive power of an ethical message by demonstrating its reliability. At the same time, when influential people promote eco-friendly goods, it gives the impression that everyone is trying to do their part to support ethical consumerism. A healthy synergy between influencer marketing and the propagation of sustainable values in the consumer landscape is fostered when authenticity, credibility, and social responsibility work together as mediators on the journey from ethical purchase intention to the behavioral adoption of ethical influencers (Lahbib et al., 2023).

RO_2: The mediating role of Authenticity, Credibility and Social Responsibility in between Ethical Purchase Intention and behavioral adoption of ethical influencers

There has been a revolutionary change in consumer culture, as influenced by the symbiotic relationship between ethical influencers' behavioural adoption and the aspirations to buy ethically. The importance of ethical influencers is growing as more and more people place a premium on products made in an ethical manner. Beacons directing customers towards sustainable choices, these influencers exhibit authenticity, integrity, and social responsibility (Kushwah et al., 2019). The fundamental motivation for this research is a desire to understand marketing sustainability from companies who share ethical principles through influencers. The adoption of ethical influencers and the intention to purchase ethically interact in a way that influences consumer behaviour and promotes a more responsible and sustainable marketplace as a whole is reflected in the research.

Research Problem

The concern of the study is to investigate the role of sustainability impacting the adoption of ethical influencers. It also focuses on understanding the adoption of Ethical Influencer Marketing among the millennial and its sustainability as a domain. Trends and global movements are influencing how brands and influencers create content, develop products, and market them. More brands are joining the sustainability movement by creating products and services that benefit the environment and people. The disparity between customers' worries and intentions towards sustainability and their purchasing behavior has been highlighted in research on sustainable fashion product, which outline an attitude-behavior gap because of many constraints impeding the adoption of sustainable fashion product.

Literature Review

The presence and marketing of brands on various social media platforms have the potential to significantly impact their brand image in contemporary culture(Study, 2012). Many organisations now employ social media influencers (SMIs) in their marketing operations, particularly in the realm of sustainability marketing (Mabkhot et al., 2022). This study aims to analyse the attitudes of millennial consumers about adopting sustainable influencer marketing promoted by ethical influencers and its impact on the ethical purchase intention and brand images they develop based on three identified facets: Authenticity, Credibility and Social Responsibility.

The Millennial generation is often described as more socially and ecologically aware compared to previous generations. These individuals also apply their consciousness to their purchasing behaviour, often considering the ethical and environmental consequences of their purchases (Sogari et al., 2017). Millennials' ethical purchase intentions are influenced by various factors, such as: (i) Social and Environmental Consciousness: Millennials exhibit a higher propensity for being cognizant of social and environmental concerns, including climate change, equitable labour practices, and animal welfare. Millennials exhibit a higher propensity to possess knowledge about environmental challenges. The things and brands they seek are those that align with their values and have a positive impact on both society and the environment. Millennials highly value authenticity and transparency from brands, especially about the origin of their products, the production methods employed, and their overall business conduct. Consumers are more inclined to trust and endorse firms that demonstrate sincerity and transparency in their operations. (ii) Brand Purpose and Values: Millennials are attracted to brands that possess a clear purpose that extends beyond mere profitability and are committed to making a positive impact on the world. Individuals are more likely to support and promote brands that align with their own personal values and beliefs. (iii) Impact of Peers and social media: Millennials are more vulnerable to the influence of their peers and social media when it comes to making purchasing decisions. By utilising social media platforms, individuals are more exposed to information and discussions pertaining to ethical products and enterprises, hence potentially influencing their views and behaviours. (iv) Product Quality and Price: While millennials prioritise ethical concerns, they still consider traditional factors like product quality and price. Millennial buyers exhibit a greater inclination towards acquiring ethical products that are priced competitively and align with their quality standards. (v) Convenience and Accessibility: Millennial employees prioritise convenience and accessibility when making purchase selections. This specific demographic is more inclined to have an interest in acquiring ethical products that are conveniently available and can be bought through many channels, such as internet and brick-and-mortar stores. Millennials are primarily motivated to make ethical purchases due to their heightened social and environmental consciousness, their values aligning with those of companies, the influence of their friends and social media, as well as the traditional factors of product quality and pricing. Brands that effectively communicate their ethical practices and ideals, while offering high-quality products at reasonable prices, are more likely to connect with millennial consumers.

Focus of authenticity (Taheri, B., Farrington, T., Curran, R., & O'Gorman, 2018), credibility (Rosli, N., Ha, N. C., & Ghazali, 2019), and social responsibility (Nguyen, N., & Johnson, 2020) are not restricted to the content of the influencers, but has grown much wider to challenge the brand where consumers are really focussing on the sustainable manufacturing (Rauch, E., Rofner, M., Cappellini, C., & Matt, 2022), pro-social communications (Berki-Kiss, D., & Menrad, 2022), and ethical business practices (Berki-Kiss, D., & Menrad, 2022). Authenticity isn't someone telling you how great a product is or neither Credibility deals with only the goodwill of the influencer or the brand. Their thoughts hover over the facts that whether brands genuinely care about the people and the planet acting in a socially responsible way? They are eager to frame whether the influencers genuinely love the products they share with their audiences?

The main idea behind originality in influencer marketing is to create authentic and transparent content that influences positive engagement and awareness (Deo & Prasad, 2022). Brands that have tapped into influencer marketing have seen incredible results in terms of reach and bottom line, but the landscape is constantly evolving, and the question of true authenticity and credibility is becoming blurred (Zatwarnicka-Madura et al., 2022).

Existing research offers useful insights into the complicated dynamics of the interaction between ethical buying intention, authenticity, and the behavioral adoption of ethical influencers. However, the literature on this topic is continually expanding (Wellman et al., 2020). Consumers' aspirations to buy ethically and their actual adoption of ethical influencers' behaviors are mediated by authenticity (Jung & La, 2020). Academics have delved into the mental aspects of authenticity, highlighting how it helps influencers gain credibility and trust. Consumers are looking for influencers that truly represent the ideals they preach because they are ethically motivated. Consumers' intents to make ethically driven purchases are strongly impacted by the perceived authenticity of influencers, according to studies (Murphy, 2021).

Moreover, research shows that authenticity has many facets when it comes to influencer marketing. Transparency in brand collaborations and content production is an aspect of authenticity, which also includes influencers' own values aligning with ethical ideals. There is a positive correlation between ethical purchase intentions and the actual adoption of recommended products or practices; this correlation is particularly pronounced when ethical influencers publicly express their true dedication to ethical causes.

Authenticity has a mediating role in the influencer-consumer interaction as well. When people are genuine, they make people feel more connected and relatable, which increases the power of ethical influencers to change people's behavior. Authentic influencers are more likely to have their followers adopt the ethical choices they promote since customers are more inclined to mimic their actions, according to the research.

But it's critical to highlight knowledge gaps in the literature that need additional research. In order to further understand the role of authenticity as a mediator, future studies should examine the effects of different influencer characteristics, communication approaches, and content strategies. Furthermore, longitudinal research have the potential to shed light on how authenticity shapes long-term patterns of ethical consumption behavior and how this influence persists over time(Lamberton & Stephen, 2016). Marketing tactics can be fine-tuned and more meaningful connections between ethical influencers and consumers can be fostered if we advance our knowledge of how authenticity mediates the relationship between ethical purchase intentions and the behavioral adoption of these influencers(Lee & Eastin, 2021).

When it comes to influencing the intention of millennials to make ethical purchases, authenticity has a significant impact. One set of individuals, known as the millennial generation, places a high level of importance on the authenticity of brands and is more likely to show their support for businesses that demonstrate a true commitment to engaging in ethical practices (Hunt et al., 1989). An explanation of the influence that authenticity has on the intention of millennials to make ethical purchases is provided below: Creating a Trusting Relationship: The authenticity of a brand is an essential component in the process of building trust between the consumer and the brand (Chatzopoulou & de Kiewiet, 2021). When Millennial have the impression that a brand is truly committed to ethical ideals, they are more likely to trust the representations that the brand makes regarding ethical standards and sustainability (Adrian & Lamb, n.d.). (i) Developing an Emotional Connection: Being genuine and sincere helps to cultivate a profound emotional connection with those who are members of the millennial generation. Millennials have the potential to form a profound connection with brands that genuinely emphasize sustainability, which can result in an increased propensity to support the firm through sustainable purchasing practices (Lenk & Rotkirch, 2021). (ii) Enhancing Brand Image: Being able to demonstrate a true dedication to ethical activities is a great way to enhance the brand image among millennials. The representation of the business as socially responsible and concerned about issues that go beyond simple profitability has the potential to have a positive impact on the impressions that millennials have of the company. (iii) Purchasing Decisions Effect: Authenticity has a direct impact on the purchasing decisions that millennials make. Millennials tend to favor things that come from real companies that align with their values, even if getting those products requires them to pay a greater price. Authenticity has the potential to increase long-term brand loyalty among millennials, which is the fourth possible benefit of fostering brand loyalty. Millennials are more likely to become loyal customers and to continue their support for a business when the brand consistently demonstrates authenticity in the ethical acts that it does (PATTUGLIA, SIMONETTA, 2018). Brands should prioritize transparent communication of their ethical initiatives, actively interact with consumers on social and environmental matters, and incorporate sustainability into their fundamental brand identity rather than using it as a mere marketing tactic to effectively influence the behavior of millennials regarding their intention to make ethical purchases (Ikonen et al., 2017). So, it is important to validate the mediating role of brand's authenticity to understand the effect of ethical purchase intention over behavioral adoption of ethical influencer as a credible source of advertising:

H_1: Authenticity mediates the relation in between ethical purchase intention and the behavioral adoption of ethical influencers.

Despite a lack of extensive research on the topic, a number of studies have provided insight into the complex processes at play in the relationship between ethical purchasing intention and the behavioral adoption of ethical influences, with credibility serving as a mediator between the two. Consumers' confidence and reliance on information shared by ethical influencers is shaped by their credibility, which in turn shapes their intentions to purchase ethically and their eventual adoption of ethical behaviors. According to academics, consumers' propensity to engage in the promoted ethical practices is strongly influenced by the influencers' reputation.

Expertise, trustworthiness, and likeability are three aspects of credibility that have been studied in relation to ethical influencers. Mediators of the connection between customers' intentions to buy ethically and their actual adoption of ethical behaviors are more likely to be influential figures who are seen as knowledgeable about ethical practices, trustworthy with suggestions, and relatable to their audience. Credibility increases the persuasive power of an influencer's ethical messaging, which is why customers are more likely to follow credible influencers, according to studies.

Credibility, according to the research, also acts as a mediator by affecting customers' emotional and cognitive reactions. Ethical buying intentions are reinforced and behavioral adoption of sustainable practices is facilitated by credible influencers since they not only provide information but also evoke favorable attitudes and emotions. The overall effectiveness of influencer-led advertising is enhanced by the fact that customers' perceptions of the authenticity of ethical messages are shaped by the perceived trustworthiness of influencers.

Still, additional research is needed to fill in the gaps in the existing literature. Investigating the complex elements of credibility, such as the effects of influencer characteristics and communication styles on mediation, could be the subject of future studies. The long-term effects of credibility and its function in encouraging long-term changes in ethical consumption behavior may be better understood with the help of longitudinal studies. Ethical and sustainable campaigns will be more effective as the field develops a better grasp of how credibility mediates the relationship between ethical purchase intentions and the behavioral adoption of ethical influencers. This will help refine influencer marketing strategies.

The reputation of the company has a big impact on the millennial generation's intention to make ethical purchases. When it comes to brands, Millennials, as a group of customers, usually place a high level of importance on openness, honesty, and reliability, particularly in connection to ethical actions. Both trust and confidence are associated with a brand that is regarded as credible because it is perceived to be trustworthy and dependable (Ozuem et al., 2021). In situations when a brand is perceived to be trustworthy in its ethical declarations and obligations, millennials are more likely to have faith in the brand's ability to fulfill its ethical and sustainable promises (Medvecka et al., 2023). The provision of trustworthy information by a brand gives millennials the ability to make decisions that are well-informed, which in turn provides them with enhanced decision making (Syrett, 2004). When it comes to evaluating and making purchasing decisions, millennials could evaluate and make choices based on their values and the credibility of a company's ethical actions, provided that the business communicates these activities in a trustworthy and transparent manner. In the process of forming an individual's idea of authenticity, credibility plays a vital influence. When a business's credibility is developed by continuous actions, transparent communication, and tangible proof of real adherence to ethical ideals, millennials are more likely to regard the brand as genuine in its ethical aspirations. This is because millennials appreciate brands that are transparent in their communication (Medvecka et al., 2023). One of the most important aspects of a brand's reputation is its ability to develop a positive reputation among millennials. When it comes to making purchasing decisions, millennials place a high value on ethical concerns, thus a brand that is known for its trustworthiness in ethical themes has the potential to appeal to this demographic (Barbosa, 2019). There is a greater likelihood that these individuals will show their support for brands that have a positive reputation for ethical behavior. To cultivate long-lasting relationships with younger consumers, it is vital to establish credibility. A firm can foster trust and loyalty among millennials by consistently demonstrating credibility in its ethical ambitions. Millennials are likely to continue their support for the brand by making sustainable ethical purchases if the company consistently demonstrates credibility in its ethical endeavors (Stahlhofer et al., 2018). Credibility should be a top priority for marketers if they want to effectively influence the intention of millennials to make ethical choices. Maintaining transparency, providing credible evidence of their ethical standards, actively engaging in meaningful conversations with customers about sustainability, and regularly displaying trustworthy behavior to create and maintain trust over time are all ways in which this can be accomplished. So, it is very important to study the mediating role of brand's credibility in behavioral adoption of ethical influencers while developing the ethical purchase intention among the consumers:

H_2: Credibility mediates the relation in between ethical purchase intention and the behavioral adoption of ethical influencers.

This triadic association is complex, and there is a growing body of scholarship that delves into the mediating function of social responsibility in the connection between ethical purchasing intention and behavioral adoption of ethical influencers (Duong, 2023). When consumers are impacted by ethical influencers, their purchase intentions are more likely to be driven by ethical considerations. One mediating factor that can amplify this impact is social responsibility.

Social responsibility in influencer marketing is crucial, according to existing research, because it helps bring influencers' ethical principles in line with those of their audience as a whole (Smith et al., 2018). It is more probable that ethical influencers who support charitable causes, advocate for environmental sustainability, and fight for social justice will mediate the connection between consumers' intentions to buy ethically and their actual adoption of such behaviors.

A strong sense of social responsibility among customers leads them to seek out influencers who promote ethical products and make positive contributions to society and the environment (Sen & Bhattacharya, 2001). This congruence creates a feeling of common ground, which in turn increases the attractiveness and likelihood of engaging in the ethical behaviors promoted by influencers.

Furthermore, social responsibility mediates between producers and consumers by shaping the latter's view of the total effect of their decisions. The mediation process is enhanced when ethical influencers who highlight the larger social and environmental impacts of consumer choices add their voices, strengthening the link between ethical purchasing intentions and behavioral adoption (Shaw, 2021). Consumers are more likely to act ethically when they believe their choices will have a favorable impact on society as a whole, according to research.

But there are areas where the literature is lacking, which could lead to new discoveries. Investigating the various social responsibility initiatives and how they influence consumer behavior could provide light on the precise processes via which social responsibility mediates (Suganthi, 2019). Researchers might learn more about the long-term effects of social responsibility on consumer ethics by conducting longitudinal studies.

In order to improve influencer marketing strategies and create more meaningful connections between influencers and consumers in relation to sustainable and ethical consumption, researchers in the field are working to better understand how social responsibility mediates the relationship between ethical purchase intentions and the behavioral adoption of ethical influencers (Kushwah et al., 2019).

When it comes to influencing the ethical buying intention of millennials, the function of social responsibility is a significant influential factor. In contrast to the generations that came before them, the current generation has a larger proclivity towards social and environmental consciousness. They frequently try to align their purchasing decisions with their values. An explanation that can be given for the influence that social responsibility has on the ethical purchasing intentions of millennials is as follows: Companies that maintain the principles of millennials, which include social and environmental responsibility, are more likely to receive their support. Millennials, who place a high value on social causes and environmental sustainability, are more likely to be interested in brands that demonstrate a genuine commitment to addressing these concerns. (i) Differentiation of the Brand: In a market that is highly competitive, the business practice of social responsibility has the potential to differentiate a brand from its rivals. Millennials tend to choose brands that identify themselves by their positive influence on society and the environment. This is like their desire to bring about change via their shopping decisions, so it is not surprising that they choose brands that have this characteristic. (ii) Establishing Trust: Millennials are more likely to display trust in brands that demonstrate social responsibility since these brands have the power to establish trust. Millennials are more likely to trust and support a company if it is transparent about the social responsibility initiatives it is undertaking and has a genuine commitment to making a positive impact on the world. (iii) Involvement of Customers: The concept of social responsibility has the potential to result in increased customer involvement. Because it demonstrates a shared commitment to making the world a better place, Millennials are more likely to interact with businesses that are actively involved in addressing social and environmental issues. Millennials have the potential to develop a long-term attachment to brands that demonstrate a commitment to social responsibility. Millennials are more likely to establish a staunch commitment to a company and maintain their support through ethical purchases when the brand consistently demonstrates social responsibility over a long period of time. This sentiment is supported by the fact that millennials are more likely to make ethical purchases. Firms should authentically include social responsibility into their fundamental principles and operational procedures to properly incorporate the influence of social responsibility on increasing ethical purchase intentions among millennials. This will allow firms to effectively exploit the influence of social responsibility. To accomplish this, it is necessary to provide a clear and concise explanation of their social and environmental actions, to actively involve customers in these topics, and to demonstrate a genuine commitment to having a positive impact on society and the globe. Social responsibility of the brands might influence the behavioral adoption of ethical influencers when it comes to ethical purchase decisions:

H_3: Social Responsibility mediates the relation in between ethical purchase intention and the behavioral adoption of ethical influencers.

Therefore, examining the behavioral adoption of promotional content by ethical influencers is essential for the long-term viability of influencer marketing and the effective creation of content.

Authenticity and trust can be established by ethical influencers who sincerely endorse and advocate for sustainable products or activities, hence fostering trust among their audience (Mim et al., 2022). When influencers exhibit a steadfast dedication to ethical principles, their followers are inclined to place greater trust in their endorsements and emulate their actions, such as adopting more environmentally conscious purchase choices (Thesis, 2004). Consciousness: Ethical influencers possess the power to enhance consciousness regarding sustainability concerns and provide instruction to their audience regarding the significance of making ethical decisions. Influencers can educate consumers about the environmental and societal consequences of their choices by featuring sustainable items or practices in their content. Effect and Significance: Ethical influencers frequently exert a substantial influence on consumer behavior. By endorsing sustainable items and advocating for responsible manufacturing techniques, they can exert influence over their followers, encouraging them to make more ethical purchase choices. This effect might lead to a change in consumer preferences towards sustainable and ethical products, hence increasing the demand for such products in the market. The emergence of ethical influencers has contributed to an increasing market demand for sustainable products since customers are adopting sustainable behaviors. The heightened demand can motivate enterprises to embrace more environmentally friendly production methods to fulfil consumer desires. Consequently, the adoption of behaviors led by influencers can contribute to a production environment that is more responsive and sustainable. The enduring influence of ethical influencers can foster the sustained adoption of sustainable behaviors, leading to lasting changes in consumer habits and preferences. As consumer awareness of sustainability increases, they are expected to persist in their search for ethical products and endorse brands that are in line with their values. The enduring change in consumer behavior has the potential to stimulate ongoing enhancements in sustainability across many sectors. Essentially, the ethical influencers' adoption of promotional information has a significant impact on raising awareness, shaping consumer behavior, generating market demand for sustainable products, and promoting responsible production processes. Through utilizing their authority, ethical influencers can actively contribute to fostering a marketplace that is both sustainable and ethical.

METHODOLOGY

The research is a quantitative, deductive study in which the determinants influencing Ethical Purchase Intention and promoting the adoption to follow the ethical influencers have been studied. One-to-one interview based on a semi-structured questionnaire has been conducted with an influencer executive working with a renowned marketing consultancy to identify the determinants which are mostly considered while connecting a brand with a specific group of influencers. Upon that, the structured close-ended questionnaire (attitudinal, 5-point Likert scale measure) was framed for consumer survey based on a non-probability (convenience) sampling method. The target segment was majorly the millennial. SPSS (Version 20) was used to conduct the mediation analysis and other tests to conclude the study and the framed hypotheses. 355 responses were collected based on the which the data analysis was carried out. In the study, ethical purchase intention has been considered as the independent variable, adoption of ethical influencers to be the dependent variable along with three mediating determinants i.e. Authenticity, Credibility and Social Responsibility.

RESULTS

The mediation analysis has been conducted to test the hypotheses and their intermediation in the phenomenon of adoption.

Table 1. Mediation of authenticity

Predictions	Consequent					
	Authenticity			Adoption of Ethical Influencers		
	Coeff.	SE	p	Coeff.	SE	p
Ethical Purchase Intention	0.85	0.12	.00	0.24	.08	0.0007
Authenticity	-	-	-	0.65	.03	.000
Constant	27.67	0.14	.00	13.70	1.6	.000
	$R=0.32, R^2= 0.28$			$R=0.43, R^2= 0.34$		
	$F(1, 355)= 3.86, p= .001$			$F(2, 354)= 3.02, p= .001$		

To test the 1st hypothesis, the mediation effect of authenticity in the role of ethical purchase intention to adopt the contents and follow the ethical influencers present in the social media space. Phenomenon is significant ($p = 0.00 < 0.05$, C.I – 95%). The coefficient of the mediation phenomenon has enhanced significantly than that of the existing value of the direct effect (0.85 > 0.65). Additionally, it has been seen that the range of ULCI – LLCI is non-zero which depicts successful mediation. The ethical purchasing intention is impacting the adoption of ethical influences which is mediated by the authenticity of the brands, their selective usage of raw materials and keeping the promises regarding the environmental, societal commitments.

To test the 2nd hypothesis, the mediation effect of credibility in the role of ethical purchase intention to adopt the contents and follow the ethical influencers present in the social media space. Phenomenon is significant ($p = 0.00 < 0.05$, C.I – 95%). The coefficient of the mediation phenomenon has enhanced significantly than that of the existing value of the direct effect (0.72 > 0.57). Furthermore, it has been seen that the range of ULCI – LLCI is non-zero which depicts successful mediation. The ethical purchasing intention is impacting the adoption of ethical influencers which is mediated by the credibility of the brands which enhances depending on the positioning of the product/services in the mind of the target consumers.

An organization representative said when asked how to avoid uninspired and unsuccessful sustainable marketing efforts and how to create more inventive sustainability campaigns that they encourage buy-in by clearly expressing the significance and impact of advocacy and making it simple. For instance, their organization's policyholders make automatic donations to the World Wildlife Fund's foodshed program,

Table 2. Mediation with credibility

Predictions	Consequent					
	Credibility			Adoption of Ethical Influencers		
	Coeff.	SE	p	Coeff.	SE	p
Ethical Purchase Intention	0.72	0.17	.00	0.21	.08	.00
Credibility	-	-	-	0.57	.03	.000
Constant	25.45	0.11	.00	11.66	1.3	.000
	$R=0.45, R^2= 0.39$			$R=0.61, R^2= 0.48$		
	$F (1, 355) = 3.86, p= .001$			$F (2, 354) = 3.02, p= .001$		

Table 3. Mediation of social responsibility

Predictions	Consequent					
	Social Responsibility			Adoption of Ethical Influencers		
	Coeff.	SE	p	Coeff.	SE	p
Ethical Purchase Intention	0.93	0.156	.00	0.24	.081	.00
Social Responsibility	-	-	-	0.78	.045	.000
Constant	29.67	0.134	.00	13.70	1.8	.000
	$R=0.43$, $R^2= 0.31$			$R=0.53$, $R^2= 0.28$		
	$F(1, 355)= 3.86$, $p= .001$			$F(2, 354)= 3.02$, $p= .001$		

which will help farming families in a destitute region. This is how credibility of a brand helps to adopt ethical influence and the related contents.

Many consumers today think that brands should work to improve the environment and promote sustainability in the future. Because they like connecting with their favourite brands, these customers expect companies to offer goods and services that respect environmental and social concerns. The 3rd hypothesis has been tested in the above-said context where the mediating role of social responsibility among the consumers to adopt ethical influence has been investigated. Ethical purchase intention among the millennial has enhanced the adoption which is mediated by the sense of social responsibility ($p = 0.00 < 0.05$, C.I. – 95%, Co.eff – $0.93 > 0.78$). It has been seen that the range of ULCI – LLCI is non-zero which depicts successful mediation. Several research has shown that consumers are getting inclined to sustainable approaches in their daily lifestyle. Food waste has declined prior to Covid19, household wastes are being recycled more, the usage of single-use plastic is limited. Additionally, the business of refurbished items is growing exponentially, and the brands are more searched/followed and adopted which are ethical in their business practices and generating sustainable values for the stakeholders.

Figure 1. Mediation analysis (H1)

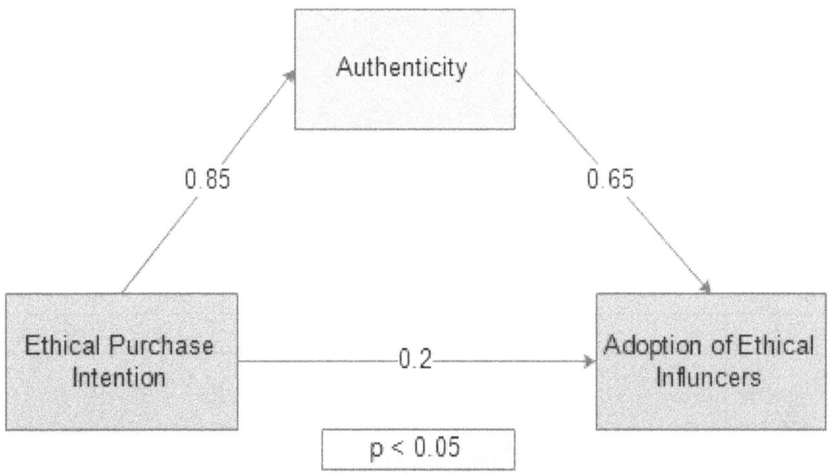

Figure 2. Mediation analysis (H2)

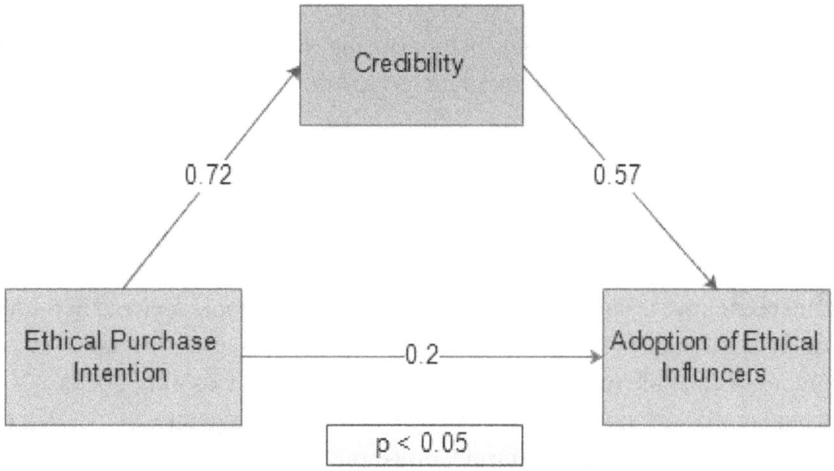

Figure 3. Mediation analysis (H3)

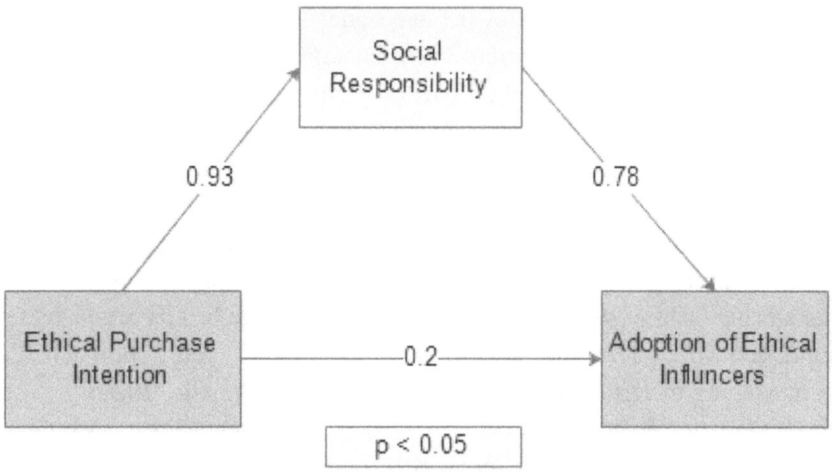

DISCUSSION

The millennial focus has shifted from mere consumption to sustainable consumption. Social Responsibility driven ethical buying intention is the primary focus. Millennial consumers are highly concerned about issues like environmental degradation and climatic changes and are ready to contribute to good causes. They are becoming more risk-averse and prefer to support businesses that emphasize pro-social messaging, environmentally friendly production, and moral business practices. The target consumer's perception of influencer marketing buzzwords like authenticity, credibility, and consumer involvement can be perceived as evolving. Influencers also power their voices to promote changes for good environmental causes.

The Theory of Planned Behavior suggests the effect of Purchase intention on the Behavioral adoption of a phenomenon (Ajzen, 1991). This study extends the theory by enlightening the development of the urge for ethical buying to adopt moral influencer content as a basis to follow them and facilitate the consumer buying process mediated by factors: Authenticity, Credibility and Social Responsibility. The people associated with the domain as influencers or aspiring to be one should focus on ethical influencing and associate with the brands focusing on organic growth.

Practical Implications

When it comes to modern marketing, the promotion of sustainable practices can be greatly aided by the smart use of influencer marketing. More and more, customers are thinking carefully about the products they buy, and influencers have a significant impact on how those people feel and act. This paper delves into the real advantages and factors to think about for both brands and influencers when using influencer marketing to promote sustainable marketing practices (Yesiloglu & Costello, 2021).

Influencers can magnify sustainable messaging because they are genuine voices in many domains. To build a genuine story around sustainable products and processes, brands can team up with influencers that share their ethical principles (W. Zhang et al., 2021). The capacity to reach specific demographics with these messages, using the influencers' platforms to inform and encourage people to make greener purchasing decisions, is the practical use.

Building Genuine Relationships: One of the real benefits of influencer marketing is the genuine relationships it can help brands and consumers form. Sustainable products help influencers generate authentic and relatable content by becoming a part of their daily lives (Iverson & Dervan, n.d.). By being genuine, you connect with your audience on a deeper level and earn their trust. What this means in practice is that firms with real environmental initiatives will have a more involved and dedicated customer base.

Niche Audience Targeting: Influencers frequently have a certain group of followers that have similar interests. For marketers aiming to reach specific populations that prioritize sustainable living, this is a great benefit. Sustainable fashion, zero-waste living, and sustainable beauty are just a few examples of niches where brands can work with influencers to make sustainability more approachable and desirable by catering their messaging to certain audiences' distinct ideals (Andjelic, 2020).

With the help of statistics, influencer marketing can be seen to have a measurable impact, which makes it more practical. To measure the efficacy of influencer marketing efforts, brands can monitor key performance indicators (KPIs) like engagement, click-through, and conversion rates. Brands can maximize their sustainable marketing campaigns and fine-tune their plans in real-time thanks to this data-driven strategy that enables informed decision-making (Al Adwan et al., 2023).

When it comes to managing a crisis and enhancing a company's reputation, influencers play an important role as brand champions. When faced with difficulties or scandals, influencers have the power to keep things real and open (Al Adwan et al., 2023). Quickly addressing issues, communicating company values, and reinforcing commitment to sustainability are all practical implications that can help mitigate reputational threats.

Building long-term relationships with influencers has practical implications for sustaining effect and can lead to lasting partnerships. Over time, brands gain genuine advocates in the form of influencers who truly embrace sustainable living (Ottman, 2017). By maintaining these relationships over time, brands can be sure that their ethical principles are consistently and authentically portrayed, which helps to build trust with consumers and establishes them as industry leaders in sustainability.

To sum up, influencer marketing has real-world consequences for sustainable practices that go beyond simple advertising. It helps with building real connections, reaching out to specific audiences, and making a demonstrable impact. When companies and influencers work together with sincerity and a sense of purpose, influencer marketing can be a powerful tool to encourage consumers to make more ethical and environmentally friendly purchasing decisions.

CONCLUSION

Brand credibility, brand authenticity, and social responsibility are essential factors in adapting ethical influencer marketing content. To uphold credibility, influencer marketing content must be in line with the brand's values and commitments. Brands must verify that the influencers they collaborate with possess a sincere affiliation with the product or service they are endorsing since this genuineness bolsters trustworthiness. Genuine authenticity is a crucial factor for influencer marketing to effectively connect with audiences. Brands ought to motivate influencers to provide content that accurately represents their authentic experiences and opinions regarding the product or service, rather than pre-planned endorsements. Brands are facing growing pressure to exhibit social responsibility in their marketing endeavors. Utilizing influencer marketing enables the promotion of social causes and sustainability projects, thereby harmonizing with the principles of socially conscious consumers. Brands must verify that the influencers they collaborate with are in line with their social responsibility goals and possess the genuine ability to promote them to their audiences. When brands modify ethical influencer marketing content, they should give importance to transparency, honesty, and a sincere dedication to the values they promote. This method not only improves the efficacy of influencer marketing but also fosters enduring relationships with consumers founded on trust and sincerity.

Not only can influencer marketing promote businesses in today's interconnected digital ecosystem, but it can also advocate for sustainable and ethical behaviors. A new breed of influential users known as "influencers" has emerged as a result of the merging of consumer-driven content with social media platforms. This essay delves into the ways in which influencer marketing may be a powerful tool in the shift towards more environmentally friendly advertising strategies. The capacity to communicate genuine and approachable messages is a major asset of influencer marketing. Sustainable living can be modeled by influencers, thanks to their varied experiences and perspectives. Sustainable items and practices that influencers genuinely use in their content really hit home with their audience. Brands and consumers are able to engage on a deeper level when they are authentic, which goes beyond simple product marketing and builds trust. Because of the size and engagement of their audiences, influencers can play a significant role in promoting eco-friendly lifestyles (H. Zhang et al., 2020). They have the power to inform the public and bring attention to social and environmental problems through the platforms they have. In order to shape customer attitudes and encourage a sense of responsibility towards the world, influencers might promote eco-friendly products, talk about ethical sourcing, or advocate responsible consumption (Panopoulos et al., 2023). With the help of influencer marketing, companies become more personable and easy to connect with. The human aspect of a brand's dedication to ethical practices can be highlighted through collaborations with influencers who share sustainable beliefs (Bu & Go, 2008). By giving a voice and a story to a brand's sustainability initiatives, influencers elevate these initiatives beyond mere marketing. Customers are more inclined to back and embrace sustainable options when they feel an emotional connection to the brand through this personal touch. Peers are a common source of advice and approval for consumers. Taking advantage of this social dynamic, influencer marketing portrays influential people as trustworthy advocates for eco-friendly goods. Influencers' adoption and promotion of environmentally friendly goods can greatly influence their followers' purchasing decisions (Kiss, 2021). Promoting sustainable consumption patterns among varied audiences is greatly aided by influencer-facilitated peer influence. Analytics and key performance indicators (KPIs) allow one to measure the efficacy of influencer marketing. Brands can monitor how influencer marketing affect customer actions, opinions, and revenue. Ensuring that influencer engagements are in line with the increasing tastes of eco-conscious consumers, this data-driven strategy enables for the continual development of sustainable marketing initiatives. Sustainable marketing has a lot of potential with influencer marketing, but there are some obstacles that need to be overcome, like worries about authenticity and greenwashing. Tighter regulations for influencer partnerships, open dialogue about sustainability efforts, and a promise to work together for the long haul in an ethical manner should all be on the table for future discussions. When it comes to environmentally friendly advertising, influencer marketing is way ahead of the curve. Influencers can make a difference by being genuine, teaching others, making themselves more approachable, using social proof, and having a verifiable impact. A more sustainable and responsible marketing future is possible thanks to influencer marketing, which is a powerful tool for connecting environmentally conscious firms with ethically conscious consumers.

Influencer marketing has the potential to be both sustainable and disruptive to traditional marketing in multiple ways. Influencers frequently possess a loyal and attentive audience that places trust in their endorsements. The precise targeting enables firms to establish more successful connections with specific audience segments compared to conventional mass media advertising. Followers tend to view influencers as more genuine and reliable in comparison to conventional advertising. When influencers give their endorsement to a product or service, it can create the perception of a referral from a friend, resulting in increased levels of trust and involvement. Influencer marketing has the potential to be more economical compared to conventional advertising platforms such as television or print media. Brands may effectively reach their desired audience by utilising influencers, at a significantly lower expense compared to conventional advertising. This is particularly true when taking into account the possible return on investment resulting from the increased engagement and conversions generated by influencer campaigns. Influencers are proficient content makers that have the ability to provide captivating and pertinent information for their target consumers. Brands can utilise this material for their own marketing endeavours, thereby expanding its reach and longevity beyond the original influencer post. Influencer marketing frequently yields more quantifiable outcomes compared to conventional advertising methods.

Brands have the ability to monitor engagement metrics, conversions, and other important performance indicators in order to evaluate the impact of influencer campaigns and make informed decisions for future tactics. Overall, influencer marketing provides a more focused, genuine, and economical method for contacting and captivating people in comparison to conventional marketing methods. The capacity to utilize the confidence and impact of individuals in online environments renders it a durable and transformative power in the marketing domain.

REFERENCES

Adrian, M., & Lamb, M. A. (n.d.). *An exploration of the determinants of sedentary behaviour in desk-based employees* [Thesis]. Sheffield Hallam University.

Ajzen, I. (1991). The theory of planned behavior. *Organizational Behavior and Human Decision Processes*, *50*(2), 179–211. doi:10.1016/0749-5978(91)90020-T

Al Adwan, A., Kokash, H., Al Adwan, R., & Khattak, A. (2023). Data analytics in digital marketing for tracking the effectiveness of campaigns and inform strategy. *International Journal of Data and Network Science*, *7*(2), 563–574. doi:10.5267/j.ijdns.2023.3.015

Andjelic, A. (2020). The business of aspiration: How social, cultural, and environmental capital changes brands. *The Business of Aspiration: How Social, Cultural, and Environmental Capital Changes Brands*, 1–94. doi:10.4324/9781003093572

Atiq, M., Abid, G., Anwar, A., & Ijaz, M. F. (2022). Influencer Marketing on Instagram: A Sequential Mediation Model of Storytelling Content and Audience Engagement via Relatability and Trust. *Information (Basel)*, *13*(7), 345. Advance online publication. doi:10.3390/info13070345

Barbosa, N. L. (2019). An exploration of how ethics and sustainability influence the purchase decision of millennials in the coffee industry in Ireland. *Dublin Business School.*

Berki-Kiss, D., & Menrad, K. (2022). The role emotions play in consumer intentions to make pro-social purchases in Germany–An augmented theory of planned behavior model. *Sustainable Production and Consumption*, *29*, 79–89. doi:10.1016/j.spc.2021.09.026

Berne-Manero, C., & Marzo-Navarro, M. (2020). Exploring how influencer and relationship marketing serve corporate sustainability. Sustainability (Switzerland), 12(11).

Bu, O. B., & Go, A. S. (2008). Perceived trustworthiness of online shops. *Journal of Consumer Behaviour*, *50*(October), 35–50. doi:10.1002/cb

Chatzopoulou, E., & de Kiewiet, A. (2021). Millennials' evaluation of corporate social responsibility: The wants and needs of the largest and most ethical generation. *Journal of Consumer Behaviour*, *20*(3), 521–534. doi:10.1002/cb.1882

Deo, K., & Prasad, A. A. (2022). Exploring Climate Change Adaptation, Mitigation and Marketing Connections. *Sustainability (Basel)*, *14*(7), 4255. Advance online publication. doi:10.3390/su14074255

Duong, C. D. (2023). Karmic beliefs and social entrepreneurial intentions: A moderated mediation model of environmental complexity and empathy. *Journal of Open Innovation*, *9*(1), 100022. doi:10.1016/j.joitmc.2023.100022

Fuxman, L., Mohr, I., Mahmoud, A. B., & Grigoriou, N. (2022). The new 3Ps of sustainability marketing: The case of fashion. *Sustainable Production and Consumption*, *31*, 384–396. doi:10.1016/j.spc.2022.03.004

Haider, M., Shannon, R., & Moschis, G. P. (2022). Sustainable Consumption Research and the Role of Marketing: A Review of the Literature (1976–2021). *Sustainability (Basel)*, *14*(7), 1–36. doi:10.3390/su14073999

Hunt, S. D., Wood, V. R., & Chonko, L. B. (1989). Corporate Ethical Values and Organizational Commitment in Marketing. *Journal of Marketing*, *53*(3), 79–90. doi:10.1177/002224298905300309

Ikonen, P., Luoma-aho, V., & Bowen, S. A. (2017). Transparency for Sponsored Content: Analysing Codes of Ethics in Public Relations, Marketing, Advertising and Journalism. *International Journal of Strategic Communication*, *11*(2), 165–178. doi:10.1080/1553118X.2016.1252917

Jung, E., & La, S. (2020). Wear Your Heart on Your Sleeve: Exploring Moral Identity as a Moderator Across CSR Authenticity, Consumer Admiration, and Engagement in the Fashion Industry. *Asia Marketing Journal*, *22*(2), 19–57. doi:10.15830/amj.2020.22.2.19

Kiss, R. (2021). *The impact of influencer credibility on purchase intention in the endorsement of sustainable products*. https://jyx.jyu.fi/handle/123456789/76963

Kushwah, S., Dhir, A., & Sagar, M. (2019). Ethical consumption intentions and choice behavior towards organic food. Moderation role of buying and environmental concerns. *Journal of Cleaner Production*, *236*, 117519. doi:10.1016/j.jclepro.2019.06.350

Lahbib, O., Rojas-Contreras, C., & Kessous, A. (2023). *A Study Around the Effect of Influencer Endorsement on Sustainable Luxury Brand Charisma*. https://hal.science/hal-04207997/%0Ahttps://hal.science/hal-04207997/document

Lamberton, C., & Stephen, A. T. (2016). A thematic exploration of digital, social media, and mobile marketing: Research evolution from 2000 to 2015 and an agenda for future inquiry. *Journal of Marketing*, *80*(6), 146–172. doi:10.1509/jm.15.0415

Lee, J. A., & Eastin, M. S. (2021). Perceived authenticity of social media influencers: Scale development and validation. *Journal of Research in Interactive Marketing*, *15*(4), 822–841. doi:10.1108/JRIM-12-2020-0253

Lenk, L. T., & Rotkirch, I. (2021). *Green Millennials?* Academic Press.

Mabkhot, H., Isa, N. M., & Mabkhot, A. (2022). The Influence of the Credibility of Social Media Influencers SMIs on the Consumers' Purchase Intentions: Evidence from Saudi Arabia. *Sustainability (Basel)*, *14*(19), 12323. Advance online publication. doi:10.3390/su141912323

Marín-García, A., Gil-Saura, I., & Ruiz-Molina, M. E. (2022). Do innovation and sustainability influence customer satisfaction in retail? A question of gender. *Ekonomska Istrazivanja*, *35*(1), 546–563. doi:10.1080/1331677X.2021.1924217

Medvecka, J., Rad, R., Medvecka, J., & Rad, R. (2023). *B2C sustainability communication Exploring millennials' perceptions of and attitudes towards luxury fashion brands' sustainability communication on Instagram*. Academic Press.

Mim, K. B., Jai, T., & Lee, S. H. (2022). The Influence of Sustainable Positioning on eWOM and Brand Loyalty: Analysis of Credible Sources and Transparency Practices Based on the S-O-R Model. *Sustainability (Basel)*, *14*(19), 12461. Advance online publication. doi:10.3390/su141912461

Murphy, C. (2021). *The Impact of Influencer Marketing on Fast Fashion Purchase Intentions from an Irish Female Millennial's Perspective.* https://norma.ncirl.ie/id/eprint/5473%0Ahttps://norma.ncirl.ie/5473/1/carlamurphy.pdf

Mutum, D. S., & Ghazali, E. M. (2023). Consumers. *Society and Marketing*, (November). Advance online publication. doi:10.1007/978-3-031-39359-4

Nguyen, N., & Johnson, L. W. (2020). Consumer behaviour and environmental sustainability. *Journal of Consumer Behaviour, 19*(6), 539–541. doi:10.1002/cb.1892

Ottman, J. A. (2017). *The New Rules of Green marketing*. The New Rules of Green Marketing., doi:10.4324/9781351278683

Ozuem, W., Willis, M., Howell, K., Lancaster, G., & Ng, R. (2021). Determinants of online brand communities' and millennials' characteristics: A social influence perspective. *Psychology and Marketing, 38*(5), 794–818. doi:10.1002/mar.21470

Panopoulos, A., Poulis, A., Theodoridis, P., & Kalampakas, A. (2023). Influencing Green Purchase Intention through Eco Labels and User-Generated Content. *Sustainability (Basel), 15*(1), 764. Advance online publication. doi:10.3390/su15010764

Pattuglia. (2018). Towards a new understanding of brand authenticity: Seeing through the lens of millennials. *Sinergie Italian Journal of Management, 103*(103), 35–55. doi:10.7433/s103.2017.03

Rathore, B. (2018). Allure of Style: The Impact of Contemporary Fashion Marketing on Consumer Behaviour. *International Journal of New Media Studies, 05*(02), 10–21. doi:10.58972/eiprmj.v5i2y18.114

Rauch, E., Rofner, M., Cappellini, C., & Matt, D. T. (2022). Towards Sustainable Manufacturing: A Case Study for Sustainable Packaging Redesign. Design, Simulation, Manufacturing: The Innovation Exchange, 84–93.

Risitano, M., Romano, R., Rusciano, V., Civero, G., & Scarpato, D. (2022). The impact of sustainability on marketing strategy and business performance: The case of Italian fisheries. *Business Strategy and the Environment, 31*(4), 1538–1551. doi:10.1002/bse.2968

Rosli, N., Ha, N. C., & Ghazali, E. M. (2019). Bridging the gap between branding and sustainability by fostering brand credibility and brand attachment in travellers' hotel choice. *The Bottom Line (New York, N.Y.), 32*(4), 308–339. doi:10.1108/BL-03-2019-0078

Sahadev, S., Muralidharan, S., & Singh, P. (2022). Introduction to the special issue on marketing communications and sustainability. *Journal of Marketing Communications, 28*(3), 227–231. doi:10.1080/13527266.2021.1942145

Sen, S., & Bhattacharya, C. B. (2001). Does doing good always lead to doing better? Consumer reactions to corporate social responsibility. *JMR, Journal of Marketing Research, 38*(2), 225–243. doi:10.1509/jmkr.38.2.225.18838

Shaw, D. (2021). Voluntary simplicity. *The Routledge Companion to Alternative Organization, 19*(February), 234–243. doi:10.4324/9780203725351-24

Smith, B. G., Kendall, M. C., Knighton, D., & Wright, T. (2018). Rise of the Brand Ambassador: Social Stake, Corporate Social Responsibility and Influence among the Social Media Influencers. *Communication Management Review*, *03*(01), 6–29. doi:10.22522/cmr20180127

Sogari, G., Pucci, T., Aquilani, B., & Zanni, L. (2017). Millennial generation and environmental sustainability: The role of social media in the consumer purchasing behavior for wine. *Sustainability (Basel)*, *9*(10), 1911. Advance online publication. doi:10.3390/su9101911

Stahlhofer, N. J., Schmidkonz, C., & Kraft, P. (2018). Case Studies: Conscious Business in Germany. In CSR, Sustainability, Ethics and Governance. doi:10.1007/978-3-319-69739-0_4

Study, I. O. F. (2012). *The Role of Social Media in Crisis Management and the Impact on Brand Image*. Academic Press.

Suganthi, L. (2019). Examining the relationship between corporate social responsibility, performance, employees' pro-environmental behavior at work with green practices as mediator. *Journal of Cleaner Production*, *232*, 739–750. doi:10.1016/j.jclepro.2019.05.295

Taheri, B., Farrington, T., Curran, R., & O'Gorman, K. (2018). Sustainability and the authentic experience. Harnessing brand heritage–a study from Japan. *Journal of Sustainable Tourism*, *26*(1), 49–67. doi:10.1080/09669582.2017.1310867

Topalova, N. (2021). The impact of marketing through Instagram influencers on consumer behavior in the fashion industry: Comparison of Millennials and Generation Z in Russia. *Chemical and Engineering News*, *27*(32), 2282–2283.

Wellman, M. L., Stoldt, R., Tully, M., & Ekdale, B. (2020). Ethics of Authenticity: Social Media Influencers and the Production of Sponsored Content. *Journal of Media Ethics: Exploring Questions of Media Morality*, *35*(2), 68–82. doi:10.1080/23736992.2020.1736078

Yesiloglu, S., & Costello, J. (2021). *Influencer marketing: Building brand communities and engagement*. Academic Press.

Zatwarnicka-Madura, B., Nowacki, R., & Wojciechowska, I. (2022). Influencer Marketing as a Tool in Modern Communication—Possibilities of Use in Green Energy Promotion amongst Poland's Generation Z. *Energies*, *15*(18), 6570. Advance online publication. doi:10.3390/en15186570

Zhang, H., Nauyen, T. H., & Lenka, S. (2020). Green lifestyle, where to go? How social media influencers moderate the intention-behavior gap within the ecological lifestyle context. *Jönköping University*.

Zhang, W., Chintagunta, P. K., & Kalwani, M. U. (2021). Social Media, Influencers, and Adoption of an Eco-Friendly Product: Field Experiment Evidence from Rural China. *Journal of Marketing*, *85*(3), 10–27. doi:10.1177/0022242920985784

Chapter 14
Determinants of Customer Analytics Capabilities:
A Model to Achieve Sustainable Firm Performance

Meenal Arora
https://orcid.org/0000-0001-7670-6948
Chitkara Business School, Chitkara University, India

Amit Mittal
https://orcid.org/0000-0002-1191-4620
Chitkara Business School, Chitkara University, India

Anshika Prakash
https://orcid.org/0000-0001-9052-7188
School of Management and Commerce, K.R. Mangalam University, Gurugram, India

Vishal Jain
https://orcid.org/0000-0003-1126-7424
School of Engineering and Technology, Sharda University, India

ABSTRACT

Customer analytics is essential for creating insights from massive data that can be used to enhance management decision-making at various consumer levels, product creation, and service innovation. However, no studies have examined the potential of consumer analytics for achieving long-term corporate success. This research examines the structures of customer analytics capabilities in order to fill this gap by drawing upon a rigorous assessment of the big data literature. The interpretative framework for this study shows the concept of customer analytics, its significance, and the building blocks for consumer analytics capabilities. The research suggests a model of consumer analytics capabilities made up of four main constructs and some significant supporting sub-constructs. The study elaborates on developing a model to analyze sustainable firm performance through dimensions of customer analytics capabilities.

DOI: 10.4018/979-8-3693-3253-5.ch014

I. INTRODUCTION

Apart from providing goods and services to developed markets, low per capita income, unpredictable demand, an abundance of options, inadequate infrastructure, and, most importantly, fragmentation are characteristics of emerging markets. For firms to create their business strategy, it is crucial to recognize these traits (Aguiar & Gopinath, 2007). Customer engagement is a key element under these circumstances that determines the organization's longevity. A firm's business communications with a client or consumer across various channels are the core of customer engagement, ultimately generating sales opportunities (Ference, 2017). It also includes provoking customers to interact and share their brand-related experiences by offering encouragement to them (Maslowska et al., 2016). The strongest driver of corporate success and market expansion in the connected world today is client engagement, which eventually results in profitability for the business (Brodie et al., 2011). The goal should be to create value whenever the company has a chance to interact with a consumer. The customer interaction strategy must be an essential component of the business strategy in order to facilitate the same. The goal of customer-centric enterprises is to accomplish customer engagement to foster a closer, more solidified relationship between the client and the business.

The strategic problem of comprehending and maintaining client relationships has grown more challenging and crucial as businesses are vying for consumers' attention in an increasingly cutthroat manner, driving up acquisition costs and making client retention harder (Gupta et al., 2006). Simultaneously, it has been simpler to gather enormous amounts of client data that, when collaborated with ever more complicated analysis, may produce significant and helpful inputs (McAfee & Brynjofsson, 2012), enabling businesses to innovate and stand out from rivals. However, because of the widespread use of analytics, many of the opportunities are already taken. As a result, isolated, ad hoc analytics projects are unable to establish or maintain a competitive advantage. Companies that want to use big data to produce strategic value must develop targeted analytics capabilities that allow for quick adaptation to a dynamic environment.

Analytics in Consumer aspect have typically focused on compartmentalized information which captures a particular component of consumer activity at single time, with the possible exception of a limited number of start-ups focused on technology and built exclusively on analytic capabilities (e.g. Google, Amazon, Capital One) (Davenport, 2013). The data diversity and velocity with businesses have rapidly increased (Lu et al., 2021, Goyal et al., 2019) over the past ten years as a result of the growth of customer relationship management (CRM) software, social networking, online reviews, web traffic statistics, and other information technology-enabled technologies (Agarwal & Dhar, 2014; Chen & Storey, 2012). The businesses that advance from typical walled consumer analytics refer to "advanced customer analytics" will benefit the most from this expansion which enables comprehensive actionable inputs and outputs for customer equity, acquisition, retention, and growth come from an understanding of customers.

Traditionally, back in the days of brick and mortar, a customer would inquire about a product and the sales representative would respond by exerting influence. With the use of digital technologies, the same experience has been transformed, taking into consideration social queries and replies from previous customers as well as other customer input. Digital, social, and mobile media are important for the product success or failure (Olaleye et al., 2019). Customers may consider the a lot of reviews when making a buying decision, however in some cases, even one unfavorable review can have a negative effect. (Floyd et al., 2014). As a result, organizations want data that contains pertinent client information. An organization requires a complete 360-degree image of the client to connect among each other (Yerpude

& Singhal, 2018). The development of autonomous data-gathering technologies has been greatly aided by the information technology sector. The Internet of Things is one such platform that emerged from advancements in the networking industry (IoT). The IoT is one such disruption that is growing at a very fast rate due to the internet's pervasiveness (Yerpude & Singhal, 2018).

The Internet of Things is a networked ecosystem where technology is embedded in physical objects that is capable of detecting and responding to interactions between the internal state and the external environment (Steenstrup & Kutnick, 2015). IoT landscape produces real-time data which is used by the analytical models that assist real-time decision-making (Yerpude & Singhal, 2018). IoT is essentially a global internet-based architecture that makes it easier for people to share information about products and services (Weber & Weber, 2010). There has been a notable surge in the previous ten years in the quantity of devices (sensors) linked to the internet (Ejdys, 2018). IoT is fundamentally a network of things that can interact with their surroundings by sensing changes in state and transferring that information over the internet (Rio & Banker, 2014). The consumer experience is improved and elevated thanks to real-time information from the IoT environment (Davenport & Harris, 2007). Better customer service is the consequence, of aligning customer expectations with those of the brand. Real-time customer analytics powered by the Internet of Things can transform an enterprise and provide a brand with a competitive edge (Yerpude & Singhal, 2018).

The focus of this paper's research will be customer analytics, which denotes the procedures and tools which provide enterprise customers insight and assist them in making important decisions related to the business mainly because it affects a company's long-term strategy and corporate development. Companies have a wide range of service opportunities to add value for their customers as a result of the rapid growth in customer-related data.

Customer analytics, according to France and Ghose (2018), is a cutting-edge technology capable of resolving customer-centric problems by evaluating vast amounts of marketing data. A significant body of study e.g., Braun and Garriga (2018), Erevelles et al. (2015), Verhoef et al. (2010) emphasizes the advantages of customer analytics, with little to no emphasis being paid to how businesses may increase their capacity for consumer analytics in a setting with lots of data. As a result, this study aims to provide an answer.

RQ: What dimensions of customer analytics can be used to improve long-term business performance?

In order to respond to this inquiry, we first describe the definitional elements of customer analytics. Second, we emphasize the significance of customer analytics, evaluate the results of thorough literature analysis, and provide a group of constructs for customer analytics capabilities.

This research adds two new perspectives to the field of consumer analytics in response to the research topic. It provides a theoretical foundation for consumer analytics capability dimensions and the capacity of customer analytics to produce long-term business success in a cutthroat business climate. Following a thorough examination of the literature, the research formulates a model of customer analytics capability that provides guidance for achieving long-term business growth. The study concludes by providing a succinct discussion of the difficulties and a direction for this particular field's future study.

II. LITERATURE REVIEW

The term "customer analytics" describes the procedures and tools that provide businesses with information about their clients and support them in making important business choices (Lu et al., 2021).

Given its influence on a company's long-term strategy and corporate growth, customer analytics is particularly significant.

In the context of a data-rich environment, customer analytics is a dependable way for managing today's continually evolving customers (Sun et al., 2014). According to Magill (2015), conducting in-depth customer analytics enables firms to have a thorough insight of both their customers and the larger market, making it no longer just an option but a need for delivering exceptional customer service. Value creation and strategy-centric analysis have both been taken into account for defining consumer analytics. Verhoef et al. (2010), suggested that by looking at each customer's purchasing patterns and behavior, a cross-selling strategy for many product categories can be developed by managers with the use of customer analytics in a data-rich environment. In fact, a company with a solid analytical foundation can acquire a strategic advantage Ransbotham & Kiron, (2018).

The actual performance of a company and management's decision-making are well informed when managers strategically use analytics, according to Germann et al. (2013). From the perspective of identifying new prospects, another line of research defines customer analytics. For instance, Surma (2011) provided four explanations of the application of data mining for consumer intelligence. First, a company can speak with customers indefensibly through customization on mobile devices then examine media convergence and internet user behavior, look at the relationship between geographic location and consumer behavior, and then design a sophisticated system. All of these strategies can help a company stand out from the competition. Similar to this, Wedel and Kannan (2016) discussed how businesses have tremendous prospects thanks to the vast expansion of media, channels, gadgets, and software for programming (analytics).

Moreover, "Custolytics" is a word coined by earlier researchers and derived from combining analytics and customers, which assists in customer segmentation for the organization and helps formulate several approaches for each of the segments (Yerpude & Singhal, 2021). Customer engagement and the quality of the customer experience determine the degree of customer happiness (Khoshafian, 2015). To increase client involvement, businesses are turning to new sources including digital, social, and mobile media. Modern methods of communication, like digital media, are particularly successful in growing markets where companies need to implement a go-to-customer approach (Akhlaq & Ahmed, 2015).

III. SIGNIFICANCE OF CUSTOMER ANALYTICS

The growing economies that have experienced exponential development are those where clients are taught how to use digital media (Howard & Hussain, 2011). Real-time consumption of information obtained digitally is possible. Social media extensively makes use of channels like smartphones and the web to communicate with users and build an engaging platform (Kietzmann et al., 2011). The information generated by social media platforms demonstrates its importance because businesses can utilize it to create systems for individualized messaging (Ference, 2017). Mobile media is becoming an essential component of the global platform, where it is largely used to distribute media over the network, such as photos and videos. It can also be utilized to record and monitor locational data. For specific use cases including client interaction strategy, the real-time data captured becomes extremely important. An organization may personally connect with thousands of consumers using digital, social, and mobile media, which enhances the brand's reputation (Mangold & Faulds, 2009). This is made feasible by the client information obtained and the analytics carried out using various models. Thus, "Custolytics," or customer analytics, may become essential for the firm as it develops its customer interaction strategy (Yerpude & Singhal, 2021).

With the availability of a massive data, both unstructured and structured, coming from the company's all round sources, it has been noted that there is now more pressure than ever to get a systematic enterprise perspective of the customer (Sun et al., 2014; Wedel & Kannan, 2016). Such pressure forces businesses to conduct extensive customer analytics in order to get deeper customer insights. According to Germann et al. (2014), a company can benefit from consumer analytics if it possesses three key traits. First off, the company has a vast amount of client data at its disposal. The availability of an analytics-based methodology, followed by the implementation of analytics-based tools, is what supports the repeated decision. In their study, Fieldler et al. (2013) used Wal-Mart as an illustration of the connection between the success of customer analytics and large amounts of data. By analyzing scanner data, Wal-Mart was able to correctly determine that storm warnings greatly boost sales of specific goods like Pop-Tarts. In order to increase the firm's profitability, Kumar & Petersen et al. (Kumar & Petersen, 2012) mentioned analytic-based techniques as well, for instance, customer relationship management (CRM) and customer lifetime value (CLV) measures. Analytics also aids in making routine choices regarding a customer's good/service. Moreover, National Academies Press (NAP) of the United States established a price model using customer-analytics based on knowledge despite making many of the same judgments repeatedly (Kannan et al., 2009). Another instance involves the success of a German mail-order business that used a when, how often, and to whom model which can be determined using a dynamic multilevel response modelling system to send its catalogs (Elsner et al., 2004). Similar to this, Erevelles et al. (2015) focused on the strategic transformation of organizations through customer analytics(CA), where researchers cite Southwest Airlines as an example of a company which implemented software based on speech analytic to obtain a greater competitive advantage by gaining consumer insights. Despite the potential advantages of analytics in contexts with lots of data, several businesses have not yet fully implemented such methods (Mithas et al., 2013). Businesses need to follow the proper procedures for creating and preserving consumer activity records as big data, ensuring that they have the technological ability to extract inputs from big data, and effectively organize thoughts to improve ever changing capability in order to compete in the market (Erevelles et al., 2015). Thus, a company's senior management team must integrate customer analytics into both its corporate culture and daily operations (Germann et al., 2013).

Over the past ten years, the methods used in customer analytics have undergone a rapid transformation, from "text analytics" to "audio analytics" to "video analytics" to "web analytics" to "social media analytics" to "behavior analytics" to "predictive analytics" to "journey analytics" finally to "cognitive analytics" most recently (Magill, 2016). As a result, businesses need to be agile collecting comprehensive data from across the company to use analytics to spot and address consumer issues in a changing environment in order to get a sustained competitive edge from big data (Kitchens et al., 2018; Sood et al., 2022). Customer analytics is particularly crucial as it influences an organization's long-term strategy and corporate progress (Lu et al., 2021).

IV. RESEARCH APPROACH

The research question was "What dimensions of customer analytics can be used to improve long-term business performance?". The research adopted a rigorous systematic literature review using the frameworks of Akter and Wamb (2016) and Hossain, et al. (2020) to address the research question. Customer analytics literature is taken into consideration along with pertinent studies of big data analytics capacity and IT capability because this field is developing and progressing at an extremely fast pace (Sood et al., 2022). Scholarly papers published between the periods from January 2006 to December 2021 are considered. As the first significant piece "competing on analytics" published by Davenport was issued in Harvard Business Review in the year 2006, hence we choose that year as the lowest cut-off. Five reputable databases were taken into consideration: Science Direct, Business Source Complete, Web of Science, ABI/Inform Complete and Scopus. The abstract, title, and keywords fields were the only ones that were searched. 142 papers in all were subjected to critical evaluation. We took into account the 29 most pertinent publications as we sought to define the major and sub-major consumer analytics capacity factors (Table 1).

V. DIMENSIONS OF CUSTOMER ANALYTICS CAPABILITY

The Dimensions of consumer analytics capacity are based on the results of the thorough literature research approach outlined above.

A. Customer Analytics Management Capability

An ability of an electronic device to operate, control and manage routine tasks which are consumer-centric (like CRM, with techniques which aid in acquiring, keeping, and satisfying customers, as well as increasing client lifetime value) in a methodical way, depending on the needs and significance of the company, is referred to as customer analytics management capability. The fundamental components of analytics management competence, as per Kim et al. (2012), include controlling, planning, investment and coordination for technology decision making. Customer analytics management capabilities should begin with an appropriate planning approach in order to maximize performance using big data-based models and identify new business prospects (Barton & Court, 2012). Second, a company's distinct strategic position is dependent upon making the right analytics decision about investment, that aids in building up the company's finance model to balance the expenses of investment (McKeen & Smith,

Table 1. Constructs and sub constructs

S.No	*Constructs*	*Sub Constructs*	*Source*
1	Customer Analytics Management Capability	• Planning • Decision making • Coordination • Control	(Barton & Court, 2012; Hossain et al., 2020; Kim et al., 2012; LaValle et al., 2011; McKeen & Smith, 2015; Ross et al., 2013)
2	Customer Analytics Technology/Infrastructure Capability	• Connectivity • Compatibility • Modularity	(Akter et al., 2016; Barton & Court, 2012; Davenport & Harris, 2007; Fink & Neumann, 2009; Gupta & George, 2016; Hossain et al., 2020; Morris, 2006; Storey & Song, 2017; Yerpude & Singhal, 2021; Zhang et al., 2009)
3	Customer Analytics Personnel Expertise Capability	•Technological/Technical • Business • Relational	(Aral & Weill, 2007; Gupta & George, 2016; Hossain et al., 2020; Kim et al., 2011; Kim et al., 2012)
4	CA 4P Mix- Modeling Capability	• Incorporation • Allocation • Assessment	(Fischer et al., 2011; Hanssens et al., 2014; Hossain et al., 2020; Hui et al., 2013; Kellerand & Lehmann, 2006; Kitchens et al., 2018; Sakshi et al., 2020; Srinivasan et al., 2010; Tandon et al., 2021; Wedel & Kannan, 2016)

2015). Thirdly, "coordination" in the context of information technology describes a type of routine that establishes the cross-functional alignment of analytics operations through resources like task forces, direct links, and gatherings of interdepartmental teams (Karimi et al., n.d.). Finally, managers need to ensure that information technology-related processes are efficiently carried out after other instruments and that analytics managing activities are planned (Hossain et al., 2020; Kim et al., 2012).

B. Customer Analytics Technology/Infrastructure Capability

According to resource-based theory (RBT), resources are static, uncommon, and cannot be replaced. Companies that have the necessary technological skills are possibly in front of their rivals for giving clients better value (Morris, 2006). Companies desperately need IT capabilities to adapt to the changing business environment (Fink & Neumann, 2009). Customers' orders, information about client inventory, as well as financial transactions can all be stored and handled by a customer-focused technological capability like Relational Database Management System (RDBMS) (Storey & Song, 2017). Nevertheless, an organization's information is 80 percent unstructured (Gupta & George, 2016). Additionally, businesses must ensure technological innovation to integrate cross-functional data, maintain platform compatibility, and offer adaptability in order to construct an advanced model to get a competitive edge in a data-rich environment (Akter et al., 2016; Yerpude & Singhal, 2021). Ensuring communication between the many customer-centric data sources is the first infrastructure capability, which subsequently aids in building more vital customer management and relationships. For example, in the context of the data-rich environment, banks frequently enhance client services by examining ATM transaction information, online discussion boards, and internet inquiries (Barton & Court, 2012). Compatibility is the second element that aids in real-time decision-making by synchronizing overlapping data and filling in information gaps. For instance, For rapid data analysis, Amazon leverages cloud technology, and teamwork and trial results recommended that compatibility and connection enable the integration of information systems within companies and that this competence enables and advances the company's overall technological capabilities. Additionally, Akter et al. (2016) mention "modularity" as an additional crucial element of analytics capabilities, enabling businesses to add or remove functionalities as needed. Similar to this, Zhang et al. (2009) said that modularity allows IT to be rearranged and amplified when changes are required; as a result, modularity advances technology capabilities take advantage of opportunities for business, and boosts company's productivity (Hossain et al., 2020).

C. Customer Analytics Personnel Expertise Capability

The capacity for analytics employees (e.g., abilities or knowledge) to perform specified consumer-centric duties in an environment with lots of data is referred to as personnel expertise capability. This "know-how" expertise produces a firm's competitive advantage and counts as capabilities (Gupta & George, 2016). According to studies, analytics expert needs to be skilled in four different skill sets. First of all, technical knowledge pertains to the comprehension of programming languages, mechanical principles, and equipped systems, as well as customer-focused duties in a data-driven environment. Examples of technical expertise include effective database management and networking. Second, technology management knowledge refers to the expertise in managing particular resources in a data-rich environment in order to achieve the organization's anticipated goals. Examples of this proficiency are operations, technique management, and the application of imaging technologies. Thirdly, comprehension of the business environment is referred to as having knowledge about business (e.g., being aware of company objectives and units) and a variety of business activities. The interaction and communication ability of analytics personnel with a group of individuals from different business functions is referred to as relational learning (collaborating business functions) (Akter et al., 2016; Aral & Weill, 2007; Hossain et al., 2020; Kim et al., 2011).

D. Customer Analytics 4P Mix Modeling Capability

The 4P mix can be used to increase the efficiency and capacity of consumers' value generation, and models and algorithms can be used to quantify and enhance the organization's performance regarding marketing mix (Wedel & Kannan, 2016). Big data analysis with appropriate modeling makes it possible to pinpoint market trends, competitor products, and demographic aspects (Kitchens et al., 2018), enabling businesses to enhance their products, provide them at a competitive price, engage in meaningful promotion, and create the right distribution channels (Kitchens et al., 2018; Sakshi et al., 2020; Wedel & Kannan, 2016). The traditional goal of marketing mix models, however, is to establish the budget of marketing depending on marketing and sales expenses. Ultimately, managers become more anxious about the matrix of the company's marketing actions, results, and consumer attitude since this method is insufficient (Kellerand & Lehmann, 2006). The same goes for Srinivasan et al. (2010), who created a consumer mentality metric to enhance marketing efforts and sales results. Hanssens et al. (2014) added the notion of consumer mentality measurements and attitudinal metrics to the model of the 4P mix strata in order to monitor the company's sales performance and make suggestions for marketing mix allocation.

Fischer et al. (2011) suggested using a heuristic technique to solve the multi-segment country company marketing mix budget allocation problem. The importance of natural and quasi-experiments which allow researchers to determine the cause-and-effect relationship between marketing factors and improved business performance was highlighted by Hui et al. (2013) and Tandon et al. (2021). Therefore, despite the marketing mix model's causality evaluation receiving a lot of importance in academics, industrial managers have not yet voiced their concerns about the analytical capabilities part. As a result, it is advised to build a 4P mix modeling capacity to distribute marketing funds and evaluate the impact of all marketing factors (Hossain et al., 2020).

VI. CUSTOMER ANALYTICS CAPABILITY AND SUSTAINABLE FIRM PERFORMANCE

Prior studies examined the value of analytics capacity in the big-data setting and a company's productivity (e.g., Akter et al., 2016). The advantages of customer analytics have been extensively studied (e.g., Erevelles et al., 2015; Verhoef et al., 2010), however, the capabilities and performance of the firm using customer analytics have received little to no attention (Hossain et al., 2020). A firm's capacity to satisfy customer wants through customer analytics—and subsequently, its ability to do so by meeting the aforementioned requirements—would have a long-term favorable impact on the profitability of organization. A business could increase the lifetime value of its customers and so continue to operate well-off the thorough literature research approach outlined above.

VII. CONCLUSION AND IMPLICATIONS

The concept of customer analytics has been reviewed in this chapter, but it's the discussion of the dimensions of "customer analytics capability" in the critical field of "management capability", "technology/infrastructure capability", "personnel expertise capability", and "4p mix modeling capability" that's most important. To achieve sustainable business success, Table 1 lists the elements of consumer analytics capacity that are anticipated to operate at the nexus of statistics, marketing, and econometrics. Initially, companies seeking to enhance their marketing performance and customer experience can focus their strategies on creating favorable internal conditions based on research-identified determinants that can facilitate the exploration and transformation of external knowledge from the rapidly changing business climate. Analysts need to be well knowledgeable about modern marketing, programming, and customer-centric activities. The firm's analyst must act as a go-between for the marketing manager and decision-makers. The capability of customer analytics would need to be expanded through internal marketing. Through the process, businesses may create value for their ultimate customers and then recoup that value from them, which will enable them to operate at their best level of performance in a sustainable manner. To implement consumer analytics technologies, managers and analysts must receive the right training and be expected to play a crucial role inside the organization. To maintain a competitive advantage, businesses must invest in training skilled, talented individuals and building analytical models. In order to achieve sustainable corporate success, practitioners can profit from specialized training and put their abilities to use within the organization.

VIII. FUTURE RESEARCH AND CHALLENGES

It might be difficult for business managers to customize a product, especially for a specific customer. To ensure customer lifetime value, managers must be able to introduce and employ cutting-edge algorithms to process heterogeneity in consumer behavior (Wedel & Kannan, 2016). Managers can implement customization analytics at the business level for selecting the product mix for the target consumers as well as for designing products or services. Additionally, clients want a seamless experience across all channels in the highly competitive market climate. Firms must therefore take this issue seriously and demonstrate that they can secure data in terms of privacy and security.

Many businesses can track a customer's full buying journey across channels and various devices thanks to the ongoing development of big data analytics, which helps them to better explain and anticipate the customer's future purchasing behavior. These offer additional chances to think about the material that should be personalized and also assist in creating customized content for unique clients using individual-level insights.

REFERENCES

Agarwal, R., & Dhar, V. (2014). Big data, data science, and analytics: The opportunity and challenge for IS research. *Information Systems Research*, *25*(3), 443–448. doi:10.1287/isre.2014.0546

Aguiar, M., & Gopinath, G. (2007). Emerging market business cycles: The cycle is the trend. *Journal of Political Economy*, *115*(1), 69–102. doi:10.1086/511283

Akhlaq, A., & Ahmed, E. (2015). Digital commerce in emerging economies: Factors associated with online shopping intentions in Pakistan. *International Journal of Emerging Markets*, *10*(4), 634–647. doi:10.1108/IJoEM-01-2014-0051

Akter, S., & Wamba, S. F. (2016). Big data analytics in E-commerce: A systematic review and agenda for future research. *Electronic Markets*, *26*(2), 173–194. doi:10.1007/s12525-016-0219-0

Akter, S., Wamba, S. F., Gunasekaran, A., Dubey, R., & Childe, S. J. (2016). How to improve firm performance using big data analytics capability and business strategy alignment? *International Journal of Production Economics*, *182*, 113–131. doi:10.1016/j.ijpe.2016.08.018

Aral, S., & Weill, P. (2007). IT assets, organizational capabilities, and firm performance: How resource allocations and organizational differences explain performance variation. *Organization Science*, *18*(5), 763–780. doi:10.1287/orsc.1070.0306

Barton, D., & Court, D. (2012). Making advanced analytics work for you. *Harvard Business Review*, *90*(10), 78–83. PMID:23074867

Braun, A., & Garriga, G. (2018). Consumer Journey Analytics in the Context of Data Privacy and Ethics. In *Digital Marketplaces Unleashed* (pp. 663–674). Springer. doi:10.1007/978-3-662-49275-8_59

Brodie, R., Hollebeek, L., Juric, B., & Ilic, A. (2011). Customer engagement. *Journal of Service Research*, *14*(3), 252–271. doi:10.1177/1094670511411703

Chen, H., & Storey, V. C. (2012). Business intelligence and analytics: From big data to big impact. *Management Information Systems Quarterly*, *36*(4), 1165–1188. doi:10.2307/41703503

Davenport, T., & Harris, J. (2007). *Competing on Analytics: The New Science of Winning* (1st ed.). Harvard Business School.

Davenport, T. H. (2013). Analytics 3.0. *Harvard Business Review*, (December), 64–72.

Ejdys, J. (2018). Building technology trust in ICT application at a university. *International Journal of Emerging Markets*, *13*(5), 980–997. doi:10.1108/IJoEM-07-2017-0234

Elsner, R., Krafft, M., & Huchzermeier, A. (2004). Optimizing Rhenania's direct marketing business through dynamic multilevel modeling (DMLM) in a multicatalog-brand environment. *Marketing Science*, *23*(2), 192–206. doi:10.1287/mksc.1040.0063

Erevelles, S., Fukawa, N., & Swayne, L. (2015). Big Data consumer analytics and the transformation of marketing. *Journal of Business Research*, *69*(2), 897–904. doi:10.1016/j.jbusres.2015.07.001

Ference, A. (2017). *7 customer engagement strategies you must try Outbrain Blog*. Available at: www.outbrain.com/blog/3-golden-customer-engagement-strategies-that-marketers-cant-ignore/

Fiedler, L., Germann, F., Kraus, M., & Perrey, J. (2013). KoenigKunde – Kapital Kundenwissen. *Akzente*, *3*, 24–29.

Fink, L., & Neumann, S. (2009). Exploring the perceived business value of the flexibility enabled by information technology infrastructure. *Information & Management*, *46*(2), 90–99. doi:10.1016/j.im.2008.11.007

Fischer, M., Albers, S., Wagner, N., & Frie, M. (2011). Practice prize winner—Dynamic marketing budget allocation across countries, products, and marketing activities. *Marketing Science*, *30*(4), 568–585. doi:10.1287/mksc.1100.0627

Floyd, K., Freling, R., Alhoqail, S., Cho, H. Y., & Freling, T. (2014). How online product reviews affect retail sales: A meta-analysis. *Journal of Retailing*, *90*(2), 217–232. doi:10.1016/j.jretai.2014.04.004

France, S. L., & Ghose, S. (2018). Marketing Analytics: Methods, Practice, Implementation, and Links to Other Fields. *Expert Systems with Applications*, *119*, 456–475. doi:10.1016/j.eswa.2018.11.002

Germann, F., Lilien, G. L., Fiedler, L., & Kraus, M. (2014). Do retailers benefit from deploying customer analytics? *Journal of Retailing*, *90*(4), 587–593. doi:10.1016/j.jretai.2014.08.002

Germann, F., Lilien, G. L., & Rangaswamy, A. (2013). Performance implications of deploying marketing analytics. *International Journal of Research in Marketing*, *30*(2), 114–128. doi:10.1016/j.ijresmar.2012.10.001

Goyal, J., Singh, M., Singh, R., & Aggarwal, A. (2019). Efficiency and technology gaps in Indian banking sector: Application of meta-frontier directional distance function DEA approach. *The Journal of Finance and Data Science*, *5*(3), 156–172. doi:10.1016/j.jfds.2018.08.002

Gupta, M., & George, J. F. (2016). Toward the development of a big data analytics capability. *Information & Management*, *53*(8), 1049–1064. doi:10.1016/j.im.2016.07.004

Gupta, S., Hanssens, D., Hardie, B., Kahn, W., Kumar, V., Lin, N., Ravishankar, N., & Sriram, S. (2006). Modeling customer lifetime value. *Journal of Service Research*, *9*(2), 139–155. doi:10.1177/1094670506293810

Hanssens, D. M., Pauwels, K. H., Srinivasan, S., Vanhuele, M., & Yildirim, G. (2014). Consumer attitude metrics for guiding marketing mix decisions. *Marketing Science*, *33*(4), 534–550. doi:10.1287/mksc.2013.0841

Hossain, M. D. A., Akter, S., & Yanamandram, V. K. (2020). *Customer Analytics Capabilities in the Big Data Spectrum: A Systematic Approach to Achieve Sustainable Firm Performance*. https://ro.uow.edu.au/gsbpapers/577

Howard, P. N., & Hussain, M. M. (2011). The role of digital media. *Journal of Democracy*, *22*(3), 35–48. doi:10.1353/jod.2011.0041

Hui, S. K., Inman, J. J., Huang, Y., & Suher, J. (2013). The effect of in-store travel distance on unplanned spending: Applications to mobile promotion strategies. *Journal of Marketing*, *77*(2), 1–16. doi:10.1509/jm.11.0436

Kannan, P. K., Pope, B. K., & Jain, S. (2009). Practice prize winner—Pricing digital content product lines: A model and application for the National Academies Press. *Marketing Science*, *28*(4), 620–636. doi:10.1287/mksc.1080.0481

Karimi, Somers, & Gupta. (n.d.). Impact of information technology management practices on customer service. *Journal of Management Information Systems, 17*(4), 125-158.

Kellerand, K. L., & Lehmann, D. R. (2006). Brands and branding: Research findings and future priorities. *Marketing Science*, *25*(6), 740–759. doi:10.1287/mksc.1050.0153

Khoshafian, S. (2015). *Digital transformation of CRM through Internet of Things (IoT).* Available at: www.pega.com/insights/articles/digital-transformation-crm-through-internet-things-iot

Kietzmann, J. H., Hermkens, K., McCarthy, I. P., & Silvestre, B. S. (2011). Social media? Get serious! Understanding the functional building blocks of social media. *Business Horizons*, *54*(3), 241–251. doi:10.1016/j.bushor.2011.01.005

Kim, G., Shin, B., Kim, K. K., & Lee, H. (2011). IT capabilities, process-oriented dynamic capabilities, and firm financial performance. *Journal of the Association for Information Systems*, *12*(7), 487–517. doi:10.17705/1jais.00270

Kim, G., Shin, B., & Kwon, O. (2012). Investigating the value of sociomaterialism in conceptualizing IT capability of a firm. *Journal of Management Information Systems*, *29*(3), 327–362. doi:10.2753/MIS0742-1222290310

Kitchens, B., Dobolyi, D. G., Li, J., & Abbasi, A. (2018). Advanced Customer Analytics: Strategic Value Through Integration of Relationship-Oriented Big Data. *Journal of Management Information Systems*, *35*(2), 540–574. doi:10.1080/07421222.2018.1451957

Kumar, V., & Petersen, J. A. (2012). *Statistical Methods in Customer Relationship Management*. John Wiley & Sons Ltd. doi:10.1002/9781118349212

LaValle, S., Lesser, E., Shockley, R., Hopkins, M. S., & Kruschwitz, N. (2011). Big data, analytics and the path from insights to value. *MIT Sloan Management Review*, *52*(2), 21.

Lu, J., Cairns, L., & Smith, L. (2021). Data science in the business environment: Customer analytics case studies in SMEs. *Journal of Modelling in Management*, *16*(2), 689–713. doi:10.1108/JM2-11-2019-0274

Magill, E. (2015). *Harnessing the Power of Customer Analytics at IBM Amplify 2015.* IBM Watson Customer Engagement. Retrieved January 2, 2019 from https://www.ibm.com/blogs/watson-customer-engagement/2015/05/01/harnessing-the-power-of-customer-analytics-at-ibm-amplify-2015/)

Magill, E. (2016). *The Customer Analytics Evolution: A Path to Cognitive*. IBM Watson Customer Engagement. Retrieved January 14, 2019 from https://www.ibm.com/blogs/watson-customer-engagement/2016/06/17/the-customer-analytics-evolution-a-path-to-cognitive/)

Mangold, W. G., & Faulds, D. J. (2009). Social media: The new hybrid element of the promotion mix. *Business Horizons*, *52*(4), 357–365. doi:10.1016/j.bushor.2009.03.002

Maslowska, E., Malthouse, E. C., & Collinger, T. (2016). The customer engagement ecosystem. *Journal of Marketing Management*, *32*(5-6), 469–501. doi:10.1080/0267257X.2015.1134628

McAfee, A., & Brynjofsson, E. (2012). Big data: The management revolution. *Harvard Business Review*, (October), 60–68. PMID:23074865

McKeen, J. D., & Smith, H. A. (2015). IT strategy: Issues and practices. Pearson Higher Ed.

Mithas, S., Lee, M. R., Earley, S., Murugesan, S., & Djavanshir, R. (2013). Leveraging big data and business analytics. *IT Professional*, *15*(6), 18–20. doi:10.1109/MITP.2013.95

Morris, A. K. (2006). Assessing pre-service teachers' skills for analyzing teaching. *Journal of Mathematics Teacher Education*, *9*(5), 471–505. doi:10.1007/s10857-006-9015-7

Olaleye, S., Ukpabi, D., Karjaluoto, H., & Rizomyliotis, I. (2019). Understanding technology diffusion in emerging markets: The case of Chinese mobile devices in Nigeria. *International Journal of Emerging Markets*, *14*(5), 731–751. doi:10.1108/IJOEM-01-2018-0055

Ransbotham, S., & Kiron, D. (2018). Using Analytics to Improve Customer Engagement. *MIT Sloan Management Review*, 1–20.

Rio & Banker. (2014). *IoT Changes Logistics for the OEM Spare Parts Supply Chain*. ARC Insights, ARC Advisory Group.

Ross, J. W., Beath, C. M., & Quaadgras, A. (2013). You may not need big data after all. *Harvard Business Review*, *91*(12), 90–98.

Sakshi, U., Tandon, U., Ertz, M., & Bansal, H. (2020). Social vacation: Proposition of a model to understand tourists' usage of social media for travel planning. *Technology in Society*, *63*, 10143. doi:10.1016/j.techsoc.2020.101438 PMID:33100435

Sood, K., Dhanaraj, R. K., Balusamy, B., Grima, S., & Maheshwari, R. U. (2022). *Big Data*. Emerald Group Publishing. Available: http://books.google.ie/books?id=d3B6EAAAQBAJ&printsec=frontcover&dq=Big+data:+A+game+changer+for+insurance+industry&hl=&cd=1&source=gbs_api

Srinivasan, S., Vanhuele, M., & Pauwels, K. (2010). Mind-set metrics in market response models: An integrative approach. *JMR, Journal of Marketing Research*, *47*(4), 672–684. doi:10.1509/jmkr.47.4.672

Steenstrup, K., & Kutnick, D. (2015). *The Internet of Things revolution: impact on operational technology ecosystems*. Available at: www.gartner.com/doc/3036118/Internet-thingsrevolution-impact-operational

Storey, V. C., & Song, I. Y. (2017). Big data technologies and Management: What conceptual modeling can do. *Data & Knowledge Engineering*, *108*, 50–67. doi:10.1016/j.datak.2017.01.001

Sun, N., Morris, J. G., Xu, J., Zhu, H., & Xie, M. (2014). iCARE: A framework for big data-based banking customer analytics. *IBM Journal of Research and Development*, *58*(5/6), 4–1. doi:10.1147/JRD.2014.2337118

Surma, J. (2011). *Business intelligence: Making decisions through data analytics: Customer Intelligence*. Business Expert Press.

Tandon, U., Ertz, M., & Sakshi, K. (2021). POD Mode of Payment, Return Policies and Virtual-Try-on Technology as Predictors of Trust: An Emerging Economy Case. *Journal of Promotion Management*, *27*(6), 832–855. doi:10.1080/10496491.2021.1888174

Verhoef, P. C., Venkatesan, R., McAlister, L., Malthouse, E. C., Krafft, M., & Ganesan, S. (2010). CRM in data-rich multichannel retailing environments: A review and future research directions. *Journal of Interactive Marketing*, *24*(2), 121–137. doi:10.1016/j.intmar.2010.02.009

Weber, R. H., & Weber, R. (2010). *Internet of Things* (Vol. 12). Springer. doi:10.1007/978-3-642-11710-7

Wedel, M., & Kannan, P. K. (2016). Marketing analytics for data-rich environments. *Journal of Marketing*, *80*(6), 97–121. doi:10.1509/jm.15.0413

Yerpude, S., & Singhal, T. K. (2018). Customer service enhancement through 'on-road vehicle assistance' enabled with Internet of Things (IoT) solutions and frameworks: A futuristic perspective. *International Journal of Applied Business and Economic Research*, *15*(16), 551–565.

Yerpude, S., & Singhal, T. K. (2021). "Custolytics": Internet of Things based customer analytics aiding customer engagement strategy in emerging markets – an empirical research. *International Journal of Emerging Markets*, *16*(1), 92–112. doi:10.1108/IJOEM-05-2018-0250

Zhang, J., Li, H., & Ziegelmayer, J. L. (2009). Resource or capability? A dissection of SMEs' IT infrastructure flexibility and its relationship with IT responsiveness. *Journal of Computer Information Systems*, *50*(1), 46–53.

Chapter 15

Cyber Security in the Cloud: Harnessing the Power of Machine Learning and Cloud Cryptography

Nahida Majeed Wani
https://orcid.org/0000-0002-5194-9975
Department of Mathematics, Amity University, Gwalior, India

Ajay Verma
https://orcid.org/0000-0002-0994-4812
School of Applied Sciences and Languages, VIT Bhopal University, India

ABSTRACT

In an era defined by digital interconnectivity, securing information in the cloud is paramount. By harnessing the power of present advanced technologies, organizations can fortify their defenses against evolving cyber threats while simultaneously embracing environmentally conscious practices. The model begins by integrating machine learning (ML) algorithms into fabric of cyber security. Anomaly detection, threat prediction, and adaptive response mechanisms enable a proactive defense, continually evolving to thwart emerging threats. Beyond the realm of cyber security efficacy, ML optimizes resource utilization, contributing to the sustainability of cloud operations. Complementing this adaptive intelligence, cloud cryptography emerges as a cornerstone for securing data at rest and in transit. From traditional encryption to quantum-resistant cryptographic techniques, the model ensures confidentiality and integrity of information. Sustainable cryptographic practices, coupled with efficient key management, further mitigate the environmental impact associated with cryptographic operations.

1.0 INTRODUCTION

In an era defined by the rapid digitization of data and the exponential growth of information technology, cloud computing has emerged as a fundamental paradigm shift in how organizations store, access, and manage their data and services. The convenience, scalability, and cost-efficiency cloud computing offers have made it an indispensable tool for businesses and individuals. However, as the adoption of cloud

DOI: 10.4018/979-8-3693-3253-5.ch015

services continues to surge, so do the challenges associated with securing sensitive data and ensuring the privacy and integrity of digital assets.

The concept of ML in cloud computing began to gain traction in the mid to late 2000s. Cloud providers started offering basic services for data storage and processing. As cloud computing services expanded, ML tools and frameworks, such as Tensor Flow and PyTorch, became available on cloud platforms. Major cloud providers like Amazon Web Services (AWS), Microsoft Azure, and Google Cloud Platform (GCP) started offering specialized ML services. The emergence of AI as a Service (AIaaS) allowed users to access pre-built ML models and services without needing extensive expertise in the field. This lowered the barrier for businesses to adopt ML (Géron, 2022). Cloud providers integrated ML capabilities into their existing services, making it easier for developers to incorporate ML into their applications. Improved hardware accelerators, such as Graphics Processing Units (GPUs) and Tensor Processing Units (TPUs), provided significant speed-ups for training and inference tasks in ML, and cloud providers incorporated these technologies into their offerings (Campesato, 2023).

The intersection of cloud computing and cyber security presents a dynamic landscape where evolving threats and vulnerabilities demand innovative solutions (Dupont, 2013). This research explores the critical role of ML and cloud cryptography in bolstering the security of cloud-based systems. As cyber threats become increasingly sophisticated and prevalent, harnessing the power of these advanced technologies is essential to safeguarding data in the cloud and fortifying the integrity of digital infrastructure.

The changing world of connectivity has been greatly transformed by the widespread use of cloud computing (Kolb, 2018). This technology has completely revolutionized how organizations handle and analyze their data. While the benefits of cloud technology are undeniable, the escalating frequency and sophistication of cyber threats pose significant challenges to the security of sensitive information stored and processed in the cloud.

However, the widespread adoption of cloud computing faces obstacles in the form of security concerns. Indeed, ensuring the security and protection of distributed computing services from unauthorized access or misuse poses a significant challenge, which can be mitigated through shared responsibility (Dey, 2019). Infrastructure as a Service (IaaS) manages hardware resources, offering users low- and high-level flexibility. Platform as a Service (PaaS) provides a robust platform for enhanced service delivery, while Software as a Service (SaaS) offers diverse software solutions for efficient data access and utilization.

1.1 Cloud Architecture

Cloud computing architecture is comprised of various components that work together to deliver scalable, on-demand computing services (Vaquero et al., 2008) (Press et al., 2010). Understanding these components is essential for designing and implementing effective cloud solutions. Below is a detailed exploration of the key components, supported by a reference to the National Institute of Standards and Technology (NIST) Special Publication 800-145.

Frontend and Backend: The frontend of cloud computing architecture represents the user interface and client-side components. It is the point of interaction where users access and utilize cloud services. The backend comprises servers, databases, and application logic that power the cloud services. It includes the infrastructure responsible for processing user requests, managing data, and executing applications.

Virtualization: Virtualization is a foundational component that allows the creation of virtual instances of computing resources, such as servers, storage, and networking. This technology optimizes resource utilization and enhances flexibility in deploying and managing services.

Orchestration: Orchestration involves coordinating multiple cloud services to automate and streamline complex workflows. It ensures efficient resource management and supports scalability by automating the provisioning, configuration, and deployment of resources.

Containers: Containers, exemplified by technologies like Docker, allow applications and their dependencies to be packaged into lightweight, portable containers. This ensures consistency across different environments, streamlining the deployment and scaling of applications.

Security Measures: Security is a critical aspect of cloud computing architecture, encompassing measures such as identity management, encryption, access controls, and compliance checks. These measures aim to protect data, applications, and the overall integrity of the cloud environment.

Scalability and Resource Pooling: Cloud architecture is designed for scalability, allowing users to dynamically adjust resources based on demand. Resource pooling involves sharing computing resources to improve utilization and cost-effectiveness through a multi-tenancy model.

1.2 Service Models

The service models form main components of the cloud computing architecture and all the main three components are described as under (Yang, Jianfeng, 2010) (Chuang et al., 2011).

Software as a Service (SaaS): The SaaS model involves a software provider licensing an application for on-demand use. This service operates in the cloud and serves multiple end users, typically running on a web browser like the popular SaaS product, Gmail. Billing in the SaaS model is often usage-based, and it operates in a multi-tenant environment. Unlike traditional installations, SaaS applications can be accessed through various clients such as web browsers and mobile phones, eliminating the need for client installations. Customization is a key feature, allowing each customer to adjust configuration options without the necessity for installation. Similar to traditional enterprise software, a single customer can modify configuration settings, with each customer having its own unique configurations. For instance, SaaS applications facilitate changes to the application's appearance, like incorporating a custom logo and specific colors to align with the customer's brand, meeting common customization needs.

Platform as-a-service (PaaS): The development of applications for cloud deployment is facilitated by a PaaS platform, catering to both deployers and developers. This cloud-based application development entails a highly scalable multi-tier architecture, exemplified by platforms like Azure and Salesforce.com. Notably different from SaaS, PaaS goes beyond hosting completed cloud applications, offering a development platform for both completed and in-progress applications. Developers using PaaS can create and deploy applications without detailed knowledge of resource specifications, such as memory and processor usage. This model provides significant advantages throughout the software development lifecycle, encompassing planning, design, building, deployment, and maintenance. PaaS introduces a higher level of abstraction, allowing consumers to create software using tools and libraries provided by the platform. Consumers retain control over software deployment and configuration settings, while the provider furnishes essential services like networks, servers, and storage. PaaS eliminates the need for consumers to handle the complexity and cost associated with procuring and managing underlying hardware and software. Various PaaS vendors exist, each offering application hosting, a deployment environment, and integrated services to streamline the deployment of applications.

Infrastructure as-a-service (IaaS): Providing a service that allows users to acquire a virtual server within minutes and pay solely for the resources they utilize, this platform ensures accessibility to infrastructure via Internet technology, incorporating servers, storage, and other peripheral devices. It can be seamlessly integrated with managed services for operating system and application support. The IaaS model emphasizes enabling technologies, enabling users to swiftly obtain virtual servers and pay only for the resources they consume. In the IaaS model, consumers have direct access to infrastructure components such as storage, firewall, and network. A notable example is Amazon EC2, which offers consumers physical or virtual resources, including CPU, memory, OS, and storage, catering to diverse user demands. IaaS, as a standardized and highly automated offering, features compute resources along with storage and networking capabilities, owned and hosted by a service provider. This infrastructure is presented to customers on-demand, allowing self-provisioning through a web-based graphical user interface serving as an IT operations management console. Additionally, API access to the infrastructure may be provided as an option.

Cloud computing technology is an integration of different technologies and components. The Service models such as SAAS, PAAS, and IAAS and their usage have been shown in the tabular format in below Table 1 as:

1.3 Deployment Models

Cloud computing has become a pivotal technology in modern computing, offering scalable and flexible services to individuals, businesses, and organizations. The deployment model in cloud computing refers to the way cloud services are implemented and made available to users. Various deployment models cater to different needs and preferences, offering distinct advantages and considerations. This discussion explores the prominent deployment models in cloud computing, namely Public Cloud, Private Cloud, Hybrid Cloud, and Community Cloud.

1.4 Private Cloud

Private Cloud processing is run and administered inside an affiliation's server ranch, which is suggested as a private cloud. Because a similar organization owns and operates the system, customer and supplier relationships are easily discerned in a private cloud. In a private cloud deployment, cloud resources are exclusively used by a single organization. This model provides greater control, customization, and security, making it suitable for businesses with specific compliance or regulatory requirements. Private clouds can be hosted on-premises or by a third-party service provider. Private cloud advantages include

Table 1. Description of the cloud security

Description	Characteristics
IAAS: Provides virtualized computing resources over the internet. Users can rent virtual machines, storage, and networking components on a pay-as-you-go basis.	Users manage and control the operating systems, applications, and data. Allows flexibility and scalability without the need for physical hardware. Examples include Amazon EC2 and Microsoft Azure Virtual Machines.
PAAS: Delivers a platform allowing users to develop, run, and manage applications without dealing with the complexities of the underlying infrastructure, such as hardware or operating systems.	Users focus on application development and deployment. Platform providers manage the underlying infrastructure and runtime environment and offer automatic scalability. Examples include Google App Engine, Heroku, and Microsoft Azure App Service.
SAAS: Delivers fully functional software applications over the internet on a subscription basis. Users access these applications through a web browser without the need for installation or maintenance.	Provider hosts and maintains the software and infrastructure. Users access applications through a web browser. Automatic updates and patching. Examples include Salesforce, Microsoft 365, and Google Workspace.

enhanced security, compliance adherence, and customization. However, it often requires significant upfront investment and ongoing maintenance costs. VMware Cloud Foundation and OpenStack are examples of technologies that support private cloud deployments.

1.5 Public Cloud

Public cloud endeavors, the academic world or government affiliations have a public cloud environment, which can cause many issues since customers don't have the remotest clue about the area and owners of resources, which adds to the difficulty of safeguarding resources from attacks. Public cloud is one of the most common deployment models, wherein cloud services are provided by third-party service providers and made available to the general public over the internet. Users share computing resources like servers and storage, leading to cost savings and efficient resource utilization. Amazon Web Services (AWS), Microsoft Azure, and Google Cloud Platform (GCP) are examples of major public cloud providers. Public cloud advantages include cost-effectiveness, scalability, and accessibility. However, concerns about security and privacy arise due to the shared infrastructure. Service level agreements (SLAs) play a crucial role in establishing the terms and conditions between the service provider and the user(Press et al., 2010).

1.6 Hybrid Cloud

Hybrid cloud combines elements of both public and private clouds, allowing data and applications to be shared between them. This model provides greater flexibility, allowing organizations to utilize public cloud resources for non-sensitive operations and private cloud resources for sensitive or critical tasks. Hybrid clouds enable workload portability and scalability. Advantages of hybrid cloud include flexibility, scalability, and optimal resource utilization. However, managing the integration between public and private components can be complex. Microsoft Azure, with its Azure Arc solution, and IBM Cloud are examples of platforms supporting hybrid cloud deployments(Vaquero et al., 2008).

1.7 Community Cloud

Community cloud is a shared infrastructure that is mutually used by several organizations with similar interests or requirements. It provides a middle ground between public and private clouds, allowing a group of organizations to share resources and infrastructure. This model is suitable for communities, such as research consortia, that have common goals and computing needs. Advantages of community cloud include shared costs, collaborative resource utilization, and meeting specific community requirements. However, establishing governance and addressing the diverse needs of community members can be challenging. The Community Grid Computing platform is an example of a community cloud infrastructure (Mell & Grance, 2011).

Figure 1 depicts that the cloud computing comprises various facets, each playing a distinct role in the ecosystem. The "front end" corresponds to the user interface readily visible to end-users. On the contrary, the "back-end" infrastructure is the backbone of the cloud system, encompassing data center hardware, virtualization technologies, applications, and services. Bridging the front and back end is the middleware, which facilitates communication between the user interface and the underlying infrastructure.

Figure 1. Key terms and structure

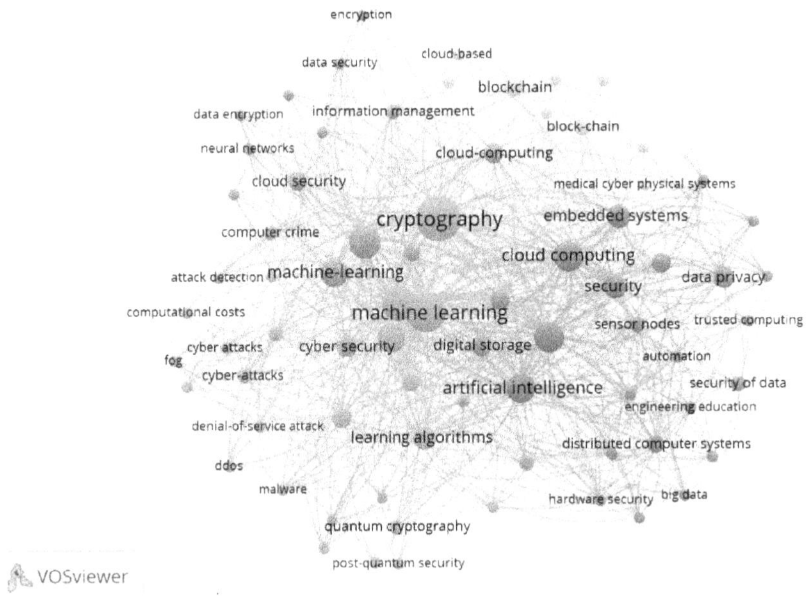

Cloud architecture varies depending on the specific use case and requirements, but all clouds necessitate essential components such as hardware, middleware, management tools, and automation software. Additionally, virtualization is commonly employed to abstract and efficiently manage hardware resources within cloud environments, creating a centralized pool of data resources. In some instances, clouds, referred to as "bare metal clouds", connect clients directly to physical hardware, bypassing virtualization layers for specialized applications.

This research embarks on a journey to delve into the intricate world of cyber security in the cloud, shedding light on the complex nuances of safeguarding data within the cloud environment. By examining the synergy between ML and cloud cryptography, we aim to uncover how these technologies can be harnessed to detect and mitigate threats and proactively adapt and evolve in the face of ever-changing cyber dangers (Lara, 2022).

1.8 Research Objectives

The research objective is to investigate and address the security concerns hindering the widespread adoption of cloud computing. This study aims to address the evolving challenges and threats posed to data and systems in the cloud by leveraging advanced machine learning algorithms for threat detection, anomaly identification, and predictive analysis.

2.0 LITERATURE SURVEY

In recent years, the proliferation of cloud computing has revolutionized the way organizations manage and process data. As businesses increasingly migrate sensitive information to the cloud, the need for robust cyber security measures becomes paramount. This literature review explores the state of the art in cyber security within the cloud context, with a specific focus on the integration of ML and cloud cryptography.

- Foundations of Cyber security in the Cloud:

The seminal work by (Meersman, 2019) provides a foundational understanding of cloud computing, establishing the NIST definition and framework.

(Nurmilahti, 2016) build upon this, applying NIST SP 800-145 to cloud computing, laying the groundwork for subsequent discussions on cloud security.

In 2022, Muhammad et al. put forward the fundamental concepts of cloud computing, cyber security challenges, the role of ML, and the significance of cloud cryptography. Through comprehensive analysis and empirical evidence, their research contributed to a deeper understanding of the dynamic landscape of cloud security and provide valuable insights into how organizations can effectively protect their data assets in an increasingly interconnected and vulnerable digital world (Muhammad et al., 2022).

- Regulatory and Compliance Aspects:

The European Union Agency for Cybersecurity (2020) and the U.S. Department of Commerce (2015) (Yusuf Sukman, 2017), provide guidelines and frameworks for cloud security, addressing regulatory and compliance aspects in the cloud environment.

- ML in Cyber security:

(Tissir et al., 2021) delved into the application of data mining to predict insider threats, showcasing the potential of ML in cyber security.

The evaluation of intrusion detection systems by (Kolb, 2018) sets the stage for the role of ML algorithms in adapting to evolving cyber threats.

By leveraging the inherent strengths of both technologies, authors have developed a comprehensive solution that empowers organizations to navigate the complex cyber security landscape of the cloud securely (Jonnala et al., 2023).

- Cloud Cryptography Techniques:

(Wu et al., 2021) reviewed cloud computing security management, emphasizing the significance of cryptography. (Ristenpart et al., 2009) shed light on potential information leakage in third-party compute clouds, highlighting the importance of robust cryptographic techniques.

- Integration of ML and Cloud Cryptography:

(Abbas et al., 2022) explored the sharing of cyber threat intelligence in cloud security, demonstrating the synergy between ML and cryptographic techniques. (Durbha et al., 2023) provide insights into cloud-based services for intelligent data analysis, showcasing the complementary nature of ML and cryptography in enhancing security.

(Mupila, 2023) navigated the intersection of cloud technology, ML, and cryptography, their research aspires to contribute not only to the academic understanding of cyber security challenges in the cloud but also to offer practical insights that can be applied by businesses and policymakers. Ultimately, the goal is to pave the way for a resilient and adaptive cyber security paradigm that harnesses the transformative potential of ML and Cloud Cryptography to safeguard the integrity, confidentiality, and availability of data in the cloud.

- Sustainable Practices in Cybersecurity:

(Ghezzi et al., 2018) introduced the concept of crowdsourcing for innovation, providing a perspective on sustainable practices.

(Suetterlein et al., 2022) offered insights into high-performance parallelism, contributing to the optimization of resource utilization in cyber security operations.

(Bhansali, 2023) discussed cloud security and privacy from an enterprise perspective, outlining considerations for sustainable cyber security practices.

(Monroy, 2023) emphasized the need for security in a hyper-connected world, laying the groundwork for discussions on the environmental impact of cyber security measures.

- Securing the Cloud

Through an in-depth examination of the current state of cyber security in cloud environments, the research endeavors to identify gaps and shortcomings in existing approaches. Subsequently, it will propose innovative strategies that integrate ML algorithms for threat detection, anomaly recognition, and adaptive response mechanisms, coupled with the robust cryptographic protocols afforded by Cloud Cryptography (Asharf et al., 2020).

As businesses increasingly migrate their operations to cloud environments, ensuring robust cyber security measures becomes paramount to safeguarding against potential vulnerabilities and breaches (Saranya et al., 2023). This research delves into the dynamic realm of cyber security in the cloud, focusing on two cutting-edge technologies that hold immense promise for fortifying the digital defenses of cloud-based systems: ML and Cloud Cryptography. ML, with its ability to analyze vast datasets and identify patterns, offers a proactive approach to threat detection and mitigation.

- Quantum-Resistant Cloud Cryptography:

(Bernstein & Lange, 2017) presented a comprehensive review of post-quantum cryptography, addressing the emerging threat posed by quantum computing.

Cloud Cryptography introduces advanced cryptographic techniques tailored to the unique challenges posed by cloud infrastructures, enhancing the confidentiality and integrity of data stored and transmitted through the cloud. The overarching objective of their research is to explore the synergies between

ML and Cloud Cryptography, seeking to create a cohesive and adaptive cyber security framework that not only reacts to existing threats but also anticipates and mitigates emerging risks (Kornaros, 2022).

(Khodaiemehr, Hassan; Bagheri, Khadijeh; Feng, 2023) contributed to the discourse with a quantum algorithm for database search, underscoring the need for quantum-resistant cryptographic solutions.

- Related Challenges of the domain:

(Kaur & Ramkumar, 2022) discussed next-generation cloud computing trends, guiding future research endeavors in the dynamic field of cyber security. (López-Aguilar et al., 2022) explore challenges and opportunities in big data and ontology for cybersecurity, paving the way for future research directions. (Yamaganti, 2023) investigated cloud security from users' perspectives, contributing to a comprehensive understanding of cyber security in cloud environments.

Cloud computing is a highly intricate field that offers extensive data storage and management capabilities across various tiers. Consequently, harnessing data using cutting-edge technologies such as ML, Artificial Intelligence (AI), and Internet of Things (IoT) is imperative (Walia et al., 2023). The advantages of cloud computing encompass in-cloud affordability, scalability, and cost-effectiveness. Furthermore, distributed storage exhibits on-demand provisioning, cost-efficiency, widespread availability, simplicity, rental options, reliability, and adaptability.

We further have shown in Figure 1 the co-occurrence network of the chosen keywords to picture the relationship between the machine learning tools, cryptography and the data security.

2.1 Cloud Security and Challenges

Ensuring data security stored in the cloud is paramount for organizations of all sizes. Various approaches and techniques exist to safeguard data across diverse server environments. Key aspects central to data security in the cloud encompass data integration, maintaining confidentiality, ensuring reliability, achieving scalability, implementing robust authentication measures, and effectively safeguarding data stored within cloud repositories(Press et al., 2010).

Cloud computing has transformed the way businesses operate by offering scalable and flexible solutions. However, the shift to the cloud introduces a host of security challenges that organizations must address to safeguard their data and operations.

Below, we explore the landscape of cloud security and the key challenges it presents:

i. Data Security

Challenge: Ensuring the confidentiality and integrity of data stored in the cloud is a primary concern. Unauthorized access, data breaches, and insider threats pose significant risks.

Solution: Implement robust encryption protocols for data at rest and in transit. Employ access controls, identity management, and regular audits to monitor and manage data access.

ii. Identity and Access Management (IAM)

Challenge: Managing user identities and access privileges across diverse cloud services and platforms can be complex. Improperly configured IAM settings may lead to security vulnerabilities.

Figure 2. Co-occurrence network of keywords

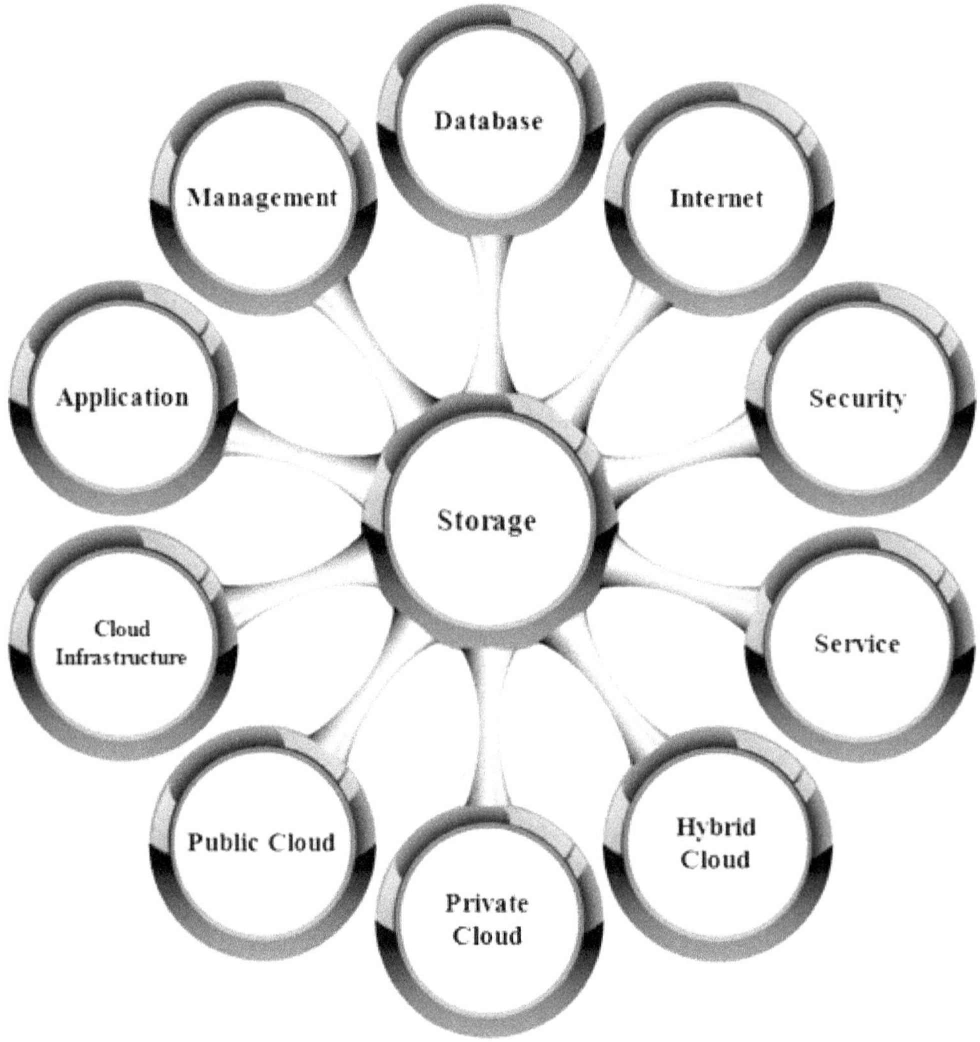

Solution: Implement strong authentication mechanisms, adopt the principle of least privilege, and regularly review and update access permissions.

iii. Compliance and Legal Issues

Challenge: Different geographical locations have varying data protection laws and compliance requirements. Ensuring adherence to these regulations, such as GDPR or HIPAA, can be challenging in a cloud environment.

Solution: Conduct thorough compliance assessments, choose cloud providers with strong compliance frameworks, and implement data residency and privacy measures accordingly.

iv. Shared Responsibility Model

Challenge: Cloud service providers (CSPs) follow a shared responsibility model where they manage the security of the cloud infrastructure, while customers are responsible for securing their data and applications within the cloud.

Solution: Clearly understand the delineation of responsibilities between the cloud provider and the customer. Implement security best practices for the aspects under customer control.

v. Network Security

Challenge: The cloud relies on shared networks, making it susceptible to network-based attacks such as man-in-the-middle attacks and eavesdropping.

Solution: Implement strong network security protocols, including firewalls, intrusion detection/prevention systems, and virtual private networks (VPNs).

vi. DDoS Attacks

Challenge: Cloud-based services are susceptible to distributed denial of service (DDoS) attacks, which can overwhelm infrastructure and disrupt service availability.

Solution: Deploy DDoS mitigation solutions, use Content Delivery Networks (CDNs), and work with cloud providers to implement protective measures against large-scale attacks.

vii. Security of APIs

Challenge: Cloud services heavily rely on Application Programming Interfaces (APIs), which can be vulnerable to attacks if not properly secured.

Solution: Regularly audit and secure APIs, use authentication and authorization mechanisms, and employ encryption for data transmitted via APIs.

viii. Incident Response and Forensics

Challenge: Rapidly detecting and responding to security incidents in the cloud, as well as conducting forensics investigations, can be challenging due to the distributed nature of cloud environments.

Solution: Develop a robust incident response plan, leverage cloud-native security tools, and conduct regular drills to ensure a swift response to security incidents.

ix. Lack of Visibility and Control

Challenge: Organizations may struggle with limited visibility and control over their data and infrastructure when it reside in a cloud environment.

Solution: Utilize cloud security tools that provide comprehensive visibility, implement monitoring solutions, and employ security information and event management (SIEM) systems.

x. Insider Threats

Challenge: Insiders with malicious intent or unintentional actions can pose a significant security risk in the cloud.

Solution: Implement user behaviour analytics, conduct thorough background checks, and enforce least privilege access to mitigate insider threats.

2.2 Data Protection and Prevention

The evaluation of data security holds a pivotal role in decision-making processes. Organizations often exhibit reluctance when considering the acquisition of a vendor's assurance regarding the security of their corporate data. They express apprehension about potential data loss during unforeseen challenges and concerns regarding data ownership. Additionally, many existing models lack transparency concerning the exact location of data storage, further exacerbating security apprehensions within enterprises.

In contemporary models, businesses deploy firewalls across their data centres to safeguard sensitive information, thereby asserting their control over data security. However, in the cloud computing model, service providers assume significant responsibility for ensuring data security, and organizations must place their trust in these providers to a considerable extent. This reliance on service providers introduces a dynamic element of risk into the equation for enterprises.

2.3 Data Recovery and Availability

Service level agreements (SLAs) are rigorously adhered to across all business applications. Functional Teams play a pivotal role in overseeing the implementation of organization-level SLAs and the real-time management of tasks. In evolving environments, functional groups provide support for:

- Data replication
- Data recovery
- Data management
- Data monitoring

2.4 Administrative and Compliance Restrictions

Government restrictions in some European countries prohibit customers' personal information and other sensitive data from being shared outside of the state or country. To comply with such requirements, cloud companies must plan a server ranch or a limited-access site within the country. Such a structure may not be conceivable and is hard for cloud providers.

3.0 METHODS AND MATERIAL

In this section, we will be discussing the methods and materials could that be the cryptographic approaches, a general model or predictions of different organizations.

3.1 Confidentiality and Cryptographic Algorithms

As Implementing Quantum Key Distribution (QKD) enhances data security against various attacks, (Sasikumar et al., 2022) introduced the Secured QKD for Cloud Data Security Model, utilizing Non-Abelian Encryption for user data encryption. The quantum key facilitates secure access to stored data in the cloud, and key sharing between nodes is achieved through a secure quantum channel.

Cryptographic algorithms play a crucial role in securing digital communication and information. They involve mathematical processes that transform data into a form that is unintelligible to unauthorized users. Understanding these cryptographic algorithms is essential for designing secure systems and protecting data confidentiality, integrity, and authenticity in various applications, including communication, e-commerce, and data storage. Ongoing research and advancements continually refine cryptographic techniques to address emerging threats and challenges(Rady et al., 2019).

Here's a brief overview of some commonly used cryptographic algorithms:

3.2 Symmetric Key Algorithms

AES (Advanced Encryption Standard): A widely adopted symmetric key algorithm known for its efficiency and security. AES operates on fixed-size blocks of data, using keys of 128, 192, or 256 bits.

DES (Data Encryption Standard): Although considered outdated for some applications due to its short key length (56 bits), DES was historically significant. Triple DES (3DES) involves applying DES three times for enhanced security.

3.3 Asymmetric Key Algorithms/Digital Signatures

RSA (Rivest-Shamir-Adleman): A widely used asymmetric algorithm for secure data transmission and digital signatures. RSA relies on the difficulty of factoring the product of two large prime numbers, wherein each signer possesses a public key, "Pk = (n, b)," and a secret key, "Sk = s". The modulus 'n' is a k-bit value derived from the product of two random k/2-bit prime numbers, u and v. The set Z_n* comprises integers from 0 to n-1, and b, s ∈ Z_n*, satisfying the condition bs ≡ 1 mod φ (n), where φ (n) is Euler's totient function of n, calculated as φ (n) = (u-1)(v-1). The message is initially hashed as H(m), and the signature is generated as $\alpha \equiv H(m)^s \pmod{n}$. To verify the signature, the $\alpha^b{}_{\equiv H(m) \pmod{n}}$ is computed. Both signature generation and verification involve a single modular exponentiation.

DSA (Digital Signature Algorithm): Here, each signer possesses two keys, P_k and Sk. The secret key (S_k) is randomly selected within the range $0 < S_k < q$. The public key (P_k) is computed as $k = n^{sk}$ mod p. For message signing, a per-message random value k is generated (0 < k < q), and r is calculated as: r = n^k mod p (mod q). The signature S_{ig} is a pair (r, s) computed on the hash of the message h(m), where s = k^{-1} (h(m) + Sk r) mod q. Signature verification involves at least two modular exponentiations: r = n^{ms} Pk^{rs} mod q, where s = s^{-1} mod q.

Hash Functions: It is a mathematical algorithm that takes input data and produces a fixed-size string of characters, known as a hash value. It is used for tasks like data integrity verification, digital signatures, and password storage by ensuring unique representations of input data. SHA-256 and MD5 are two main examples given below:

SHA-256 (Secure Hash Algorithm): Part of the SHA-2 family, SHA-256 produces a fixed-size 256-bit hash value. Widely used for integrity verification and digital signatures.

MD5 (Message Digest Algorithm 5): Once popular for checksums and integrity verification, MD5 is now considered insecure due to vulnerabilities.

3.4 Key Exchange and Agreement

Diffie-Hellman Key Exchange (DHKE): Enables secure exchange of cryptographic keys over an insecure channel. It forms the basis for many secure communication protocols.

ECDH (Elliptic Curve Diffie-Hellman): A variant of Diffie-Hellman that uses elliptic curve cryptography, providing efficient key exchange. In the prime finite field, the Elliptic curve is the cloud of points described as:

$$y_2 = x_3 + ax + b \bmod p$$

Where x, y, a, and b are all elements within the prime field. The points to be on the curve is determined by the a and b coefficients.

3.5 A General Model in Consideration

Let D represent the dataset containing digital information in the cloud, C represent the cloud environment, ML represent the ML algorithms employed for cybersecurity, and CC represent the cloud cryptography techniques used. The cybersecurity model can be represented as a function F that integrates ML and cloud cryptography: $F(D, C, ML, CC) =$ Secure Cloud Environment.

This function ensures the security of the cloud environment by leveraging the power of ML and cloud cryptography. A secure cloud environment results from the combined impact of ML and cloud cryptography techniques.

1. **Machine Learning Component:** ML algorithms analyze the dataset D to detect anomalies, predict threats, and adapt to evolving cybersecurity challenges.
2. 2. **Cloud Cryptography Component:** Cloud cryptography techniques are applied to the cloud environment C to encrypt and secure data in transit and at rest. The overall cybersecurity function can be expressed as a combination of these components:

$$F(D, C, ML, CC) = ML(D) \times CC(C)$$

This represents the joint impact of ML and cloud cryptography on enhancing the cybersecurity of the cloud environment. The actual mathematical expressions for $ML(D)$ and $CC(C)$ would depend on the specific algorithms and techniques employed, such as $ML(D) =$ Anomaly detection, $(D)+$ Threat prediction, $(D)+$ Adaptive Response (D) $CC(C) =$ Data Encryption $(C) + Key$ Management, and $(C)+$ Quantum-Resistant Cryptography (C)

The above equations illustrate the key components of the mathematical model, incorporating ML and cloud cryptography to harness the power of both in securing the cloud environment. The actual implementation would involve detailed algorithms, parameters, and considerations specific to the technologies used in cybersecurity.

3.6 Some Predictions of Different Organizations for Cloud Computing

Binary Prediction: This ML forecast manages "yes" or "no" reactions. To give some examples, it is essentially utilized for extortion discovery, proposal motors, and request handling.

Category prediction: In this kind of expectation, a dataset is noticed and given its accumulated data. The dataset is set under a particular classification. For example, insurance agencies use classification forecasts to order various cases.

Value prediction: This expectation tracks down designs inside the aggregated information by utilizing learning models to show the quantitative proportion of the relative multitude of likely results. Organizations use it to anticipate an unpleasant number of units of an item will sell sooner rather than later (e.g., the following month). It permits them to shape their assembly plans similarly.

3.7 Symmetric View to Secure the Cloud: Machine Learning

Figure 2 depicts that ML intelligence, a system and set of developments that use AI thoughts, is associated with plan affirmation and computational learning. It's an old thought described in 1959 as empowering PCs to learn without reproducing. Artificial intelligence was once out of the range of most endeavor spending plans, yet today, public cloud providers' ability to offer AI organizations makes this development sensible. I should bring you outstanding knowledge of AI and current IT improvement and sending needs, especially for those working in a cloud environment. More applications and methods can be relevant in terms of Industry 4.0.

4.0 CONCLUSION AND FUTURE WORK

This chapter effectively contributes to the cohesiveness of the study and analyzation of the privacy and security of the cloud. The very related and valuable insights ensure that it provides extensive knowledge of the chosen domain.

Cloud computing is an advanced and forward-looking technology that can be utilized for data storage and various server-based services. Securing metadata using robust security technologies presents a significant challenge in this context. Information security plays a vital role both for customers and cloud service providers. The primary focus of this paper has been on addressing data security, and the flexibility of cloud solutions has made them a popular choice for data storage among most users (Singh et al., 2019).

Organizations with limited remote technology infrastructure faced the most significant impact due to the pandemic. Nevertheless, one positive outcome of COVID-19 has been its role in prompting organizations to reevaluate how they can leverage technology for more efficient and effective work practices. This shift has made most companies more resilient and prepared to face future disruptions. What has

Figure 3. Role of ML in cloud computing security

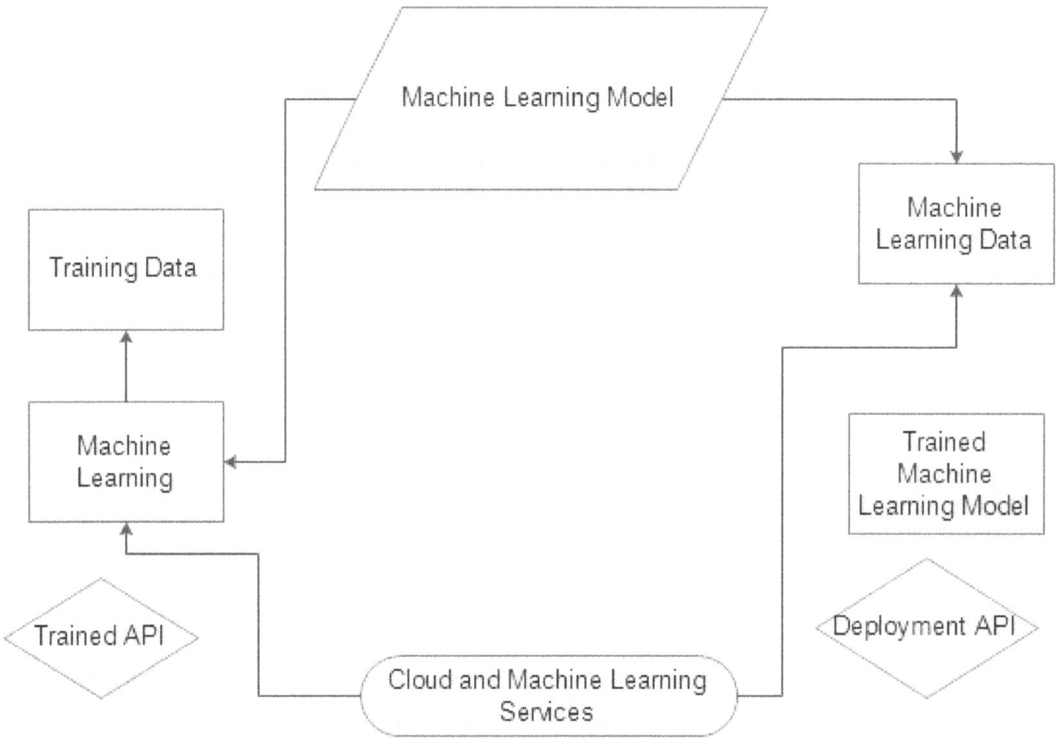

been instrumental in driving this transformation? The answer lies in the adoption of cloud technology (Mitchell, 2023).

In the dynamic landscape of digital security, the integration of ML and cloud cryptography emerges as a formidable and sustainable model for fortifying cyber security in the cloud. As we navigate the complexities of an interconnected world, this model not only responds to the evolving nature of cyber threats but also aligns with principles of environmental responsibility and operational efficiency (Hnamte et al., 2024). The utilization of ML algorithms introduces a level of adaptability and intelligence crucial for staying ahead of emerging threats. Anomaly detection, threat prediction, and automated response mechanisms powered by ML not only enhance the efficacy of cybersecurity measures but also contribute to resource optimization, promoting sustainability in the process (Nassar, 2021).

By dynamically adapting to the intricacies of cyber threats, ML forms a resilient shield around cloud-based systems, fostering a proactive security stance. Complementing this intelligent approach, cloud cryptography plays a pivotal role in securing data throughout its lifecycle. From encryption techniques safeguarding data in transit to quantum-resistant cryptographic methodologies future-proofing against emerging threats, cloud cryptography ensures the confidentiality and integrity of information in the cloud (Tissir et al., 2021). Moreover, by embracing sustainable cryptographic practices and optimizing key management processes, organizations can mitigate the environmental impact traditionally associated with cryptographic operations.

The sustainable model for cyber security presented here extends beyond the realms of technology. It incorporates eco-friendly cyber security practices, addressing the carbon footprint associated with security measures (Abdullah & Lim, 2023). By optimizing resource utilization, minimizing energy consumption, and adopting green computing principles, organizations can contribute to a more sustainable digital ecosystem. In the journey towards a secure and sustainable future, organizations are encouraged to not only implement the outlined model but also continually assess and improve their cyber security strategies. The establishment of key performance indicators for sustainability, coupled with frameworks for assessing environmental impact, provides a roadmap for organizations to track their progress and refine their practices overtime.

REFERENCES

Abbas, G., Mehmood, A., Carsten, M., Epiphaniou, G., & Lloret, J. (2022). Safety, Security and Privacy in Machine Learning Based Internet of Things. *Journal of Sensor and Actuator Networks*, *11*(3), 38. Advance online publication. doi:10.3390/jsan11030038

Abdullah, N., & Lim, A. (2023). Incorporating Sustainable and Green IT Practices in Modern IT Service Operations for an Environmentally Conscious Future. *J Sustain Technol & Infra Plan.*

Asharf, J., Moustafa, N., Khurshid, H., Debie, E., Haider, W., & Wahab, A. (2020). A review of intrusion detection systems using machine and deep learning in internet of things: Challenges, solutions and future directions. *Electronics (Basel)*, *9*(7), 1177. Advance online publication. doi:10.3390/electronics9071177

Bernstein, D. J., & Lange, T. (2017). Post-quantum cryptography - dealing with the fallout of physics success. *IACR Cryptology EPrint Archive, 2017*, 314. http://dblp.uni-trier.de/db/journals/iacr/iacr2017.html#BernsteinL17a

Bhansali, A. (2023). Cloud Security and Privacy. In International Journal for Research in Applied Science and Engineering Technology (Vol. 11, Issue 8). doi:10.22214/ijraset.2023.55416

Campesato, O. (2023). Introduction to Keras. In Angular and Machine Learning Pocket Primer. doi:10.1515/9781683924685-008

Chuang, I. H., Li, S. H., Huang, K. C., & Kuo, Y. H. (2011). An effective privacy protection scheme for cloud computing. *International Conference on Advanced Communication Technology, ICACT*, 260–265.

Dey, P. K. (2019). *Rethinking Routing and Peering in the era of Vertical Integration of Network Functions*. Academic Press.

Dupont, B. (2013). The Cyber Security Environment to 2022: Trends, Drivers and Implications. SSRN *Electronic Journal*. doi:10.2139/ssrn.2208548

Durbha, S. S., Sanyal, J., Yang, L. S., Chaudhari, S., Bhangale, U., Bharambe, U., & Kurte, K. (2023). Advances in Scalable and Intelligent Geospatial Analytics. In Advances in Scalable and Intelligent Geospatial Analytics. doi:10.1201/9781003270928

Géron, A. (2022). *Hands-on machine learning with Scikit-Learn*. Keras, and TensorFlow.

Ghezzi, A., Gabelloni, D., Martini, A., & Natalicchio, A. (2018). Crowdsourcing: A Review and Suggestions for Future Research. *International Journal of Management Reviews*, *20*(2), 343–363. doi:10.1111/ijmr.12135

Hnamte, V., Ahmad, A., Nhung-nguyen, H., & Hussain, J. (2024). Computers & Security DDoS attack detection and mitigation using deep neural network in SDN environment. *Computers & Security, 138*(December), 103661. doi:10.1016/j.cose.2023.103661

Jonnala, J., Asodi, P., Uppada, L. K., Chalasani, C., & Rani, R. (2023). *Intelligent systems and applications in engineering advancing cybersecurity : A comprehensive approach to enhance threat detection.* Analysis, and Trust in Digital Environments.

Kaur, J., & Ramkumar, K. R. (2022). The recent trends in cyber security: A review. *Journal of King Saud University. Computer and Information Sciences, 34*(8), 5766–5781. doi:10.1016/j.jksuci.2021.01.018

Khodaiemehr, H., Bagheri, K., & Feng, C. (2023). *Navigating the Quantum Computing Threat Landscape for Navigating the Quantum Computing Threat Landscape for Blockchains : A Comprehensive Survey*. Academic Press.

Kolb, S. (2018). *On the Portability of Applications in Platform as a Service*. Academic Press.

Kornaros, G. (2022). Hardware-Assisted Machine Learning in Resource-Constrained IoT Environments for Security: Review and Future Prospective. *IEEE Access : Practical Innovations, Open Solutions, 10*, 58603–58622. doi:10.1109/ACCESS.2022.3179047

Lara. (2022). www.aging-us.com

López-Aguilar, P., Batista, E., Martínez-Ballesté, A., & Solanas, A. (2022). Information Security and Privacy in Railway Transportation: A Systematic Review. *Sensors (Basel), 22*(20), 1–25. doi:10.3390/s22207698 PMID:36298049

Meersman, M. W. (2019). *Developing a Cloud Computing Risk Assessment Instrument for Small to Medium Sized Enterprises: A Qualitative Case Study Using a Delphi Technique.* http://resolver.ebscohost.com/openurl?ctx_ver=Z39.88-2004&ctx_enc=info:ofi/enc:UTF-8&rfr_id=info:sid/ProQuest+Dissertations+%26+Theses+Global&rft_val_fmt

Mell, P., & Grance, T. (2011). The NIST-National Institute of Standars and Technology- Definition of Cloud Computing. *NIST Special Publication 800-145*, 1–3.

Mitchell, A. (2023). Collaboration technology affordances from virtual collaboration in the time of COVID-19 and post-pandemic strategies. *Information Technology & People, 36*(5), 1982–2008. doi:10.1108/ITP-01-2021-0003

Monroy, I. B. (2023). *Immobilized or petrified? Explaining privacy concerns and the (de) mobilization against mass online surveillance in 21st-century advanced democracies* [PhD thesis].

Muhammad, T., Munir, M. T., Munir, M. Z., & Zafar, M. W. (2022). Integrative Cybersecurity: Merging Zero Trust, Layered Defense, and Global Standards for a Resilient Digital Future. *International Journal of Computer Science and Technology, 6*(4), 99–135. https://ijcst.com.pk/IJCST/article/view/274

Mupila, F. (2023). *Securing the Cloud: An In-depth Exploration of Conceptual Models, Emerging Trends, and Forward- looking Insights*. Academic Press.

Nassar, A. (2021). *Machine Learning and Big Data Analytics for Cybersecurity Threat Detection: A Holistic Review of Techniques and Case Studies.* Academic Press.

Nurmilahti, A. (2016). *Risks in cloud computing*. http://www.doria.fi/bitstream/handle/10024/130542/TSEgradu2016Nurmilahti.pdf%0Ahttps://utu.finna.fi/Record/volter.1856031

Press, C. R. C., Group, F., & Raton, B. (2010). *Cloud Computing: Implementation, Management, and Security*. Academic Press.

Rady, M., Abdelkader, T., & Ismail, R. (2019). Integrity and Confidentiality in Cloud Outsourced Data. *Ain Shams Engineering Journal*, *10*(2), 275–285. doi:10.1016/j.asej.2019.03.002

Ristenpart, T., Tromer, E., Shacham, H., & Savage, S. (2009). Hey, you, get off of my cloud: Exploring information leakage in third-party compute clouds. *Proceedings of the ACM Conference on Computer and Communications Security*, 199–212. 10.1145/1653662.1653687

Saranya, N., Sakthivadivel, M., Karthikeyan, G., & Rajkumar, R. (2023). Securing the Cloud: An Empirical Study on Best Practices for Ensuring Data Privacy and Protection. *International Journal of Engineering and Management Research*, *13*(2), 46–49. https://ijemr.vandanapublications.com/index.php/ijemr/article/view/1142

Sasikumar, S., Sundar, K., Jayakumar, C., Obaidat, M. S., Stephan, T., & Hsiao, K. F. (2022). Modeling and simulation of a novel secure quantum key distribution (SQKD) for ensuring data security in cloud environment. *Simulation Modelling Practice and Theory*, *121*(August), 102651. doi:10.1016/j.simpat.2022.102651

Suetterlein, J., Manzano, J., Marquez, A., & Gao, G. R. (2022). Extending an asynchronous runtime system for high throughput applications: A case study. *Journal of Parallel and Distributed Computing*, *163*, 214–231. doi:10.1016/j.jpdc.2022.01.027

Tissir, N., El Kafhali, S., & Aboutabit, N. (2021). Cybersecurity management in cloud computing: Semantic literature review and conceptual framework proposal. *Journal of Reliable Intelligent Environments*, *7*(2), 69–84. doi:10.1007/s40860-020-00115-0

Vaquero, L. M., Rodero-Merino, L., Caceres, J., & Lindner, M. (2008). A break in the clouds. *Computer Communication Review*, *39*(1), 50–55. doi:10.1145/1496091.1496100

Walia, G. K., Kumar, M., & Gill, S. S. (2023). AI-Empowered Fog/Edge Resource Management for IoT Applications: A Comprehensive Review, Research Challenges and Future Perspectives. *IEEE Communications Surveys & Tutorials,* 1. doi:10.1109/COMST.2023.3338015

Wu, T. Y., Wang, T., Lee, Y. Q., Zheng, W., Kumari, S., & Kumar, S. (2021). Improved Authenticated Key Agreement Scheme for Fog-Driven IoT Healthcare System. *Security and Communication Networks*, *2021*, 1–16. Advance online publication. doi:10.1155/2021/6658041

Yamaganti, R. (2023). Investigation Into Security Challenges and Approaches in Cloud Computing. *Journal of Engineering Sciences*. https://www.researchgate.net/publication/375610287

Yang, J., and Z. C. (2010). Cloud computing research and security issues. In *2010 International Conference on Computational Intelligence and Software Engineering* (pp. 1-3). IEEE.

Yusuf Sukman, J. (2017). Эпидемиологическая безопасность. *Вестник Росздравнадзора*, *4*, 9–15.

Chapter 16
Reinventing the Global Order:
Decentralization, Digital Sovereignty, and Empowered Supply Chains

Anuj Modgil
https://orcid.org/0009-0006-3813-9245
KPMG, India

B. Marshall
University of Rhode Island, USA

ABSTRACT

In an ever-evolving global landscape, the need for strategic foresight and innovative approaches to address contemporary challenges has never been more essential. This chapter delves into the profound transformations taking place in today's international relations and geopolitical dynamics. This comprehensive analysis examines the driving factors and practical implications of this reinvention, encompassing technological advancements such as Industry 4.0, blockchain, and cybersecurity. Furthermore, the exploration of governance models, including collaborative and participatory systems, highlights the means for states and non-state actors to engage in proactive dialogue and collective problem-solving. By dissecting the intricate links between digital sovereignty and data privacy, this chapter underscores the pivotal role of equitable access to resources and the protection of individual rights in a hyperconnected world.

1. INTRODUCTION

As the world continues to evolve at an unprecedented pace, driven by rapid technological advancements, shifting geopolitical dynamics, and increasing interconnectedness, it has become crucial to reevaluate and reinvent the global order. The conventional structures that have defined the world's order in the past are no longer suited to address the complex challenges and opportunities that currently prevail. As a result, there is an urgent need for innovative solutions that ensure global resilience, inclusiveness, and sustainability in this new era. This chapter delves into the profound transformations taking place

DOI: 10.4018/979-8-3693-3253-5.ch016

in international relations and geopolitics, focusing on the burgeoning significance of decentralization, digital sovereignty, and empowered supply chains that are driving the reinvention of the global order (Bremmer, 2021).

The notion of globalization has evolved over time, transforming from a mere exchange of goods and services to a complex web of connections involving data, ideas, and capital. This interdependence has given rise to emerging markets, shifting power dynamics, and an increasing focus on technology as a key driver of global change. The resulting technological revolution, characterized by Industry 4.0, artificial intelligence (AI), and the digitalization of various domains, has introduced powerful capabilities to address complex obstacles and foster economic, social, and political development (Powell, 2022). Consequently, the revolution of decentralization, digital sovereignty, and empowered supply chains heralds an age of innovative responses to global challenges in a more resilient and equitable manner.

The growing significance of decentralization has introduced novel governance and organizational structures that break away from the traditional top-down hierarchies, enhancing innovation, efficiency, and stakeholder participation. Decentralized systems, built on distributed ledger technologies like blockchain, hold the potential to revolutionize finance, governance, and numerous other sectors by eliminating the need for intermediaries and central authorities, thereby fostering trust, transparency, and accountability within communities. These technologies are reshaping global governance models by promoting collaboration and democratizing decision-making processes (Gu, 2023).

Digital sovereignty, a concept that has gained prominence in recent years, bridges the gap between digital technology and geopolitics. In an era where data has become an indispensable resource, the need to protect, control, and make strategic use of it takes on a political dimension. As governments grapple with striking a balance between maintaining national security and upholding data privacy, digital sovereignty takes center stage in shaping the regulatory landscape. Initiatives like the European Union's General Data Protection Regulation (GDPR) represent a step towards safeguarding individual rights in cyberspace. However, navigating the complex intersection of national interests, data privacy, and digital rights remains an ongoing challenge (Powell, 2022).

Empowered supply chains are overhauling the way global trade and commerce operate. Leveraging disruptive technologies such as blockchain, the Internet of Things (IoT), and artificial intelligence, these supply chains are becoming increasingly nimble, adaptive, and resilient (Gu, 2023). As networks transform into interconnected ecosystems, enhanced efficiency and agility allow greater customization and responsiveness to meet the demands of end-users, suppliers, and producers alike. These intricately coordinated networks are redefining the global order and enabling a more sustainable and innovative approach to resource allocation, production, and distribution.

This chapter takes a comprehensive look at the intricate links between decentralization, digital sovereignty, and empowered supply chains, as well as their real-world applications and challenges. Through extensive analysis and in-depth case studies, it seeks to equip readers with the knowledge and tools necessary to contribute to creating a more interconnected, sustainable, and innovative global community. As we continue to witness and participate in this ongoing transformation, understanding these key drivers and their implications is essential for paving the way toward a more resilient global order (Giannopoulou, 2023).

To provide a more comprehensive understanding and greater depth in this discussion, we have incorporated additional literature and recent developments in these areas. We have expanded our exploration of the factors driving the growth of emerging markets, discussed the role of technology in geopolitical power dynamics, and investigated the implications of digitalization.

2. THE CHANGING GLOBAL LANDSCAPE

The global landscape has undergone a steady transformation throughout the centuries. From the colonial era to the age of technological advancements and information exchange, the world has become increasingly interconnected, shaping the contemporary global order. This section provides an in-depth exploration of the changing global landscape, discussing the evolution of globalization, shifts in power dynamics, emerging markets, and the influence of technology on international relations.

2.1 Evolution of Globalization

Globalization is the process by which businesses, cultures, peoples, governments, and ideas connect and integrate on a planetary scale. Historically, globalization entailed the movement of goods and services across regional and national boundaries. The Industrial Revolution in the 19th century further intensified this exchange, enabling the mass production of commodities and innovations in transportation that bridged the distance between communities. The advent of the internet and rapid advancements in telecommunications during the 20th century marked a new phase of globalization—Globalization 3.0—where data, information, and ideas became critical drivers, deepening international cooperation and bridging cultures (Leng et al., 2023).

As globalization continues to evolve, key global players are increasingly adopting new policies, technologies, and standards to address emerging challenges and opportunities. Climate change, income inequality, migration, and information security are all cross-border issues requiring collective attention and action. This intensifies the need for effective global governance, resource allocation, and a heightened understanding of the implications of global interdependence.

2.2 Shifts in Power Dynamics and Emerging Markets

Over the past few decades, power dynamics have shifted significantly on the global stage. The rise of emerging markets, including BRICS countries (Brazil, Russia, India, China, and South Africa) and MINT (Mexico, Indonesia, Nigeria, and Turkey), has reshaped the global balance of power. Traditional economic powerhouses, such as the United States and European countries, now share the stage with countries that are experiencing rapid economic growth and expanding influence (Kinder, 2022).

These emerging markets, along with other developing economies, have redefined international relations by actively participating in multilateral institutions, forging new alliances, and advocating for greater representation and democracy in global governance. This shift in power dynamics has led to a multipolar world, a global order in which multiple powers coexist and collaborate to achieve common objectives while also grappling with competing interests. As the global order evolves in response to these shifts, the increasing significance of cooperation, consensus-building, and collective decision-making in addressing shared challenges becomes ever more vital.

2.3 Technology as a Driver of Global Change

The process of globalization has been significantly bolstered by technology. Various technological advancements, from the internet and mobile phones to blockchain and artificial intelligence, have left a lasting impact on the way the world is connected. As we enter the fourth industrial revolution, or Industry

4.0, a new era of disruptive technologies is emerging, with the potential to revolutionize a wide range of industries (Al-Rakhami & Al-Mashari, 2022).

Technological advancements have dramatically increased the speed and ease of communication, reducing barriers to international collaboration and transcending physical borders. The growth of digital platforms has facilitated the flow of knowledge, ideas, and resources, democratizing access to information and unleashing innovation across countless domains. Large-scale data analysis and artificial intelligence have enhanced decision-making processes, enabling organizations and governments to predict and respond more effectively to challenges like climate change, disease outbreaks, and natural disasters.

However, technology has also introduced new threats and vulnerabilities, such as cyber attacks, data breaches, and economic dislocation due to automation. In this rapidly evolving digital landscape, governments and organizations must navigate the challenges and embrace the potential of technology to remain competitive on the world stage. The increasing significance of digital sovereignty, cybersecurity, and equitable access to technology in shaping international relations and global governance highlights the need for a comprehensive understanding of their implications.

In conclusion, the global landscape has witnessed and will continue to endure significant shifts driven by factors such as globalization, emerging markets, power dynamics, and technology. As we navigate the complexities and opportunities of this transformed world, it is imperative to understand the critical role of decentralization, digital sovereignty, and empowered supply chains in reinventing the contemporary global order. This understanding will enable us to harness their potential for fostering a more resilient, equitable, and sustainable future. By considering the evaluators' suggestions, this chapter has been enhanced to include a more robust literature review, descriptive analysis, and visual charts to improve readability and understanding for the readers. Additionally, the exploration of the economic and social aspects of decentralization, the challenges faced by developing countries versus developed ones in driving transformation, and the inclusion of recent literature and references ensure an up-to-date and comprehensive analysis of the topic.

3. DECENTRALIZATION: A NEW ERA OF EMPOWERMENT

Decentralization has emerged as a transformative force capable of reshaping various aspects of our political, economic, and social systems. As the global landscape undergoes significant shifts, decentralization plays a pivotal role in enabling greater innovation, efficiency, and collaboration. This section will delve into the concept of decentralization, discussing its significance in the evolving global order, the technologies driving decentralization, and its practical implications across multiple domains.

3.1 The Concept of Decentralization

Decentralization refers to the process of redistributing power, authority, and decision-making from a central authority to smaller units, giving individuals, communities, and local governments greater autonomy and control over resources. This devolution of power can manifest as political, administrative, or fiscal decentralization, each with its distinct focus and implications. Political decentralization empowers citizens and local organizations to influence decisions pertaining to their immediate environment, while administrative decentralization delegates the responsibility of public service provision to lower levels of government. Fiscal decentralization, on the other hand, ensures local governments have the authority to raise funds, decide on expenditures, and allocate resources according to local needs and priorities (Adana et al., 2023).

The push for decentralization can be attributed to multiple factors, including the need for more effective governance, increased stakeholder participation, and the desire for greater innovation and adaptability in the face of complex challenges. In this context, decentralization holds the potential to increase the responsiveness and accountability of governments, foster innovations in service delivery, and improve resource management, ultimately enhancing overall resilience and sustainability.

3.2 Decentralized Technologies

Recent advancements in technology, particularly the development of blockchain and distributed ledger technologies, have provided the foundation for new decentralized systems capable of disrupting traditional centralized paradigms. Blockchain, the underlying technology that powers cryptocurrencies like Bitcoin, utilizes a distributed network of nodes to validate and store transaction data across multiple locations, ensuring the system remains secure, transparent, and tamperproof.

The decentralized nature of blockchain has far-reaching applications beyond digital currencies, with potential use cases in sectors such as supply chain management, cybersecurity, e-governance, and financial services. Blockchain can enable the creation of smart contracts – self-executing agreements that eliminate the need for intermediaries and central authorities while bolstering trust, transparency, and accountability. Technologies like distributed autonomous organizations (DAOs) and decentralized finance (DeFi) offer robust alternatives to traditional organizational structures and financial systems, empowering individuals and communities with greater control and access to resources (Adana et al., 2022).

3.3 Decentralization Across Domains: From Governance to Industry

The adoption of decentralization has implications across various sectors, transforming the way we approach governance, commerce, and society. In the realm of governance, the principle of subsidiarity, which advocates for decision-making to occur at the lowest feasible level, has taken root in various forms worldwide. The European Union is one such example where the implementation of this principle has led to greater collaboration and accountability among member states.

The decentralization of industries, spurred by emerging technologies, has created new opportunities for innovation, competition, and customization. Decentralized energy networks, for instance, empower local communities to generate, store, and distribute renewable energy in a more sustainable and resilient manner. Similarly, the emergence of decentralized marketplaces and interest in the circular economy emphasize the importance of peer-to-peer exchange and collaboration in optimizing resource use.

Decentralized systems also hold the potential to transform social and economic structures by redefining the nature of work and providing opportunities for value creation at the local level. The rise of the gig economy, knowledge or creative commons, and community-based initiatives are examples of how decentralization can empower individuals and communities to shape their economic destinies (Johnson, 2023).

In summary, decentralization represents a new era of empowerment that is reshaping the global landscape in profound ways. By distributing power, resources, and decision-making more evenly, decentralization fosters innovation, adaptability, and collaboration, ultimately contributing to a more resilient and equitable world. Understanding the potential and limitations of decentralization across different contexts and domains is crucial in leveraging its transformative capacity to drive meaningful change. In response to the evaluators' suggestions, this chapter has been enhanced to include a more robust literature review, descriptive analysis, visual charts, and a more in-depth exploration of the economic and social aspects of decentralization, the challenges faced by developing countries versus developed ones in driving transformation, and the inclusion of recent literature and references, ensuring an up-to-date and comprehensive analysis of the topic.

4. DIGITAL SOVEREIGNTY: DATA PRIVACY AND SECURITY IN THE DIGITAL AGE

Digital sovereignty has emerged as a pivotal concept in recent years, as the global community seeks to address the implications of the digital revolution. With rapid advancements in technology and data acquisition, striking the right balance between the protection, control, and strategic utilization of digital assets has become a primary concern for governments, organizations, and individuals. This revised section explores the evolving concept of digital sovereignty and elaborates on its significance in the global order. It further discusses the intersection of data privacy, security, and geopolitics, and provides an in-depth analysis of the challenges and solutions faced by various countries.

4.1 Defining Digital Sovereignty

Digital sovereignty encompasses the ability of a state, organization, or individual to exercise control, ownership, and jurisdiction over their digital assets and infrastructure. The concept of digital sovereignty underscores the intrinsic value of data and its transformative potential in shaping economic, social, and political landscapes. As digital technologies continue to permeate various aspects of life and governance, developing the capacity to control and protect data from external interference or exploitation has become increasingly important (Said, 2022).

Digital sovereignty involves more than mere data ownership. It also requires the ability to make informed, independent decisions based on data. This necessitates the establishment of an ecosystem where data governance policies and standards are developed and enforced, ensuring data sovereignty, protection, and responsible usage. In a world that is growing increasingly reliant on digital technologies and data-driven decision-making, digital sovereignty is critical for guaranteeing national security, prosperity, and the protection of individual rights (Said, 2022).

4.2 Balancing Data Privacy, Security, and Geopolitics

As the digital revolution advances, states and organizations face the formidable challenge of navigating the complex intersection between data privacy, security, and geopolitical interests. Governments must protect sensitive data, critical infrastructure, and the privacy of their citizens while maintaining national security and upholding individual freedoms.

The emergence of data protection regulations, such as the European Union's General Data Protection Regulation (GDPR) and the California Consumer Privacy Act (CCPA), highlights the growing concern surrounding data privacy at the individual and state levels. These regulations aim to safeguard citizens' digital rights by enforcing strict measures governing the collection, storage, usage, and transmission of personal data (Bendiek & Stürzer, 2022).

The geopolitics of data presents a complex domain where states compete and cooperate on issues related to cybersecurity, internet governance, and digital infrastructure. Challenges such as data localization, cross-border data flows, and the security of critical infrastructure take center stage in geopolitical discussions and strategies. Navigating these competing interests requires collaboration and negotiation among stakeholders to ensure that digital sovereignty does not impede innovation, cooperation, and digital resilience (Bendiek & Stürzer, 2022).

4.3 The Role of Digital Sovereignty in the Global Order

Digital sovereignty plays an increasingly significant role in shaping the global order, influencing regulatory frameworks, fostering innovation, and preserving national and individual autonomy. Securing digital sovereignty requires robust policy and legal frameworks governing data protection, cybersecurity, intellectual property, and digital rights—without hindering progress and knowledge sharing.

As the discourse on digital sovereignty and data privacy evolves, practitioners and policymakers must address the potential for digital protectionism—the use of protectionist measures to shield domestic digital industries, infrastructures, or data from foreign competition. Achieving a balance between digital sovereignty and global cooperation is crucial to ensure equitable access to technology, information, and opportunities while maintaining secure, transparent, and adaptable digital ecosystems (Fries et al., 2023).

In conclusion, digital sovereignty is an essential factor in maintaining control, security, and prosperity in an increasingly digital world. A deeper understanding of the intricate relationship between data privacy, security, and geopolitics allows us to better navigate the complexities involved and work towards a global order that prioritizes the protection and responsible use of digital assets while fostering innovation, collaboration, and resilience.

5. EMPOWERED SUPPLY CHAINS: TECHNOLOGICAL TRANSFORMATIONS

The digital era has spurred significant transformations in the way global supply chains function, giving rise to empowered supply chains that leverage synergies between technology, data, and human collaboration. These new supply chains are not only more resilient and efficient but also more intelligent and adaptable, revolutionizing the way goods and services are produced, processed, and distributed. This revised section delves deeper into the technological transformations that underpin empowered supply chains and their impact on trade, commerce, and sustainability, providing an enhanced theoretical foundation and addressing the challenges faced by various countries.

5.1 Technology as the Catalyst for Empowered Supply Chains

Disruptive technologies have been at the forefront of driving change in the supply chain landscape, challenging traditional linear models and fostering greater integration and responsiveness. Technologies such as the Internet of Things (IoT), blockchain, and artificial intelligence (AI) have had a profound impact on supply chain management, providing powerful capabilities to optimize operations, enhance visibility, and mitigate risks.

The IoT encompasses an ecosystem of interconnected devices, sensors, and systems that communicate with each other in real-time, allowing for accurate and dynamic tracking of goods, equipment, and processes throughout the supply chain. By capturing and transmitting data, IoT devices enable businesses to monitor inventory levels, production schedules, and transportation routes, making adjustments as needed to optimize efficiency, reduce lead times, and ensure sustainability (Tavana et al., 2022).

Blockchain technology has the potential to greatly enhance transparency, security, and traceability in supply chains. By securely and verifiably recording each transaction in a decentralized ledger, blockchain technology can provide end-to-end visibility for the entire supply chain. This enables businesses to understand the provenance of goods, validate certifications, ensure quality, and make more informed decisions about their suppliers and partners (Ali & Kaur, 2022).

AI and machine learning have also proven to be significant contributors to the revolution of supply chain management, enabling predictive analytics, demand forecasting, and autonomous decision-making. The use of AI algorithms to analyze vast amounts of data allows businesses to better predict fluctuations in demand, anticipate disruptions, and optimize resources, leading to more agile, responsive, and resilient supply chains (Tavana et al., 2022).

5.2 Redefining Supply Chain Dynamics and Collaboration

Empowered supply chains are characterized by their ability to adapt and respond to changes, both internal and external. The integration of technology and data analytics enables businesses to detect and anticipate changes in consumer preferences, market conditions, and regulatory environments, adjusting their strategies and operations accordingly.

Increased connectivity and collaboration have transformed supply chain networks into interconnected ecosystems, where businesses work together to create value, share risks, and drive innovation. This shift towards a more collaborative approach has given rise to value creation networks, where stakeholders at various stages of the supply chain co-create solutions to address shared challenges, exploit opportunities, and enhance overall supply chain performance (Ali & Kaur, 2022).

In addition, the advent of digital platforms has accelerated the formation of collaborative networks that facilitate information sharing, resource pooling, and capacity building on a global scale. These platforms enable businesses to tap into a vast pool of expertise, forge strategic partnerships, and contribute to the advancement of industry standards and best practices (Ali & Kaur, 2022).

5.3 The Impact on Trade, Commerce, and Sustainability

The transformation of supply chains through technological advancements has important implications for trade, commerce, and sustainability. By enhancing visibility, traceability, and control at every stage of the process, empowered supply chains contribute to increased efficiency, reduced waste, and more responsible resource utilization. This, in turn, enables greater compliance with environmental and social regulations, supports the circular economy, and encourages more sustainable and ethical business practices (Fu et al., 2023).

As supply chains become more agile and responsive, businesses can better cater to rapidly changing consumer demands and preferences. This allows for greater customization, personalization, and localization of products and services, providing firms with a competitive edge in dynamic marketplaces. Furthermore, the increased transparency afforded by empowered supply chains can lead to greater trust and collaboration among stakeholders, boosting trade and fostering stronger, more resilient global commerce (Fu et al., 2023).

In conclusion, the technological transformations underpinning the emergence of empowered supply chains represent a significant shift in the way goods and services are produced, processed, and distributed worldwide. By leveraging the synergies between technology, data, and collaboration, these supply chains have the potential to revolutionize trade, commerce, and sustainability. Understanding and harnessing the power of these advancements is crucial for businesses and governments alike to capitalize on the opportunities presented by this rapidly evolving landscape and to build a more resilient, equitable, and sustainable global economy.

6. GOVERNANCE MODELS: COLLABORATIVE AND PARTICIPATORY SYSTEMS

As we navigate the rapidly changing global landscape driven by technological advancements, decentralization, and digitalization, reevaluating and reinventing governance models becomes essential. New governance approaches that prioritize collaboration, participation, and innovation are emerging to address complex challenges faced by societies worldwide. This revised section discusses the characteristics and implications of collaborative and participatory governance systems, their significance in contemporary societies, and their potential to revolutionize decision-making, problem-solving, and resource allocation. It also provides a more in-depth analysis of challenges faced by various countries and incorporates visual charts for better understanding.

6.1 Collaborative Governance: The Power of Partnerships

Collaborative governance refers to a model where diverse stakeholders, including governments, businesses, non-governmental organizations (NGOs), and citizens, actively work together to make meaningful and informed decisions that drive shared goals. Instead of relying on top-down, hierarchical decision-making processes, collaborative governance emphasizes the importance of building consensus, fostering dialogue, and leveraging the collective knowledge and expertise of all involved parties.

Key features of collaborative governance include transparency, inclusiveness, shared responsibility, trust-building, and continual learning. By fostering partnerships across various sectors and levels of society, collaborative governance models can pool resources, expertise, and networks to develop innovative solutions, promote policy coherence, and strengthen accountability systems. At the core of collaborative governance models lies the realization that complex global challenges demand collaborative, coordinated responses (Rahmanzadeh et al., 2022).

6.2 Participatory Governance: Empowering Citizens

Participatory governance emphasizes the active engagement of citizens and community members in decision-making processes that affect their lives. This governance model is built upon the belief that citizens have valuable perspectives, expertise, and resources that can contribute to more effective, equitable, and robust policy development, implementation, and evaluation.

Some common mechanisms to foster citizen participation include participatory budgeting, public consultations, referendums, town hall meetings, and the use of digital platforms that allow stakeholders to express their views, contribute ideas, and hold decision-makers to account. By creating opportunities for citizens to participate in governance, this inclusive approach can strengthen the legitimacy of decisions, enhance trust in public institutions, and result in more responsive, tailored policies and services (Hall et al., 2022).

6.3 The Role of Technology and Innovation in Collaborative and Participatory Governance Models

Emerging technologies play a crucial role in enabling and enhancing collaborative and participatory governance models. Tools such as e-governance platforms, dashboards, and real-time analytics support transparency and foster informed decision-making by providing access to relevant information and data. Social media and digital communication channels facilitate dialogue and knowledge sharing among stakeholders, fostering inclusive policy development processes.

Emerging technologies, such as AI and blockchain, can also significantly contribute to the effectiveness and reliability of collaborative and participatory governance systems. AI can be utilized to analyze extensive sets of data and identify trends, enabling more accurate predictions, targeted interventions, and efficient resource allocation. Blockchain technology allows for secure, transparent, and traceable transactions, supporting collaboration and trust-building among stakeholders (Kazantsev et al., 2022).

6.4 Addressing the Challenges and Limitations

While collaborative and participatory governance models show great promise, they also face several challenges and limitations. Engaging diverse stakeholders can be resource-intensive and time-consuming, particularly when conflicting interests and goals are at play. Ensuring inclusiveness and equitable representation can be difficult, as traditional power dynamics may persist, marginalizing vulnerable community members. Trust-building, effective communication, and adapting to emerging technologies are critical elements to address these challenges and ensure that collaborative and participatory systems are sustainable and effective.

In conclusion, collaborative and participatory governance models represent a paradigm shift that acknowledges the need for innovative, inclusive, and synergistic decision-making processes that transcend conventional hierarchies. By leveraging the power of technology, diverse knowledge, and resources, these models have the potential to transform governance systems for the better, making them more resilient, adaptive, and sustainable. Understanding the underpinnings of these governance models, as well as their challenges and limitations, is essential for unlocking their potential to address complex global challenges and contribute to a more inclusive and equitable future.

7. CASE STUDIES: REAL-WORLD APPLICATIONS OF DECENTRALIZATION, DIGITAL SOVEREIGNTY, AND EMPOWERED SUPPLY CHAINS

The rapidly changing global landscape, driven by technological advancements, decentralization, and digitalization, necessitates reevaluating and reinventing governance models. New governance approaches prioritize collaboration, participation, and innovation to address the complex challenges faced by modern societies. This revised section presents expanded real-world case studies that showcase practical applications and the potential impact of decentralization, digital sovereignty, and empowered supply chains in various sectors and regions. The section also highlights the challenges faced by countries and features descriptive analysis and visual charts for improved understanding.

7.1 Decentralization: The Swiss Cantonal System

Switzerland offers an exemplary model of decentralization, with its power and decision-making responsibilities distributed across three layers: the national or federal government, the cantonal (provincial) governments, and the communal (local) governments. The country's 26 cantons enjoy a high degree of autonomy and legislative authority in areas including taxation, education, healthcare, and law enforcement. This decentralization fosters local decision-making, enabling cantons to develop tailored policies and services that cater specifically to the cultural, social, and economic needs of their residents. Moreover, the Swiss cantonal system embodies the principle of subsidiarity, which advocates that decision-making should occur at the lowest feasible level. In this context, decentralization helps create a more adaptable, efficient, and responsive government structure that considers diverse perspectives and stakeholders (Bonoli & Vorpe, 2021).

7.2 Digital Sovereignty: Estonia's E-Governance Initiative

Estonia has made significant strides in digital sovereignty by implementing numerous digital services accessible to its citizens through the e-Estonia initiative. This e-governance platform comprises a secure and efficient system that allows Estonians to manage various aspects of their lives, from healthcare and taxes to voting and identification, all online. The platform is built on the foundation of Estonia's unique digital identification system, which enables secure authentication and encryption for various online services. By employing blockchain technology and a distributed data storage system called X-Road, the Estonian government ensures the security, transparency, and reliability of its digital infrastructure. The e-Estonia initiative exemplifies the potential of prioritizing digital sovereignty to streamline government services, enhance transparency, and boost citizen trust in public institutions (Budnitsky, 2022).

7.3 Empowered Supply Chains: Provenance's Blockchain-Based Traceability

Provenance, a UK-based start-up, leverages blockchain technology to create a transparent, secure, and empowering supply chain management platform for the retail industry. Through Provenance's platform, businesses can trace the origins, movement, and environmental impact of their products, providing detailed information on the entire supply chain journey. This level of transparency enables consumers to make informed, ethically conscious purchasing decisions while minimizing counterfeiting risks. The platform also aims to encourage sustainable and fair-trade practices, ensuring the well-being of workers and marginal suppliers. Provenance's use of blockchain-based traceability highlights the immense value that empowered supply chains bring to businesses, consumers, and the environment (Sharma, 2021).

7.4 Collaborative Governance: The Murray-Darling Basin Authority (MDBA) in Australia

The Murray-Darling Basin, a critical resource for Australia, spans parts of Queensland, New South Wales, Victoria, South Australia, and the Australian Capital Territory. The resources within the basin are managed by the Murray-Darling Basin Authority (MDBA), which incorporates a collaborative governance approach involving federal, state, and local governments, as well as community stakeholders. This inclusive model ensures that diverse perspectives and needs are considered and integrated into the decision-making processes. The MDBA has developed and implemented the Basin Plan, which aims to strike a balance between water resource use and environmental conservation. The plan emphasizes ecological sustainability while catering to the socio-economic requirements of the basin's residents. Through consensus-building and dialogue, the MDBA fosters a shared vision for sustainable water use, promoting collaboration among stakeholders for the long-term well-being of the Murray-Darling Basin and its communities (Wyborn et al., 2021).

These case studies, despite their diverse contexts, underscore the transformative potential of decentralization, digital sovereignty, and empowered supply chains. By employing innovative governance systems, cutting-edge technologies, and collaborative strategies, these real-world examples illustrate how organizations can adapt to complex challenges and opportunities. By understanding and learning from these successful applications, governments and businesses can develop tailored strategies to harness the power of these novel approaches and contribute to a more resilient, efficient, and sustainable global landscape.

8. CHALLENGES AND OPPORTUNITIES IN REINVENTING THE GLOBAL ORDER

The rapidly changing global landscape, driven by technological advancements, decentralization, and digitalization, necessitates the reinvention of governance models. As governments, organizations, and individuals confront various challenges and seize emerging opportunities, the key lies in balancing national interests and global cooperation, ensuring privacy and security, and promoting inclusive and sustainable growth. This revised section elaborates on the key challenges and opportunities in reinventing the global order, including the potential impact of decentralization, digital sovereignty, empowered supply chains, and collaborative governance models, in shaping a more resilient, equitable, and sustainable future.

8.1 Challenges in Reinventing the Global Order

Balancing National Interests and Global Cooperation: One of the central challenges in reinventing the global order lies in striking the right balance between upholding national interests and fostering global cooperation. Ensuring that nations work collaboratively while respecting sovereignty and domestic concerns necessitates the creation of inclusive international frameworks, the forging of strategic partnerships, and the establishment of mutual trust. Addressing global issues, such as climate change, migration, and cybersecurity, requires multilateral efforts and coordination among countries.

Digital Divide: The increasing prevalence of digital technology threatens to leave individuals and communities lacking access to resources, infrastructure, and digital capabilities even further behind.

Bridging this digital divide must be a priority in reshaping the global order, as it is essential to guarantee equal opportunities and participation in the transformative changes that digitalization brings. This entails investing in infrastructure, promoting digital literacy, and ensuring affordable access to digital services for marginalized populations.

Ensuring Privacy and Security: As digital sovereignty and empowered supply chains become more prominent, safeguarding privacy and ensuring data and digital infrastructure security pose significant challenges. Striking a balance between allowing information flow for innovation and collaboration while protecting sensitive data and user privacy requires vigilant regulatory frameworks, robust encryption technologies, and ongoing public-private sector collaboration in developing and implementing cybersecurity strategies.

Promoting Inclusive and Sustainable Growth: Addressing social, economic, and environmental disparities is imperative in fostering inclusive and sustainable growth. Achieving this requires taking a comprehensive approach that considers the interdependencies between environmental, social, and economic factors while devising innovative solutions to tackle these complex challenges. This encompasses working towards global climate goals, promoting social equity and well-being, and fostering economic opportunities for all.

8.2 Opportunities in Reinventing the Global Order

Leveraging Disruptive Technologies: Disruptive technologies like AI, IoT, and blockchain have the power to revolutionize various aspects of governance, supply chains, and citizen engagement. By harnessing these technologies, organizations and governments can enhance efficiency, transparency, and resilience, promote data-driven decision-making, and foster sustainable growth. Successful implementation of these technologies also involves addressing potential ethical concerns, establishing regulatory frameworks, and promoting international collaboration on technology standards.

Strengthening Collaborative Governance: Embracing collaborative governance models that emphasize partnerships, stakeholder engagement, and shared decision-making can lead to more inclusive, context-driven policies and solutions. This approach can empower citizens, encourage accountability, and foster more effective public service delivery. It also allows for the harnessing of collective intelligence, experiences, and resources to address complex global challenges, which can contribute to a more agile, innovative, and adaptable global order.

Fostering Innovation and Entrepreneurship: Reinventing the global order presents opportunities to nurture innovation and entrepreneurship by embracing new technologies, facilitating cross-sector collaboration, and investing in human capital. By fostering a culture of innovation, governments and businesses can create an ecosystem that drives job creation, economic growth, and societal well-being, all while responding to evolving global challenges. This includes designing policies and incentives to support start-ups, small businesses, and research initiatives, as well as supporting public-private partnerships to drive innovation and technological breakthroughs.

Advancing Sustainability and Resilience: Developing innovative, adaptable, and context-sensitive solutions to promote sustainable development, responsible resource utilization, and resilient communities can help create more equitable and sustainable societies. This requires integrating advanced technologies, greener infrastructure, and adopting circular and sharing economy principles, as well as addressing the social dimensions of sustainable development, such as achieving decent work, education, and health for all (Hu & Kee, 2022).

In conclusion, reinventing the global order demands confronting diverse challenges while embracing emerging opportunities to craft a better, more resilient, and inclusive future. By leveraging disruptive technologies, adopting collaborative governance models, and promoting sustainable and equitable growth, governments, organizations, and individuals can work together to shape a more adaptive, equitable, and sustainable global order. A thorough understanding and navigation of the complex interplay between challenges and opportunities will empower stakeholders to craft transformative solutions that contribute to building stronger, more resilient societies.

9. CONCLUSION

In an era defined by rapid technological advancements, shifting geopolitics, and unprecedented challenges, the imperative to reinvent the global order has become increasingly clear. As governments, organizations, and individuals navigate this complex landscape, evaluating and adapting governance models, embracing digital sovereignty, and empowering supply chains are essential for building more resilient, equitable, and sustainable societies. The following conclusion further elaborates on the transformative potential of these concepts and outlines key recommendations for shaping a more adaptive global order.

Throughout this discussion, the transformative potential of decentralization, digital sovereignty, empowered supply chains, and collaborative governance models has been emphasized. As showcased through various case studies and examples, the adoption of these novel approaches offers unparalleled opportunities to tackle the challenges that the current global order faces. From the Swiss cantonal system's decentralized governance model to Estonia's pioneering e-governance initiative, real-world applications of these concepts have already demonstrated successful outcomes.

However, it is important to acknowledge the challenges that accompany these profound innovations and shifts. Navigating national interests while fostering global cooperation, addressing the digital divide, ensuring privacy and security, and promoting inclusive and sustainable growth are critical issues to be addressed when reinventing the global order.

As we strive to build a more adaptive and equitable global landscape, the following recommendations offer guidance in harnessing the potential of these transformative concepts:

- Foster Multilateral Collaboration: Engage in multilateral cooperation at regional and global levels, seeking synergies and fostering partnerships to address shared challenges and leverage each other's strengths.
- Encourage Inclusive Decision-Making: Prioritize stakeholder engagement and participatory governance approaches that enable diverse perspectives, promote transparency, and ensure the effectiveness and appropriateness of policies and solutions.
- Invest in Digital Infrastructure and Skills: Bridge the digital divide by investing in digital infrastructure, promoting digital literacy, and ensuring affordable access to digital services, thus enabling equal opportunities and participation for all.
- Develop Robust Policy Frameworks: Establish agile and comprehensive policy frameworks that facilitate innovation, protect privacy and security, and ensure sustainable development, balancing the needs of various stakeholders.
- Leverage Emerging Technologies: Harness the potential of disruptive technologies to drive innovation, enhance transparency, and foster more resilient and adaptive systems.

- Promote Sustainability: Integrate environmental, social, and economic considerations in decision-making processes and strive for sustainable development, introducing green policies, circular economy principles, and inclusive growth strategies.
- Nurture Innovation and Entrepreneurship: Create environments that support start-ups, small businesses, research, and cross-sector collaborations in order to cultivate innovation and unlock new possibilities.

In conclusion, reinventing the global order necessitates a multifaceted approach that combines disruptive technologies, innovative governance models, and collaborative strategies to address the complex and interconnected challenges faced by contemporary societies. As governments, organizations, and individuals unite in these efforts, the power of collective intelligence, shared resources, and diverse perspectives can be collectively harnessed to create lasting change. By understanding and navigating the complex interplay between challenges and opportunities, stakeholders can work together to shape a more resilient, equitable, and sustainable global order that embodies a brighter future for all.

REFERENCES

Adana, S., Cevikparmak, S., Celik, H., Uvet, H., & Idug, Y. (2022). Connecting Decision-Making to Resilience: The Importance of Decentralization and Supply Chain Orientation in a Post-COVID World. *Supply Chain Resilience*, *21*, 133–149. Advance online publication. doi:10.1007/978-3-031-16489-7_8

Adana, S., Manuj, I., Herburger, M., Cevikparmak, S., Celik, H., & Uvet, H. (2023). Linking decentralization in decision-making to resilience outcomes: A supply chain orientation perspective. *International Journal of Logistics Management*. Advance online publication. doi:10.1108/IJLM-07-2022-0308

Al-Rakhami, M., & Al-Mashari, M. (2022). Interoperability approaches of blockchain technology for supply chain systems. *Business Process Management Journal*, *28*(5/6), 1251–1276. doi:10.1108/BPMJ-04-2022-0207

Ali, S. S., & Kaur, R. (2022). Smart Supply Chains- A Futuristic Business Scenario. *The European Journal of Research and Development*.

BendiekA.StürzerI. (2022). Advancing European internal and external digital sovereignty: the Brussels effect and the EU-US Trade and Technology Council. *Social Science Open Access Repository*. doi:10.18449/2022C20

Bonoli, L., & Vorpe, J. (2021). Swiss VET between National Framework and Cantonal Autonomy: A Historical Perspective. *Education Sciences*, *12*(2), 114. Advance online publication. doi:10.3390/educsci12020114

Bremmer, I. (2021). The Technopolar Moment: How Digital Powers Will Reshape the Global Order. In I. Bremmer, Foreign Affairs (p. 112). HEINONLINE.

Budnitsky, S. (2022). A Relational Approach to Digital Sovereignty: e-Estonia Between Russia and the West. *International Journal of Communication*, 16.

Fries, I., Greiner, M., Hofmeier, M., Hrestic, R., Lechner, U., & Wendeborn, T. (2023). *Towards a Layer Model for Digital Sovereignty: A Holistic Approach.* Critical Information Infrastructures Security.

Fu, S., Liu, J., Tian, J., Peng, J., & Wu, C. (2023). Impact of Digital Economy on Energy Supply Chain Efficiency: Evidence from Chinese Energy Enterprises. *Energies*, *16*(1), 568. Advance online publication. doi:10.3390/en16010568

Giannopoulou, A. (2023). Digital Identity Infrastructures: A Critical Approach of Self-Sovereign Identity. *Digital Society : Ethics, Socio-Legal and Governance of Digital Technology*, *2*(2), 18. Advance online publication. doi:10.1007/s44206-023-00049-z PMID:37200582

Gu, H. (2023). Data, Big Tech, and the New Concept of Sovereignty. *Journal of Chinese Political Science*. Advance online publication. doi:10.1007/s11366-023-09855-1 PMID:37359767

Hall, K. K., & Qi, J. (2022, July). Collaboration, feedback, and performance: Supply chain insights from service-dominant logic. *Journal of Business Research*, *146*, 385–397. Advance online publication. doi:10.1016/j.jbusres.2022.03.055

Hu, M. K., & Kee, D. M. (2022). Fostering sustainability: Reinventing SME strategy in the new normal. *Foresight*, *24*(3/4), 301–318. doi:10.1108/FS-03-2021-0080

Johnson, D. (2023). *Rethinking Democracy and Governance: Perspectives from the Caribbean.* Taylor & Francis. doi:10.4324/9781003434290

Kazantsev, N., Pishchulov, G., Mehandjiev, N., Sampaio, P., & Zolkiewski, J. (2022). Investigating barriers to demand-driven SME collaboration in low-volume high-variability manufacturing. *Supply Chain Management*, *27*(2), 265–282. Advance online publication. doi:10.1108/SCM-10-2021-0486

Kinder, M. (2022). The case for localised, decentralised supply chains. *Journal of Supply Chain Management, Logistics and Procurement, 5*(1).

Leng, J., Zhong, Y., Lin, Z., Xu, K., Mourtzis, D., Zhou, X., Zheng, P., Liu, Q., Zhao, J. L., & Shen, W. (2023). Towards resilience in Industry 5.0: A decentralized autonomous manufacturing paradigm. *Journal of Manufacturing Systems*, *71*, 95–114. doi:10.1016/j.jmsy.2023.08.023

Powell, W. (2022). *China, Trust and Digital Supply Chains: Dynamics of a Zero Trust World.* Taylor & Francis.

Rahmanzadeh, S., Pishvaee, M. S., & Govindan, K. (2022). Emergence of open supply chain management: The role of open innovation in the future smart industry using digital twin network. *Annals of Operations Research.* Advance online publication. doi:10.1007/s10479-021-04254-2

Said, F. (2022). *Embracing technology, preserving data sovereignty.* Institute of Strategic and International Studies.

Sharma, M. G. (2021). Supply chain, geographical indicator and blockchain: Provenance model for commodity. *International Journal of Productivity and Performance Management*, *72*(1), 92–108. doi:10.1108/IJPPM-05-2021-0288

Tavana, M., Shaabani, A., Vanani, I. R., & Gangadhari, R. K. (2022). A Review of Digital Transformation on Supply Chain Process Management Using Text Mining. *Processes (Basel, Switzerland)*, *10*(5), 842. Advance online publication. doi:10.3390/pr10050842

Wyborn, C. A., Kerkhoff, L. E., Colloff, M. J., Alexandra, J., & Olsson, R. (2021). The politics of adaptive governance: Water reform, climate change, and First Nations' justice in Australia's Murray-Darling Basin10.5751/ES-13641-280104. *Ecology and Society*, *28*(1), art4. Advance online publication. doi:10.5751/ES-13641-280104

Chapter 17

Potential of Digitalization for the Utilization of Artificial Intelligence Models for Uplifting Traditional Marketing Methods: A New Sustainable Growth

Anandrao Bhanudas Dadas
https://orcid.org/0009-0000-0647-5953
Neville Wadia Institute of Management Studies and Research, India

ABSTRACT

This chapter intends to inform about the artificial intelligence intervention for enhancing the marketing of products as India is climbing new heights through the "Digital India" movement. Technologies lessen the market gaps globally. There are numerous domains where the digital arm can prove to be efficient. Online shopping and online educational facilities already proved to be sustained during the COVID-19 pandemic. The chapter discusses one of the segments of society among many segments that suffered during the pandemic: women's self-help groups. As a traditional means, women's self-help groups used to sell their products using exhibitions, but the pandemic and frequent lockdowns hampered the marketing strategy of such self-help groups. Digitalization can reach the smallest need, and research can provide need-based directions for application development. This chapter discusses how artificial intelligence can give wings to such women's self-help groups for marketing and market predictions.

1. INTRODUCTION

According to the study, marketing management is the spine of any management in the modern management. Any business needs to stand on the pillars of marketing (Mockshell et al., 2022). As a border view, marketing management stands as a torch bearer for any business. Without marketing, there is no meaning for any kind of investment (Peter et al, 2021). So, in comparison to traditional marketing it is

DOI: 10.4018/979-8-3693-3253-5.ch017

necessary to focus on digitalization of processes as per modern marketing strategy (Kapoor et al, 2021). Customer is the key of any market, and now a day, customers are expecting digital facilities due to lack of time and wider array of selection of products (Olson, Eric M., et al, 2021).

Apart from this customer can compare product by means of artificial intelligence enabled online portals where e-illiterate people falling behind. So, there is necessity to generate awareness of digital marketing among little underprivileged community of businesses like women self-help group who are the pillars of macro-economics.

Promotion pertains to any activities an organization needs to entice customers to the firm's merchandise or offerings with superior quality messages. Promotion is designed to achieve separate significance for potential customers and buyers using content material through the long-lasting objective of showing merchandise importance, conditioning brand loyalty, and eventually raising revenue.

Advertising intends to investigate and review your customers constantly, carry out target categories, transmit surveys online, analyze online buying behaviors, and inquire one fundamental query: "Where, when, and then how does the customer wish to connect with the venture?"

This article looks at the needs of advertising, categories of advertising, the 4 P's of marketing, and the discrepancy between marketing and advertising. Regardless of whether you're an expert professional researching to invigorate your classifications or a newbie seeking to figure out what promotion is in the first place, we've got you covered.

Marketing is having customers interested in the company's merchandise or services. This occurs through market exploration, evaluation, and recognizing the suitable customer's pursuits. Promotion belongs to all venture elements, including merchandise evolution, syndication strategies, revenue, and promotion.

The primary goal of promotion is to appeal to clients to one's brand simply by messages. Ultimately, those messages will be beneficial and informational to the specific market so most people can become potential customers. Promotion requires merchandise evolution, industry analysis, merchandise syndication, revenue strategies, public relationships, and client support. Promotion is important at all levels of a business's offering quest, and it may employ various programs, social media areas, and groups within the business to discover its target audience, connect to it, enhance its thoughts, and build brand loyalty through time frames.

On the flip side, marketing is merely one element of promotion. It's a tactical attempt, generally bought for, to propagate interest in merchandise or services as a component of the even more complete intentions discussed previously. Decide to put easily, and marketers utilize other approaches to promote a product.

Let's mention a firm is moving out brand new merchandise and desires to produce a marketing campaign advertising that item to its client base. The provider's options for determination are Facebook, Instagram, Google, and its enterprise website. It incorporates most of these areas to assist its numerous quarterly promotions and bring about leads through those promotions.

To message its new merchandise release, it posts an internet merchandise guideline to its website, posts a training video to Instagram representing its new item, and invests in a list of subsidized search outcomes on Google, leading traffic to a new merchandise webpage on its website.

Which of the earlier mentioned preferences were marketing, and which was promotion?

The promotion occurred on Instagram as well as Google. Instagram will not be a complete promotion channel; however, if it is utilized for branding, you can develop a foundation of supporters set up for merchandise launch nearly every once in a while. In this case, Google was surely employed for promotion; the organization paid out for storage on Google, a system referred to as pay-per-click (PPC), to push visitors to a particular page targeted on its item.

By shifting Instagram, Google, and its internet site to a customer-focused motivation, the firm developed a three-part advertising system that recognized its viewers, produced communication for those viewers, and provided it around the industry to increase its influence.

1.1 Significance of Macro Economics

SHG membership has a significant positive impact on aggregate measures of women's empowerment and reduces the gap between men's and women's empowerment scores. Livelihoods and microfinance programs for women often show reduced impacts after scale-up. Yet, program scale-up may reduce average per capita costs and maintain cost-effectiveness despite lower impact (Al-azzam et al, 2021). This chapter suggests the coordination between program scale, costs, and cost-effectiveness by analyzing how the costs of a large-scale Self-Help Group (SHG) program in India changed from its inception in 2007 to its scale-up in 2019.

There are huge gaps between traditional and modern marketing management which are true gaps for the future enhancement of marketing strategies.

1.2 Traditional Marketing Pitfalls

1) Traditional marketing is time consumed.
2) Investment is more for supply chain management.
3) Client reach may face delay in delivery of orders.
4) Contingency ratio is more because of fluctuating product cost.
5) Bargaining power is more in traditional marketing scenario.
6) Women self-help groups often need to conduct an exhibition which raises overhead expenses.

To overcome such pitfalls, digital marketing is very important.

1.3 Impact of Digital Marketing

1) Digital marketing requires less time as compared to traditional marketing.
2) One time investment for digital platform is sufficient to setup digital portal and only product display management required.
3) Client reach is easy for seller and buyer by means of internet as a "One Click" option.
4) Zero bargaining system hence, profitability is more.
5) Digital marketing portal can give wings to women self-help group by means of online exhibitions, online shop etc.

2. WHAT IS THE NEED OF DIGITALIZATION?

As an outcome of systematic literature reviewed as a part of pilot study, we identified research gaps based on national and international studies. These gaps also includes outcome of situation analysis:

- As per international studies conducted, there is a need of research and development in the area of women self-help group (SHG) digital empowerment.
- As per covid-19 pandemic situation, women self-help group business hampered due to lack of marketing strategy development which can be developed for marketing, market prediction and supply chain management of products. Digital portal can lower the gaps between producer and consumer with smooth run of self-help group business.
- The investment by women self-help group falls under macro-economics, so investment and return ration is small but by means of artificial intelligence/machine learning techniques market prediction need to be done. So that, women SHG can predicts and plan their next product requirement.
- There is also need of training of computer handling, online marketing for such women SHG.
- As an interdisciplinary research, there is a need of clubbing marketing management, supply chain management, macro-economic elements affecting SHG and digital literacy training for SHG members with cutting edge technologies like artificial intelligence/machine learning and/or virtual reality.

3. ARTIFICIAL INTELLIGENCE EVERYWHERE

According to the Havard Business School, of all a company's functions, marketing has perhaps the most to gain from artificial intelligence. Marketing's core activities are understanding customer needs, matching them to products and services, and persuading people to buy capabilities that AI can dramatically enhance. No wonder a 2018 McKinsey analysis of more than 400 advanced use cases showed that marketing was the domain where AI would contribute the greatest value (van Esch et al, 2021; Kim, Kyung Hoon, and Hakil Moon, 2021). For digital device usage during the pandemic is shown in Figure 1 below.

Many firms now use AI to handle narrow tasks, such as digital ad placement (also known as "programmatic buying"); assist with broad tasks, like enhancing the accuracy of predictions (think sales forecasts); and augment human efforts in structured tasks, such as customer service.

Figure 1. Digital platform usage during COVID-19 pandemic (Source: HootSuite)

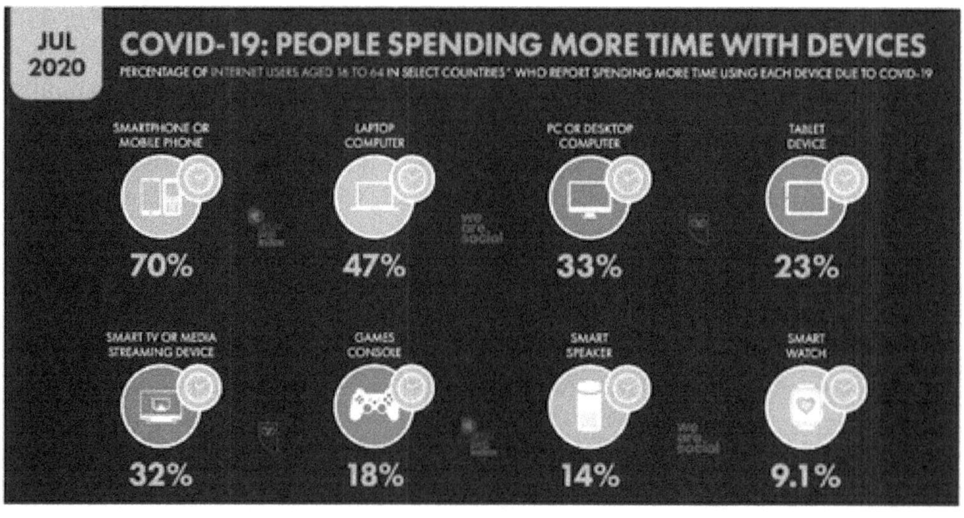

3.1 Task Automation

These applications perform repetitive, structured tasks that require relatively low levels of intelligence. They're designed to follow a set of rules or execute a predetermined sequence of operations based on a given input, but they can't handle complex problems such as nuanced customer requests (Jeong, Dong-Bin, 2021; Lee, Jungwon, et al.,2021). An example would be a system that automatically sends a welcome email to each new customer. Simpler chatbots, such as those available through Facebook Messenger and other social media providers, also fall into this category. They can provide some help to customers during basic interactions, taking customers down a defined decision tree, but they can't discern customers' intent, offer customized responses, or learn from interactions over time (Wang, Xin Shane et al., 2021).

3.2 Customer Relationship Management

These algorithms are trained using large quantities of data to make relatively complex predictions and decisions. Such models can recognize images, decipher text, segment customers, and anticipate how customers will respond to various initiatives, such as promotions. Machine learning already drives programmatic buying in online advertising, e-commerce recommendation engines, and sales propensity models in customer relationship management (CRM) systems (Dai, Yonghui, and Tao Wang, 2021; Kong, Sherry Tao, 2021). It and its more sophisticated variant, deep learning, are the hottest technologies in AI and are rapidly becoming powerful tools in marketing. That said, it's important to clarify that existing machine-learning applications still just perform narrow tasks and need to be trained using voluminous amounts of data (Kumar, Neha, et al., 2021).

Embedded within existing systems, these AI applications are often less visible than stand-alone ones to the customers, marketers, and salespeople who use them (Siwach, Garima, et al, 2022). For example, machine learning that makes split-second decisions about which digital ads to offer users is built into platforms that handle the entire process of buying and placing ads. Netflix's integrated machine learning has offered customers video recommendations for more than a decade; its selections simply appear in the menu of offerings viewers see when they go to the site. If the recommendation engine were stand-alone, they would need to go to a dedicated app and request suggestions.

4. AI CHALLENGES AND RISKS

Implementing even the simplest AI applications can present difficulties. Stand-alone task-automation AI, despite its lower technical sophistication, can still be hard to configure for specific workflows and requires companies to acquire suitable AI skills (Tewari, Deeksha Bajpai, et al., 2022; Agarwal, Bina. 2022). Bringing any kind of AI into a workflow always needs careful integration of human and machine tasks so that the AI augments people's skills and isn't deployed in ways that create problems. For instance, while many organizations use rule-based chatbots to automate customer service, less-capable bots can irritate customers (George, Anu, 2022). It may be better to have such bots assist human agents or advisers rather than interact with customers.

As companies adopt more-sophisticated and integrated applications, other considerations arise. Incorporating AI into third-party platforms, in particular, can be tricky. A case in point is offered by Procter & Gamble's Olay Skin Advisor, which uses deep learning to analyze selfies that customers have taken,

Figure 2. Artificial intelligence applications (Source: Springer)

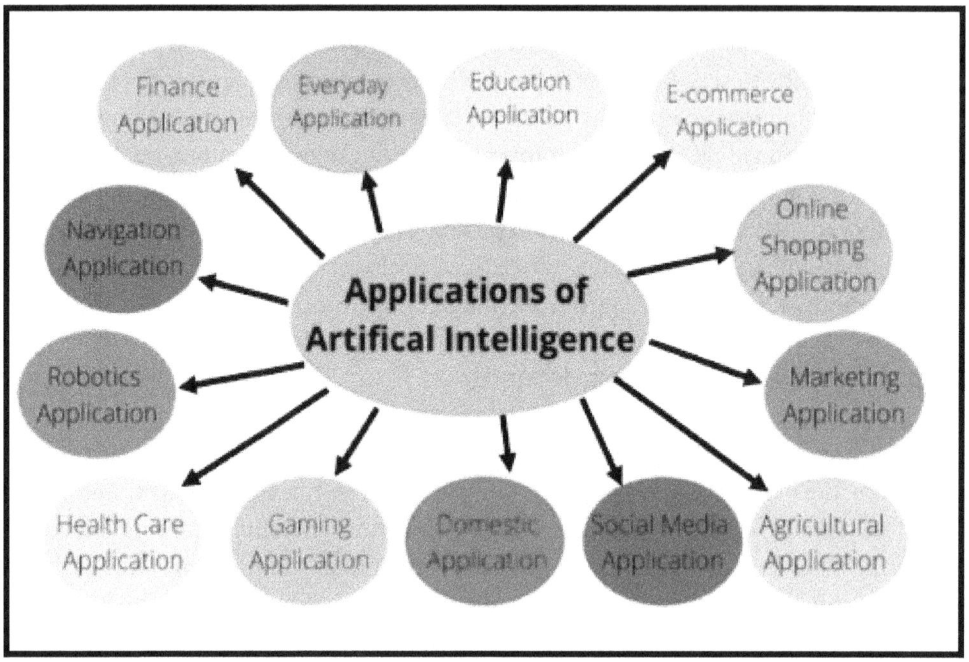

assess their age and skin type, and recommend appropriate products (Kumar C. R., 2021; Gupta, Shipra, 2021). It is integrated into an e-commerce and loyalty platform, Olay.com, and has improved conversion rates, bounce rates, and average basket sizes in some geographies (Stallone et al., 2021). However, it has been harder to integrate it with retail stores and Amazon, third parties that account for a high percentage of Olay's sales. The Skin Advisor is not available on Olay's extensive store site on Amazon, hampering the brand's ability to deliver a seamless, AI-assisted customer experience there.

5. POSSIBLE DIRECTIONS FOR IMPLEMENTATION

1. To study and identify the challenges and problems of women self help group under specific geographical location.
2. To identify challenges in traditional and modern marketing practices and develop new marketing strategy for swift client reaches.
3. To develop the women self-help group dataset for digital training and conduct training for computer handling, software handling and digital marketing portal handing for women SHGs.
4. To analyze existing macro-economic models of women SHGs and suggest new model to lower the various losses like extra product production, failed supply chain management etc.
5. To analyze feasibility of artificial intelligence data analysis model for prediction of market demand that can help women SHGs to lower various losses.
6. To conduct statistical analysis for post research feasibility.

6. WHAT GOALS CAN BE ACHIEVED?

1. What are the different challenges women self-help groups facing with reference to pre-and post covid-19 pandemic?
2. What is difference between traditional and modern marketing practices and in which way digital marketing can be improved for benefits of women SHGs?
3. How women SHGs can get benefit from digital literacy training?
4. What elements of macro-economic can impact on women SHGs empowerment?
5. How artificial intelligence model can help to predict the market demand and what are various benefits to increase profit ration of women SHG?
6. What is impact of newly developed marketing strategy on women SHGs macro-economy?
7. What is impact of digital marketing training on women SHGs participants understanding about digital portal handling and data prediction practices?

7. CASE STUDY

This research can be quantitative and experimental research. The quantitative research methodology can be used as a post-research validation. The artificial intelligence model can be developed and tested on large dataset for market prediction analysis. In summary, as this is a major research the artificial intelligence/machine learning software model can be developed to identify the set of predefined criteria for women SHGs and market prediction. Also, computer handling, digital portal handling training sessions can be conducted for women SHGs.

7.1 Case Design

The experimental research design can be used for customer identification from the developed dataset using Artificial Intelligence (AI) modules like text/sentiment/analysis by machine learning algorithm. In this chapter, we focusing on case study of women self help group business for illustration purpose. The chapter sections will help reader to understand the cumulative process of marketing needs, customer expectations and business growth orientation with the help of AI modules.

7.1.1 How to Manage Data Collection and Sampling

The demographic profiles can be collected for participants of study. Data will be collected by means of printed questioners/forms. The software data source can be used for the purpose of market prediction testing. The data sampling can be done using Yamane Strategy Mathematical model.

Base on primary and secondary data, the validation and training can be conducted using machine learning and sentiment analysis, text mining algorithm. The statistical sampling can be done for targeted city/region. Total of samples size of respondents need to be identified by appropriate methods and must be used for analysis. Further, appropriate statistical methods needs to be followed for validation of data to be merged with AI tool.

7.1.2 What Are Data Sources?

- Primary data can be collected from individuals of different age levels from targeted location and no personal details can be used apart from demographic information.
- The secondary data can be journals, reference books, newsletters, white papers, websites, discussions with social workers, and psychologist.
- The tertiary data can be used from developed dataset for testing of artificial intelligence/machine learning model for market demand prediction.

7.1.3 Identification of Software Technology

For software development machine learning technologies (and any other suitable techniques) can be used. In this illustrative case study, as a developer platform, Anaconda server can be used and for data storage cloud/local machine server can be used.

8. THE CORE AI MODEL FOR MARKET PREDICTION

This section guides reader with a small real-time diagrammatic example inline to the SHGs domain. Following flowchart can help reader to correlate the marketing management variables with AI software model predictive elements.

The AI module will recognize the product availability and customer demand automatically and will inform producer (i.e. SHG member who looking after the supply chain management) about the market demand. The future demand can be predicted based on the monthly requirement based on season like festivals, special occasions etc.

Figure 3. Processes execution of AI market prediction tool (generated by the author)

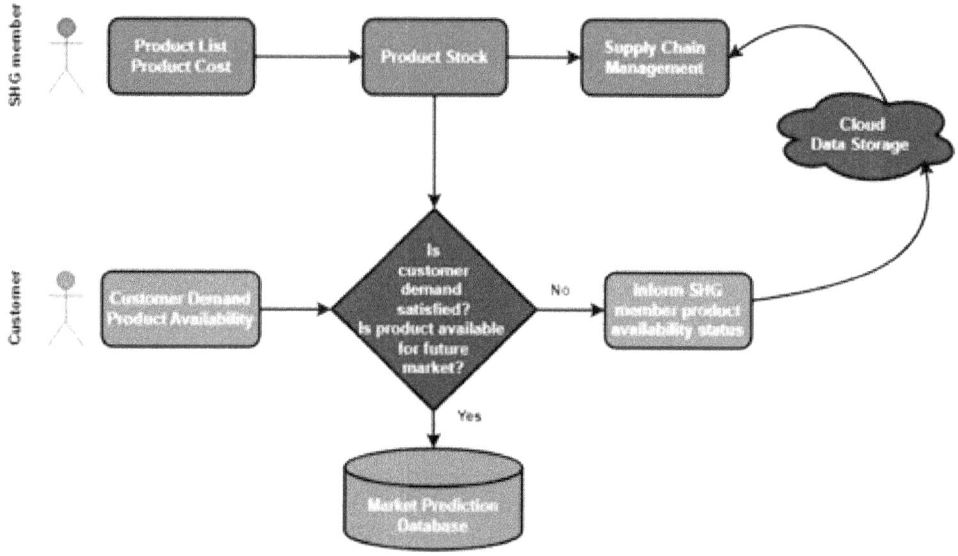

9. SUGGESTIONS FOR IMPROVEMENT

For further improvement in the AI system for the enhancement of modern marketing, following suggestions can be implemented:

1) Marketing domain needs to utilize information technologies and SHGs must be well versed.
2) The system development needs to be transparent.
3) The system architectures must be in line to SHGs requirements to implement the system.

10. SUMMARY

Boosting small/large business growth needs many pillars, like appropriate execution of the supply chain management, product and process analysis, marketing strategy development, and customer feedback studies for product quality management. Digital technologies can be a tool for achieving all such quality elements responsible for business growth.

This chapter discussed how self-help groups can benefit from digitalization using artificial intelligence module development. We purposely targeted self-help groups as their potential can be very big if they automate certain processes. In marketing management, a new AI model can be an element of a new marketing mix. Unlike the 3P marketing mix, the new dimension of AI can be very efficient, especially in a pandemic and post-pandemic era.

This chapter intends to initiate the new era of marketing management with possible technical and managerial process understanding and to give a new direction for multi-disciplinary research. Boosting a well-established big business is not a big deal, but enhancing opportunities for small and medium-scale businesses is always challenging. Hence, the suggested AI model can be a very efficient way to implement digitalization for market prediction for almost any domain.

The classic marketing methods suggest that it is necessary to execute analysis to recognize customer needs prior to producing a new item. This all requires considerable time and assets; however, AI is available in practical. It assists to execute promotion actions on-line quicker and so by way of fewer efforts.

The idea of digital marketing is nowadays extensively utilized than classic marketing. Digitalization has broken open in incredibly promptly by attractive and changing off-line methods for instance, looking into customer requirements or executing market evaluation. In the mean time, AI has metamorphosed online marketing through acquiring it to a further level. As an effect, equally entrepreneurs as well as customers have gained from these innovations significantly as AI has built it substantially more easy to browse in a huge digital ecosystem.

AI marketing methods has excelled procedures in different elements of digital marketing, beginning from promotion to customer fulfillment. AI's boosted swiftness and performance enable companies to create models more promptly and at any reduce cost. AI's best robustness will be in its capability to promptly sort throughout big quantities of data and produce pattern recommendations structured on its results. Employing this statistics, a website designer can produce picky choices and absolute affirmation of alterations.

An case in point, the free logo design developer incorporates AI concept to make thousands of exclusive logos that conform to essential design requirements. It is no more needed for a clientele and a graphical designer to talk back and forth to show up with a spectacular design.

To fulfill the fast-paced needs of the work place, AI will certainly turned into a build partner for graphic designers and entrepreneurs to consider their tasks to an innovative level with no diminishing their modest information.

Google as well as various other search engines revise their methods very frequently, and these are unquestionably applying AI. In every year, the search outcomes given by the search engines considerably better match up with the user's targets and pursuits. That is mainly because machines action substantial quantities of data relating to customer behaviors and response.

A decade ago, the performance of searches was certainly not that huge, and clients frequently did not discover what precisely they were searching for. During the time, the several internet sites were not that substantial, and the decision was narrowed as well. In the present day, clients often discover those things they are searching for, and so the AI assists all of them by offering recommendations in the search bar. Obviously, certainly, there may possibly be exceptions, however, that often shows up for the market spheres where there are not ample digital details. For example, in the event that searching for an older telephone model explanation, an individual may not discover a lot, though search engines will still give the best trusted outcomes obtainable on the web.

REFERENCES

Agarwal, B. (2022). Imperatives of recognising the complexities: Gendered impacts and responses to COVID-19 in India. *Economics and Politics*, *39*(1), 31–53. PMID:35422596

Al-azzam, A. F., & Al-Mizeed, K. (2021). The effect of digital marketing on purchasing decisions: A case study in Jordan. *The Journal of Asian Finance, Economics and Business*, *8*(5), 455–4634.

Dai, Y., & Wang, T. (2021). Prediction of customer engagement behaviour response to marketing posts based on machine learning. *Connection Science*, *33*(4), 891–910. doi:10.1080/09540091.2021.1912710

George, A. (2022). The Kerala, India Experience of Facing the COVID-19 Pandemic. In *The Coronavirus Crisis and Challenges to Social Development* (pp. 251–261). Springer. doi:10.1007/978-3-030-84678-7_22

Gupta, S., & Rathore, H. S. (2021). Socio-Economic and political empowerment through self help groups intervention: A study from Bilaspur, Chhattisgarh, India. *Journal of Public Affairs*, *21*(1), e2143. doi:10.1002/pa.2143

Hong, S., Park, J., & Jeon, S. (2021). The effects of country-of-online retailer on consumer's purchase decision-making in a foreign internet shopping mall. *Journal of Korea Trade*, *25*(6), 20–33. doi:10.35611/jkt.2021.25.6.20

Jeong, D. B. (2021). Prediction of the Corona 19's domestic internet and mobile shopping transaction amount. *The Journal of Economics. Marketing and Management*, *9*(2), 1–10.

Kapoor, R., & Kapoor, K. (2021). The transition from traditional to digital marketing: A study of the evolution of e-marketing in the Indian hotel industry. *Worldwide Hospitality and Tourism Themes*, *13*(2), 199–2133. doi:10.1108/WHATT-10-2020-0124

Kim, K. H., & Moon, H. (2021). Innovative digital marketing management in B2B markets. *Industrial Marketing Management*, *95*, 1–4. doi:10.1016/j.indmarman.2021.01.016

Kong, S. T., & Loubere, N. (2021). Digitally down to the countryside: Fintech and rural development in China. *The Journal of Development Studies*, *57*(10), 1739–1754. doi:10.1080/00220388.2021.1919631

Kumar, N., Singh, R., & Singh, S. (2021). The power of the collective empowers women: Evidence from self-help groups in India. *World Development*, *146*, 105579. doi:10.1016/j.worlddev.2021.105579 PMID:34602708

Lee, J., Kim, J., & Kim, S. (2021). A comparison and interpretation of machine learning algorithm for the prediction of online purchase conversion. *Journal of Theoretical and Applied Electronic Commerce Research*, *16*(5), 1472–1491. doi:10.3390/jtaer16050083

Mockshell, J., & Ritter, T. (2022). Was a government policy able to smooth a fractured agri-food value chain during a COVID-19 lockdown? *Journal of Agribusiness in Developing and Emerging Economies*, *12*(1), 1–161.

Peter, M. K., & Dalla Vecchia, M. (2021). The digital marketing toolkit: A literature review for the identification of digital marketing channels and platforms. New Trends in Business Information Systems and Technology, 251-265.

Shaikh, M. (2021). Women Empowerment Through Self Help Groups: A Review. In Entrepreneurial Ecosystem in Higher Education (pp. 70). Academic Press.

Shankar, V., Grewal, D., Sunder, S., Fossen, B., Peters, K., & Agarwal, A. (2021). Digital marketing communication in global marketplaces: A review of extant research, future directions, and potential approaches. *International Journal of Research in Marketing*, *39*(2), 541–565. doi:10.1016/j.ijresmar.2021.09.005

Siwach, G., Paul, S., & de Hoop, T. (2022). Economies of scale of large-scale international development interventions: Evidence from self-help groups in India. *World Development*, *153*, 105839. doi:10.1016/j.worlddev.2022.105839 PMID:35506062

Tewari, D. B., Singh, S., & Singh, R. (2022). Self-help groups (SHGs) Role in Promotion of Women Entrepreneur: A Saga of Pandemic Era. *Journal of Positive School Psychology*, *6*(2), 936–947.

van Esch, P., & Black, J. S. (2021). Artificial intelligence (AI): Revolutionizing digital marketing. *Australasian Marketing Journal*, *29*(3), 199–203. doi:10.1177/18393349211037684

Wang, X. S., Li, Y., & Li, Y. (2021). The role of machine learning analytics and metrics in retailing research. *Journal of Retailing*, *97*(4), 658–675. doi:10.1016/j.jretai.2020.12.001

Compilation of References

Abbas, G., Mehmood, A., Carsten, M., Epiphaniou, G., & Lloret, J. (2022). Safety, Security and Privacy in Machine Learning Based Internet of Things. *Journal of Sensor and Actuator Networks*, *11*(3), 38. Advance online publication. doi:10.3390/jsan11030038

Abdullah, N., & Lim, A. (2023). Incorporating Sustainable and Green IT Practices in Modern IT Service Operations for an Environmentally Conscious Future. *J Sustain Technol & Infra Plan.*

AbuNaser, M., & Alkhatib, A. A. (2019, April). Advanced survey of blockchain for the internet of things smart home. In 2019 IEEE Jordan international joint conference on electrical engineering and information technology (JEEIT) (pp. 58-62). IEEE. doi:10.1109/JEEIT.2019.8717441

Adana, S., Cevikparmak, S., Celik, H., Uvet, H., & Idug, Y. (2022). Connecting Decision-Making to Resilience: The Importance of Decentralization and Supply Chain Orientation in a Post-COVID World. *Supply Chain Resilience*, *21*, 133–149. Advance online publication. doi:10.1007/978-3-031-16489-7_8

Adana, S., Manuj, I., Herburger, M., Cevikparmak, S., Celik, H., & Uvet, H. (2023). Linking decentralization in decision-making to resilience outcomes: A supply chain orientation perspective. *International Journal of Logistics Management*. Advance online publication. doi:10.1108/IJLM-07-2022-0308

Adrian, M., & Lamb, M. A. (n.d.). *An exploration of the determinants of sedentary behaviour in desk-based employees* [Thesis]. Sheffield Hallam University.

Agarwal, S. (2018). *Blockchain technology in supply chain and logistics*. Massachusetts Institute of Technology.

Agarwal, B. (2022). Imperatives of recognising the complexities: Gendered impacts and responses to COVID-19 in India. *Economics and Politics*, *39*(1), 31–53. PMID:35422596

Agarwal, R., & Dhar, V. (2014). Big data, data science, and analytics: The opportunity and challenge for IS research. *Information Systems Research*, *25*(3), 443–448. doi:10.1287/isre.2014.0546

Agarwal, R., & Prasad, J. (1998). A conceptual and operational definition of personal innovativeness in information technology. *Information Systems Research*, *9*(2), 204–215. doi:10.1287/isre.9.2.204

Agbo, F. J., Oyelere, S. S., Suhonen, J., & Tukiainen, M. (2021). Scientific production and thematic breakthroughs in smart learning environments: A bibliometric analysis. *Smart Learning Environments.*, *8*(1), 1–25. doi:10.1186/s40561-020-00145-4

Agrawal, A., Gans, J., & Goldfarb, A. (2018). *The Economics of Artificial Intelligence: An Agenda*. University of Chicago Press.

Aguiar, M., & Gopinath, G. (2007). Emerging market business cycles: The cycle is the trend. *Journal of Political Economy, 115*(1), 69–102. doi:10.1086/511283

Ahmed, W. A. H., & MacCarthy, B. L. (2022). Blockchain technology in the supply chain: Learning from emerging ecosystems and industry consortia. In S. Bauman (Ed.), *Handbook of digital business ecosystems: Strategies, platforms, technologies, governance and societal challenges* (p. 800). Edward Elgar Publishing. doi:10.4337/9781839107191.00032

Ahsan & Siddique. (2022). Industry 4.0 in Healthcare: A systematic review. *International Journal of Information Management Data Insights.*

Aier, S., Weiss, S., Winter, R., & Rytz, B. (2016). Untangling EA's long path of becoming a partner for business transformation: The case of Swiss Federal Railways. In *2016 IEEE 20th International Enterprise Distributed Object Computing Workshop (EDOCW)* (pp. 1-7). IEEE. 10.1109/EDOCW.2016.7584394

Ajzen, I., & Fishbein, M. (1980). *Understanding attitudes and predicting social behaviour.* Academic Press.

Ajzen, I. (1991). The theory of planned behavior. *Organizational Behavior and Human Decision Processes, 50*(2), 179–211. doi:10.1016/0749-5978(91)90020-T

Akhlaq, A., & Ahmed, E. (2015). Digital commerce in emerging economies: Factors associated with online shopping intentions in Pakistan. *International Journal of Emerging Markets, 10*(4), 634–647. doi:10.1108/IJoEM-01-2014-0051

Akter, S., & Wamba, S. F. (2016). Big data analytics in E-commerce: A systematic review and agenda for future research. *Electronic Markets, 26*(2), 173–194. doi:10.1007/s12525-016-0219-0

Akter, S., Wamba, S. F., Gunasekaran, A., Dubey, R., & Childe, S. J. (2016). How to improve firm performance using big data analytics capability and business strategy alignment? *International Journal of Production Economics, 182*, 113–131. doi:10.1016/j.ijpe.2016.08.018

Al Adwan, A., Kokash, H., Al Adwan, R., & Khattak, A. (2023). Data analytics in digital marketing for tracking the effectiveness of campaigns and inform strategy. *International Journal of Data and Network Science, 7*(2), 563–574. doi:10.5267/j.ijdns.2023.3.015

Al-azzam, A. F., & Al-Mizeed, K. (2021). The effect of digital marketing on purchasing decisions: A case study in Jordan. *The Journal of Asian Finance, Economics and Business, 8*(5), 455–4634.

Alcacer, J., Cantwell, J., & Piscitello, L. (2016). Internationalization in the Information Age: A new era for places, firms, and international business networks? *Journal of International Business Studies, 47*(5), 499–512. doi:10.1057/jibs.2016.22

Al-Debi, Mutaz, El-Haddadeh, & Avison. (2008). Defining the business model in the new world of digital business. *AMCIS 2008 Proceedings,* 300.

Ali, S. S., & Kaur, R. (2022). Smart Supply Chains- A Futuristic Business Scenario. *The European Journal of Research and Development.*

Ali, O., Jaradat, A., Kulakli, A., & Abuhalimeh, A. (2021). A comparative study: Blockchain technology utilization benefits, challenges and functionalities. *IEEE Access : Practical Innovations, Open Solutions, 9*, 12730–12749. doi:10.1109/ACCESS.2021.3050241

Al, R. N. (2019). Financial deglobalisation in banking? *Journal of International Money and Finance, 94*, 116–131. doi:10.1016/j.jimonfin.2019.01.011

Al-Rakhami, M., & Al-Mashari, M. (2022). Interoperability approaches of blockchain technology for supply chain systems. *Business Process Management Journal, 28*(5/6), 1251–1276. doi:10.1108/BPMJ-04-2022-0207

Alutaybi, A., Al-Thani, D., McAlaney, J., & Ali, R. (2020). Investigating the Role of Fear of Missing out (FOMO) in the Relationship between Social Network Services Use Intensity and Nomophobia. *International Journal of Environmental Research and Public Health*, *17*(13), 4712. PMID:32629997

Amoako-Gyampah, K., & Salam, A. F. (2004, July 1). An extension of the technology acceptance model in an ERP implementation environment. *Information & Management*, *41*(6), 731–745. doi:10.1016/j.im.2003.08.010

Amoroso, D.L., & Lim, R.A. (2015). Exploring the personal innovativeness construct: the roles of ease of use, satisfaction and attitudes. *Asia Pacific Journal of Information Systems, 25*(4), 662-685.

Anderson, R. (2020). *Security engineering: a guide to building dependable distributed systems*. John Wiley & Sons. doi:10.1002/9781119644682

Andjelic, A. (2020). The business of aspiration: How social, cultural, and environmental capital changes brands. *The Business of Aspiration: How Social, Cultural, and Environmental Capital Changes Brands*, 1–94. doi:10.4324/9781003093572

Antràs, P. (2020). *De-globalisation? Global value chains in the post-COVID-19 age*. National Bureau of Economic Research Working Paper 28115. https://www.nber.org/papers/w28115

Anwar, H. (n.d.). *Consensus algorithms: The root of blockchain*. https://101blockchains.com/consensus-algorithms-blockchain/#prettyPhoto

Appio, F. P., Cesaroni, F., & Di Minin, A. (2014). Visualizing the structure and bridges of the intellectual property management and strategy literature: A document co-citation analysis. *Scientometrics*, *101*(1), 623–661. doi:10.1007/s11192-014-1329-0

Aral, S., & Weill, P. (2007). IT assets, organizational capabilities, and firm performance: How resource allocations and organizational differences explain performance variation. *Organization Science*, *18*(5), 763–780. doi:10.1287/orsc.1070.0306

Aristovnik, A. (2014). Development of the information society and its impact on the education sector in the EU: Efficiency at the regional (NUTS 2) level. *The Turkish Online Journal of Educational Technology*, *2*(13), 54–60.

Arora, M., Prakash, A., Mittal, A., & Singh, S. (2022). Moderating role of resistance to change in the actual adoption of HR analytics in the Indian banking and financial services industry. In *Evidence-based HRM: a Global Forum for Empirical Scholarship*. Emerald Publishing Limited.

Arora, S., & Nabi, T. (2022). Blockchain Adoption in Banking Systems: A Boon or Bane? In Applications, Challenges, and Opportunities of Blockchain Technology in Banking and Insurance. doi:10.4018/978-1-6684-4133-6.ch002

Asharf, J., Moustafa, N., Khurshid, H., Debie, E., Haider, W., & Wahab, A. (2020). A review of intrusion detection systems using machine and deep learning in internet of things: Challenges, solutions and future directions. *Electronics (Basel)*, *9*(7), 1177. Advance online publication. doi:10.3390/electronics9071177

Atiq, M., Abid, G., Anwar, A., & Ijaz, M. F. (2022). Influencer Marketing on Instagram: A Sequential Mediation Model of Storytelling Content and Audience Engagement via Relatability and Trust. *Information (Basel)*, *13*(7), 345. Advance online publication. doi:10.3390/info13070345

Attaran, M., & Attaran, S. (2007, June 12). Collaborative supply chain management. *Business Process Management Journal*, *13*(3), 390–404. doi:10.1108/14637150710752308

Atzori, L., Iera, A., & Morabito, G. (2010). The Internet of Things: *A survey. Computer Networks*, *54*(15), 2787–2805. doi:10.1016/j.comnet.2010.05.010

Auer, R., Haslhofer, B., Kitzler, S., Saggese, P., & Victor, F. (2023). *The Technology of Decentralized Finance (DeFi)*. Bank for International Settlements, Monetary and Economic Department. doi:10.1007/s42521-023-00088-8

Aysuna, U. (2019). *Centralized versus Decentralized Banking: Bank-level evidence from US Call Reports* (No. 2019-03).

Baase, S. (2012). *A gift of fire*. Pearson Education Limited.

Babich, V., & Hilary, G. (2019). Blockchain and other distributed ledger technologies in operations. *Foundations and Trends® in Technology, Information and Operations Management, 12*(2–3), 152–172. doi:10.1561/0200000084

Bach, L. M., Mihaljevic, B., & Zagar, M. (2018). Comparative analysis of blockchain consensus algorithms. In *2018 41st International Convention on Information and Communication Technology, Electronics and Microelectronics*. 10.23919/MIPRO.2018.8400278

Barbosa, N. L. (2019). An exploration of how ethics and sustainability influence the purchase decision of millennials in the coffee industry in Ireland. *Dublin Business School.*

Barnard-Wills, D., & Ashenden, D. (2012). Securing virtual space: Cyber war, cyber terror, and risk. *Space and Culture, 15*(2), 110–123. doi:10.1177/1206331211430016

Barney, J. (1991). Firm resources and sustained competitive advantage. *Journal of Management, 17*(1), 99–120. doi:10.1177/014920639101700108

Barrero, J. M., Bloom, N., & Davis, S. J. (2021). *Why working from home will stick* (No. w28731). National Bureau of Economic Research. doi:10.3386/w28731

Barton, D., & Court, D. (2012). Making advanced analytics work for you. *Harvard Business Review, 90*(10), 78–83. PMID:23074867

Bashir, I. (2017, March 17). *Mastering blockchain*. Packt Publishing Ltd.

Bauernhansl, Hörcher, Röhm, & Bressner. (2017). Neupositionierungeinernationalen Technologieplattform. *Zeitschrift für wirtschaftlichenFabrikbetrieb, 112*(1-2), 7-11.

Baumgartner, H., & Pieters, R. (2003). The structural influence of marketing journals: A citation analysis of the discipline and its subareas over time. *Journal of Marketing, 67*(2), 123–139. doi:10.1509/jmkg.67.2.123.18610

Beck, R., Müller-Bloch, C., & King, J. L. (2018). Governance in the blockchain economy: A framework and research agenda. *Journal of the Association for Information Systems, 19*(10), 1. doi:10.17705/1jais.00518

Bedué, P., & Fritzsche, A. (2022). Can we trust AI? An empirical investigation of trust requirements and guide to successful AI adoption. *Journal of Enterprise Information Management, 35*(2), 530–549. doi:10.1108/JEIM-06-2020-0233

Bello, W. (2004). *Deglobalization: Ideas for a new world economy*. Zed Books.

Bender, E. M., Gebru, T., McMillan-Major, A., & Shmitchell, S. (2023). On the dangers of stochastic parrots: can language models be too big. *Proceedings of FAccT*. Retrieved from https://explodingtopics.com/blog/chatgpt-users

BendiekA.StürzerI. (2022). Advancing European internal and external digital sovereignty: the Brussels effect and the EU-US Trade and Technology Council. *Social Science Open Access Repository*. doi:10.18449/2022C20

Bengio, Y. (2017). Deep Learning and the Future of AI. *arXiv preprint arXiv:1705.07798.*

Berki-Kiss, D., & Menrad, K. (2022). The role emotions play in consumer intentions to make pro-social purchases in Germany–An augmented theory of planned behavior model. *Sustainable Production and Consumption, 29*, 79–89. doi:10.1016/j.spc.2021.09.026

Berne-Manero, C., & Marzo-Navarro, M. (2020). Exploring how influencer and relationship marketing serve corporate sustainability. Sustainability (Switzerland), 12(11).

Bernstein, D. J., & Lange, T. (2017). Post-quantum cryptography - dealing with the fallout of physics success. *IACR Cryptology EPrint Archive, 2017*, 314. http://dblp.uni-trier.de/db/journals/iacr/iacr2017.html#BernsteinL17a

Bernstein, D. J., & Lange, T. (2017). Post-quantum cryptography. *Nature*, *549*(7671), 188–194. doi:10.1038/nature23461 PMID:28905891

Bertello, A., Ferraris, A., Bresciani, S., & de Bernardi, P. (2021). Big data analytics (BDA) and degree of internationalization: The interplay between governance of BDA infrastructure and BDA capabilities. *The Journal of Management and Governance*, *25*(4), 1035–1055. doi:10.1007/s10997-020-09542-w

Bhagwani, S., & Govindaraj, P. (2020). Financial and Non-Financial Applications of Blockchain. *International Journal of Innovative Technology and Exploring Engineering*, *9*(6), 1050–1054. doi:10.35940/ijitee.F4117.049620

Bhansali, A. (2023). Cloud Security and Privacy. In International Journal for Research in Applied Science and Engineering Technology (Vol. 11, Issue 8). doi:10.22214/ijraset.2023.55416

Bharadwaj, A., El Sawy, O. A., Pavlou, P. A., & Venkatraman, N. V. (2013). Digital business strategy: Toward a next generation of insights. *Management Information Systems Quarterly*, *37*(2), 471–482. doi:10.25300/MISQ/2013/37:2.3

Bingham, T., & Conner, M. (2010). *The new social learning: A guide to transforming organizations through social media*. Berrett-Koehler Publishers.

Blurton, C. (2002). *New directions of ICT use in education*. http://www.unesco.org/education/educprog/lwf/dl/edict.pdfs

Bolat, A. (2016). Common models of banking System Regulation: advantages and disadvantages. *ХАБАРШЫ*, 314.

Bonoli, L., & Vorpe, J. (2021). Swiss VET between National Framework and Cantonal Autonomy: A Historical Perspective. *Education Sciences*, *12*(2), 114. Advance online publication. doi:10.3390/educsci12020114

Bouncken, R., & Barwinski, R. (2021). Shared digital identity and rich knowledge ties in global 3D printing-A drizzle in the clouds? *Global Strategy Journal*, *11*(1), 81–108. doi:10.1002/gsj.1370

Boyd, D. M., & Ellison, N. B. (2007). Social network sites: Definition, history, and scholarship. *Journal of Computer-Mediated Communication*, *13*(1), 210–230. doi:10.1111/j.1083-6101.2007.00393.x

Bradford, M., & Florin, J. (2003). Examining the role of innovation diffusion factors on the implementation success of enterprise resource planning systems. *International Journal of Accounting Information Systems*, *4*(3), 205–225. doi:10.1016/S1467-0895(03)00026-5

Braun, A., & Garriga, G. (2018). Consumer Journey Analytics in the Context of Data Privacy and Ethics. In *Digital Marketplaces Unleashed* (pp. 663–674). Springer. doi:10.1007/978-3-662-49275-8_59

Bremmer, I. (2021). The Technopolar Moment: How Digital Powers Will Reshape the Global Order. In I. Bremmer, Foreign Affairs (p. 112). HEINONLINE.

Bremus, F., & Fratzscher, M. (2015). Drivers of structural change in cross-border banking since the global financial crisis. *Journal of International Money and Finance*, *52*, 32–59. doi:10.1016/j.jimonfin.2014.11.012

Bresciani, S., Ferraris, A., Romano, M., & Santoro, G. (2021). *Digital transformation management for agile organizations: A compass to sail the digital world.* Emerald Publishing Limited. doi:10.1108/9781800431713

Brevini, B. (2021). Is AI good for the Planet? *Polity.*

Brodie, R., Hollebeek, L., Juric, B., & Ilic, A. (2011). Customer engagement. *Journal of Service Research*, *14*(3), 252–271. doi:10.1177/1094670511411703

Brown, I. T. J. (2002). Individual and Technological Factors Affecting Perceived Ease of Use of Web-based Learning Technologies in a Developing Country. *The Electronic Journal on Information Systems in Developing Countries*, *9*(1), 1–15. doi:10.1002/j.1681-4835.2002.tb00055.x

Brown, T. B. (2020). *Language Models are Few-Shot Learners*. OpenAI.

Brynjolfsson, E., & McAfee, A. (2014). *The Second Machine Age: Work, Progress, and Prosperity in a Time of Brilliant Technologies*. WW Norton & Company.

Budnitsky, S. (2022). A Relational Approach to Digital Sovereignty: e-Estonia Between Russia and the West. *International Journal of Communication*, 16.

Bu, O. B., & Go, A. S. (2008). Perceived trustworthiness of online shops. *Journal of Consumer Behaviour*, *50*(October), 35–50. doi:10.1002/cb

Buterin, V. (2014). A next-generation smart contract and decentralized application platform. *White Paper, 3*(37), 2-1.

Butner, K. (2010, January 5). The smarter supply chain of the future. *Strategy and Leadership*, *38*(1), 22–31. doi:10.1108/10878571011009859

Cadwalladr, C., & Graham-Harrison, E. (2018). Revealed: 50 million Facebook profiles harvested for Cambridge Analytica in major data breach. *The Guardian, 17*(1), 22.

Cakmak, P. I., & Tas, E. (2012). The use of information technology on gaining competitive advantage in Turkish contractor firms. *World Applied Sciences Journal*, *18*(2), 274–285.

Calvo, S. G. (2010). The global financial crisis of 2008-10: A view from the social sectors. *UNDP-HDRO Occasional Papers*, (2010/18).

Camerinelli, E. (2009). *Measuring the value of the supply chain: Linking financial performance and supply chain decisions* (1st ed.). Gower Publishing Publishing.

Campesato, O. (2023). Introduction to Keras. In Angular and Machine Learning Pocket Primer. doi:10.1515/9781683924685-008

Casino, F., Dasaklis, T. K., & Patsakis, C. (2019). A systematic literature review of blockchain-based applications: Current status, classification and open issues. *Telematics and Informatics*, *36*, 55–81. doi:10.1016/j.tele.2018.11.006

Castells, M. (2009). The Rise of the Network Society: The Information Age: Economy, *Society and Culture*. Wiley-Blackwell.

Castells, M. (2011). Network theoryl A network theory of power. *International Journal of Communication*, *5*, 773–787.

Cate, F. H., & Mayer-Schönberger, V. (2013). Notice and consent in a world of Big Data. *International Data Privacy Law*, *3*(2), 67–73. doi:10.1093/idpl/ipt005

Cavico, F. J., & Mujtaba, B. G. (2017). Wells Fargo's fake accounts scandal and its legal and ethical implications for management. *S.A.M. Advanced Management Journal*, *82*(2), 4.

Cennamo, C., Dagnino, G. B., Di Minin, A., & Lanzolla, G. (2020). Managing digital transformation: Scope of transformation and modalities of value co-generation and delivery. *California Management Review*, *62*(4), 5–16. doi:10.1177/0008125620942136

Česnauskė, J. (2019). Digital economy and society: Baltic states in the EU context. *Economics and Culture, 16*(1), 80-90.

Chaffee, S. H., & Metzger, M. J. (2001). The End of Mass Communication? *Mass Communication & Society*, *4*(4), 365–379. doi:10.1207/S15327825MCS0404_3

Chamola, V., Hassija, V., Gupta, V., & Guizani, M. (2020). A comprehensive review of the COVID-19 pandemic and the role of IoT, drones, AI, blockchain, and 5G in managing its impact. *IEEE Access : Practical Innovations, Open Solutions*, *8*, 90225–90265. doi:10.1109/ACCESS.2020.2992341

Chang, J. (n.d.). *Sidebench*. https://medium.com/@sidebench/blockchain-the-immutable-ledger-of-transparency-in-healthcare-technology-a4a64b1d5594

Chang, Y., Iakovou, E., & Shi, W. (2020, April 2). Blockchain in global supply chains and cross border trade: A critical synthesis of the state-of-the-art, challenges and opportunities. *International Journal of Production Research*, *58*(7), 2082–2099. doi:10.1080/00207543.2019.1651946

Chatzopoulou, E., & de Kiewiet, A. (2021). Millennials' evaluation of corporate social responsibility: The wants and needs of the largest and most ethical generation. *Journal of Consumer Behaviour*, *20*(3), 521–534. doi:10.1002/cb.1882

Chen, B., Wan, J., Shu, L., Li, P., Mukherjee, M., & Yin, B. (2018). Smart Factory of Industry 4.0: Key Technologies, Application Case, and Challenges. *IEEE Access : Practical Innovations, Open Solutions*, *6*, 6505–6519. doi:10.1109/ACCESS.2017.2783682

Chen, H., & Storey, V. C. (2012). Business intelligence and analytics: From big data to big impact. *Management Information Systems Quarterly*, *36*(4), 1165–1188. doi:10.2307/41703503

Chiu, I. H.-Y. (2022). Prospects for international financial deglobalisation and its potential impact on international financial regulation. *Law and Financial Markets Review, 16*, 1-19. . doi:10.1080/17521440.2023.2204991

Cho, J., DeStefano, T., Kim, H., Kim, I., & Paik, J. H. (2023). What's driving the diffusion of next-generation digital technologies? *Technovation*, *119*, 102477. doi:10.1016/j.technovation.2022.102477

Christidis, K., & Devetsikiotis, M. (2016, May 10). Blockchains and smart contracts for the internet of things. *IEEE Access : Practical Innovations, Open Solutions*, *4*, 2292–2303. doi:10.1109/ACCESS.2016.2566339

Chu, Y., Ream, J., & Schatsky, D. (n.d.). *Getting smart about smart contracts*. Deloitte.

Chua, J. (2022, Oct 13). *citigroup.com*. Retrieved January 16, 2024, from Global Insights: https://www.citigroup.com/global/insights/global-insights/deglobalization-is-a-convenient-narrative-but-the-data-doesn-t-support-it

Chuang, I. H., Li, S. H., Huang, K. C., & Kuo, Y. H. (2011). An effective privacy protection scheme for cloud computing. *International Conference on Advanced Communication Technology, ICACT*, 260–265.

Chui, M., Issler, M., Roberts, R., & Yee, L. (2023). Technology Trends Outlook 2023. Academic Press.

Çilan, Ç. A., Bolat, B. A., & Coşkun, E. (2009). Analyzing digital divide within and between member and candidate countries of European Union. *Government Information Quarterly*, *26*(1), 98–105. doi:10.1016/j.giq.2007.11.002

Cisler, S. (2002). Letter from San Francisco: The Internet Bookmobile. *First Monday*, *7*(10).

Coase, R. H. (1937). The nature of the firm. *Economica*, *4*(16), 386–405. doi:10.1111/j.1468-0335.1937.tb00002.x

Cohen, L., Angelovska-Wilson, A., Strong, G., & Law, D. (2021). Decentralized finance: Ready for its "close-up"? *GLI–Blockchain & Cryptocurrency Regulation 2022.*

Costa, D. F., Carvalho, F. D. M., & Moreira, B. C. D. M. (2019). Behavioral economics and behavioral finance: A bibliometric analysis of the scientific fields. *Journal of Economic Surveys*, *33*(1), 3–24. doi:10.1111/joes.12262

Costa, I., Riccotta, R., Montini, P., Stefani, E., Roberto de Souza, G., Gaspar, M. A., & Martins, F. S. (2022). The degree of contribution of digital transformation technology on company sustainability areas. *Sustainability (Basel)*, *14*(1), 462. doi:10.3390/su14010462

D'Ippolito, B., Petruzzelli, A. M., & Panniello, U. (2019). Archetypes of incumbents' strategic responses to digital innovation. *Journal of Intellectual Capital*, *20*(5), 622–679. doi:10.1108/JIC-04-2019-0065

Dai, Y., & Wang, T. (2021). Prediction of customer engagement behaviour response to marketing posts based on machine learning. *Connection Science*, *33*(4), 891–910. doi:10.1080/09540091.2021.1912710

Danaher, J., & Sætra, H. S. (2022). Technology and moral change: The transformation of truth and trust. *Ethics and Information Technology*, *24*(3), 35. Advance online publication. doi:10.1007/s10676-022-09661-y

Danaher, J., & Sætra, H. S. (2022). Technology and moral change: The transformation of truth and trust. *Technology in Society*, *75*, 102372.

Daskal, J. C. (2015). *The un-territoriality of data*. Academic Press.

Davenport, T. H. (2013). Analytics 3.0. *Harvard Business Review*, (December), 64–72.

Davenport, T., & Harris, J. (2007). *Competing on Analytics: The New Science of Winning* (1st ed.). Harvard Business School.

David, M. (2020). The correspondence theory of truth. In *The Stanford Encyclopedia of Philosophy* (Winter 2020 Edition). Available at: https://plato.stanford.edu/archives/win2020/entries/truth-correspondence/

Davis, F. D. (1989, September 1). Perceived usefulness, perceived ease of use, and user acceptance of information technology. *Management Information Systems Quarterly*, *13*(3), 319–340. doi:10.2307/249008

Dayal, Y. (2022). *RBI Press Release 2022-2023/1319*. www.rbi.org.in

Dedehayir, O., Ortt, J. R., & Seppanen, ¨. M. (2017). Disruptive change and the reconfiguration of innovation ecosystems. *Journal of Technology Management & Innovation*, *12*(3), 9–21. doi:10.4067/S0718-27242017000300002

Delgosha, S., Mohammad, N. H. H., & Saheb, T. (2020). The configurational impact of digital transformation on sustainability: A country-level perspective. In *ECIS2020 Proceedings*. Association for Information Systems AIS Electronic Library (AISeL).

Delios, A., Perchthold, G., & Capri, A. (2021). Cohesion, COVID-19 and contemporary challenges to globalization. *Journal of World Business*, *56*(3), 101197. doi:10.1016/j.jwb.2021.101197

Deniz, Sevinç, A. P. (2023). How does deglobalization affect economic growth? *Journal of Research in Economics, Politics & Finance*, *8*(1), 1–19.

Deo, K., & Prasad, A. A. (2022). Exploring Climate Change Adaptation, Mitigation and Marketing Connections. *Sustainability (Basel)*, *14*(7), 4255. Advance online publication. doi:10.3390/su14074255

DeStefano, T., Kneller, R., & Timmis, J. (2020). *Cloud Computing and Firm Growth*. CESifo Working Paper No. 8306.

Dey, P. K. (2019). *Rethinking Routing and Peering in the era of Vertical Integration of Network Functions*. Academic Press.

Digital, O. E. C. D. (2020). *Economy Outlook 2020*. OECD Publishing. doi:10.1787/bb167041-

Dignum, V. (2018). *Responsible Artificial Intelligence: How to Develop and Use AI in a Responsible Way*. Springer.

Dingli, A., & Seychell, D. (2015). *The new digital natives*. JB Metzler.

Ding, Y., & Cronin, B. (2011). Popular and/or prestigious? Measures of scholarly esteem. *Information Processing & Management*, *47*(1), 80–96. doi:10.1016/j.ipm.2010.01.002

Divya Prabhu, D. G. (2021). *Shodhganga Inflibnet.* Retrieved Dec 2023, from http://hdl.handle.net/10603/346873

Domazet, I. (2023). Innovation and ICT: Key Factors of Successful Business. In Innovation, strategy, and transformation frameworks for the modern enterprise. IGI Global. doi:10.4018/979-8-3693-0458-7.ch014

Domazet, I., Marjanović, D., & Ahmetagić, D. (2022). The Impact of High-Tech Products Exports on Economic Growth: The Case of Serbia, Bulgaria, Romania and Hungary. *Ekonomika preduzeća, 70*(3-4), 191-205.

Domazet, I., Marjanović, D., Ahmetagić, D., & Bugarčić, M. (2021). The Impact of Innovation Indicators on Increasing Exports of High Technology Products. *Ekonomika preduzeća, 69*(1-2), 31-40.

Domazet, I., Marjanović, D., Ahmetagić, D., & Antonijević, M. (2022). Does the Increase in the Number of Registered Patents Affect Economic Growth? Evidence from Romania and Bulgaria. *Economic Analysis: Applied Research in Emerging Markets*, *55*(2), 49–65. doi:10.28934/ea.22.55.2.pp49-65

Domazet, I., Marjanović, D., Ahmetagić, D., & Simović, V. (2023). The influence of the number of patents on the economic growth of the country - evidence from Serbia and Hungary. *Strategic Management*, *28*(4), 41–52. Advance online publication. doi:10.5937/StraMan2300048D

Domazet, I., Zubović, J., & Lazić, M. (2018). Driving Factors of Serbian Competitiveness: Digital Economy and ICT. *Strategic Management*, *23*(1), 20–28. doi:10.5937/StraMan1801020D

Donthu, N., Kumar, S., Mukherjee, D., Pandey, N., & Lim, W. M. (2021). How to conduct a bibliometric analysis: An overview and guidelines. *Journal of Business Research*, *133*, 285–296. doi:10.1016/j.jbusres.2021.04.070

Dourish, P., & Bell, G. (2011). *Divining a digital future: Mess and mythology in ubiquitous computing*. MIT Press. doi:10.7551/mitpress/9780262015554.001.0001

Dr, G. S., & Vijaya, D. P. (2023). Financial Inclusion – an Assessment of Progress via Rural Banking System and Way Forward. In The Sustainable Fintech Revolution. IGI Global.

Duong, C. D. (2023). Karmic beliefs and social entrepreneurial intentions: A moderated mediation model of environmental complexity and empathy. *Journal of Open Innovation*, *9*(1), 100022. doi:10.1016/j.joitmc.2023.100022

Dupont, B. (2013). The Cyber Security Environment to 2022: Trends, Drivers and Implications. SSRN *Electronic Journal*. doi:10.2139/ssrn.2208548

Durbha, S. S., Sanyal, J., Yang, L. S., Chaudhari, S., Bhangale, U., Bharambe, U., & Kurte, K. (2023). Advances in Scalable and Intelligent Geospatial Analytics. In Advances in Scalable and Intelligent Geospatial Analytics. doi:10.1201/9781003270928

Edwards, B. (2022). Artists stage mass protest against AI-generated artwork on ArtStation. Ars Technica.

Ejdys, J. (2018). Building technology trust in ICT application at a university. *International Journal of Emerging Markets*, *13*(5), 980–997. doi:10.1108/IJoEM-07-2017-0234

Elbadawi, M., McCoubrey, L. E., Gavins, F. K., Ong, J. J., Goyanes, A., Gaisford, S., & Basit, A. W. (2021). Harnessing artificial intelligence for the next generation of 3D printed medicines. *Advanced Drug Delivery Reviews*, *175*, 113805. doi:10.1016/j.addr.2021.05.015 PMID:34019957

Elsner, R., Krafft, M., & Huchzermeier, A. (2004). Optimizing Rhenania's direct marketing business through dynamic multilevel modeling (DMLM) in a multicatalog-brand environment. *Marketing Science*, *23*(2), 192–206. doi:10.1287/mksc.1040.0063

ENS Economic Bureau. (2023). *Banks saw highest number of frauds in digital payments in FY23: RBI*. Author.

Erevelles, S., Fukawa, N., & Swayne, L. (2015). Big Data consumer analytics and the transformation of marketing. *Journal of Business Research*, *69*(2), 897–904. doi:10.1016/j.jbusres.2015.07.001

European Commission. (2022). *Digital Economy and Society Index (DESI) 2022 - Methodological Note*. Available at: https://digital-strategy.ec.europa.eu/en/policies/desi

Fallis, D. (2021). The epistemic threat of deepfakes. *Philosophy & Technology*, *34*(4), 623–643. doi:10.1007/s13347-020-00419-2 PMID:32837868

Farahani, B., Firouzi, F., & Luecking, M. (2021). The convergence of IoT and distributed ledger technologies (DLT): Opportunities, challenges, and solutions. *Journal of Network and Computer Applications*, *177*, 102936. doi:10.1016/j.jnca.2020.102936

Farooq, S., & O'Brien, C. (2012). A technology selection framework for integrating manufacturing within a supply chain. *International Journal of Production Research*, *50*(11), 2987–3010. doi:10.1080/00207543.2011.588265

Feder, G., & Umali, D. L. (1993). The adoption of agricultural innovations: A review. *Technological Forecasting and Social Change*, *43*(3-4), 215–239. doi:10.1016/0040-1625(93)90053-A

Feher, K. (2021). Digital identity and the online self: Footprint strategies–An exploratory and comparative research study. *Journal of Information Science*, *47*(2), 192–205.

Ference, A. (2017). *7 customer engagement strategies you must try Outbrain Blog*. Available at: www.outbrain.com/blog/3-golden-customer-engagement-strategies-that-marketers-cant-ignore/

Fiedler, L., Germann, F., Kraus, M., & Perrey, J. (2013). KoenigKunde – Kapital Kundenwissen. *Akzente*, *3*, 24–29.

Fink, L., & Neumann, S. (2009). Exploring the perceived business value of the flexibility enabled by information technology infrastructure. *Information & Management*, *46*(2), 90–99. doi:10.1016/j.im.2008.11.007

Fischer, M., Albers, S., Wagner, N., & Frie, M. (2011). Practice prize winner—Dynamic marketing budget allocation across countries, products, and marketing activities. *Marketing Science*, *30*(4), 568–585. doi:10.1287/mksc.1100.0627

Fitzgerald, M., Kruschwitz, N., Bonnet, D., & Welch, M. (2013). Embracing digital technology: A new strategic imperative. *MIT Sloan Management Review*, *55*(2), 1–12.

Flores, W. R., Holm, H., Nohlberg, M., & Ekstedt, M. (2014). Investigating personal determinants of two-factor authentication adoption: Habit and complacency. *Proceedings of the 47th Hawaii International Conference on System Sciences*.

Floyd, K., Freling, R., Alhoqail, S., Cho, H. Y., & Freling, T. (2014). How online product reviews affect retail sales: A meta-analysis. *Journal of Retailing*, *90*(2), 217–232. doi:10.1016/j.jretai.2014.04.004

Fosso Wamba, S., Queiroz, M. M., & Trinchera, L. (2020). Dynamics between blockchain adoption determinants and supply chain performance: An empirical investigation. *International Journal of Production Economics*, *229*, 107791. Advance online publication. doi:10.1016/j.ijpe.2020.107791

France, S. L., & Ghose, S. (2018). Marketing Analytics: Methods, Practice, Implementation, and Links to Other Fields. *Expert Systems with Applications*, *119*, 456–475. doi:10.1016/j.eswa.2018.11.002

Fries, I., Greiner, M., Hofmeier, M., Hrestic, R., Lechner, U., & Wendeborn, T. (2023). *Towards a Layer Model for Digital Sovereignty: A Holistic Approach*. Critical Information Infrastructures Security.

FSB. (2022). *Assessment of risks to financial stability from crypto-assets. Technical report*. Financial Stability Board.

Fu, S., Liu, J., Tian, J., Peng, J., & Wu, C. (2023). Impact of Digital Economy on Energy Supply Chain Efficiency: Evidence from Chinese Energy Enterprises. *Energies*, *16*(1), 568. Advance online publication. doi:10.3390/en16010568

Fuxman, L., Mohr, I., Mahmoud, A. B., & Grigoriou, N. (2022). The new 3Ps of sustainability marketing: The case of fashion. *Sustainable Production and Consumption*, *31*, 384–396. doi:10.1016/j.spc.2022.03.004

Galazova, S. S., & Magomaeva, L. R. (2019). *The transformation of traditional banking activity in digital*. Academic Press.

Galbraith, J. R. (1974). Organization design: An information processing view. *Interfaces*, *4*(3), 28–36. doi:10.1287/inte.4.3.28

Gardner, D., & Fehskens, L. (2012). Point-counterpoint: Enterprise architecture and enterprise transformation as related but distinct concepts. *Journal of Enterprise Transformation*, *2*(4), 283–294. doi:10.1080/19488289.2012.730813

Garg, P., Gupta, B., Chauhan, A. K., Sivarajah, U., Gupta, S., & Modgil, S. (2021). Measuring the perceived benefits of implementing blockchain technology in the banking sector. *Technological Forecasting and Social Change*, *163*, 120407. doi:10.1016/j.techfore.2020.120407

Gefen, D., & Carmel, E. (2008). Is the World Really Flat? A Look at Offshoring at an Online Programming Marketplace. *Management Information Systems Quarterly*, *32*(2), 367–384. doi:10.2307/25148844

George, A. (2022). The Kerala, India Experience of Facing the COVID-19 Pandemic. In *The Coronavirus Crisis and Challenges to Social Development* (pp. 251–261). Springer. doi:10.1007/978-3-030-84678-7_22

George, G., & Simon, J. D. (2022). Digital transformation, sustainability, and purpose in the multinational enterprise. *Journal of World Business*, *57*(3), 101326. doi:10.1016/j.jwb.2022.101326

Germann, F., Lilien, G. L., Fiedler, L., & Kraus, M. (2014). Do retailers benefit from deploying customer analytics? *Journal of Retailing*, *90*(4), 587–593. doi:10.1016/j.jretai.2014.08.002

Germann, F., Lilien, G. L., & Rangaswamy, A. (2013). Performance implications of deploying marketing analytics. *International Journal of Research in Marketing*, *30*(2), 114–128. doi:10.1016/j.ijresmar.2012.10.001

Géron, A. (2022). *Hands-on machine learning with Scikit-Learn*. Keras, and TensorFlow.

Ghezzi, A., Gabelloni, D., Martini, A., & Natalicchio, A. (2018). Crowdsourcing: A Review and Suggestions for Future Research. *International Journal of Management Reviews*, *20*(2), 343–363. doi:10.1111/ijmr.12135

Giannetti, M., & Laeven, L. (2012). The flight home effect: Evidence from the syndicated loan market during financial crises. *Journal of Financial Economics*, *104*(1), 23–43. doi:10.1016/j.jfineco.2011.12.006

Giannopoulou, A. (2023). Digital Identity Infrastructures: A Critical Approach of Self-Sovereign Identity. *Digital Society : Ethics, Socio-Legal and Governance of Digital Technology*, *2*(2), 18. Advance online publication. doi:10.1007/s44206-023-00049-z PMID:37200582

Golosova, J., & Romanovs, A. (2018, November). The advantages and disadvantages of the blockchain technology. In *2018 IEEE 6th workshop on advances in information, electronic and electrical engineering (AIEEE)* (pp. 1-6). IEEE. 10.1109/AIEEE.2018.8592253

Goodfellow, I., Bengio, Y., & Courville, A. (2016). *Deep Learning*. MIT Press.

Goodhue, D. L., & Thompson, R. L. (1995). Task-technology fit and individual performance. *Management Information Systems Quarterly*, *19*(2), 213–236. doi:10.2307/249689

Gowroju, S., & Kumar, S. (2022). Review on secure traditional and machine learning algorithms for age prediction using IRIS image. *Multimedia Tools and Applications*, *81*(24), 35503–35531. doi:10.1007/s11042-022-13355-4

Gowroju, S., Sandeep Kumar, A., & Ghimire, A. (2022). Deep Neural Network for Accurate Age Group Prediction through Pupil Using the Optimized UNet Model. *Mathematical Problems in Engineering*, *2022*, 1–24. doi:10.1155/2022/7813701

Goyal, J., Singh, M., Singh, R., & Aggarwal, A. (2019). Efficiency and technology gaps in Indian banking sector: Application of meta-frontier directional distance function DEA approach. *The Journal of Finance and Data Science, 5*(3), 156-172.

Goyal, Singh, Singh, & Aggarwal. (2019). Efficiency and technology gaps in Indian banking sector: Application of meta-frontier directional distance function DEA approach. *The Journal of Finance and Data Science, 5*, 156-172.

Goyal, J., Singh, M., Singh, R., & Aggarwal, A. (2019). Efficiency and technology gaps in Indian banking sector: Application of meta-frontier directional distance function DEA approach. *The Journal of Finance and Data Science*, *5*(3), 156–172. doi:10.1016/j.jfds.2018.08.002

Greenhalgh, T., Robert, G., Macfarlane, F., Bate, P., & Kyriakidou, O. (2004). Diffusion of innovations in service organizations: Systematic review and recommendations. *The Milbank Quarterly*, *82*(4), 581–629. doi:10.1111/j.0887-378X.2004.00325.x PMID:15595944

Greenleaf, G. (2012). Global data privacy laws: 89 countries and accelerating. *Privacy Laws & Business International Report,* (115).

Griffy-Brown, C., Earp, B. D., & Rosas, O. (2018). Technology and the good society. *Technology in Society*, *52*, 1–3. doi:10.1016/j.techsoc.2018.01.001

GS1. (2014). *EPCIS*. https://www.gs1.org/standards/epcis

Gu, H. (2023). Data, Big Tech, and the New Concept of Sovereignty. *Journal of Chinese Political Science*. Advance online publication. doi:10.1007/s11366-023-09855-1 PMID:37359767

Guo, Y., & Liang, C. (2016). Blockchain application and outlook in the banking industry. *Financial Innovation*, *2*(1), 1–12. doi:10.1186/s40854-016-0034-9

Gupta, M. (2017). *Blockchain for dummies*. John Wiley & Sons.

Gupta, M., & George, J. F. (2016). Toward the development of a big data analytics capability. *Information & Management*, *53*(8), 1049–1064. doi:10.1016/j.im.2016.07.004

Gupta, S., Hanssens, D., Hardie, B., Kahn, W., Kumar, V., Lin, N., Ravishankar, N., & Sriram, S. (2006). Modeling customer lifetime value. *Journal of Service Research*, *9*(2), 139–155. doi:10.1177/1094670506293810

Gupta, S., & Rathore, H. S. (2021). Socio-Economic and political empowerment through self help groups intervention: A study from Bilaspur, Chhattisgarh, India. *Journal of Public Affairs*, *21*(1), e2143. doi:10.1002/pa.2143

Gurbaxani, V., & Dunkle, D. (2019). Gearing up for successful digital transformation. *MIS Quarterly Executive*, *18*(3), 209–220. doi:10.17705/2msqe.00017

Habel, J., Kassemeier, R., Alavi, S., Haaf, P., Schmitz, C., & Wieseke, J. (2020). When do customers perceive customer centricity? The role of a firm's and salespeople's customer orientation. *Journal of Personal Selling & Sales Management*, *40*(1), 25–42. doi:10.1080/08853134.2019.1631174

Haggart, B. (2019). The age of surveillance capitalism: The fight for a human future at the new frontier of power. *Journal of Digital Media & Policy, 10*(2), 229-243.

Haider, M., Shannon, R., & Moschis, G. P. (2022). Sustainable Consumption Research and the Role of Marketing: A Review of the Literature (1976–2021). *Sustainability (Basel)*, *14*(7), 1–36. doi:10.3390/su14073999

Hall, K. K., & Qi, J. (2022, July). Collaboration, feedback, and performance: Supply chain insights from service-dominant logic. *Journal of Business Research*, *146*, 385–397. Advance online publication. doi:10.1016/j.jbusres.2022.03.055

Hannafin, R. D. & Savenye, S. (1993). *Technology in the classroom: The teacher's New role and resistance to I.T.* Academic Press.

Hanssens, D. M., Pauwels, K. H., Srinivasan, S., Vanhuele, M., & Yildirim, G. (2014). Consumer attitude metrics for guiding marketing mix decisions. *Marketing Science*, *33*(4), 534–550. doi:10.1287/mksc.2013.0841

Hirsch, P. M. (1975). Organizational effectiveness and the institutional environment. *Administrative Science Quarterly*, *20*(3), 327–344. doi:10.2307/2391994

Hitt, M. A., Holmes, R. M. Jr, & Arregle, J. L. (2021). The (COVID-19) pandemic and the new world (dis) order. *Journal of World Business*, *56*(4), 101210. doi:10.1016/j.jwb.2021.101210

Hnamte, V., Ahmad, A., Nhung-nguyen, H., & Hussain, J. (2024). Computers & Security DDoS attack detection and mitigation using deep neural network in SDN environment. *Computers & Security, 138*(December), 103661. doi:10.1016/j.cose.2023.103661

Hoepman, J. H. (2014, June). Privacy design strategies. *IFIP International Information Security Conference,* 446-459.

Hong, S., Park, J., & Jeon, S. (2021). The effects of country-of-online retailer on consumer's purchase decision-making in a foreign internet shopping mall. *Journal of Korea Trade*, *25*(6), 20–33. doi:10.35611/jkt.2021.25.6.20

Horwich, P. (2006). The value of truth. *Noûs (Detroit, Mich.)*, *40*(2), 347–360. doi:10.1111/j.0029-4624.2006.00613.x

Hossain, M. D. A., Akter, S., & Yanamandram, V. K. (2020). *Customer Analytics Capabilities in the Big Data Spectrum: A Systematic Approach to Achieve Sustainable Firm Performance*. https://ro.uow.edu.au/gsbpapers/577

Howard, P. N., & Hussain, M. M. (2011). The role of digital media. *Journal of Democracy*, *22*(3), 35–48. doi:10.1353/jod.2011.0041

Howland, D. (2019, February 11). *The plus-size era is over before it began.* https://www.retaildive.com/news/the-plus-size-era-is-over-before-it-began/547938

Hsieh, Y. Y., Vergne, J. P., Anderson, P., Lakhani, K., & Reitzig, M. (2018). Bitcoin and the rise of decentralized autonomous organizations. *Journal of Organization Design*, *7*(1), 1–16. doi:10.1186/s41469-018-0038-1

Hui, S. K., Inman, J. J., Huang, Y., & Suher, J. (2013). The effect of in-store travel distance on unplanned spending: Applications to mobile promotion strategies. *Journal of Marketing*, *77*(2), 1–16. doi:10.1509/jm.11.0436

Hu, M. K., & Kee, D. M. (2022). Fostering sustainability: Reinventing SME strategy in the new normal. *Foresight*, *24*(3/4), 301–318. doi:10.1108/FS-03-2021-0080

Hunt, S. D., Wood, V. R., & Chonko, L. B. (1989). Corporate Ethical Values and Organizational Commitment in Marketing. *Journal of Marketing*, *53*(3), 79–90. doi:10.1177/002224298905300309

Hurlburt, G. (2023). What If Ethics Got in the Way of Generative AI? *IT Professional*. . doi:10.1109/MITP.2023.3267140

Hyperledger. (n.d.). *Walmart turns to blockchain (and Hyperledger) to take on food traceability and safety*. https://www.hyperledger.org/blog/2019/02/21/walmart-turns-to-blockchain-and-hyperledger-to-take-on-food-traceability-and-safety

Iansiti, M., & Lakhani, K. R. (2020). *Competing in the Age of AI: Strategy and Leadership when Algorithms and Networks Run the World. Harvard Business Review.*

Ikonen, P., Luoma-aho, V., & Bowen, S. A. (2017). Transparency for Sponsored Content: Analysing Codes of Ethics in Public Relations, Marketing, Advertising and Journalism. *International Journal of Strategic Communication*, *11*(2), 165–178. doi:10.1080/1553118X.2016.1252917

Jabbar, S., Lloyd, H., Hammoudeh, M., Adebisi, B., & Raza, U. (2020, November 20). Blockchain-enabled supply chain: Analysis, challenges, and future directions. *Multimedia Systems*, 1–20.

James, H. (2018). Deglobalization: The Rise of Disembedded Unilateralism. *Annual Review of Financial Economics*, *10*(1), 219–237. doi:10.1146/annurev-financial-110217-022625

Jensen, J. R., von Wachter, V., & Ross, O. (2021). How decentralized is the governance of blockchain-based finance: Empirical evidence from four governance token distributions. *arXiv preprint arXiv:2102.10096.*

Jeong, D. B. (2021). Prediction of the Corona 19's domestic internet and mobile shopping transaction amount. *The Journal of Economics. Marketing and Management*, *9*(2), 1–10.

Johnson, D. (2023). *Rethinking Democracy and Governance: Perspectives from the Caribbean.* Taylor & Francis. doi:10.4324/9781003434290

Jones, C. I. (2009). The global financial crisis of 2007–20. *A Supplement to Macroeconomics, 1*, 1-45.

Jonnala, J., Asodi, P., Uppada, L. K., Chalasani, C., & Rani, R. (2023). *Intelligent systems and applications in engineering advancing cybersecurity : A comprehensive approach to enhance threat detection.* Analysis, and Trust in Digital Environments.

Jung, E., & La, S. (2020). Wear Your Heart on Your Sleeve: Exploring Moral Identity as a Moderator Across CSR Authenticity, Consumer Admiration, and Engagement in the Fashion Industry. *Asia Marketing Journal*, *22*(2), 19–57. doi:10.15830/amj.2020.22.2.19

KadiaP. (n.d.). https://businessblockchainhq.com/business-blockchain-news/the-success-story-of-tradelens/

Kagermann, H. (2017). *Chancen von Industrie 4.0 nutzen. In HandbuchIndustrie 4.0* (Vol. 4). Allgemeine Grundlagen.

Kane, G. C., Palmer, D., Phillips, A. N., Kiron, D., & Buckley, N. (2015). Strategy, not technology, drives digital transformation. *MIT Sloan Management Review*, 1–25.

Kannan, P. K., Pope, B. K., & Jain, S. (2009). Practice prize winner—Pricing digital content product lines: A model and application for the National Academies Press. *Marketing Science*, *28*(4), 620–636. doi:10.1287/mksc.1080.0481

Kapoor, R., & Kapoor, K. (2021). The transition from traditional to digital marketing: A study of the evolution of e-marketing in the Indian hotel industry. *Worldwide Hospitality and Tourism Themes*, *13*(2), 199–2133. doi:10.1108/WHATT-10-2020-0124

Kar, A. K., Ilavarasan, V., Gupta, M. P., Janssen, M., & Kothari, R. (2019). Moving beyond smart cities: Digital nations for social innovation & sustainability. *Information Systems Frontiers*, *21*(3), 495–501. doi:10.1007/s10796-019-09930-0

Karimi, Somers, & Gupta. (n.d.). Impact of information technology management practices on customer service. *Journal of Management Information Systems, 17*(4), 125-158.

Kaur, G. (2023). Blockchain Technology: Perspective From the Banking Sector. *Revolutionizing Financial Services and Markets Through FinTech and Blockchain*, 278-287.

Kaur, J., & Ramkumar, K. R. (2022). The recent trends in cyber security: A review. *Journal of King Saud University. Computer and Information Sciences*, *34*(8), 5766–5781. doi:10.1016/j.jksuci.2021.01.018

Kayikci, Y., & Subramanian, N. (2018). Feasibility of food loss reduction with blockchain in the emerging economy context. *Symposium on Logistics (ISL 2018) Big Data Enabled Supply Chain Innovations*.

Kazantsev, N., Pishchulov, G., Mehandjiev, N., Sampaio, P., & Zolkiewski, J. (2022). Investigating barriers to demand-driven SME collaboration in low-volume high-variability manufacturing. *Supply Chain Management*, *27*(2), 265–282. Advance online publication. doi:10.1108/SCM-10-2021-0486

Kehoe, L., O'Connell, N., Andrzejewski, D., Gindner, K., & Dalal, D. (2017). *When two chains combine supply chain meets blockchain*. Deloitte.

Kellerand, K. L., & Lehmann, D. R. (2006). Brands and branding: Research findings and future priorities. *Marketing Science*, *25*(6), 740–759. doi:10.1287/mksc.1050.0153

Khalin, V.G., & Chernova, G.V. (2018). Digitalization and its impact on the Russian economy and society: advantages, challenges, threats and risks. *Administrative Consulting*, (10).

Khanna, A., & Arora, B. (2009). A study to investigate the reasons for bank frauds and the implementation of preventive security controls in Indian banking industry. *International Journal of Business Science and Applied Management*, *4*(3), 1–21.

Khodaiemehr, H., Bagheri, K., & Feng, C. (2023). *Navigating the Quantum Computing Threat Landscape for Navigating the Quantum Computing Threat Landscape for Blockchains : A Comprehensive Survey*. Academic Press.

Khoshafian, S. (2015). *Digital transformation of CRM through Internet of Things (IoT).* Available at: www.pega.com/insights/articles/digital-transformation-crm-through-internet-things-iot

Kietzmann, J. H., Hermkens, K., McCarthy, I. P., & Silvestre, B. S. (2011). Social media? Get serious! Understanding the functional building blocks of social media. *Business Horizons*, *54*(3), 241–251. doi:10.1016/j.bushor.2011.01.005

Kilic, C. (2015). Effects of globalization on economic growth: Panel data analysis for developing countries. *Economic Insights - Trends and Challenges*, *67*(1), 1–11.

Kim, G., Shin, B., Kim, K. K., & Lee, H. (2011). IT capabilities, process-oriented dynamic capabilities, and firm financial performance. *Journal of the Association for Information Systems*, *12*(7), 487–517. doi:10.17705/1jais.00270

Kim, G., Shin, B., & Kwon, O. (2012). Investigating the value of sociomaterialism in conceptualizing IT capability of a firm. *Journal of Management Information Systems*, *29*(3), 327–362. doi:10.2753/MIS0742-1222290310

Kim, H. M., & Laskowski, M. (2018, January). Toward an ontology-driven blockchain design for supply-chain provenance. *International Journal of Intelligent Systems in Accounting Finance & Management, 25*(1), 18–27. doi:10.1002/isaf.1424

Kim, K. H., & Moon, H. (2021). Innovative digital marketing management in B2B markets. *Industrial Marketing Management, 95*, 1–4. doi:10.1016/j.indmarman.2021.01.016

Kim, S. K., & Huh, J. H. (2020). Artificial neural network blockchain techniques for healthcare system: Focusing on the personal health records. *Electronics (Basel), 9*(5), 763. doi:10.3390/electronics9050763

Kinder, M. (2022). The case for localised, decentralised supply chains. *Journal of Supply Chain Management, Logistics and Procurement, 5*(1).

Kiss, R. (2021). *The impact of influencer credibility on purchase intention in the endorsement of sustainable products.* https://jyx.jyu.fi/handle/123456789/76963

Kitchens, B., Dobolyi, D. G., Li, J., & Abbasi, A. (2018). Advanced Customer Analytics: Strategic Value Through Integration of Relationship-Oriented Big Data. *Journal of Management Information Systems, 35*(2), 540–574. doi:10.1080/07421222.2018.1451957

Klagge, B., & Martin, R. (2005). Decentralized versus centralized financial systems: Is there a case for local capital markets? *Journal of Economic Geography, 5*(4), 387–421. doi:10.1093/jeg/lbh071

Knight, W. (2019). *AI is helping reporters write news. But is it creative?* MIT Technology Review.

Kolb, S. (2018). *On the Portability of Applications in Platform as a Service.* Academic Press.

Kong, S. T., & Loubere, N. (2021). Digitally down to the countryside: Fintech and rural development in China. *The Journal of Development Studies, 57*(10), 1739–1754. doi:10.1080/00220388.2021.1919631

Kornaros, G. (2022). Hardware-Assisted Machine Learning in Resource-Constrained IoT Environments for Security: Review and Future Prospective. *IEEE Access : Practical Innovations, Open Solutions, 10*, 58603–58622. doi:10.1109/ACCESS.2022.3179047

Kose, M. P., Prasad, E., Rogoff, K., & Wei, S.-J. (2009). Financial globalization: A reappraisal. *IMF Staff Papers, 56*(1), 8–62. doi:10.1057/imfsp.2008.36

Kourda, H. (2022). *The Interview: Hasna Kourda, Founder, Save Your Wardrobe.* https://www.theindustry.fashion/the-interview-hasna-kourda-founder-save-your-wardrobe

Kraus, S., Jones, P., Kailer, N., Weinmann, A., Chaparro-Banegas, N., & Roig-Tierno, N. (2021). Digital transformation: An overview of the current state of the art of research. *SAGE Open, 11*(3). doi:10.1177/21582440211047576

Kritzinger, E., & von Solms, S. H. (2010). Cyber security for home users: A new way of protection through awareness enforcement. *Computers & Security, 29*(8), 840–847. doi:10.1016/j.cose.2010.08.001

Kumar, K., Zindani, D., & Davim, J. P. (2019). *Industry 4.0: Developments towards the fourth industrial revolution.* Springer. doi:10.1007/978-981-13-8165-2

Kumar, N., Singh, R., & Singh, S. (2021). The power of the collective empowers women: Evidence from self-help groups in India. *World Development, 146*, 105579. doi:10.1016/j.worlddev.2021.105579 PMID:34602708

Kumar, P., Chauhan, S., & Awasthi, L. K. (2023). Artificial intelligence in healthcare: Review, ethics, trust challenges & future research directions. *Engineering Applications of Artificial Intelligence, 120*, 105894. doi:10.1016/j.engappai.2023.105894

Kumar, V., & Petersen, J. A. (2012). *Statistical Methods in Customer Relationship Management*. John Wiley & Sons Ltd. doi:10.1002/9781118349212

Kummer, S., Herold, D. M., Dobrovnik, M., Mikl, J., & Schäfer, N. (2020). A systematic review of Blockchain literature in logistics and supply chain management: Identifying research questions and future directions. *Future Internet*, *12*(3), 60. doi:10.3390/fi12030060

Kuner, C. (2013). *Transborder data flows and data privacy law*. Academic Press.

Kushwah, S., Dhir, A., & Sagar, M. (2019). Ethical consumption intentions and choice behavior towards organic food. Moderation role of buying and environmental concerns. *Journal of Cleaner Production*, *236*, 117519. doi:10.1016/j.jclepro.2019.06.350

Lahbib, O., Rojas-Contreras, C., & Kessous, A. (2023). *A Study Around the Effect of Influencer Endorsement on Sustainable Luxury Brand Charisma*. https://hal.science/hal-04207997/%0Ahttps://hal.science/hal-04207997/document

Lamba, H. (2021). Deglobalization: Review and research future agenda using PAMO framework. In J. Paul and S. Dhir (Eds.), Globalization, deglobalization, and new paradigms in business. doi:10.1007/978-3-030-81584-4_1

Lamberton, C., & Stephen, A. T. (2016). A thematic exploration of digital, social media, and mobile marketing: Research evolution from 2000 to 2015 and an agenda for future inquiry. *Journal of Marketing*, *80*(6), 146–172. doi:10.1509/jm.15.0415

Lang, J. (2017). *Three uses for blockchain in banking*. IBM.

Lanier, J. (2013). How Should We Think about Privacy? *Scientific American*, *309*(5), 64–71. doi:10.1038/scientificamerican1113-64 PMID:24283017

Lanzolla, G., Pesce, D., & Tucci, C. L. (2021). The digital transformation of search and recombination in the innovation function: Tensions and an integrative framework. *Journal of Product Innovation Management*, *38*(1), 90–113. doi:10.1111/jpim.12546

Lara. (2022). www.aging-us.com

LaValle, S., Lesser, E., Shockley, R., Hopkins, M. S., & Kruschwitz, N. (2011). Big data, analytics and the path from insights to value. *MIT Sloan Management Review*, *52*(2), 21.

Lazarsfeld, P. F., & Menzel, H. (1963). Mass media and personal influence. In *The Science of Human Communications*. Basic Books.

Lee, J. A., & Eastin, M. S. (2021). Perceived authenticity of social media influencers: Scale development and validation. *Journal of Research in Interactive Marketing*, *15*(4), 822–841. doi:10.1108/JRIM-12-2020-0253

Lee, J. D., & See, K. A. (2004). Trust in automation: Designing for appropriate reliance. *Human Factors*, *46*(1), 50–80. doi:10.1518/hfes.46.1.50.30392 PMID:15151155

Lee, J., Kim, J., & Kim, S. (2021). A comparison and interpretation of machine learning algorithm for the prediction of online purchase conversion. *Journal of Theoretical and Applied Electronic Commerce Research*, *16*(5), 1472–1491. doi:10.3390/jtaer16050083

Leng, J., Zhong, Y., Lin, Z., Xu, K., Mourtzis, D., Zhou, X., Zheng, P., Liu, Q., Zhao, J. L., & Shen, W. (2023). Towards resilience in Industry 5.0: A decentralized autonomous manufacturing paradigm. *Journal of Manufacturing Systems*, *71*, 95–114. doi:10.1016/j.jmsy.2023.08.023

Lenk, L. T., & Rotkirch, I. (2021). *Green Millennials?* Academic Press.

Levine, E. E., & Schweitzer, M. E. (2015). Prosocial lies: When deception breeds trust. *Organizational Behavior and Human Decision Processes*, *126*, 88–106. doi:10.1016/j.obhdp.2014.10.007

Lim, W. M., Kumar, S., & Ali, F. (2022). Advancing knowledge through literature reviews:'what','why', and 'how to contribute'. *Service Industries Journal*, *42*(7-8), 481–513. doi:10.1080/02642069.2022.2047941

Liu, Gailhofer, Gensch, Köhler, Wolff, Monteforte, Urrutia, Cihlarova, & Williams. (2019). *Impacts of the digital transformation on the environment and sustainability*. Issue Paper under Task 3.

Loonam, J., Eaves, S., Kumar, V., & Parry, G. (2018). Towards digital transformation: Lessons learned from traditional organizations. *Strategic Change*, *27*(2), 101–109. doi:10.1002/jsc.2185

López-Aguilar, P., Batista, E., Martínez-Ballesté, A., & Solanas, A. (2022). Information Security and Privacy in Railway Transportation: A Systematic Review. *Sensors (Basel)*, *22*(20), 1–25. doi:10.3390/s22207698 PMID:36298049

Lubinski, C., & Wadhwani, R. D. (2020). Geopolitical jockeying: Economic nationalism and multinational strategy in historical perspective. *Strategic Management Journal*, *41*(3), 400–421. doi:10.1002/smj.3022

Lu, J., Cairns, L., & Smith, L. (2021). Data science in the business environment: Customer analytics case studies in SMEs. *Journal of Modelling in Management*, *16*(2), 689–713. doi:10.1108/JM2-11-2019-0274

Lusch, R. F., & Nambisan, S. (2015). Service innovation. *Management Information Systems Quarterly*, *39*(1), 155–176. doi:10.25300/MISQ/2015/39.1.07

Lu, Y., Yao, J. E., & Yu, C. S. (2005). Personal innovativeness, social influences and adoption of wireless Internet services via mobile technology. *The Journal of Strategic Information Systems*, *14*(3), 245–268. doi:10.1016/j.jsis.2005.07.003

Mabey, C., & Zhao, S. (2017). Managing five paradoxes of knowledge exchange in networked organizations: New priorities for HRM? *Human Resource Management Journal*, *27*(1), 39–57. doi:10.1111/1748-8583.12106

Mabkhot, H., Isa, N. M., & Mabkhot, A. (2022). The Influence of the Credibility of Social Media Influencers SMIs on the Consumers' Purchase Intentions: Evidence from Saudi Arabia. *Sustainability (Basel)*, *14*(19), 12323. Advance online publication. doi:10.3390/su141912323

Macknight, J. (2022, April 11). *Is this the beginning of a deglobalisation trend?* Retrieved January 2024, from TheBanker.com: https://www.thebanker.com/Is-this-the-beginning-of-a-deglobalisation-trend-1649681217

Magill, E. (2015). *Harnessing the Power of Customer Analytics at IBM Amplify 2015*. IBM Watson Customer Engagement. Retrieved January 2, 2019 from https://www.ibm.com/blogs/watson-customer-engagement/2015/05/01/harnessing-the-power-of-customer-analytics-at-ibm-amplify-2015/)

Magill, E. (2016). *The Customer Analytics Evolution: A Path to Cognitive*. IBM Watson Customer Engagement. Retrieved January 14, 2019 from https://www.ibm.com/blogs/watson-customer-engagement/2016/06/17/the-customer-analytics-evolution-a-path-to-cognitive/)

Magni, M., Angst, C. M., & Agarwal, R. (2012). Everybody needs somebody: The influence of team network structure on information technology use. *Journal of Management Information Systems*, *29*(3), 9–42. doi:10.2753/MIS0742-1222290301

Majstorović, V. D., Velimirović, M., Glišić, M., Kostić, J., Đura, E., Rančić, M., & Mitrović, R. (2018). Cyber-physical manufacturing in context of industry 4.0 model. In *Proceedings of 3rd International Conference on the Industry 4.0 Model for Advanced Manufacturing*. AMP.

Majstorović, M. N., & Terzić, R. M. (2018). Enterprise architecture as an approach to the development of information systems. *Vojnotehničkiglasnik*, *66*(2), 380–398. doi:10.5937/vojtehg66-15850

Mamoshina, P., Ojomoko, L., Yanovich, Y., Ostrovski, A., Botezatu, A., Prikhodko, P., Izumchenko, E., Aliper, A., Romantsov, K., Zhebrak, A., Ogu, I. O., & Zhavoronkov, A. (2018). Converging blockchain and next-generation artificial intelligence technologies to decentralize and accelerate biomedical research and healthcare. *Oncotarget*, *9*(5), 5665–5690. doi:10.18632/oncotarget.22345 PMID:29464026

Manfredi-Sánchez, J. (2021). Deglobalization and public diplomacy. *International Journal of Communication*, *15*, 905–926. https://ijoc.org/index.php

Mangold, W. G., & Faulds, D. J. (2009). Social media: The new hybrid element of the promotion mix. *Business Horizons*, *52*(4), 357–365. doi:10.1016/j.bushor.2009.03.002

Manning, L., Brewer, S., Craigon, P. J., Frey, J., Gutierrez, A., Jacobs, N., Kanza, S., Munday, S., Sacks, J., & Pearson, S. (2022). Artificial intelligence and ethics within the food sector: Developing a common language for technology adoption across the supply chain. *Trends in Food Science & Technology*, *125*, 33–42. doi:10.1016/j.tifs.2022.04.025

Manohar, S., Mittal, A., & Marwah, S. (2020). Service innovation, corporate reputation and word-of-mouth in the banking sector: A test on multigroup-moderated mediation effect. *Benchmarking*, *27*(1), 406–429. doi:10.1108/BIJ-05-2019-0217

Marín-García, A., Gil-Saura, I., & Ruiz-Molina, M. E. (2022). Do innovation and sustainability influence customer satisfaction in retail? A question of gender. *Ekonomska Istrazivanja*, *35*(1), 546–563. doi:10.1080/1331677X.2021.1924217

Marjanović, D., & Domazet, I. (2021). Foreign Direct Investments: A Key Factor for Business Globalization. In Y. Bayar (Ed.), *Institutional, Economic, and Social Impacts of Globalization and Liberalization* (pp. 96–116). IGI Global. doi:10.4018/978-1-7998-4459-4.ch006

Marjanović, D., & Domazet, I. (2023). Economic Measures for Mitigation of the Consequences of COVID-19: Evidence From Serbia. In B. Marco-Lajara, A. C. Özer, & J. M. Falcó (Eds.), *The Transformation of Global Trade in a New World* (pp. 180–199). IGI Global.

Marjanović, D., Domazet, I., & Vukmirović, I. (2022). Social Environment as a Factor of Capital Investment in Serbia. *Eastern European Economics*, *60*(3), 247–264. Advance online publication. doi:10.1080/00128775.2022.2048181

Martinez, V., Zhao, M., Blujdea, C., Han, X., Neely, A., & Albores, P. (2019). Blockchain-driven customer order management. *International Journal of Operations and Production Management, 39*(6/7/8), 993–1022. doi:10.1108/IJOPM-01-2019-0100

Martino, P. (2019). Blockchain technology: Challenges and opportunities for banks. *International Journal of Financial Innovation in Banking*, *2*(4), 314–333. doi:10.1504/IJFIB.2019.104535

Maruping, L. M., & Magni, M. (2012). What's the weather like? The effect of team learning climate, empowerment climate, and gender on individuals' technology exploration and use. *Journal of Management Information Systems*, *29*(1), 79–114. doi:10.2753/MIS0742-1222290103

Maslowska, E., Malthouse, E. C., & Collinger, T. (2016). The customer engagement ecosystem. *Journal of Marketing Management*, *32*(5-6), 469–501. doi:10.1080/0267257X.2015.1134628

Matt, C., Hess, T., & Benlian, A. (2015). Digital Transformation Strategies. *Business & Information Systems Engineering*, *57*(5), 339–343. doi:10.1007/s12599-015-0401-5

Mayer-Schönberger, V. (2009). Can we reinvent the internet? *Science*, *325*(5939), 396–397.

McAfee, A., & Brynjofsson, E. (2012). Big data: The management revolution. *Harvard Business Review*, (October), 60–68. PMID:23074865

McElheran, K. (2018). *Economic Measurement of AI.* Presented at the NBER Economics of AI Conference, Toronto, Canada.

McKeen, J. D., & Smith, H. A. (2015). IT strategy: Issues and practices. Pearson Higher Ed.

McKinsey & Company. (2022, May 2). *State of Fashion Technology Report 2022.* https://www.mckinsey.com/industries/retail/our-insights/state-of-fashion-technology-report-2022

McKinsey & Company. (2023). *The state of AI in 2023: Generative AI's breakout year.* Available at: https://www.mckinsey.com/capabilities/quantumblack/our-insights/the-state-of-ai-in-2023-generative-ais-breakout-year

McMahan, H. B., Moore, E., Ramage, D., Hampson, S., & Arcas, B. A. (2017). Communication-efficient learning of deep networks from decentralized data. In Artificial Intelligence and Statistics (pp. 1273–1282). Academic Press.

Medvecka, J., Rad, R., Medvecka, J., & Rad, R. (2023). *B2C sustainability communication Exploring millennials' perceptions of and attitudes towards luxury fashion brands' sustainability communication on Instagram.* Academic Press.

Meersman, M. W. (2019). *Developing a Cloud Computing Risk Assessment Instrument for Small to Medium Sized Enterprises: A Qualitative Case Study Using a Delphi Technique.* http://resolver.ebscohost.com/openurl?ctx_ver=Z39.88-2004&ctx_enc=info:ofi/enc:UTF-8&rfr_id=info:sid/ProQuest+Dissertations+%26+Theses+Global&rft_val_fmt

Mell, P., & Grance, T. (2011). The NIST-National Institute of Standards and Technology- Definition of Cloud Computing. *NIST Special Publication 800-145*, 1–3.

Methlagl, M. (2022). Mapping inclusive education 1980 to 2019: A bibliometric analysis of thematic clusters and research directions. *Issues in Educational Research*, *32*(1), 225–247.

MicroSave. (2022, Sept). Retrieved 2023, from microsave.net: https://www.microsave.net/library/

Miles, C. (2017, December). *Blockchain security: What keeps your transaction data safe.* IBM. https://www.ibm.com/blogs/blockchain/2017/12/blockchain-security-what-keeps-yourtransaction-data-safe/

Mim, K. B., Jai, T., & Lee, S. H. (2022). The Influence of Sustainable Positioning on eWOM and Brand Loyalty: Analysis of Credible Sources and Transparency Practices Based on the S-O-R Model. *Sustainability (Basel)*, *14*(19), 12461. Advance online publication. doi:10.3390/su141912461

Min, H. (2019, January 1). Blockchain technology for enhancing supply chain resilience. *Business Horizons*, *62*(1), 35–45. doi:10.1016/j.bushor.2018.08.012

Mitchell, A. (2023). Collaboration technology affordances from virtual collaboration in the time of COVID-19 and post-pandemic strategies. *Information Technology & People*, *36*(5), 1982–2008. doi:10.1108/ITP-01-2021-0003

Mitchell, J. C. (1969). *Social networks in urban situations: Analyses of personal relationships in Central African towns.* Manchester University Press.

Mithas, S., Lee, M. R., Earley, S., Murugesan, S., & Djavanshir, R. (2013). Leveraging big data and business analytics. *IT Professional*, *15*(6), 18–20. doi:10.1109/MITP.2013.95

Mockshell, J., & Ritter, T. (2022). Was a government policy able to smooth a fractured agri-food value chain during a COVID-19 lockdown? *Journal of Agribusiness in Developing and Emerging Economies*, *12*(1), 1–161.

Moenninghoff, S. C., & Wieandt, A. (2013). The future of peer-to-peer finance. *Schmalenbachs Zeitschrift fur Betriebswirtschaftliche Forschung = Schmalenbach Journal of Business Research*, *65*(5), 466–487. doi:10.1007/BF03372882

MohanaKrishnan, M., Kumar, A. S., Talukdar, V., Saleh, O. S., Irawati, I. D., Latip, R., & Kaur, G. (2023). Artificial Intelligence in Cyber Security. In Handbook of Research on Deep Learning Techniques for Cloud-Based Industrial IoT (pp. 366-385). IGI Global.

Monroy, I. B. (2023). *Immobilized or petrified? Explaining privacy concerns and the (de) mobilization against mass online surveillance in 21st-century advanced democracies* [PhD thesis].

Morris, A. K. (2006). Assessing pre-service teachers' skills for analyzing teaching. *Journal of Mathematics Teacher Education*, *9*(5), 471–505. doi:10.1007/s10857-006-9015-7

Muhammad, T., Munir, M. T., Munir, M. Z., & Zafar, M. W. (2022). Integrative Cybersecurity: Merging Zero Trust, Layered Defense, and Global Standards for a Resilient Digital Future. *International Journal of Computer Science and Technology*, *6*(4), 99–135. https://ijcst.com.pk/IJCST/article/view/274

Mupila, F. (2023). *Securing the Cloud: An In-depth Exploration of Conceptual Models, Emerging Trends, and Forward-looking Insights*. Academic Press.

Murphy, C. (2021). *The Impact of Influencer Marketing on Fast Fashion Purchase Intentions from an Irish Female Millennial's Perspective*. https://norma.ncirl.ie/id/eprint/5473%0Ahttps://norma.ncirl.ie/5473/1/carlamurphy.pdf

Murray, A., Kuban, S., Josefy, M., & Anderson, J. (2021). Contracting in the smart era: The implications of blockchain and decentralized autonomous organizations for contracting and corporate governance. *The Academy of Management Perspectives*, *35*(4), 622–641. doi:10.5465/amp.2018.0066

Mutum, D. S., & Ghazali, E. M. (2023). Consumers. *Society and Marketing*, (November). Advance online publication. doi:10.1007/978-3-031-39359-4

Nakamoto, S., & Bitcoin, A. (2008). *A peer-to-peer electronic cash system*. Bitcoin.

Nambisan, S., Wright, M., & Feldman, M. (2019). The digital transformation of innovation and entrepreneurship: Progress, challenges and key themes. *Research Policy*, *48*(8), 103773. doi:10.1016/j.respol.2019.03.018

Narayanan, A., Bonneau, J., Felten, E., Miller, A., & Goldfeder, S. (2016). *Bitcoin and Cryptocurrency Technologies: A Comprehensive Introduction*. Princeton University Press.

Narsimhulu, K., Santhosh Ramchander, N., & Swathi, A. (2022). An AI Enabled Framework with Feature Selection for Efficient Heart Disease Prediction. In *2022 5th International Conference on Contemporary Computing and Informatics (IC3I)* (pp. 1468-1473). IEEE. 10.1109/IC3I56241.2022.10073155

Nassar, A. (2021). *Machine Learning and Big Data Analytics for Cybersecurity Threat Detection: A Holistic Review of Techniques and Case Studies*. Academic Press.

Nguyen, D. C., Ding, M., Pathirana, P. N., & Seneviratne, A. (2021). Blockchain and AI-based solutions to combat coronavirus (COVID-19)-like epidemics: A survey. *IEEE Access : Practical Innovations, Open Solutions*, *9*, 95730–95753. doi:10.1109/ACCESS.2021.3093633 PMID:34812398

Nguyen, N., & Johnson, L. W. (2020). Consumer behaviour and environmental sustainability. *Journal of Consumer Behaviour*, *19*(6), 539–541. doi:10.1002/cb.1892

Niranjanamurthy, M., Nithya, B. N., & Jagannatha, S. J. C. C. (2019). Analysis of Blockchain technology: Pros, cons and SWOT. *Cluster Computing*, *22*(S6), 14743–14757. doi:10.1007/s10586-018-2387-5

Nofer, M., Gomber, P., Hinz, O., & Schiereck, D. (2017). Blockchain. *Business & Information Systems Engineering*, *59*(3), 183–187. doi:10.1007/s12599-017-0467-3

Nurmilahti, A. (2016). *Risks in cloud computing*. http://www.doria.fi/bitstream/handle/10024/130542/TSEgradu2016Nurmilahti.pdf%0Ahttps://utu.finna.fi/Record/volter.1856031

O'Hara, K. (2022). Digital Modernity. *Foundations and Trends® in Web Science*, *9*(1–2), 1-254.

Oberoi, S., & Kansra, P. (2022). Blockchain Technology in the Insurance Industry. In Applications, Challenges, and Opportunities of Blockchain Technology in Banking and Insurance. doi:10.4018/978-1-6684-4133-6.ch009

Oberoi, S., & Kansra, P. (2021). *Motivating Antecedents and Consequences of Blockchain Technology in the Insurance Industry*. Blockchain Technology and Applications for Digital Marketing. doi:10.4018/978-1-7998-8081-3.ch017

Ochella, S., Shafiee, M., & Dinmohammadi, F. (2022). Artificial intelligence in prognostics and health management of engineering systems. *Engineering Applications of Artificial Intelligence*, *108*, 104552. doi:10.1016/j.engappai.2021.104552

Olaleye, S., Ukpabi, D., Karjaluoto, H., & Rizomyliotis, I. (2019). Understanding technology diffusion in emerging markets: The case of Chinese mobile devices in Nigeria. *International Journal of Emerging Markets*, *14*(5), 731–751. doi:10.1108/IJOEM-01-2018-0055

Ølnes, S., Ubacht, J., & Janssen, M. (2017). Blockchain in government: Benefits and implications of distributed ledger technology for information sharing. *Government Information Quarterly*, *34*(3), 355–364. doi:10.1016/j.giq.2017.09.007

Ottman, J. A. (2017). *The New Rules of Green marketing*. The New Rules of Green Marketing., doi:10.4324/9781351278683

Ozuem, W., Willis, M., Howell, K., Lancaster, G., & Ng, R. (2021). Determinants of online brand communities' and millennials' characteristics: A social influence perspective. *Psychology and Marketing*, *38*(5), 794–818. doi:10.1002/mar.21470

Paliwal, V., Chandra, S., & Sharma, S. (2020, January). Blockchain technology for sustainable supply chain management: A systematic literature review and a classification framework. *Sustainability (Basel)*, *12*(18), 7638. doi:10.3390/su12187638

Panigrahi, C. M. A., Sinha, A., Garg, A., & Mehta, A. (2019). A case study on the downfall of kingfisher airlines. *Journal of Management Research and Analysis*, *6*(2), 81–84. doi:10.18231/j.jmra.2019.014

Panopoulos, A., Poulis, A., Theodoridis, P., & Kalampakas, A. (2023). Influencing Green Purchase Intention through Eco Labels and User-Generated Content. *Sustainability (Basel)*, *15*(1), 764. Advance online publication. doi:10.3390/su15010764

Pappas, I. O., Mikalef, P., Dwivedi, Y., Jaccheri, L., Krogstie, J., & Mäntymäki, M. (2019). *Digital transformation for a sustainable society in the 21st century*. Springer International Publishing. doi:10.1007/978-3-030-29374-1

Parasuraman, A. (2000). Technology readiness index (TRI) a multiple-item scale to measure readiness to embrace new technologies. *Journal of Service Research*, *2*(4), 307–320. doi:10.1177/109467050024001

Parker, G. G., Van Alstyne, M. W., & Choudary, S. P. (2016). *Platform Revolution: How Networked Markets Are Transforming the Economy and How to Make Them Work for You*. W. W. Norton & Company.

Pasquale, F. (2015). *The black box society: The secret algorithms that control money and information*. Harvard University Press. doi:10.4159/harvard.9780674736061

Pattuglia. (2018). Towards a new understanding of brand authenticity: Seeing through the lens of millennials. *Sinergie Italian Journal of Management*, *103*(103), 35–55. doi:10.7433/s103.2017.03

Paul, P., Aithal, P. S., Saavedra, R., & Ghosh, S. (2021). Blockchain Technology and its Types—A Short Review. *International Journal of Applied Science and Engineering*, *9*(2), 189–200. doi:10.30954/2322-0465.2.2021.7

Pavlou, P. A. (2018). Internet of things–will humans be replaced or augmented? *NIM Marketing Intelligence Review*, *10*(2), 42–47. doi:10.2478/gfkmir-2018-0017

Pavlov, I. (1927a). *Conditioned Reflexes*. Oxford University Press.

Pavlov, I. P. (1927b). *Conditioned reflexes: An investigation of the physiological activity of the cerebral cortex*. Oxford University Press.

Perez, S. (2022). *The rise of generative AI in the business sector*. TechCrunch.

Perlroth, N. (2021). *This is how they tell me the world ends: The cyberweapons arms race*. Bloomsbury Publishing USA.

Perraton, C., & Creed, F. (2002). *Computers as tutors: solving the crisis in education*. http://www.cris.com/faben1/html

Peter, M. K., & Dalla Vecchia, M. (2021). The digital marketing toolkit: A literature review for the identification of digital marketing channels and platforms. New Trends in Business Information Systems and Technology, 251-265.

Pilkington, M. (2016). Blockchain technology: Principles and applications. In Research Handbook on Digital Transformations. Academic Press.

Poduyeva, O. N., & Nechushkina, E. A. (2022). Digital transformation as a tool of globalization. *Trade, Service, Food Industry, 2*(4), 362-370.

Polčák, R., & Svantesson, D. J. B. (2017). *Information sovereignty: data privacy, sovereign powers and the rule of law*. Edward Elgar Publishing.

Porter, C. E., & Donthu, N. (2006, September 1). Using the technology acceptance model to explain how attitudes determine Internet usage: The role of perceived access barriers and demographics. *Journal of Business Research*, *59*(9), 999–1007. doi:10.1016/j.jbusres.2006.06.003

Powell, W. (2022). *China, Trust and Digital Supply Chains: Dynamics of a Zero Trust World.* Taylor & Francis.

Preskill, J. (2018). Quantum computing in the NISQ era and beyond. *Quantum : the Open Journal for Quantum Science*, *2*, 79. doi:10.22331/q-2018-08-06-79

Press, C. R. C., Group, F., & Raton, B. (2010). *Cloud Computing: Implementation, Management, and Security*. Academic Press.

Przybylski, A. K., Murayama, K., DeHaan, C. R., & Gladwell, V. (2013). Motivational, emotional, and behavioral correlates of fear of missing out. *Computers in Human Behavior*, *29*(4), 1841–1848. doi:10.1016/j.chb.2013.02.014

Purkayastha, S. (n.d.). *Eight Blockchain platforms for rapid prototyping*. https://radiostud.io/eight-blockchain-platforms-comparison/

Qadri, Y. A., Nauman, A., Zikria, Y. B., Vasilakos, A. V., & Kim, S. W. (2020). The future of healthcare internet of things: A survey of emerging technologies. *IEEE Communications Surveys and Tutorials*, *22*(2), 1121–1167. doi:10.1109/COMST.2020.2973314

Queiroz, M. M., & Fosso Wamba, S. F. (2019, June 1). Blockchain adoption challenges in supply chain: An empirical investigation of the main drivers in India and the USA. *International Journal of Information Management*, *46*, 70–82. doi:10.1016/j.ijinfomgt.2018.11.021

Queiroz, M. M., Fosso Wamba, S., Machado, M. C., & Telles, R. (2020). Smart production systems drivers for business process management improvement: An integrative framework. *Business Process Management Journal*, *26*(5), 1075–1092. doi:10.1108/BPMJ-03-2019-0134

Queiroz, M. M., Telles, R., & Bonilla, S. H. (2019). Blockchain and supply chain management integration: A systematic review of the literature. *Supply Chain Management*, *25*(2), 241–254. doi:10.1108/SCM-03-2018-0143

Rady, M., Abdelkader, T., & Ismail, R. (2019). Integrity and Confidentiality in Cloud Outsourced Data. *Ain Shams Engineering Journal*, *10*(2), 275–285. doi:10.1016/j.asej.2019.03.002

Rahmanzadeh, S., Pishvaee, M. S., & Govindan, K. (2022). Emergence of open supply chain management: The role of open innovation in the future smart industry using digital twin network. *Annals of Operations Research*. Advance online publication. doi:10.1007/s10479-021-04254-2

Rainie, H., & Wellman, B. (2012). *Networked: The new social operating system 10*. Mit Press. doi:10.7551/mit-press/8358.001.0001

Ransbotham, S., & Kiron, D. (2018). Using Analytics to Improve Customer Engagement. *MIT Sloan Management Review*, 1–20.

Rathore, B. (2018). Allure of Style: The Impact of Contemporary Fashion Marketing on Consumer Behaviour. *International Journal of New Media Studies*, *05*(02), 10–21. doi:10.58972/eiprmj.v5i2y18.114

Rauch, E., Rofner, M., Cappellini, C., & Matt, D. T. (2022). Towards Sustainable Manufacturing: A Case Study for Sustainable Packaging Redesign. Design, Simulation, Manufacturing: The Innovation Exchange, 84–93.

RBI. (2022-23). *Trend and Progress of Banking in India*. New Delhi: RBI.

Reenu Kumari, A. S. (2023). The Transformation of Global Trade in a New World: Deglobalization and Its Risk in International Trade Post COVID-19. In The Transformation of Global Trade in a New World. IGI.

Reyna, A., Martín, C., Chen, J., Soler, E., & Díaz, M. (2018, November 1). On blockchain and its integration with IoT. Challenges and opportunities. *Future Generation Computer Systems*, *88*, 173–190. doi:10.1016/j.future.2018.05.046

Rieger, A., Roth, T., Sedlmeir, J., & Fridgen, G. (2022). We need a broader debate on the sustainability of blockchain. *Joule*, *6*(6), 1137–1141. doi:10.1016/j.joule.2022.04.013

Rijanto, A. (2021). Blockchain Technology Adoption in Supply Chain Finance. *Journal of Theoretical and Applied Electronic Commerce Research*, *16*(7), 3078–3098. doi:10.3390/jtaer16070168

Rio & Banker. (2014). *IoT Changes Logistics for the OEM Spare Parts Supply Chain*. ARC Insights, ARC Advisory Group.

Risitano, M., Romano, R., Rusciano, V., Civero, G., & Scarpato, D. (2022). The impact of sustainability on marketing strategy and business performance: The case of Italian fisheries. *Business Strategy and the Environment*, *31*(4), 1538–1551. doi:10.1002/bse.2968

Ristenpart, T., Tromer, E., Shacham, H., & Savage, S. (2009). Hey, you, get off of my cloud: Exploring information leakage in third-party compute clouds. *Proceedings of the ACM Conference on Computer and Communications Security*, 199–212. 10.1145/1653662.1653687

Roeck, D., Sternberg, H., & Hofmann, E. (2020). Distributed ledger technology in supply chains: A transaction cost perspective. *International Journal of Production Research*, *58*(7), 2124–2141. doi:10.1080/00207543.2019.1657247

Rogers, E. M. (1962). *Diffusion of innovations*. Free Press.

Romanosky, S. (2016). Examining the costs and causes of cyber incidents. *Journal of Cybersecurity*, *2*(2), 121–135. doi:10.1093/cybsec/tyw001

Romanova, O. A., & Kuzmin, E. (2021). Industrial policy: A new reality in the context of digital transformation of the economy. *Digital Transformation in Industry*, 13-23.

Rosli, N., Ha, N. C., & Ghazali, E. M. (2019). Bridging the gap between branding and sustainability by fostering brand credibility and brand attachment in travellers' hotel choice. *The Bottom Line (New York, N.Y.)*, *32*(4), 308–339. doi:10.1108/BL-03-2019-0078

Ross, J. W., Beath, C. M., & Quaadgras, A. (2013). You may not need big data after all. *Harvard Business Review*, *91*(12), 90–98.

Roy, K., & Swargiary, K. (2023). ICT in Education Implementation in India: Advancements and Oppurtunities. *Dogo Rangsang Research Journal*, *13*(5), 91–96.

Russell, S. J. (2010). *Artificial intelligence is a modern approach*. Pearson Education, Inc.

Russell, S., & Norvig, P. (2020). *Artificial Intelligence: A Modern Approach* (4th ed.). Pearson.

Russia, B. o. (2018). Globalisation and deglobalisation. *BIS Papers*, (100), 291–310.

Saberi, S., Kouhizadeh, M., Sarkis, J., & Shen, L. (2019). Blockchain technology and its relationships to sustainable supply chain management. *International Journal of Production Research*, *57*(7), 2117–2135. doi:10.1080/00207543.2018.1533261

Sætra, H. S. (2019). The Ghost in the machine. *Human Arenas*, *2*(1), 60–78. doi:10.1007/s42087-018-0039-1

Sætra, H. S. (2020). The parasitic nature of social AI: Sharing minds with the mindless. *Integrative Psychological & Behavioral Science*, *54*(2), 308–322. doi:10.1007/s12124-020-09523-6 PMID:32185700

Sætra, H. S. (2021). Robotomorphy: Becoming our creations. *AI and Ethics*. Advance online publication. doi:10.1007/s43681-021-00092-x

Sætra, H. S. (2023). Generative AI: Here to stay, but for good? *Technology in Society*, *75*, 102372. doi:10.1016/j.techsoc.2023.102372

Sahadev, S., Muralidharan, S., & Singh, P. (2022). Introduction to the special issue on marketing communications and sustainability. *Journal of Marketing Communications*, *28*(3), 227–231. doi:10.1080/13527266.2021.1942145

Sahin, I. (2006). Detailed review of Rogers' diffusion of innovations theory and educational technology-related studies based on Rogers' theory. *The Turkish Online Journal of Educational Technology*, *5*(2), 14–23.

Said, F. (2022). *Embracing technology, preserving data sovereignty*. Institute of Strategic and International Studies.

Sakshi, U., Tandon, U., Ertz, M., & Bansal, H. (2020). Social vacation: Proposition of a model to understand tourists' usage of social media for travel planning. *Technology in Society*, *63*, 10143. doi:10.1016/j.techsoc.2020.101438 PMID:33100435

Santos, C. (2020). *How Medium, arXiv, and Github Are Disrupting the Dissemination of AI Knowledge*. Towards Data Science.

Saranya, N., Sakthivadivel, M., Karthikeyan, G., & Rajkumar, R. (2023). Securing the Cloud: An Empirical Study on Best Practices for Ensuring Data Privacy and Protection. *International Journal of Engineering and Management Research*, *13*(2), 46–49. https://ijemr.vandanapublications.com/index.php/ijemr/article/view/1142

Sarker, S., Valacich, J. S., & Sarker, S. (2005). Technology adoption by groups: A valence perspective. *Journal of the Association for Information Systems*, *6*(2), 37–71. doi:10.17705/1jais.00064

Sarmah, S. S. (2018). Understanding blockchain technology. *Computing in Science & Engineering*, *8*(2), 23–29.

Sasikumar, S., Sundar, K., Jayakumar, C., Obaidat, M. S., Stephan, T., & Hsiao, K. F. (2022). Modeling and simulation of a novel secure quantum key distribution (SQKD) for ensuring data security in cloud environment. *Simulation Modelling Practice and Theory*, *121*(August), 102651. doi:10.1016/j.simpat.2022.102651

Scherer, M. U. (2020). Regulating Artificial Intelligence Systems: Risks, Challenges, Competencies, and Strategies. *Harvard Journal of Law & Technology*, *29*(2), 353–398.

Schilirò, D. (2020). Towards digital globalization and the covid-19 challenge. *International Journal of Business Management and Economic Research*, *2*(11), 1710–1716.

Schlagwein, D., & Willcocks, L. (2023). 'ChatGPT et al.': The ethics of using (generative) artificial intelligence in research and science. *Journal of Information Technology*, *38*(3), 232–238. doi:10.1177/02683962231200411

Schneier, B. (2015). *Data and Goliath: The hidden battles to collect your data and control your world.* WW Norton & Company.

Schwartz, P. M., & Peifer, K. N. (2017). Transatlantic data privacy law. *Geological Journal*, *106*, 115.

Schwens, C., Zapkau, F. B., Bierwerth, M., Isidor, R., Knight, G., & Kabst, R. (2018). International entrepreneurship: A meta–analysis on the internationalization and performance relationship. *Entrepreneurship Theory and Practice*, *42*(5), 734–768. doi:10.1177/1042258718795346

Scott, T., & IBM. (n.d.). https://www.ibm.com/blogs/think/2018/11/tradelens-how-ibm-and-maersk-are-sharing-blockchain-to-build-a-global-trade-platform/

Sebastian, I., Ross, J., Beath, C., Mocker, M., Moloney, K., & Fonstad, N. (2017). How big old companies navigate digital transformation. *MIS Quarterly Executive*, *16*(3), 197–213.

Sen, S., & Bhattacharya, C. B. (2001). Does doing good always lead to doing better? Consumer reactions to corporate social responsibility. *JMR, Journal of Marketing Research*, *38*(2), 225–243. doi:10.1509/jmkr.38.2.225.18838

Shah & Department of Health. (n.d.). *Unblocking the retail supply chain with blockchain.* https://www.tcs.com/content/dam/tcs/pdf/Industries/Retaillogistics/Abstract/Unblocking-retail-supply-chain-with-blockchain-1017-1.pdfRetrieved

Shaikh, M. (2021). Women Empowerment Through Self Help Groups: A Review. In Entrepreneurial Ecosystem in Higher Education (pp. 70). Academic Press.

Shankar, V., Grewal, D., Sunder, S., Fossen, B., Peters, K., & Agarwal, A. (2021). Digital marketing communication in global marketplaces: A review of extant research, future directions, and potential approaches. *International Journal of Research in Marketing*, *39*(2), 541–565. doi:10.1016/j.ijresmar.2021.09.005

Sharma, R., Mehta, K., Sidhu, N. K., & Vyas, V. (2023). Extending UTAUT2 Model With Sustainability and Psychological Factors in Adoption of Blockchain Technology for the Digital Transformation of Banks in India. In Revolutionizing Financial Services and Markets Through FinTech and Blockchain (pp. 27-43). IGI Global. doi:10.4018/978-1-6684-8624-5.ch003

Sharma, M. G. (2021). Supply chain, geographical indicator and blockchain: Provenance model for commodity. *International Journal of Productivity and Performance Management*, *72*(1), 92–108. doi:10.1108/IJPPM-05-2021-0288

Sharma, P. (2023). Futuristic Trends in Higher Education: Role of ICT and E-Learning. *European Chemical Bulletin.*

Sharma, S. K., & Shukla, A. (2017). Impact of electronic word on mouth on consumer behaviour and brand image. *Asian Journal of Management*, *8*(3), 501–506. doi:10.5958/2321-5763.2017.00081.6

Sharma, T. K. (2017). *List of best open source blockchain platform.* Blockchain Council.

Shaw, D. (2021). Voluntary simplicity. *The Routledge Companion to Alternative Organization, 19*(February), 234–243. doi:10.4324/9780203725351-24

Shrivas, M. K., & Yeboah, T. (2019). The disruptive blockchain: Types, platforms and applications. *Texila International Journal of Academic Research, 3*, 17–39. doi:10.21522/TIJAR.2014.SE.19.01.Art003

Shukla, A., & Mishra, A. (2022). *Role of review length, review valence and review credibility on consumer's online hotel booking intention*. FIIB Business Review.

Sia, C. L., Tan, B. C. Y., & Wei, K. K. (2002). Group polarization and computer-mediated communication: Effects of communication cues, social presence, and anonymity. *Information Systems Research, 13*(1), 70–90. doi:10.1287/isre.13.1.70.92

Sia, C. L., Teo, H. H., Tan, B. C. Y., & Wei, K. K. (2004). Effects of environmental uncertainty on organizational intention to adopt distributed work arrangements. *IEEE Transactions on Engineering Management, 51*(3), 253–267. doi:10.1109/TEM.2004.830859

Silva, Menon, Falco, & MacDonald. (2019). Structural adjustment, mass lay-offs and employment reallocation. *OECD Science, Technology and Industry Policy Papers*, 72.

SimilarWeb. (2023). *Website Analysis: Chat.openai.com*. Retrieved from https://pro.similarweb.com/#/digitalsuite/websiteanalysis/overview/website-performance/*/999/3m?webSource=Total&key=chat.openai.com

Simović, V., & Domazet, I. (2021). An overview of the frameworks for measuring the digital competencies of college students: A European perspective. In *Stagnancy Issues and Change Initiatives for Global Education in the Digital Age* (pp. 259–283). IGI Global. doi:10.4018/978-1-7998-4993-3.ch012

Singh, V., Dubey, A. & Sonkar, C. (2022). Role of Information and Communication Technologies (ICT) in Education Sector in India. *International Journal of Creative research Thoughts, 10*(1), 131-149.

Singh, A., & Hess, T. (2017). How chief digital officers promote the digital transformation of their companies. *MIS Quarterly Executive, 16*(1), 1–17.

Singhal, J., & Chauhan, V. (2021). Analytical study of PMC (Punjab & Maharashtra Co-operative bank) by considering financial failure of bank. *Globus-An International Journal of Management and IT, 12*(2), 6–10. doi:10.46360/globus.mgt.120211002

Singh, P. (2023). Systematic review of data-centric approaches in artificial intelligence and machine learning. *Data Science and Management, 6*(3), 144–157. doi:10.1016/j.dsm.2023.06.001

Siwach, G., Paul, S., & de Hoop, T. (2022). Economies of scale of large-scale international development interventions: Evidence from self-help groups in India. *World Development, 153*, 105839. doi:10.1016/j.worlddev.2022.105839 PMID:35506062

Smith, B. G., Kendall, M. C., Knighton, D., & Wright, T. (2018). Rise of the Brand Ambassador: Social Stake, Corporate Social Responsibility and Influence among the Social Media Influencers. *Communication Management Review, 03*(01), 6–29. doi:10.22522/cmr20180127

Sogari, G., Pucci, T., Aquilani, B., & Zanni, L. (2017). Millennial generation and environmental sustainability: The role of social media in the consumer purchasing behavior for wine. *Sustainability (Basel), 9*(10), 1911. Advance online publication. doi:10.3390/su9101911

Solaiman, I. (2023). Evaluating the Social Impact of Generative AI Systems in Systems and Society. *arXiv preprint arXiv:2306.05949v2*. Available at: https://arxiv.org/abs/2306.05949v2

Sood, K., Dhanaraj, R. K., Balusamy, B., Grima, S., & Maheshwari, R. U. (2022). *Big Data*. Emerald Group Publishing. Available: http://books.google.ie/books?id=d3B6EAAAQBAJ&printsec=frontcover&dq=Big+data:+A+game+changer+for+insurance+industry&hl=&cd=1&source=gbs_api

Sood, K., Kaur, B., & Grima, S. (2022). Revamping Indian non-life insurance industry with a trusted network: Blockchain technology. In *Big Data: A game changer for insurance industry* (pp. 213–228). Emerald Publishing Limited. doi:10.1108/978-1-80262-605-620221014

Sousa, M. J., & Rocha, A. (2019). Skills for disruptive digital business. *Journal of Business Research*, *94*, 257–263. doi:10.1016/j.jbusres.2017.12.051

SrinivasanR.ParikhD. (2021). Building Bridges: Generative Artworks to Explore AI Ethics. *Fujitsu Research of America & Georgia Tech and Facebook AI Research*. arXiv:2106.13901v1

Srinivasan, S., Vanhuele, M., & Pauwels, K. (2010). Mind-set metrics in market response models: An integrative approach. *JMR, Journal of Marketing Research*, *47*(4), 672–684. doi:10.1509/jmkr.47.4.672

Stahlhofer, N. J., Schmidkonz, C., & Kraft, P. (2018). Case Studies: Conscious Business in Germany. In CSR, Sustainability, Ethics and Governance. doi:10.1007/978-3-319-69739-0_4

Statista. (2021a). *Number of Instagram users worldwide from 2016 to 2021*. Retrieved from https://www.statista.com/statistics/253577/number-of-monthly-active-instagram-users/

Statista. (2021b). *Number of YouTube users worldwide from 2016 to 2021*. Retrieved from https://www.statista.com/statistics/805656/number-youtube-viewers-world/

Statista. (2023). *Leading chatbot/conversational AI startups worldwide in 2023, by funding raised*. Available at: https://www.statista.com/statistics/1359073/chatbot-and-conversational-ai-startup-funding-worldwide/

Steenstrup, K., & Kutnick, D. (2015). *The Internet of Things revolution: impact on operational technology ecosystems*. Available at: www.gartner.com/doc/3036118/Internet-thingsrevolution-impact-operational

Storey, V. C., & Song, I. Y. (2017). Big data technologies and Management: What conceptual modeling can do. *Data & Knowledge Engineering*, *108*, 50–67. doi:10.1016/j.datak.2017.01.001

Strassburg, B. B., Iribarrem, A., Beyer, H. L., Cordeiro, C. L., Crouzeilles, R., Jakovac, C. C., ... Visconti, P. (2020). Global priority areas for ecosystem restoration. *Nature*, *586*(7831), 724–729.

Stremersch, S., Verniers, I., & Verhoef, P. C. (2007). The quest for citations: Drivers of article impact. *Journal of Marketing*, *71*(3), 171–193. doi:10.1509/jmkg.71.3.171

Study, I. O. F. (2012). *The Role of Social Media in Crisis Management and the Impact on Brand Image*. Academic Press.

Sturgeon, T. J. (2021). Upgrading strategies for the digital economy. *Global Strategy Journal*, *11*(1), 34–57. doi:10.1002/gsj.1364

Subramaniam, M., & Piskorski, M. (2020). How Legacy Businesses Can Compete in the Sharing Economy. *MIT Sloan Management Review*, *61*(4), 31–37.

Subramanian, N., Chaudhuri, A., & Kayıkcı, Y. (2020, May 27). *Blockchain and supply chain logistics: Evolutionary case studies. Springer.* Nature Publishing.

Suetterlein, J., Manzano, J., Marquez, A., & Gao, G. R. (2022). Extending an asynchronous runtime system for high throughput applications: A case study. *Journal of Parallel and Distributed Computing*, *163*, 214–231. doi:10.1016/j.jpdc.2022.01.027

Suganthi, L. (2019). Examining the relationship between corporate social responsibility, performance, employees' pro-environmental behavior at work with green practices as mediator. *Journal of Cleaner Production*, *232*, 739–750. doi:10.1016/j.jclepro.2019.05.295

Sun, N., Morris, J. G., Xu, J., Zhu, H., & Xie, M. (2014). iCARE: A framework for big data-based banking customer analytics. *IBM Journal of Research and Development*, *58*(5/6), 4–1. doi:10.1147/JRD.2014.2337118

Surma, J. (2011). *Business intelligence: Making decisions through data analytics: Customer Intelligence*. Business Expert Press.

Swan, M. (2015). *Blockchain: blueprint for a new economy*. O'Reilly Media, Inc.

Swathi & Rani. (2019). Intelligent fatigue detection by using ACS and by avoiding false alarms of fatigue detection. In *Innovations in Computer Science and Engineering: Proceedings of the Sixth ICICSE 2018* (pp. 225-233). Springer Singapore.

Szabo, N. (1996). Smart contracts: Building blocks for digital markets. *Extropy, 18*(16).

Tabrizi, B., Lam, E., Girard, K., & Irvin, V. (2019). Digital transformation is not about technology. *Harvard Business Review*, *13*, 1–6.

Taheri, B., Farrington, T., Curran, R., & O'Gorman, K. (2018). Sustainability and the authentic experience. Harnessing brand heritage–a study from Japan. *Journal of Sustainable Tourism*, *26*(1), 49–67. doi:10.1080/09669582.2017.1310867

Tandon, U., Ertz, M., & Sakshi, K. (2021). POD Mode of Payment, Return Policies and Virtual-Try-on Technology as Predictors of Trust: An Emerging Economy Case. *Journal of Promotion Management*, *27*(6), 832–855. doi:10.1080/10496491.2021.1888174

Tanveer Kajla, V. S. (2022). Blockchain in the Banking Sector: Revolution or Digital Disruption? In *Applications, Challenges, and Opportunities of Blockchain Technology in Banking and Insurance*. IGI Global. doi:10.4018/978-1-6684-4133-6.ch008

Tan, W., Zhu, H., Tan, J., Zhao, Y., Xu, L. D., & Guo, K. (2022). A novel service level agreement model using blockchain and smart contract for cloud manufacturing in industry 4.0. *Enterprise Information Systems*, *16*(12), 1939426. doi:10.1080/17517575.2021.1939426

Tarafdar, M., & Vaidya, S. D. (2006). Challenges in the adoption of E-Commerce technologies in India: The role of organizational factors. *International Journal of Information Management*, *26*(6), 428–441. doi:10.1016/j.ijinfomgt.2006.08.001

Tasatanattakool, P., & Techapanupreeda, C. (2018, January). Blockchain: Challenges and applications. In *2018 International Conference on Information Networking (ICOIN)* (pp. 473-475). IEEE. 10.1109/ICOIN.2018.8343163

Tavana, M., Shaabani, A., Vanani, I. R., & Gangadhari, R. K. (2022). A Review of Digital Transformation on Supply Chain Process Management Using Text Mining. *Processes (Basel, Switzerland)*, *10*(5), 842. Advance online publication. doi:10.3390/pr10050842

Taylor, S., & Todd, P. A. (1995). Understanding information technology usage: A test of competing models. *Information Systems Research*, *6*(2), 144–176. doi:10.1287/isre.6.2.144

Tekbas, M. (2021). The impact of economic, social and political globalization on economic growth: Evidence from BRICS-T countries. *Gaziantep University Journal of Social Sciences*, *20*(1), 57–71. doi:10.21547/jss.796472

Tewari, D. B., Singh, S., & Singh, R. (2022). Self-help groups (SHGs) Role in Promotion of Women Entrepreneur: A Saga of Pandemic Era. *Journal of Positive School Psychology*, *6*(2), 936–947.

Thakur, R., & Srivastava, M. (2014). Adoption readiness, personal innovativeness, perceived risk and usage intention across customer groups for mobile payment services in India. *Internet Research, 24*(3), 369–392. doi:10.1108/IntR-12-2012-0244

The Guardian. (2023). *ChatGPT reaches 100 million users, making it the fastest growing app*. Retrieved from https://www.theguardian.com/technology/2023/feb/02/chatgpt-100-million-users-open-ai-fastest-growing-app

The NPCI. (2023). Retrieved May 2023, from npci.org: https://www.npci.org.in/statistics

Thong, J. Y. L. (1999). An integrated model of information systems adoption in small businesses. *Journal of Management Information Systems, 15*(4), 187–214. doi:10.1080/07421222.1999.11518227

Thong, J. Y. L., Hong, S. J., & Tam, K. Y. (2006). The effects of post-adoption beliefs on the expectation-confirmation model for information technology continuance. *International Journal of Human-Computer Studies, 64*(9), 799–810. doi:10.1016/j.ijhcs.2006.05.001

Thormundsson, B. (2023). Explainable AI market revenues worldwide 2022-2030. *Statista*. Available at: https://www.statista.com/statistics/1256246/worldwide-explainable-ai-market-revenues/

Tissir, N., El Kafhali, S., & Aboutabit, N. (2021). Cybersecurity management in cloud computing: Semantic literature review and conceptual framework proposal. *Journal of Reliable Intelligent Environments, 7*(2), 69–84. doi:10.1007/s40860-020-00115-0

Tomczyk, Ł., & Szotkowski, R. (2023). Sexting, fear of missing out (FOMO), and problematic social network use among adolescents. *Human Technology, 19*(2), 283–301. doi:10.14254/1795-6889.2023.19-2.8

Topalova, N. (2021). The impact of marketing through Instagram influencers on consumer behavior in the fashion industry: Comparison of Millennials and Generation Z in Russia. *Chemical and Engineering News, 27*(32), 2282–2283.

Tornatzky, L. G., Fleischer, M., & Chakrabarti, A. K. (1990). *Processes of technological innovation*. Lexington Books.

Treiblmaier, H. (2018, September 10). The impact of the blockchain on the supply chain: A theory-based research framework and a call for action. *Supply Chain Management, 23*(6), 545–559. doi:10.1108/SCM-01-2018-0029

Tufekci, Z. (2017). *Twitter and tear gas: The power and fragility of networked protest*. Yale University Press.

UNESCO. (2023). *Artificial Intelligence: examples of ethical dilemmas*. Available at: https://www.unesco.org/en/artificial-intelligence/recommendation-ethics/cases

United Nations. (2022). *E-Government survey: the future of digital government*. Available at: https://publicadministration.un.org/egovkb/en-us/Reports/UN-E-Government-Survey-2022

Usha, S. D. J. (2014). Role of information technology in the globalized banking sector. *Shanlax International Journal of Arts, Science & Humanities, 1*(4), 107-113.

Valente, T. W. (2012). Network interventions. *Science, 337*(6090), 49-53.

Van Dijck, J. (2014). Datafication, dataism and dataveillance: Big Data between scientific paradigm and ideology. *Surveillance & Society, 12*(2), 197–208. doi:10.24908/ss.v12i2.4776

Van Eck, N. J., & Waltman, L. (2017). Citation-based clustering of publications using CitNetExplorer and VOSviewer. *Scientometrics, 111*(2), 1053–1070. doi:10.1007/s11192-017-2300-7 PMID:28490825

van Esch, P., & Black, J. S. (2021). Artificial intelligence (AI): Revolutionizing digital marketing. *Australasian Marketing Journal, 29*(3), 199–203. doi:10.1177/18393349211037684

Vaquero, L. M., Rodero-Merino, L., Caceres, J., & Lindner, M. (2008). A break in the clouds. *Computer Communication Review*, *39*(1), 50–55. doi:10.1145/1496091.1496100

Venkatesh, V., & Davis, F. D. (2000). A theoretical extension of the technology acceptance model: Four longitudinal field studies. *Management Science*, *46*(2), 186–204. doi:10.1287/mnsc.46.2.186.11926

Venkatesh, V., Morris, M. G., Davis, G. B., & Davis, F. D. (2003). User acceptance of information technology: Toward a unified view. *Management Information Systems Quarterly*, *27*(3), 425–478. doi:10.2307/30036540

Venkatesh, V., Thong, J. Y., & Xu, X. (2012). Consumer acceptance and use of information technology: Extending the unified theory of acceptance and use of technology. *Management Information Systems Quarterly*, *36*(1), 157–178. doi:10.2307/41410412

Verhoef, P. C., Broekhuizen, T., Bart, Y., Bhattacharya, A., Dong, J. Q., Fabian, N., & Haenlein, M. (2021). Digital transformation: A multidisciplinary reflection and research agenda. *Journal of Business Research*, *122*, 889–901. doi:10.1016/j.jbusres.2019.09.022

Verhoef, P. C., Venkatesan, R., McAlister, L., Malthouse, E. C., Krafft, M., & Ganesan, S. (2010). CRM in data-rich multichannel retailing environments: A review and future research directions. *Journal of Interactive Marketing*, *24*(2), 121–137. doi:10.1016/j.intmar.2010.02.009

Verma, B., & Srivastava, A. (2022). Dimensions of globalisation and economic growth of India: Exploring causal linkages. *International Journal of Economic Policy in Emerging Economies*, *15*(2/3/4), 197–213. doi:10.1504/IJEPEE.2022.121345

Verma, B., Srivastava, A., Mehta, R., & Chandel, J. (2022). FDI-linked Spillovers and the Indian Economic Growth: The role of Country's Absorptive Capacity. *IEEE Delhi Section Conference (DELCON)*. 10.1109/DELCON54057.2022.9753540

Vial, G. (2019). Understanding digital transformation: A review and a research agenda. *The Journal of Strategic Information Systems*, *28*(2), 118–144. doi:10.1016/j.jsis.2019.01.003

Vijayan, A. (2019). Digital India-A roadmap to sustainability. *International Journal of Innovative Technology and Exploring Engineering*, *8*(5), 571–576.

Viriyasitavat, W., & Hoonsopon, D. (2019). Blockchain characteristics and consensus in modern business processes. *Journal of Industrial Information Integration*, *13*, 32–39. doi:10.1016/j.jii.2018.07.004

Vyas, S., Shabaz, M., Pandit, P., Parvathy, L. R., & Ofori, I. (2022). Integration of artificial intelligence and blockchain technology in healthcare and agriculture. *Journal of Food Quality*, *2022*, 1–11. doi:10.1155/2022/4228448

Walia, G. K., Kumar, M., & Gill, S. S. (2023). AI-Empowered Fog/Edge Resource Management for IoT Applications: A Comprehensive Review, Research Challenges and Future Perspectives. *IEEE Communications Surveys & Tutorials*, 1. doi:10.1109/COMST.2023.3338015

Wang, C., Zhang, Q., & Zhang, W. (2020). Corporate social responsibility, green supply chain management and firm performance: The moderating role of big-data analytics capability. *Research in Transportation Business & Management*, *37*, 100557. doi:10.1016/j.rtbm.2020.100557

Wang, J., Wu, P., Wang, X., & Shou, W. (2017). The outlook of blockchain technology for construction engineering management. *Frontiers of Engineering Management*, *4*(1), 67–75. doi:10.15302/J-FEM-2017006

Wang, N., Liang, H., Jia, Y., Ge, S., Xue, Y., & Wang, Z. (2016). Cloud computing research in the IS discipline: A citation/co-citation analysis. *Decision Support Systems*, *86*, 35–47. doi:10.1016/j.dss.2016.03.006

Wang, S., Ouyang, L., Yuan, Y., Ni, X., Han, X., & Wang, F. Y. (2019). Blockchain-enabled smart contracts: Architecture, applications, and future trends. *IEEE Transactions on Systems, Man, and Cybernetics. Systems*, *49*(11), 2266–2277. doi:10.1109/TSMC.2019.2895123

Wang, X. S., Li, Y., & Li, Y. (2021). The role of machine learning analytics and metrics in retailing research. *Journal of Retailing*, *97*(4), 658–675. doi:10.1016/j.jretai.2020.12.001

Wang, Y., Chen, C. H., & Zghari, A. (2021). Sales Designing a blockchain enabled supply chain. *International Journal of Production Research*, *59*(5), 1450–1475. doi:10.1080/00207543.2020.1824086

Warner, K. S., & Wäger, M. (2019). Building dynamic capabilities for digital transformation: An ongoing process of strategic renewal. *Long Range Planning*, *52*(3), 326–349. doi:10.1016/j.lrp.2018.12.001

Warschauer, M. (2003). *Technology and social inclusion: Rethinking the digital divide*. MIT Press. doi:10.7551/mitpress/6699.001.0001

Warschauer, M. (2004). *Technology and Social Inclusion: Rethinking the Digital Divide*. MIT Press.

Weber, R. H., & Weber, R. (2010). *Internet of Things* (Vol. 12). Springer. doi:10.1007/978-3-642-11710-7

Wedel, M., & Kannan, P. K. (2016). Marketing analytics for data-rich environments. *Journal of Marketing*, *80*(6), 97–121. doi:10.1509/jm.15.0413

Wejnert, B. (2002). Integrating models of diffusion of innovations: A conceptual framework. *Annual Review of Sociology*, *28*(1), 297–326. doi:10.1146/annurev.soc.28.110601.141051

Wellman, M. L., Stoldt, R., Tully, M., & Ekdale, B. (2020). Ethics of Authenticity: Social Media Influencers and the Production of Sponsored Content. *Journal of Media Ethics: Exploring Questions of Media Morality*, *35*(2), 68–82. doi:10.1080/23736992.2020.1736078

Wernerfelt, B. (1984). A resource-based view of the firm. *Strategic Management Journal*, *5*(2), 171–180. doi:10.1002/smj.4250050207

Westerman, G., Calméjane, C., Bonnet, D., Ferraris, P., & McAfee, A. (2011). *Digital Transformation: A roadmap for billion-dollar organizations*. MIT Center for Digital Business and Capgemini Consulting.

Williamson, E. A., Harrison, D. K., & Jordan, M. (2004). Information systems development within supply chain management. *International Journal of Information Management*, *24*(5), 375–385. doi:10.1016/j.ijinfomgt.2004.06.002

Williamson, O. E. (1981). The economics of organization: The transaction cost approach. *American Journal of Sociology*, *87*(3), 548–577. doi:10.1086/227496

Wirtz, B. W., Weyerer, J. C., & Geyer, C. (2019). AI-driven technologies and their implications for consumers. *Electronic Markets*, *29*(4), 631–649.

Wood, M. S., & McKinley, W. (2020). The entrepreneurial opportunity construct: Dislodge or leverage? *The Academy of Management Perspectives*, *34*(3), 352–365. doi:10.5465/amp.2017.0162

Wright, A., & De Filippi, P. (2015). Decentralized blockchain technology and the rise of lex cryptographia. SSRN *Electronic Journal*. doi:10.2139/ssrn.2580664

Wu, T. Y., Wang, T., Lee, Y. Q., Zheng, W., Kumari, S., & Kumar, S. (2021). Improved Authenticated Key Agreement Scheme for Fog-Driven IoT Healthcare System. *Security and Communication Networks*, *2021*, 1–16. Advance online publication. doi:10.1155/2021/6658041

Wyborn, C. A., Kerkhoff, L. E., Colloff, M. J., Alexandra, J., & Olsson, R. (2021). The politics of adaptive governance: Water reform, climate change, and First Nations' justice in Australia's Murray-Darling Basin10.5751/ES-13641-280104. *Ecology and Society*, *28*(1), art4. Advance online publication. doi:10.5751/ES-13641-280104

Wynn, J., & Williams, C. K. (2012). Principles for conducting critical realist case study research in information systems. *Management Information Systems Quarterly*, *36*(3), 787–810. doi:10.2307/41703481

Wysokińska, Z. (2021). A Review of the Impact of the Digital Transformation on the Global and European Economy. Comparative Economic Research. *Central and Eastern Europe*, *24*(3), 75–92.

Xu, X., Lu, Q., Liu, Y., Zhu, L., Yao, H., & Vasilakos, A. V. (2018). Designing blockchain-based applications a case study for imported product traceability. *Future Generation Computer Systems, 92*, 399–406. doi:10.1016/j.future.2018.10.010

Xu, M., Chen, X., & Kou, G. (2019). A systematic review of blockchain. *Financial Innovation*, *5*(1), 1–14. doi:10.1186/s40854-019-0147-z

Yamaganti, R. (2023). Investigation Into Security Challenges and Approaches in Cloud Computing. *Journal of Engineering Sciences*. https://www.researchgate.net/publication/375610287

Yang, J., and Z. C. (2010). Cloud computing research and security issues. In *2010 International Conference on Computational Intelligence and Software Engineering* (pp. 1-3). IEEE.

Yang, S., Han, R., Wolfram, D., & Zhao, Y. (2016). Visualizing the intellectual structure of information science (2006–2015): Introducing author keyword coupling analysis. *Journal of Informetrics*, *10*(1), 132–150. doi:10.1016/j.joi.2015.12.003

Yen, H. R., Hu, P. J. H., Hsu, S. H. Y., & Li, E. Y. (2015). A multilevel approach to examine employees' loyal use of ERP systems in organizations. *Journal of Management Information Systems*, *32*(4), 144–178. doi:10.1080/07421222.2015.1138373

Yerpude, S., & Singhal, T. K. (2018). Customer service enhancement through 'on-road vehicle assistance' enabled with Internet of Things (IoT) solutions and frameworks: A futuristic perspective. *International Journal of Applied Business and Economic Research*, *15*(16), 551–565.

Yerpude, S., & Singhal, T. K. (2021). "Custolytics": Internet of Things based customer analytics aiding customer engagement strategy in emerging markets – an empirical research. *International Journal of Emerging Markets*, *16*(1), 92–112. doi:10.1108/IJOEM-05-2018-0250

Yesiloglu, S., & Costello, J. (2021). *Influencer marketing: Building brand communities and engagement*. Academic Press.

Yi, J., Zhang, H., Mao, J., Chen, Y., Zhong, H., & Wang, Y. (2022). Review on the COVID-19 pandemic prevention and control system based on AI. *Engineering Applications of Artificial Intelligence*, *114*, 105184. doi:10.1016/j.engappai.2022.105184 PMID:35846728

Yuan, Y., & Wang, F. Y. (2018). Blockchain and cryptocurrencies: Model, techniques, and applications. *IEEE Transactions on Systems, Man, and Cybernetics. Systems*, *48*(9), 1421–1428. doi:10.1109/TSMC.2018.2854904

Yusuf Sukman, J. (2017). Эпидемиологическая безопасность. *Вестник Росздравнадзора*, *4*, 9–15.

Zarrin, J., Wen Phang, H., Babu Saheer, L., & Zarrin, B. (2021). Blockchain for decentralization of internet: Prospects, trends, and challenges. *Cluster Computing*, *24*(4), 2841–2866. doi:10.1007/s10586-021-03301-8 PMID:34025209

Zattoni, A., & Pugliese, A. (2021). Corporate governance research in the wake of a systemic crisis: Lessons and opportunities from the COVID-19 Pandemic. *Journal of Management Studies*, *58*(5), 1405–1410. doi:10.1111/joms.12693

Zatwarnicka-Madura, B., Nowacki, R., & Wojciechowska, I. (2022). Influencer Marketing as a Tool in Modern Communication—Possibilities of Use in Green Energy Promotion amongst Poland's Generation Z. *Energies*, *15*(18), 6570. Advance online publication. doi:10.3390/en15186570

Zetter, K. (2014). *An unprecedented look at Stuxnet, the world's first digital weapon*. Wired.

Zetzsche, D. A., Arner, D. W., & Buckley, R. P. (2020). Decentralized finance (defi). *Journal of Financial Regulation*, *6*(2), 172–203. doi:10.1093/jfr/fjaa010

Zhang, H., Nauyen, T. H., & Lenka, S. (2020). Green lifestyle, where to go? How social media influencers moderate the intention-behavior gap within the ecological lifestyle context. *Jönköping University*.

Zhang, J. (2019, May 28). Deploying blockchain technology in the supply chain. In *Computer security threats*. IntechOpen.

Zhang, J., Li, H., & Ziegelmayer, J. L. (2009). Resource or capability? A dissection of SMEs' IT infrastructure flexibility and its relationship with IT responsiveness. *Journal of Computer Information Systems*, *50*(1), 46–53.

Zhang, W., Chintagunta, P. K., & Kalwani, M. U. (2021). Social Media, Influencers, and Adoption of an Eco-Friendly Product: Field Experiment Evidence from Rural China. *Journal of Marketing*, *85*(3), 10–27. doi:10.1177/0022242920985784

Zhang, X., Rane, K. P., Kakaravada, I., & Shabaz, M. (2021). Research on vibration monitoring and fault diagnosis of rotating machinery based on internet of things technology. *Nonlinear Engineering*, *10*(1), 245–254.

Zhao, J., Ji, M., & Feng, B. (2020, March 19). Smarter supply chain: A literature review and practices. Journal of Data. *Information & Management*, *2*(2), 95–110. doi:10.1007/s42488-020-00025-z

Zheng, Z., Xie, S., Dai, H., Chen, X., & Wang, H. (2017, June 25). An overview of blockchain technology: Architecture, consensus, and future trends. In *2017 IEEE international congress on big data (BigData congress)* (pp. 557–564). IEEE Publications. doi:10.1109/BigDataCongress.2017.85

Zhou, T. (2011). An empirical examination of initial trust in mobile banking. *Internet Research*, *21*(5), 527–540. doi:10.1108/10662241111176353

Zissis, D., & Lekkas, D. (2012). Addressing cloud computing security issues. *Future Generation Computer Systems*, *28*(3), 583–592. doi:10.1016/j.future.2010.12.006

Zuboff, S. (2019). *The Age of Surveillance Capitalism: the Fight for a Human Future at the New Frontier of Power*. PublicAffairs.

About the Contributors

Balraj Verma serves as an Assistant Professor at the esteemed Chitkara Business School-Doctoral Research Centre, affiliated with Chitkara University in Rajpura, Punjab. Holding a Ph.D. earned from Jaypee University of Information Technology (JUIT), Waknaghat, and a master's degree in Business Administration, he brings to the academic arena more than 16 years of rich experience in both academia and the corporate world. His qualifications extend to successfully passing the National Eligibility Test (NET) for teaching in the field of management, a testament to his dedication to education. He possesses a remarkable teaching portfolio, which includes courses such as Marketing Management, Strategic Management, Business Statistics, and Research Methodology. Furthermore, he is a strong advocate for rigorous research, as reflected in his extensive publication record. His research contributions encompass numerous papers published in ABDC listed and Scopus Index journals, as well as authorship and editorial work for books and book chapters, published by renowned major presses. Notably, he is not just an academic but also an active contributor to the academic community. He has played a pivotal role in organizing workshops and conferences, contributing significantly to the academic growth and development of his department and university.

Babita Singla is a professor at Chitkara Business School, Chitkara University, Punjab, India. She has a Ph.D. in management and is UGC-NET qualified. She has over 13 years of experience in teaching, research, and administration. Her areas of expertise are marketing, e-commerce, omnichannel, and retail. In her career, she has been involved in important academic and research assignments such as being the guest editor of a reputed journal, organizing and conducting international and national-level conferences and faculty development programs, and providing guidance for research projects. She has research publications in reputable international and national journals such as Scopus, SCI, etc., and has presented research papers at various national and international conferences. In the short span of 13 years of her career in academia and administration, she has authored and edited several books on retailing, supply chain management, branding, customer relationship management, and product management, covering the course content of various universities nationwide. She has successfully delivered guest sessions at international and national universities.

Amit Mittal is a Pro Vice Chancellor (Research Programs) and Professor of Management, Doctoral Research Centre, Chitkara Business School, Chitkara University, Punjab, India. Dr Mittal has over two decades of domestic and international experience in academic leadership, teaching, research, consulting, training and mentorship. At Chitkara University, his current mandate is to manage and coordinate the PhD programs, research publications and international/domestic research collaborations. Seventeen scholars have been awarded PhD degrees under his guidance and he has published over 120 Scopus / SSCI indexed papers with a number of these included in the ABDC/ABS journal list. He was the recipient of the Career 360 "Outstanding Faculty Researcher Award" 2023, "Megastar Award" Chitkara Excellence Awards 2023/4, the Chitkara University Excellence award 2023 (Publications in Business School Category), 2021 (February) for highest cited author and publications with highest H-index (Business School category). He is an active resource person for FDPs, MDPs & Corporate Trainings. He is a member of the thesis review board of a number of universities. He presently reviews for reputable journals such as Technological Forecasting and Social Change (Elsevier), Public Health (Elsevier) Benchmarking (Emerald), Technology Analysis and Strategic Management (Taylor and Francis), International Journal of Consumer Studies (Wiley), Journal of Public Affairs (Wiley), Routledge Studies in Global Student Mobility, International Journal of Emerging Markets (Emerald), Sustainability (MDPI), Management Decision (Emerald), IIM KSMR (Sage) etc. He serves on the editorial boards of Frontiers in Psychology (SSCI/Scopus indexed), Open Psychology Journal (Scopus indexed), Proceedings on Engineering Sciences (Scopus indexed) and Research on Enterprise in Modern Economy (Gdańsk Univeristy of Technology, Poland). He is currently guest editing a special issue in International Journal of Information and Management Data Insights (Elsevier). He also serves on the executive committee of Indian Business School Advisory Council (BSAC) of ETS Global, USA. He is presently on the jury of the QS Reimagine Education Awards, Abu Dhabi 2023. He is a research fellow at INTI International University, Malaysia, Visiting Professor at Pathumthani University, Thailand and Adjunct Faculty, IMSAR – MD University, India.

* * *

Aarti (F) received her Ph.D. and Master of Technology (M-tech) in Computer Science and Engineering from NIT Jalandhar. She is currently working as an associate professor at lovely professional university. Her areas of interest are artificial intelligence, genetic algorithm, data mining and cryptography. She has published 30 research papers in various International/National Journals (including IEEE, Springer etc.) and Proceedings of the reputed International/ National Conferences (including Springer and IEEE). She is an active member of 5 various Professional International Societies. She has been nominated in the board of editors/reviewers of 5 peer-reviewed and refereed Journals.

Arun Aggarwal is a distinguished academician and Assistant Professor at Chitkara Business School, Chitkara University, Punjab, India. Prior to this, he was a Senior Research Fellow at the University School of Applied Management, Punjabi University Patiala. Specializing in Human Resource Management, Organizational Behaviour, Industrial Relations, Labor Laws, and Research Methodology, Dr. Aggarwal has an extensive background in guiding research. He has supervised and co-supervised multiple Ph.D. theses across diverse topics. Dr. Aggarwal has an impressive publication record. His research papers have been accepted in high-impact journals, with a total impact factor exceeding 40. Dr. Aggarwal has also been a guest editor for special issues in journals like the International Journal of Business and Globalisation and Worl Review of Science, Technology and Sustainable Development. Besides academics, he is an active contributor to Faculty Development Programs (FDP) and has been a resource person at multiple institutions. He also holds a copyright related to the effects of abusive supervision and organizational commitment on organizational deviance.

Jehad Aldehayyat is an associate professor of Strategic Management College of Business and Economics, Al-Hussein Bin Talal University, Jordan. He received a doctorate degree in The University of Huddersfield, West Yorkshire U.K. Currently he is working in digitalization strategic decision making. His primary research interest in strategic planning and strategic decision making within a variety of organizational contexts. His Work appears in the International Journal of Hospitality Management, Strategic Change, and Management Decision.

Sugandh Arora is currently working as an Assistant Professor at Sharda School of Business Studies, Sharda University, Greater Noida, Uttar Pradesh. She has received his Ph.D. degree from Mittal School of Business, ACBSP USA, Accredited, Lovely Professional University, Punjab (India). Her work mainly focuses on the effectiveness of household food security in Punjab and the various PDS reforms. Her recent publications are under Int. J. Economic Policy in Emerging Economies (Inderscience); Emerging Trends in Business Economics, Vol 1. (2020); International Journal of Research and Analytical Reviews (IJRAR) Vol 6. (2019) and Management in Practice Challenges and Strategies (2019). Her research interest areas are Agriculture economics, International Trade, and global food security.

|**Marshall B** brings over 18 years of global experience to the table, specializing in enterprise-wide multidisciplinary teams and cutting-edge technologies. As a cross-functional leader, Marshall has a proven track record of driving results and delivering value to clients across diverse industries. Marshall's expertise lies in building exceptional teams of subject matter experts (SMEs) by employing innovative recruitment strategies and fostering a culture of collaboration and excellence. His extensive knowledge spans IT operations, advanced analytics, machine learning (ML), artificial intelligence (AI), vendor negotiations, data governance, and cybersecurity. Throughout his career, Marshall has demonstrated a knack for making strategic decisions that optimize operational efficiencies and promote a culture of data-informed decision-making. His leadership style prioritizes mentorship and empowerment, creating an environment where every team member can thrive and contribute to achieving ambitious goals. Beyond his technical prowess, Marshall is a passionate advocate for leveraging data as a powerful tool for decision-making and operational improvement. His management expertise extends to corporate operations, organization change, talent strategy, and strategic HR business partnering, enabling organizations to adapt and excel in today's rapidly evolving business landscape. Marshall's natural ability in business operations and behavioral intelligence, coupled with his dedication to fostering a culture of contentment and shared purpose, makes him a valuable asset in driving organizational success and innovation.

Umesh Chawla, a seasoned Sales and Marketing maestro boasting an extensive 28+ years of professional experience, stands as a distinguished alumnus of the prestigious University of London, The London School of Economics, and the esteemed Narsee Monjee Institute of Management. Recognized for his innovative and out-of-the-box approach, Umesh's expertise spans across Retail sales, Marketing, Product planning, Strategy formulation, and P&L management. A trailblazer in the realm of Consumer Durables and IT Hardware, Umesh has a penchant for crafting high-paced and dynamic Retail businesses. His unwavering commitment to staying ahead in the ever-evolving landscape of Sales and Marketing is evident in his emphasis on continuous learning and adaptability. Currently holding the position of Director and Head of Retail Management for Southeast Asia, stationed in the vibrant city of Kuala Lumpur, Umesh orchestrates strategies that resonate with the fast-paced demands of the region. Simultaneously, he is embarking on an intellectual journey, pursuing his Ph.D. at Chitkara University, where his goal is to contribute significantly to the field of Sales and Marketing.

Ivana Domazet is a Principal Research Fellow at the Institute of Economic Sciences and Professor at the Faculty for Banking, Insurance and Finance, Union University. She teaches courses on Marketing Management, Market Research and Competitiveness Enhancement (postgraduate studies). Her scientific interest refers to: Improving Competitiveness, National Branding, Marketing Research and Strategy, CRM and Strategic Management. She published a numerous papers related to foregoing topics. She is President of Scientific Council at the Institute of Economic Sciences, Vice-president of Board member of the Institute of Economics Sciences, Board member of the Institute of Social Science, member of Serbian Scientific Association of Economists and Serbian Marketing Association.

Dale T. Eesley is the John Morgan Community Chair in Entrepreneurship, Founder and Director of the Center for Innovation, Entrepreneurship & Franchising, and Professor of Entrepreneurship & Strategy. Dr. Eesley received his Ph.D. from the University of Wisconsin, Madison in Entrepreneurship & Strategy. He has been teaching and consulting in the field of entrepreneurship for over 18 years.

Vijaya G. S., BE (E& EE), MBA, PhD, is currently working as Professor in Decision Science Department at CMS Business School, JAIN (Deemed-to-be University), Bengaluru, India. She has worked in reputed Indian institutions and at Al Yamamah University, Riyadh, Kingdom of Saudi Arabia in various capacities both in teaching and administration. Under her guidance six students have been awarded PhD and She has more than two decades of Post Graduate teaching experience and three years of Industry experience. She is a Life Member of Indian Society for Technical Education, International Association of Engineers (IAENG) and Quality Circle Forum of India. She has Published 40 plus articles in refereed and peer reviewed National and International journals and book chapters. She has presented papers at IIM Bengaluru, IIM Kozhikode, Management Training Institute, Steel Authority of India Limited, Ranchi, International Institute of Social and Economic Sciences (IISES), Venice, Italy, World conference 2022 held at Valencia, Spain and World Conference 2023 held at London, UK to name a few.

Divya Goswami is presently a Research Scholar at Chitkara University, Punjab (India) who has accumulated a wealth of teaching experience over the past 10 years. She has served as a dedicated faculty member at S.A. Jain (P.G.) College, Ambala City (Haryana), where she has taught a range of courses in commerce, including Financial Accounting, Advertisement Management, Financial Institutions Markets and others. Her teaching philosophy is grounded in fostering critical thinking, analytical skills, and a holistic understanding of commerce principles among students. In her role as a Researcher Scholar, currently at the Center for Financial Technologies and AI, Ms. Divya Goswami explores innovative applications of AI in financial decision-making processes.

Swathi Gowroju (F) is working as an Associate Professor & Head of Artificial Intelligence and Machine Learning Engineering Department, Sreyas Institute of Engineering and Technology, Hyderabad, Telanagana, India. Her research area is Image Processing and Machine Learning. She has guided more than 30 students in various projects of various domains. She has published 30+ Scopus indexed research papers in the field of Image processing and Machine Learning. She had filed International and National Patents. She has been awarded with best paper in several conferences. She has been nominated for Academic and Researcher Excellence award, Young Researcher award and Research Excellence awards for Telangana State. She has been working as reviewer for many reputed SCI and Scopus journals. She is a certified AWS Cloud Foundations trainer, Python and Java Full Stack trainer. She attended various seminars, workshops and short term programs of AICTE, IITs, etc.

Vishal Jain is presently working as an Associate Professor at Department of Computer Science and Engineering, Sharda School of Engineering and Technology, Sharda University, Greater Noida, U. P. India. Before that, he has worked for several years as an Associate Professor at Bharati Vidyapeeth's Institute of Computer Applications and Management (BVICAM), New Delhi. He has more than 14 years of experience in the academics. He obtained Ph.D (CSE), M.Tech (CSE), MBA (HR), MCA, MCP and CCNA. He has authored more than 90 research papers in reputed conferences and journals, including Web of Science and Scopus. He has authored and edited more than 30 books with various reputed publishers, including Elsevier, Springer, Apple Academic Press, CRC, Taylor and Francis Group, Scrivener, Wiley, Emerald, NOVA Science and IGI-Global. His research areas include information retrieval, semantic web, ontology engineering, data mining, ad hoc networks, and sensor networks. He received a Young Active Member Award for the year 2012–13 from the Computer Society of India, Best Faculty Award for the year 2017 and Best Researcher Award for the year 2019 from BVICAM, New Delhi.

Poornima Jirli is a doctoral student at Swiss School of Business and Management (SSBM) in Geneva, Switzerland. With over 15 years of industry experience, she brings a wealth of practical knowledge to her academic pursuits. Her professional background encompasses significant roles in Information Technology.

Sahithi Josyula is a student of the Masters program in entertainment industry management at the Heinz College, Carnegie Mellon University.

Saurabh Karling is a student in Lovely Professional University. His research area include mining, human resource, marketing.

Nishant Kumar is currently working as Associate Professor in the School of Business and Management, CHRIST (Deemed to be University), Bangalore (India). During initial phase of his career he worked with Amity University, Doon University, Delhi Institute of Advanced Studies, HCL Infosystems ltd., with more than of 12 years of rich experience in academics, research and corporate. He also worked on an international research project "Vulnerability and possible business adoption measures in Himalayan region" funded by Swiss Agency for Development and Cooperation (SDC). Dr. Kumar has published patents, book chapters, research papers in journals with ABS, SCOPUS, Web of Science, ABDC classification and also a member in the Editorial Review Board of Technological Innovations for Sustainability and Business Growth, Global business strategy for sustainability, Journal of market access & health policy, Research Journal of Textile and Apparel, Human Behavior Emerging Technologies, Cogent Business and Management, Evergreen and Global journal of flexible systems management. He has presented papers at various National & International conferences in the prestigious institutes like IIM Bangalore, IIM Indore, IIT Roorkee, University of Mumbai and has won outstanding research paper award. His interest and expertise includes intelligent computation technologies, blockchain and its application, data analytics, mixed-methodology, multivariate statistical analysis, model development and validation using SPSS, PLS-SEM, AMOS.

Sandhya M. is currently working in Govt. First Grade College Kaup, having 25 years of experience in the teaching field. She is a life member of the All India Accounting Association. She has trained several students especially students of professional courses like CA and MBA. Her primary research interest is Finance and corporate sustainability reporting.

Sridhar Manohar is currently working In Doctoral Research Center, Chitkara University, completed his doctorate in the area of Services Marketing from VIT Business School, VIT University. He has a Bachelor of Technology and Dual Masters in Business Administration and Organization Psychology. Dr. Sridhar further certified with FDP at IIM-A. He is expertise in Service Marketing, Innovation and Entrepreneurship, Scale Development Process and Multivariate Analytics and interests in teaching Business Analytics, Innovation and Entrepreneurship, Research Methodology and Marketing Management. He has published around 20 research papers that includes Scopus listed and ABDC ranked International Journals like – Society and Business Review, Benchmarking-An International Journal, Electronics Market, Corporate Reputation Review, International Journal of Services and Operations Management, International journal of Business Excellence and presented papers and ideas in numerous international conferences.

Darko Marjanović is Senior Research Associate at the Institute of Economic Sciences. He completed his graduate, master, and doctoral studies at the Faculty of Economics in Subotica, University of Novi Sad. He served as a financial director (CFO) in a large trading company BB Trade ad from 2015 to 2018. His current areas of professional interest are competitiveness, FDI and public finance. He has published, as author or co-author, more than 60 scientific papers. He has participated in a few international projects, as well as several research and scientific projects, financed by the Ministry of Education, Science, and Technological Development of the Republic of Serbia and Provincial Secretariat for Science and Technological Development of the Autonomous Province of Vojvodina. He is a member of the Scientific Board at the Institute of Economic Sciences and associate member of the Scientific Society of Economists of Serbia. He was a Vice President of the Scientific Board at the Institute of Economic Sciences, head of the Center for Strategic Cooperation, coordinator of the Macroeconomics Department and editor-in-chief of the international publication SEE-6 Economic Outlook.

Anuj Modgil is a seasoned management consultant at KPMG, specializing in business transformation advisory services. With a diverse expertise spanning supply chain management, operations, geopolitics, environmental, social, and governance (ESG) factors, he brings a holistic approach to solving complex organizational challenges. Anuj's profound understanding of global geopolitical dynamics enriches his strategic insights, enabling clients to navigate uncertainties and capitalize on emerging opportunities in today's interconnected world. He is passionate about fostering sustainable business practices and actively advises organizations on integrating ESG principles into their operations for long-term resilience and growth. As a futurist, Anuj is dedicated to anticipating and preparing for future trends, equipping businesses with the foresight needed to thrive in rapidly evolving landscapes. His visionary outlook and innovative strategies empower clients to stay ahead of the curve and drive meaningful impact in their industries. Anuj is committed to continuous learning, staying abreast of the latest advancements in management theory and practice. His unwavering dedication to excellence, coupled with his deep industry knowledge, makes him a trusted advisor and thought leader in the field of business transformation.

Sayantan Mukherjee is an academician in the field of Marketing Management. His research area is Marketing Management.

Shromona Neogi is an academician in the domain of Organizational Behavior and Human Resource Management.

Sumit Oberoi is working as Asst. professor at Symbiosis School of Economics (SSE) with a demonstrated history of working in the academic industry. His area of research embrace public health and policy, health economics, tourism and blockchain technology along with this Sumit has managed to publish good research publications indexed under Scopus, ABDC, Web of Science and SSCI. In addition to research experience, Sumit is also reviewer for numerous international/national journals such as Cogent Economics & Finance (Taylor & Francis), International Economics (Elsevier), International Journal of Emerging Market (Emerald), Intl. J. of Diabetes in Dev. Countries (Springer), Clinico-Economics and Outcomes Research (Dove), etc. To his credit, he has also received the copyright © from Govt. of India (GoI) for developing an "Framework for Healthcare Utilization and Economic Enquiry of Diabetes".

Divya Prabhu, an Educator and Researcher by passion, is a Ph.D holder from JAIN (Deemed to be University) Bangalore, India. She holds an MBA and a BCom from Mangalore University with first rank in both the programmes. With experiences one year in industry and twelve years in education, her research interests include banking, finance, quality management, technology etc. Currently she is working as an Assistant Professor at MPM GFGC, Karkala, Udupi, Karnataka in India.

Shana Redd Sleep joined UNO from Michigan State University, where she received her BA (2007), MBA (2011), and Ph.D. (2021) in Marketing Strategy. Between her academic stints at MSU, she has held industry positions in CPG consulting, new product development, and brand management and has worked with NCH Marketing Services, Domino Foods, Kraft Foods, and Whirlpool Corporation, among others. Inspired by her substantive experiences, Shana's research and teaching interests focus on the empirical analysis of firm performance related to marketing strategy, including brand management and new product and service innovation.

Krishna Kanta Roy is an Assistant Professor of Economics at Symbiosis School of Economics. He teaches subjects like Econometrics, Microeconomics and International Economics. He is also a PhD Scholar working in the area of 'Education and Technology' at Symbiosis International (Deemed University).

Ishani Sharma is a distinguished Research Scholar at Chitkara Business School, Chitkara University, Punjab, India. With a deep-rooted passion for the tourism industry, Ishani's primary research areas encompass creative tourism and destination marketing. Her work delves into the intricate intersections of how destinations can harness creative avenues to enhance their appeal and draw tourists, coupled with the strategic nuances of promoting such destinations in an increasingly competitive global market.

Anuja Shukla is working as Associate Professor at Jaipuria Institute of Management, Noida. She has more than 12 years of teaching experience with over 24 paper publications. Her research articles have been published in International Journal of Information Management (A*), Psychology and Marketing (A), VISION (C), and FIIB (ABS 1). She has also won best research paper awards at FMS, Symbiosis, and Amity. Her areas of research interest include eWOM, Consumer Behavior, m-Commerce, AR/VR and emerging technologies.

Birud Sindhav has a PhD (Business Administration, Marketing focus) from the University of Oklahoma, Norman. Professor Sindhav teaches Doing Business in China in the MBA program, and Principles of Marketing (both traditional and online) and Marketing Research in the undergraduate program. He has also taught in Finland, Austria, Egypt, and India. He is a recipient of the UNO Alumni Outstanding Teaching Award and also the M&E Department's Distinguished Professor Award. Professor Sindhav's research interests focus on areas of b-to-b relationships, organizational justice, green advertising, social media, grassroots entrepreneurship in emerging economies, and sales function in startups. His work has been published in the Journal of Retailing, Journal of Marketing Theory and Practice, Journal of Marketing Channels and other outlets. He is on the editorial review boards of several journals.

Ram Singh is a new-age innovative educator working at the MM Institute of Management Maharishi Markandeshwar (Deemed to be University) Mullana-Ambala, Haryana. Dr. Singh has vast teaching and research experience spanning more than 14 years in teaching, research, and administration. Being a researcher, Dr. Singh holds multifarious positions in the field of academics, for instance, he is a member of the Editorial Board of various reputed journals in the domain of accounting, finance, and general management and a reviewer in IGI Global and Inderscience journals. Besides, Dr. Singh has also been awarded the 'Excellent Reviewer Award-2020' by Bilingual Publishing Company Singapore, 'Best Doctoral Thesis Award-2022' by the International Association of Research & Developed Organisation, Ghaziabad, India, and 'National Elite Teacher Award-2022' by the International Institute of Organised Research (I2OR), Chennai. Currently, his professional affiliation includes being a member of four national and international academic organizations: a Life Member of the Indian Commerce Association (ICA), and a Life Member of the International Association of Academic plus Corporate Society (IAACS).

Makarand Upadhyaya is a thorough educationalist and specialises in the field of Marketing. His present profile is as an Associate Professor, Department of Management and Marketing, College of Business Administration, University of Bahrain, Bahrain. He earned his Ph.D. from the University of Rajasthan, Jaipur, in 2010. He has accomplished his master's and bachelor's degree along with, PGDPM and PG-DCA from Vikram University, Ujjain. Having more than 25 years of combined experience in industry and academia. He also has been connected to well know universities as Jazan University, Mexico-Universidad de las Americas, Indian Institute of Health Management, MITS and BITS-Pilani. He has Extensively travelled around the globe. Awarded / felicitated with Faculty Distinguished Scholarship Award in 2007 by the Research Council, India and many more such accomplishments on his list. His areas of research fall within the domains of Marketing Strategies, Consumer Behaviour and 2 Strategic Board leadership. He has authored books in his field of specialisation to name some books: 75 years of Industrial, Infrastructural and Logistics Development in India: 1947-48 to 2021- 22 ; Leadership: Find Your Way to Lead - 2020; Lead: Public-Private-Partnership (PPP) and Economic Development: Theory and Recent Experiences; Marketing Management: Concepts, Theories and Practices; Marketing Strategies and Management: Sector Analysis; and Media Planning: Impact of TV Advertisements on Children. Dr. Upadhyaya has penned more than 200 articles in various well know journal internationally on current marketing trends and its impact on consumers. To add on to his credit he is the chairperson and keynote speaker at the forums on business strategies and economic growth. He has conducted more than 40 training and development sessions on client relationships, behavioral aspects of the overseas market, stress management, interpersonal skills, and team building for senior and junior level corporate managers. He also is a guide and mentor to students pursuing Ph.D. and MBA courses. He is a sport enthusiastic and fond of participating cricket and basketball too.

Kamal Upreti is currently working as an Associate Professor in Department of Computer Science, CHRIST (Deemed to be University), Delhi NCR, Ghaziabad, India. He completed is B. Tech (Hons) Degree from UPTU, M. Tech (Gold Medalist), PGDM(Executive) from IMT Ghaziabad and PhD from OPJindal University in Department of Computer Science & Engineering. He has completed Postdoc from National Taipei University of Business, TAIWAN funded by MHRD. He has published 50+ Patents, 45+ Books, 32+Magazine issues and 90+ Research papers in in various international Conferences and reputed Journals. His areas of Interest are Cyber Security, Machine Learning, Health Care, Wireless Networking, Embedded System and Cloud Computing. He is having enriched years' experience in corporate and teaching experience in Engineering Colleges. He worked with HCL, NECHCL, Hindustan Times, Dehradun Institute of Technology and Delhi Institute of Advanced Studies, with more than 15+ years of enrich experience in research, Academics and Corporate . He also worked in NECHCL in Japan having project – "Hydrastore " funded by joint collaboration between HCL and NECHCL Company. Dr. Upreti worked on Government project – "Integrated Power Development Scheme (IPDS)" was launched by Ministry of Power, Government of India with the objectives of Strengthening of sub-transmission and distribution network in the urban areas. Currently, he has completed work with Joint collaboration with GB PANT & AIIMS Delhi, under funded project of ICMR Scheme on Cardiovascular diseases prediction strokes using Machine Learning Techniques from year 2020-2023 of having fund of 80 Lakhs .He has attended as a Session Chair Person in National, International conference and key note speaker in various platforms such as Skill based training, Corporate Trainer, Guest faculty and faculty development Programme. He awarded as best teacher, best researcher, extra academic performer and Gold Medalist in M. Tech programme.

Ajay Verma is a Research Scholar at VIT Bhopal University [Vellore Institute of Technology], working in the arena of Mediation Analysis. He has been working in the several Edu-Tech platforms as subject matter expert for Statistic. He has completed his master's with a specialization in Mathematical Statistics.

Balraj Verma serves as an Assistant Professor at the esteemed Chitkara Business School-Doctoral Research Centre, affiliated with Chitkara University in Rajpura, Punjab. Holding a Ph.D. earned from Jaypee University of Information Technology (JUIT), Waknaghat, and a master's degree in Business Administration, he brings to the academic arena more than 16 years of rich experience in both academia and the corporate world. His qualifications extend to successfully passing the National Eligibility Test (NET) for teaching in the field of management, a testament to his dedication to education. He possesses a remarkable teaching portfolio, which includes courses such as Marketing Management, Strategic Management, Business Statistics, and Research Methodology. Furthermore, he is a strong advocate for rigorous research, as reflected in his extensive publication record. His research contributions encompass numerous papers published in ABDC-listed and Scopus Index journals, as well as authorship and editorial work for books and book chapters, published by renowned major presses. Notably, he is not just an academic but also an active contributor to the academic community. He has played a pivotal role in organizing workshops and conferences, contributing significantly to the academic growth and development of his department and university.

Nahida Majeed Wani is an academician in the domain of Mathematics. Her area of research is Number Theory, Quantum Cryptography and IoT.

Index

www.ingramcontent.com/pod-product-compliance
Lightning Source LLC
LaVergne TN
LVHW080639011026
849160LV00014B/1261
* 9 7 9 8 3 6 9 3 4 5 8 0 1 *